Political Parties of Eastern Europe, Russia and the Successor States

edited by

Bogdan Szajkowski

STOCKTON

Political Parties of Eastern Europe, Russia and the Successor States

Published by Longman Information & Reference
Longman Group Limited, Westgate House, The High, Harlow,
Essex CM20 1YR, United Kingdom.

Telephone: (01279) 442601
Facsimile: (01279) 444501

First Published 1994

A catalogue record for this book is available from the British Library.

ISBN 0-582-25531-7

Co-published in the United States and Canada by Stockton Press,
49 West 24th Street, New York, NY 10010-3206, USA
Telephone: 212-627 5757
Facsimile: 212-627 9256

ISBN 1-56159-079-7.

Printed and bound in Great Britain by Bookcraft (Bath) Ltd.

CONTENTS

INTRODUCTION

The dismantling of the communist regimes in Central Eastern Europe and the former Soviet Union has created a substantial vacuum, particularly of robust political institutions capable of dealing with the social, economic and political challenges of post-totalitarianism. It has been relatively easy to accomplish structural changes in terms of proclaiming legal provisions and arrangements for political pluralism. However, structural change without the necessary social change clearly makes those structures unworkable, or at least leaves them lagging behind. Thus the desired effects of structural change cannot be achieved, and the end result appears to lead to dissolution, confusion, negation and finally an inevitable challenge to the whole system. In the long run all of these have destructive consequences not only for the structures themselves but more importantly for the process of transformation itself. The slow progress of social change has been particularly evident in the reconstruction of political parties in the former communist states. The legacy of communism has placed a particular stress on these institutions and produced almost insurmountable challenges in dealing with the past, present and future complex problems and issues of post-totalitarianism.

One of the main features of the communist political system was its marginalization of effective party politics. Starting with the Bolshevik revolution in 1917, communist practice led to the eradication of existing party systems and a consequent centralization and strict administration of party politics. In all the communist countries the ruling communist parties claimed to be the leading force in both society and the state, the "vanguard of the proletariat", comprising the most conscious sections of society and representing the views of the majority. The parties' privileged role was guaranteed by all constitutions of the former communist countries. In reality, however, these parties were élite organizations, marked by very small memberships, narrow social support and little legitimacy. Despite this, however, they functioned in effect as the "Ministry of Politics", beyond reproach and beyond reform.

The fundamental changes that have taken place at an astonishing speed in Central Eastern Europe and the former Soviet Union since 1989, resulted in reconstitution of old parties, the creation of new political parties and an explosion of popular support for party politics, coupled with an abandonment of restrictions and controls, the flowering of new ideas and the airing of old concepts which under communist rule had existed only beneath the surface. A multitude of political parties and movements has been created in the 27 countries analysed in this volume (*see* Table 1). The only exception is Turkmenistan where the old communist party pattern of a dominant party, the Democratic Party of Turkmenistan, and its auxiliary organizations still prevails.

In historical retrospect the event which must be seen as a watershed in the development of independent mass political action in opposition to communist party rule was the formation of the Independent Self-governing Trade Union "Solidarity" in Poland in August 1980. Solidarity, of course, utilized a whole range of ideas developed earlier by the Committee for the Defence of Workers in Poland, Charter-77 in Czechoslovakia and other smaller dissident groups, as well as individuals elsewhere in Eastern Europe. It, however, grew into a vast social and political movement mobilizing the various strands of opposition

INTRODUCTION

to the communist regime, and even included a large number of members of the ruling Polish United Workers' Party. Solidarity had a profound impact on the development of independent party politics not only in Poland but also in the rest of Eastern Europe and Hungary and Czechoslovakia in particular. At the end of the 1980s the bankrupt regimes of Eastern Europe sought to incorporate the ideas of Solidarity into the political process through negotiated settlements reached at the various Round Table agreements, in Poland, Hungary, Czechoslovakia, the former German Democratic Republic and Albania, that led to formation of new political parties.

Two other developments were crucial to the process of the formation of political parties in the closing stages of communist rule and its immediate aftermath. Firstly, the removal of constitutional provisions guaranteeing the respective communist parties monopoly of representation and power instituted *structural democratization* and, secondly, formalized political pluralism. These allowed the process of structural change to begin. The first set of parliamentary elections, during 1989–90, in which the electorates were offered a choice of candidates (who in many cases were still the nominees of the ruling communist parties), laid the operational foundations for political parties. The subsequent, second, fully democratic elections in several Eastern European countries during 1991–94, not only consolidated the process of party formation but also proved decisive for the emergence of a working party system by effectively reducing the number of parties in the parliaments to the strongest, most supported and best organized.

Prior to the demise of communism in the former USSR the party system in the constituent republics was entirely based on the Communist Party of the Soviet Union (CPSU). Although republican communist parties existed, these were, to all intents and purposes, the effect branches of the CPSU and functioned under its tight control. The emergence during 1989 of Popular Fronts in several of the republics challenged the monopoly of communist parties. These processes had particularly significant impacts on Estonia, Latvia, Lithuania and Moldova where Popular Front candidates defeated communist candidates in the first semi-democratic elections (1989–90) to the republican Supreme Soviets. In other republics, including Russia, informal alternatives to the CPSU emerged which were based on the urban intelligentsia and which gathered together individuals opposed to communist party rule and communists who saw the need for democratization. Often formed in a haphazard way, in many cases these groups were able to survive and, once they attracted and retained supporters, have gradually been transformed into political parties and movements. During 1989–91 two issues appear to have been critical to the formation of party systems in the former Soviet republics: the attitudes of republican communist parties to the nationalist challenge and to the August 1991 coup attempt in Moscow. In Lithuania the renamed communist party — the Lithuanian Democratic Labour Party — successfully associated itself with Lithuanian nationalist politics. In Moldova the Communist Party of Moldova supported the *coup*. Shortly thereafter its activities were suspended and all its assets confiscated, but it was able to reconstitute itself as the Socialist Party.

A glance at the political parties listed in this volume that have emerged in Central Eastern Europe, Russia and the Successor States, suggests the following eight broad categories: historic parties; parties descended from dissident groups; nationalist parties; issue parties; religious parties; reformed former communist parties; extremist right-wing parties; and traditional hard line communist parties.

The first category comprises parties of nostalgia, historic parties that existed before the communist takeovers, that were refounded on the old well-established traditions, mostly with the support of their old members. With few exceptions they have avoided major internal splits but appear to have been unable to increase their membership and popular appeal.

The secondary category includes parties that have emerged from dissident groups and opposition movements. Some, such as Charter-77 in Czechoslovakia or Solidarity in Poland, have had a long and distinguished history throughout the 1970s and 1980s of opposition to the communist regimes in their respective countries. Other parties have their roots in the liberalization process linked with Gorbachev's policies of *glasnost* and *perestroika*. Initial public exposure of environmental damage permitted under *glasnost*, in for example Bulgaria, Estonia and Latvia, gave rise to opposition groupings which subsequently formed the nuclei of political parties. *Perestroika* also permitted the exposure of falling living standards, unfulfilled promises and the burgeoning social and political crisis in many states. These disclosures led to the formation of reformist communist groups that subsequently became the basis of political parties such as Hungarian Democratic Forum and the Alliance of Free Democrats.

Since 1989 Solidarity, Civic Forum and Public Against Violence, all initially based on mass popular movements, have shown the greatest tendency to splits and divisions as they readjusted to the realities of power. Civic Forum, Public Against Violence and Solidarity were useful and convenient umbrellas for uniting many diverse views and ideologies while in opposition to communist rule but subsequent policy differences, and more importantly personality clashes, have led to disunity and discord. While the splits in the civic Forum produced three parties which nevertheless have remained together in coalition, the fissures within Solidarity and Public Against Violence were marked by a far greater fracturing accompanied by more pronounced conflicts on the level of both policies and personalities.

The third group of nationalist parties encapsulates the nationalist aspirations of diverse ethnic groups long denied by the communist rulers. Since these parties often represent homogeneous and vociferous ethnic constituencies, they present a considerable challenge to the new post-communist political authorities. In several countries, particularly in the former Soviet republics, the cohesiveness of the ethnic groups, including the Russian minority, is reflected in the strongly nationalistic outlooks, programmes and demands of their political organizations. This is particularly evident, for example, in the cases of the Edynstvo movements in both Kazakhstan and Moldova, or the Party of Democratic Progress and the Slavic movement *Lad* in Kazakhstan. These Russian and/or Slavic movements embrace cultural groups, veteran associations, pensioners, trade unions and even Cossacks, with the overriding aim of economic, cultural and political protection of ethnic interests. Similarly in all the Union republics of the present Russian Federation the nationalist movements and parties of the titular peoples embrace whole ranges of social groups and ideologies, with an overall goal of national self-determination. In East Central Europe, no matter how homogenous the ethnic group may or appears to be, the ethnic parties on the whole represent a diversity of views and ideological complexions: left, centre and right. This is particularly evident among the Hungarian parties in Slovakia, the Roma parties in Bulgaria and Macedonia and the Albanian parties in Kosovo and Macedonia.

The fourth category includes parties inspired by their western counterparts, such as the Green and Feminist movements and other less serious equivalents like Friends of the Beer Party, the Independent Erotic Initiative and the Monster Loony Party. While the Greens and Feminists have brought environmental and gender issues into the wider political agenda and contributed considerably to the development of party politics, despite their limited resources, the three latter examples are of course mere curiosities.

INTRODUCTION

The fifth category includes religious parties devoted specifically to the advancement of religious views and the social, political and moral teaching of various denominations. They also aim at reversing the separation between church and state and demand the adoption by the state of religious values and doctrines as a safeguard against moral and social disintegration.

The sixth category includes the former ruling communist parties that have rejected the last vestiges of Marxism-Leninism and declared their conversion to Western-style social democracy. As they lost their grip on power they were at first often subjected to acrimonious divisions and quarrels over their legacy, claims to properties and finances as well as policies in the new post-communist environment. During 1993 and 1994 however, the reformed communists, operating under revised names and with much reduced membership, have become the mouthpiece for the frustrations and disappointments caused by the increasingly obvious social costs of transition. They have been returned to power in Lithuania, Poland and Hungary. They have also made strong gains elsewhere in Eastern Europe and Russia, establishing the so-called "rejection fronts" aiming at slowing down or indeed reversing the whole process of change.

The seventh category comprises extreme parties of the right. In countries where for decades democratic traditions and institutions were unable to develop, the extreme right did not find it difficult to find a place within the political spectrum. The absence of democratic culture is further strengthened by a tradition of anti-Semitism, confusion over what in the new post-communist world constitutes nationhood, demands for the revisions of borders and increased irredentism, and the role of politicized ethnicity. All these issues have served as breeding grounds for the growth of extreme right-wing, fascist and neo-fascist parties in most of the former communist states. In this category one should also include the extreme nationalist parties exploiting xenophobia and the perceived threat from ethnic minorities. These have found increasing appeal in Romania, Serbia, Ukraine, Bulgaria and Slovakia. The extreme right often shares affinity with the unreformed communists producing the menacing spectre of the "red–brown" alliance.

The final category comprises the remnants of the communist parties which still adhere to Marxism-Leninism. Their membership includes the old hardline communist elements, people who found themselves unable to adjust to change. Deprived of their former privileged positions, properties and resources, these parties now operate on the fringes of society.

There are considerable similarities in many of the programmes of political parties in Eastern Europe and the former Soviet Union. Voters often have had to decide between them by concentrating on the personalities of their leaders and their competence to deliver promises rather than on any policy differences. In the overwhelming majority of countries, parties and movements have found it difficult to produce distinct ideological content in their programmes. The divergences between their platforms are more quantitative than qualitative. With the exception of the old unreformed communists and the extreme right-wing groups, virtually all parties have "catch-all" platforms that support a market or social-market economy, privatization and either closer relations with the European Union, NATO and the Western European Union or full membership of these organizations and their institutions. The platforms only vary in the emphasis placed on the priorities in social policy, on the desirable degree of state intervention in the economy, on pace of privatization and on integration into Western European institutions. More substantial differences can be observed in terms of the importance given to individual liberties versus collective obligations to family, church and nation.

INTRODUCTION

Table 1 Numbers of political parties and movements in 1994

Country	Parties	Movements	Total
Albania	28	1	29
Armenia	40	2	42
Azerbaijan	7	2	9
Belarus	23	3	26
Bosnia-Herzegovina	33		33
Bulgaria	79	14	93
Croatia	23	1	24
Czech Republic	52	26	78
Estonia	11	2	13
Georgia	34	3	37
Hungary	101	4	105
Kazakhstan	10	4	14
Kyrgyzstan	11	6	17
Latvia	5	3	8
Lithuania	11	2	13
Macedonia	51	3	54
Moldova	19	7	26
Poland	39	4	43
Romania	194	5	199
Russian Federation	127	38	165
Adygea	9	7	16
Dagestan	6	1	7
Kabardino-Balkaria	5	7	12
Karachaevo-Cherkessia	8	14	22
Tatarstan	22	11	33
Slovakia	38	19	57
Slovenia	23	3	26
Tajikistan	6	2	8
Turkmenistan	4	2	6
Ukraine	57	6	63
Uzbekistan	8	6	14
Yugoslavia			
Serbia and Vojvodina	87	19	106
Kosovo	6		6
Montenegro	19	2	21
TOTAL	1,196	229	1,425

Note: Excluded from this table are political parties and movements in the "Serbian Republic of Bosnia and Hercegovina" (three parties and two movements) and in the "Republic of Serbian Krajina" (five parties).

INTRODUCTION

An overwhelming majority of the political parties are small with a narrow support base, and few have social roots or public recognition. By and large they are unknown and up to now have failed to capture the public's interest. They appear to have been unable to develop communications with the society at large and distinctive group political interests in particular. They possess few resources to spread their message to an electorate with little experience of democratic practice. Moreover, it should be remembered that after 1989 perhaps an overwhelming majority of the populations of the former communist countries have shown a great deal of scepticism about parties as an institution and a concept. Political parties still do not inspire sufficient confidence, acclaim and support as all too often they are associated with the former communist parties and their arbitrary and discredited rule. All of this has produced the phenomenon of transitory political parties, with constant changes, regrouping, splits and mergers into coalitions, alliances and blocs. The exceptions, but only to a limited extent, are the Czech Republic, Poland, Hungary, Estonia, Latvia, Lithuania, Slovenia and Slovakia where the development of political parties has advanced quite considerably in the direction of their consolidation and the creation of a working party system. In these countries four broad ideological categories of parties have emerged: social-liberal; nationalist-Christian; social democratic; and unreformed communist.

This book presents a comprehensive picture of the development and current state of political parties and party politics in Central Eastern Europe, Russia and the Successor States. Every effort has been made to give accurate and up-to-date information and analysis wherever possible. In the overwhelming number of cases contributors to this volume have been able to obtain a complete set of data on history, membership, programme, structure and affiliations, and electoral behaviour.

The list of abbreviations and a comprehensive index will help guide the reader through the labyrinth of organizations and associations and make the book more accessible.

The speedy publication of this book would not have been possible without the help and co-operation of Lorimer Poultney and Shane Hooper. I am grateful for their patience, advice and support.

I wish to express my appreciation to Krystyna Vere-Bujnowski for her research assistance, Dr Tamara Dragadze for her critical comments and suggestions on part of the manuscript, and Rasmus Bing for his co-operation and the excellent material on Romania. I am also grateful to IT Services of the Faculty of Social Studies of the University of Exeter and Mr Neil Mathieson in particular for help and co-operation. Dr Charles King wishes to express his appreciation and thanks to Igor Botan and Valeriu Opinca for their assistance.

The Editor and Authors wish to acknowledge the following publications which have been helpful: Research papers published by the RFE/RL Research Institute; Keesings Contemporary Archives; BBC Summary of World Broadcasts.

Bogdan Szajkowski
Department of Politics
University of Exeter

ABBREVIATIONS

Albania
AAP	Albanian Agrarian Party
ADAP	Albanian Democratic Alliance Party
ANUP	Albanian National Unity Party
APL	Albanian Party of Labour
ARP	Albanian Republican Party
ASP	Albanian Socialist Party
DP	Democratic Party
SDPA	Social Democratic Party of Albania

Armenia
AAM	All-Armenia Movement
ARF	Armenian Revolutionary Federation
DLP	Democratic Liberal Party of Armenia

Azerbaijan
APF	Azerbaijan Popular Front
PRR	Party of Revolutionary Revival
SDP	Social Democratic Party

Belarus
BPF	Belarusian Popular Front
BZV	Belarusian Association of Servicemen
CPB	Communist Party of Belarus
LDP	Liberal Democratic Party
MDSPJ	Movement for Democracy, Social Progress and Justice
PMB	Popular Movement of Belarus

Bulgaria
ASA	Alternative Socialist Association
ASP	Alternative Social-Liberal Party
BANU	Bulgarian Agrarian National Union
BANUNP	Bulgarian Agrarian National Union-Nikola Petkov
BCP	Bulgarian Communist Party
BNDU	Bulgarian National Democratic Union
BPP	Bulgarian People's Party
BSDP	Bulgarian Social Democratic Party
BSP	Bulgarian Socialist Party
CRP	Christian Republican Party
CI	Citizens' Initiative
DP	Democratic Party

LDP	Liberal Democratic Party
MRF	Movement for Rights and Freedoms
RDP	Radical Democratic Party
RP	Republican Party
UDF	Union of Democratic Forces

Bosnia-Hercegovina

CDUBH	Croatian Union of Bosnia and Hercegovina
DLG-EKO	Democratic League of Greens-EKO
DPS	Democratic Party of Socialists
MBO	Liberal-Bosnian Organization
PDA	Party of Democratic Action
SDP-BH	Social Democratic Party of Bosnia-Hercegovina
UBSD	Union of Bosnian Social Democrats
CDP	Civic Democratic Party
CPP	Croatian Peasant Party
MDP	Muslim Democratic Party
RP	Republican Party

Croatia

CDU	Croatian Democratic Union
CID	Croatian Independent Democrats
CNP	Croatian National Party
CPR	Croatian Party of Rights
CPP	Croatian Peasant Party
CSLP	Croatian Social Liberty Party
DA	Dalmatian Action
IDA	Istrian Democratic Assembly
RDL	Rijeka Democratic League
SNP	Serbian National Party
SDP	Serbian Democratic Party of Croatia
CCDU	Croatian Christian Democratic Union

Czech Republic

CMSS	Bohemian-Moravian Centre Party
CSSD	Czech Social Democratic Party
DEU	Democratic Union
DL	Democratic Left
KAN	Club of Committed Non-Party Members
KDS	Christian Democratic Party
KDU-CSL	Christian Democratic Union-Czechoslovak People's Party
KSCM	Communist Party of Bohemia and Moravia
LNSP	Liberal National Social Party
LSU	Liberal Social Union
MNS	Moravian National Party
ODA	Civic Democratic Alliance
ODS	Civic Democratic Party

ABBREVIATIONS

SDL	Democratic Left Party
sLB	Left Bloc Party
SPR-RSC	Association for the Republic-Republican Party of Czechoslovakia
SPZR	Party of Entrepreneurs, Tradesmen and Farmers of the Czech Republic
SZ	Green Party
ZS	Agrarian Party

Estonia

ENIP	Estonian National Independence Party

Hungary

AA	Agrarian Alliance
AFD	Alliance of Free Democrats
AP	Active Party
AYD	Alliance of Young Democrats
CDPP	Christian Democratic People's Party
DC	Democratic Coalition
DP	Democratic Party
DSP	Democratic Smallholders and Citizens' Party
EP	Entrepreneurs Party
FIDESZ	Alliance of Young Democrats
HDF	Hungarian Democratic Forum
HGP	Hungarian Green Party
HISP	Historic Independent Smallholders Party
HJLP	Hungarian Justice and Life Party
HNP	Hungarian National Party
HPP	Hungarian People's Party
HSDP	Hungary's Social Democratic Party
HSP	Hungarian Socialist Party
HSWP	Hungarian Socialist Workers' Party
IHDP	Independent Hungarian Democratic Party
ISP	Independent Smallholder, Land Labourer and Citizens' Party
NDA	National Democratic Alliance
NSBP	National Smallholder and Bourgeois Party

Kazakhstan

KPK	Communist Party of Kazakhstan
KS	Co-ordinating Council of Public Associations
NDPK	National Democratic Party of Kazakhstan
NKK	People's Congress of Kazakhstan
PDPK	Party of Democratic Progress of Kazakhstan
RPK	Republican Party of Kazakhstan
SDPK	Social Democratic Party of Kazakhstan
SPK	Socialist Party of Kazakhstan
SNEK	Union of People's Unity of Kazakhstan

ABBREVIATIONS

Kosovo

ADP	Albanian Demo-Christian Party
DLK	Democratic League of Kosovo
PPK	Parliamentary Party of Kosovo
PPK	Peasant Party of Kosovo
SDP	Social Democratic Party
TPP	Turkish People's Party

Latvia

DCP	Democratic Centre Party (Latvia)
KDS	Latvian Christian Democratic Union
LNNK	Latvian National Independence Movement
SLAT	Harmony for Latvia
WFFL	World Federation of Free Latvians

Lithuania

LDP	Lithuanian Democratic Party
LDLP	Lithuanian Democratic Labour Party

Macedonia

DP	Democratic Party
DPS	Democratic Party of Serbs
IMRO-DPMNU	Internal Macedonian Revolutionary Organization-Democratic Party for Macedonian National Unity
LP	Liberal Party of Macedonia
MAAK	Movement for Pan-Macedonian Action
PCER	Party for Complete Emancipation of the Roma
PDP	Party of Democratic Prosperity in Macedonia
PYRM	Party of Yugoslavs in the Republic of Macedonia
SDAM	Social Democratic Alliance of Macedonia
SPM	Socialist Party of Macedonia
SDPM	Social Democratic Party of Macedonia

Montenegro

ARFM	Alliance of Reform Forces for Montenegro
DC	Democratic Coalition
DPS	Democratic Party of Socialists
LAM	Liberal Alliance of Montenegro
NP	National Party
NSP	New Socialist Party of Montenegro

Moldova

AF	Association of Women
AFDP	Association of Former Political Prisoners
ATL	Alliance of Free Peasants
AV	Ecological Party "Green Alliance"
AVRTC	Association of Victims of the Totalitarian Communist Regime

ABBREVIATIONS

CI	Congress of the Intelligentsia
LNT	National Youth League
MV	Movement of Volunteers
OTCD	Christian Democratic Youth Organization
PCD	Christian Democratic Party
PD	Democratic Party
PDA	Agrarian Democratic Party
PDM	Democratic Labour Party
PFCD	Christian Democratic Popular Front
PNL	National Liberal Party
PNS	National Christian Party
PPG	Gaugauz People's Party
PR	Republican Party
PRef	Party of Reform
PS	Socialist Party
PSD	Social Democratic Party
UE	Edinstvo Movement
UT	Union of Youth

Poland

BBWR	Non-Party Bloc for the Support of Reform
CD	Christian Democracy
KLD	Liberal Democratic Congress
KPN	Confederation for Independent Poland
PC	Centre Accord
PCD	Party of Christian Democrats
PK	Conservative Party
PPG	Polish Economic Programme
PPPP	Polish Friends of Beer
PSL	Polish Peasant Party
PSL-PL	Peasant Accord
PSL-W	Polish Peasant Party-Wilanow
PZPR	Polish United Workers' Party
PZZ	Polish Western Union
RdR	Movement for the Republic
RDS	Democratic Social Movement
RTR	Third Republic Movement
SD	Democratic Party
SdRP	Social Democracy of the Republic of Poland
SLCh	Christian Peasant Alliance
UD	Democratic Union
UP	Union of Labour
UPR	Union of Political Realism
WAK	Catholic Electoral Committee
ZChN	Christian National Union
ZSL	United Peasant Party

ABBREVIATIONS

Romania

ADN	Alliance for National Dignity
ADPR	Agrarian Democratic Party of Romania
ASD	Social Democratic Alliance
CDR	Conventia Democratica din Romania
CSS	Convention of Social Solidarity
DCR	Democratic Convention of Romania
DNSF	Democratic National Salvation Front
DP-NSF	Democratic Party-National Salvation Front
DUP	Democratic Unity Party
FSN-PD	Partidul Democrat
GRP	Greater Romania Party
HDUR	Hungarian Democratic Union of Romania
MER	Romanian Ecological Movement
MPR	Movement for Romania
NDP	National Democratic Party
NPP-CD	National Peasants' Party-Christian Democrat
NSF	National Salvation Front
PAC	Civic Alliance Party
PADRR	Democratic Alliance Party of Romania
PCCDR	Conservative Christian Democratic Romanian Party
PCD	Christian Party of Justice
PDM	Democratic Labour Party
PDP	Progressive Democratic Party
PDR	Romanian Democratic Party
PDS	Social Justice Party of Romania
PER	Romanian Ecologist Party
PL-1993	Liberal Party 1993
PLD	Free Democratic Party
PLDR	Freedom and Romanian Democracy Party
PLMR	Liberal Monarchist Party of Romania
PLR	Free Republican Party
PLS	Free Change Party
PNA	Agrarian National Party
PNDC	Christian Democratic National Party
PNDD	National Democratic Party of Romania for Justice
PNL	National Liberal Party
PNL-CD	National Liberal Party-Democratic Convention
PNP	National Progressist Party
PNR	National Reunification Party
PNR	National Royalist Party
PNR	Romanian National Party
PNRC	New Christian Romanian Party
PNT	National Peasants' Party
PRCD	Christian Democratic Revolution Party
PRCR	Christian Republican Party of Romania
PRR	Romanian Revolution Party

ABBREVIATIONS

PSDI	Independent Social Democratic Party
PUC	Conservative Humanist Party
PUR	Republican Union Party
PUSD	Social Democratic Unity Party
PVDP	Democratic Future of the Homeland Party
RCP	Romanian Communist Party
RNUP	Romanian National Unity Party
RSDP	Romanian Social Democratic Party
SPDR	Social Democracy Party of Romania
SPL	Socialist Party of Labour
UDC	Christian Democratic Union Party
ULB	Bratianu Liberal Union
ULDRR	Democratic and Free Union of Romanis of Romania
UNVR	National Union for the Victory of the Revolution
VR	Vatra Romaneasca Union

Russian Federation

APR	Agrarian Party of Russia
ATTO	Association of Tatars of Tyumen Oblast
AUTY	Azatlyk Union of Tatar Youth
BNC	Bulgar National Congress
CDP-PPF	Constitutional Democratic Party-Party of People's Freedom
CKP	Congress of the Karbadin People
CPRF	Communist Party of the Russian Federation
DCB	Dignity and Charity Bloc
DPR	Democratic Party of Russia
IDPT	Islamic Democratic Party of Tatarstan
LDPR	Liberal Democratic Party of Russia
MWP-PDP	Marxist Workers Party-Party of the Dictatorship of the Proletariat
NCBP	National Council of the Balkar Peoples
PEF	Party of Economic Freedom
PPFR	People's Party of Free Russia
PRUA	Party of Russian Unity and Accord
RCDM	Russian Christian Democratic Movement
RCWP	Russian Communist Workers' Party
RMDR	Russian Movement for Democratic Reforms
RUIE	Russian Union of Industrialists and Entrepreneurs
SDPR	Social Democratic Party of the Russian Federation
TOT	Tatar Public Centre
VTOT	All-Union Tatar Public Centre

Serbia

AYDI	Association for a Yugoslav Democratic Initiative
CA	Civic Alliance
DACV	Democratic Alliance of Croats in the Vojvodina
DUMV	Democratic Union of Magyars of Vojvodina
DP	Democratic Party

ABBREVIATIONS

DPA	Democratic Party of Albanians
DPS	Democratic Party of Serbia
DRPM	Democratic Reform Party of Muslims
DEPOS	Democratic Movement of Serbia
NPP	National Peasant Party
ND	New Democracy
PPS	Peasant Party of Serbia
PDA	Party of Democratic Action
PSU	Party of Serbian Unity
PY	Party of Yugoslavs
SLP	Serbian Liberal Party
SMR	Serbian Movement for Renewal
SRP	Serbian Radical Party
SPS	Socialist Party of Serbia
LC-MY	League of Communists-Movement for Yugoslavia

Slovakia

RSS	Agrarian Party of Slovakia
KDH	Christian Democratic Movement
KSU	Christian Social Union
HCDM	Hungarian Christian Democratic Movement
MFDS	Movement for a Democratic Slovakia
SNP	Slovak National Party
PDL	Party of the Democratic Left
CDM	Christian Democratic Movement (Sl)
PAV	Public Against Violence

Slovenia

DP	Democratic Party
G-ESP	Greens-Ecological Social Party
LDP	Liberal Democratic Party
SCD	Slovene Christian Democrats
SNP	Slovene National Party
SPP	Slovene People's Party
SDPS	Social Democratic Party of Slovenia
UL	United List

Tajikistan

CPT	Communist Party of Tajikistan
IRP	Islamic Renaissance Party
RPM	Rastokhez (Rebirth) Patriotic Movement
TDP	Tajik Democratic Party

Turkmenistan

DPT	Democratic Party of Turkmenistan

ABBREVIATIONS

Ukraine

CDARU	Christian Democratic Alliance of Romanians in Ukraine
CDPU	Christian Democratic Party of Ukraine
CPC	Communist Party of the Crimea
CPU	Communist Party of Ukraine
CNDF	Congress of National Democratic Forces
CUN	Congress of Ukrainian Nationalists
DMD	Democratic Movement of the Donbas
DPC	Democratic Party of the Crimea
DPU	Democratic Party of Ukraine
GPU	Green Party of Ukraine
IBR	Interregional Bloc for Reforms
LCU	Labour Congress of Ukraine
LabPU	Labour Party of Ukraine
LDPU	Liberal Democratic Party of Ukraine
LibPU	Liberal Party of Ukraine
NMCT	National Movement of the Crimean Tatars
OCNM	Organization of the Crimean Tatar National Movement
PDRU	Party of Democratic Rebirth of Ukraine
PERC	Party of the Economic Rebirth of Crimea
PPU	Peasants' Party of Ukraine
PPC	People's Party of Crimea
PPU	People's Party of Ukraine
RMC	Republican Movement of the Crimea
RusPC	Russian Party of the Crimea
SDPU	Social Democratic Party of Ukraine
SNPU	Social National Party of Ukraine
SocPU	Socialist Party of Ukraine
SIU	Statehood and Independence for Ukraine
SRP	Subcarpathian Republican Party
UCDP	Ukrainian Christian Democratic Party
UCCC	Ukrainian Civic Congress of the Crimea
UCRP	Ukrainian Conservative Republican Party
UNU	Ukrainian Nationalist Union
UNA	Ukrainian National Assembly
UNCP	Ukrainian National Conservative Party
UNP	Ukrainian National Party
UPDP	Ukrainian Peasants' Democratic Party
URP	Ukrainian Republican Party
UDR	Union for Democratic Reforms
USRC	Union in Support of the Republic of Crimea
USDPU	United Social Democratic Party of Ukraine

Uzbekistan

PDP	People's Democratic Party (Uzbek)
FPP	Free Peasants' Party
IRP	Islamic Renaissance Party

ABBREVIATIONS

EDP	Erk (Freedom) Democratic Party
BPM	Birlik (Unity) People's Movement

Other abbreviations

AVNOJ	Anti-fascist Council for the National Liberation of Yugoslavia
BH	Bosnia-Hercegovina
CPSU	Communist Party of the Soviet Union
CSCE	Council on Security and Co-operation in Europe
EC	European Community
EU	European Union
IMF	International Monetary Fund
NATO	North Atlantic Treaty Organization
NCSR	National Council of the Slovak Republic
RSFSR	Russian Soviet Federation of Socialist Republics
SNC	Slovak National Council
USSR	Union of Soviet Socialist Republics

LIST OF CONTRIBUTORS

Dr John B. Allcock	Research Unit in South East European Studies, University of Bradford.
Mr Rasmus Bing	Centre for Slavonic Studies, University of Copenhagen.
Mr Peter Bugge	Slavisk Institut, Aarhus University.
Dr Tamara Dragadze	School of Slavonic and East European Studies, University of London.
Dr Zhanylzhan Dzhunusova	Department of International Relations, Centre of Oriental Studies of Kazakh National Academy of Sciences, Almaty.
Dr Karen Henderson	Department of Politics, University of Leicester.
Mr Lars Johannsen	Institute of Political Science, Aarhus University.
Dr Charles King	New College, University of Oxford.
Dr Ustina Markus	Radio Free Europe — Radio Liberty Research Institute, Munich.
Dr Martin McCauley	School of Slavonic and East European Studies, University of London.
Dr Frances Millard	School of Social and Historical Studies, University of Portsmouth.
Dr Ole Nørgaard	Institute of Political Science, Aarhus University.
Ms Anette Pedersen	Institute of Political Science, Aarhus University.
Mr Mark Pittaway	Department of Social and Economic History, University of Liverpool.
Ms Domitilla Sagramoso	School of Slavonic and East European Studies, University of London.
Mr Markar Sarafyan	ex-BBC World Service, London.
Dr Rustem Sartaev	Information and Analysis Centre of the Supreme Soviet of Kazakhstan, Almaty.
Dr Nigel Swain	Centre for Central and East European Studies, University of Liverpool.
Dr Bogdan Szajkowski	Department of Politics, University of Exeter.
Ms Krystyna Vere-Bujnowski	Department of Sociology, University of Exeter.
Dr Andrew Wilson	Sidney Sussex College, University of Cambridge.

ALBANIA

Bogdan Szajkowski

Albania was the last nation in Eastern Europe to undertake the transition from totalitarianism to democracy. The slow process of tangible change in Albania began in January 1990. The 9th plenum of the Central Committee of the Albanian Party of Labour (APL), held between Jan. 22 and 23, 1990, produced a 25-point programme advocating greater decentralization of the economy and more democracy in political and social institutions. In the economic sphere this included limiting centralized management, improvements in wage and price regulations, and the introduction of supply and demand mechanisms. At that time Ramiz Alia, leader of the APL, still argued that because of the country's specific conditions, traditions and even "national psychology", its future would be different from that of the other former communist states.[1] Alia emphasized that Albania had no democratic traditions and that it did not need a Western style multi-party system. Significantly, however, perhaps to compensate for the lack of political pluralism, the plenum agreed to accept measures guaranteeing legal defence for citizens under police investigation and during trials. It also decided to restore the Ministry of Justice, abolished at the height of the cultural revolution in Albania in 1966.

At the next (10th) plenum of the APL, in April, Alia announced a major shift in Albania's foreign policy. This included a willingness to establish relations with the Soviet Union and the United States, and to join the Conference on Security and Co-operation in Europe (CSCE). It was a belated but clear attempt by Albania to adopt a more realistic policy in the new post-Cold War European environment in order to protect the country's interests. On July 30, 1990, Albania and the USSR resumed diplomatic relations after a break of 29 years.[2] The CSCE, however, let it be known that in order to join democratic Europe Albania needed to improve its human rights record and its democratic credentials. Negotiations on the establishment of diplomatic relations with the USA dragged on for almost a year before the appropriate memorandum of understanding was signed in Washington by the two governments on March 15, 1991.[3]

Ramiz Alia demonstrated his determination to increase the democratization process and comply with CSCE standards when on May 7 and 8, 1990, the assembly passed a series of new laws on human rights, travel and religion.[4] These decrees gave ordinary citizens the right to apply for and obtain passports for travel abroad. Defection was no longer to be considered an act of treason but simply "illegal border trespassing". Agitation and propaganda against the state were also re-classified, and only acts aimed at "overthrowing the social and state order" were to be considered crimes. "Religious propaganda", considered a crime since the 1968 pronouncement declaring Albania the first atheist state in the world, was now removed from the list of crimes.[5]

1

In the summer of 1990 the Albanian regime became engulfed in a major refugee crisis reminiscent of that faced by the Honecker regime in East Germany during the summer of 1989. On July 2, 1990, after a demonstration by a group of young people in Tirana (still officially illegal at that time) several thousand people sought refuge in the Western embassies.[6] After several days of confusion, some 4,786 were allowed to leave the country under UN supervision. The exodus prompted the government to decide to issue passports to all Albanian citizens on request. The crisis, which shook the foundations of the Albanian regime, took the political élite by surprise. It showed, however, that Ramitz Alia had opted for a conciliatory approach rather than a show of force in order to avoid a bloody scenario similar to that in Romania.

On July 6 Alia convened the 11th plenum of the APL Central Committee, which made numerous important changes in both the Politburo and the government that allowed him to consolidate his position.[7] The appointments in the reshuffle included Kico Mustaqi, the Chief of the Army General Staff since 1982, who was appointed Minister of Defence and promoted to full membership of the Politburo.

On Dec. 8 between 500 and 1,000 students marched from the University of Tirana (at that time still called the Enver Hoxha Tirana University) through the streets of the capital shouting slogans such as: "Reforms", "No Dictatorship", and "Don't Lie". Other slogans supported Mikhail Gorbachev and Ramiz Alia. The unrest, which had grown out of a dispute over living conditions at the university's halls of residence,[8] soon turned into a political one.[9] The unrest continued for three days and the majority of students did not attend classes on Dec. 10.[10] By resisting the inevitable for far too long the communists had let discontent build up to the boiling point. Following the three days of student's unrest the APL 13th Central Committee plenum took place on Dec. 11, 1990. In addition to the dismissal of four prominent hardliners in the Politburo it made the dramatic announcement that: "The plenum expressed the opinion that it is to the benefit of the further democratization of the country's life and of pluralism to create independent political organizations in accordance with the laws in force."[11]

By allowing what was in essence the creation of a multi-party system, the communists took a calculated risk. However, incorporating dissent into organized forms and into the party–state structural relations was perhaps one of the very few options open for a peaceful diffusion of an increasingly explosive situation. The leadership of the APL assumed that the opposition to the regime could be more easily controlled if it was confined to political organizations. Another factor in favour of the unexpected decision to allow a multi-party system was the fact that the opposition was too weak and divided to demand any substantial part in the decision-making process or fundamental changes to the system, particularly since most of the leading figures in the opposition circles were former members of the APL. The Albanian communists, like their reformed counterparts in Bulgaria earlier, made a major mistake in their assumption that the opposition could be safely ignored, except for what they themselves would be prepared to share with it. They, like their Bulgarian colleagues, miscalculated the mood of revolt of a large section of the population against the system and its symbols.

On Dec. 18, 1990, the Presidium of the People's Assembly formally approved a Decree no. 7442 "On the Creation of Political Organizations and Associations", that provided for a multi-party system in the country. The first party to emerge, the Democratic Party, was formed by a group of students and intellectuals at Tirana University only a day after the Central Committee announcement of the legalization of other political parties. Most of the new party senior members had to resign from the communist party in order to start the job of making Albania a multi-party state.[12] This was clearly done with Ramiz Alia's tentative support. The President trod a delicate line as he cautiously proceeded with the awkward task of ending the Hoxha legacy of poverty and xenophobia, under the watchful eyes of angry old Stalinist colleagues on the one hand and even angrier workers, young people and intellectuals on the other.

The communists' attempt at controlling discontent by allowing the formation of new political parties proved unsuccessful. The December unrest in Tirana triggered widespread riots later that month in four of the largest cities in northern Albania (the Geg region); Shkoder, Elbasan, Durrës, and Kavaja. Shkoder, which has always been considered the centre of Roman Catholic intellectualism, has had a long history of organized discontent and opposition to the regime. In early 1990 protesters in the city tried to remove a statute of Stalin which was eventually taken down a few months later. The violent clashes between demonstrators and the police this time lasted for several hours and caused considerable damage, estimated at around 18,000,000 leks (US$1,800,000). The demonstrators dynamited (but did not destroy) the statue of Enver Hoxha and attacked two other hated institutions of the regime, the newly built radio and television stations.[13] In Elbasan, an important heavy industry centre where the "Steel of the Party" plant is located, demonstrators vented their anger against Hoxha by ransacking bookshops and throwing copies of his books onto the streets. In the second largest city, Durrës, extensive looting of shops took place and bookshops selling Hoxha's writings were destroyed. The security services, following instructions from the central authorities, responded with restraint in order to avoid further escalation of violence and possible bloodshed.

Further indications of the Albanian leadership's attempts to dissociate itself from the past dominated by Hoxha's legacy came on Dec. 21 when the Council of Ministers declared: ". . . taking into consideration that historic circumstances have changed when decisions were adopted in our country to honour J. V. Stalin, it has been decided: 1) To deprive the state enterprises, objects and institutions bearing the name of J. V. Stalin of his name and remove his symbols; 2) Concerning the agricultural co-operatives and dwelling centres named after J. V. Stalin, their inhabitants should decide upon according to the laws in force.[14] At the end of December Albania witnessed another exodus of refugees, this time to Greece. It is estimated that some 6,000 people crossed the southern frontier, apparently with little if any obstruction from Albanian border guards.[15]

Between December 1990 and March 1991 five political parties were created reflecting the emerging social and political differentiation of the country.[16] Their membership, although growing steadily, as well as their social base, were, however very fragile reflecting their limited financial, physical and manpower resources. The holding of parliamentary elections only four months after the legalization of opposition parties was another attempt by the communists to retain control of the transition process. Opposition parties demanded at least six months in order to prepare themselves for the elections and the resolution of some of the outstanding issues, such as the withdrawal of the APL cells from workplaces, the depoliticization of the media, the judiciary, the security forces and the disbanding of the secret police, the Sigurimi, prior to the elections. The regime flatly refused to agree to opposition demands except to postpone the date of the elections from February to March.

Eleven parties and organizations registered candidates to contest the elections to be held on March 31, 1991. On the government's side, in addition to the Albanian Party of Labour, candidates were submitted by the Trade Union Federation (*Bashkimi*), the Youth

Table 1 1991 Parliamentary Elections: Number of Candidates and Party Affiliation

Democratic Party	250
Albanian Party of Labour	243
Republican Party	164
Democratic Front	124
Trade Unions	108
Youth Union	94
Women's Union	71
Agrarian Party	36
Independent candidates	17
National Veterans' Committee	7
OMONIA Organization	5
Ecological Party	2

Source: Authors' calculation from various issues of
Zeri i Popullit (Voice of the People).

Organization, the Women's Organization, the Democratic Front and the National Veterans' Committee. The latter five have operated as APL front organizations throughout almost the entire period of Albania's post-war history and therefore did not offer meaningful alternatives to the communist party. An alternative was offered by opposition parties founded after Dec. 11, 1990: the Democratic Party, the Republican Party, the Agrarian Party, the Ecological Party, and the Democratic Union of the Greek Minority (OMONIA).

A major issue of contention between the opposition and the APL was access to enlisted military personnel. No outside groups were allowed into military barracks and the opposition could not therefore conduct election campaigning there, while the APL was able to continue political education among the military. Another crucial problem for the opposition parties was access to the state-controlled mass media. During the campaign the opposition parties were able to secure only limited reporting of their mass meetings and other events while the APL and the communist-backed candidates enjoyed overwhelming use of state resources. This was particularly evident in the case of the state-controlled television which regularly presented extended coverage of APL rallies. Similarly, the communists and their allies had at their disposal the printed media while the six-page newspaper of the Democratic Party, *Rilindja Demokratike*, and the four-page paper of the Republican Party, *Republike*, were published twice-a-week in a print run of only 50,000.

Altogether 1,074 candidates contested 250 seats in the National People's Assembly (*see* Table 1). The first, and decisive, round of the elections was held on March 31, 1991. The election results reflected the high degree of polarization between urban residents and peasants (*see* Table 2). The APL won a two-thirds majority in the People's Assembly (*see* Table 3) by capturing almost all of the seats in the rural areas where over 70 per cent of the country's population live. This was largely due to the all-powerful communist machinery in the countryside, the traditionalism and conservatism of the rural constituency, and the nature of the social structures based on clan and family loyalty. On the other

Table 2: Election results — first round, March 31, 1991

	Villages	Small towns	Middle-sized towns	Cities
Number of constituencies	158	31	10	50
Registered voters	1,160,120	260,841	93,081	463,474
Percentage of registered voters	58.7	13.2	4.7	23.4
Number of constituencies with conclusive results	144	31	7	49
Seats won by Albanian Party of Labour	126	28	5	3
Percentage	87.5	90.3	71.4	6.1
Seats won by Democratic Party	14	3	2	46
Percentage	9.7	9.7	28.6	93.9
Seats won by OMONIA	3	—	—	—
Percentage	1	—	—	—
Seats won by Veterans' Committee	1	—	—	—
Percentage of voters for Albanian Party of Labour	64.9	67.8	49.9	33.6
Percentage of voters for Democratic Party	30.2	29.9	48.2	63.4

Source: *Bashkimi*, April 8, 1991.

hand, the Democratic Party received overwhelming support in the cities. Virtually all the main urban areas, and Tirana in particular, voted solidly for the DP. Several of the prominent functionaries of the APL,[17] including Ramiz Alia who stood in Tirana, were defeated.[18] The OMONIA organization, which presented its candidates in the Greek heartland in southern Albania, won each of the five constituencies there.

The elections are perhaps best described as free but not fair. The conduct of elections was observed by 117 foreign parliamentarians from 31 countries and although they agreed that there were no systematic abuses in the voting process, scattered electoral irregularities did occur, including ballots without official stamps, early opening of polling stations and

Table 3: 1991 parliamentary elections: Number of votes and seats

	Seats First round (March 31)	Seats Second round (April 7 and 14)	Total votes %	Total seats	Seats %
Albanian Party of Labour	162	7	56.17	169	7.3
Democratic Party	65	10	38.71	75	30.3
Republican Party	—	—	1.77	—	—
Ecology Party	—	—	0.03	—	—
Agrarian Party	—	—	0.07	—	—
OMONIA Organization	3	2	0.73	5	2.0
National Veterans' Committee	1	—	0.28	1	0.4
Total	231	19		250	100

Sources: *Bashkimi*, April 8, *Zeri i Popullit*, April 10, 16, 18, 1991.

voting by some unregistered people. Perhaps the most unusual departure from established democratic electoral practice was the appointment of Prof. Rexhep Mejdani as Chairman of the Central Electoral Commission when he was also a candidate of the Youth Union in Tirana.

The real political struggle, however, began only after the elections. During the next two months Albania witnessed a period of intense political competition which eventually led the communists to a fundamental re-thinking of their past and resulted in a power-sharing administration. Albania's first multi-party parliament in more than six decades met on April 19, 1991, but had to adjourn its first session after only 30 minutes because of a Democratic Party boycott in protest of the government's failure to investigate the killings of its supporters in Shkoder on April 2. A compromise was eventually reached when the DP deputies were assigned seats on the Credential Commission and on a Commission created to investigate the Shkoder incidents. On April 30 the assembly adopted an interim constitution and elected Ramiz Alia as the President of the Republic. The Democratic Party declined to present a candidate for the presidency and voted against Alia. He succeeded by the combined votes of the APL and OMONIA MPs. Alia was subsequently released from his post of First Secretary of the Central Committee of the APL.

At the beginning of May the country slowly began to be paralysed by labour unrest. On May 3 the miners of the chrome mines Bater and Kraste in Mat district went on strike demanding an improvement in working and living conditions. The government responded by meeting some of their demands, increased the number of buses and sent more food, while others were to be fulfilled within an agreed timetable, but during the next few days the unrest among miners spread to the mines in Bulqize in Diber district. About 1,000 miners of Valias mine decided to join the Independent Miners' Union. In response to the fast deteriorating situation, the Prime Minister, Fatos Nano, during separate meetings on May 7 with representatives of all the political parties discussed the possibilities of forming a government of national unity consisting of experts. Apart from the APL, the Ecological and Social Democratic parties, all the others refused Nano's suggestion.[19]

In the middle of May the miners' strike escalated into a general strike in Durrës, Shkoder, Tirana and Kavaje involving 250,000 people. The crisis deepened when on May 25 a group of miners in the Valias mine went on hunger strike. They were later joint by hunger strikers in other cities. By the beginning of June the strike movement grew to 350,000, half of the country's workforce. By now it had become obvious that the legitimacy of the reforming communist regime was in fact beyond repair. The six months of attempts to revamp it since December 1990 had in fact led to its further erosion.

Left with little if any authority, the leadership of the APL had no option but to search for a genuine political solution. The grounds for such were laid by deputies of the Democratic Party and the OMONIA organization during a debate in the People's Assembly on June 1, when they proposed the creation of a new government "with the participation of all political forces". This government would have a "temporary mandate" until the holding of a general election at an early date.

After lengthy consultations the leaders of the APL, Democratic Party, Republican Party, Social Democratic Party, the OMONIA organization and the Independent Trade Union Federation formulated on June 3 a six-point agreement aimed to resolve, albeit temporarily, the most acute crisis in the country's post-war history. The parties agreed that the government should resign and a new prime minister nominated by the APL should form a government consisting of persons detached from political parties, and that new elections should be held in May–June 1992. The Independent Trade Union Federation agreed not to stage strikes during the tenure of the new government.[20]

The Nano government resigned during the night of the 3 to 4 June. It was replaced on June 11 by "the government of personalities", proposed by the new Prime Minister, Ylli Bufi. It consisted of representatives "known for their technical abilities", of five political parties to which 21 ministerial posts and three posts of secretaries of state at ministerial level were allocated under a somewhat complex arrangement by which the affiliation with respective parties was identified not only in terms of an actual membership but also in terms of nomination for the post. Thus the government included 15 members (including the three secretaries of state) from four political parties and nine non-party members proposed by five parties. The Albanian Party of Labour received seven portfolios. In addition to the post of Prime Minister, it controlled six ministries: Foreign Affairs, Mineral Resources and Energy, Agriculture, Foreign Economic Relations, Education and Health. The Democratic Party was allocated the posts of one Deputy Prime Minister — who was also the Minister of the Economy, and the ministries of Finance, Domestic Trade and Tourism, Construction, and Culture Youth and Sports. The Agrarian Party received the post of Secretary of State for Agriculture. Among the nine ministerial posts allocated to non-party members four were proposed by the APL, two by the DP (including the Ministry of Defence), one (Ministry of Justice) by the Social Democratic Party, and one (Ministry of Transport) by the Republican Party.[21] The striking fact was that the APL controlled some of the most important portfolios concerned with foreign relations, public order, agriculture, energy, food and education while the DP was responsible for almost all ministries concerned with economic matters and youth affairs — areas entirely mismanaged by the communists in the past and requiring a complete turn-around in terms of policies and gigantic efforts to put the economy on its feet.

The 10th Congress of the APL, held on June 10–13, 1991, marked a radical departure from past practice. The main report of the APL Central Committee for the first time acknowledged the disastrous state of affairs in the country. It attacked some of the cornerstones of the past policies of the Albanian regime under Enver Hoxha: "The model we chose opened up the road to a centralized, administrative and commanding bureaucratic policy in all fields of life. These ran contrary to the objective laws of social development, especially the economic one, and the democratic tendency of the socialist ideal itself. The concept that social ownership eliminated the exploitation of man by man, led to an excessive ideologization in the policy of nationalization. Alongside the banks, enterprises, the estates of the big feudal lords, small private activities which in fact did not violate anybody's interests, were nationalized."

Referring to the very essence of Hoxha's economic doctrine of self-reliance the report acknowledged, for the first time, its absurdity. "The self-enclosed system of economic relations did serious harm, especially from the end of the seventies onward. The principle of relying on our own resources . . . was quite unjustified . . . Closing off the economy did not harm the world, but harmed Albania." Class struggle, the cardinal precept of Marxism-Leninism "had significant negative consequences". "The aim was to strengthen the unity of the people through the class struggle, but the result was an accumulation of silent fury and rage among different strata of the people against the party." The Congress defined the main points of the party's policies: political pluralism, support for agricultural co-operatives, "property pluralism" but with state control of land and natural resources, and help for the Albanians in Kosovo.

To mark the APL's final departure from its Stalinist past, the Congress also decided to change the party's name to the Socialist Party of Albania — ASP,[22] and alter its leadership structure by creating a Steering Committee in place of the Central Committee and a Presidency of the Managing Committee, headed by a chairman, instead of a Political Bureau. Fatos Nano, known for his reformist views, was elected chairman of the Presidency.

The Bufi National Stability Government survived with considerable difficulties until December 1991. On Dec. 6, the chairman of the Democratic Party, Sali Berisha, announced during a press conference that the DP was withdrawing its representatives from the government. He blamed the Socialists for the lack of progress in tackling the country's enormous economic and social problems and for unwillingness to co-operate with other groups in the search for a solution. Significantly Berisha made his announcement to withdraw when the deputy chairman of the party, Dr Gramoz Pashko, was on an official visit to London. Pashko was opposed to such a move on the grounds that the departure of DP representatives from the administration would lead to its collapse and plunge the country into even deeper anarchy and chaos. Pashko's view proved to be right.

Berisha's action marked the beginning of a split in the DP ranks which subsequently led to the expulsion of many of its prominent members, including Gramoz Pashko, and the formation of the Albanian Democratic Alliance Party. Amidst all the chaos and political turmoil that followed the withdrawal of the seven DP ministers from the National Stability Government, Ylli Bufi resigned and a caretaker administration was appointed under the premiership of the former Minister of Food, Vilson Ahmeti. His government continued until the general elections in March 1992.

The date of the elections had been postponed several times because the People's Assembly could not agree on the text of the Electoral Law for several months. It was finally approved by the parliament on Feb. 4, 1992.

The election campaign was dominated by the problems of the fast-disintegrating economy and an almost complete breakdown in law and order. In the spring of 1992 Albania had

Table 4: 1992 Parliamentary Elections: Number of Candidates and Party Affiliation

Socialist Party	100
Democratic Party	97*
Social Democratic Party	97**
Republican Party	94
Agrarian Party	46
Communist Party	31
Human Rights Union	29
Christian Democratic Party	11
Ecology Party	7
Independent candidates	5
Popular Alliance	3
Universal Party	1
Total	521

Source: Author's calculation from various issues of *Zeri i Popullit, Rilindja Demokratike* and ATA Bulletins.

*In four constituencies the Democratic Party presented joint candidates with the Green Party.

**In one constituency the Social Democratic Party, Republican Party and Democratic Party presented a joint candidate.

registered an inflation rate of 260 per cent a month. Some 70 per cent of the workforce was idle, but by government decree continued to collect 80 per cent of their salaries. The issue of Albanians living outside the borders of the country attracted particular attention. The chairman of the Democratic Party, Sali Berisha, explained that the party guaranteed "our brothers living in their territories in the former Yugoslavia and wherever they are that the DP will not stop fighting until her great dream of uniting the Albanian nation comes true".[23] The DP even proposed to "strive for dual nationality for all those with Albanian blood, wherever they are".[24] As in the 1991 elections the problems of the rural population figured prominently in the election campaign. In particular the question of land distribution to the peasants and compensation for previously confiscated land, and future taxation for individual farmers proved to be the most difficult. The Socialist Party accused the Democratic Party of wanting to bring back the landlords and impose taxes on peasants who had recently acquired land. The DP denied these accusations stressing that the old title deeds were invalid and that the landowners would be compensated in cash. It also promised not to levy taxes for at least two or three years and provide help with tractors and machinery. Organized emigration was also put forward as another way of helping the densely populated countryside. The DP proposed to ask Western countries to give priority to accept Albanian immigrants for at least five or 10 years in order to alleviate unemployment in the country.

In all 11 parties and five independent candidates — total 521 candidates — were registered with the Central Electoral Commission (*see* Table 4). The Electoral Law which banned the formation of parties on "ethnic principles" prevented the participation in the election of Albania's biggest minority organization, the Democratic Union of Greek Minority

Table 5   1992 Parliamentary Election Results — first round, March 22, 1992

Party	Votes	%	Deputies
Democratic Party	1,046,193	62.8	79
Socialist Party	433,602	25.73	6
Social Democratic Party	73,820	4.38	1
Republican Party	52,471	3.11	1
Human Rights Union Party	48,923	2.90	2
Agrarian Party	10,648	0.63	—
Communist Party	8,264	0.49	—
Christian Democratic Party	5,906	0.35	—
Independent candidates	3,976	0.24	—
Ecology Party	823	0.04	—
Popular Alliance	284	0.01	—
Universal Party	121	0.00	—

Source: Communiqué from the Central Electoral Commission, March 26, 1992.

(OMONIA). Another minority organization unable officially to take part in the election was Prespa, representing the Macedonian community. However, both groups put forward their candidates on the list of the Human Rights Union Party.

During the first round of voting, held on March 22, 1,826,142 of the 2,021,169 registered voters (90.35 per cent) cast their votes. The results (*see* Table 5) were a clear victory for the Democratic Party which received almost three times as many votes as the Socialist Party, capturing virtually all the seats in major towns and cities as well as the rural constituencies in the northern part of the country. Only 18 of the DP's 97 candidates failed to win outright during the first round. The Socialist Party, which had proposed candidates in 100 constituencies, won only six in the south, the traditional power base of the communists (two in Fier, one in Kucove, two in Skrapar and one in Berat).

The smaller parties received little backing from the electorate. The Social Democratic Party, which had submitted 97 candidates, gained only one seat in the industrial city of Elbasan. Similarly, of the 95 candidates proposed by the Republican Party only one was elected in Elbasan district.

Perhaps the most unexpected result was the decline in popular support for the Human Rights Union Party which had been expected to build on the ethnic Greek and Macedonian vote. It succeeded in winning only two constituencies, Sarande and Gjirokastër, out of the 29 in which it had submitted candidates. Both constituencies are in the south of the country and have a high percentage of the ethnic minority population.

Of the 140 deputies, 100 were elected directly under the first-past-the-post system and the remaining 40 on the basis of proportional representation. Parliamentary seats were distributed proportionally to every party that had won more than 4 per cent of the votes, on the basis of the percentages of votes won nationwide during the first round. The votes gained by parties that did not achieve the 4 per cent threshold were distributed proportionately to those parties gaining more that 4 per cent. The DP, ASP and SDP thus gained the votes of

Table 6: 1992 Parliamentary Elections: Final election results — number of seats won

Party	Directly elected seats		Seats from proportional representation list	Total
	I round	II round		
Democratic Party	79	11	2	92
Socialist Party	6	—	32	38
Social Democratic Party	1	—	6	7
Human Rights Union Party	2	—	—	2
Republican Party	1	—	—	1
TOTAL				140

Source: Communiqué from the Central Electoral Commission, March 26 and 31, 1992.

Table 7: 1992 Parliamentary Elections: Final election results — percentage of votes and seats

Party	% of votes	% of Assembly seats
Democratic Party	62.08	65.71
Socialist Party	25.70	27.14
Social Democratic Party	4.30	5.00
Human Rights Union Party	2.90	1.43
Republican Party	3.11	0.71

Source: Communiqué from the Central Electoral Commission, March 26 and 31, 1992.

other parties that did not succeed in winning seats under proportional representation (*see* Tables 6 and 7).

However, despite its victory the Democratic Party failed to attain the two-thirds majority in parliament that would allow the clear passage of controversial legislation, including the new constitution. Since 1992 it has therefore had to rely on the support of smaller parties of the anti-communist coalition. At the same time the Socialists, with their presence reduced to less than a third of the chamber, have been a noisy but rather ineffective opposition. Their fast evaporating credibility was further undermined by the revelations from the trials of the former communist leadership that took place in 1993.

Much of the success of the Democratic Party and the other former opposition parties was due to growing political maturity and the increasing democratic experience of the Albanian electorate. But equally important was the fact that the democratic parties have vastly improved their organization and expertise with the electoral process, compared with 1991.

The DP has understandably claimed that its victory at the polls meant the final end for communism in Albania. However, despite the euphoria there were substantial doubts whether the party would be able to preserve its organizational cohesion, keep its electoral promises and thereby preserve its credibility with the electorate. Berisha's calls for the unification of all the Albanians living across the borders in neighbouring states and for the granting of dual nationality for all those with Albanian blood, appealed to many voters' nationalist feelings but alarmed both moderate Democrats and many foreign governments. The poor showing of the smaller parties appears to be largely due to the high degree of polarization of the electorate and the assumption that the defeat of communism could only be achieved by voting for the large Democratic Party.

President Ramiz Alia resigned on Apr. 3, 1992, and on Apr. 9 the parliament elected Sali Berisha to be his replacement. In the new government, led by Aleksander Meksi, the Democratic Party, in addition to the post of Prime Minister, held 14 portfolios. The SDP and the Republican Party received one portfolio each while two independent technocrats were appointed to head the ministries of Industry and Justice.

The new government, faced with mounting problems of falling industrial and agricultural production, a high level of unemployment the breakdown of state authority, responded very cautiously. In the July 1992 local elections the percentage of voters' support for the Democratic Party fell to 43.25 per cent while the Socialist Party's share of the vote increased to 40.91 per cent (see Table 8). The increased popularity of the Socialists not only reflected the degree of control that they still had at the local level but also how quickly a volatile and highly politicized electorate can change its preferences.

The administration's difficulties were compounded by the boycott of parliament by the deputies of the Social Democratic Party in June 1993 in protest at the delay in adopting a new constitution. They were joined by the Socialists and members of the Union for Human Rights Party. However, the government withstood what appeared to be an attempt to force a new general election and the boycott ended at the end of August.

The long-awaited new constitution is still in preparation despite the fact that a special commission comprised of representatives of all political parties and chaired by the Prime Minister has been working on the document since 1992. The slow process of change, and in particularly the lack of progress over the constitution, has met with increasing criticism from the Social Democratic and Republican parties, the DP's coalition partners. Despite almost insurmountable difficulties and severe criticisms from within its ranks, as well as from its opponents, the Democratic Party government has continued its slow programme of the de-communization of Albanian social, political and economic structures and steering the country towards liberal-democratic values and a market economy. Dismantling the communist structures may prove to be the easy bit for Albania's new rulers. Coping with the mess they left behind will prove to be much harder than the Democratic Party has been prepared to admit thus far.

Table 8: Results of Local Elections, July 24, 1992

Party	Municipal Councils		District Councils		Commune Councils		% of votes	Mayors of Municipalities	Chairmen of Communes
	% of votes	seats	% of votes	seats	% of votes	seats			
Democratic Party	43.25	266	41.24	363	38.95	1357	35.76	18	113
Socialist Party	40.91	281	43.57	417	44.74	1774	46.75	23	177
Social Democratic Party	4.36	31	4.81	42	4.51	233	6.14		2
Republican Party	3.42	25	3.88	32	3.43	169	4.45		1
Human Rights Union Party	4.30	32	4.96	53	5.69	159	4.19	1	13
Party of National Unity		5	0.78	8	0.86	25	0.66		3
Christian Democratic Party		3	0.47	7	0.75	26	0.69		
Agrarian Party		1	0.16	5	0.54	26	0.69		
Ecology Party						3	0.03		
Democratic Union		1	0.16	5	0.54	23	0.61		1
Independent candidates									4
TOTAL	100	645	100	932	100	3795	100	42	314

Source: Author's calculations from ATA Bulletins, July 27 and Aug. 13, 1992.

13

Directory of Parties

Albanian Agrarian Party (AAP)
Partie Agrar Shqipërisë

Address. Rruga Budi 6, Tirana.

Telephone. (355) 42 27481.

Foundation. February 1991.

Leadership. Prof. Lufter Xhuveli (pres.)

Membership. 20,000 (est.)

History. The party was founded in 1991 in the run-up to the first multi-parliamentary elections. Despite the fact that an overwhelming majority of the Albanian population live in the countryside the party has only managed to attract limited support from the rural population. This is probably as much due to the strong conservatism of the peasants who still remain the major power base for the former communists, as it is due to the miniscule resources at the party's disposal.

Programme. The AAP proposes a comprehensive programme for the rescuing of Albania's agricultural sector and the peasant population devasted by over four decades of collectivization. It demands new laws to regulate the privatization of former collectivized property and land; the setting up of credit arrangements for farmers; the establishment of the right to form new and voluntary arrangements, including co-operatives; and a concerted effort to create new jobs for the large percentage of unemployed, particularly youth, in the countryside.

Albanian Communist Party
Partia Komuniste Shqiptare

Foundation. December 1991, outlawed June 1992.

Membership. Several thousands.

History. The party was formed by hardline communists opposed to the policies of the reformed Albanian Socialist Party. It produced a political platform for the 1992 parliamentary elections. In the summer of 1992 the Albanian parliament imposed a ban on the activities of the Albanian Communist Party and on the formation of similar organizations in the future.

Programme. The party's programme issued at the time of the 1992 parliamentary elections warned of "danger on the doorstep" as a result of the "counter-revolution taking place in the country". It appealed to the electorate to follow the "teachings and instructions of the genius, Enver Hoxha, who contributed to the freedom, independence and sovereignty of the homeland as nobody before in the history of this nation. The betrayal of Enver Hoxha does not in any way mean that Albania is finished". Clearly trying to mobilize nationalist appeal, the Communist Party expressed "support for the Republic of Kosovo and the territorial autonomy of Albanians in Macedonia, Montenegro and South Serbia, with the prospect of uniting all these territories in a single national state, as well as support for the legitimate human and national rights of the Albanians violently expelled from, or living under discrimination in, their territories in Cameria".

Albanian Democratic Alliance Party (ADAP)
Aleanca Demokratike

Address. Rruga Msylym Shyri, Pallati 40 Shkalla 1 Ap. 1, Tirana.

Telephone. (355) 42 424 68; 42 320 10; 42 331 03.

Foundation. July 1992.

Leadership. Neritan Çeka (pres.)

Membership. 20,000.

History. The party was founded as a result of a split with the Albanian Democratic Party (DP). Following Sali Berisha's announcement on Dec. 6, 1991, that the DP was withdrawing from the Ylli Bufi government — an announcement made against the view of the party's deputy chairman, Gramoz Pashko — the DP parliamentary leader, Neritan Çeka, left the party. He was supported by six other members of parliament: Pashko; Perikli Teta, former Minister of Defence; Arben Imami, former Secretary-General of the DP; Ridvan Peshkepia, Teodor Keko and Afrim Jupi. All were formally expelled from the DP in July 1992. The ADPA members of parliament are not recognized as a separate parliamentary caucus but as a group of independents.

In October 1993 the party leadership paid a controversial visit to Belgrade aimed at opening dialogue during which they held talks with Serbian government officials. The visit was sharply criticized by the DP on the grounds that "their mission gives world-isolated Milošević an argument to claim he is talking with Albanians".

Programme. The ADAP programme is not dissimilar to that of the DP. The party is critical of what it calls authoritarian tendencies within the Democratic Party's leadership. It advocates a faster pace for reforms and their widening in scope. It opposed Albania joining the Islamic Conference Organization.

Albanian Democratic Party (DP)
Partia Demokratike e Shqipërisë

Address. Rruga Konferenca e Perez, Tirana.

Telephone. (355) 42 235 25.

Fax. (355) 42 284 63.

Foundation. December 1990.

Leadership. Eduard Selami (ch.); Ali Spahia (dep. ch.); Tomor Dosti (s. g.)

Membership. 105,000.

History. Originally part of a dissident intelligentsia group largely made up of disillusioned ex-communists, the founders of the DP followed the example of their unofficial leader, Ismail Kadare.[26] A well-known Albanian writer and at that time Secretary of the Albanian Academy of Sciences, during 1989–90 Kadare used the institutions of Albanian Party of Labour to undermine the APL from within. In March 1990 *Zëri i Rinsë* (Voice of the Youth), the organ of the Union of Labour Youth of Albania, published an outspoken and extremely influential interview with Kadare who openly called for the overthrow of the APL regime. This is now generally taken to mark the beginning of the revolt of the intellectuals in Albania. In May 1990 *Drita*, the weekly newspaper of the Union of Albanian Writers and Artists of the Albanian Academy of Sciences, a pro-Kadare stronghold, published Sali Berisha's first major interview, significantly entitled "The Intellectual Faces the Tasks of the Times". In it Berisha called for an autonomous and intellectually honest intelligentsia, whose major social role at that time was to act as an embryonic opposition movement in a country destroyed by communist totalitarianism.

The movement was led by Kadare until his defection to France in October 1990, and depended on the country's radicalized university and high school students to use mass street politics to force the APL regime to make major concessions.

The Democratic Party of Albania was founded on Dec. 12, 1990, immediately after the mass student demonstrations in Tirana, and only a day after the APL Central Committee pronounced on the legislation of independent political groups. It was launched by a group of intellectuals and students at Tirana University which included Dr Sali Berisha, a cardiologist; Dr Gramoz Pashko, an economist; Azem Hajdari, a student activist; Dr Eduard Selami, a professor of the philosophy of aesthetics; and Arben Imami, a professor of drama. It was the first opposition party to be registered on Dec. 17.

With little financial and material resources the DP struggled to build up its membership and infrastructure. In February 1991 it claimed a membership of 60,000. By the time of the first parliamentary elections in March 1991, barely three months after its foundation, the DP had managed to establish branches in both the northern (Gegs area) and southern (Tosk area) parts of the country thus becoming a genuinely national party.

In the first multi-party elections the DP won 75 seats in the People's Assembly (*see* Table 3). However, a year later, during the second parliamentary elections it increased its representation to 92 (*see* Table 5) and became the main party in the first post-war non-communist government.

At the end of 1991 policy differences over its continued participation in the Bufi National Stability Government marked the beginning of a split in the DP ranks that subsequently led to the expulsion of many of its prominent members, including Gramoz Pashko, and the formation of the Albanian Democratic Alliance Party in July 1992. Another split occurred in August 1993 when two prominent members of a right-wing faction, known as *Balli Kombëter*, were dismissed from the party. This led in March 1994 to the formation of the Democratic Party of the Right.

Programme. The party has pledged to "fight for the accomplishment of the century-long hopes and dreams: the realization of democracy based on human rights and fundamental freedoms, prosperity through economic freedom and social justice, and the unification of our nation with the new historic developments that will take place in Europe". The programme denounces as wholly anti-democratic, anti-national and anti-human the Enverist pattern of Stalinism and promises the eradication from Albanian society of the premises that led to the establishment of this "savage dictatorship". "The DP aims to have democracy in Albania established on the basis of the United Nations Universal Declaration of Human Rights, the latest Helsinki agreement, the latest document of Copenhagen, the Paris Charter and the CSCE accords." It recognizes "as righteous and legitimate the returning of private property to the expropriated, or providing compensation for property that was unjustly confiscated by the communist regime, as far as possible". The DP's foreign policy is based on the "internationalization of the all-Albanian question". In foreign policy the DP aims at "observing all the international obligations to integrate Albania in the new epoch of democracy, peace and unity". It considers it a basic condition for its solution the relations with the USA and with the democratic countries of Western Europe. It plans "to work towards creating the conditions that would enable Albania eventually to join the European Community".

Organization. According to the party's statutes, at the top of its hierarchy is the National Conference comprising of 600 delegates elected at bi-annual intervals. It meets once or twice a year. The National Council consists of 107 members. It comprises chairmen of party branches and about half of its total number is directly elected for two years by secret ballot by delegates to the National Conference. The Council, which meets four times a year, is headed by a chairman. The executive body of the party is the Steering Committee consisting of 19 members elected for a two-year period.

Albanian Ecological Party
Partia Ekologjike

Telephone. (355) 42 34413.

Foundation. Jan. 1, 1991.

Leadership. Namik Hoti (pres.)

Membership. Between 1,500 and 2,000.

Albanian Green Party
Partia e Blerte Shqiptare

Leadership. Nasi Bozhegu (ch.).

Membership. 3,000.

Albanian Liberal Party
Partia Libetarle Shqiptare

Foundation. Oct. 1, 1991.

Leadership. Valter File (pres.)

History. The Liberal Party declined to put forward candidates during the 1992 parliamentary elections because of the lack of financial resources. It also claimed that "anti-democratic Electoral Law" had placed "insurmountable obstacles" on its activity. Its supporters were advised to vote for the Democratic Party.

Albanian National Democratic Party
Partia Nacional Demokrate Shqipërisë

Telephone. (355) 42 34446.

Foundation. 1991.

Leadership. Fatmir Çekani.

History. The party did not participate in the 1992 parliamentary elections.

Albanian National Unity Party (ANUP)
Partia Bashkimi Kombëtare Shqipërisë

Leadership. Idajet Beqiri (ch.)

History. The National Unity Party is an extreme pan-Albanian nationalist organization which also operates in Kosovo. It did not take part in the 1992 parliamentary and local elections, claiming that the electoral law was "anti-democratic". It also asserted that the state did not create "even the most minimal conditions for the normal development of the election campaign". More specifically, the ANUP complained that it received no financial support, that its postal service was affected because of the "indifference of postal workers", and that it was unable to print its newspaper and election material because of the shortage of newsprint.

The party's leader, Idajet Beqiri, was sentenced on July 12, 1993, to six months' imprisonment for insulting and slandering President Sali Berisha by suggesting that Berisha was installing a fascist dictatorship in Albania.

Programme. Re-unification of lands inhabited by Albanians.

Albanian Republican Party (ARP)
Partia Republikana Shqipërisë

Address. Bulevardi Deshmoret e Kombit, Tirana.

Telephone. (355) 42 325 11.

Fax. (355) 42 283 61.

Foundation. Jan. 10, 1991.

Leadership. Sabri Godo (ch.); Fatmir Mediu (vice-ch.); Çerçiz Mingomataj (s. g.)

Membership. 10,000 (est.)

History. The ARP is one of the minor opposition parties that emerged in the upsurge of mass political activity during 1991. Until 1992 the Republicans appeared to have adopted a rather cautious role of wait-and-see to events. After the 1992 parliamentary elections, in which they won one seat, the party joined the Democratic Party dominated government with one minister (Transport) and two deputy ministers. The RP held its first congress in June 1992 during which major divisions within the party emerged. These subsequently led to splits and the creation of two parties: the Right-Wing Republican Party and the Party of Republican Alliance.

Programme. "Land will belong to those who work it." The party proposes rebuilding the countryside with credits, without levying taxes on the peasants for two or three years. In the meantime, legal emigration, communication and employment through infrastructure, tourism and the development of natural resources must be ensured. It supports rapid privatization with less interference from the state.

Organization. A National Council elects the Steering Committee which is headed by chairman, deputy chairman and secretary-general. Until 1992 the party was largely urban-based with branches in many major towns, including Durrës, Burrel, Berat and Gjirokastër. It claims that subsequently it has also built a rural following with branches in 60 per cent of the villages. The party's main power base is the Tosk area in the south of the country.

Albanian Socialist Party (ASP)
Partia Socialiste Shqipërisë
formerly Albanian Party of Labour (APL) Partia ë Punës e Shqipërisë.

Address. Bulevardi Deshmoret e Kombit, Tirana.

Telephone. (355) 42 23408.

Fax. (355) 42 27417.

Foundation. Nov. 8, 1941, as Albanian Communist Party, renamed Party of Labour of Albania in September 1948, adopted present name in June 1991.

Leadership. Fatos Nano (ch. of the presidency). Namik Dokle (dep. ch.); Servet Pellumbi (dep. ch.); Illr Meta (dep. ch.).

Membership. 100,000–110,000 (ste.).

Organization. Managing Committee of 81 members, headed by a presidency of 15 members. Despite his arrest and sentencing to 12 years' imprisonment, Fatos Nano remains the chairman of the party's presidency.

History. The Albanian Communist Party (ACP) was founded on Nov. 8, 1941, when two agents of the Yugoslav Communist Party (YCP), acting on instructions from Belgrade, convened a meeting of 20 delegates which elected the party's Central Committee headed by a former school teacher, Enver Hoxha. The party, which was in fact no more than an offshoot of the YCP, until 1948 operated under the "guidance" of Josip Broz Tito. Like its Yugoslav counterparts, the Albanian communists dominated the nationalist movement. The Anti-Fascist National Liberation Council, under their control, in October 1944 transformed itself into the Provisional Democratic Government of Albania, with Enver Hoxha as its Prime Minister. After the liberation elections took place in December 1945 in which only candidates of the communist-dominated Democratic Front were allowed to stand. The newly elected Constituent Assembly formally abolished the monarchy and on Jan. 11, 1946, proclaimed Albania a People's Republic and promulgated its first constitution modelled on Stalin's constitution of 1936. The Albanian Communist Party was renamed the Albanian Party of Labour in September 1948 and purged of Yugoslav supporters.

Following the Soviet–Yugoslav split in June 1948, the APL became dominated by the Communist Party of the Soviet Union (CPSU) and followed religiously the Soviet pattern of development. The relations between the two parties prospered until the 20th Congress of the CPSU in February 1956. The strong denunciation of Stalin and Stalinism at the Congress disturbed the Albanian leadership and Enver Hoxha who supported both vigorously. During the closing session of the congress the Soviet Party leader, Nikita Khrushchev, attacked the Albanian leadership for despotism and misuse of power and called on the Albanian people to overthrow it.

The APL then began to consolidate its ties with the Chinese Communist Party (CCP), which also opposed de-Stalinization. From 1961 to 1977 the APL copied the Chinese model. In 1966 Enver Hoxha initiated the Albanian Cultural Revolution aiming to "preserve Marxist-Leninist purity in all aspects of Albanian life". This, according to Hoxha, included elimination of all traces of religion, the emancipation of women and the eradication of undesirable foreign influences such as long hair, lack of respect for authority, and modern styles in clothing. The special relationship with CCP came to end after the reconciliation between China and the United States, the downfall of the Gang of Four and rehabilitation of Deng Xiaoping. In 1978 China announced the ending, with immediate effect, of all aid and all civilian and military credits to Albania and the withdrawal of all Chinese specialists.

With the ending of the Chinese phase the APL became isolated. Hoxha, who regarded himself as the only true Marxist-Leninist in the world, embarked on a policy of self-reliance. His ideologically inspired fantasies reduced to country to ruin. Hoxha died in 1985 and the APL and country's leadership was taken over by his chosen successor, Ramiz Alia. Alia wanted to preserve the essential elements, if not the violent excesses, of the rigid Stalinist system. The initial changes he made in 1990 were clearly forced upon him by the dismantling of communism throughout Eastern Europe and the disastrous state of the country's economy. Alia's attempts at controlled change led quickly to social and political explosion beyond the APL's control.

Perhaps one of the most difficult and decisive points in the history of the APL was its 10th Congress held on June 11–13, 1991. The Congress approved the main points of the party's policies: political pluralism, support for agricultural co-operatives, "property pluralism" but with state control of land and natural resources, and help for the Albanians in Kosovo. At the same time, the report of the Central Committee marked a radical departure from the past practice of self-congratulatory sycophantic speeches delivered at previous party congresses by making a critical assessment of the current political and economic situation of the country and even more importantly by apportioning blame for the state of affairs. It attacked some of the cornerstones of the past policies of the Albanian regime under Enver Hoxha and blamed the former leader personally.

Referring to the very essence of Hoxha's economic doctrine of self-reliance the report acknowledged, for the first time, its absurdity. "The self-enclosed system of economic relations did serious harm, especially from the end of the seventies onward. The principle of relying on our own resources ... was quite unjustified ... Closing off the economy did not harm the world, but harmed Albania."

In responding in some way to the demands of the opposition for an account of who was responsible for Albania's dismal state of affairs, the report embarked on an unprecedented criticism of Hoxha himself. "His merits are indisputable but the question posed today is whether Enver Hoxha, the party's founder and leader, had any direct or indirect responsibility for all the baggage of the party's shortcomings and mistakes . . . The weight of his comments led to the deformation of democracy within and outside the party. The cult of orders, instructions and commands from above grew. The spirit of command replaced the spirit of discussion."

The Central Committee report also criticized Ramiz Alia, present at the congress, for his "sentimental stand towards some of his close companions and collaborators, who were part of the senior party and state leadership". However, the most direct responsibility for the grave situation of the country was levelled at a group of Politburo members, "figures stained with privileges and unmerited profits" who "combined old age with incompetence".

The issue of Enver Hoxha's role and his responsibility for the catastrophic situation in the country displayed the deep divisions within the party and resistance to reforms. Not only was the Central Committee' report received in stony silence, but when one delegate from Tirana criticized "the violation of human rights and the cult of Enver Hoxha", his speech led to uproar. "Whispering began in the hall and crescendoed into noise that prevented the speaker from continuing. An elderly delegate rose to his feet and shouted: "Albanian Party of Labour". At this delegate's signal many others stood up, shouting: "Albanian Party of Labour", "Enver, we are always ready". The chairman intervened to calm the hall."[27]

In an unprecedented display of self-criticism (in Albanian communist history), and in the new spirit of openness President Ramiz Alia also admitted that "the party and mainly its leadership are responsible for the economic, spiritual crisis and the crisis of confidence".[28] He confessed that, "the violation of human rights, in the name of the class struggle, the slogans on the manifold imperialist-revisionist blockade and encirclement, the enlargement of the circles of enemies based on family ties, at a time when we talked of unity in ideo-political homogeneity etc., are mistakes of grave consequences". He acknowledged the degree of privileges enjoyed by the ruling élite. These "unjust acts" involved "medical treatment abroad" for "leaders and some other cadres, as well as of their children", and the existence of special residential quarter of plush residences in the middle of Tirana, separated by a wall from the rest of the city. "For the excesses and abuses", said Alia, "I have my responsibility. I only have made criticism in the meetings of the Political Bureau but I did not take measures to put an end to these acts". He advised that "the party must get used to pluralism. There can be no more talk of its absolute influence on the masses. The APL is one of the alternative parties in society. The people are encouraged, but not obliged, to support it. Let the party realize where it has its support". To mark the ALP's final parting from its Stalinist past, the Congress also decided to change the party's name to the Socialist Party of Albania, and alter its leadership structure.

After the congress the criticism of Enver Hoxha intensified further and prompted his widow to write a letter to the party's daily *Zeri i Popullit*. In the letter she claimed that neither Hoxha nor his family enjoyed any special privileges and that they lived a simple life. Nehmije Hoxha's intervention was an attempt to rally some of the party's faithful behind the hardliners. Within a few days, however, *Zeri i Popullit* contradicted her claims by publishing an article describing the lavish style, certainly by Albanian standards, of the Hoxha household. It included 25 refrigerators, 28 colour televisions and 19 telephone lines.[29]

The APL won the first multi-party parliamentary elections in 1991 with 169 of the 250 seats in the People's Assembly (*see* Table 3). It finally lost power after the 1992 elections and became the main opposition party in the parliament. During 1993 and 1994 the APL was shaken by a series of arrests and trials of former members of the communist establishment. In July 1993, the chairman of the presidency, Fatos Nano, was arrested and charged with corruption during his term as Prime Minister from April to June 1991. His parliamentary immunity was withdrawn the following month. Nano, who is alleged to have appropriated US$8 million, has repeatedly declared his innocence. The Socialists alleged that the arrest and subsequent trial were politically motivated by the DP. In protest Socialist Party MPs boycotted parliament for two months (July–August 1993). After Nano's arrest a mass rally attended by some 20,000 people was held in Tirana demanding new elections. He was convicted on Apr. 3, 1994, of misappropriating state funds, of dereliction of duty and of falsifying official documents, and sentenced to 12 years' imprisonment. No evidence that Nano benefited directly from the alleged fraud was offered in court. His imprisonment may have negative consequences for political stability in Albania. He apparently enjoys wide support among the Albanian public and particularly within his party. In September 1993 when Nano was still awaiting trial, a petition was organized for his release, apparently signed by 700,000 people, and submitted to the Ministry of Justice.

During 1993 several former high-ranking party officials were arrested, including the former president Ramiz Alia, former prime minister Adil Carcani, his deputy Manush Myftiu and the majority of the members of the former APL Politburo (Foto Cami, Besnik Bekteshi, Vangejl Cerrava and Pali Miska). They were all charged with violation of citizens' rights while in office and in July 1994 sentenced to several years of imprisonment.

Programme. The party is committed to the defence of democracy, freedoms and human rights and a fight for a new democratic constitution for Albania. The ASP pledges itself to radical reform of the economy, for its transition into a market economy with social provisions. It supports "an economy open to the world, naturally integrated and capable of co-operating with and rivalling it". Economic and social progress of Albania is impossible without its integration into Europe. The country's interests demand the *rapprochement* of Albania towards European structures, the Council of Europe, the European Parliament, and the European Union. The ASP is also committed to the active development of relations with the USA.

Christian Democratic Party
Partia Demokristiane

Telephone. (355) 42 24615.

Foundation. Oct. 10, 1991.

Leadership. Gjergj Ndoja (pres.)

Democratic Party of the Right
Partia Demokratike e Djathte

Foundation. March 1994.

Leadership. Abdi Baleta and Petrit Kalakula (ch.)

History. The party emerged as a result of a split within the Democratic Party when two prominent members of a right-wing faction, known as *Balli Kombëter*, Abdi Baleta and

Petrit Kalakula, left the DP. On Aug. 15, 1993, Kalakula was dismissed as Minister of Agriculture and Food (after barely five months in the cabinet) after making an allegedly pro-fascist statement in the Albanian parliament. Initially, the Ministry of Justice refused to register the party on the grounds that its programme advocated the return of the former landowners. However, the Supreme Court ruled at the beginning of 1994 that the party's programme did not contradict the law.

Programme. The complete return of property nationalized in 1945, including land to its former owners. Support for the Republic of Kosovo and Greater Albania "without which there would be no stability in the Balkans".

Affiliation. The party has close links with the Association of the Formerly Expropriated "Ownership with Justice".

Publication. E Djathte (The Right).

Democratic Union of Greek Minority (OMONIA)
(also known as OMONIA Socio-Political Organization)
OMONIA–Bashkimia Demokratik i Minoritet Grek

Foundation. December 1990.

Leadership. Sotiris Kyriazatis (pres.); Theodori Bezhani, (ch.)

Membership. 60,000 (est.)

History. OMONIA is Albania's largest minority organization, representing the Orthodox Christian ethnic Greek community of Albania. The Greek minority in Albania, estimated at 59,000 by Tirana and more than 300,000 by Athens, in the main inhabits the hillside villages of southern Albania, an area known to Greeks as Northern Epirus (a name widely believed by Albanians to disguise irredentist claims). The region, which borders the Greek province of Southern Epirus, was incorporated into the modern Albanian state in 1925.

The Greek minority was savagely oppressed by the local Tosks communist authorities throughout the post-war period and in particular after 1967 when the practice of religion was prohibited by the Albanian authorities. Those who attempted to express their ethnicity, religious beliefs, or support for Greece were sentenced to long prison terms or endured years of internal exile. As early as December 1989 Greek Albanians had organized small protests against the communist regime. In the March 1991 elections OMONIA presented its candidates in the Greek heartland in southern Albania and won each of the five constituencies it contested there, thus becoming the third largest political party in the Albanian parliament. Under the 1992 Electoral Law which banned the formation of parties on "ethnic principles" it was prevented from participating in the parliamentary and local elections of that year. However, it put forward its candidates on the list of the Human Rights Union Party. In 1992, when Albania's first democratic government assumed power, the Greek minority had hoped for an improvement in their condition. However, according to them, matters worsened as conflict spread across the Balkans. The estimated 25,000 Greeks who live outside "minority zones" enjoy no minority rights at all. Since the collapse of communism in Albania humanitarian groups have, on numerous occasions, denounced the severe religious and educational discrimination suffered by the country's ethnic Greeks. In turn, the minority has become increasingly vociferous in its demands for self-determination and closer links with Greece. Tirana says Athens has incited the Greek minority to separatism. The position of OMONIA and the ethnic Greeks appears to be closely related to the state of official Albanian–Greek relations. Since 1992 these relations have been steadily deteriorating and brought the two countries to the brink of open confrontation. Relations between Greece and Albania worsened in the middle of April 1994, when two Albanian conscripts were killed in a cross-border raid on a military training camp. The attack was blamed by Tirana on ethnic Greek separatist gunmen. In the wake of the attack the Albanian army quickly dismissed its last ethnic Greek officer. He joined a multitude of other ethnic Greeks sacked from the civil service or barred from senior posts in private companies. Subsequently Albania announced the trial of six ethnic Greeks for spying. In a tit-for-tat move the Greek government said it had used its powers to suspend 35 million ECU (£27 million) of EU aid to Albania. On May 26, 1994, Albania arrested more than 50 ethnic Greek politicians, intellectuals and journalists (mostly in the southern Albanian town of Dervitsani), members of OMONIA, on suspicion of "anti-state" activities, including the possession of arms and espionage. As the tension has grown thousands of ethnic Greeks have abandoned their homes and attempted to cross into Greece.

Programme. As a purely ethnic Greek party, OMONIA is a regional organization, exclusively concerned with local Greek minority issues.

Green Party
Partia e Blerte

Telephone/Fax. (355) 42 33309.

Foundation. Oct. 2, 1991.

Leadership. Nevroz Paluka (pres.)

Human Rights Union Party
Partia Bashkimi i te Drejtava te Njeriut

Telephone. (355) 42 27170.

Fax. (355) 42 28361.

Foundation. Feb. 24, 1992.

Leadership. Vasil Melo (pres.)

Programme. The party's programatic documents emphasize the need to work for "full democratization of the social order in Albania, to realize democracy based on the basic human rights and liberties in the framework of constitutional and international law". The party advocates a profound economic reform leading towards the market economy which would ensure a fast rate of development for Albania and a higher standard of living for the population. It stresses the need to make the peasants owners of land, with technical and financial help from the state to assist farmers. The Union's programme supports close economic relations with foreign countries, bilateral relations with all states, and the encouragement of foreign investment.

Independent Centre Party
Partia Indipendente Centriste

Address. Rruga "Qemal Stafa" nr 120. Tirana.

Foundation. Aug. 7, 1991.

Leadership. Edmond Gjokrushi (ch.)

History. During the 1992 election campaign the party stated that it could not enter the electoral campaign on equal terms as a result of "a serious shortage of the most elementary resources for the normal conduct of its activities". It advised its supporters to vote for Democratic Party candidates.

Movement of Legality Party
Partia Lëvizja e Legalitetit

Address. Rruga "P. Shkurti", pallati 5/1. Tirana.

Foundation. Feb. 20, 1991.

Leadership. Agustin Shashaj (pres.)

Membership. 4,000 (est.)

History. The Movement of Legality Party is the political arm of the monarchist movement founded during World War II. It only has a miniscule following inside Albania. During the 1992 local elections a handful of its candidates were elected to district and communal councils. The Movement, however, does have some wider support among the Albanian expatriate community in Europe and the United States. It refused to participate in the 1992 parliamentary elections on the grounds that republicanism as a political system in Albania was a foregone conclusion. The Movement's 50th anniversary celebrations in November 1993 were attended by the exiled pretender to the Albanian throne, King Leka I (the only son of the self-proclaimed King Zog who fled Albania in 1939). He arrived in Albania on Friday and left on Saturday, after being asked by the authorities to leave the country. During 1993 major divisions emerged within the party's ranks which could lead to a formal split.

Programme. The party demands the restoration of the monarchy in Albania.

Party of National Progress
Partia e Progresit Kombetar

Address. Rruga "8 Nentori" pallati 1282, Vlora.

Foundation. Sept. 26, 1991.

Leadership. Myrto Xhaferri (pres.)

Party of National Unity
Partia e Unitetit Kombëtar

Address. Rruga Alqi Kondi, Tirana.

Telephone. (355) 42 274857.

Fax. (355) 42 274898.

Leadership. Idajet Beqiri (ch.)

Membership. 7,000 (est.)

Party of Republican Alliance
The party emerged in the summer of 1992 as a result of a split within the Republican Party.

People's Party
Partia Popullore

Foundation. Aug. 31, 1991.

Leadership. Bashkim Driza (pres.)

Membership. 5,000 (est.)

Programme. The main aim of the party is to eradicate communism and all its vestiges.

Right-Wing Republican Party
Partia Republikane e Djathte

Foundation. March 10, 1992.

Leadership. Hysen Cobani (pres.)

History. The party emerged as a result of a split within the Republican Party when its leader, Hysen Cobani, walked out and formed a new organization. The party did not take part in the 1992 parliamentary elections.

Republican Alternative Party

Leadership. Shemshedin Memia (pres.)

Social Democratic Party of Albania (SDPA)
Partia Socialdemokratike ë Shqipërisë

Address. Bulevardi Deshmoret e Kombit, Tirana.

Telephone/Fax. (355) 42 27485.

Foundation. March 1991.

Leadership. Prof. Skënder Gjinushi (ch.); Lisien Bashkurti (sec.)

Membership. 20,000.

Organization. Managing Council consisting of 11 members.

Social Labour Party of Albania
Partia Socialpuntore Shqiptare

The Party was founded on March 4, 1992. It did not take part in the 1992 parliamentary elections.

Universal Party
Partia Universale

Telephone/Fax. (355) 42 33449.

Notes

1 Louis Zanga, "Watershed Year", *Report on Eastern Europe*, RFE/RL Research Institute, vol. 2, no. 6, Feb. 8, 1991. p. 2.
2 Albania broke off diplomatic ties with the Soviet Union in 1961 at the height of the Sino–Soviet dispute. The Hoxha regime refused to support Soviet condemnations of China. As a result of the break, Soviet aid to Albania ceased and Soviet advisers and technicians were recalled and replaced by Chinese specialists. Between 1961 and 1979 Albania was a *de facto* Chinese satellite. It followed closely China's pattern of social and political development, including a version of the Chinese cultural revolution.
3 The United States like Britain never had diplomatic relations with the post-war regime in Tirana. Proposals made in November 1945 by American and British governments to normalize relations with Tirana were scorned by the Hoxha regime.
4 Full membership of the CSCE became the Albanian government's most important foreign policy objective. Albania was allowed to attend the CSCE summit meeting in Paris on Nov. 19 and 20, 1990, as an observer, but was refused full membership. It was finally accepted as a full member of the CSCE in June 1991.
5 Louis Zanga, "Watershed Year", *Report on Eastern Europe*, RFE/RL Research Institute, vol. 2, no. 6, Feb. 8, 1991, p. 3.
6 A decree issued only on July 31, 1990, allowed public meetings, assemblies and demonstrations on the condition of prior notification to the appropriate authorities.
7 Several unpopular old-guard lost their positions on July 11. Simon Stefani lost his post of Deputy Chairman of the Council of Ministers and Minister of Internal Affairs, he became Chairman of the State Control Commission, only to be finally removed from all posts on Dec. 22, 1990; Manush Myftiu was released from the post of Deputy Chairman of the Council of Ministers and Chairman of the State Control Commission due to retirement; Prokop Murra was released from the post of Minister of People's Defence due to retirement. In addition four other ministers were also removed from their posts and retired.
8 According to official reports, the actual cause of discontent was an electrical failure during an evening dinner in two dormitories which lasted for several hours. The breakdown in the supply of electricity, it was suspected, resulted from an overloading of the grid, following massive use of electric heaters because the central heating system did not function properly. (*BBC SWB*, EE/0945 B/1, Dec. 12, 1990).

9 In addition to the economy, young people have been the main worry of the Albanian leadership. Youth constitutes the largest social group in Albania with the average age being only 26, the lowest in Europe.
10 ATA, Dec. 11, 1990.
11 ATA, Dec. 12, 1990.
12 *The Economist*, Feb. 16, 1991.
13 Louis Zanga, "A candid report on demonstrations", *Report on Eastern Europe*, RFE/RL Research Institute, vol. 2, no. 2, Jan. 11, 1991, p. 5.
14 ATA, 21 Dec. 1990.
15 By February the number of refugees escaping to Greece rose to 16,000.
16 *New political parties in Albania December 1990–March 1991*

Name	Date of foundation	Membership claimed
Democratic Party	12 Dec. 1990	80,000
Democratic Union of the Greek Minority (OMONIA)	Dec. 1990	60,000
Republican Party	Jan. 1991	8,000
Ecology Party	Jan. 1991	1,000
Agrarian Party	Feb. 1991	30,000
Social Democratic Party	Mar. 1991	3,000
Total		182,000

17 In a statement on April 3, 1991, the Central Committee of the AWP admitted: "Some of our party's candidates did not win in some constituencies, especially in the large towns. This shows that the party's work in these constituencies, especially its ties with the working class, young people and the intelligentsia has been poor. Comrade Ramiz Alia was among the candidates who failed to win in Tirana"; *Zeri i Popullit*, April 3, 1991.
18 Ramiz Alia stood as a candidate in constituency No. 218 in Tirana, the capital's most privileged district. He received only 32 per cent of the vote. The seat was won by the virtually unknown Franko Gjon Krroqi, an engineer, DP candidate during the first round.
19 ATA, May 7, 1991.
20 *BBC SWB*, EE/1900 B/1, June 5, 1991.
21 The distribution of posts in the 24-member government among the five political parties in percentage terms was as follows (including the nine non-party but party proposed posts): APL 50 per cent, DP 29.2 per cent, SDP 8.0 per cent, RP 8.3 per cent, AP 4.2 per cent.
22 *Ibid.*
23 The issue of changing the name revealed deep divisions among the delegates to the Congress, with some arguing strongly for the retention of the name APL, others suggesting the Renovated Workers' Party or Party of Socialist Future of Albania. After the lengthy deliberations of a specially appointed commission it was decided to adopt the name "Socialist Party of Albania" to link the party with the "European left wing" movement.
24 *BBC SWB*, EE/1336 B/3. March 23, 1992.
25 *BBC SWB*, EE/1338 B/1. March 25, 1992.
26 The account of the earlier history of the Albanian Democratic Party is based on Marko Milivojevic, "Albania" in Bogdan Szajkowski (ed.), *New Political Parties of Eastern Europe and the Soviet Union*. Longman, Harlow, 1991, p. 8.
27 *BBC SWB*, EE/1098 B/2, June 14, 1991.
28 ATA, June 12, 1991.
29 *Reuter*, July 7, 1991.

ARMENIA

Mark Sarafyan

Among the newly independent nations of the former Soviet Union, Armenia stands out in one important respect: it has a *bona fide* non-communist leadership. Armenia is the smallest of the former republics of the Soviet Union, landlocked and mountainous. It has few sources of natural wealth and even less in the way of fossil fuels. It still suffers from the effects of the disastrous earthquake of 1988. Last but not least, over the past five years it has been in dispute with neighbouring Azerbaijan over Nagorno-Karabakh, the 80 per cent Armenian-populated enclave in Azerbaijan, which has led to open conflict between the two countries. As a result of the hostilities, Azerbaijan has imposed a blockade and cut off Armenia's main trade routes with Russia, causing severe shortages of food and fuel in Armenia and bringing Armenia's industry to all but a standstill.

The Armenians have a distinctive language and culture, and a strong sense of nationhood. There has been an Armenian national church since the fourth century, which has often served to provide institutional support in periods when Armenian statehood was eclipsed. The longest such period lasted until World War I, culminating in the terrible holocaust of 1915, when a million and a half Armenians perished at the hands of the Turkish state. As a result of forced deportations and massacres Western Armenia was denuded of its entire Armenian population. In May 1918, the first Armenian state for nearly 600 years was established in Eastern Armenia. It covered a tenth of the historical land of Armenia and had a population of less than 1 million. In 1920, it succumbed to Lenin's resurgent Soviet Russia and the area eventually became a Soviet Republic.

The traumatic effects of the events of 1915, and the fear of national extinction following from it, colour every aspect of Armenian political life to this day. Between the two world wars, traditional Armenian cultural and political institutions — and the memory of the 1915 holocaust — were kept alive by the survivors. They did this in countries where they had taken refuge in the Middle East and in the West at a time when that heritage was being suppressed or subverted in Soviet Armenia under the policies of Stalin.

There was never complete isolation between Soviet Armenia and the Armenian diaspora, mainly because Moscow hoped and sometimes succeeded in exploiting the diaspora for its own purposes. Ironically, by a system of cultural and political reverse-osmosis, the opposite also occurred. Thus, over the years, Soviet Armenians became better informed about the West than other peoples of the Soviet Union who had no diaspora of their own.

In 1945 Moscow made territorial demands on Turkey on behalf of Armenia and Georgia. These demands eventually came to nothing and were officially withdrawn, but at the time they generated intense enthusiasm among Armenians of the diaspora. In the heady period that followed, Moscow arranged for the "repatriation" of some 100,000 to 150,000

Armenians from abroad. It was the largest voluntary mass emigration in the history of the Soviet Union. Once in Soviet Armenia, however, the new arrivals had to face the horrors of life under the Stalinist regime and were also subjected to discrimination in the choice of jobs and careers. Over the years, this kept the "repatriates" and their children out of the *nomenklatura*, thus creating a pool of people untainted by communism and sowing fresh seeds of Armenian nationalism.

In 1965, when the Armenian diaspora was commemorating the 50th anniversary of the 1915 massacre, unauthorized anti-Turkish mass demonstrations were held in Yerevan, the Armenian capital. Bloodshed was narrowly avoided in containing them. One of the arrested demonstrators was Levon Ter-Petrosyan, a youth born in Syria and "repatriated" with his family at the age of one in 1945. In 1988, he emerged as one of the leaders of the "Karabakh Committee" which demanded the annexation of Nagorno-Karabakh to Armenia. Together with other members of the "Karabakh Committee", he was jailed and sent to Moscow early at the end of 1988, only to be freed six months later to return to a triumphant reception in Yerevan.

Under Ter-Petrosyan's deft leadership, the "Karabakh Committee" was quickly transformed into a loose but effective organization calling itself the "All-Armenian Movement" (AAM). In elections to the Supreme Soviet, held in May – July 1990, the AAM became the largest single party and Ter-Petrosyan was elected chairman of the Soviet. Following the failure of the August 1991 *coup*, a referendum on independence was held on Sept. 21 which resulted in an overwhelming vote in support of independence for Armenia. Armenia duly declared itself independent on Sept. 23, 1991. In the first democratic elections to be held after the collapse of the CP of the Soviet Union in October 1991, Ter-Petrosyan was elected President of Armenia with 80 per cent of the votes cast.

In the post-independence period four major parties in Armenia have emerged, in addition to a large number of smaller minor parties. The political scene is dominated by President Ter-Petrosyan and the All-Armenian Movement (AAM) which is the instrument of his will in parliament. Ter-Petrosyan's regime strongly supports a free market economy and has carried out a comprehensive privatization of agriculture. Under his administration Armenia has repaired its relations with Russia and has not lost the contest with Azerbaijan over Nagorno-Karabakh; and, despite extreme shortages of food and fuel, deaths from starvation, cold or epidemics in Armenia have been avoided. Above all, civil strife has been conspicuous by its absence. All this has been achieved without any serious censorship or political repression.

The main opposition to the All-Armenian Movement comes from the Democratic Party of Armenia (DPA), formerly The Communist Party of Armenia (CP) which commands the second largest block of votes in parliament. However, due to long used reliance on orders from Moscow, the party suffers from a lack of self-confidence and strong local leadership. From time to time, the opposition comes close to mustering enough votes to upset the pro-government balance in parliament. Rumours in Yerevan imply that at such times President Ter-Petrosyan invites the parliamentary leadership of the DPA to a friendly meeting and at the next round of voting in parliament, the DPA bloc abstains. The implication is that President Ter-Petrosyan raises the spectre of past indiscretions during the communist party's long tenure in office and the DPA takes fright. In any case, it is clear that the CP lacks the determination to seek to regain power at this stage.

In addition to these two major "home-grown" parties, there are also offshoots of the two main Armenian parties of the diaspora, the Armenian Revolutionary Federation (ARF) and the Democratic Liberal Party of Armenia (DLP). The ARF, known popularly as either *"Dashnaktsoutyoun"* or as the *"Dashnak"* Party, is over 100 years old. It was in power when the first independent Armenian Republic was formed in 1918 and was banned when the Bolsheviks seized control in 1920. Since then, the ARF has flourished in the Armenian diaspora as the strongest and best-organized Armenian party. It is indisputably nationalist in practice but, as defined by its constitution, it is also socialist in principle. It also commands fanatical loyalty among its members.

The ARF has made strategic mistakes in the recent past — for example when it fielded Sos Sargsyan, a highly popular actor, as the ARF candidate against Levon Ter-Petrosyan in the presidential elections. Sargsyan ended up with a derisory 4 per cent of the vote. The ARF has since learnt its lesson and for the past two years has been actively engaged in creating a grassroots organization in Armenia and in Karabakh — where it is particularly strong — with a range of auxiliary organizations. The ARF also sponsors units in the Armenian armed forces. The recruits in these units are young local members of the ARF and they receive better food, better equipment, and better leadership and training than other recruits. This is a somewhat ominous development in view of the fact that there have been occasions in the past when the ARF has used strong-arm methods in pursuit of its political aims.

The DLP, also known as the *"Ramkavar"* party, is mainly the party of professionals and intellectuals of a moderate right-of-centre outlook like its counterpart in the diaspora. It is occasionally critical of the government but always supports it in the end.

The ARF and the DLP publish their own newspapers in Armenia which are of high quality. It is an open secret that the ARF and the DLP in Armenia are funded by their respective counterparts in the diaspora and, despite claims to the contrary, have their policies broadly dictated by the latter.

With 39 registered political parties in the Republic none of the four leading parties can hope to win a working majority at the next parliamentary elections due in spring 1995. The way ahead, therefore, seems to lie in electoral pacts. This process is already underway. On Sept. 7, 1994, the AAM and the DLP issued a joint declaration together with four other minor parties — Republican Organization of Armenia, the Christian Democratic Party of Armenia, the Intellectual Armenian Union and the Social Democratic Hnchakian Party — praising the achievements of the Armenian Republic, pointing out its failings, and outlining their demands from the government. As this joint declaration includes the AAM as a signatory, it is clear that it carries President Ter-Petrosyan's blessing. Equally, it may presage the beginnings of an electoral pact and a joint platform by these parties, led by the AMM, at the next elections.

It is very uncertain whether either the CP or the AFP can mount similar initiatives of their own. On the other hand, an ARF–CP electoral pact — however unlikely it may be — has intriguing possibilities of the two ends of the political spectrum meeting against the middle.

Directory of Parties

Agrarian Democratic Party of Armenia

Date of registration. 25.9.1992.

Leader. Telman Dilanyan.

Armenian Christian Democratic Union

Date of registration. 19.8.1991.

Leader. Azat Arshakyan.

Armenian Labour Union

Date of registration. 1.3.1993.

Leader. Hamlet Karayan.

Armenian Monarchists' Party

Date of registration. 25.10.1992.

Leader. Aghasi Yesayan.

Armenian National Congress

Date of registration. 13.1.1992.

Leader. Miasnik Hakobyan.

Armenian Revolutionary Federation

Date of registration. 2.7.1991

Leader. Hrayr Karapetyan.

Armenian Revolutionary Federation of Armenia

Date of registration. 2.7.1991.

Leader. Haroutyoun Aristakesyan.

Armenian Royalist Party

Date of registration. 15.4.1992.

Leader. Tigran Petrosyants.

Communist Party of Armenia

Date of registration. 29.7.1991.

Leader. Sergey Badalyan.

Constitutional Rights Union

Date of registration. 19.8.1991.

Leader. Hrand Khachatryan.

Democratic Forces of Dilijan Union

Date of registration. 12.3.1993.

Leader. Zhora Madatyan.

Democratic Liberal Party of Armenia

Date of registration. 10.6.1991.

Leader. Rouben Mirzakhanyan.

Democratic Party of Armenia

Date of registration. 25.10.1991.

Leader. Aram Sargsyan.

"Hoveta" Alliance for Spiritual Uprise and Economic Freedom Social-Political Organization

Date of registration. 9.3.1994.

Leader. A. Yereghyan.

"Intellectual Armenia" Union

Date of registration. 22.6.1994.

Leader. H. Tokmajyan.

Labour Party of Armenia

Date of registration. 5.5.1994.

Leader. L. Yesayan.

National Conservative Party of Armenia

Date of registration. 10.6.1991.

National Renaissance Party

Date of registration. 26.12.1991.

Leader. Hovik Vasilyan.

National Self-Determination Union

Date of registration. 29.7.1991.

Leader. Parouyr Hayrikyan.

"National Social-Democratic Union" of Abovyan

Date of registration. 19.8.1991.

Leader. Valeri Sargsyan.

"National State" Social-Political Organization

Date of registration. 5.5.1994.

Leader. Th. Soghomonyan.

National Unity Party

Date of registration. 21.4.1993.

Leader. Tigran Nikoghosyan.

"New Path of the Armenian Republic" Social-Political Organization

Date of registration. 21.4.1993.

Leader. Ashot Bleyyan.

Nzhtehyan Chauvinist Party

Date of registration. 15.7.1991.

Leader. Gevorg Hovsepyan.

Racist Party of Armenia

Date of registration. 2.7.1991

Leader. Shant Haroutyounyan.

Radicals' Party of Armenia

Date of registration. 3.12.1991.

Leader. Valery Vardanyan.

"Renaissance of Gyumri" Social-Political Organization

Date of registration. 9.3.1994.

Leader. K. Haroutyounyan.

Republican Party of Armenia

Date of registration. 14.5.1991

Leader. Ashot Navasardyan.

"Salvation" National Party

Date of registration. 15.9.1992.

Leader. Anton Vardanyan.

Social Democratic Hnchak Party

Date of registration. 14.10.1991.

Leader. Yeghia Najaryan.

The "Artsakh-Armenia" Social-Political Organization

Date of registration. 15.9.1992.

Leader. Lenser Aghalovyan.

The "Fatherland" Social-Political Organization

Date of registration. 12.12.1991.

Leader. Jasmen Asryan.

The "Heritage" Club

Date of registration. 16.9.1991.

Leader. Igor Mouratyan.

The "Mission" Social-Political Organization

Date of registration. 12.11.1991.

Leader. Artoush Papoyan.

The "National Democratic Union" Social-Democratic Organization

Date of registration. 19.3.1992.

Leader. Davit Vardanyan.

The Pan-Armenian Movement

Date of registration. 15.7.1991.

Leader. Rev. Housik Lazaryan.

Traditionalist Democratic "Armwomall" (Armenian Womens' Alliance) Party

Date of registration. 21.2.1994.

Leader. Armenouhi Ghazaryan.

Universal Prosperity Party

Date of registration. 30.4.1992.

Leader. Armen Kirakosyan.

"Varazdat Sports-Cultural" Social-Political Organization

Date of registration. 9.3.1994.

Leader. K. Hambaryan.

AZERBAIJAN

Bogdan Szajkowski
Krystyna Vere-Bujnowski

Two years after independence from the Russian Empire, Azerbaijan once again came under Russian domination when it became a Soviet Socialist Republic in 1920. It lost its status as a separate Soviet republic between 1922 and 1936 when together with Armenia and Georgia it formed the Transcaucasian Soviet Socialist Republic. The territory of Azerbaijan includes the Nakhichevan Autonomous Republic, separated from Azerbaijan by Armenia; and the Nagorno-Karabakh Autonomous *Oblast*, populated largely by ethnic Armenians, although it lies wholly within Azerbaijan. These territorial and ethnic anomalies are legacies of Stalin's "divide and rule policy" over ethnic and nationalist groups and have been highly influential in the development of Azerbaijan since the collapse of the Soviet Union.

Even before the disintegration of the USSR, Azerbaijan was in dispute with Armenia over Nagorno-Karabakh. The region's autonomy was abolished by the Azerbaijan Supreme Soviet on Nov. 26, 1991, but the *oblast* immediately declared itself a republic. Fighting has continued in the region and has spread on occasion to surrounding areas. Policy decisions concerning the handling of the violent dispute in Nagorno-Karabakh have dogged successive governments and failure to resolve the question has supplied welcome political fodder for successive opposition groups.

Since 1989 the Nakhichevan exclave has attempted to become wholly independent of the Azerbaijani leadership in Baku and though unsuccessful its separatist claims have helped to politicize the population. The exclave's electorate has been cultivated by Nakhichevan politicians such as Abulfaz Elchibey[1] and Geidar Aliyev who have aspired to leadership in Azerbaijan proper. Their Nakhichevan following has helped them to assert themselves on the wider stage.

The 1989 census shows the total population of Azerbaijan to be just over 7 million, composed of Azeris (82.7 per cent), Russians (5.6 per cent), Armenians (5.6 per cent) and Lezghins (2.4 per cent). Since the census, however, many Armenians have fled the ethnic violence spilling out of the Nagorno-Karabakh conflict. Azerbaijan is overwhelmingly Muslim (87 per cent), with the Russian and Armenian populations following Christianity; language, too, reflects the ethnic division, Azeri is spoken by 82 per cent of the population, Russian by 7 per cent and Armenian by 5 per cent. The territory of Azerbaijan is bordered by Armenia, Georgia, Russia and Iran but the capital, Baku, is situated away from all land borders by the Caspian Sea. Some Azerbaijanis desire absorption of or unification with the ethnically Azeri portion of northern Iran; there have been minor irredentist disputes along the Georgian border and the unsettled political situation has given rise to nationalist claims to autonomy from elements of the Lezghin population which straddles the border with Russia.

Despite the unfolding of nationalist squabbles, Azerbaijan in 1989 continued to be controlled by the Communist Party which retained its links with the CPSU in Moscow. Like most of the Soviet republics, Azerbaijan had no coherently organized political alternative that had both popular support and the ability to assume the reins of power. The Azerbaijani Popular Front, *Khalq Jibhasi*, came closest to unsettling the incumbent regime but in January 1990 made a gross tactical error. The party had calculated that the Nagorno-Karabakh dispute was the best means available to mobilize support for the Front and against the government. Some elements of the APF, however, organized a pogrom against Armenians in Baku and elsewhere that led to bloodshed. The army was brought out on to the streets of Baku to quell the riots and 150 civilians were killed. The communists successfully blamed the APF for fomenting the unrest and provoking the military reaction.[2]

It has been claimed that the government orchestrated the backlash against the APF and that the riots had subsided by the time the army was called in on Jan. 19, 1990.[3] It is certainly true that these events led to the promotion of the hardline Ayaz Mutalibov, who became First Secretary of the Communist Party in January and in May was elected President by the communist-controlled Supreme Soviet. Mutalibov kept the republic in line with the CPSU programme. The direct parliamentary elections that were held on Sept. 30 and Oct. 14, 1990, could have been turned to the advantage of an opposition more disciplined than the APF, though this remains speculative since the ruling communists had control of the media and the electoral process. The coalition of opposition groups, including the APF, managed to win only 45 seats (12.5 per cent) out of the 360 seats available in the Supreme Soviet while the Communist Party returned 280 deputies (78 per cent). Because of difficulties over security elections were not held in 11 areas and this left 20 seats vacant.[4]

The recent history of political development in Azerbaijan has rested on the ability of individual politicians to maintain their credibility in the face of a worsening economic situation and a failure to provide a lasting solution to the Nagorno-Karabakh dispute. The two factors are linked. While the hostilities continue in and around Nagorno-Karabakh and while they have the potential to spread to the rest of Azerbaijan, financial, political and military resources are concentrated on the conflict to the detriment of Azerbaijan as a whole. The poor economic situation in itself might not lead to profound anxiety if it were not coupled with political uncertainty. Political stability, in turn, would enhance the prospect for attracting aid to the economy.

Ayaz Mutalibov, Abulfaz Elchibey and Geidar Aliyev came to power on the back of people's anxiety about the spread of hostilities. By the same token, Mutalibov and Elchibey lost credibility largely when their policies on Nagorno-Karabakh were seen to have failed. The yardsticks for failure were the loss of civilian lives and the loss of territory; and the resulting political instability made it less likely that foreign investment would risk backing the Azerbaijan economy. Politicians who successfully pinned responsibility for the failure on the incumbent president became the next in line to take office and the rewards of power remained high enough for political figures to risk their reputations as they manoeuvred their way towards the top. In such situations, however, the end is not progression towards democracy but a consolidation of personal power; and the means become measures of repression. Aliyev, for example, currently relies on intimidating opposition groups and on media censorship to consolidate his power and depends on the personal trust invested in him by various foreign powers to provide economic and political backing for his regime.

Back in August 1991, Abulfaz Elchibey capitalized on Mutalibov's initial support for the failed Moscow coup. In spite of recanting his support, Mutalibov was under pressure to accommodate the APF. He suspended the Supreme Soviet and formed the National Council, half of whose 50 members were APF supporters. Mutalibov was still in sufficient control of the political process, however, to be the only candidate in the presidential elections in September 1991, less than one month after he had proclaimed Azerbaijan's independence from the Soviet Union on Aug. 30, 1991.

After the Act of Independence was ratified on Oct. 18, 1991, and confirmed almost unanimously in a national referendum on Dec. 29, Mutalibov further angered the APF by his decision to join the CIS in contradiction to a unanimous decision of the National Council. Mutalibov's high-handedness was confirmation if it were needed that in spite of the dissolution of the Communist Party after the Moscow coup in August, Mutalibov favoured close federation with Russia and saw Azerbaijan's future within some semblance of the old Soviet Union. Such examples of disdain for the democratic process might have continued unchecked and Elchibey's campaign to restrict Mutalibov's power might have been futile if Mutalibov had had some military success in Nagorno-Karabakh. In February 1992, however, Elchibey and the APF managed to hold the ex-communist leader responsible for the delay in forming the National Azerbaijani Army which enabled Armenian forces to overrun Khodjaly, an Azerbaijani-populated town within the enclave of Nagorno-Karabakh. The killing of several hundred civilians was laid at Mutalibov's door and he was forced to resign on March 6, 1992.[5]

Although there was an attempt to offer the country democratic presidential elections, Elchibey was forced to engineer a coup when Mutalibov endeavoured to make a comeback in May 1992[6] and after successfully countering Mutalibov the APF-dominated government took steps to curb other opposition. They restricted the age of presidential candidates to 65, which removed Geidar Aliyev, who was 69, from taking part in the presidential elections where he posed the greatest threat to Elchibey. Aliyev, although less personally popular than Elchibey in national opinion polls, was seen as the individual most likely to sort out Azerbaijan's difficulties.[7] In the presidential elections on June 7, 1992, without the participation of Aliyev, Elchibey won 59 per cent of the vote against four other candidates.[8]

Whatever Elchibey's intentions when he stood for office, and he campaigned on a platform of civil rights and democratic liberties, after his election he found it impossible to pursue the development of democratic institutions and practices. Unable to consolidate his position he deemed it expedient to delay legislation on a new constitution, on a pluralist political party system and on direct parliamentary elections which he had initially promised for the autumn of 1992.

Elchibey's difficulties escalated in March 1993 when the European Bank of Reconstruction and Development stipulated a settlement of the Nagorno-Karabakh conflict as a necessary requirement for investment. When the Bank's conclusions were made public the Lezghin separatist movement *Sadval* began demonstrations on the Russian border and by March 31 Etibar Mamedov was calling for popular demonstrations against the Baku government. In early April, the Armenian and Karabakh forces launched an offensive and captured 10 per cent of Azerbaijani territory. Aliyev, meanwhile, achieved his own diplomatic coup by making an agreement with Armenia on a ceasefire along the Nakhichevan border and the lifting of economic sanctions against the exclave. On June 4, 1993, Elchibey was forced to bring troops and tanks onto the streets of Baku after Iksander Hamidov, Elchibey's ex-Minister of Internal Affairs, threatened to stage a demonstration.[9] On the same day, troops led by the deposed military commander of the Azerbaijani forces in Nagorno-Karabakh, Surat Huseinov, began to advance on Baku. Ten days later, Elchibey's government was in tatters and Geidar Aliyev had taken on the role of mediator between Elchibey and Huseinov. The National Council elected Aliyev parliamentary chairman on June 16, Huseinov pledged his loyalty to Aliyev (and in return was given the role of prime minister) and Elchibey fled to Nakhichevan. Elchibey refused to return although he maintained that he was still in control of the government, but on June 24 the National Council officially transferred all of his presidential powers to Aliyev.

Aliyev's first steps in office were to safeguard his position and he has brought back a politburo style of government to ensure he remains in power. He introduced press censorship, at first on a temporary emergency basis; but with a view to allowing the new chairman of parliament, Rasul Guliyev, time to steer through a bill on media censorship of military matters. Opposition forces have been harrassed in attempts to render them ineffective: initial harrassment of *Musavat*, the most organized of the factions in the APF, was followed by a further crackdown in February 1994 when the Baku offices of the APF and its newspaper *Azadlyq* were searched for arms. Members of the APF and *Musavat* were arrested.[10]

The construction of legitimacy for Aliyev's rule echoes that found consistently under totalitarian regimes. A 93 per cent turn-out in a referendum on public confidence in Elchibey returned an overwhelming 97 per cent vote against him. Parliament endorsed the result, promptly tabled presidential elections for Sept. 3, 1993, and repealed the legislation on the upper age limit for candidates. Geidar Aliyev polled 98.8 per cent of the vote against two other candidates.[11] To underpin his authority, Aliyev quickly sought and achieved trade and commerce agreements with Iran and signed a document on principles of friendship and co-operation; by February 1994 he had also negotiated a rapprochement with Turkey and declared his support for NATO's Partnership for Peace.

During 1994 Aliyev has played an increasingly delicate game in his search for a resolution to the Nagorno-Karabakh conflict. Like others before him, he has found that difficulties in this area of policy tends to concentrate the forces of opposition. Aliyev initially refused to participate with CSCE's attempts to conduct peace negotiations and held out for a peace brokered by Russia, but the protocol he signed in Bishkek, Kyrgyzstan, threatened to unite public opinion against him. Thus, in an abrupt turnaround, Aliyev called for CSCE involvement in negotiations and CSCE ratification of the peace plan proposed by the Russian Defence Minister, Pavel Grachev. Aliyev is facing the same difficulties as his predecessors over Nagorno-Karabakh and his preference for dealing with Russia has increased fears of a return to Russian domination. The amendments he has felt obliged to make to the Grachev plan have all been designed to restrict the deployment of Russian troops on Azerbaijani soil and, in a further attempt to stave off increasingly violent opposition, Aliyev met with the Turkish Chief of Staff on July 7 to negotiate the deployment of Turkish troops to act as peacekeepers in Nagorno-Karabakh.[12]

The violent conflict and the legacy of a political culture used to being dominated by strong personalities have hampered rapid movement towards democratic rule along liberal lines. Neither the Act of Independence of Oct. 16, 1991, nor the referendum which endorsed it nor the inauguration of the first popularly elected president on June 6, 1992, heralded the

AZERBAIJAN

"true path to democracy". Brezhnev's 1978 Constitution has not yet been superseded and the formulation of a new constitution has been delayed by the exigencies of the political situation. The ratification of a new constitution together with a firm date for multi-party parliamentary elections scheduled for 1995 have been deemed less urgent than searches for political and economic alliances designed to consolidate the President's hold on power. This stability is seen as essential to attract foreign investment.

Although there are many different political organizations in Azerbaijan, the main parties have been neither able nor willing to institute a fully pluralist system. Their programmes set out their commitment to civic freedoms, economic reform and democratic rule but because of the war none of the main contenders to power have been able to make any significant steps towards implementing the rule of law, equality for all citizens and free and fair elections. Indeed, the trend has been the other way and political factions and personalities have manoeuvred in the old style to gain and consolidate power. Peace, the political will and strong economic inducements will be needed for an infrastructure to be built which safeguards democratic development and economic liberalization.

Directory of Parties

Azerbaijan Popular Front (APF) *Khalq Jibhasi*

Foundation. 1989

Leadership. Ibrahim Ibrahimov.

History The APF was originally an organization of individuals who came together to support the aims of *perestroika*. Members came from a variety of backgrounds and did not have a coherent programme, nor did they have a substantial popular following. They were gaining ground, however, when they put up an undisciplined showing in victimizing Armenians in Baku. This was used to the government's advantage and the APF suffered in the direct parliamentary elections. The APF made a comeback when they were able to capitalize on mistakes over Nagorno-Karabakh by President Mutalibov. They were to fall foul of the Nagorno-Karabakh problem themselves, however, in 1993, when President Abulfaz Elchibey was ousted by a coup led by Huseinov, the deposed and dissatisfied commander of Azeri troops in Nagorno-Karabakh. During 1994 their opposition to Aliyev's government has centred on his policy to bring peace to Nagorno-Karabakh which, the APF claims, is based on giving in to pressure to deploy Russian soldiers back onto Azerbaijani soil. They have found popular support for their anti-Russian stance and have forced Aliyev onto the defensive.

Programme. The APF embraces a number of political viewpoints. It is essentially a pro-Turkic movement and it included radical right-wing members of "The Grey Wolves", a pan-Turkic nationalist organization. It has also supported irredentist calls for unity with the Tabriz and Azerbaijani provinces in Iran. It supports equality in its relations with Russia but is not in favour of federation. The APF espouses a commitment to democratic reform, civil liberties, and equality for all citizens and it avows the principle of a pluralist party system. When in office, however, it was unable to pursue its programme and keep its promises

41

to institute a new constitution and democratic parliamentary elections. Its policy towards Nagorno-Karabakh is to achieve a negotiated settlement but hardliners within the Front advocate offensives against the enclave in order to negotiate from a position of strength.

Independent Azerbaijan Party

Leadership. Nizami Suleymanov.

History. Suleymanov was an ally of Aliyev and ran as a presidential candidate in the June 1992 elections. At that time he was the leader of the Democratic Union of the Intelligentsia of Azerbaijan.

Islamic Party of the Republic of Azerbaijan

Foundation. Dec. 6, 1992.

Membership. 50,000.

Programme. Revival of Islamic culture, aims to maintain the independence of the republic of Azerbaijan and maintain its national culture.

Muslim Democratic Party — *Musavat* (Equality)

Foundation. 1992.

Leadership. Isa Gambarov.

History. The original *Musavat* party was founded in 1911 and existed until Azerbaijan became a Soviet Socialist Republic. The present party's leadership disclaims links with this historical party but like the earlier *Musavat* it is a nationalist party advocating the tenets and values of Islam and is in favour of pan-Turkic unity. *Musavat* had been the main grouping within the APF. Gambarov was chairman of the National Council under Elchibey until he resigned on June 13, 1993.

National Independence Party — *Istiklal*

Leadership. Etibar Mamedov.

History. Etibar Mamedov was a leader in the APF but fell out with others over his position on Nagorno-Karabakh and political tactics. He advocated negotiating only from strength and this implied maintaining the offensive and escalating the conflict. Although others who agreed with him seem to have remained in the APF, Mamedov left to found his own party.

Programme. The National Independence Party is the main opposition party. Mamedov has been a constant critic of the APF, especially when it was in power in 1992–93. At that time there was talk of Mamedov and Aliyev forming an alliance, but when Aliyev came to power, Mamedov refused a position in his government. *Istiklal* maintains a hard line on Nagorno-Karabakh and this has caused difficulties when alliances have been mooted. The National Independence Party is firmly against federation with Russia and against any Russian attempts at peacekeeping in Nagorno-Karabakh.

New Azerbaijan Party — *Yeni Azerbaijan*

Foundation. September 1992.

History. The party was founded by Geidar Aliyev as an alternative to the ruling APF after his unsuccessful attempts to be nominated as a presidential candidate in the June 1992 elections and used it as a base to develop popular support against Elchibey and the APF.

Programme. The party's stated aims are the defence of the rights of all individuals, regardless of nationality and the creation of a law-based state. Aliyev claims that his party is "a party of the parliamentary type" which will be used as a political debating platform and will only develop a definitive manifesto when elections are called in 1995.[13]

Party of Revolutionary Revival (PRR)

Foundation. Nov. 2, 1993.

Leadership. Sayad Afes Ogly Sayadov (g.s.).

History. The PRR is the successor to the Communist Party. Its reconstituent congress was held in Baku after Aliyev secured the presidency.

Social Democratic Party (SDP)

Address. 370014 Baku, 28 May St. 3-11.

Telephone. 8922-933378.

Foundation. 1989.

Leadership. Araz Alizadeh.

Membership. 2,000.

United Azerbaijan

Leadership. Kerrar Abilov (ch.).

History. Abilov stood against Aliyev in the September 1993 elections, where he appeared to be a token candidate.

Notes

1 Abulfaz Elchibey was born in Nakhichevan in 1938 and attended Baku University 1957–63 where he read Arabic Philology. He followed an academic career, teaching at Baku University after he had obtained his doctorate in 1968. He specialised in oriental philosophy, religion, history and literature. He was arrested and imprisoned in 1975 for slandering the Soviet Union and released in 1977. He resumed his academic career at the Azerbaijan Soviet Socialist Republic Academy of Sciences where he worked in the Institute of Manuscripts. His full-time political career started after he had been elected chairman of the Azerbaijani Popular Front in 1989.

2 Elizabeth Fuller, "Azerbaijan After the Presidential Elections" *RFE/RL Research Report* vol. 1 no. 26, 26 June 1992.

3 *Human Rights and Democratization in the Newly Independent States of the Former Soviet Union*, compiled by the Staff of the Commission on Security and Co-operation in Europe, Washington, D.C., January 1993, p. 109.

4 That the opposition could have done better is given some credence by their performance in Nakhichevan, where the APF supported separation from Azerbaijan. The APF won 31 (28 per cent) out of 110 seats in the Nakhichevan parliament.

5 Elizabeth Fuller "Azerbaijan After the Presidential Election" *ibid.*

6 On May 14, 1992, Mutalibov's majority in the Supreme Soviet, which had been suspended through APF pressure, declared his resignation in March to be unconstitutional and therefore void. They also voted to postpone the parliamentary elections indefinitely and to dissolve the National Council which had been used to minimize the influence and legislative powers of parliament. Since power was slipping away from them, the APF managed a successful coup on May 15 supported by popular demonstrations on the streets of Baku and by factions of the army. The reinstated National Council put together a coalition government where the APF figured prominently and presidential elections were scheduled for June 7, 1992.

7 Geidar Aliyev, born in 1923, joined the CPSU in 1945 and was active in the politics of his native Nakhichevan. He became leader of the republic of Azerbaijan when he was made First Secretary of the Azerbaijani Communist Party in 1969. His career led him to Moscow where he eventually became First Deputy Chairman on the Soviet Union's Council of Ministers. He was sacked by Gorbachev in 1987 after allegations of corruption and returned to Nakhichevan where he began to rebuild his political career. Since his return from Moscow, he had been distrusted by members of the Nakhichevan parliament but had worked on perfecting his image among the populace not only of Nakhichevan but also of Azerbaijan. He became chairman of the Nakhichevan Supreme Soviet in September 1991.

Elchibey was not the only politician to fear Aliyev. Mutalibov and the communists in the Supreme Soviet had also tried to limit Aliyev's influence. On Oct. 16, 1991, the Nakhichevan deputies were obliged to walk out in support of Aliyev when the Supreme Soviet attempted to remove the article from the 1978 constitution which declared the chairman of the Nakhichevan Supreme Soviet an *ex officio* deputy chairman of the Azerbaijani Supreme Soviet. The move was dropped because the walk out removed the quorum needed for a change to the constitution.

Even before Aliyev was prevented from standing in the June 1992 elections he was pursuing an independent foreign policy on behalf of Nakhichevan. He proceeded to form political and personal alliances within and outside Azerbaijan that added to his credibility as a successful politician. In particular he was able to forge political and economic agreements with governments as diverse as Turkey, Iran and Russia. In September Aliyev founded the New Azerbaijani Party and proceeded to harry Elchibey on his failure to resolve the Nagorno-Karabakh dispute; on the absence of parliamentary elections which had been promised for the autumn but had been postponed until spring 1993; and on the continuing decline of the economic situation.

8 The election candidates were Tamerlan Kareyev, vice-chairman of the Azerbaijani parliament, who had left the APF to found the True Path Party in April 1992; Rafik Abdullayev of the small Azerbaijan National-Democratic Group; Ilyas Ismailov, of the Movement for Democratic Reforms in Azerbaijan; Nizami Suleimanov of the Democratic Union of Intelligentsia of Azerbaijan and an ally of Geidar Aliyev; Yagub Mamedov, the former interim president after Mutalibov's resignation; Etibar Mamedov, a former leader of the APF but now a strong critic of it and founder of the National Independence Party — *Istiklal*; and Abulfaz Elchibey of the Azerbaijani Popular Front. Only Elchibey had any substantial popular support and Etibar Mamedov withdrew on June 2 claiming that the ballot and security arrangements favoured Elchibey and were unconstitutional. Kareyev withdrew the day before the election urging his supporters to vote for Elchibey. There was a 70 per cent turn-out.

9 Iksander Hamidov had been a liability to Elchibey for some time. He was a member of the right wing pan-Turkic movement "The Grey Wolves" and he advocated strong measures against Nagorno-Karabakh. He did not seem to be interested in a negotiated peace. Hamidov was prone to delivering inflammatory statements particularly against opposition figures and by the time he was forced to resign he had publicly insulted the government and the opposition, and fought with a member of the Azerbaijani Socialist Party.

10 *RFE/RL News Briefs* 1 March 1994. The news report stated that the Azerbaijani government had been tipped off that the APF were planning a coup for March 5. The APF denied this, claiming that the government were trying to avert attention from their own political failures.

11 Zakir Tagiyev and Kerar Abilov were the other candidates, they polled 0.5 per cent and 0.3 per cent respectively. The Helsinki Watch declared the elections undemocratic because the major political opposition parties did not field candidates.

12 *RFE/RL News Briefs* 8 July 1994. Aliyev invited the Turkish Chief of Staff to Baku, four days after a bomb exploded on a metro train in Baku. Seven people were killed and 30 were seriously injured. This was not the first serious explosion, there had been a similar bombing in March when 12 people were killed.

13 Elizabeth Fuller "Azerbaijan: Geidar Aliyev's Political Comeback" *RFE/RL Research Report* vol. 2 no. 5, 29 January 1993, p. 10.

THE BALTIC REPUBLICS
ESTONIA, LATVIA AND LITHUANIA:
The Development of Multi-party Systems

Ole Nørgaard

Lars Johannsen

Anette Pedersen

It is a widespread myth that the three Baltic states — Estonia, Latvia, and Lithuania — are quite similar in their basic social and political features. However, the wide differences between the three countries in economic and political development, which can be observed today a mere three years after emancipation from Soviet hegemony, are clear evidence to the contrary. Firstly, these differences epitomize historical differences implanted into the collective memory of the titular nations of the three states. Secondly, they reflect their previous experience as free and independent national states between the two world wars. Thirdly, they are a symbol of the national identities that survived the levelling experience of the Soviet period.

Lithuania is the only one of the three Baltic nations with a long period of independent statehood. For more than 500 years, from the middle of the 13th to the end of the 18th century, Lithuania was allied with Poland as an important European power. This experience places national self-esteem and national symbols much more central on the political stage in Lithuania than is the case in Estonia and Latvia, which did not obtain their first independence until after World War I. Until then these countries and their native populations had been conquered and oppressed by foreign rulers: Danes, Swedes, Germans, and Russians. For Latvia, in particular, this troubled history made it difficult to find a national identity. That state and nation had been separated until 1920 constituted only part of the problem. The second problem was that Latvia, within present-day borders, is composed of regions with different history and cultural identities.

In addition to this, the three countries are separated by their cultural identity and orientation. The main dividing line is here between Lithuania, on the one hand, and Estonia and Latvia, on the other. Lithuania remained a deeply Catholic country as the only Baltic state, while Estonia and Latvia were deeply rooted in North European tradition and culture. These links with Northern Europe were born when German knights settled in these areas, first as missionaries, later as a feudal landed gentry, "the German Barons". Even when foreign rulers changed over the centuries, the German barons remained a privileged élite until the land reform, which followed independence after World War I. It was this privileged élite that maintained a close relationship with North European culture, philosophy, and economy. As a consequence, Estonia and Latvia followed the pattern of North European economic and cultural modernization, while Lithuania remained a backward, rural, and inward-oriented country.

Baltic independence between 1920 and 1940 remains of great importance in the political consciousness of the three countries. The common Baltic identity which was created during that period was to play a renewed role both before and after independence in 1991.

Firstly, the legal continuity back to the first independence was emphasized to demonstrate that the Soviet period constituted an illegal occupation through the illegal Molotov–Ribbentrop Pact of 1939. Secondly, personal continuity was assured through the older generation, who preserved a collective memory of an alternative society, and with a few surviving politicians from that period, who re-entered the political stage for a short while.

However, the major importance of the inter-war years is of a symbolic nature. For Estonia and Latvia it was their first experience as a nation-state, and hence the major focal point in their uprising against the Soviet system. Furthermore, the inter-war years are for most Balts testimony to the economic and political viability of their independent states. In many ways the political and economic difficulties faced by the Baltic states in the early 1920s remind them of present-day challenges. Their economic dependence on Russia was on a similar scale as today, at the same time as the major Western powers expressed reservations over economic and political viability of these small states on the fringe of a major power. That the Baltic states survived for 20 years against all odds, and at the same time modernized close to European standards, is for many Baltic politicians proof that they can succeed today.

The Soviet period in the Baltic states began with the Molotov–Ribbentrop Pact of Aug. 23, 1939, when Nazi Germany accepted the three Baltic states as falling within the Soviet sphere of influence. After a masquerade of external pressure and internal manipulation, the three states acceded "voluntarily" into the Soviet Union in June 1940. The first Soviet occupation of the three states was, however, terminated by the outbreak of war between Russia and Nazi Germany in the summer of 1941, which led to the rapid occupation of the three states by German forces. When the Soviet forces returned to the Baltic states in 1944, the second phase of sovietization, which was to last for the next 47 years, started.

Soviet policy in the Baltic states followed the same pattern as in other occupied countries. The local political and economic élites, who had already been heavily reduced through deportation during the first phase of occupation, through casualties during the war, and through a huge emigration to the West in front of the advancing Soviet army, were now further exposed to deportation and repression. It is estimated that the Baltic states lost about 30 per cent of their populations during the war and the forced sovietization after the war.

Today, the Baltic states share the same general obstacles on the road to market economy and liberal democracy with other countries from the former Soviet bloc. At the same time, they occupy a kind of middle position between Central and Eastern European countries and the other former Soviet republics. On the one hand, they were "only" exposed to the Soviet system for about 45 years. On the other hand, the social, political, economic and cultural impact of the Soviet period was as intense in the Baltic states as in the other republics of the former Soviet Union.

The most severe political problem left behind by the Soviet period is the huge number of immigrants from other former Soviet republics. This also has implications for the development of the present party system in the Baltic states. This immigration took place in two waves. The first wave was launched in the late 1940s, when a large group

THE BALTIC REPUBLICS: ESTONIA, LATVIA, AND LITHUANIA

Table 1: Immigration of the Baltic States from Other Soviet Republics

	Estonia 1946–1989	Latvia 1947–1988	Lithuania 1951–1989
Immigration	1,158,600	1,517,800	1,093,500
Immigration per year	26,300	36,100	28,000
Net immigration	365,900	445,200	311,000
Net immigration per year	8,300	10,600	8,000

Source: Sakkeus, Luule (1993), "Post-War Migration Trends in the Baltic States", *RU-series B*, no. 20, Tallinn: Estonian Interuniversity Population Research Centre, Appendix.

of administrators and party apparachiks was sent to the Baltic republics to manage the economic and political transformation.

However, the effects of this first immigration were mainly political. The major impact to the demographic situation followed only after the second immigration which began in the early 1960s. The scale of the immigration from other Soviet republics to the three Baltic republics is shown in Table 1.

Economically the immigration was motivated by the relatively highly developed infra-structure of the Baltic states, by their skilled workforce and their geographical proximity to the Eastern European and Western markets. However, the influx of Soviet workers and specialists clearly had a political background, indicated by the fact that jobs in the new industries were often announced only in Moscow and Leningrad — not in the Baltic states. By changing the demographic structure of the three countries, and eventually making the titular nationalities minorities in their own countries, the Soviet leadership hoped to prevent any attempt to regain national independence once and for all. The strategy was almost successful. By independence, the Russian-speaking part of the population of Estonia was approximately 37 per cent, and of Latvia approximately 48 per cent. In Lithuania, the picture was different. Here, due to a large labour reserve in the countryside, and a deliberate policy on the part of the nationalist communist party, the titular nationality made up 80 per cent of the population, whereas Russian speakers made up only about 10 per cent and Poles about 7 per cent. The dynamics of the demographic composition of the three countries is shown in Table 2.

These demographic changes were to leave a profound mark on the political system of the post-Soviet independent Baltic republics of Estonia and Latvia. The issue of nationality would for a while overwhelm all other political issues. Only in Lithuania, where citizenship was offered to all residents even before independence, did more traditional issues conquer the political stage.

Political opposition in the three Baltic states has a long and tragic history, which dates back to the guerrilla movements that fought against the Soviet regime until the early 1950s. The armed opposition was, however, crushed after collectivization had removed the social infrastructure that had been the basis of their strength. At the same time, the communist parties of Estonia and Latvia were almost exclusively dominated by immigrant Russians (or sovietized Balts), leaving no room for institutionalized opposition. In Lithuania,

Table 2: Demographic Development in the Three Baltic States

	Estonia		Latvia		Lithuania	
	1934	1989	1935	1993	1923	1993
Estonians/Latvians/Lithuanians	88.2	61.5	77.0	54.0	69.2	80.6
Russians	8.2	30.3	10.6	33.4	2.5	8.7
Ukrainians	—	3.1	0.1	3.2	—	1.1
White Russians	—	1.8	1.4	4.2	0.4	1.6
Poles	—	—	2.5	2.3	15.3	7.1
Other nationalities	3.6	3.3	8.4	2.9	12.6	0.9
Inhabitants in millions	0.14	1.57	1.91	2.61	2.62	3.74

Sources: *The Baltic States. A Reference Book* (1991), Tallinn: Estonian, Latvian, and Lithuanian Encyclopedia Publishers, p. 16, pp. 91–92, p. 178.
Lithuanian Department of Statistics (1993), *Lithuania in Figures 1992*, Vilnius: Information and Publishing Centre, p. 12.
Karaliene, Marija (1993), *Migration: Evolution of Direction, Number and Composition of Movers*, Vilnius: Lithuanian Department of Statistics.
Department of Citizenship and Migration (1993), *Information Reading the Latvian Civil Population Register as at 20 April 1993*, Riga.
Note: Researchers estimate that the share of Estonians is around 63 per cent today, and that the Russians now constitute less than 30 per cent.
Kirch, A., Kirch and Tuisk (1992), *The Non-Estonian Population Today and Tomorrow. A Sociological Overview*, Preprint, Tallinn: Estonian Academy of Sciences, Department of Humanities and Social Sciences.

unlike the two other republics, national communists managed to gain control over the communist party due to the absence of Lithuanian emigrés in the Soviet Union and to the ensuing language problems of the Russian officials. Pursuing a national-oriented policy, the Lithuanian Communist Party achieved a certain legitimacy among the general population, who gradually started to regard it as the lesser of two evils.

The popular opposition to the Soviet regime was closely linked to Gorbachev's reforms of the Soviet system. The opposition found its first expression in protests against the environmental degradation: in Estonia against phosphorite mining, which also attracted tens of thousands of Soviet immigrants to the country; in Latvia against monstrous hydro-power projects, which would have destroyed sensitive areas of the Latvian heartland; and in Lithuania against the chemical industry and against the Chernobyl-type nuclear power station in Ignalina. In step with political developments in Moscow, the ecological movements were soon replaced by movements preoccupied with broader issues, at first economic but later political.

However, it was the nationalist groups, started by former political prisoners and dissidents, which first put the independence issue on the political agenda. Furthermore, they also forced the popular movements to adopt more radical positions.

In Estonia, the Estonian National Independence Party — ENIP, was established on Aug. 20, 1988, as the first political party in the whole Soviet Union besides the CPSU.

From the start, the political style of ENIP was radical compared to that of the Estonian Popular Front which caused several clashes between the two. ENIP did not participate in the official election, but was one of the promoters behind the Estonian Congress (*Eesti Kongress*), an alternative parliament with strong nationalist tendencies. The Latvian National Independence Movement was founded on July 10, 1988, and was in many ways similar to ENIP, but was politically more co-operative. In Lithuania, the Lithuanian Freedom Union never had the same influence as the opposition groups in the other two countries because the Lithuanian Popular Front *Sajudis* (*Lietuvos Persitvordys Sajudis*) was radical in its demands from the very beginning and left no room for a second nationalist movement.

In Estonia and Latvia, it was the national intelligentsia, journalists, writers and university teachers who were the first to be engaged in the protest movement. Numerous reform-oriented members of the local communist parties also supported the protests. The communist parties of the three Baltic states were, however, up to 1988 ruled by conservative leaders, who opposed any support for the new movements. To move further, the communist parties had to replace their leadership.

June 1988 saw the dismissal of Karl Vaino, first secretary of the Estonian Communist Party. He had been appointed by Leonid Brezhnev in 1978 and was sacked because he tried to rig the election of his own candidates to the People's Congress in contradiction to orders from Moscow. He was replaced by Vaino Väljas, the former Soviet Ambassador to Nicaragua. As intense conflicts evolved within the Latvian and Lithuanian communist parties, in August 1988 Moscow sent Alexander Yakovlev, a member of the Politburo, to settle the conflicts. After his visit, Moscow gave the green light for the local communist parties to proceed with their involvement in the reform movement.

The first consequence was the discharge of the previous communist leaders. In Lithuania, the reform-oriented Algirdas Brazauskas was elected owing to the dominance of national communists. In the beginning, he and the party were on friendly terms with the local popular front, "Sajudis", but later were in constant conflict. Brazauskas' popularity reached enormous heights both in Lithuania and abroad when in December 1989 he declared the Communist Party independent of the mother party, the CPSU.

In Latvia, Latvians only made up a third of the communist party membership. This made the election of Anatolij Gorbunovs, the reform-minded ideological party secretary who had openly supported the protest movement, impossible. Instead Janis Vagris, an anonymous apparachik without any public appeal, was elected. The conservative wing of the party formed Interfront in January 1989 as a political counterweight to the Popular Front with the mayor of Riga Alfred Rubiks, as a leading figure. However, after having lost the election in the spring of 1990, a split could no longer be avoided. At a congress in April 1990, a group of delegates left the meeting to form their own party: the Democratic Labour Party, LDLP. From now on, the rump of the Communist Party was nothing but a conservative communist bastion with a steady declining membership and political influence. The party was dissolved in 1991 by order of the Latvian Supreme Council (former Supreme Soviet) after the failed coup. Despite the prohibition against communist activities, some hardline communists reorganized during 1992, but this turned out to be a temporary distraction. In Estonia and Lithuania, the national communists achieved the majority and broke all party links to the Soviet Communist Party.

When the reform-oriented communists started to support the protest movements, they, in turn, also started to build a firmer organizational basis. During the summer and autumn of 1988, "popular fronts", which were to form the framework of the protests as umbrella organizations, were created in all three countries. Thus, in Estonia the mobilization in connection with environmental protests meant that already by April 1988 reformist forces within the Estonian Communist Party could call for the creation of a broad movement that could function as a local support for the reformist politicans in Moscow. Among its participants were Edgar Savisaar, a former chairman of the Estonian Planning Committee (Gosplan), and Marju Lauristin, a well-known critically minded journalist. Of the seven members of the initiative committee which was established, five were members of the Estonian Communist Party. The founding congress of the Estonian Popular Front (*Estimaa Rahvarinne*) was held in October 1988. In Latvia, the idea of a popular front was formulated at an open meeting held by the society of authors on June 1–2, 1988. At this meeting, a number of speeches dealt with the many lies and suppressions in Latvian historiography and the social and economic conditions in the country, and a majority demanded that Latvia should be recognized as an autonomous state within the Soviet federation with sovereign control of internal affairs. After the meeting, a working group was set up, and on Oct. 8, 1988, the founding congress was held. It was also during the summer and autumn of 1988 that a group of intellectuals from the Academy of Sciences established "initiative groups for the perestroika movement in Lithuania", later known as "*sajudis*" — the Lithuanian word for movement. In all three countries, the immediate aim of the popular fronts was economic and political autonomy within a looser Soviet federation. Independence was not at that point regarded as a realistic objective. In this respect, the popular fronts differed from the radical groups, which — as well within as outside the popular fronts — only regarded sovereignty as a first step on the road to full independence.

During the first phase, the popular fronts concentrated on reform of the economic system. It was frustration over the centralized and economically deeply irrational control of Moscow that had motivated many young communist leaders and intellectuals to join the protest movements, and therefore reform of this system became their immediate goal. In this economic phase, Estonia led the way. The idea of economic liberation had already been formulated in September 1987, when a number of economists had drawn up the so-called IME programme, an economic reform programme the purpose of which was to create an autonomous Estonian economy within the Soviet Union. The proposal was based on the idea that Estonia itself should become responsible for the economic activities taking place within the country's territory, while maintaining a common financial and monetary community with Moscow. However, the demand of autonomy, formulated in the IME programme and in similar projects in the other two republics, soon transcended the limits acceptable to the Soviet bureaucracy, and the proposal was never implemented.

The blocking of these economic autonomy ideas led to a gradual radicalization of the popular fronts. It soon became evident that real economic autonomy presupposed a simultaneous political liberation. This political phase, when the demand for independence gradually came into focus, appeared in the Baltic popular fronts during the autumn of 1989 and the spring of 1990. During this phase, Lithuania, which up until then had been the most moderate of the three countries, came to the fore. This was largely the result of the country's internal political development.

From its start the development of *Sajudis* can be briefly described as a continuous radicalization. This trend was reflected in the parliamentary elections in February 1990 when Vytautas Landsbergis was elected as a compromise candidate between the moderate and the nationalist groups. Immediately after *Sajudis*' overwhelming victory, Parliament passed a resolution on March 11, 1990, in which it was declared that Lithuanian independence had been re-established. The inexperienced parliamentarians were convinced that the declaration of independence would soon be followed by Western recognition that could function as a defence against the expected reaction from Moscow. However, Western recognition did not materialize. The most important Western countries still supported Mikhail Gorbachev, and feared that a dissolution of the Soviet Union could threaten his position *vis-à-vis* reactionary groups in the Soviet leadership.

Moscow, however, reacted strongly. After a number of half-hearted negotiations and attempts to compromise, Moscow imposed an economic blockade of Lithuania at the beginning of April which put a stop to all supplies from the rest of the Soviet Union. Lithuania retaliated by discontinuing her exports — mainly of food articles — to Soviet cities. However, the struggle was heavily uneven. Though a black market was created quickly, in which local Soviet troops were active participants, Lithuania was soon forced to give in to the Soviet pressure. After strong requests from Western leaders, the declaration of independence was suspended in May as an attempt to reach a compromise with Moscow.

During this political phase, Estonia and Latvia acted much more carefully. The declarations of independence passed by their parliaments in the spring of 1990 anticipated a long period of transition. The reason for this cautiousness was evident. Both countries had large groups of Soviet immigrants, who were far more critical towards the desire for independence than titular nationalities. However, the pressure from the national opposition groups and the growing awareness among the more moderate politicians that the Soviet system was not able to carry out really radical reforms also radicalized the reform movements in Estonia and Latvia.

One result of this gradual movement towards more radical positions was a growing conflict of interest with the Russian-speaking immigrants. As a reaction to the growing nationalist orientation of the popular fronts, the Russian-speaking community in Estonia created "Interfront" as early as in 1988. This kind of organization emerged in most republics where Russian (and other Russian-speaking) immigrants felt their position threatened by the titular nationalities' demands for national sovereignty and independence. In Estonia, the organization had its base in the north-eastern industrial areas, especially in the town of Narva where less than 10 per cent of the inhabitants are Estonians. However, Interfront in Estonia became distinctly the party of the industrial leaders. It turned out to be difficult to mobilize large groups in protest actions against the policy of the Estonian Popular Front. In Latvia, Interfront was concentrated in the industrial cities which felt the political pressure from the country and smaller towns with a homogenous Latvian population. The main driving force behind Interfront in Latvia was partly the communists, and partly the large group of retired Soviet officers who had settled in Riga.

During the autumn and winter of 1990, the political climate in Moscow changed and Gorbachev sought political support from conservative groups. The price was a tougher line against the rebellious Baltic republics. This was reflected especially in the negotiations about independence which had been planned to start after the Lithuanian suspension of its declaration of independence. These negotiations never got off the ground. At the same time, rumours started to flourish about an imminent military intervention into the Baltic states, during which Gorbachev could take advantage of the new emergency measures that had been incorporated into the Soviet constitution. The threats from Moscow against the Baltic independence movements gradually became still more outspoken, and it is likely that the new alliance in Moscow had already decided upon a military solution to the "Baltic problem" in the early autumn of 1990. The actions had been planned to coincide with the expiration of UN's ultimatum to Iraq and the start of the Gulf War on Jan. 12, 1991, when the world's attention was believed to be directed elsewhere.

With this background, Soviet paratroopers who had been flown in from Pskov, attacked a number of public buildings and communication centres in Vilnius during the night of Jan. 12 and 13, while an anonymous "committee for the rescue of the nation" declared that it had seized power. In the course of a chaotic night, 13 people lost their lives, and several hundred were wounded when the paratroopers attacked and occupied the TV-tower. Most people expected the next target to be parliament. Defences made in haste, combined with a crowd numbering thousands who had gathered outside parliament to hinder the advance of the Soviet tanks, prevented further actions. Moscow had shown that it no longer had the ruthlessness necessary to suppress popular movements. The period up to August thus became one long war of attrition, in which parliament — as the only "liberated" area in Lithuania — became the framework of resistance against the Soviet occupying power, which retorted with random harassments, attacks on, and killings of Lithuanian officials. The attempt to find a military solution in the Baltic states had definitely failed. When Soviet special forces attacked the Ministry of the Interior in Riga a week later, it was thus more an expression of the frustration of the local Soviet troops, than part of a co-ordinated action.

The spring of 1991 was characterized by continued political confrontation with Moscow. In February, Gorbachev organized a referendum, which was meant to demonstrate continuous support of a Soviet union. However, the Baltic authorities refused to hold the referendum and instead they organized a referendum on Baltic independence. Naturally, this referendum showed an overwhelming support of independence, and even among the Russian-speaking minorities in Estonia and Latvia between 30 and 40 per cent of the people voted for independence.

The Baltic states regained their independence after the unsuccessful *coup d'état* in Moscow in August 1992. After gaining independence, the three countries were faced with two fundamental constitutional issues: should the countries adopt presidential or parliamentary systems of government and who should be citizens of the states? These questions had to be resolved before the first free elections could take place.

A reintroduction of the constitutions from the period of independence between the two world wars carried an obvious strong symbolic value. However, with the exception of the Latvian constitution, they were undemocratic and had legitimatized the authoritarian systems of the dictators Päts and Smetona of Estonia and Lithuania respectively. By reintroducing these constitutions Baltic politicians could, on the basis of international law, deny the Russian immigrants citizenship, since they could be seen as occupiers. Hence, the two constitutional issues were closely interconnected.

In Estonia, which was the first to adopt a new constitution, the two issues were successfully separated by a compromise between representatives of the Supreme Council and the alternative parliament, the Estonian Congress (*Eesti Kongress*), which was dominated by representatives of the Estonian National Independence Party (*Eesti Rahvusliku Soltumatuse Partei*). ENIP recognized that a new constitution had to take its point of departure from existing institutions — the Supreme Council — and the Supreme Council on their part made concessions to ENIP on the question of citizenship. A separate referendum on voting rights to the Russian immigrants was held prior to the constitutional referendum in the summer of 1992, in which roughly 40 per cent of the inhabitants of the territory were *de facto* denied citizenship.

After the question of citizenship was settled, the Estonian politicians reached an agreement on other constitutional issues. Already from the first draft constitution selected on Oct. 11, 1991, it was clear that Estonia was heading for a parliamentary system of government. Late in the campaign prior to the referendum a maverick right-wing movement, "Restitution", appeared which campaigned for a "No" to the new constitution and advocated the reinstatement of the 1938 constitution instead, in which political parties had been outlawed and the media had been censored. In a surprising show of unity the 13 political parties behind the new constitution issued a common appeal to the electors in which they launched a counterattack against the arguments of Restitution and urged them to vote for the new constitution. Restitution's campaign failed and the new constitution was adopted by a referendum on 28 July 1992 with 91 per cent of the vote.

If the Estonian constitutional struggle was characterized by exclusion of the minority and compromise and consensus on the system of government, the Lithuanian constitutional struggle can be characterized by inclusion and confrontation. The question of citizenship in Lithuania had never been a political issue because of the size and the long historical affiliation with the country of the Polish minority. Instead the question of presidency or parliamentarism divided the political parties in a battle that paralysed Parliament.

Sajudis, headed by the popular leader Vytautas Landsbergis, favoured a strong presidency in which the president could appoint or dismiss the government without the approval of parliament. The president should further be vested with strong veto rights and lead the work of the government. *Sajudis* fought for a strong presidency under the slogan: "Anarchy or a steady, firm hand in the reforms".

The Lithuanian Democratic Labour Party — LDLP, headed by the former leader of the Lithuanian Communist Party, Algirdas Brazauskas, favoured a stronger parliament than *Sajudis*, in which the role of the president in direct policy would be limited to foreign policy. The slogan was: "Parliamentary democracy or beginning of authoritarian rule".

However, the political slogans disguised the different organizational structures, interests and opportunities of *Sajudis* and LDLP at that time. The LDLP, which had inherited the organization of the communist party, believed that its organization would offer better opportunities in a parliament where its members would be the best organized. *Sajudis*, with a loose organizational structure, could on its hand mobilize for a presidential election, but due to the fact that *Sajudis* was less developed as a political party, the parliamentary group of *Sajudis* would be more prone to internal anarchy than the parliamentary group of the LDLP. Furthermore, *Sajudis* feared the strong links between LDLP and the former *nomenklatura* of agriculture, industry and many of the intellectuals. *Sajudis* feared that these links would terminate the reforms if LDLP were to become the major political party in parliament. In return *Sajudis* believed that it could win a presidential election given the popularity of Vytautas Landsbergis.

In the spring of 1992 *Sajudis* lost its majority in Parliament and in the constitutional committee, and *Sajudis* took the question of a strong president to the streets and started a petition for a referendum. The referendum was held on 23 May, 1992, but the result was a defeat for *Sajudis*. Although a majority of the voters (69.5 per cent) had voted for a strong presidency, the participation was too low (57.5 per cent) to fulfil the criterion that a majority of all citizens entitled to vote cast their votes in favour of the proposal.

Sajudis and the LDLP therefore negotiated a compromise during the autumn that was put into effect only two weeks prior to Oct. 25, 1992, when a new referendum on the compromise constitution and the first round of the parliamentary elections had been scheduled. The compromise constitution, in which the president is still a substantial actor in the Lithuanian political system reflects the relations between *Sajudis* and LDLP. The sheer number of built-in checks and balances showes the distrust between these two principal political forces.

Latvia's constitutional struggle was characterized by an apparent lack of struggle and debate and, except for a brief period in the spring of 1992, there has been a general consensus among the political parties about the restitution of the 1922 constitution. This consensus has ensured that the first freely elected parliament was dominated by ethnic Latvians according to a decision by the Supreme Council in October 1991 when it was decided that only those who had citizenship in 1940 and their descendants could immediately become citizens of Latvia. As a result immigrants, numbering approximately 25 per cent of the population, were barred from acquiring citizenship and hence from voting. In reality, Latvia has no coherent constitution. Some of the articles in the 1922 constitution have been suspended and new constitutional laws have replaced or supplemented the 1922 constitution.

After the first free elections in June 1993 a constitutional revision was suggested by Harmony for Latvia (SLAT), but received no support in Parliament. However, there are signs that a new round of constitutional struggle and discussion will begin. First, the restitution of the 1922 constitution has served its purpose by ensuring ethnic Latvians the leading role in parliament. Secondly, the political parties (Equal Rights and SLAT) which claim to represent the non-citizens have gained representation in Parliament. And, thirdly, political parties such as the Farmers' Union, which is represented in the government and to which President Guntis Ulmanis belongs, have raised their voices in favour of a revision of the powers of the president and the way he is elected.

Before the first elections the Baltic politicians had to make the important decision on what electoral system to use. In doing this they have been keen to avoid the mistakes of the inter-war period when adopting new election laws. The inter-war election laws contained no rules about the minimum percentage of votes required for representation, a system that resulted in fragmented parliaments. In the early 1930s 27 political parties were represented in the Latvian parliament. This political fragmentation was a factor which had contributed to the breakdown of democracy and installation of dictatorship. In consequence of these memories, the new election laws all operate with lower threshold requirements (see Table 3).

In Estonia small parties can gain representation if they obtain seats in the multi-seat constituencies but can only receive additional compensation seats if they either pass the 5 per cent lower threshold requirement or win at least three seats in the multi-seat constituencies.

The Latvian election law divides the country into five multi-seat constituencies in which seats are distributed proportionally by the Sainte-Lagüe method. Since candidates are allowed to enroll on the list in more than one of the five constituencies, the system is close to resembling one national multi-seat constituency. This rule ensures that popular candidates can draw votes for the party nationwide by running in all or several of the constituencies. At the election in June 1993 Gorbunovs from Latvia's Way — the former and present chairman of the Supreme Council — could therefore pass on votes to less successful candidates by being elected in more than one constituency.

The Latvian and Estonian systems resemble to a large degree the systems known in Scandinavia. Lithuania has chosen a third way which is a mixture of the proportional system and first-past-the-post system in single seat constituencies. The 141 seats in the

Table 3: Election Laws, the Baltic states 1993

	Estonia	Latvia	Lithuania
Election period (years)			
-parliament	4	3	4
-president	5	3	5
Franchise (years)	18	*18	18
Eligibility (years)			
-parliament	21	21	25
-president	40	40	40
Threshold (per cent)	5	4	4
Electoral System	proportional, modified d'Hondt	proportional, Sainte-Lague	Mixture of single seat constituencies and proportional system

Lithuanian Parliament are divided into two groups: one comprising 70 seats for the national list and the other comprising 71 seats distributed across single seat constituencies. The election is organized by giving each voter two ballots, one for the national list and one for the constituency. The result of the national list can only be compiled after the single seat constituencies are settled, because the winning candidate in the constituency is struck off the national list. The national list operates with a 4 per cent lower threshold requirement, with exception of parties and organizations which are recognized as representing ethnic minorities. This allowed the Union of Poles to be represented by two seats won on the national list in addition to the two seats won in single seat constituencies.

The lesson taught from the inter-war period was well received in the Baltic states. Of the 16 different political parties running for the first Estonian election only nine were successful and gained representation. In Latvia 23 parties ran for the election and eight parties gained seats, and in Lithuania there were 17 lists which sought representation but only five were successful. In this respect the lower threshold requirements have worked. Even so, establishing a lower threshold requirement does not ensure the smooth working of parliament nor that the political parties themselves will not split and obstruct the work of parliament.

The development of the Baltic party systems can be divided into two stages: before and after independence. Parties or party-like organizations before independence were basically divided by their attitudes towards independence. The political space developed from a one-party to a two-party system with the communists at the one end and the popular front at the other. Today the independence issue has been transformed into questions of citizenship and minority rights.

After independence, the political parties faced a totally new situation. Suddenly they were expected to behave as "real" parties with detailed programmes and solutions to mounting economic and political problems — a task which the parties undertook with varying degrees of success. With the first general elections in all three countries, a multi-party system appeared. In Estonia nine different political groupings and political parties obtained seats in the new parliament (see Table 4). None of them obtained a majority and the government is a coalition between Pro Patria, the Moderates and ENIP, which together obtained 51 of the 101 seats in parliament. The government aims at transforming the Estonian economy into a market economy, even though there are disagreements on how radically the reform process should be carried out. Furthermore, the government parties are united in their wish to keep former communists out of power. This is perhaps the strongest factor uniting a government whose only alternative would have been a coalition led by Edgar Savisaar, the former Prime Minister and Arnold Rüütel, the former head of the Estonian Supreme Soviet. The government has pursued a strict fiscal and monetary policy and throughout the central civil service the old apparatchiks have been replaced by a younger generation.

In Latvia eight political groupings and political parties were represented in the new parliament. Latvia's Way won the election but failed to secure a majority (see Table 5) and has set up a minority government in coalition with the Farmers' Union. The government faces opposition from both sides of the political spectrum but since the opposition is unable to co-operate due to fundamental disagreements on the question of citizenship and attitudes towards the past, the government can govern by shifting majorities on different issues. Since the elections in June 1993 Latvian politics have focused on two issues: the treaty with Russia for troop withdrawal and a new citizenship law, which have made the political climate between the two opposition groups tense. Furthermore, the same issues have threatened to split the government, especially Latvia's Way, which was formed shortly before the election to give the popular politicians a platform.

In Lithuania the 1992 election produced an absolute majority for the Lithuanian Democratic Labour Party and in January 1993 the leader of the party, Algirdas Brazauskas, was elected president. The LDLP came to power on a programme based on a gradual transition to a market economy. The election admitted seven political groupings and coalitions representing ten different political parties to Parliament (see Table 6). The opposition consists of the Union of Poles to the left of LDLP and the Social Democratic Party to the right. The right-wing opposition has created a formal political coalition in the Fatherland Fraction, but maintains separate parliamentary fractions in order to ensure full access to parliamentary staff. *Sajudis*, which lost the elections, now tries to use the Fatherland Fraction as a platform to form a new Conservative Party.

Comparing the three Baltic countries, Lithuania is the only country with an influential post-communist party. In a way, Latvia's Equal Rights is also a survival of the previous Latvian Communist Party, but its political influence at present is insignificant. The majority of Latvia's intellectuals and reformist communists are today organized in Latvia's Way. In Estonia the former communists have no influence at the moment. However, many top politicians from the Estonian Communist Party are leading figures in political opposition parties.

The crucial divide in the three Baltic countries today could be termed a post-Soviet conflict. It includes many political problems that are all rooted in the process of state-building which the three Baltic countries are undergoing: the presence of Russian troops, the question of citizenship, the incipient reprivatization of collectivized land and property,

Table 4: **Results of the Estonian parliamentary election 1992**

	% of votes	Seats
Pro Patria	22.0	29
Secure Home	13.6	17
Popular Front	12.2	15
Moderates	9.7	12
Estonian National Independence Party	8.7	10
Independent Royalists	7.1	8
Estonian Citizens' Coalition	6.8	8
Entrepreneurs' Party	2.6	1
Greens	2.3	1
Total	85.0	101

Note: Only political parties which gained representation are listed.
Source: Ott Mihkel Tammepuu, *Baltic Discussion List*, 1/10 1992.

Table 5: **Results of the Latvian parliamentary election 1993**

	% of votes	Seats
Latvia's Way	32.38	36
National Independence Movement of Latvia	13.35	15
Harmony for Latvia – Rebirth of the Economy	11.99	13
Latvia's Farmers' Union	10.64	12
Equal Rights	5.78	7
For the Fatherland and Freedom	5.36	6
Latvia's Christian Democratic Party	5.01	6
Democratic Centre Party	4.76	5
Total	89.26	100

Note: Only parties which received above 4 per cent of the votes are included.
Source: RFE/RL Research Report, vol. 2, No. 28, 1993, p. 2.

and the pace and direction of the de-sovietization. The unwinding of the Soviet planned economy is another problem with a strong potential for future conflict because of the questions of distribution of assets which to a large extent reinforce other cleavages. A normal left–right perspective cannot be applied to the political parties of the Baltic countries since the coherence between ideas and attitudes known from Western systems is absent. The dimensions of the party systems are therefore of another character.

After August 1991, the former dividing line between the parties over the question of independence has been transformed into a new dimension: the nationality issue, which includes the problem of citizenship and the attitude towards immigrants in general. This

Table 6: Results of the Lithuanian parliamentary election, 1992

	National List (proportional, 70 of 141)		Single-seat (71 of 141)	Total
	per cent	seats		
Lithuanian Democratic Labour Party	42.61	36	37	73
Sajudis Coalition	20.52	17	13	30
Lithuanian Christian Democratic Party Coalition	12.22	Total of which 10	Total of which 8	Total of which 18
-LCDP		LCDP 3	LCDP 6	LCD 9
-ULPPD		ULPPD 3	ULPPD 2	ULPPD 5
-LDP		LDP 4	LDP 0	LDP 4
Lithuanian Social Democratic Party	5.86	5	3	8
Union of Poles	2.07	2	2	4
National Union of Lithuania	1.92	0	Total of which 4	Total of which 4
-NUL			NUL 3	NUL 3
-IP			IP 1	IP 1
Centre Movement			2	2
Coalition for a United Lithuania	3.44	0	1	1
Independent Candidate	—	—	1	1
Total				

Note: The percentage in the first column is based on the total number of ballots cast and not those recognized as valid. In the two rows where more than one political party is listed, the political parties ran as coalitions. Only political parties which gained representation are listed.

LCDP = Lithuanian Christian Democratic Party, ULPPD = Union of Lithuanian Political Prisoners and Deportees, LDP = Lithuanian Democratic Party, NUL = National Union of Lithuania, IP = Independence Party.

Source: *RFE/RL Research Report*, Vol. 1, NO. 48, 1992 pp 8–9.

dimension is not parallel to the one on economic questions that is shown in Figures 1 and 2 for Estonia and Latvia.

The two dimensions paint a more detailed picture of the political situation in Estonia and Latvia. Two of the governing parties in Estonia, ENIP and Pro Patria, are radical when it comes to the question of nationality, but divided on the economic question, in which ENIP is left-wing and more socially orientated, while Pro Patria is more radical and therefore placed as a right-wing party. Estonia and Latvia have many similarities when it comes to political cleavages, but there are differences as well. In Estonia, it is expected that the nationality dimension will disappear when the problems concerning that

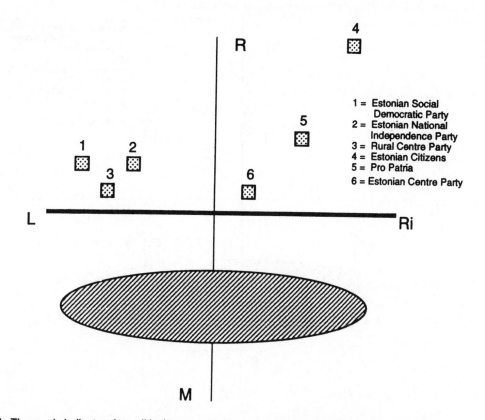

Legend: The x-axis indicates the political-economic dimension. The y-axis indicates the nationality dimension. L = Left; Ri = Right; M= Moderate; R = Radical. The hatching indicates the possible position of non-citizens if they should get the opportunity of participating actively in political life.

Figure 1: The party spectrum of Estonia, 1993

dimension have been solved. Since some of these problems have already been dealt with, it is the economic dimension that is dominant today. In Latvia, however, these problems are still on the political agenda and the two dimensions are equally important.

The figures also show that the scope of the party system in the two countries is different. No political parties in Estonia represent the big group of non-citizens. Non-citizens are simply not allowed to form parties. In Latvia, we find Equal Rights, representing immigrants with Latvian citizenship, and a Latvian party, Harmony, which represents the interests of immigrants and non-citizens. Both Estonia and Latvia exclude large groups of the political system, which may give a false picture of the political interests as they are not articulated in the party spectrum. This situation is most obvious in Estonia, but if and when non-citizens are allowed to participate in political life, the spectrum will change in both countries, probably most in Estonia.

In Lithuania, things look different compared with the other two countries. Here the nationality dimension is absent. Instead, this question is one among many which together

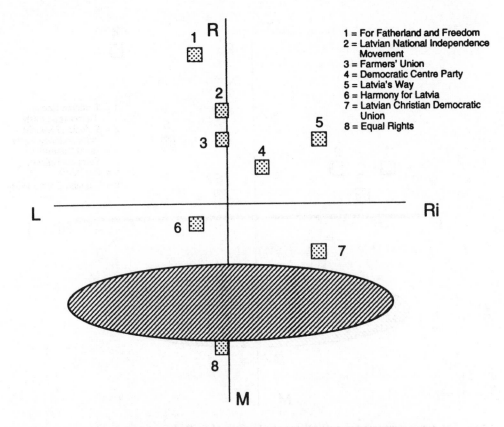

Legend: The x-axis indicates the political-economic dimension. The y-axis indicates the nationality dimension. L = Left; Ri = Right; M = Moderate; R = Radical. The hatching indicates the possible position of non-citizens if they should get the opportunity of participating actively in political life.

Figure 2: The party spectrum of Latvia, 1993

illustrate the Lithuanian party spectrum. As shown in Figure 3, the spectrum is made up of at least seven dimensions. An additional one is the question of social guarantees, which is defended by both right-wing and left-wing parties in parliament. Only the centre parties (not represented in parliament) argue for no or only very small social guarantees. The complex left–right scale is a good illustration of the political situation in Lithuania at present. When the nationality dimension disappears in Estonia and Latvia, their party systems are expected to approach that of Lithuania, with the religious dimension as the only major difference.

The multi-party systems of the Baltic states are still in a formative stage. However, a common feature of all three countries is that no political party currently in power can expect to hold office after the next election. That makes predictions about the future strength of the political parties difficult. The voters have been given the power to re-elect or punish the current leaders and change government by the ballot. They use this power to show their dissatisfaction with falling living standards, rising crime and rising differences in incomes, which redefine social structures and status. At the same time no political party

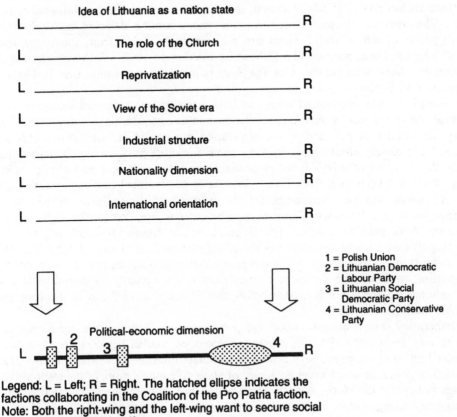

Legend: L = Left; R = Right. The hatched ellipse indicates the factions collaborating in the Coalition of the Pro Patria faction.
Note: Both the right-wing and the left-wing want to secure social guarantees and social welfare.
Source: Inspired by an interview with Vladas Gaidys.

Figure 3: The party spectrum of Lithuania, 1993

has yet developed an affiliation to specific groups in the population. Furthermore, for most Balts democracy has from the start carried the promise of rising welfare and material improvement. So far, however, democracy has been accompanied by a steep decline in living standards, and socio-political reactions are already detectable.

Firstly, the *Sajudis* government in Lithuania was severely punished in the 1992 election when an absolute majority was won by LDLP. The local elections in Latvia in May 1994 were a disaster for the leading government party, Latvia's Way, which only received about 3.4 per cent of the votes compared to 32 per cent at the national election a year before. And in Estonia opinion polls show that the government coalition is expected to receive between 10 and 20 per cent of the votes at the next election.

Secondly, as the economic reforms begin to work, a new pattern of interest groups will form. Some political parties will of course try to develop a "catch all" platform but the elections laws, particularly in Estonia and Latvia, leave plenty of room for newcomers and small political parties representing specific interests.

Thirdly, a move to the left is to be expected as the social costs of the market economy continue to increase. The Soviet system implanted strong egalitarian values among many Balts. The wish to develop modern welfare states can be detected not only from the constitutions in which social rights are guaranteed but also from the programmes of the different political parties. The Lithuanian election in 1992, which brought the former communists back into power, was the first example of a pattern that is likely to be reproduced in Estonia and Latvia.

In Estonia it is the question of when and how to integrate the Russian immigrants into the political life of the state which, besides the economic issue, dominates the political agenda today. In Estonia 40 per cent of the population are denied citizenship and this division follows very closely ethnic lines, making room for cross-pressure on the individual and opens the prospect of ethnic-based political organizations at best and ethnic violence at worst. As it can been seen from Figure 1, none of the political parties currently represent the immigrants and the immigrants are not members of the political parties. According to page 48 of the Estonian Constitution non-citizens are denied the right to form or be members of political parties. The Estonian Social Democrat youth organization are avoiding this by naming themselves a social organization. It is unlikely that the Russians will support political parties that are against their political integration and hence their integration would change the current party pattern dramatically. A period of inter-ethnic and national reconciliation is needed before the "Russian factor" can be incorporated into a stable multi-party system.

Furthermore, much depends upon the power struggle between the presidency and the government. In January 1994 this developed into open conflict between President Meri and Premier Laar over the president's power to nominate ministers and Meri's earlier attempts, as a skillful politician and former Secretary of State, to capture more of the responsibility for foreign policy. So far Meri has been unsuccessful, but with a government that is becoming increasingly more divided, Meri is left with more power to operate. If the president's office becomes more powerful, the stake for the individual political party to win the presidency will increase. That would prompt new mergers and close alliances between the Estonian political parties in order to try to minimize the risks and maximize the prospects of losing and winning the presidency respectively.

The development of the multi-party system in Latvia is also, as in Estonia, primarily determined by the question of when and how the Russian immigrants should acquire citizenship and become integrated into political life. The citizenship law which was passed by Parliament in late June 1994 foresees a quota system which dramatically limits the number of immigrants that can acquire citizenship, irrespective of their fulfillment of other criteria. The Council of Europe has protested against this system, and the law was referred back to parliament by President Ulmanis. But in two ways the situation in Latvia differs from that of Estonia. Firstly, the division in Latvia between citizens and non-citizens does not follow ethnic lines to the same degree as in Estonia. It is true that the non-citizens in Latvia consist mainly of Russians but half of the Russian population have citizenship because they have family roots in Latvia. Secondly, two of the political parties (SLAT and Equal Rights) in the Latvian Parliament try to speak for and represent the non-citizens (see Figure 2). An integration of the Russian immigrants would therefore be mainly to the benefit of these two parties. But the question of citizenship is powerful enough to tear the political parties apart as long as it remains on the agenda. Together with a sensitive agreement on the withdrawal of the Russian troops and continued Russian control over the radar station in Skrunda,

Latvian politics has tended to become even more divided between a nationalistic block, on the one hand, and a corporative/integrationist on the other with a dwindling centre between these two poles.

On top of this there is the start of a constitutional struggle. However, given the magnitude of practical political problems with the reform process it is most unlikely that an enforced debate over constitutional issues will engage many people. Most likely Latvia will remain without a coherent constitution for years to come and if changes are introduced, it will be a strengthening of the president's office in order to make the decision-making process quicker and easier.

Lithuania is different from Latvia and Estonia first of all because of the absence of the citizenship question. About 80 per cent of the population is Lithuanian with the remainder split equally between ethnic Russians and Poles who have acquired citizenship. Secondly, Lithuanian politics is very polarized, a situation stemming from the division between former communists and those with "clean hands". Unparalleled in the other Baltic states, the former communists managed successfully to reform their policy and reorganize what was left of the Lithuanian branch of the Soviet Union's Communist Party.

The polarization between LDLP on the one hand and the *Sajudis*-led forces on the other, is reinforced by the Lithuanian presidential system. In order to compete with LDLP it is necessary that the rightist parties become better organized. The realization of this may be one of the reasons for the creation or transformation of *Sajudis* into the Conservative Party, which is regarded as the new all-embracing right-wing political party. However, there is a reluctance among the other right-wing parties, such as the Christian Democrats, to abandon their own organization, while many regard the Conservative Party as Landsbergis's last attempt to regain power.

Even so, the Lithuanian election system is flexible enough to leave room for several other political parties. Besides the LDLP and the Conservatives, the Polish minority seems to be strongly organized in the Polish Union, which benefits from the exception from the lower threshold requirement. The LDLP is currently held together by Brazauskas' prestige and it seems likely to continue its transformation into a social democratic party along the lines of the British Labour Party, although the left faction within LDLP may try to break away and establish a new leftist socialist party.

In a few years the Baltic states have managed the transition from communism to workable democracies in which political parties can compete freely. In this period a tremendous number of political parties and organizations have been established, but the parties and organizations still lack a solid foundation in their societies. It can be difficult to see which interests the parties represent as they have not yet fully developed programmes and coherence between proposals, interests and ideology.

While the political parties try to consolidate their programmes and organizations, the majority of the population are still waiting for the promised results of democracy — increased welfare. So far the political parties have failed to fulfil the promises. The ensuing apathy among a still larger part of the population — as in other post-communist systems — poses the greatest threat to the emerging democracies of the Baltic states.

BELARUS

Ustina Markus

During the Soviet era Belarus was noted for being the most passive republic of the Soviet European states. There were few dissidents or mass movements calling for dramatic change. It was only after the Chornobyl disaster in 1986, which affected Belarus more than any other republic, and the discovery of the mass graves at Kurapaty, that people began to agitate for changes in the political structure. Mostly what was demanded at this time was that Moscow officials be accountable for their policies towards Belarus. It was on the crest of this popular feeling that the nationalist movement, the Belarusian Popular Front (BPF), was born in 1989. While not a political party it united various groups and organizations who felt Belarus's interests would best be served if Belarus were governed by its own authorities rather than Moscow. Following the break-up of the Soviet Union, the BPF became the representative organization of the groups and parties which upheld Belarusian independence. Its opposite number is the Popular Movement of Belarus (PMB) founded in 1992. This organization encompasses the hardliners who believe that maintaining close ties with Russia, and even uniting with the Russian Federation, is the best guarantee for Belarus's future. The country's three communist parties belong to this movement, along with the active left-wing and right-wing pro-Russian groups in Belarus. There is little middle ground between the BPF and PMB and most political parties fall into one camp or the other. Within the ranks of these two organizations the various parties differ in their stands on questions concerning economic reforms, but otherwise Belarus's political spectrum is defined over the issue of the country's relationship with its large eastern neighbour.

As Belarus's governing body, the Supreme Soviet, was elected under the Soviet regime in 1990, it is not considered to be representative of Belarus's citizenry or of the political spectrum. Only around the capital Minsk was there anything resembling competitive, democratic elections. Otherwise the elected deputies were largely Communist Party (CP) members belonging to the country's *nomenklatura*. Despite calls by the BPF and strike committees for early parliamentary elections following Belarus's independence, the Supreme Soviet succeeded in avoiding setting a date for the elections and drafting the enabling legislation. The retention of the government and legislature in the hands of the old guard is reflected in the slow pace of economic and political reform in Belarus. Thus Belarus continues to behave as passively as it had under the Soviet regime.

No parties or movements which made any appreciable impact materialized in Belarus prior to the last years of *perestroika*. The reasons behind this lack of politicization were largely historical. Most political movements which emerged during the last years of Soviet rule in the non-Russian republics of the USSR were initiated by the republic national intelligentsias and rooted in the politics of nationalism. As the intelligentsia in Belarus had been more stifled than in other Soviet European state this handicapped the country in its formation of political parties.[1]

Strictly speaking, in modern history there had never been a Belarusian state before the creation of the Belarusian Soviet Socialist Republic (BSSR). Nevertheless, the existence of a distinct ethnic group with cultural traditions and a common language residing within a certain radius created the potential for the formation of a modern Belarusian state. The earliest principalities on Belarusian territories were the dominions of Polocak, Tarau and Navahradek. These asserted their independence, or semi-independence, from Kiev towards the end of the tenth century. The lands ruled from Polacak included the cities of Minsk and Vitebsk. These areas shared the written Church Slavonic language with Kiev and the Christian religion. In the thirteenth century a new confederated state emerged on the territories of eastern Lithuania and western Belarus named the Duchy of Lithuania and Rus. Although never known as the kingdom of Belarus, the Grand Duchy of Lithuania was not a subjugation of the Belarusian people by Lithuanians, but a typical medieval kingdom in which the various nations living between the Baltic and Black Seas were grouped together under one ruling house. Under the Duchy the old Belarusian language was the official court language and educated native speakers of the language formed a class of nobility at court. In 1387 the Grand Duke of Lithuania entered into an alliance with Poland. This alliance developed into a federation by 1569 when the Grand Duchy of Lithuania, Rus and Samogotia signed a union creating the Commonwealth of Poland.

With the formation of the Commonwealth, Poland began exerting pressure on the area to convert to Catholicism and become polonized. In 1696 the old Belarusian language was replaced by Polish as the official court language. Following the 1772 partition of Poland many cities and towns in the area of Belarus were deprived of their self-governing status as granted by the Magdeburg Statutes when it was revoked in 1776. With the second and third partitions of Poland in 1793 and 1795, the area of Belarus came almost entirely under Russian rule with the exception of a small western corner which was incorporated into Prussia. The nineteenth century was a period of russification for the area. It was decreed that the term "Belarusian" was not to be used in reference to the north-western districts of the Russian empire, and the use of the Latin script in Belarusian literary works was prohibited by Russian censors. Through these processes of polonization and russification the group which serves as the usual vehicle for politization, the native intelligentsia, was very small and did not control any governing structures so it could exert only a limited amount of influence on state policy. None the less, as in the rest of nineteenth century Europe, nationalism was emerging as a political issue in Belarus. In 1902 the Belarusian Revolutionary *Hramada* was founded. It was to spearhead the movement for the establishment of a Belarusian state.[2]

The First World War and the Russian Revolution changed the political landscape of East and Central Europe and saw the creation of the Belarusian state. Its external supporters had less interest in the Belarusian national identity, however, than in courting allies to support their side in the war. On March 25, 1918, the Executive Committee of the Council of the First All-Belarusian Congress in Minsk declared that Belarus was an independent Democratic Republic. The following year in January the Bolsheviks in Smolensk declared the creation of the BSSR. This was followed in February 1919 by the creation of a short-lived Lithuano-Belarusian Soviet Socialist Republic. With the end of the Polish–Russian War in 1921 Belarus was divided between the two. Under this arrangement western Belarus was incorporated into Poland, while the eastern part of the country retained its separate status as the BSSR.

The inter-war years were marked by the gradual repression of Belarusian political groups and publications in Poland. By 1935 Belarusian deputies were no longer even represented in the Polish parliament. In contrast, Belarusian language and literature were allowed to flourish in the BSSR through most of the 1920s. In 1929, however, just as in the rest of the USSR, the national intelligentsia of the BSSR was subject to such severe repression that by 1937 this sector of Belarusian society had effectively been eliminated. The national persecution policies of the Poles and Soviets guaranteed that the Belarusian intelligentsia would remain small and inhibited in their political activities.[3]

Following the Rippentrop–Molotov Pact of 1939 the Soviets moved into Poland and took over western Belarus. In keeping with his usual policy of removing all possible elements of opposition, the Soviet leader Joseph Stalin established a detention/execution centre in Kurapaty close to Minsk which functioned from 1937–41 and where it is estimated that as many as 250,000 people were killed. The Second World War further devastated Belarus and its national intelligentsia. German policy was to exterminate this sector of society in occupied territories. In addition, as much of the fighting took place in Belarus when the German forces attacked Russia and then were forced to retreat, the whole country was devastated and suffered the highest casualties in proportion to its population of all of the Soviet republics. By the end of the war Belarus had lost over 2 million inhabitants out of a pre-war population of 9.34 million.[4] Under such circumstances it was a simple matter for the Soviets to place their own cadres in administrative positions in Belarus after the war. A very high proportion of the republic's administrative positions were, in fact, filled by former Soviet partisans who had operated in Belarus during the war and were intimately familiar with the areas they were appointed to administrate. This delegation of authority immediately placed the republic under tight Soviet control.[5]

As the only legal party in the USSR was the Communist Party (CP) there was little organized political opposition after the war. The country's national intelligentsia had been annihilated and russification was more complete in Belarus than in other republics. By Khrushchev's era the Soviet leader could boast that there was not a single Belarusian language school left in Minsk. It was not until the mid-1960s that dissent began to be voiced. The agitators were scholars and students who were mainly united by nationalist appeals. The first secretary of the CP of Belarus (CPB), Piotr Masherau, dealt with the problem by expelling the agitators from their positions or schools. In 1979 a student movement calling for the renewal of Belarusian culture was established in Minsk under the name of "The Belarusian Workshop." A few years later a movement called *Talaka* (Together) was formed. Its adherents advocated preserving Belarusian monuments and traditions. That same year another organization, *Spadachyna*, became active. It too called for the recovery of Belarusian culture.[6]

Not surprisingly, the increasingly vocal calls in support of Belarusian nationalism elicited a response from the CPB. In April 1986 a group of Afghan war veterans (*Afgantsy*) beat young participants at a folk festival in Minsk for their nationalistic inclinations. The *Afgantsy* had acted at the instigation of the CPB. The following year in November participants in an unauthorized rally in Minsk accused the Soviet regime of genocidal policies in Belarus. In 1988 the archaeologist Zyanon Paznyak published evidence of the mass graves at Kurapaty. This set off more demonstrations and gave further impetus to calls that the authorities in Moscow be held accountable for their policies in Belarus. That same year an organizational committee began setting up the BPF. As the authorities were denying nationalist agitators permission to hold meetings in Minsk, the committee met in the

Lithuanian capital, Vilnius, in June 1989. At that meeting the BPF was formally established and Paznyak was elected as its president.[7]

1990 was an eventful year as a prelude to the beginning of a multi-party system in Belarus. In January Belarusian became the official language of the republic. Elections to the Supreme Soviet were held in March. Although non-CP candidates were allowed to run in the elections, as the CP controlled the media and its members managed the industrial enterprises and collective farms, CP candidates won the majority of the seats. The opposition BPF candidates gained only some 10 per cent of the 365 seats and 13 remained unfilled because, despite the holding of several rounds of voting, enough voters did not turn out to make the elections in those districts valid. That same month Article 6 of the Soviet constitution guaranteeing the CP a monopoly on power was abrogated. In July the democratic opposition bloc in the Supreme Soviet was established with 34 members. Later that month the Supreme Soviet of the BSSR adopted the declaration of state sovereignty. Politics unfolded in much the same way in Belarus as in other Soviet republics until the August 1991 putsch. The hardliners warned against rising nationalism and chauvinism, while the national democrats called for political reform. When the putsch did take place on Aug. 19, the Belarusian authorities called for calm and did not condemn the coup leaders. As a result, when the coup failed the Chairman of the Supreme Soviet, Mikalai Dzementsei, was forced to resign for having taken the side of the coup leaders. He was replaced by his first deputy, the physicist Stanislau Shushkevich. On Aug. 25 Belarus declared independence. Following Belarus's declaration of independence the CPB was suspended and its assets frozen on Aug. 29. The Prime Minister Vyacheslau Kebich and his cabinet had suspended their party membership the day before.[8]

In September Shushkevich and Kebich competed for the post of Chairman of the Supreme Soviet. Shushkevich was an exception on the Belarusian political scene as he had not made his career in politics. He had only become involved in politics in the late 1980s when he took up the issue of the government's neglect and mishandling of the consequences of the Chornobyl disaster in Belarus. His activities struck a chord among Belarusians, where 23 per cent of the country had been contaminated by the accident, and won him a parliamentary seat in the 1990 elections to the Supreme Soviet of the USSR and to the Supreme Soviet of the BSSR. Kebich, on the other hand, was a career politician and hardliner who, despite having suspended his CP membership, was supported by the communists and former communists in the parliament. After several rounds of run-off elections between the two in which neither was able to secure the necessary majority vote, Kebich acceded the post to Shushkevich. Despite the cavalier gesture, as time went on it became apparent that there was a deep rift between the two men that eventually erupted into an open war-of-words in the newspapers. In 1991, however, this antagonism between the two was not yet being aired publicly. By the end of that year the signing of the Belavezha agreement by Russia, Ukraine and Belarus established the Commonwealth of Independent States (CIS) and the Soviet Union became a dead letter. Once the country's *de facto* independence was established nationalism began to be replaced as the main concern motivating political groups with economics.

Despite the election of a non-*nomenklatura* person as head of state, the pace of political and economic reforms in Belarus remained sluggish. Shushkevich himself advocated only a moderate economic reform programme and his powers were limited. He was, however, committed to the concept of an independent Belarusian state and for this reason was supported on many issues by the opposition in parliament. As the ministries fell under the jurisdiction of the Prime Minister, Kebich was the real authority in Belarus while Shushkevich played largely a figurehead role. In addition, as the largest faction in parliament, the 120-strong "Belarus" group comprised of conservatives and communists supported the Prime Minister, he effectively controlled the parliament's vote.

In regards to both economic and political reform Kebich had been reluctant to implement any programme which called for drastic change. This attitude reflected that of the Soviet elected parliament which reacted to any reform proposals as a threat to its position. This was well demonstrated when calls for early parliamentary elections went out in 1992. Between February and April of that year the BPF initiated a signature collection campaign to hold a referendum on new parliamentary elections. In all 442,000 signatures were collected. Although a number were invalidated, over 384,318 were still good, well above the 350,000 necessary to have a referendum. Rather than setting a date for elections, however, when parliament reconvened in October it rejected the petition as invalid because of minor technicalities.[9] Signatures were again collected on a petition to have early elections, this time at the initiative of the Federation of Belarusian Trade Unions, in 1993. Once again, the parliament ignored the appeal.[10] The parliament's term will end in 1995, but until then the conservative body has effectively blocked economic reform choosing instead to try and preserve ties with Russia as a means of keeping the country afloat economically.

Although Shushkevich's position was largely symbolic he was enough of an irritant to the conservative parliament that deputies voted him out of office in January 1994. This move had been predicted for some time. In July 1993 a no-confidence vote was held which Shushkevich narrowly failed to lose. Only because the opposition deputies had refused to participate in the voting was parliament short of the necessary quorum. The issue over which it was proposed that Shushkevich should be removed was his refusal to sign the CIS Collective Security Pact. As Belarus had proclaimed itself to be a neutral state in its declaration of independence, Shushkevich argued that the country could not join any military blocs as entailed in the CIS pact. Conservative deputies who favoured a military alliance with Russia and who dominated the parliament ordered him to sign the agreement on numerous occasions. Finally it was decided to hold the unsuccessful no-confidence vote in him. When parliament reconvened in November both Shushkevich and Kebich came under attack from the head of parliament's anti-corruption committee, Alyaksandr Lukashenka. Lukashenka charged both men with abusing their offices and using state services for their personal benefit. The charges didn't stick, but a couple of months later, in January 1994, Lukashenka again raised them. This time the parliament held a no-confidence vote in both Shushkevich and Kebich over the matter even though most observers did not believe the corruption charges against Shushkevich had any real foundation. Kebich survived the vote, but Shushkevich was voted out of office even though the opposition again refused to take part in the voting hoping that the quorum tactic would be effective. However, too many deputies were present at the session for the tactic to work.[11]

Shushkevich was succeeded by Mechyslau Hryb. Like Shushkevich, Hryb had not made his career in politics but had been a legal expert and had risen in the interior ministry to the rank of general. Unlike Shushkevich, Hryb is a conservative who heartily supported Belarusian participation in the CIS Collective Security Pact and is not in disagreement with Kebich over the pace and means of economic reform. On the contrary, he is reputed to be very much Kebich's man.[12]

The stale atmosphere of the Belarusian political scene is only likely to change when a new, democratically elected parliament replaces the current one, or if a reformer should be elected president. On March 30, 1994, the country's new constitution which established the office of President came into force.[13] The opposition had been against the establishment of a presidency at this early date in Belarus's independent history because they feared that the republic's democratic system and electorate was still immature and any strong president could turn into a despot. They also feared that as Kebich controlled the government and media he would have been the most likely victor in the presidential race.[14]

Presidential elections were held on 23 June. In a result which surprised many Western observers, the maverick Lukashenka won the most votes in the first round of voting and even came close to an outright victory with some 45 per cent of all votes being cast in his favour (candidates needed 50 per cent of all votes cast to be elected president, and the voter turnout had to be over 50 per cent), while the political "heavy" Kebich, received just over 17 per cent. Paznyak placed third with 12.7 per cent of the vote.[15] Apparently Lukashenka had gained considerable popularity with his anti-corruption in government crusade. Although he was highly unpopular with the government officials whom he has accused of corruption, Lukashenka's fiery campaign rhetoric appealed to the electorate which viewed him as the crusader who had been instrumental in removing Shushkevich from office and as a man who would get down to business and do something about the country's deteriorating economic situation.[16]

Directory of Parties

Officially there were 14 registered parties in Belarus in February 1994. Most fell either under the BPF or PMB umbrella. The BPF has claimed that roughly one third of the country supports it, while the PMB chairman, Syarhey Haydukevich, has said that his movement has over 500,000 adherents. There are also over 100 organizations, movements and unions in Belarus which also tend to fall under one of the two umbrella organizations. With the exception of the communist parties most political parties are small and exert little political influence.

Agrarian Union of Belarus

Telephone. 015-2-47-29-34.

Leadership. Alyaksandr Dubko (ch.)

History. Dubko ran as a presidential candidate and succeeded in collecting enough signatures to be placed on the first ballot. He advocated a conservative economic reform programme calling for a state regulated market economy.

Belarusian Association of Servicemen
Belaruskae Zhurtavanne Vaiskoutsau (BZV).

Leadership. Mikola Statkevich.

History. Statkevich was demoted from active service into the reserves in the summer of 1993 because the union's advocacy of Belarusianizing the armed forces was causing tension within the military, particularly among the officers, 80 per cent of whom are Russians. It sides with the BPF. This is the nationalist union within the armed forces of Belarus.

Belarusian Christian Democratic Union

Telephone. 017-2-46-77-46.

Leadership. Piotr Silko (ch.)

Programme. It is right-wing party meant to succeed the Christian Democratic Association based in western Belarus in the 1930s.

Affiliation. Falls under the BPF umbrella.

Belarusian Peasants' Party

Telephone. 017-2-34-38-35.

Foundation. 1991.

Leadership. Yauhen Luhin (ch.); Mikhail Antanenka (dep. ch.)

Programme. The party favours private farming.

Affiliation. Falls under the BPF umbrella.

Belarusian Popular Front

Telephone. 017-2-29-61-52.

Foundation. The BPF formed its own party in May 1993.

Leadership. Zyanon Paznyak (ch.); Yuriy Khodyko (dep. ch.).

Programme. It advocates Belarusianization and market economic reforms.

Belarusian Social Democratic Party

Telephone. 017-2-49-70-30.

Foundation. Also known as the *Hramada*. The party was founded in 1991.

Leadership. Aleh Trusau (ch.).

Programme. It promotes democratic reform and a socialist programme in the economic sphere.

Affiliation. Falls under the BPF umbrella.

Communist Party of Belarus

Foundation. The party was relegalized in February 1993.

Leadership. Viktor Chykin (ch.) who also heads the Movement for Democracy, Social Progress and Justice.

Membership. It claims to be the largest party with some 26,000 officially registered members. This figure is doubtful.

Programme. It is at odds with the Party of Communists of Belarus although both parties have similar stands over issues. The conflict between the communist parties is over the question of leadership.

Affiliation. Falls under the PMB umbrella.

Historical and Cultural Society
Also known as *Pakhodnia.*

Telephone. 015-2-47-36-31.

Leadership. Mikola Taranda (ch.).

Independent Trade Unions of Belarus

Leadership. Henadz Bykau (ch.).

Membership. It reportedly has some 10,000 members.

Labour Party

Affiliation. The party does not associate itself as being under either the BPF or PMB umbrella. Considers itself centrist.

League of Women of Belarus

Telephone. 017-2-33-34-89.

Leadership. Halina Kazlova Svetlana.

The Liberal Democratic Party (LDP)
Falls under the PMB umbrella. The sister party of Vladimir Zhirinovsky's Russian LDP. It is headed by Vasil Kryvenkiy.

Minsk Strike Committee

Leadership. The co-chairmen are Syarhey Antonchyk (tel: 71-83-73 or headquarters numbers 27-57-78 or 27-13-16).

Programme. The committee was created to organize mass protest strikes and was active in organizing the February 1994 strikes to protest Shushkevich's removal and demand early parliamentary elections.

Movement for Democratic Reforms
(Also known as Democratic Belarus)

Telephone. 017-2-62-87-69.

Leadership. Olha Abramova (ch.) and Leonid Zlatnikau (dep. ch.)

Affiliation. The organization falls under the BPF umbrella.

Movement for Democracy, Social Progress and Justice (MDSPJ)

Foundation. Founded in October 1993.

Leadership. Its chairman is Viktor Chykin. It unites seven communist organizations.

Programme. A Stalinist and Russian-supremist party.

Affiliation. Falls under the PMB umbrella.

National Democratic Party

Telephone. 017-2-27-43-76.

Foundation. The party was founded in 1990.

Leadership. Anatoly Astapenka, Viktar Naumenko (joint ch.).

Programme. It aims to promote political and economic reform and Belarusianization. The party is very right wing and devoted to Belarusian national causes.

Affiliation. Falls under the BPF umbrella.

Party of Communists of Belarus

Foundation. The party was created in June 1992 to take the place of the banned CPB.

Leadership. Vasil Novikau (ch.).

History. Novikau ran as a presidential contender in the June 1994 elections and succeeded in being placed on the ballot for the first round of elections.

Programme. The party stands for close ties with Russia, politically and economically, the restoration of the Soviet Union or at least a Slavic union, having both Russian and Belarusian as official state languages, and a state controlled economy.

Affiliation. Falls under the PMB umbrella.

Party of Popular Accord

Leadership. Henadz Karpenka (ch.).

History. The party is supported by technocrats and is more concerned with economic reform than the issue of nationalism and has refused to be grouped in either the BPF or PMB camp. Karpenka has been courted by both sides. It was reported in late 1993 that Kebich was considering proposing the first deputy premiership to Karpenka as a way of neutralizing him and placing him on his own team. Karpenka tried to get on the presidential ballot but failed after a number of the signatures he collected from the electorate were invalidated and eleven deputies retracted their signatures of support leaving him short of the necessary 100,000 citizens' signatures or the 70 deputies' signatures to make the slate. After dropping out of the presidential race as he announced his support for Paznyak in the elections.

Affiliation. The party does not associate itself as being under either the BPF or PMB umbrella.

Republican Party

Foundation. This party was registered in February 1994 and is so far the most recent party to be officially registered.

Leadership. Viktar Talmachou (ch.).

Programme. The party has a strictly economic platform and does not concern itself with the issue of Belarus's political relationship with Russia or nationalism. It thus reflects the increasing importance attached to economic reform in the country over other issues.

Affiliation. The party does not associate itself as being under either the BPF or PMB umbrella.

Slavic Assembly Belaya Rus

Programme. This is a pro-Russian organization which says it does not espouse communist economics.

Affiliation. It falls under the PMB umbrella and stands for the union of the three major Slavic nations: Russia, Ukraine and Belarus.

Social Democratic Party of Belarus

Foundation. Founded in 1991.

Programme. Similar to the *Hramada* in its objectives.

Affiliation. Falls under the BPF umbrella.

Trade Union Federation of Belarus

Telephone. 017-2-23-89-88.

Leadership. Uladzimir Hancharyk; Mikola Rosh (dep. ch.).

Membership. Officially it claims to represent some 5 million workers.

History. As the official union organization during the Soviet era it is the largest of the labour unions. Its record of supporting the national democratic reformists is mixed. Although it has called for early parliamentary elections it has not used its muscle to try and enforce them on the conservative parliament. Following the removal of Shushkevich from office as the chairman of the Supreme Soviet, the Independent Trade Union organization called for mass strikes to protest against the action. The Federation, however, did not participate in the strikes. They have been more active in striking over the removal of social subsidies and threat of closure of bankrupt enterprises in the summer of 1993 than in political strikes.

Union of Officers of Belarus

Programme. This is the pro-Russian union within the military which endorses the CIS Collective Security Pact, wants Russian to be the main language used in the military and does not want the officer corps to be Belarusianized.

Affiliation. It supports the PMB.

United Democratic Party of Belarus

Telephone. 017-2-49-99-64.

Foundation. Founded in 1990 when three pro-democratic reform parties merged.

Leadership. Alyaksandr Dabravolski (ch.); Stanislau Husak (dep. ch.).

Programme. Its main supporters are the technical/scientific intelligentsia and it is more committed to democratic reform than issues concerning nationalism.

Affiliation. Falls under the BPF umbrella.

Writers' Union of Belarus

Telephone. 017-2-36-56-07.

Leadership. Vasil Zuyonak (ch.).

Affiliation. Sides with the BPF.

Notes

1 *Novoye Vremya*, no. 7, February 1994.
2 V. Lastouski, *Kratkaya Historiya Belarusi*, (Minsk: 1993).
3 ed. Vitaut Kipel and Zora Kipel, *Byelorussian Statehood*, (Belarusian Institute of Arts and Science, New York: 1988); N. Vakar, *Belorussia: The Making of a Nation, a Case Study* (Harvard University Press, Cambridge, MA: 1956).
4 Jan Zaprudnik, *Belarus at the Crossroads*, (Boulder, CO: 1993), p. 101.
5 Ivan Lubachko, *Belorussia Under Soviet Rule, 1917–57*, (Lexington, KY; 1972).
6 Zaprudnik, p. 240.
7 Vasil Bykau, *Na Kryzhakh*, (Minsk: 1992), p. 114–17.
8 Kathleen Mihalisko, "Belorussia: Setting Sail Without a Compass," *RFE/RL Research Report*, vo. 1, no. 1, 3 Jan. 1992.
9 Kathleen Mihalisko, "Political Crisis in Postcommunist Belarus," *RFE/RL Research Report*, vol. 1, no. 22, 29 May 1992; Alexander Lukashuk, "Belarus: a Year on a Treadmill," *RFE/RL Research Report*, vol. 2, no. 1, 1 Jan. 1993.
10 Interfax, 8 November 1993; Ustina Markus, "Belarus: Slowly Awakening to New Realities," *RFE/RL Research Report*, vol. 3, no. 1, 7 Jan. 1994.
11 Ustina Markus, "Conservatives Remove Belarusian Leader," *RFE/RL Research Report*, vol. 3, no. 8, 25 Feb. 1994.
12 *The Independent*, 29 Jan. 1994; *The Guardian*, 29 Jan. 1994.
13 *Sovetskaya Belorussiya*, 30 March 1994.
14 *East European Constitutional Review*, Fall 1993/Winter 1994.
15 Belarusian radio, 1 July 1994.
16 Belarusian radio, 6 April 1994; Belarusian television, 12 June 1994; Ustina Markus, "Belarusians Elect a President," *RFE/RL Research Report*, vol. 3, no. 30, 31 July 1994.
17 All phone numbers are from ed. Vladimir Pribylovsky, *A Guide to Political Parties in the Newly Independent States*, (Panorama, Moscow: 1994); ed. Bogdan Szajkowski, *New Political Parties of Eastern Europe and the Soviet Union*, (Longman, Essex: 1991), pp. 279–80; "Belarus," in The Economist Intelligence Unit, *EIU Country Profile 1993/94*, (The Economist Intelligence Unit, Ltd., London: 1993); Ustina Markus, "Belarus," *RFE/RL Research Report*, vol. 3, no. 16, 22 April 1994; Belarusian television, 12 March 1994; Belarusian radio, 8 February 1994; *Sovetskaya Belorussiya*, 29 April 1993.

BOSNIA AND HERCEGOVINA

John B. Allcock

Formerly a part of the Ottoman Empire, Bosnia and Hercegovina were occupied by the Austrians in 1878, formally annexed in 1908, and united into the newly formed Kingdom of Serbs, Croats and Slovenes in 1918 (renamed "Yugoslavia" in 1929). During World War II the area was incorporated into the "Independent State of Croatia", under joint Italian/German military control, but reconstituted as a republic within Yugoslavia following liberation in 1945. With a surface area of 51,129 km sq the Republic of Bosnia and Hercegovina was the third largest of the six republics of the former federation (20 per cent of the total) with a population (census of 1991) of 4,542,014 (19 per cent of the total). The most numerous (and the most rapidly growing during the post-war period) ethnic group in the republic was the Muslims, with 41 per cent of the population, followed by Serbs, with 30.7 per cent, and Croats, with 18.1 per cent. No single group has an absolute majority, although particular areas of the republic may be dominated by any one of these three groups.

The size and composition of the population of the republic has been drastically affected by war, with in mid-1994 some 2.78 million people believed to be displaced within the republic itself; more than a million refugees estimated to be in other republics of the former Yugoslavia; and many thousands more settled in other countries, either officially or unofficially. The toll of the war in deaths and casualties is unknown.

Before the outbreak of war and the infamous process of "ethnic cleansing", Serbs were generally most heavily concentrated in the north-west and in eastern Hercegovina, Croats in the south-west (eastern Hercegovina) and Muslims in the central and eastern regions, although no clear territorial segregation along ethnic lines was ever possible. At the time of the pre-war census, only nine municipalities had Croat majorities of 75 per cent or more, and there were eight with similar majorities of Muslims and six with Serb majorities of this order. More than 8 per cent of the population of Bosnia and Hercegovina refused to declare their identity in national terms to the census of 1991, suggesting the sensitivity of this issue in the republic, while 8 per cent declared themselves to be "Yugoslavs".

Although contemporary advocates of the division of Bosnia and Hercegovina have insisted upon its artificiality as a political unit, interpreting its creation as a post-war republic as a communist device to divide and contain the Serbs, the boundaries adopted in 1945 are among the oldest in the Balkans.

Four factors created the intense severity of conflict here: the entrenchment of a highly conservative Communist hierarchy, which inhibited the possibilities of developing civic politics as an alternative to the League of Communists more than in any other republic; the mineral and industrial wealth of the republic, which made control over Bosnia and

Hercegovina an especially valuable prize for any successor states to Yugoslavia; its location at the heart of former Yugoslavia, astride the essential lines of communication between areas which would be important to both Serbs and Croats in the event of a disintegration of the former federation; and the lack of clear spatial differentiation of the ethnic groups. These factors have been far more significant than the fact of ethnic diversity itself in promoting the disaster of the war.

Many defenders of the integrity of the republic have insisted that before the outbreak of war ethnic consciousness was minimal; but this overlooks several essential facts about the republic's social and political life. Sociologically speaking it is true that differences between Croats, Muslims and Serbs were not typically conceptualized in "ethnic" terms: nevertheless, ordinary people were usually aware of their own *confessional* identity, and that of others. The two important exceptions to this would be the relative anonymity of a large city such as Sarajevo, and among the educated middle class, especially those whose social mobility had been tied in with the socialist order. When the first multi-party elections took place in November–December 1990, the vote split overwhelmingly along confessional lines (see Table 1). All seven seats in the republic's collective presidency were taken by explicitly confessional candidates. If we compare the results of the Yugoslav republics in this first round of multi-party elections, the percentage of the electorate voting for explicitly confessional parties in Bosnia and Hercegovina was *higher* than in any other republic. The vote for the inheritor of the mantle of the former LC was *lower* here than anywhere else — even in Croatia and Slovenia, in which the victories of the CDU and the DEMOS coalition respectively have been interpreted as evidence of a sweeping rejection of communism in these republics.

This paradoxical point has been noted previously although it has yet to be adequately explained.[1] In order to find such an explanation it seems probable that attention will need to be devoted to the period leading up to the elections. Here four factors appear to be potentially worth investigation. Firstly, although Ante Marković launched his Alliance of Reform Forces in Bosnia, believing it to be the locus of the most "Yugoslav" population, he underestimated the influence of the economic dimension, in that as a largely underdeveloped republic many voters perceived his reform programme as favouring the more-developed regions of the federation. Secondly, the former Communists were more clearly discredited here than anywhere else, not only because of their general hard line, but possibly more significantly because of their association with corruption. In 1987–88 the republic had been shaken by the "Agrokomerc" scandal, in which Fikret Abdić (a leading Communist from Velika Kladuša) had been implicated in a massive swindle. Thirdly, the growing significance of a specifically Muslim ethnic consciousness had been underestimated. The 1983 trial of Sarajevo intellectuals for the publication of the "Islamic Declaration" represented a confrontation between the staunchly anti-nationalist line of the republic's communist party and a genuinely widespread crystallization of identity. Lastly, in the period leading up to the elections Serbia rural and small town groups became rapidly politicized in relation to the anticipated break-up or confederalization of Yugoslavia, in which they (possibly even more than Croatian Serbs) were brought to see themselves as potential victims of the disintegration process. In turn, the spread of stories about the accumulation of weapons by Serbs had a profoundly destabilizing effect upon other groups.

Whereas in other republics of Yugoslavia the LC was in a position to act as a balancing force between emerging ethnic/confessional interests, in Bosnia its emasculation prevented it from playing this role. Recognizing the dangers of this situation, however, the

Table 1: The vote for ethnic/confessional parties in the republics of Yugoslavia, November–December 1990 (%)

Republic	Ethnic/ confessional parties	Legatees of the former LC	Non-Communist all-Yugoslav parties	Others*
Bosnia and Hercegovina	85	8	6	1
Croatia	64	27	3	6
Macedonia	48	34	8	10
Montenegro	20	66	14	
Serbia†	18	78	2	2
Slovenia	49	21	15**	15

Notes: * The category "Others" includes independents whose orientation is not known. In every case it is possible that more detailed knowledge might have distributed these across the other three columns.

** This number is unusually large in the case of Slovenia because of an admittedly questionable decision to place the Liberals in this group, on the basis that they represent a specifically *ideological* approach to politics, even though the party is confined in its activities to Slovenia.

† The decision to place the SPS in the column of the "Legatees of the former LC", rather than to identify it as an "ethnic" party might be challenged. Within the context of the 1990 elections, however, a major item of its platform was the defence of the integrity of Yugoslavia.

leaders of the three principal ethnic parties (the PDA, the SDP and the CDU) initially agreed to a collaborative administration, in which posts would be shared among them. This arrangement rapidly turned out to be unworkable as on successive issues the Serb representatives found themselves to be isolated, yet the requirement of unanimity enabled them to prevent action on policies that otherwise had majority support in the republican Assembly.

Whether some kind of *modus vivendi* might have been reached eventually remains hypothetical, as political development within the republic was subsequently shaped by events elsewhere in Yugoslavia. The secessionist movement of Serbs in Croatia (which depended heavily for support and especially communications upon Bosnia and Hercegovina was felt as especially threatening. The deterioration of ethnic relations within the republic was marked throughout September by a series of declarations of "Autonomous Serbian Regions", along the lines of those in Croatia.

Both before and following the declarations of independence in Slovenia and Croatia in June 1991, President Izetbegović (in concert with the Macedonians) attempted some strenuous last-minute brokerage for a looser confederal structure for Yugoslavia, but without success. Even this position was seen by Bosnian Serbs as insufficiently committed to the integrity of Yugoslavia. As the war in Croatia intensified, the republican presidency of Bosnia and Hercegovina shifted its position, and in October 1991 proposed to the Assembly that the republic declare its independence of the federation (following a similar declaration

Table 2: Results of elections to the Assembly of Bosnia and Hercegovina, November 1990

Party	Seats
Chamber of Citizens	
Party of Democratic Action	43
Serbian Democratic Party	34
Croatian Democratic Union	21
Party of Democratic Changes (LCBH)	15
Alliance of Reform Forces	12
Muslim-Bosnian Organisation	2
Democratic Socialist Party	1
Democratic Leagues of Greens – EKO	1
Liberal Party	1
Total	130
Chamber of Municipalities	
Party of Democratic Action	43
Serbian Democratic Party	38
Croatian Democratic Union	23
Party of Democratic Changes (LCBH)	4
Democratic Socialist Party	1
Serbian Movement for Renewal	1
Total	110

Source: Ministry of Information, Republic of Bosnia and Hercegovina.

in Macedonia the previous month). The Serb representatives promptly withdrew from the Assembly in Sarajevo and established their own "Assembly of the Serb Nation of Bosnia and Hercegovina" in Pale. This body organized a referendum of the republic's Serbs, which on Nov. 9–10 overwhelmingly supported the retention of Bosnia within a Yugoslav state. On Feb. 29 and March 1, 1992, the official government referendum was conducted on the issue of independence. This was boycotted by the Serbs. An estimated 63 per cent of the electorate did participate, however, and 99 per cent of those voting supported the independence of the republic from the federation. After minor constitutional changes the new state was recognized by the EC and the USA on April 7, 1992, even though two weeks earlier the Serbs had declared their own "Serbian Republic of Bosnia and Hercegovina".

Although there had been intermittent fighting in several parts of the republic throughout the autumn and early spring, in which Serb forces (with the assistance of the YNA) had gradually extended their control over territory, the formal secession of Bosnia and Hercegovina from Yugoslavia produced an intensification of hostilities. Sarajevo was besieged, and a general state of emergency was declared.

Table 3: Presidential Election in Bosnia and Hercegovina, 1990

Ethnic group	Candidate	Party	% of vote*
Muslim	Fikret Abdić	Party of Democratic Action (PDA)	44
	Alija Izetbegović	" " "	37
Serb**	Nikola Koljević	Serbian Democratic Party	25
	Biljana Plavšić	" " "	24
Croat	Stjepan Kljuić	Croatian Democratic Union	21
	Franjo Boras	" " "	19
Other (Yugoslav)	Ejup Ganić	Party of Democratic Action (PDA)	

Notes * Votes at the second round, Dec. 2, 1990.
** A third Serb (Nenad Kecmanović) stood for the Alliance of Reform Forces, but secured only 21 per cent of the vote.

From this point onwards it is increasingly difficult to provide an account of political life in Bosnia and Hercegovina in which political parties play a meaningful role. Initially politics became polarized between the Serbs, led by Radovan Karadžić, and those remaining loyal to the Presidency, under Alija Izetbegović. In spite of the nominal activity of parties around the Serb Assembly in Pale, Karadžić's Serbian Democratic Party came to be identified with the Serb struggle, providing in caricatured form a counterpart to the role of the SPS in Serbia itself, or even of Tudjman's CDU. Croatian politics within the republic soon became deeply divided between those who remained loyal to the idea of a multi-ethnic state under its elected leadership and those who (in July 1992) gave their support to the setting-up of a secessionist Croat "Herceg-Bosna" (western Hercegovina) under the leadership of Mate Boban. This division represented as much a split within the CDU as between Croats supporting different parties. The compromised position of the CDU in this respect, however, has given a stimulus both to the Croatian Peasant Party within Bosnia and Hercegovina, and to Croats who have adopted ethnically neutral parties, such as the Social Democrats or Stjepan Kljuić's's Republican Party, launched in the spring of 1994.

The Party of Democratic Action (PDA) has generally come to be seen as the flag-bearer of the cause of the integrity of Bosnia and Hercegovina, both within the republic and abroad. In practice, however, this has been a difficult position to sustain, as the party was elected primarily as the voice of ethnic Muslims within Bosnia. Consequently it has found itself vacillating between defence of the constitutional order (and insistence upon the multi-ethnic character of the state) and support for the creation of a new and specifically Muslim state within whatever territory can be salvaged after the secession of Serb and Croat units. This path has been rendered particularly difficult for two reasons. Politics within Croatia since 1992 has veered wildly between support for the integrity of the republic and the secession of "Herceg-Bosna". Between July 1992, when the autonomy of "Herceg-Bosna" was declared, and February–March 1994, when the accord was signed setting up a Bosnian federation, the government was under extreme pressure to favour the option of a Muslim state. Successive attempts by outside bodies to broker peace (especially the joint UN–EU negotiators) backed various versions of "cantonization", and the primary source of international backing came from various Islamic countries. Even during 1994, when the Clinton administration in the

USA was drawn more closely into the diplomatic effort. American representatives typically spoke of using the lifting of the UN army embargo of 1991 *in the case of the Muslims* as a lever to bring the Serbs into line with negotiating positions agreed to by other parties. This has been a constant embarrassment to the Presidency of Bosnia and Hercegovina at a time when they have been attempting to build a *rapprochement* with Croatia, emphasizing the importance of the republic's multi-ethnic composition.

Party political opposition to the PDA has been weakened by two other factors. Opposition has tended to become identified with the interests of specific *regions*, and consequently fragmented. It has found itself in the awkward position of needing to balance opposition with affirmations of loyalty to the state, thus inevitably blurring its own identity.

The area of north-western Bosnia surrounding the town of Bihać, ethnically one of the most homogeneous in the republic with a massive preponderance of Muslims, became a fief of Fikret Abdić — the former boss of Akrokomerc in Velika Kladuša. Until the summer of 1994, when he was ousted by forces loyal to the Izetbegović presidency, the region was under the nominal political control of Abdić's Muslim Democratic Party. The key to his survival, surrounded by Serb-controlled territory, but dependent also upon good communications with Zagreb, was an extremely pragmatic approach to his situation based upon a mixture of business principles and personal patronage rather than any ideological commitment. The autonomy of the Bihać enclave weakened the Presidential/Muslim camp without adding anything to the dynamic of democratic opposition elsewhere. Similarly the Liberals have been generally confined in their influence to Sarajevo, and the Union of Bosnian Social Democrats (the former ARF) has become identified with Tuzla.

There has been a very gradual development of ethnically neutral, ideological parties in the republic. The weakness of the LC has been succeeded by the stunted growth of a Social Democratic Party. Liberal opposition has been divided between the Liberal Party and a Liberal Bosnjak Organization. Like the PDA, the latter has never fully resolved its identity problem *vis-à-vis* Islam. Originally named the Muslim Bosnjak Organization, it soon split into two wings under its founders, the successful Swiss-based business magnate Adil Zulfikarpašić and the philosopher Muhamed Filipović.

Dominated by the conduct of the war and attitudes towards the international effort to negotiate peace agreements, Bosnian politics has had no opportunity to develop significant differences, expressed in party terms, over issues such as the privatization of social property, the reform of the banking system, or the freedom of mass communication. The political differences which do divide people within the republic have been pursued more typically through what Marx once called the "criticism of weapons". Not only the psychological impact of the war, with its imperative simplification of issues, but also the sheer practical difficulties of communication in the region have made anything approaching a "normal" political life impossible.

There have been no electoral contests since November 1990, so that any clear picture of changes in the strength or organization of parties is impossible. The difficulty of forming a judgement about the future direction of party politics is underlined by the drastic changes in the demography of the republic that have taken place since the outbreak of the war. By the end of August 1994 it was estimated that the population recorded at the 1991 census, of 4.4 million, had declined to around 2.9 million.

Directory of Parties

Croatian Democratic Union of Bosnia and Hercegovina (CDUBH)
Hrvatska Demokratska Zajednica Bosne i Hercegovine (HDZ BiH)

Foundation. Aug. 18, 1990.

Leadership. Mate Boban (pres.); Ignac Kostroman (g.s.); Mile Akmadžić.

History. It appears that the initiative for the party's foundation came from the parent body in Croatia, and the party's ambivalence with respect to the independent state of Bosnia and Hercegovina has persisted throughout. Initially participating in the ruling coalition, the CDU withdrew in 1992, and was the motivating force behind the setting up of the secessionist state of "Herceg-Bosna", backed by the "Hercegovina lobby" within the Zagreb CDU. For a time it attempted to run an alternative Croatian Assembly in Western Hercegovina town of Grude. When the Tudjman government changed its line yet again, supporting the creation of a federal state, this project collapsed. The CDU is both literally and metaphorically in the wilderness, since outside of Western Hercegovina the CPP has emerged as a more effective voice for the Croats of Bosnia and Hercegovina.

Organization. In the elections of 1990 the party contested seats in 65 constituencies where there were substantial numbers of Croats. With 18 per cent of the vote, it secured a total of 44 seats in both chambers of the Assembly, and is the smallest partner of the three-party ethnically balanced coalition which forms the government of the republic.

Programme. See the CDU entry in the chapter on Croatia. The party sees itself explicitly as the defender of the interests of the Croat population of the republic.

Affiliations. The CDU in Bosnia–Hercegovina is in effect a branch of the main party in Croatia.

Democratic League of Greens–EKO (DLG–EKO)
Demokratski Savez Zelena – EKO (DSZ–EKO)

Dražen Petrović was elected as member of the republic's Assembly in 1990. No contact address, published programme or other details of the party are known, and it is uncertain whether the party still functions.

Democratic Party of Socialists (DPS)
Demokratska Stranka Socijalista (DSS)
(formerly Demokratski Socijalistički Savez Bosne i Hercegovine — DSS BiH)

Foundation. June 30, 1990.
The party is an adaptation of the former Communist popular front organization, the Socialist Alliance, to the new conditions of party pluralism, but at the time of the elections its programme could be considered as more "communist" than the Communists! It gained representation in the Assembly, but nothing is known of its capacity to continue functioning.

Liberal–Bosnian Organization (MBO)
Liberalno-Bošnjačka Organizacija (MBO)
(Formerly the Muslim–Bosnian Organization
Muslimansko–Bošnjačka Organizcija)

Foundation. Oct. 19, 1990; changed title 1992.

Leadership. Rasim Kadić (pres.); Muhamed Filipović (vice-pres.)

History. The MBO broke with the "Party of Democratic Action" in September 1990, objecting to its alleged "clericalism", and attempting to secure a platform for the electoral representation of all "Bosnians". In 1992 it merged with the former smaller Liberal Party. Its founder, Adil Zulfikarpašić, was appointed as the republic's Ambassador to Switzerland and he left the party, accused of compromising his position.

Organization. Although a relatively late creation, formed on the eve of the elections of 1990, the MBO secured two seats in the republican Assembly. The party developed initially as the personal following of Zulfikarpašić (a very wealthy businessman who made his fortune outside the country) who provided its finance, and Muhamed Filipović, who provided its ideology. The Liberals enjoyed a certain popularity within Sarajevo itself, but it is doubtful whether it is effective outside of the capital.

Programme. The MBO presented itself as the voice of distinctively *Bosnian* (*Bošnjak*) nationality — "all who belong to the three great cultural-religious traditions of Bosnia and Hercegovina and who consider this to be their homeland" — and in its new form continues this tradition. A primary ideological concern has been the nature and means of developing a Bosnian cultural identity. The LBO stresses the autonomy of institutions from the state, especially the law and education; the subordination of administration and the police to the law. It is staunchly committed to a market economy and the privatization of social property.

Party of Democratic Action (PDA)
Stranka Demokratske Akcije (SDA)

Foundation. May 26, 1990.

Leadership. Alija Izetbegović (pres.); Muhamed Čengić and Ejup Ganić, (vice-pres.); Haris Siladžić, Prime Minister.

Organization. Although this fact is not acknowledged in its title, the PDA is a self-consciously nationalist organization representing Bosnian Muslims. Consequently it only contested 65 seats in the elections within the republic where Muslims were a substantial element of the population. With 36 per cent of the popular vote, the party secured 86 seats in the two chamber republican Assembly, where it forms the largest party.

Programme. The PDA's programme presents itself as the party of Yugoslav Muslims. It gives central place to demands for parliamentary democracy and the defence of human rights and the rights of ethnic or religious minority groups, specifically insisting that the Kosovo problem cannot be resolved by the use of force. In the economic field it is content to give support to the Marković programme. Its manifesto gives a prominent place to the defence of the family.

Affiliations. The party also successfully contested elections in the Sandžak area of Serbia, and has offices in Novi Pazar (see chapter on Serbia). It is believed to have links with several Arab countries, and with Malaysia, but nothing is known for certain about these.

Social Democratic Party of Bosnia–Hercegovina (SDP–BH)
Socijalistička-Demokratska Partija Bosna i Hercegovina
(Formerly the League of Communists of Bosnia and Hercegovina – Party of Democratic Changes (LCBH–PDC))
Savez Komunista Bosne i Hercegovine – Stranka Demokratskih Promjena (SK BiH–SDP)

Foundation. November 1948.

Leadership. Nijaz Duraković (pres.)

History. Continues the work of the former League of Communists of Bosnia and Hercegovina, although now as a social democratic party.

Organization. As with most other communist parties in Yugoslavia, the PDC inherited the apparatus of the former LC, with branches throughout the republic. In 1990 it was able to contest only 14 seats successfully on its own account, with another five in association with other socialist groups. This made it the largest opposition group in the first multi-party Assembly. War, and the subsequent rise of other opposition groups, have progressively marginalized it.

Programme. The party describes itself as a "modern party of left orientation", which specifically disavows association with any particular nationality. It seeks the development of a modern market economy, including reform of the taxation system, but several points presuppose the continuing active economic intervention of the state — an active programme of infrastructure development; housing reform. It also advocates return of formerly confiscated land to the peasantry.

Affiliations. It is not known to what extent the collapse of the LCY has been followed by any reconstitution of links between the various republican organizations.

Union of Bosnian Social Democrats (UBSD)
(Formerly the Alliance of Reform Forces of Yugoslavia for Bosnia and Hercegovina (ARFYBH))
Savez Reformskih Snaga Jugoslavije za Bosnu i Hercegovinu (SRSJ BiH)

Foundation. Sept. 15, 1990 as the ARF.

Leadership. Currently led by Selim Beslagić, mayor of Tuzla.

History. In the late summer of 1990 the president of the Executive Council (Prime Minister) of the federal government, Ante Marković, decided that he would contest the coming elections through his own party. In deliberately setting out to create an image of a party free from specific ethnic loyalties, Marković chose to launch the new Alliance in Bosnia — ethnically the most diverse of the republics. The ARF later spread throughout the

87

federation, but its heartland and one of its greatest electoral successes has been in Bosnia and Hercegovina. With the collapse of the Yugoslav federation the ARF remained in being in Bosnia, although with a change of name.

Organization. In spite of its late launch, the ARF secured the election of 12 candidates to the Assembly. The war has left the party rather physically isolated, with its headquarters in Tuzla.

Programme. The UBSD seeks the establishment of full parliamentary democracy, and the replacement of various forms of collectivism (class, nation and religion) with a society of free citizens. It advocates the modernization of the state and the legal system, and the complete reconstruction of the economic order in terms of its regulation through market mechanisms. It proposes corresponding reform of the systems of banking, taxation, education, communication and social security. It has consistently opposed all attempts to divide the republic into ethnic states, insisting upon the integrity of a multi-ethnic Bosnia.

Four possibly significant parties have emerged in the republic since the elections of 1990.

Civic Democratic Party (CDP)

Led by Marko Pejanović, the CDP's origins are obscure, but it seems to be a merger of several smaller political fractions. Pejanović has a seat in the collective Presidency.

Croatian Peasant Party (CPP)
Hrvatska Seljačka Stranka (HSS)

This is a branch of the major Croatian party of the same title. Its history in Bosnia and Hercegovina is curious, in that it is now led by Ivo Komšvić, a former vice-president of the LC. As with the Croatian mother-party, the CPP in Bosnia–Hercegovina is strongly committed to the market economy, and has clerical links. Its strength lies among Croats outside of Western Hercegovina, which is still dominated by the CDU.

Muslim Democratic Party (MDP)

This organization split from the PDA, largely under the impact of the war. It represents the following of former member of the republican presidency, Fikret Abdić. Isolated within the enclave of north-western Bosnia (surrounding the city of Bihać), Abdić successfully defended the area from the surrounding Serbs by virtue of two factors: his economic prowess and capacity for compromise; and the fact that the solidly Muslim character of the region made for dogged resistance. Acute differences over policy developed between Abdić and Izetbegović, which surfaced in 1992. In 1994 forces loyal to Izetbegović managed to take control of the Bihać enclave by force. At the time of writing it is not known whether this has meant the definitive collapse of the MDP, which existed largely as the personal following of Abdić.

Republican Party (RP)

This party is led by Stjepan Kljuić, a former member of the republican presidency, representing the Croatian Democratic Union. He has now set out to establish a party which is firmly committed to a multi-ethnic state. The differences between the RP and the UBSD are unclear at present.

The following minor parties also registered within the republic of Bosnia and Hercegovina at the time of the 1990 elections. The extent to which this information is now reduced to the level of historical curiosity by the war is unknown.

Association for a Yugoslav Democratic Initiative (AYDI): *Udruženje za Jugoslovensku Demokratsku Inicijativu (UJDI)*: a branch of the Belgrade-based organization of the same name, in Mostar, and reported under Serbia. **Bosnian Democratic Party (BDP)**:*Bosanska Demokratska Stranka* (BDS): registered in Bihać. **Democratic Party (DP)**: *Demokratska Stranka* (DS). Parties with this title were registered in Bosanski Brod, Mostar and Tuzla, although it is not known whether they are branches of the Belgrade party of the same name. **Democratic Party of Freedom (DPF)**: *Demokratska Stranka Slobode* (DSS): registered in Mostar. **Democratic Union of Bosnia and Hercegovina (DUBH)**: *Demokratska Zajednica Bosne i Hercegovine* (DZBiH): registered in Bosanski Šamac. **Hercegovina Democratic Union (HDU)**: *Hercegovačka Demokratska Zajednica* (HDZ): registered in Čitluk. The initials make it sound suspiciously like a spoiling party against the Croatian Democratic Union. **National Council for the Defence of the Peoples of Bosnia and Hercegovina (NCDPBH)**: *Narodno Vijeće za Zaštitu Naroda Bosne i Hercegovine* (NVZN BiH): registered in Gradačac. **National Party of Bosnia (NPB)**: *Narodna Stranka Bosne* (NSB): registered in Sarajevo. **Party for Democracy and a Just State (PDJS)**: *Stranka za Demokratiju i Pravnu Državu* (SDPD): registered in Nevesinje. **Party of Democratic Agreement (PDA)**: *Stranka Demokratskog Dogovora* (SDD): registered in Bosanski Brod. **Party of Democratic Reforms of Bosnia and Hercegovina (PDRBH)**: *Stranka Demokratskih Reforma Bosne i Hercegovine* (SDR BiH): registered in Banja Luka. **Party of Private Initiative (PPI)**: *Stranka Privatne Inicijative* (SPI): registered in Doboj. **Party of Progressively Oriented Yugoslavs (PPOY)**: *Stranka Progresivno Orijentisanih Jugoslovena* (SPOJ): registered in Teslić. **Party of Yugoslavs for Bosnia and Hercegovina (PYBH)**: *Stranka Jugoslovena za Bosnu i Hercegovinu* (SJ BiH): registered in Sarajevo. **Peasant-Workers' Party (PWP)**: *Seljačko-Radnička Stranka* (SRS): registered in Bosanska Dubica. **Peasant Yugoslav Party (PYP)**: *Seljačka Jugoslovenska Stranka* (SJS): registered in Bosanska Gradiška. **Republican Party of Bosnia and Hercegovina (RPBH)**: *Republička Stranka Bosne i Hercegovine* (RSBiH): registered in Sarajevo. **Social Democratic League of Bosnia and Hercegovina (SDLBH)**: *Socijaldemokratski Savez Bosne i Hercegovine* (SDS BiH). This is undertood to be a branch of the Belgrade-based Yugoslav Social Democratic Party, in Mostar. **United Socialist Party of Yugoslavia (USPY)**: *Jedinstvena Socijalistička Partija Jugoslavije* (JSPJ): registered in Jajce. **Yugoslav Democratic Party (YDP)**: *Jugoslovenska Demokratska Stranka* (JDS): registered in Banja Luka. **Yugoslav Democratic Party "Fatherland Front" (YDPFF)**: *Jugoslovenska Demokratska Stranka "Otadžbinski Front"* (JDSOF): registered in Kukulje kod Srpca. **Workers' Democratic Party – Party of Federalists (WDP–PF)**: *Radnička Demokratska Stranka – Stranka Federalista* (RDS–SF): registered in Sarajevo.

BULGARIA

Bogdan Szajkowski

Bulgarian party politics since the end of World War II followed a similar pattern to that of other Central and Eastern European countries. Communist control was established initially through the Bulgarian Communist Party's (BCP) dominance of the Fatherland Front government, formed after a bloodless coup on Sept. 9, 1944. The communists filled the key positions in the new government including the crucially important Interior and Justice Ministries. Gradually other political groups within the Front were purged of incompatible individuals which led to increasing dominance of the Front by the communists. The Front's successes in the first post-war elections on Nov. 18, 1945 when it won 88.2 per cent of the vote, led to another victory on Sept. 8, 1946 in the referendum on the abolition of the monarchy. This allowed for the proclamation of the People's Republic on Sept. 15, 1946. Attempts to resist the slide into communist totalitarianism by a group within the Bulgarian Agrarian National Union (BANU) which participated in the Fatherland Front, came to an end in 1947. On July 7, 1947, Nikola Petkov, an outstanding leader of BANU and principal opponent of the communists, was arrested on trumped-up charges of conspiracy together with 23 other Agrarian deputies in the Grand National Assembly. Petkov was expelled from the parliament, tried and inevitably found guilty. The execution of Petkov on Sept. 23, 1947 marked the effective end of resistance to the BCP-dominated Fatherland Front. The arrest and trial of Petkov and his associates formed part of a much larger process of the so-called war crimes trials which began in 1945, which in effect was a particularly ruthless and bloody consolidation of power, perhaps the most brutal in post-war Eastern Europe. Between 180,000–200,000 people were repressed, about 18,000 were killed without trial and 2,500 were executed under death sentences. Almost one million people were forced to join co-operative farms.

The BCP established its total domination within the Fatherland Front in the elections of Oct. 27, 1946. Thereafter all political groups and parties were absorbed within the Front. The only exception was BANU which was allowed to function as a separate political party but within the Front and as an appendix to the BCP.

For the rest of the post-war period the Fatherland Front changed from its initial function as an anti-fascist umbrella coalition and became a major organ, mobilizing, controlling and monitoring social and political development at neighbourhood, district, town and city level. It encompassed BANU, the Communist Youth League (*Komsomol*), the Trade Unions, the Women's Organization and, theoretically, the BCP. In practice, however, the Communist Party controlled the activities of the Front which were in essence and scope determined by the party.

91

The BCP faithfully carried out the Soviet model of development, nationalization of industry and banking, industrialization, collectivization of agriculture, central control of the economy, emasculation of any forms of dissenting trends, and in terms of external relations complete subjugation to Soviet foreign policy. Similarly, the development of political structures to a large extent followed closely that of the USSR.

The death of Stalin in March 1953 was followed in Bulgaria by the adoption of a "New Course" which incorporated many of the political and economic features of the de-Stalinization process in the Soviet Union. In keeping with the developments in Moscow the government and party leadership in Sofia was divided in 1954 and Todor Zhivkov was appointed the Secretary-General of BCP. Initially portrayed as a reformer, Zhivkov consolidated his position over the next six years and in 1962 also became the Prime Minister. In 1971 he gave up this position to become the President of the newly created Council of State and continued to unite the chief government and party posts until 1987.

Zhivkov ruled Bulgaria for 35 years in an increasingly sycophantic way. He even proposed to the Soviet Union that Bulgaria should be incorporated into the USSR as a constituent republic. In an attempt to silence Bulgarian exiles and frightened opponents inside the country, he ordered the use of the secret police in assassinations carried out in Britain and France. The Bulgarian Secret Service was also implicated in the attempted assassination of Pope John Paul II in 1981. All this caused immeasurable damage to Bulgaria's international reputation. Moreover, from 1984 the Turkish minority was subjected to what was officially called "regeneration process".

In order to enforce the ethnic homogeneity of the country, the regime embarked on the policy of "promotion and consolidation of an emphatic Bulgarian self-consciousness" by declaring that the 1.5 million ethnic Turks in Bulgaria were not Turks at all but Turkicized Bulgarians. They were forced to renounce their Islamic names and adopt new Bulgarian ones. The use of the Turkish language in public and on the telephone was forbidden. The regime imposed new lay burial rituals to eliminate any vestiges of tradition and faith and a representative was instructed to follow the funeral to ensure that it was carried out correctly. Furthermore, Turkish cemeteries were closed down and the circumcision of infants as required by the Muslim faith punishable by law. Zhivkov and his regime paid lip service to *perestroika* but his version amounted merely to tinkering with the system rather than genuine reforms. Over the years he became increasingly out of touch with reality and the regime was paralysed within its own straightjacket.

The fast-deteriorating economic situation coupled with the regime's massive abuses of human rights — particularly against the Turkish minority — and the worsening environmental situation, all results of BCP policies, gave impetus to the fledgling dissident movement. Various groups began to appear between 1988 and 1989. The Independent Association for Human Rights formed in January 1988; the Club for the Support of Perestroika and Glasnost organized at Sofia University in November 1988; the Citizens' Initiative formed in December 1988; *Podkrepa* (Support) Independent Trade Union organized in February 1989; the Committee for Religious Rights, Freedom of Conscience and Spiritual Values, established in March 1989; and *Ecoglasnost*, formed in April 1989, all played an important role in mobilizing public opinion and articulating demands for change. They also laid the foundations for the subsequent working party system in Bulgaria.

At the beginning of May 1989 four ethnic Turks began a hunger strike to protest against the compulsory changing of Muslim names. At the end of the month thousands demonstrated in Sofia and other parts of the country against the regime's national assimilation policy. Zhivkov responded by announcing that the law allowing Bulgarians to travel abroad, which was to come into force in September 1989, applied with immediate effect to the Turkish minority. On May 20, the regime began to expel the leaders of the ethnic Turks' hunger strikes and demonstrations. Several waves of expulsions followed later. The flood of refugees forced the Turkish authorities to close its borders with Bulgaria on Aug. 22. By then some 310,000 people had left Bulgaria. The regime's sponsored exodus of ethnic Turks not only substantially undermined Bulgaria's international reputation because of its appalling human rights record, but also had a devastating effect on the depopulation of the rural areas since most of the ethnic Turks worked on the land and consequently in agricultural production.

The regime suffered a further dent in its already bad international standing when demonstrations organized by *Ecoglasnost* during the CSCE conference on the environment in Sofia in October were brutally suppressed by the police.

On Nov. 10, 1989, a communiqué from the Central Committee plenum announced that Todor Zhivkov had resigned from all his posts. The fiction of his resignation became apparent within a few days. What had brought about Zhivkov's departure was not a popular revolution, as elsewhere in Eastern Europe, but a carefully staged coup. The crucial factors in the conspirator's calculations were clearly the disintegration of the communist regimes in Poland, Hungary and the GDR in particular, Gorbachev's abandonment of the old guard and their support for change, the worsening economic situation of the country and Bulgaria's increasing international isolation because of its human rights record. Moreover Zhivkov's attempts to promote his playboy son Vladimir (in July he was appointed head of the Central Committee's Department of Culture) further eroded support among his colleagues. In the tidal wave sweeping across Eastern Europe, Bulgaria's communist leaders tried to save themselves and their party.

The coup, which was in the making for some three months, was organized by the then Prime Minister Georgi Atanasov, Foreign Minister Petur Mladenov, who visited Moscow just before the Central Committee meeting, and the Minister of Foreign Economic Relations, Andrei Lukanov. A crucial role was also played by the Minister of Defence, Gen. Dobri Dzurov, an old supporter of Zhivkov who at the critical stage of the Central Committee's deliberations refused to back him up.

Mladenov replaced Zhivkov as a state and party leader. Together with the purged Politburo and government he pledged to promote political pluralism and respect the rule of law. On Dec. 29, the government repudiated the "Bulgarization" campaign and invited the ethnic Turks who had fled the country to return. However, the decision was greeted with protests, particularly in the region of Khaskovo with the largest Muslim and Turkish speaking population. The protests reflected deep divisions over ethnic issues in Bulgarian society.

At the end of November 1989 the contours of a working multi-party system began to emerge with foundation of the Union of Democratic Forces (UDF). The Union was launched on Nov. 23, during a meeting at Sofia University. It initially consisted of 10 parties and organizations connected with the struggle against the totalitarian regime: the Bulgarian Social Democratic Party; the Bulgarian Agrarian National Union, Nikola Petkov; *Ecoglasnost*; the Federation of Clubs for Glasnost and Democracy; the Committee for Religious Rights, Freedom of Conscience and Spiritual Values; the Club for the Victims of Repression after 1945; Citizens' Initiative; the Federation of Independent Students' Societies; the Independent Association for the Defence of Human Rights; and the Independent Labour

Federation, *Podkrepa*. Dr Zhelyu Zhelev, the country's most prominent dissident, was elected chairman of the UDF Co-ordinating Council.

The Union began to press the BCP to enter into round-table negotiations, similar to those that took place in Poland and Hungary, in order to determine the future shape of the country's political institutions and its pluralistic framework. The communists prevaricated. It took the threat of a general strike in December before the BCP agreed on the composition of the parties in the negotiations and general procedures.

The democratization process moved a step further when on Jan. 15, 1990 the Grand National Assembly removed parts of Article 1 of the Bulgarian constitution which defined the BCP as the leading force in society and state. There followed a decision by the BCP Politburo on Jan. 24 to disband the party and *Komsomol* organizations in the armed forces.

Between Jan. 30 and Feb. 2, 1990 the BCP held its 14th "Congress of Renewal" which became a scene of a bitter inner-party disputes and periodic turmoil. It revealed the deep divisions among Bulgaria's communists and younger reformers. Radicals organized into three principal factions — the Bulgarian Road to Europe, the Alternative Socialist Organization and the Movement for Democratic Socialism — threatened to split the party until the last moments of the Congress proceedings. They claimed that some 37 per cent of the party members had showed interest and sympathy with their ideas. The delegates produced few innovations, none of particular significance. The Congress accepted the resignation of Petur Mladenov from his party post and elected Aleksandur Lilov, Politburo member under Zhivkov who fell out of favour in 1983, as the chairman of the party's new Presidium. The Manifesto on Democratic Socialism adopted by the Congress described the party as Marxist and not Marxist-Leninist. This alarmed a large proportion of the delegates who thought that it represented too much of a concession to social democracy. In the new statute the principle of democratic unity was substituted for the Leninist principle of democratic centralism. The Central Committee was replaced by a Supreme Council and the Politburo by a Presidium composed of 11 persons and headed by a chairman and two deputies, rather than the secretary-general as in the past. Some of the most bitter exchanges among the delegates were made when the results of the secret elections to the Supreme Council were made public. It excluded the reformers. Subsequently, in order to avoid "the unhappy experience of the communist parties in the other socialist countries", the membership of the Council was increased by 22 (from 131 to 153) to include representatives of the BCP factions. It was an obvious attempt at a compromise between the reformists and hard-liners and a frantic attempt to preserve the organizational unity of the party. The Congress also decided to hold a referendum among its members on changing the party's name. Some 64 per cent of the total membership (86 per cent of those who participated in the referendum) voted to rename the BCP as the Bulgarian Socialist Party (BSP), which became its official name on April 3, 1990.

The round-table negotiations conducted intermittently since the middle of January until May resulted in the signing of several separate agreements over the period of five months. On March 12 the first three documents were signed setting out preliminary agreements on the introduction of a multi-party system, "free and competitive" parliamentary elections, to take place by the end of June, and equality of all forms of ownership. On March 30 a further package of documents on political reforms was signed. These included agreement on amendments to the constitution, Law on Political Parties and Electoral Law, all subsequently approved by the Grand National Assembly. The Constitutional Amendment

Law abolished the Council of State and replaced it by the post of President as a head of state (not to be a member of leadership of any party), whose extensive prerogatives included also that of the Commander-in-Chief of the Armed Forces. The participants of the round table agreed that Petur Mladenov should be elected as the President of the Republic. Other amendments stipulated that the Grand National Assembly was to operate as a permanent working legislature and consist of 400 deputies.

Some of the most tedious and difficult debates of the round table concerned the provisions of the Electoral Law passed by parliament on April 3. The compromise reached provided for elections of half of the 400 deputies by majority vote in 200 single-seat constituencies, while the other half of the chamber would be elected by proportional representation from party lists in 28 multi-seat constituencies. Each voter had the right to two votes, one to elect a candidate in a one-mandate election region and another to make a choice from party lists. Political parties, political blocks and coalitions of at least 500 voters had the right to nominate their candidates for the elections. The Law on Political Parties legalized political pluralism and guaranteed the citizen's right to form political parties. However, it prohibited the creation of political organizations on religious or ethnic basis, those that incite racial, national, ethnic or religious hatred and/or seek to achieve their ends through violence. Meeting one of the constant demands of the opposition, which was the eradication of the intimidating influence of communist party cells in places of work, the law also stipulated that political parties and other organizations and movements were forbidden to carry out organized political activity at workplaces. These included rallies, demonstrations, meetings, canvassing and other forms of public campaigns. Moreover, the Law stipulated that political parties would have equal rights to state support in terms of premises and other basic infrastructure necessary for its proper functioning. But they could not be financed by state bodies, institutions, other organizations, economic enterprises and anonymous sources at home and abroad. Foreign citizens were allowed to make private or collective donations to the maximum of US$500. The acquisition and management of party property would be scrutinized by special parliamentary committee.

All parties entered the election campaign with a high level of confidence. The UDF emphasized that the elections were a referendum on communist rule during the past 46 years, while the BSP campaigned as a party of "responsible conservative change".

The first round of voting took place on June 10. The results (see Table 1) gave the BSP twice as many seats as the UDF in the single-seat constituencies, while the difference narrowed significantly in the multi-seat constituencies where the proportional system was used. The proportional system also benefited BANU through which it won their only seats in the parliament. The other beneficiary of the proportional system turned out to be the MRF which emerged with the third largest number of seats.

The second round of elections in 81 single-seat constituencies in which no candidate had won an absolute majority took place on June 17 (see Table 2). The trend established during the first round was followed with a considerable degree of consistency with the BSP, UDF and MRF receiving roughly a similar number of votes to those of the first round.

The results were disappointing for almost all the parties. Although the BSP, largely because of the mixed electoral system, emerged with an absolute majority in the Grand National Assembly, it received less than 50 per cent of all the votes. The UDF captured a large number of votes in the cities but it trailed rather badly in the countryside. The results placed BANU with only 16 seats in fourth place in terms of parliamentary representation and thus undermined its claims to be a significant political force in the country. The

Table 1: Distribution of seats among political parties after first round of parliamentary elections, 1990

Party	Single seat constituencies	Multiple seat constituencies	Total
Bulgarian Socialist Party	75	97	172
Union of Democratic Forces	32	75	107
Bulgarian Agrarian National Union		16	16
Party of Rights and Freedoms	9	12	21
Fatherland Front	1	1	1
Social Democrats	1	1	1
Independent	1	1	1
TOTAL	119	200	319

Source: *Duma*, 14 June 1990.

Table 2: Election results, 1990

Party	Votes	%	Seats
Bulgarian Socialist Party	2,886,363	47.15	211
Union of Democratic Forces	2,216,127	36.20	144
Bulgarian Agrarian National Union	491,500	8.03	16
Party of Rights and Freedoms	368,929	6.03	23
Others	1,588,279	2.59	6
Total	6,121,198	100.0	400

Sources: Author's calculation from various editions of *Duma* between June 12–22, 1990.

unexpected winner of the electoral process was the Movement for Rights and Freedoms which surprisingly won 23 seats.

Although the elections were free, there was considerable evidence of intimidation of voters and manipulation of public resources by the BSP. Foreign observers catalogued threats against UDF members and said some opposition activists were dismissed or warned that they would lose their jobs if they did not support the BSP. Army conscripts were disciplined for expressing support for the UDF and the country's one million Gypsies were told that they would lose their homes and jobs under a UDF government.

Accusations of bully-boy tactics, intimidation and manipulation by the BSP focused in particular on rural areas, where diehard communists exercised a substantial amount of control over villagers. The peasants were told by government officials that they would lose their jobs and pensions and that they would have to pay for hospitals and education if the UDF came to power and brought in a market economy.

The results of the June elections, instead of stimulating the process of transition in Bulgaria, in fact produced a prolonged political stalemate which despite several attempts has not been resolved at the time of writing. Since the elections, the BSP has adopted an increasingly obstructive attitude to political and economic reforms while the UDF on the other hand has refused to be drawn into coalition. The result has been an ever-deepening mistrust between the two principal political blocks and prolonged delays in the enactment of major legislation required for the fundamental restructuring of Bulgaria's political, social and economic institutions.

The political impasse has been punctuated by the resurfacing of ethnic conflict. Demonstrators met the MRF deputies when the Grand National Assembly conveyed its meeting in Veliko Turnovo, the historical seat of the Bulgarian governments, in July 1990. Further mass protests and strikes took place in the regions of Kurdzhali, Khaskovo, Razgrad, Shumen, Aytos and other areas the same month. Although ostensibly against the formation of parliamentary groups on an ethnic principle, in fact these protests were against the existence of MRF and the Jan. 15, 1990 Act rescinding the policies of the "Bulgarization" process and allowing Bulgarian ethnic Turks to return from Turkey and reclaim their property.

In July 1990 Petur Mladenov was forced to resign the Presidency of the Republic over a videotape showing that in December 1989 he advocated the use of tanks against demonstrators. In the Grand National Assembly, five ballots of three candidates, Chavdov Kyuranov (BSP), Petur Dertliev (UDF) and Viktor Vulkov (BANU), failed to elect a successor. Finally the impasse was broken when Dr Zhelyu Zhelev, the chairman of the Co-ordinating Council of the UDF, was accepted as the sole candidate and elected by 284 votes on Aug. 1. As the position of President requires that he may not be affiliated with a political party or group, Zhelev officially left the UDF. The choice of Zhelev was interpreted as the beginning of a breakthrough in the long political impasse.

On the insistence of the new President the hotly disputed Depolitization Act demanded by the UDF was finally approved by the Parliament on Oct. 24, 1990. Under the Act, members of the Armed Forces, paramilitary employees of the Ministry of Internal Affairs, the Security Protection Service, the Intelligence Service, judges, public prosecutors, investigation magistrates, diplomats and the staff members of the Presidency may not be members of political parties, organizations, movements and coalitions with political purposes. They had to relinquish party membership within a month of the Act coming into force and declare themselves to have done so in writing. Failure to do this would result in dismissal from individual posts.

During 1990, three successive governments, consisting of BSP members and two or three figures unaffiliated with any political party or group, tried without success to tackle the country's increasing political, social and economic problems. In the autumn the rising tide of discontent culminated in a general strike organized by university students and trade union organizations. The strike coincided with the presentation in parliament of an economic reform programme by Prime Minister Andrei Lukanov. The programme was voted down by the Grand National Assembly, despite the socialist majority, and consequently forced Lukanov's resignation on Nov. 29. His resignation was generally interpreted as a sign of the final demise of one-party BSP-dominated governments.

On Nov. 29 President Zhelev convened a meeting of representatives of the main political parties and groups, which led on Dec. 7 to the appointment of Dimitur Popov (non-party) as Prime Minister and to the initialling on Dec. 14 of an Agreement Guaranteeing a Peaceful Transition to Democratic Society. (The signing of the Agreement took place only on Jan. 3, 1991.) With the Agreement, political forces resolved to guarantee further peaceful transition to a democratic society based on political pluralism. They declared that all contradictions connected with the transition were to be resolved on the basis of the law and through the institution of parliamentary democracy. The Agreement contained a detailed legislative programme and timetable for the Grand National Assembly. It envisaged that by the end of 1990 seven bills, including legislation on local government and territorial organization, and a bill on the election of local government organs, were to be submitted to the parliament. This package of legislation would enable local government elections in February or March 1991. In January 1991 another set of bills was to be considered by the Assembly, including one on the sale, privatization and transformation of state and municipal enterprises. Finally, by March 1991, a new constitution was to be adopted and a new general election held by the end of May or the first days of June 1991. The Agreement also included the consent of the political forces to the composition of the government with a limited term of office until new parliamentary elections, as well as a guarantee of a moratorium on political actions, including strikes.

The intention of the Agreement was to give a certain degree of impetus to the processes of change and to identify a much needed wider common framework for all political actors. When it came to the signing, seven of the political groups gave their signatures with reservations, while the *Podkrepa* Independent Trade Union refused to sign it altogether. Moreover, the extremely ambitious legislative programme fell behind virtually from the day the Agreement was signed.

On Dec. 19, 1990, after 12 days of extensive consultations, Dimitur Popov presented at the last moment before the expiry of the already extended parliamentary dateline, the composition of the new interim government. The cabinet included for the first time since 1944 three representatives of the opposition Union of Democratic Forces. The UDF was given the key economic ministries of Finance and Industry, Trade and Services and the post of one of the Deputy Prime Ministers. Seven posts, including that of Defence Minister, were allocated to the Bulgarian Socialist Party, two including the Ministry for Foreign Affairs to the Bulgarian Agrarian National Union, while five posts, including that of the Minister of Interior, were allocated to non-party members.

An indication of the precarious nature of the Bulgarian politics of transition is the fact that the three UDF members of the government were, within days of its formation, expelled from the respective political parties, despite the consent for their participation that had been given by the party leaders during the negotiations on the cabinet composition.

The issue of acceptance of political responsibilities during the post-war history of Bulgaria, which has dominated the country's politics since the overthrow of Zhivkov, was at least partially resolved by the declaration of the BSP. The Supreme Council of the BSP issued on March 27, 1991, a declaration extending sympathy and apologies to all communists, members of other political parties and non-party people who had suffered unlawful and unfair physical, moral and professional harassment under totalitarianism. The declaration pointed out that political responsibility and guilt could not be confined to a handful of people, however great their guilt may be. The party's collective bodies, such as the Politburo and the Secretariat of the Central Committee, as well as the leaderships of other party bodies, the former government, the Council of State, parliament and the top apparat, had played an important part in the decision-making and in the actual exercise of power. The BSP also accepted its responsibility for the grave mistakes and setbacks in the economic policy which had led to the present acute economic crisis in the country. Furthermore, the declaration also stated that in the ideological sphere, the most serious abuses were connected with the establishment of Marxism-Leninism as the monopoly ideology and of dogmatism in the theory and treatment of Marxism. Accordingly, the BSP found the roots of the crisis in the Stalinist-style political system imposed and accepted in Bulgaria. The formulations of the dictatorship of the proletariat, democratic centralism, the absolutization of class struggle, the party's ideological and political monopoly, the total state control and centralization of economic management, were seen to underlie the grave abuses of the socialist ideal. The declaration clearly stated that these formulations were incompatible with democracy under the new conditions.

The BSP's admission of responsibility for the country's economic and political problems has improved somewhat the prospect for the acceleration of the transition process. The ambitious legislative programme contained in the Agreement on Peaceful Transition to Democratic Society, which has substantially fallen behind schedule, was revived again when on April 4, 1991 the Grand National Assembly approved its revision. The new Agreement accelerated the modified legislative process. On July 12 the new constitution was finally approved by parliament.[2] It provides for a parliamentary form of government, with all state power derived from the people and separation of the legislature, the executive and the judiciary. The citizens are guaranteed equal rights and freedom of speech, religion, assembly, conscience and the press. It prohibits the formation of political parties along separatist, ethnic or religious lines. The parliament, renamed the National Assembly, consists of 240 members elected for a four-year term. Perhaps some of the more controversial provisions of the constitution determine the role and powers of the president. Although the president is Supreme Commander-in-Chief of the Armed Forces and presides over the Consultative National Security Council, he does not have the power to veto legislation. The limited emergency action available to the president must be approved by the Chairman of the Council of Ministers. Binding interpretation of the constitution is provided by the Constitutional Court consisting of 12 justices, four of whom are elected by the National Assembly, four appointed by the president and four elected by the justices of the two Supreme Courts — the Supreme Court of Cassation, and the Supreme Administrative Court. At the end of August, after months of often acrimonious discussion, the parliament adopted a new electoral law which established 4 per cent threshold for gaining seats in the National Assembly.

The period between the 1990 and 1991 parliamentary elections is best described as one of political stalemate in the country as a whole and also in the development of political parties. The UDF appeared to have lost the political initiative and adopted the posture of an opposition, rather than continuing its earlier role as an initiator of reforms. The main reasons for this were lack of experience, the fluid nature of the Union, and its immature leadership. The main beneficiary was the former communist political bureaucracy, quick to take advantage of private business arrangements and diverting a substantial amount of state funds to its own benefit. The UDF's confused responses of the "no, but yes" style led to a multitude of political compromises; the most striking example of this was the UDF's attitude to the post-June 1990 government. At first it refused to enter a coalition government, then it rejected the president's idea of a caretaker cabinet, but later it facilitated the resignation of the Lukanov BSP administration instead of making Lukanov take the responsibility for the failure of limited reforms, and finally — at the most unfavourable moment — it entered the coalition government. Amidst all this confusion the UDF gave credence to the erroneous idea that it was ruling and the communists were in opposition.

This assertion was exploited by the communists to the detriment of the UDF whose political credit diminished quickly.[3]

By mid-1991, one year after the parliamentary elections, Bulgaria's political institutions were barely functioning and as a consequence little progress was made in laying the necessary legal, social and political foundations for effective economic and political reform. Growing social dissatisfaction with the failure of the parliamentary process, coupled with economic hardship, social deprivation, and rapidly rising levels of unemployment and crime, was also reflected in the further proliferation of political parties with strong nationalist tendencies. In the summer of 1991 the UDF split into three groups. The UDF proper, also known as UDF–Movement, claimed the middle ground and retained some of the eclectic ideological and structural nature of the original Union. At the time of the October 1991 elections it comprised 19 political parties and groups (see Table 3). The UDF–Centre claimed the left-of-centre ground, while the UDF–Liberals comprised the right-of-centre parties. As a result of the UDF's split two of the Union's founding members, *Ecoglasnost* and the Federation of Clubs for Democracy, as well as the Bulgarian Social Democratic Party, also broke into two parts. The break-up of the original amorphous Union sharpened political cleavages. The UDF–Movement became a more coherent, more streamlined organization, more capable of implementing a radical economic and political programme.

The 1991 parliamentary election campaign accelerated the creation and consolidation of other coalitions: the Election Alliance of the BSP, the Tsarstvo of Bulgaria Confederation, and the Sovoba Coalition for the Turnovo Constitution. Of the total of 86 parties that took part in the elections, 53 (62 per cent) chose the umbrellas of seven coalitions.[4] The "explosion of coalitions" (from one in 1990 to seven in 1991) is perhaps one of the most striking facets of Bulgarian party politics. It reflects the preponderance and continuation of the "primitive collectivist tendencies" of a post-totalitarian party system.[5]

The election campaign of 1991 again gave an opportunity to the nationalist and right-wing parties to amplify their anti-ethnic minority views. The principal target for these groups being the MRF. At first the Central Electoral Commission even banned the MRF from participating in the elections. The ban was ostensibly based on the new Bulgarian Constitution which explicitly forbids the creation of parties on ethnic grounds. The ban was lifted after a direct appeal by the Turkish Prime Minister, Mezut Yilmaz, to his Bulgarian counterpart Dimiter Popov in August 1991. Similar diplomatic pressure was asserted by the United States ambassador in Sofia. Subsequently the Central Electoral Commission granted the MRF's registration not as a "party" but as a "movement". However, despite the Commission's ruling several district and municipal electoral commissions (Kardjali, Smolian, Suvorovo, Glaviniza, Pleven, Karlovo and Madan) still refused to register MRF candidates. Although local courts subsequently ruled against such refusals, the problem of recognition of the MRF still remained in Pleven, Karlovo, Glaviniza and Madan. In the end these were resolved by election day, except in Madan where MRF candidates were not registered at all.

The long-awaited and hotly discussed new parliamentary election took place on Oct. 13, 1991. Thirty-eight coalitions,[6] separate political parties and organizations nominated candidates for the 240 seats in the National Assembly. However, only three parties managed to pass the threshold (see Table 3). The elections represented a modest victory for the Union of Democratic Forces, which despite internal divisions and increased factionalism won 110 seats. Its share of the vote decreased by only 1.64 per cent — from 36.20 per cent in 1990 to 34.36 per cent in 1991. The Bulgarian Socialist Party won 106 seats, but its vote fell by 13.01 per cent from 47.15 per cent in 1990, to 34.14 per cent in 1991. The real winner as the Movement for Rights and Freedom, which managed to increase its share of the vote by 1.51 per cent from 6.03 per cent in 1990, to 7.55 per cent in 1991 and gained 24 seats. The election results, while reversing the BSP majority in the former parliament and giving a four-seat majority to the UDF–Movement, essentially confirmed the pre-election bipolar arrangement. Despite an attempt to prevent the MRF and the ethnic-Turks issue from

Table 3: Results of Bulgarian Parliamentary Elections, Oct. 13, 1991

Party/Coalition	Votes	%
Union of Democratic Forces*	1,903,567	34.36
Election Alliance of the Bulgarian Socialist Party†	1,836,050	33.14
Movement for Rights and Freedoms	418,168	7.55
Bulgarian Agrarian National Union — United	214,052	3.86
Bulgarian Agrarian National Union (Nikola Petkov)	190,454	3.44
Union of Democratic Forces (Centre)‡	177,295	3.20
Union of Democratic Forces (Liberal)§	155,902	2.81
Tsarstvo Bulgaria Confederation¶	100,883	1.82
Bulgarian Business Bloc	73,379	1.32
Bulgarian National Radical Party	62,462	1.13
Bulgarian Business Party	51,497	0.93
Svoboda Coalition for the Turnovo Constitution ‖	39,719	0.72
Bulgarian Communist Party	39,386	0.71
Preobrazhenie Political Forum	30,442	0.55
Non-Party for Democracy Movement	22,588	0.41
Liberal Party (Pernik)	18,577	0.34
Bulgarian National Union Coalition**	17,262	0.31
Bulgarian National Democratic Party	15,339	0.28
Liberal Congress Party	14,454	0.26
National Patriotic Alliance Party	14,288	0.26
Bulgarian Democratic Party	13,767	0.25
Independent Democratic Party	12,770	0.23
Free Co-operative Party	12,150	0.22
Union of Non-Party Warrants	9,945	0.18
Bulgarian Revolutionary Youth Party	8,133	0.15
Bulgarian Communist Party (Marxist)	7,663	0.14
Christian Radical Party	6,399	0.12
Bulgarian Workers' Social Democratic Party	5,961	0.11
Bulgarski Orel Party	4,853	0.09
Bulgarian Workers' and Peasants' Party (Varna)	3,793	0.07
Organization of Cardiac Patients and the Socially Disadvantaged in Bulgaria	3,362	0.06
Free Democratic Party	1,758	0.03
Bulgarian Democratic Party for European and World States	984	0.02

Table 3: Cont.1

Party/Coalition	Votes	%
Party of Free Democrats (Centre)	866	0.02
Party of Justice United Democratic Alliance	30	0.00
Party of Proprietors in Bulgaria	8	0.00
Christian Radical Democratic Party	5	0.00
Constitutional Forum Political Club	0	0.00
Independent candidates (19)	52,617	0.95
TOTAL	5,540,837	100.00

Source: Author's calculations from various issues of *Demokratsija, Duma* and Bulletins of the Bulgarian Telegraph Agency.

*The Union of Democratic Forces coalition included the following parties: Alternative Social Liberal Party, Bulgarian Democratic Forum, Bulgarian Social Democratic Party — Ivan Kourtev, Christian Democratic Front, Civic Initiative Movement, Democratic Party, *Ecoglasnost* National Movement — Edvin Sougarev, Federation of Clubs for Democracy — Yordan Vassilev, Federation of Independent Students Associations, Independent Society for Human Rights Protection, New Social Democratic Party, Radical Democratic Party, Republican Party, Roma Union, Spasenie Christian Union, Union of Free Democrats, Union of Non-party Members, Union of the Repressed, United Democratic Centre.

†The Election Alliance was registered on Sept. 9, 1991, with the Central Electoral Commission. According to an agreement signed by its members, the parties of the coalition preserved their political independence and ideological differences. They were united by common goals: the preservation of peace in the country, protection of democracy, preservation of Bulgarian spirit and culture, guarantees of personal security, and protection of the national security in Bulgaria. The Alliance comprised the following groups and parties: Bulgarian Communist Party, Bulgarian Liberal Party, Bulgarian Socialist Party, Christian Republican Party, Christian Women's Movement, Fatherland Party of Labour, Federation of Socialist Youth, People's Liberal Party — Stefan Stambolov, Socialist Youth's Union.

‡The Union of Democratic Forces–Centre coalition included: Alternative Socialist Association — Independent, Bulgarian Social Democratic Party, Democratic Party — Plovdiv, *Ecoglasnost* Political Club.

§The coalition of the Union of Democratic Forces–Liberal included: Democratic Party — Conservative Concord, Federation of Clubs for Democracy, Green Party.

¶The Confederation, the objective of which is the restoration of the Turnovo Constitution and King Simeon II, and the transformation of Bulgaria into a stable democratic state based on the rule of law, with a market economy integrated into the European economic system, included: Committee for the Restoration of Parliamentary Monarchy, Constitutional Union of Plovdiv, Crown Movement of Gabrovo, Kingdom of Bulgaria Union of Rousse, Prosvetlenie Association of Sofia, St John of Rila Club of Sofia, Third Bulgarian Kingdom Committee of Sofia, Union–Nadezhda of Dobrich, Union–Simeon the Great of Lovech.

‖The coalition included: Bulgarian Democratic Party for European Federation, Bulgarian People's Party, Conservative Party, Liberal Democratic Party, Party of Freedom and Progress, United Agrarian Party.

**The coalition included: Bulgarian Fatherland Party, Bulgarian National Union, New Democracy.

Table 4: Comparative election results, 1990 and 1991

Party/Coalition	1990		1991	
	Votes	%	Votes	%
Union of Democratic Forces	2,215,874	36.20	1,903,567	34.36
Election Alliance of the Bulgarian Socialist Party*	2,886,145	47.15	1,836,050	33.14
Movement for Rights and Freedoms	369,108	6.03	418,168	7.55
Bulgarian Agrarian National Union — United**	491,532	8.03	214,052	3.86
Others	158,539	2.59	1,169,000	21.09
TOTAL	6,121,198	100.00	5,540,837	100.00

* In the 1990 elections the BSP took part as a single party.

** The Bulgarian National Union — United claims to be the the continuator of the old BANU which throughout the post-war period participated in communist-dominated governments.

Sources: Author's calculations from various issues of *Demokratsija, Duma* and Bulletins of the Bulgarian Telegraph Agency.

NOTE The discrepancy of 580,361 votes between the 1990 and 1991 total number of votes is mainly due to the changes in the Electoral Law. The 1990 provisions permitted Bulgarian citizens resident abroad to vote in Bulgarian Embassies abroad. These provisions were not incorporated into the 1991 Law. Expatriates were allowed to vote only if they returned to Bulgarian territory. It is estimated that nearly one million Bulgarians reside outside the country.

occupying a central role in Bulgarian politics the elections again demonstrated its crucial position.

Despite the emergence of the UDF/BSP bipolarity, Bulgarian party politics has remained fluid. An analysis of the proliferation of political parties and coalitions, which may suggest an enlargement of the political spectrum and political debate, are contradicted by electoral results. Two solid blocs dominated the post-election political scene, and have continued to do so, with a third party based on an even tighter ethnic bloc of votes, holding the balance of power.

A careful look at the issues and identification of cleavages that dominate party political debate focus on five major issues: firstly, the need for a new revival of the Bulgarian nation; secondly, the place and role of ethnic minorities (Turks and Macedonians in particular); thirdly, the fear of the "revenge of democracy"; fourthly, the economic and social costs of transition; and fifthly, the variability and risks of opening to the West with all the national, economic and social consequences. These areas form the cornerstones of party political programmes and have dominated political debate since the 1991 elections. The lack of resolution of these problems has had, and will continue

Table 5: Distribution of seats in the National Assembly, 1990 and 1991

Party/Coalition	1990		1991	
	Seats	%	Seats	%
Union of Democratic Forces	144	36.00	110	45.80
Election Alliance of the Bulgarian Socialist Party*	211	52.75	106	44.20
Movement for Rights and Freedoms	23	5.75	24	10.00
Bulgarian Agrarian National Union — United**	16	4.00	–	–
Others	6	1.50	–	–
Total	400	100.00	240	100.00

* In the 1990 elections the BSP took part as a single party.

** The Bulgarian National Union — United claims to be the continuator of the old BANU.

Sources: Author's calculations from various issues of *Demokratsija, Duma* and Bulletins of the Bulgarian Telegraph Agency.

to have, a fundamental influence on the post-1991 and future shape of Bulgarian party politics.

Following the October 1991 elections the UDF formed a minority government, headed by its chairman, Filip Dimitrov, as Prime Minister. The new government, although comprised only of UDF members, had strong backing from the MRF, however. The historic victory of UDF over the BSP was the result of a complicated equation which in the long run had increasingly negative consequences on the operation and policies of the government. Dimitrov made an effort to appoint ministers with specialized knowledge in the respective fields, but he had to yield to pressure from major factions and member organizations within the UDF in making his selection. When the bargaining ended, most major political groups found themselves represented in the government, sometimes by their leaders. But in the process, decision-making and governance were obstructed owing to the lack of directional unity. It should be remembered that the whole UDF — the so called blue idea (derived from the party's colour) — is based more on organizational cohesion than on ideological affinity.[7]

In the first post-war democratic presidential elections in January 1992, the incumbent president, Zhelyu Zhelev, and his running mate, the poet Blaga Dimitrova, won the elections with the backing of the ruling Union of Democratic Forces. Although they defeated 21 other teams, their victory was secured only after the second round. In the first round on Jan. 12, the Zhelev–Dimitrova team, received 44.58 per cent of the popular vote, while the candidates backed by the BSP, Velko Valkanov and Rumen Vodenicharov, won 30.52 per cent of the vote. The second round of voting which took place on Jan. 19 gave the Zhelev–Dimitrova team the required absolute majority when they managed to secure 52.8 per cent of the votes. However, 47.1 per cent of the ballots were cast in favour of the Valkanov–Vodenicharov team. The very narrow margin by which Zhelev and Dimitrova won indicated not only the continued level of support for the communists in the country, but more importantly the degree of disappointment of the population with the politics of transformation and in particular those pursued by the UDF government.

Over the months the Dimitrov government managed to alienate its supporters, including the powerful Independent Trade Union Federation *Podkrepa* which blamed the administration for the slow pace of reform, the fast-deteriorating economic situation and rising crime. There was also increasing tension between President Zhelev and the government over the conduct of foreign policy, particularly the Macedonian question, and the issue of the publication of secret files. Most importantly, however, the government began losing the support of the UDF's traditional ally, the Movement for Rights and Freedoms. The rural areas in the south of the country inhabited predominantly by MRF's supporters had been extremely hard hit by the economic downturn, with very high unemployment and devastating social consequences for close-knit peasant communities. As a result, tens of thousands of ethnic Turks began to leave Bulgaria for Turkey in a second spate of emigration. The Turkish government was again forced to impose tough border and emigration controls in order to prevent the exodus. Had this trend continued it would have deprived the MRF of many of its votes. The MRF therefore sided with the BSP in the National Assembly and sealed the fate of the UDF administration.

The Dimitrov government was eventually forced to resign on Oct. 28, 1992, having lost a vote of confidence by a small margin of 120 to 111 votes. It took the National Assembly two months to agree on Dimitrov's successor as prime minister. After complex negotiations, on Dec. 30 a 67-year-old economics professor and adviser to President Zhelev, Lyuben Berov, managed to receive sufficient backing in the parliament. His cabinet of mainly non-party technocrats had support from the MRF, the majority of the BSP and a small section of dissident members of the UDF who formed a small New Union for Democracy (NUD) parliamentary faction. At first the UDF expressed strong doubts that an administration depending on what they called an "unholy coalition" between the BSP and the MRF could be sufficiently strong and stable to promote adequate policies. These doubts soon turned into outright and determined opposition to the government. The Union charged the Berov administration with incompetence, anti-social policies, partial "recommunization" of society, and of being under the control of the communists. Although Lyuben Berov has ordered the sacking of several pro-UDF state officials and experts, actions that inevitably slowed down the process of "decommunization", the UDF's claims of restoration of communism were somewhat exaggerated.

On April 15, 1993, members of 12 political parties and groups sharing centrist views, including the Movement for Rights and Freedoms, the Alternative Social Liberal Party, the Bulgarian Social Democratic Party and the Green Party, established the Council for Co-operation. The aim of this loose coalition was to support President Zhelyu Zhelev, who after the break with the Union of Democratic Forces had been lacking organized political support of his own.

The serious rift between President Zhelev and his former power base, the UDF, widened further in 1993. In June one of the UDF's leaders, Edvin Sugarev, went on hunger strike demanding the President's resignation. He was supported by mass rallies in Sofia and some of the UDF mayors throughout the country. A tent city was erected outside the presidential office in the capital. On June 13, President Zhelev accused the UDF of seeking "to destroy constitutional order and democratic institutions". Although the hunger strike and mass protest was called off at the end of June heeding the President's calls for solving political problems through political involvement rather than through passive resistance, the Vice-President, Blaga Dimitrova, tended her resignation to the Constitutional Court. She cited a number of reasons that had led to her decision, including feelings of being deliberately shut out of the decision making-process and her belief that "preparations are under way for dictatorship in this country".[8]

Throughout 1993 and 1994 the Lyuben Berov government enjoyed the support of three of the four parliamentary factions in the National Assembly. In spite of managing to survive seven no-confidence motions, it resigned on Sept. 2, 1993, thus precipitating yet another stage in the country's on-going political crisis. This is likely to continue unless there is a substantial internal realignment among the political parties constituting the UDF/BSP polarity and the third force, the MRF.

Directory of Parties

Agrarian Youth League
Zemedelski Mladezhki Sayuz

Foundation. December 1989.

Leadership. Minchev Plamen (ch.).

History. The League is a youth section of the Bulgarian Agrarian National Union–Nikola Petkov. The original League was banned in 1947.

Alternative Social-Liberal Party (ASP)
Alternativna Sotsialiberlna Partiya

Address. 1000 Sofia, Blvd. V. Levski 10A.

Telephone. 44 19 31; 44 21 98.

Foundation. Feb. 11, 1990.

Leadership. Prof. Nikolay Vasilev (ch. of the Political Council).

History. The party was founded by a group which left the BCP in February 1990 at the time of the second conference of the Alternative Socialist Association, a reformist faction within the former BCP, now the Bulgarian Socialist Party.

Programme. The ASP supports the struggle of the UDF for the immediate dismantling of the totalitarian social, political and economic structures and for the persistent democratization of society. The party supports the radical reforming forces in the BSP and BANU.

Affiliation. From October 1990 to April 15, 1993, the party belonged to the Union of Democratic Forces. It subsequently joined the Council for Co-operation.

Alternative Socialist Association
Alternativo Socialistichesko Obedinienie

Address. 1000 Sofia, 12 Vitosha Blvd.

Leadership. Manol Manolov (pres.).

Membership. 5,000.

History. The Association was originally created in the spring of 1990 as a faction within the BSP. In the summer of 1991 it became a member of the Union of Democratic Forces–Centre. During the October 1991 elections its candidates ran within the UDF–Centre coalition.

Programme. The establishment of a left-wing democratic centre in Bulgaria. The Association sees the Bulgarian Social Democratic Party as its natural ally.

Associated Roma Union

Foundation. October 1992.

Leadership. Vasil Chaprazov.

Bulgarian Agrarian National Union (BANU)
Bulgarski Zemedelski Naroden Sayuz (BZNS)

Address. 1000 Sofia, ul. Yanko Zabunov 1.

Telephone. 88 19 51.

Foundation. 1900.

Membership. 120,000.

Leadership. Anastasia Dimitrova-Moser (ch.).

History. Since the beginning of the 1950s the party has been effectively controlled by the BCP, which virtually vetted new members recruited from the Komsomol and imposed a membership ceiling of 120,000. Throughout the post-war period it participated in communist-dominated governments which allowed the BCP to maintain the fiction that Bulgaria was a two-party state. After the overthrow of Zhivkov in November 1989 the BANU tried to shed its image as the faithful ally of the communists. On Dec. 2, 1989, it dismissed its compromised leader, Petar Tanchev, and decided to act as an independent opposition party. It refused to take part in the Lukanov administration formed on Feb. 1, 1990. It did, however, agree to take part in the Popov interim government named on Dec. 19, 1990. One of the unresolved problems for the party is its merger with BANU–NP. On Aug. 27, 1990, the BANU Standing Committee stated that the unification of the two Agrarian parties was possible. It suggested that after the merger the new agrarian party should be an independent political organization in alliance with all democratic forces and working with the UDF in united opposition for the complete dismantling of the totalitarian system. However, despite several attempts to negotiate the merger no progress has been made on this issue principally because of the distrust and contempt with which the party is viewed by the BANU–NP.

Publication. Zemedelsko Zname (Agrarian Banner).

Bulgarian Agrarian National Union–Nikola Petkov (BANU–NP)
Bulgarski Zemedelski Naroden Sayuz–Nikola Petkov (BZNS–NP)

Address. 1000 Sofia, 4-A Slaveikov Sq.

Telephone. 80 03 67; 87 57 41.

Foundation. Nov. 9, 1989. (Revival of the original BZNS established in 1945 and banned in 1947.)

Leadership. Milan Drenchev (s. g.); Nikodim Popov, Vielin Kirimov, Krum Nevrokopski, Mihail Mihailov (members of the secretariat).

Membership. 117,000.

History. The BANU–NP is separate from the Bulgarian Agrarian National Union, compromised since 1947 by its association with the communists. It was the survivors of the communist repression who in the spring of 1989 took the first steps towards restoring an uncompromised representation of the Bulgarian agrarian movement. Almost immediately after the fall of Todor Zhivkov, on Nov. 10, 1989, a new BANU was formally revived. The Union is named after Nikola Petkov, the party's outstanding leader in the 1940s and the principal opponent of the communists, who was hanged on Sept. 23, 1947. The party's 26th regular congress (the first in 58 years) was held in Sofia on April 19–25, 1991. The party has repeatedly stated that the unification of BANU and BANU–Nikola Petkov can and should take place only within the framework of the UDF. On Feb. 8, 1992, the leaders of the BANU–United and BANU–Nikola Petkov signed an agreement to hold a joint congress at which they would unite their respective parties. The agreement, however, only proved one of numerous paper attempts to bring together structurally the deeply divided peasant movement in Bulgaria.

Programme. To provide a democratic agrarian alternative to the official Bulgarian Agrarian National Union; to win the rehabilitation of Petkov and other members of the Union persecuted during the 1940s and 1950s; and to campaign for democracy and a market economy, based on private agriculture.

Affiliation. Member of an opposition alliance, the Union of Democratic Forces, since its foundation in December 1989.

Publication. Naradno Zemedelsko Zname (National Agrarian Banner).

Bulgarian Agrarian National Union–United

Address. 1000 Sofia, 1 Yanko Zabounov Str.

Telephone. 88 19 51.

Foundation. July 27, 1991.

Leadership. Tsenko Barev (pres.).

History. The Union was created by dissident members from BANU, BANU–Nikola Petkov, and BANU–Vrachba-1. It claims to be the heir of the historical BANU founded in 1899. In Feb. 8, 1992, the leaders of the BANU–United and BANU–Nikola Petkov signed an agreement to hold a joint congress at which they would unite their respective parties. The agreement, however, only proved one of countless paper attempts to bring together structurally the deeply divided peasant movement in Bulgaria.

Bulgarian Business Bloc
Bulgarski Biznes Blok

Foundation. Nov. 5, 1990.

Leadership. George Ganchev (pres.).

History and Programme. Founded by Valentin Mollov, a leading private businessman, the Bloc describes itself as a right-wing Anglo-Saxon and Thatcherite-type political formation which seeks to attract Bulgaria's best economic and intellectual brains. The Bloc aims to turn Bulgaria into a free-trade zone. It argues that the country's geographical proximity to the former USSR makes Bulgaria a natural bridgehead for the invasion of West European and North American capital into the "boundless" Russian market.

Bulgarian Business Party
Bulgarska Biznes Partyia

Address. 1000 Sofia, "Sredec", Blvd. Al., Stambolinski 2A.

Leadership. Aleksandur Cherpokov (pres.).

Bulgarian Communist Party (BCP)
Bulgarska Komunisticheska Partiya (BKP)

Foundation. 1891.

Membership. 1,000,000 (January 1990).

History. The BCP had its origins in the Bulgarian Social Democratic Party which split in 1903, the result of which was the formation of the Workers' Social Democratic Party. This group renamed itself the Bulgarian Communist Party in 1919. Ordered by the courts to disband in 1924 it reappeared as the legal Workers' Party in 1927. After the dissolution of all political parties by the Military League–Zveno government in 1934 it continued its activities underground as the Bulgarian Workers' Party (Communist), its policies being directed from Moscow. After the seizure of power in 1944 it changed its name to Bulgarian Communist Party in 1948. The BCP ruled Bulgaria with the support of the Bulgarian Agrarian National Union until Dec. 19, 1990. In 1954 Todor Zhivkov became the party's Secretary-General, a post he combined with that of Prime Minister between 1962 and 1971, and since 1971 President of the Council of State until he was overthrown by an internal *coup* on Nov. 10, 1989. The BCP held its 14th "Congress of Renewal" between Jan. 30 and Feb. 1, 1990. In September 1990 the BCP changed its name to the Bulgarian Socialist Party.

Bulgarian Communist Party
Bulgarska Komunisticheska Partiya

Address. 1404 Sofia, Blvd. Mladezhki prohod bl. 5, B.

Telephone. 59 16 73.

Leadership. Ivan Spasov.

History. Originally formed as the Party of the Working People on April 25, 1990. It adopted its present name on June 21, 1990, and was formally re-founded in September 1990.

Bulgarian Communist Party (Marxist)
Bulgarska Komunisticheska Partiya (Marksismu)

Address. 1000 Sofia, p. k. 21 ul. Pozitano 20, et. II.

Telephone. 85 141 (ext. 299).

Leadership. Boris Petkov.

History. The party held its 15th Congress in Panagyurishte on Nov. 4, 1990, at which a First Secretary and the Central Committee were elected. The party, consisting of orthodox communists, considers itself as the only party based on Marxist-Leninist ideas and the legal successor to the BCP property including the buildings in Sofia. It has initiated legal proceedings against the BSP for material and financial assets. The refounded BCP split into groups on March 27, 1991.

Bulgarian Communist Party (Revolutionary)
Bulgarska Komunisticheska Partiya (Revoliucionna)

Address. 9000 Varna, Beloslav, ul. Sava 39.

Telephone. 52 42 36.

Foundation. March 8, 1991.

Leadership. Angel Tsonev.

History. Formerly known as the Bulgarian Revolutionary Youth Party, the party was founded in Varna and registered in April 1990. It claims that "there is no other party in Bulgaria based on true Marxism-Leninism" but itself. The party decided to "accept the communist Todor Zhivkov as one of its members on account of the great merit he has earned in serving the International Workers' and Communist Movement if he wishes to join the party".

Bulgarian Democratic Forum
Bulgarski Demokraticheski Forum

Address. 1505 Sofia, ul. G.S. Rakovski 82.

Telephone. 89 02 85; 75 64 50.

Leadership. Vasil Zlatarov (pres.); Nikola Yanachkov, Hristo Yonov, Ivan Evlogiev, (vice-pres.).

History. A right-wing organization, the successor to the Union of Bulgarian National Legions disbanded in 1944. The Forum has an observer status with the Union of Democratic Forces.

Bulgarian Democratic Party
Bulgarska Demokraticheska Partyia

Address. 1528 Sofia, Druzhba 1, bl. 42, vh. 5, et. 3.

Telephone. 79 66 18.

Bulgarian Democratic–Constitutional Party
Bulgarska Demokrat–Konstitucionna Partyia

Address. 4000 Plovdiv, ul. Chataldzha 6.

Telephone. 43 79 1; 55 61 35.

Leadership. Ivan Ambarev (leader); Aleksandur Dolev, Nikolai Buchkov.

Bulgarian Democratic Youth Federation
Bulgarska Demokratichna Mladezh

Address. 1000 Sofia, Blvd. Al Stamboliski 11.

Telephone. 87 26 89.

Foundation. Feb. 27, 1990.

Leadership. Rosen Karadimov (ch.).

History. The Federation emerged as a result of the dissolution of the Dimitrov Young Communist League.

Bulgarian Labour Social Democratic Party
Bulgarska Rabotnicheska Sotsialdemokraticheska Partyia

Address. 1373 Sofia, Zapaden Park, ul. Suhodolska 2, bl. 32, ap. 5.

Telephone. 22 81 58.

Leadership. Mahol Dimitrov (sec.).

Bulgarian Liberal Party
Bulgarska Liberalna Partyia

Address. 1000 Sofia, p.k. 819, ul. Haidushka gora 4, bl. 35 A, vh. A, et. 9, ap. 29.

Telephone. 58 51 19.

Leadership. Vlkan Vergev (pres.); Ekaterina Zahareva (s. g.).

Bulgarian National Democratic Union (BNDU)
Bulgarski Natsionalen Demokraticheski Sayuz (BNDS)

Foundation. Dec. 8, 1989.

Leadership. Nikolay Genchev (ch.); Ventsislav Nachev, Luko Zahariev, Mincho Minchev, Georgi Genov, Licho Gogov, Mariya Yankova.

Bulgarian National Party
Bulgarska Narodna Partyia

Address. 1000 Sofia, ul. Tsar Samuil 115.

Telephone. 80 21 16.

Leadership. Dimitur Brankov (pres.); Stroimir Minkov (sec.).

Bulgarian National Democratic Party
Bulgarska Nasionalna Demokraticheska Partyia

Address. 1000 Sofia, Blvd. Vitosha 25.

Telephone. 80 15 10.

Leadership. Lchezar Stoyanov (pres.).

Bulgarian National Radical Party
Bulgarska Natsionalna Radikalna Partiya

Address. 1000 Sofia, ul. Alen mak 6.

Telephone. 65 51 19; 88 46 52.

Leadership. Ivan Georgiev (pres.); Zdravko Bakalov, Ivan Krctev (secs.).

Programme and Organization. Small group with extreme nationalist platform. It supports Bulgarian territorial claims against its neighbours and Turkey in particular; the revision of international agreements and the emigration to Turkey of Bulgaria's Turkish minority. The party is suspected of having strong links with the *nomenklatura* of the BSP.

Publication. Bulgarski Glas (Bulgarian Voice).

Bulgarian People's Party (BPP)
Bulgarska Narodna Partiya (BNP)

Address. 1343 Sofia, Ljulin, Bloc 214.

Foundation. Feb. 5, 1990.

Programme. To support the ideals of equal opportunities, equal rights, freedom, and a just, humane and cohesive society, as well as federal Europe.

Affiliation. Union of Democratic Forces.

Bulgarian Social Democratic Party
Bulgarska Sotsialdemokraticheska Partyia

Address. 1303 Sofia, Blvd. Al Stambolinski 87.

Telephone. 39 01 12.

Leadership. Atanas Moskov (pres.).

Affiliation. The Council for Co-operation since April 15, 1993.

Bulgarian Social Democratic Party (BSDP)
Bulgarska Sotsial-demokraticheska Partiya (BSDP)

Address. 1000 Sofia, 37 Exarch Yossif Street.

Foundation. 1891, refounded Jan. 10, 1990.

Leadership. Dr Peter Dertliev (ch.).

Membership. 50,000.

History. The party was suppressed after 1948 but never actually banned. It held its first congress since revival (38th in its history) on March 23–25, 1991. The congress approved the party's programme and a political statement. In the summer of 1991 it became a member of the Union of Democratic Forces–Centre. During the October 1991 elections its candidates ran within the UDF–Centre coalition.

Programme. The party categorically distances itself from Marxism-Leninism and its relapses; it opposes communism, eastern socialism and all other forms of totalitarianism and extremism; and it sees the democratic state committed to the rule of law as the only form of political system of Bulgarian society. The BSDP campaigns for democracy, for a welfare market economy, for the equitability of three types of ownership (private, co-operative and state). Co-operatives are viewed as the most suitable form of privatization for Bulgaria.

Organization. Rules approved by the 38th congress give the central leadership an imposing presence in the work of the party's branches.

Affiliation. Member of the Union of Democratic Forces since its foundation in December 1989, and also of the Socialist International.

Publication. The BSPD has its own newspaper *Svoboden Narod* (Free People) which resumed publication after a break of 43 years on Feb. 1, 1990.

Bulgarian Socialist Party (BSP)
Bulgarska Sotsialisticheska Partiya (BSP)

Foundation. Dec. 31, 1989.

Leadership. Ivan Velkov (ch.).

Membership. 10,000.

History. The BSP emerged from a political circle formed at the end of 1988. It disputes the BCP right to rename itself as the Bulgarian Socialist Party in April 1990.

Programme. To promote democracy and end the "Stalinist and Brezhnevist political, ideological, and economic system" of socialism. The BSP renounces class-based politics and defends the rights of the individual.

Bulgarian Socialist Party (BSP)
Bulgarska Sotsialisticheska Partiya (BSP)

Address. 1000 Sofia, 1 Dondoukov Blvd.

Telephone. 84 01.

Leadership. Jean Videnov (ch. of the Supreme Council).

Membership. 370,333 (June 1994).

History. The BSP is a continuation of the BCP which changed its name in April 1990 as a result of a referendum conducted among its members in the spring of 1990. The change of name was officially approved by the 15th Congress of the BCP which became the 39th consecutive Congress of the BSP. The claim of the BCP to assume the name of the Bulgarian Socialist Party is disputed by the Bulgarian Socialist Party founded on Dec. 31, 1989 (*see* above). At its 40th Congress in December 1991 the party claimed membership of 480,000. In November 1992 it declared that the membership was some 420,000. Both figures proved to be overestimated when the June 1994 membership was finally released clearly showing a downwards trend. In 1994 the BSP acknowledged that only 30 per cent of its present members are below 44 years of age, while as many as 40 per cent are pensioners. The party's 41st congress was held on June 3–6, 1994. The 749 delegates re-elected Jean Videnov as chairman of the 106-member Supreme Council.

Programme. The party's programme as adopted at its 39th Congress held between Sept. 22 and 25, 1990, and restated by subsequent declarations, stipulates that the BSP is a mass parliamentary party which expresses the interests of the working people and which attains its goals by democratic means and in compliance with the constitution and the law of the land. Its activities are based on the values of Marxism, of the experience and traditions of the socialist movement and the contemporary left democratic parties and movements. As a party of democratic socialism it is a part of the world socialist left.

Organization. Several prominent factions have emerged within the party since November 1989. The most vocal include:

Alternative Socialist Association (ASA), led by Prof. Ivan Nikolov. The faction was established on Jan. 12, 1990, and has 100 clubs throughout the country. It aims to promote democracy by campaigning for the radical democratization of the BSP. The ASA objects to the results of the extraordinary congress of BCP held between Jan. 30 and Feb. 1, 1990.

Alternative Socialist Organization is led by Valentin Vatsev. The faction is highly critical of the BSP leadership claiming that genuine reformers have been systematically removed from responsible positions in the party.

Bulgarian Road to Europe, led by Rumen Georgiev, who is the chairman of a 12-person Co-ordinating Committee. The faction was formed on Jan. 4, 1990, at Sofia University as an anti-Stalinist wing of the BCP. At the extraordinary BCP congress (Jan. 30–Feb. 1, 1990) the group won significant representation in party's leadership. The platform claims to have co-ordinating committees in 52 towns throughout the country. It supports the democratic understanding of socialism, pluralism of property, de-Stalinization of the BCP/BSP, the eradication of Zhivkovism, the separation of the BSP from the state and the establishment of a multi-party system, transition to a market economy, and the promotion of Bulgaria's interaction within the European Community.

Democratic Forum is a small faction formed in the spring of 1990.

Marxist Alternative Movement, led by Prof. Mitryu Yankov, claims several thousand members.

Movement for Democratic Socialism is the most significant faction within the BSP. It claims to have 13,000 members in Sofia and over 9,000 members in the provinces. The movement aims to rally broad social circles around a platform of democratic socialism based on the principle of market economy, political pluralism, the people's self-government, social justice, and freedom of the individual.

Movement for Radical Changes in the Socialist Party is a small but very active faction demanding fundamental restructuring of the BSP.

Christian Democratic Front
Hristiyan-Demokraticheska Fronta

Leadership. Nikolai Vasilev.

Membership. Predominantly intellectuals, former members of the BCP, now vehemently anti-communist.

Affiliation. Member of the Union of Democratic Forces since October 1990.

Christian Republican Party (CRP)
Hristiyan-Republikanska Partiya (HRP)

Address. 1066 Sofia, p.k. 113.

Telephone. 52 24 06.

Foundation. Nov. 24, 1989, in Plovdiv.

Leadership. Konstantin Adzharov (ch.); Dimitar Petkanov (sec.); Elisaveta Adzharov, Ekaterina Petkanova.

Membership. Several thousands.

Programme. To combine the virtues of Christianity with republican principles. In February 1990 the party proposed the holding of a referendum on whether Bulgaria should be a republic or a monarchy.

Organization. 24 branches and a youth league.

Affiliation. Member of the Political Opposition Block.

Citizens' Initiative (CI)
Grazhdanska Initsiativa (GI)

Address. 1000 Sofia, Blvd. Dondukov 39.

Telephone. 39 01 93.

Foundation. Dec. 25, 1988, in Ruse, relaunched on Nov. 27, 1989 in Sofia.

Leadership. Lyubomir Sobadjiev (ch.); Dimitar Todorov Angelov, Totyu Totov, Hristo Peev, Emil Stumbov.

Membership. 8,500.

History. The CI has its roots in two earlier organizations. The Ruse section of the Independent Association for the Defence of Human Rights, and the Committee 273 (named after an article in the penal code used to imprison opponents of the regime). A year later it became a national organization.

Programme. Defence of human rights and the promotion of public debate and political awareness. Support for *glasnost* and the speedy end of the command administrative system. The movement supports the socially weak and homeless and is also involved in investigating communist crimes.

Affiliation. Member of the Union of Democratic Forces since its foundation in December 1989.

Club for the Victims of Repression after 1945
Klub na Represiranite sled 1945 Godina

Address. 4000 Plovdiv.

Telephone. 22 700 71.

Foundation. September 1989.

Leadership. Dimitur Bakalov (ch.); Vangel Gorev, Todor Kavaldzhiev, Tako Karaivanov, Ivan Nevrokopski.

History. Set-up by ex-political prisoners, most of them Agrarian Union activists, the Club was responsible for the discovery of mass graves of opponents of communism killed in the 1940s. The Club's national conference took place on April 1, 1990, in Plovdiv.

Programme. The gradual rehabilitation of all democrats, socialists, agrarians, and non-party people who suffered repression after 1945; to win constitutional guarantees of the freedom of research and publication on Bulgaria's post-war history; to construct a memorial to the victims of communist persecution; to win indemnities for surviving relatives.

Affiliation. Member of the Union of Democratic Forces since its foundation in December 1989.

Committee for Religious Rights, the Freedom of Conscience, and Spiritual Values
Komitet za Zashtita na Religioznite Prava Svobodata na Savestta i Duhovnite Tsenosti

Foundation. March 9, 1989, in Veliko Turnovo.

Leadership. Rev Hristofor Subev (ch.); Petar Kanev Petrov (sec.).

Programme. To campaign for an end to political interference in Church affairs and religious life; to promote religious education, publishing, and broadcasting; to campaign for the legislation of religious charitable work; to promote religious tolerance in Bulgaria.

Organization. Although the Committee was established by an Orthodox priest, both clergy and lay people are its members. It is more of a political than a religious organization and is characterized by extreme anti-communism.

Affiliation. Union of Democratic Forces.

Confederation of Roma in Bulgaria

Foundation. May 8, 1993.

Programme. To pressurize the government into improving the living conditions and standing of Bulgarian Gypsies. At the time of its formation the Confederation called on the government to prepare a development scheme for the Roma community, to elaborate a special education plan which envisages the optional teaching of Romany in schools and to allocate a building that could serve as a Roma Cultural Centre.

Conservative Party
Konservativna Partyia

Address. 1505 Sofia, kv. Reduta, ul. Ribarica 22, bl. 4.

Telephone. 72 02 82.

Leadership. Ivan Edisonov (pres.); Stefan Kospartov (dep. pres.).

Constitutional Alliance
Konstitucionen Sayuz

Address. 4000 Plovdiv, ul. Oplchenska 10-A.

Foundation. Jan. 5, 1991, in Plovdiv.

Leadership. Manol Zhurnalov (pres.).

History. The Constitutionalists had one of the longest battles of any party in Bulgaria over their registration. The Sofia City Court refused to register the party in January objecting to its programme which challenges the republican framework of the state system. The party appeals against the decision eventually went to the Supreme Court which on May 7 reversed the decision of the lower courts and thus allowed the party's registration.

Programme. The party challenges the validity of the 1946 referendum on the abolition of monarchy. It considers the referendum as an "unlawful, coercive and unprecedented act in the history of democratic states".

Democratic Forum
Demokratichen Forum

Foundation. January 1990.

Leadership. Dragomir Draganov.

Programme. To revive the BCP and the Bulgarian economy essentially by promoting austerity and efficiency and eliminating the power of the *nomenklatura*; to create a democratic civil society and to separate the party from the state.

Organization. The Forum is a radical-left group within the BCP.

Democratic League for the Defence of Human Rights
Demokratichnata Liga za Zashtita na Pravata na Choveka

Foundation. November 1988, in the village of Drashan, near Vratsa.

Leadership. Mustafa Yumerov (ch.); Sabri Iskenderov and Ali Ormanliev.

Membership. Over 10,000.

Programme. To campaign for human rights in Bulgaria; to restore democratic principles in public life.

Organization. The League's membership consists largely but not exclusively of ethnic Turks. Its leadership was expelled to Turkey after the formation of the organization.

Democratic Movement for Constitutional Monarchy
Demokratichno Dvizhenie za Konstytucjonalna Monarhia

Address. 1463 Sofia, ul. Tsar Asen 55, vh. 5.

Telephone. 89 75 45.

Foundation. Jan. 17, 1990.

Leadership. Bozhnka Milusheva, Konstantin Halachev, Hristo Metaniev.

Programme. The party campaigns for the restoration of the civil rights of Simeon II of Turnovo (the last king of the Bulgarians, currently living in Madrid) and for the establishment of a democratic state based on the principles of constitutional monarchy.

Democratic Party (DP)
Demokraticheska Partiya (DP)

Address. 1000 Sofia, Blvd. Dondukov 34, et. IV, st. 8.

Telephone. 80 01 87; 88 20 46.

Foundation. 1886, refounded Jan. 1990.

Leadership. Stefan Savon (ch.); Georgi Markov (dep. ch.).

History. A traditional right-wing party, the DP held power several times prior to the communist takeover in 1944. The DP never entered into any agreements with the communists. It was banned by the communist regime in 1947 and at the end of 1948 liquidated all together.

Programme. Political and economic pluralism.

Affiliation. Member of the Union of Democratic Forces since February 1990.

Democratic Party in Bulgaria
Demokraticheska Partiya v Bulgaria

Address. 1000 Sofia, Mladost 2, bl. 226, vh. G.

Telephone. 74 48 22.

Leadership. Konstantin Georgiev (ch.); Bogdana Zhelyazka (sec.).

Democratic Party–Conservative Concord

Address. 1000 Sofia, 3 Alabin Str.

Telephone. 54 49 06.

Foundation. July 23, 1991.

Leadership. Stefan Vassilev Stoyanov (ch.).

Democratic Party–Plovdiv

The party was founded in Plovdiv on Jan. 7, 1990, and registered on Feb. 2, 1990. Its membership is estimated at 3,000, with sections operating in Varna, Bourgas, Plovdiv, Razgrad and Sofia. In the summer of 1991 it became a member of the Union of Democratic Forces–Centre. During the October 1991 elections its candidates ran within the UDF–Centre coalition.

Democratic Union of Gypsies — ROMA

Leadership. Manush Romanov

Membership. 50,000

History. This is the largest of the nine Gypsy organizations in Bulgaria. It gained a measure of political importance when its leader, Manush Romanov, was elected to parliament in 1990 on the list of the Union of Democratic Forces. Subsequently, however, the Democratic Union of Gypsies was denied the status of a political party on the grounds that this would violate the constitution, which explicitly prohibits the creation of parties on ethnic grounds. The Democratic Union thus was banned from participating in the 1991 elections.

Democratic Women's Movement
Demokratichen Sayuz Zhenite

Address. 1463 Sofia, Blvd. Patriarch Evtimin 82.

Telephone. 52 53 18.

Leadership. Emilia Maclarova, Nora Ananieva, Rumiana Modeva.

Programme. The Movement established on March 17, 1990, aims at the protection of women's rights.

Dimitrov Communist Youth Union
Dimitrovski Komunisticheski Mladezhki Sayuz

Foundation. 1947.

Membership. 750,000 (early 1990, rapidly declining)

History. The union has been known previously as the People's Youth Union (*Sayuz na Narodna Mladezh*) and the Proletarian Youth Union (*Rabotnicheski Mladezhki Sayuz*) before adopting the current name in 1958. Membership has been steadily declining since 1987. After the overthrow of Todor Zhivkov in November 1989 the Union became increasingly independent and critical of the BCP leadership. Its congress in February 1990 severed all institutional links with the BCP and adopted the name of the Bulgarian Democratic Youth Federation.

Programme. To organize youth activities.

Ecoglasnost

Address. 1504 Sofia, 28 Marin Drinov Str.

Foundation. April 13, 1989.

Leadership. Petur Slabakov (ch. of National Council); Georgi Avramov (sec. of National Council).

Membership. Over 50 clubs and organizations throughout the country.

History. The roots of the group lie in the so-called Committee of Ruse, Bulgaria's first dissent formation, a spontaneous movement of intellectuals — predominantly film makers and writers — for ecological preservation of the town of Ruse. In October 1989 Ecoglasnost organized demonstrations in Sofia during the Conference on Security and Co-operation in Europe conference on the environment which were brutally suppressed by the police. These events precipitated Zhivkov's downfall and marked the beginning of the democratization process. After the February 1990 congress of the BCP many of the communist party members withdrew from Ecoglasnost and the alliance became politically anti-communist movement defined by environmentalism. The first national conference of the movement took place on April 1, 1990, in Sofia.

Programme. To campaign for the implementation of ecological laws; to promote *glasnost* and educate the public on ecological issues. The priority of the movement is the socio-ecological self-protection of the population, the control over management decisions on which the people's health and state of their living environment depends.

Organization. A nationwide environmental pressure group it has branches throughout the country, many of which have announced that they are autonomous and some of which have taken different names, such as Eco-Voice in Plovdiv.

Affiliation. Member of the Union of Democratic Forces since its foundation in December 1989.

Ecoglasnost — Political Club

Address. 1000 Sofia, 37 Exarch Yossif St, 8th floor.

Foundation. March 1990.

Leadership. Boris Kolev (ch.)

History. In the summer of 1991 it became a member of the Union of Democratic Forces — Centre. During the October 1991 elections its candidates ran within the UDF–Centre coalition.

Federation of Christian Parties and Movements

Formed on Dec. 30, 1990, as a grouping of three small parties: the Christian Democrats, the Christian Radicals and the New Christian Democrats.

Fatherland Party of Labour

Leadership. Dimitur Arnandov (ch.)

Extreme nationalist party, an offshoot of the People's Committee for Defending National Interests. It stresses Bulgaria's role as a barrier against Islam.

Federation of Clubs for Glasnost and Democracy
Federatsiya na Klubove za Glasnost i Demokratsiya

Address. 1000 Sofia, 134 Rakovski Street.

Foundation. Jan. 20, 1990.

Membership. 67 clubs around the country.

Leadership. Prof. Ivan Dzhadzhev (ch.)

History. Originally founded on Nov. 30, 1988, as a discussion club at Sofia University by 120 leading writers, poets, film-makers, philosophers, sociologists and scientists under the name "Club to Support *Glasnost* and *Perestroika*". They suffered harassment from the authorities and several were dismissed from their jobs. Many of the Club's founders were prominent members of the BCP, and were expelled from the party. The Club's first chairman was Dr Zhelyu Zhelev. On Jan. 20, 1990, 19 clubs from Sofia and other parts of the country formed the Federation. A split within the leadership of the organization in early 1990 led to the departure of a number of its BCP members.

Programme. To conduct a free public debate on the major problems facing Bulgaria and to promote *glasnost* and democracy.

Organization. Some 20 provincial branches, including Plovdiv, Bourgas, Pazardzhik and Smolyn.

Affiliation. Member of the Union of Democratic Forces since its foundation in December 1989.

Federation of Independent Students' Societies
Federatsiya na Nezavisimi Studentski Druzhestva

Address. 1000 Sofia, Blvd. Dondukov 39.

Telephone. 39 00 18.

Foundation. January 1990.

Leadership. Stlian Stoichev (pres.); Zahari Nikolov (sec.)

History. The Federation emerged from the Independent Students' Society founded in Sofia University on Nov. 15, 1989. The students organized two occupational strikes in the universities. The first in June and July 1990 proved to be instrumental in bringing about the fall of President Petar Mladenov. The second strike in the autumn of 1990 contributed significantly to the bringing down of Andrei Lukanov and his government.

Programme. To encourage free expression and democratization in higher education, to campaign for the freedom of association for young people and the removal of ideological constraints on academic life.

Affiliation. Member of the Union of Democratic Forces since its foundation in December 1989.

Green Party
Zelena Partiya

Address. 1000 Sofia, Blvd. Yanko Saksov 30.

Telephone. 44 21 85.

Foundation. Dec. 28, 1989.

Leadership. Aleksander Karakachanov (ch.); Dimitri Novakov (dep. ch.); Lyubomir Ivanov, (dep. ch.)

Membership. 1,000 in Sofia alone.

History. Formed by a group of former Ecoglasnost members of whom Aleksander Karakachanov, the mayor of Sofia, is the most prominent member.

Programme. To establish a pluralistic democracy in which legislative and executive power are decentralized to the maximum extent possible; to base the economy on ecological principles and promote local and private initiative.

Organization. 15 branches in Sofia and eight branches in the provinces. The party lacks a specific social base.

Affiliation. From January 1990 to April 15, 1993, the party was a member of the Union of Democratic Forces. In the summer of 1991 it became a member of the Union of Democratic Forces — Centre. During the October 1991 elections its candidates ran within the UDF–Centre coalition. Subsequently it joined the centrist Council for Co-operation.

Independent Association for the Defence of Human Rights in Bulgaria
Nezavisimo Druzhestvo za Zashtita na Choveshkite Prava v Bulgariya

Foundation. Jan. 16, 1988.

Leadership. Ilya Minev (ch.); Stefan Vulkov (dep. ch.)

Membership. Over 1,000 in early 1990.

History. The Association, the oldest dissident group in the country, was established after six Bulgarian dissidents sent an appeal to a Conference on Security and Co-operation in Europe follow-up conference in Vienna, in which they protested against human rights violations by the communist regime. Its members were subjected to some of the harshest persecution of any dissident groups and several were forced into exile. Many of the group's initial members were ethnic Turks joining in protest against the communist regime process of "Bulgarization". The membership of the group fell after June 1989 when some 310,000 of the ethnic Turkish population left Bulgaria. The issue of the Turkish minority was a source of major divisions within the Association, with some members advocating strongly that this should not be a subject of concern for its activities. During 1990 the Association more or less disintegrated due to the controversial behaviour of Rumen Vodenicharov, who left the parliamentary group of the UDF and declared himself independent.

Programme. To collect information on political prisoners and other cases of abuse of human rights; to campaign for legal reforms; to protect minority rights.

Affiliation. Founding member of the Union of Democratic Forces.

Independent Trade Union Federation *Podkrepa*
Nezavisima Federatsiya na Truda Podkrepa

Address. 1000 Sofia, 134 Rakovski Street.

Foundation. Feb. 11, 1989, in Plovdiv.

Leadership. Dr Konstantin Trenchev (ch.); Todor Gagalov (dep. ch.); Plamen Darakchiev (sec.)

Membership. Over 500,000

History. Originally conceived as a trade union for scientific, technical, educational, and cultural professions, the Federation later broadened its scope of membership and activities. *Podkrepa's* foundation congress (March 17–24, 1990) approved the Federation's statute and political resolution. *Podkrepa* has subsequently emerged as a powerful organization and has played an increasingly important role in Bulgarian politics, in some respects comparable to that of Solidarity in Poland. The general strike organized by the Federation in November 1990 helped to bring down the Lukanov's cabinet and made it possible for the key economic ministries to be given to UDF experts.

Programme. To defend workers' rights.

Affiliation. Member of the Union of Democratic Forces from December 1989 until the autumn of 1990. Since then it has an observer status only. A member of the International Confederation of Trade Unions and the World Confederation of Labour.

Liberal Congress Party
Partyia Liberalen Kongres

Address. 1000 Sofia, Blvd. Dondukov 39.

Telephone. 39 00 18.

Leadership. Yanko Yankov (pres.); Bozhidar Palyushev (dep. pres.), Lyulian Kocev (dep. pres.)

History. Formerly known as the Social Democratic Party (Non-Marxist) the party was re-named on Jan. 12, 1991.

Liberal Democratic Party (LDP)
Liberalno-Demokraticheska Partiya (LDP)

Address. Stara Zagora, 26A Karadsha Str.

Foundation. Nov. 27, 1989.

Leadership. Hristo Santulov (ch.)

History. The party was founded in Stara Zagora as the Union of Free Democrats, and adopted the current name in January 1990.

Programme. To work for a democratic society based on the rule of law. The state president should be elected directly by the population.

Affiliation. Political Opposition Bloc.

Liberal Democratic Party in Bulgaria
Liberalno-Demokraticheska Partyia v Bulgaria

Address. 1113 Sofia, ul. Chehov 10.

Telephone. 70 60 40.

Liberal Party
Liberalna Partyia

Address. 2300 Piernik, ul Radomir 1.

Telephone. 2 34 98; 7 59 64.

Liberal Union
Liberalnyi Sayuz

Foundation. April 1990.

History. Originally formed on Jan. 11, 1990, as the Political Opposition Bloc, it adopted the present name in order to attract wider popular support during the June 1990 parliamentary elections.

Organization. Opposition alliance of six political parties and groups, including the Christian Republican Party and Liberal Democratic Party.

Monarchic Conservative Union
Monarhichsko-Konservativen Sayuz

Address. Veliko Turnovo, p.k. 334.

Telephone. 3 13 04.

Movement for Rights and Freedoms (MRF)
Dvizhenie za Prava i Svobodi (DPS)

Address. 1408 Sofia, Ivan Vazov ul., Petar Topalov Shmid bl., 50, vh. B, ap. 55.

Telephone. 51 98 22; 65 8 32.

Foundation. Jan. 4, 1990.

Leadership. Ahmed Dogan (ch.)

Membership. 100,000.

History. The Movement has its roots in the resistance of the Turkish minority to the "Bulgarization" process conducted with particular ferocity by the communist regime between 1985 and 1989. The MRF began its activities underground in the spring of 1985. Exposed by the authorities in June 1986, its leadership (including Ahmed Dogan) was sentenced to long prison terms. Between 1986 and December 1989 its activities were planned and directed from prison. Originally formed in December 1989 as the Movement for the Rights and Freedoms of the Turks and Moslems in Bulgaria, the MRF Co-ordinating Council resolved that the Movement should undertake to protect the universal rights and freedoms of all individuals and communities, rather than just those of local Turks and Moslems. Officially registered on April 26, 1990, the MRF conducted an extremely well-organized electoral campaign prior to the June 1990 parliamentary elections and won 23 seats in the Grand National Assembly, thus becoming the third largest political force in the country. The first national conference of the MRF was held on March 26–27, 1990 in Sofia. Prior to the October 1991 parliamentary elections, the Central Electoral Commission at first banned the Movement from participating. The ban was ostensibly based on the new Bulgarian Constitution which explicitly forbids the creation of parties on ethnic grounds. The ban was lifted after a direct appeal by the Turkish Prime Minister, Mezut Yilmaz, to his Bulgarian counterpart, Dimiter Popov, in August 1991. Similar diplomatic pressure was exerted by the United States ambassador in Sofia. Subsequently the Central Electoral Commission granted the MRF's registration not as a "party" but as a "movement". In the election the MRF increased its share of vote by 1.51 per cent from 6.03 per cent in 1990, and gained 24 seats. Its second national conference was held in Sofia on Nov. 27–28, 1993. Although it re-elected Ahmed Dogan as MRF chairman, his leadership was strongly criticized by Mehmed Hodzha, member of parliament from Kardzhali, an MRF stronghold. Kardzhali bombasted Dogan for backing the Lyuben Berov government and therefore joining an informal alliance with the Bulgarian Socialist Party. After alleging that several top MRF members are former state security collaborators, Hodzha and other Kardzhali delegates staged a walkout from the conference.

Programme. The MRF calls for respect for all civil rights and freedoms of individuals and that of communities as enshrined in the Bulgarian Constitution and international instruments. It opposes all forms of segregation in education, the economy or culture. It rejects any form of separatism, nationalism or fundamentalism as well as attempts to fuel ethnic hatred and calls for hostility.

Organization. Membership of the party is open to all Bulgarian citizens regardless of their language, ethnic identity and party affiliation. Some 80 per cent of the MRF's members are

Bulgarian Turks. Members of the BSP are eligible for membership but cannot hold senior posts in the organization.

Affiliation. The Council for Co-operation.

Publication. Weekly newspaper *Prava i Svobodi* (Rights and Freedoms).

National Committee for the Defence of National Interests
Obshtonaroden Komitet za Zashtita na Natsionalnite Interesi

Foundation. January 1990.

Leadership. Dimitar Arnaudov (ch.); Mincho Minchev (spokesman); Kiril Haramiev, Kamen Garelov.

History. The Committee was formed as an alliance of provincial nationalist groups in the wake of the 29 Dec., 1989, decision of the BCP Politburo condemning the "Bulgarization" process of the Turkish minority by the Zhivkov regime. The decision to restore names and rights of this minority was, however, greeted by rallies, strikes and street violence across the country.

Programme. To represent the interests of the ethnic Bulgarian community in areas of mixed population; to promote public discussion of national questions; to oppose separatist and autonomous movements among ethnic minorities.

National Liberal Party "Stefan Stambolov"
Narodnoliberalna Partyia "Stefan Stambolov"

Address. 5000 Veliko Turnovo.

Telephone. 2 73 98.

Leadership. Zafir Vielinov.

National Union "Zveno"
Naroden Sayuz "Zveno"

Telephone. Sofia 89 13 40.

Leadership. Vera Peicheva (sec.)

National Youth Union

Foundation. May 5, 1991.

Organization. The union is an umbrella organization of most of the youth organizations of parties and groups that comprise the UDF. The founding members of the Union include: Union of Young Social Democrats, Union of Macedonian Associations, the Internal Macedonian Revolutionary Organization, the Nikola Petkov Agrarian Youth Union, the

Club of Friends of Jesus Christ, Union of the Democratic Party, and the Federation of Independent Students Associations.

New Social Democratic Party
Nova Sotsialdemokraticheska Partyia

Address. 1504 Sofia, p.k. 14.

Telephone. 44 99 47; 22 24 40.

Leadership. Vasil Mihailov (pres.); Petar Atanasov (dep. pres.)

Radical Democratic Party (RDP)
Radikalna Demokraticheska Partiya (RDP)

Address. 1000 Sofia, Blvd. Dondukov 34, et. III, st. 6–8.

Telephone. 80 02 69; 80 03 45; 80 02 91; 80 02 99.

Foundation. 1902, refounded Dec. 4, 1989.

Leadership. Elka Konstantinova (pres.); Aleksander Yordanov, Mikhail Nedelchev (co-pres.). Other prominent members of the leadership include: Boycho Petrov, Asen Kolushki, Aleksandar Tarkalanov.

History. The RDP is a successor of a small centrist party which existed unil 1944.

Programme. To establish a secular, democratic republic with a mixed economy

Organization. A powerful right-wing party with a strong influence among educated urban population.

Affiliation. Member of the Union of Democratic Forces since December 1989.

Publication. The party publishes an influential paper *Bek XXI* (21st Century).

Republican Party (RP)
Republikanska Partiya (RP)

Address. 1606 Sofia, Blvd. Gen. Ckobelev 46.

Telephone. 54 25 91.

Foundation. Jan. 22, 1990.

Leadership. Lenko Roussanov (pres.); Ivan Sotirov (sec.)

Programme. To establish Bulgaria as a democratic parliamentary and law-governed republic with a mixed economy. The RP advocates the separation of party and state and the depoliticization of the Ministries of Internal Affairs and Defence, the courts, the Chief Prosecutor's Office, radio and television organizations and the official news agency.

Affiliation. Observer status with the Union of Democratic Forces.

Republican Party in Bulgaria
Republikanska Partyia v Bulgaria

Address. 1000 Sofia, ul. Graf Ignatiev 2.

Telephone. 88 22 35; 87 47 64.

Leadership. Aleksandur Popov (pres.); Olga Ivanovna (dep. pres.)

Socialist Youth Union
Socialisticheski Mladezhki Sayuz

Address. 1000 Sofia, Blvd. Al. Stambolinski 11.

Telephone. 87 25 26.

Svoboda
Freedom

Also known as the Coalition for the Turnovo Constitution (referring to the constitution of 1879) the group was formed on Dec. 30, 1990. It consists of 13 small political parties that had been members of the Liberal Union, the National Democratic Forum and the Christian Social Union.

Union for Civic Economic Initiative
Sayuz za Grazhdanska Stopanska Initsiativa

Foundation. Dec. 22, 1989.

Leadership. Prof. Zahari Staykov.

Programme. The union's founding document is based on the statutes of the British and Belgian chambers of commerce: to support private enterprise; to oppose state monopolies in the economy; to provide legal assistance to members and represent them in discussion with the government.

Union of Democratic Forces (UDF)
Sayuz na Demokratichni Sili (SDS)

Address. 1000 Sofia, 134 Rakovski Street.

Telephone. 88 25 01.

Foundation. Nov. 23, 1989.
Leadership. Filip Dimitrov (ch. of Co-ordinating Council); Mihan Drenchev (dep. ch.); Hristofor Sbev (dep. ch.)

History. The UDF was established by ten groups and organizations connected with the struggle against the totalitarian regime. Its founding members were: the Bulgarian Social Democratic Party; Bulgarian Agrarian National Union — Nikola Petkov; *Ecoglasnost*; the Federation of Clubs for Glasnost and Democracy; the Committee for Religious Rights, the Freedom of Conscience and Spiritual Values; the Club for the Victims of Repression after 1945; Citizens' Initiative; the Federation of Independent Students' Societies; the Independent Association for the Defence of Human Rights; and the Independent Labour Federation *Podkrepa*. The latter withdrew from the UDF in the autumn of 1990. The first chairman of the Union was Dr Zhelyu Zhelev. He resigned the chairmanship after being elected President of Bulgaria on Aug. 1, 1990. In December, 1989 the Radical Democratic party joined the UDF, followed by the Green Party in January 1990, the United Democratic Centre in February 1990, the Democratic Party in February 1990, the Christian Democratic Front in October 1990, and the Alternative Socialist Party in October 1990. Three organizations had observer status: the Independent Labour Federation *Podkrepa*, the Bulgarian Democratic Forum, and the Republican Party. In the summer of 1991 the UDF split into three groups. The UDF proper, also referred to as UDF–Movement, claimed the middle ground and retained some of the eclectic ideological and structural nature of the original Union. At the time of the October 1991 elections it comprised 19 political parties and groups (see Table 3, footnote 1). The UDF–Centre claimed the left-of-centre ground, while the UDF–Liberals comprised of the right-of-centre parties.

Organization. The union is a coalition that cuts across almost the entire political spectrum of Bulgarian party politics with the exclusion of left-wing or pro-communist parties and those associated with the Zhivkov regime. The backbone of the UDF are opposition movements and organizations formed in 1988 and 1989 as well as political parties outlawed by the communists and restored after the fall of Zhivkov. There have been two basic trends since the formation of the Union. The first is one of the coalition of spontaneously formed organizations that were not interconnected under the totalitarian regime. This perhaps explains their number. The other is the movement trend — people joining the organizations not so much because of a doctrinaire allegiance but because they were accessible.

Structurally the UDF has a broad network of organizations throughout the country. At the central level power appears to be dispersed across the Co-ordinating Commission, the parliamentary group and the Presidency of the Republic. Perhaps the single most important factor in the survival of the UDF as an umbrella organization comprising groups very diverse in strength is the shared opposition to the communists.

Programme. To establish a democratic political system and a market economy; to unite the democratic opposition. The Union is defined, however, not by a programme or policy statement but by the common opposition of its constituent organizations and their members to the Bulgarian Socialist Party.

Publication. Daily newspaper *Demokratsija* (Democracy).

Union of Democratic Forces — Centre

The coalition emerged as a splinter group from the UDF in the summer of 1991. The dividing issue was whether the new constitution should be adopted by the BSP dominated parliament, or whether a newly elected assembly should have the final say on the content of the document. The UDF–Centre, like the BSP, were in favour of adopting the constitution before holding elections. The coalition comprised the following parties: Alternative Socialist Association — Independent, Bulgarian Social Democratic Party, Democratic Party — Plovdiv and *Ecoglasnost* Political Club.

Union of Democratic Forces — Liberals

Address. 1000 Sofia, 3 Alabin Street.

Telephone. 54 49 06.

Foundation. July 18, 1991.

Leadership. Petko Simeonov and Alexander Karakachanov (co-ch.)

History. The coalition emerged in the summer of 1991 as a result of a split within the Union of Democratic Forces. It comprises: the Democratic Party — Conservative Concord, the Green Party and the Federation of the Clubs for Democracy.

Union of Democratic Moslems
Sayuz na Demokratichni Myusyulmani

Foundation. 1989.

Leadership. Dimitar Chaushev, Yuli Mladenov Bakardzhiev.

Programme. To involve the Moslem minorities in creating democracy in Bulgaria.

United Democratic Centre

Leadership. Lyubomir Pavlov and Stoyan Ganev (co-pres.)

Membership. The party has practically no rank-and-file members. It was formed by a group of UDF economists and lawyers who were instrumental in developing the UDF's programme.

Affiliation. Member of the Union of Democratic Forces since February 1990.

United Front for the Restructuring and Defence of Socialism
Edinen Front za Preustroistvo i Zashtita na Sotzialisma

Foundation. Jan. 18, 1990.

Leadership. Prof. Vasil Ivanov, Prof. Asen Katov, Col. Mitriu Yanchev, Gen. Stoyan Kutsarov.

Programme. To foster a revival of the moral and political strength of the BCP in order to prevent a capitalist restoration in Bulgaria and to resist the challenge of the Union of Democratic Forces; to promote democratization and political pluralism.

Organization. The Front is a conglomerate of four main BCP factions: Alternative Forum (*Alternativen Forum*) founded on Jan. 4, 1990; the Movement for Developing Marxism and Renewing Socialism (*Dvizhenie za Razvitie na Marksizma i Obnovlenie na Sotsializma*) founded in January 1990; the Public Forum (*Obshtestven Forum*) founded in January 1990; and Unity-Movement for a Socialist Revival (*Edinstvo-Dvizhenie za Sotsialistichesko Vazrazhdane*) founded in January 1990.

The following minor parties and political groups have also been registered:

Alev is an organization of Bulgaria's Muslims which aims for the preservation and promotion of cultural and religious traditions and values of the Turkish and Muslim population.

Christian Democratic Community established in Veliko Turnovo on April 2, 1991, is led by Rev Hristofor Suber.

Civic Alliance for the Republic (CAR). Formed on June 1, 1993, by 15 members of parliament of the Bulgarian Socialist Party and other left-wing politicians and intellectuals, including the former deputy chairman of the Bulgarian Socialist Party and former deputy Prime Minister in the interim government formed in December 1990, Aleksandar Tomov, and the former UDF deputy, Slavyan Saparev. The Alliance pledged to improve social and political climate in Bulgaria by putting an end to confrontation. At its first national conference, held on Oct. 24, 1993, the Civic Alliance decided to seek registration as a "movement" and not as a party to allow its sympathizers to retain membership of other political organizations. The conference elected Aleksandar Tomov as the CAR chairman and appointed a 79-member National Council, of whom 21 are members of the BSP.

Confederation of Independent Syndicates in Bulgaria.

Confederation of Independent Trade Unions, led by Krustyn Petkov.

Dobrudzka **All-Bulgarian Union,** founded on Sept. 24, 1990, seeks to re-awaken, preserve and promote the Bulgarian national spirit.

Ecoforum for Peace Association, is led by Pavel Georgiev.

General Assembly of the Union of Economic Leaders, chaired by Stoyan Drundarov. Its programme supports market economy but not the "shock therapy" which it considers to be socially too costly.

Internal Macedonian Revolutionary Organization–Union of Macedonian Associations (IMRO–UMA) rejects the existence of Macedonian nationality in Bulgaria and therefore has the support of the Bulgarian authorities.

Ilinden, **the Alternative Movement of Those Resettled from Aegean, Vardar and Pirin Macedonias,** founded on Nov. 14, 1989, is devoted to the protection of the rights of Macedonians in Bulgaria. It was originally accepted as a member of the Union of Democratic Forces but after strife broke out in January 1990 it was ejected from the UDF as an organization set up along purely ethnic lines. The leader of the UDF at that time, Dr Zhelyu Zhelev, declared on Jan. 21, 1990, that there was no Macedonian minority in Bulgaria. The organization was declared illegal by the Bulgarian Supreme Court in August 1990.

Independent 19 November Club is a left-wing organization established in the city of Burgas.

Movement for Civic Peace, founded on June 29, 1990, comprises representatives of several political parties and public organizations, the Orthodox Church and the Chief Mufti's Office. It aims to enroll all public and political forces and all people who are striving to create a democratic, humane and law abiding state in Bulgaria.

Movement for the Promotion of Marxism and the Renewal of Socialism declares itself in favour of Marxism free of Stalinist dogmas and upgraded to a modern level. It held its national conference in Sofia on Jan. 22, 1990.

Progressive People's Party was founded in Sofia on March 2, 1990. It seeks to continue the establishment of an economically stable, intellectual free, law-governed and democratic civil society with equal opportunities for all.

Union of Free Democrats was co-founded by the Forum of Free Democrats, the Free Democratic Party and the Union for Civil Society on Feb. 9, 1990. It declares itself in favour of total privatization, a monetary reform, a confiscation of misappropriated property and a fair distribution of the burdens of market economy. The Union also advocates that the BSP which succeeded the BCP should repay the country's foreign debt and public debt.

Union for the Prosperity of Pirin Macedonia, formed in September 1993, aims to secure the official recognition of a Macedonian, as well as a Pomak minority in Bulgaria.

Notes

1 The current constitution is Bulgaria's fourth since the country's foundation in 1879.
2 Nikolai Genchev, "The liberal alternative to the post-totalitarian society", *Bulgarian Quarterly*, vol. 1, no. 3 (Winter 1991), pp. 46–47.
3 The grouping of the parties into coalitions and alliances reduced the number to 38 blocs and individual parties that offered candidates.
4 Evgenia Ivanova, "Current forces in Bulgarian life and politics", *East European Reporter*, vol. 5, no. 1 (Jan.–Feb. 1992), pp. 74.
5 Altogether 86 parties and organizations put forward candidates for the elections. However, 53 were grouped into seven coalitions — thus reducing the total number of organizations with lists of candidates to 38.
6 Kjell Engelbrecht, "Bulgaria's Cabinet shake-up: A lasting compromise?", *RFE/RL Research Report*, vol. 1, no. 28, pp. 2 & 5.
7 *RFE/RL News Briefs*, vol. 2, no. 28, 1993, p. 17.

CROATIA

John B Allcock

For an analysis of the developments prior to the declaration of the Republic of Croatia, see the chapter entitled "Yugoslavia (The Socialist Federal Republic of Yugoslavia)" on pages 615–632.

The area historically known as Croatia since the twelfth century has had a chequered history, in which the greater part was associated with the Hungarian crown (principally Slavonia and central Croatia); the larger part of Dalmatia was attached to Austria, but parts remained Italian territory. These were only reunited in the settlement of 1918 (although Istria and parts of Dalmatia remained Italian). As the result of sustained nationalist agitation, a semi-autonomous *banovina* of Croatia (which incorporated some areas now in Bosnia and Hercegovina) was established in 1938. Following the attack by the Axis powers in 1941 an "Independent State of Croatia" was formed, governed by the indigenous fascist *Ustaša* movement, but under the military control of Italy/Germany. Croatia was returned to Yugoslavia (with additional territories ceded from Italy) in 1945. With a surface area of 56,538 sq km the Republic of Croatia was the second largest of the six republics of the federation (22 per cent of the total). Its population (census of 1991) was 4,688,507 (20 per cent of the total).

The most numerous ethnic group in the republic are the Croats, with 74.6 per cent of the pre-secession population of the republic, followed by the Serbs, with 11.3 per cent. The extent to which these figures have been changed significantly by the war is unknown; but Croatia has been the host to more than 500,000 refugees (primarily from Bosnia–Hercegovina) and persons displaced from other parts of the republic: an unknown number of Serbs have left for Serbia. There are small, locally significant minorities of Muslims, Slovenes, Magyars, Italians and Czechs.

The largest concentrations of Serbs have been located historically in the areas south of Zagreb, known as Kordun and Banija, and along the western border of Bosnia, especially in the region of Lika. This latter, containing about a half of Croatia's Serb minority, in 1990 declared itself to be independent of the Croatian republic as an autonomous "Serbian Republic of Krajina" centred on the town of Knin. In addition to these areas a substantial area of eastern Slavonia, extending along the west bank of the Danube, was still under Serb control in 1994. Altogether almost a third of the former territory of Croatia remained outside the control of the republic's government. These territories largely coincided with the UN "Protected Areas" established in January 1992.

Before the outbreak of war an estimated 100,000 Serbs lived in Zagreb itself. Nine and a half per cent of the population of Croatia (the highest proportion in the whole federation) refused to declare their nationality to the census of 1991. Nine per cent of the population declared themselves to be "Yugoslavs" — the highest proportion to do so in the federation.

The first contested elections in Croatia were held before the disintegration of the Yugoslav federation in two rounds on April 22 and May 6, 1990. These returned an overwhelming majority for the presidential candidate of the Croatian Democratic Union (CDU), Franjo Tudjman, and substantial majorities for his party in each house of the tricameral *Sabor* (Assembly). As these elections took place before the reform of the constitution the Assembly still comprised a "Socio-Political Chamber", a "Chamber of Associated Labour" and a "Chamber of Municipalities". In the first, the CDU held 54 of the 78 seats; in the second 84 of the 156 seats; and in the third 70 of the 115 seats. In each case the reformed League of Communists (Party of Democratic Change) occupied second place, with 16, 36 and 23 seats respectively, and there were 16 successful independent candidates. (See Table 1, page 81)

Following the landslide victory of the CDU a referendum was held on May 19, 1991, which sought the opinion of the citizens on the question of the autonomy of the republic within Yugoslavia. The purpose of this was ostensibly to strengthen the hand of President Tudjman in his negotiations with the other republics over the restructuring of the federal constitution. Croatia and Slovenia argued for a revision which would have produced a much looser confederation. The referendum returned a "Yes" vote of 94 per cent (although it was boycotted by many of the Serb minority). The failure of these negotiations resulted in a declaration of independence by the Croatian *Sabor* on June 25, 1991, this coinciding with a similar declaration by the Slovenes.

This was followed by a brief war in which the Yugoslav National Army (YNA) was compelled to withdraw from Slovenia. Following the intervention of the European Community a cease-fire was also negotiated in Croatia. Under the provisions of the cease-fire agreement, which was policed by a UN Protection force (UNPROFOR), Serb forces were left in control of those areas that had declared their own independence from Croatia, and these areas have subsequently followed their own political development. Comment on this is developed on pages 633–634.

A new constitution was introduced in December 1990, attempting to eliminate the influence of the earlier Communist concept of the state. A new electoral law was subsequently passed in December 1991, making provision for fresh elections. A new electoral system was also created by a law of December 1992. This created a unicameral *Sabor*, elected on a mixed principle of local representation and national lists: 64 representatives of territorial constituencies and 60 from national lists, and representatives of national minorities, who may or may not associate themselves with specific parties.

On the basis of this new law elections to the *Sabor* were held in August 1992. Once again the CDU was returned with a clear majority, although there were several key changes in composition in relation to the former Assembly.

In contrast to other republics of former Yugoslavia, a process of the concentration of parties had taken place. Whereas in 1990 45 parties had put up candidates for election (not including numerous independents), by 1992 the field had been effectively halved. Parties whose existence had been rooted in the continuing existence of Yugoslavia (such as the Alliance of Reform Forces and the Party of Yugoslavs) had disappeared, there had been a degree of consolidation of left-wing factions, and a reduction in the number of minor ethnic parties. Curiously also, the Greens had disappeared. It is an oddity of party politics in the republic that the Green agenda seems to have been (at least for the time being) entirely submerged.

In the two-year interval since the first multi-party elections the focus of opposition moved from the former Communists and the bearers of the tradition of the "Croatian Spring" (the CNP) to the Liberals and the far right (especially the Croatian Peasant Party — CPP). For the first time regional identities began to assert themselves within a Croatia which had previously occupied itself entirely with the independence of the state (Istria and Dalmatia).

This pattern was also reflected in the contest for the presidency. Here the general fragmentation of party structure was indicated by the fielding of eight candidates. Tudjman was returned with a reduced majority (57 per cent). His nearest rival (Budiša of the Liberals — CSLP) polled 22 per cent.

A further modification of the constitutional structure took place in February 1993, when the new order was completed in the form of elections for an "Upper House" — the *Županijski Dom*, or Chamber of Counties. This body combines the principle of territorial representation with that of élite sponsorship. It may initiate legislation, suggest amendment to legislation initiated in the lower house, and refer it back for further consideration.

Candidates for seats in the Upper House compete for three places in each of 21 geographical constituencies, including two areas having "special status"; and five members are nominated by the President — 68 members in all. ("Special status" refers to the regions centred upon Glina and Knin, with a heavy preponderance of Serbs, and in fact at the time of the elections under secessionist Serb control within the "Serbian Republic of Krajina".)

Conflict over the structure and functions of this body delayed the elections for five months. In the event the D'Hondt method was adopted, introducing an element of proportionality. Minor parties are systematically excluded and their vote distributed. The five nominated members are supposed to introduce an element of independent reflection on legislation on the part of people who take their seats on their own merits. At the time of writing, one of the five nominees (the speaker Josip Manolić) is a former close associate of Tudjman, who in the spring of 1994 left the CDU, and one other is linked to the CPP.

In the elections for the *Županijski Dom* the general processes which emerged in the elections to the *Zastupnički Dom* (Lower House) are seen more clearly. The reduction in the predominance of the CDU continued (37 seats); there was a growth in the influence of the Liberals as its major left-of-centre rival; a further eclipse of the explicitly socialist parties; and a consolidation of the right around the CPP. Unlike in Slovenia, the traditional European opposition between "left" and "right" makes some sense in Croatia. The left agenda is to some extent distributed, however, in that the Liberals and socialists concentrate more on its social welfare aspects, whereas the centralized control over the economy is sustained (paradoxically) by the otherwise right-of-centre ruling party.

Although there has been some reduction in the degree of fragmentation of parties since 1990, the continuing importance of this feature is intelligible in the light of the lack of traditions of political identification, and the absence of any established track record of performance on the part of those in power. The belief of political activists in the instability of party support among the electorate (and the demonstrable realism of this belief) means that in principle everything is possible in future, even for parties which now appear to have no hope.

This pattern will probably remain in force for as long as war persists. Whereas in Slovenia no interviewees mentioned the war spontaneously unless pressed for comment, in Croatia it featured as an explicit concern for everybody, and was only rivalled in saliency as a political issue by the process of privatization. Indeed, the lack of real progress with economic restructuring was characteristically attributed to the impact of war. The consensus among political actors was that the war blocks totally the conduct of "normal politics" in Croatia, a central consequence of which is that opposition to the government on any issue can too easily be represented as treachery. Real decisions about the allocation of resources are thus set aside, as more than a quarter of the state budget goes for military purposes.

The Croatian Democratic Union is a highly unstable entity, which has drawn a great deal of its power and prestige from its early dominance as the movement which led the bid for independence. In the early post-independence period considerable anxiety was expressed as to whether the CDU was turning Croatia into a one-party state. Whereas the patronage of the party continues to be important this concern is probably less well-founded than it used to be. From the outset it was clear that the party was in effect a coalition of rather pragmatic middle-of-the-road and moderate nationalists (such as Slipe Mesić), more ideologically oriented Christian Democrats, and the personal following of Franjo Tudjman. Over time, three issues have served gradually to prise apart this combination: the conduct of the war; the conduct of the economic reform; and the position and political role of Tudjman himself.

In relation to the war, two issues have strained support for the government. No real progress has been made in restoring to Croatian control the territories of the "Serbian Republic of Krajina" (which amount nearly a third of the area of Croatia). The one attempt made to secure real strategic gains, in the establishment of control over the Maslenica bridge in January 1993, produced only a marginal alleviation of the problem of the effective isolation of southern Dalmatia from Zagreb. The influence of the infamous "Hercegovina Lobby" associated with Defence Minister Gojko Šušak, which committed Croatia for a time to open support for an independent state of "Herceg-Bosna", and open war in Bosnia–Hercegovina between Croats and Presidential forces, was bitterly criticized as losing Croatia a key ally in the superordinate struggle against Serbia. Both of these policies were attacked as diminishing international support for Croatia, and undermining Croatia's case that it was among the parties injured by "Serb aggression".

In the economy (as in cultural life) the CDU was criticized for stepping too readily into the shoes vacated by the Communists, substituting one *nomenklatura* for another, and politicizing economic decision-making without really addressing economic issues. War was an excuse for the lack of progress in economic restructuring, not an overriding reason for it.

These two issues have been linked by the third: in that both have been explained in part by Tudjman's unwillingness/inability to share responsibility and listen to independent advice.

The CDU, as the ruling party with (initially) a clearly dominant position in politics came to be the unwitting victim of a significant continuity in Croatian political culture. As under the Communists, it came to be believed that if you want to do well you need connections in government. A series of press scandals have suggested that there is a streak of venality in Croatian politics, partly linked to party activity. Should the CDU be ousted from power in future elections one might expect the rats to desert the sinking ship.

The strains within the CDU came to a head in April 1994 when two very senior figures in the party, Josip Manolić (one of its founders, and Speaker of the Upper House) and

Slipe Mesić (Speaker of the Lower House, and a former member of the federal Praesidium) left the party to set up their own Croatian Independent Democrats (CID). They have been supported by several other CDU representatives in both Houses of the Assembly, but at the time of writing have not been sufficiently strong to bring down the government by voting with the opposition. The grounds for the split appear to cover a very wide range of policy issues — including the conduct of the war (especially in Bosnia), the party's stance towards the republic's Serb minority and (above all) economic policy — as well as dissatisfaction with Tudjman's personal style of handling the party and government.

In spite of the war party allegiance is not distributed exclusively along ethnic lines. Of the 13 Serbs in the Assembly only three represent the Serbian National Party (SNP). The others ally themselves with the Social Democrats and the Croatian National Party. This reflects two things about urban Serbs in Croatia. They were identified with the former power structure, and consequently tend to ally themselves with the socialists. Also they are more educated, secular and "modernist" in their orientation even than most Croats. Among the 13 representatives in the Assembly who are identifiable as Serbs only two reported their religion as "Orthodox". The rest claim to have no religious allegiance or to be explicitly atheist. The proportion of Croats who distance themselves from Roman Catholicism is much smaller: only four members of the Upper and 13 members of the Lower House who identified themselves as Croats failed to mention that they are Roman Catholics. Although the CDU is far from being a "clerical" party, it does count a priest among its parliamentary representatives.

The manner in which Serb representation in the Assembly has been achieved has been the subject of some debate. It has been alleged that a kind of magic produced a statistical match between ethnicity and representation which is too neat to be an artefact of the elements of proportionality in the electoral system, and that the SNP is a creature of Tudjman. It is worth noting that around the time of independence those Serbs in Croatia who wished to identify their political aspirations with their ethnicity voted for the Serbian Democratic Party. This fell apart after the death of its founder, Dr Jovan Rašković. Resort to conspiracy theory does not seem to be strictly necessary here. Rašković was a figure who attracted a very personal following (he was rather extravagantly referred to on several occasions as "the Serbian Gandhi"). There is also a deep social and cultural difference between urban Serbs in Croatia, represented by the SNP, and the predominantly rural status of Krajina Serbs. The former by no means give their support to the secession of the latter, and indeed see it as threatening their own security in Croatian society. It seems more likely that the SNP does simply represent the outlook of urban Serbs in the political culture of contemporary Croatia.

The right is noticeably more unstable than any other segment of politics in Croatia, with splits and some notable defections, and the reconstruction of parties. This is possibly because hitherto the CDU has pre-empted most of the space in this sector of politics. The CPP will probably survive, however, as one of the few parties having a distinctive ideological position. The rest are hampered by conflicts of personal loyalty/ambition, degrees of chauvinism/militancy and differences over elements of the Christian Democratic agenda.

The structure of local government also underwent reform in 1992, but it is too early to judge the impact of this upon party development in Croatia.

Directory of Parties

Croatian Democratic Union (CDU)
Hrvatska Demokratska Zajednica (HDZ)

Address. Trg Hrvatskih Velikana 4, 41000, Zagreb.

Telephone. 41 452-500; 452-600; 453-000.

Fax. 41 435-314.

Foundation. Feb. 28, 1989.

Membership. The party does not publish membership figures.

Leadership. Franjo Tudjman (pres.) President of the Croatian Republic; Ivić Pašalić (pres. of exec. council); Nediljko Matić (sec.). The party is the majority party in both houses of the Assembly, and of 20 ministerial posts, 14 are in the hands of CDU members, including Nikica Valentić (Prime Minister), Mate Granić (Foreign Sec.), Gojko Šušak (Defence), Vladimir Šeks and Borislav Škegro.

History. The party traces its effective existence to mid-1988 (before its nominal foundation) and it was undoubtedly extremely significant as the flag-bearer for multi-party democracy in Croatia as well as the spearhead of Croatian independence from the Yugoslav federation. It has suffered from the natural strains of being a broad umbrella movement, and in April 1994 suffered the defection of a number of its leading figures to found the Croatian Independent Democrats.

Organization. The CDU is organized in all communes of the republic. It is the principal political organization of Croats in Bosnia and Hercegovina as well as Croatia, and has an extensive and effective network of fund-raisers abroad. Its greatest strength is found in the Croatian Zagorje, parts of Slavonia and Dalmatia — in fact in areas characterized by massive ethnic uniformity — and is conspicuously weak in Istria and other regions characterized by large ethnic minorities. The party is highly centralist in spirit. It has its own youth organization, CDU Youth.

Programme. The CDU is an explicitly anti-communist expression of Croatian nationality. It presents itself as a centre party in the Christian democratic tradition, envisaging a pluralistic transformation of the state, the development of a market economy, and the institutionalization of civil and human rights, including the freedom of labour organization. Concern is expressed about the decline of the Croatian population, and this is related to a range of policies including the stimulation of return migration and pro-natality measures. Curiously, as time has passed its manifesto has become visibly less concrete in the kinds of proposals which it offers. Representatives of the party attribute this to the difficulty of making concrete legislative plans under war conditions.

Croatian Independent Democrats (CID)
Hrvatski Nezavisni Demokrati (HND)

Address. Kačićeva 16, 41000, Zagreb.

Foundation. May 1994.

Leadership. Stipe Mesić (pres.), Josip Manolić, Slavko Degorica, Perica Jurić, Tomislav Duka, Dragutin Hlad.

History. Formed by split of the leadership of the CDU.

Programme. At the time of writing it is not entirely clear the extent to which the secession of this group is stimulated by major ideological differences with the CDU, as opposed to disagreements over the leadership of Franjo Tudjman. Both seem to be significant, as comments at their founding press conference about the importance of "legality" point in a somewhat coded way towards the former, while there have been evident policy differences over the conduct of the war in Bosnia.

Croatian National Party (CNP)
Hrvatska Narodna Stranka (HNS)

Address. Gajeva 12/II, 41000, Zagreb.

Telephone. 41 427-749; 425-335.

Fax. 41 425-332.

Foundation. Oct. 13, 1990.

Membership. Claims around 25,000.

Leadership. Savka Dabčević-Kučar (pres.); Krešimir Džeba (vice-pres.).

History. The leadership core date back to the Croatian party struggles of 1971–72 as a relatively coherent political clique. The party in its present form is a relatively new phenomenon.

Organization. Has six representatives in the Lower House of the Assembly, and one in the Upper House. There is some indication that although the core of the party is very loyal to its leadership, its support in the electorate is hard pressed by the rise of other modernizing centre groups, especially Liberals.

Programme. The key concept in the programme of the CNP is probably "modernity". Its individualism is therefore presented not in "right–left" terms, but as a distancing from traditionalistic collectivisms of various kinds (religious or ethnic as well as socialist). This is reflected in its support among Croatian Serbs (two of its members of the Upper House and two in the Lower House are Serbs). The creation of strong private enterprise in the economy is only one dimension of a wider project of building a vigorous "civil society". To this end also the party is outspoken in its demands for a free press, and for regionalism. The role of the state is seen as regulatory rather than operative.

Croatian Party of Rights (CPR)
Hrvatska Stranka Prava (HSP)

Address. Trg Sv. Marka 7, 41000, Zagreb.

Telephone. 41 444-000 ext. 33-14.
(Both the address and the telephone number are those of the party's office in the Assembly, as at the time of the research their former offices had been reappropriated by the government)

Foundation. Feb. 25, 1990.

Membership. Claims around 76,000 in Croatia and Bosnia–Hercegovina, although this seems unlikely.

History. It is not known to what extent its claimed descent from the party of the same name which existed before the war is justified. This may well be the case, as it has certainly a highly active following outside Croatia — more so than in the republic. The party was refounded by Dobroslav Paraga as an extremely nationalist and militant organization which eventually developed its own paramilitary wing, HOS. Although the party secured five seats in the 1992 elections to the Lower House, it had no success in the elections to the Upper House. Dissatisfaction with the leadership of Paraga resulted in his removal from the party in the autumn of 1993.

Organization. The party claims more than 20 branches in Croatia, and 20 overseas. The adverse publicity attracted by the activities of HOS (which was especially active in Hercegovina), tarring the entire Croatian nationalist project with the brush of fascism, eventually led to the abrogation of the independence of HOS and the integration of its units under the direct control of the Defence Ministry.

Programme. The published programme of the party makes it difficult to distinguish it from other nationalistic, centre-right groupings in Croatia, such as the Croatian Democratic Party, or even the CDU. It does have a reputation, however, for extreme nationalism. Possibly this is hinted at in its concern for "Croatian national-state sovereignty throughout the whole of its historical and ethnic space", which can be read as meaning not only western Hercegovina but the whole of Bosnia–Hercegovina.

Affiliations. These are unclear, although it does have a reputation for links with terrorist groups.

Croatian Peasant Party (CPP)
Hrvatska Seljačka Stranka (HSS)

Address. Trnskoga 8, 41000, Zagreb.

Telephone. 41 212-325; 412-471

Fax. 412 513; 217-411.

Foundation. Originally founded by the brothers Radić in 1904. Re-established in Croatia, Nov. 20, 1989.

Membership. Claims 50,000.

Leadership. Drago Stipac (pres.). The party has three seats in the Lower and five in the Upper House. Zlatko Tomčić is Minister for Construction and the Environment.

History. The party is the oldest in the whole of former Yugoslavia. It is the only party currently in operation which can legitimately claim continuity with a pre-war organization. Founded in 1904, it became during the inter-war years the principal political expression of Croatian nationalism. Its leaders were interned by the fascists during the last war, and after the war fled to Canada, where the party was kept in being. Returned to register in Zagreb when party pluralism was again permitted in 1989.

Organization. The CPP claims to have around 200 branches, but as this exceeds the number of communes in Croatia, the figure probably includes affiliates abroad. In addition to the conventional apparatus of the party, an attempt is afoot to recreate the network of co-operatives and related organizations which were the strength of the party in the pre-war years. This has been hampered by the lack of economic "normality" as a result of war. The party has three seats in the Lower and five in the Upper House, reflecting its growing strength over the period between elections.

Programme. The CPP stresses the continuity of its links with the party of Maček and the brothers Radić — it is still distributing copies of their speeches, and led the celebrations in 1991 of the bicentenary of the birth of Stjepan Radić. In this respect it sees itself as offering a vision of Croatian society as much as a programme, which combines radical libertarianism, pacifism and a commitment to localism and mutual co-operation. Although in one sense a "nationalistic" party, it has opposed Croatian territorial claims in Bosnia. The CPP advocates complete privatization and reprivatization of economic resources, but combines this economic individualism with a sense of local solidarity in the provision of comprehensive welfare. In spite of its radical aims it is gradualist in temper. Strongly opposed to the authoritarianism of the CDU. The affairs of both agriculture and small business figure high on their agenda.

Croatian Social Liberal Party (CSLP)
Hrvatska Socijalno-Liberalna Stranka (HSLS)

Address. Galovićeva 8, 41000, Zagreb.

Telephone. 41 215-704; 235-222.

Fax. 41 214-444.

Foundation. May 20, 1989.

Membership. 8,000.

Leadership. Dražen Budiša (pres.); Jozo Radoš, Ljubomir Antić, Zlatko Kramarić, Goran Dodig.

Organization. Claims branches in most municipalities. Has a highly regionalized structure, by counties. With 14 representatives in the Lower House, and 16 in the Upper House of the Assembly, the party is the strongest force in opposition. The CSLP claims to be particularly strong in the Zagreb area, in Medjumurje and eastern Slavonia, controlling local councils in both Osijek and Našice. It has extensive support among youth.

Programme. In many ways the CSLP can be described as a nineteenth-century Liberal party. It emphasizes the "democratic and European tradition and orientation of Croatia". In one way or another the European context features prominently in the party's literature, although rhetorically rather than in relation to concrete proposals. The party presents itself as being every bit as Croatian and Catholic as the CDU, from which it is not conspicuously different in policy. It is different in style, however, with a strongly critical stance *vis-à-vis* the government from the point of view of its ineffectiveness and corruption. Consequently its greatest success is in those areas which feel that their regional interests are being neglected by the capital.

Dalmatian Action (DA)
Dalmatinska Akcija (DA)

Address. Kružićeva 2/II, 58000, Split.

Telephone. 58 362-060

Fax. 58 517-036.

Foundation. Dec. 16, 1990.

Membership. Around 4,000.

Leadership. Mira Ljubić-Lorger (pres.), Srdan Benzon, Nikša Ivanišević, Ivan Rudež.

Organization. The party is based in Split, and confines its activities to the Dalmatian region. One representative (the president) sits in the Lower House.

Programme. The programmatic priorities of the party centre on the issues of regional interests, stimulated by the sense of increased isolation felt by many in the Dalmatian region as a consequence of the difficulties of communication imposed by the war and the attempted secession of the Krajina. Co-operates closely with the Istrian Democratic Assembly and the Rijeka Democratic League.

Istrian Democratic Assembly (IDA)
Istarski Demokratski Sabor (IDS)
Sieta Democratica Istriana (SDI)

Address. Flanatička 29/I, 52000, Pula.

Telephone. 52 43-702.

Fax. 52 43-707.

Organization. The party confines its activities to the Istrian region, from which it returned members in the elections to the Lower House, and three to the Upper House (two additional members of the party were nominated to the Upper House by the President). It co-operates closely with the other regional parties: Dalmatian Action, the Rijeka Democratic League, and also the Serbian National Party.

Programme. In practice the party's programmatic concerns have been framed primarily in terms of regional issues, and generally speaking it is a slightly left-of-centre critic of the government. The IDA has been especially exercised over the developing conflict with Slovenia over border definition, and the dispute with Italy regarding compensation for the property of Italian "optants" and "expellees" after World War II.

Rijeka Democratic League (RDL)
Riječki Demokratski Savez (RDS)

Address. Ciottina 19, 51000, Rijeka.

Telephone. 51 34-743.

Membership. 900.

Leadership. Vladimir Smešny (pres.); Nikša Vitković, Ferrucio Glavina, Marijan Turina.

Organization. Although not exclusively a party of the Italian-speaking minority in Croatia it has very strong links with it, and has a special committee for Italian affairs. The RDS has its own youth organization, *"Mlada Rijeka"* (Young Rijeka). The RDS has one seat in the Lower House.

Programme. Its identification with the interests of the region, and consciousness of the importance of the Italian minority, makes the party primarily concerned with issues of cultural expression, minority rights and education. On the whole the RDS is left-of-centre, co-operating with other regional and minority parties on several issues of common concern.

Serbian National Party (SNP)
Srpska Narodna Stranka (SNS)

Address. Trg. Mažuranića 3, 41000, Zagreb.

Telephone. 41 451-090.

Foundation. May 18, 1991.

Membership. Claims around 18,000.

Leadership. Milan Dukić (pres.); Veselin Pejnović (vice-pres.); Veljko Milijević, Dragan Hinić.

History. At the time of the first multi-party elections in Croatia a Serbian Democratic Party was established, under the leadership of Dr Jovan Rašković. The Serb community was deeply split by the creation of the Serbian "Krajina", and many Serbs, especially those in Zagreb, were opposed to the separatist solution to the problems of the republic's Serb population. The new party represents this accommodationist stance.

Organization. The party only operates in the regions still controlled by the Croatian government, where it has well-established branches in eight areas, and active representation in 11 others, all with significant Serb minorities. Three representatives of the party sit in the Lower House of the Assembly, all elected on the national list rather than for specific constituencies, as one might expect with minority parties. The SNP publishes its own magazine, *NIT* (The Thread).

Programme. While explicitly representing Serbs in Croatia, the party is clear that its role is to act as the voice of those Serbs who regard Croatia as their homeland. Its dominant active concerns therefore have, naturally, had to do with constitutional issues, and securing an adequate representation for Serbs and other minorities. In this respect it claims to have made effective inputs into constitutional and legislative drafting. It has been loudly critical of the gerrymandering of constituency boundaries, especially in relation to the new *Županije*. It has concerned itself with issues relating to the cultural heritage and rights of cultural expression of Serbs within Croatia, and has participated actively in the formulation of proposals for the resolution of the problem of the Krajina. Reflecting the rural location of the great majority of the republic's Serbs, the SNP expresses particular and active concern about Croatia's underdeveloped regions and agrarian issues.

Social Democratic Party of Croatia (SDP)
Socijaldemokratska Stranka Hrvatske (SDP)
(formerly Savez Komunista Hrvatske – Stranka Demokratskih Promjena)

Address. Iblerov trg 9, 41000, Zagreb.

Telephone. 41 452-055; 412-109.

Foundation. Aug. 1, 1937. In its present form Nov. 3, 1990.

Membership. 35–40,000.

Leadership. Ivica Račan (pres.); Davorko Vidović, Snježana Biga-Friganović, Sime Lučin, Mirko Pačarek.

History. The Croatian Communist Party, in one form or another, has been in continuous existence ever since its reorganization in 1937 by Josip Broz "Tito". It has also been characterized by a succession of important attempts to liberalise and reform the party, especially in 1971–72. With the change to a multi-party system, the former League of Communists of Croatia changed its name initially to the Party of Democratic Change, settling subsequently upon its present title.

Organization. The PDC (as it was) suffered enormously from the rise of the CDU, losing an estimated 100,000 members to the CDU bandwagon in the early days of the independence movement. The party was regarded as too compromised with "Yugoslavism". Following electoral defeat, however, it underwent a comprehensive shake-up, but still retains its greatest strength in the larger industrial towns and among former administrators. It has six representatives in the Lower House; but the protracted crisis of the party is reflected in its failure to secure any seats in the Upper House. There has been a degree of organizational consolidation of left parties over the past two years, from which the SDP has benefited.

Programme. The party describes itself as a "contemporary political organization of the left in Croatia, European in its orientation, which is committed to political democracy and a market economy", and attempts to hold together the imperatives of economic modernization with a strong emphasis on "solidarity" — the defence of welfare state measures. While deferring to the dominant nationalism, and acknowledging that Croatia is the "national state of the Croatian people", the party stresses the need to accommodate other groups for whom the republic is an "historic homeland".

Affiliations. As with other former LC organizations, it is unclear to what extent an effective federal network of links remains in existence.

In addition to these parties which are currently represented in the Assembly, the following party merits detailed mention because of the size of its following and its impact on political debate.

Croatian Christian Democratic Union (CCDU)
Hrvatska Kršćanska Demokratska Unija (HKDU)

Address. Tkalčićeva 4, 41000, Zagreb.

Telephone. 41 422-062.

Fax. 41 421-969.

Foundation. Dec. 20, 1992.

Membership. Claims 40–50,000.

Leadership. Marko Veselica (pres.); Ivan Cesar, Željko Olujić, Anto Kovačević, Pavao Barišić.

History. The party was formed by the merger of two right-wing groups which were both created around the time of the first multi-party elections in Croatia: the Christian Democratic Party, formerly led by Ivan Cesar, and the Croatian Democratic Party, led by Marko Veselica. The first of these managed to secure the election of two representatives in the first Assembly, and the second had nine. Both fared disastrously in the second elections of August 1992, however, following which a merger between the two was agreed. Although they had no greater success in the elections to the Upper House, the party remains a significant voice on the right of Croatian politics.

Organization. Has organizations in all counties and municipalities.

Programme. The party claims to be based upon the Christian principles of faith, hope and love. A good part of its programme is devoted to the exposition of very general ideals of an ethical nature. Staunchly anti-communist, it demands the depoliticization of the organs of administration and justice; the creation of a market economy based upon private property and the encouragement of Croat emigrants to return to Croatia. A high priority is given to the perceived decline of the Croat population, and the traditional Catholic focus on "pro-life" issues figures substantially in its manifesto.

Affiliations. The European Christian Democratic Union.

The following minor parties are also registered in Croatia in 1994. They are all registered in Zagreb, unless otherwise stated. This information has been obtained from the Croatian Ministry of Information.

Albanian Christian Democratic Party (ACP): *Albanska Demokršćanska Stranka* (ADS). This is believed to be a branch of the Kosovo party of the same name, representing principally Catholic Albanians. **Christian National Party (CNP):** *Kršćanska Narodna Stranka* (KNS). **Croatian Democratic Party of Rights (CDPR):** *Hrvatska Demokratska Stranka Prava* (HDSP). This group contests the same ground and claims the same political heritage as the CPR. Its leader is Krešimir Pavelić. **Croatian Movement for State-building (CMS):** *Hrvatski Državnotvorni Pokret* (HDP). The principal claim to fame of this extreme nationalist faction is that its leader, Nikola Štedul, was the victim of an assassination attempt by the Yugoslav secret service in Kirkaldy, in Scotland, where he lived for many years. **Croatian Muslim Democratic Party (CMDP):** *Hrvatska Muslimanska Demokratska Stranka* (HMDS). **Croatian Natural Law Party (CNLP):** *Hrvatska Stranka Naravnog Zakona* (HSNZ). As its title suggests, this represents the followers of the Maharishi, and is affiliated to the European Council of Natural Law Parties. **Croatian Party (CP):** *Hrvatska Stranka* (HS). Although this group has had no significant electoral success its president, Dr Hrvoje Šošić, sits in the Upper House as one of the members nominated by the President of the Republic. This is in recognition of his personal expertise in economic affairs rather than as a tribute to his party. **Croatian Socialist Party (CSP):** *Stranka Socijalista Hrvatske* (SSH). This group is one of the successors to the former Socialist Alliance which secured representation in the first multi-party elections, but which has subsequently lost ground rapidly, possibly because of its relatively "hard left" stance. **Party of Democratic Action (PDA):** *Stranka Demokratske Akcije* (SDA). Registered in Zagreb, but a Croatian branch of the Sarajevo-based party. **Social Democratic Party of Croatia (SPC):** *Socijaldemokratska Stranka Hrvatske* (SDH). This is not to be confused with the SDP or the SDU, in spite of the close similarity of their titles. Another of the left factions to emerge from the former Socialist Alliance, it had one representative in the first multi-party Assembly. **Social Democratic Union (SDU):** *Socijaldemokratska Unija Hrvatske* (SDU). The programmatic basis for the separation between the three parties all using the title "social democratic" is unclear. This is not to be confused with the SDP or the SPC. It is in this particular political wilderness, however, that the eminent Croatian economist Branko Horvat has chosen to find his home. **Transnational Radical Party (TRP):** *Transnacionalna Radikalna Stranka* (TRS). The leadership group of the TRP suggests a multi-ethnic appeal; it has an address in Rome and declares affiliation to the Italian *Partito Radicale*.

THE CZECH REPUBLIC

Peter Bugge

The partition of Czechoslovakia — or the Czech and Slovak Federative Republic as the country was officially called from March 1990 — and the creation of two independent successor states, the Czech Republic and the Slovak Republic, on Jan. 1, 1993, presented the last Czechoslovak federal government and the cabinets of the two emerging states with the difficult task of splitting up a unitary economy, and the loss of an integrated market with a common currency has had negative repercussions on the economics of both countries. By contrast, the party political structure of disappearing Czechoslovakia was remarkably little affected by the division, since two almost fully separate party systems had already developed in the Czech and the Slovak republics between 1989 and 1992.

This trend was stimulated by the federative structure of Czechoslovakia. Federalism had already been introduced in 1968 in what was probably the only surviving reform initiated during the "Prague Spring". A constitutional law of Oct. 27, 1968, that took effect on Jan. 1, 1969, turned Czechoslovakia into a federation of two republics with equal rights, the Czech Socialist Republic and the Slovak Socialist Republic. The National Assembly of old was replaced by a bicameral Federal Assembly, consisting of a House of the People, in which the seats were distributed in proportion to the size of the electorate in the two newly created republics, and a House of the Nations with an equal number of seats for each republic. The new republics had their own parliaments, the Czech National Council and the Slovak National Council, with legislative powers in matters that did not belong to the competence of the Federal Assembly, and although their autonomy was significantly reduced — *de jure* and *de facto* — during the so-called "normalization" of Czechoslovakia under Gustav Husák, Alexander Dubček's successor as leader of the Communist Party, the parliamentary structure introduced in 1969 was preserved until the end of 1992, when the Federal Assembly was dissolved along with Czechoslovakia.

Under Communist rule elections were held in single-member constituencies with only one contender standing in each constituency, but a new Electoral Law of Feb. 27, 1990 introduced a system of proportional representation as used in Czechoslovakia until the Communist seizure of power in February 1948. The principle of proportionality was, however, subjected to one major restriction: to win a seat in one of the two chambers of the Federal Assembly a party or political movement would have to obtain at least 5 per cent of the vote cast at the elections to that chamber (since 1969 voters were to vote separately for each chamber in the Federal Assembly). On Jan. 29, 1992, an amendment to the Electoral Law raised this threshold to 7 per cent for coalitions of two or three parties and to 10 per cent for coalitions of four or more parties. In 1992, these thresholds also applied in elections to the Czech and Slovak National Councils while in 1990 a lower,

3 per cent threshold had been introduced in the elections to the Slovak parliament. The Federal Assembly had 300 seats, equally shared by its two chambers. In the House of the Nations, 75 deputies were elected from each republic, while in the House of the People the distribution was altered from 1990 to 1992 as the census of 1991 registered a slight growth in the Slovak Republic's share of the Czechoslovak population. In 1990, 101 seats were allocated to the Czech Republic and 49 to the Slovak republic, while in 1992 the numbers were 99 and 51 respectively.

The 5 per cent threshold was applied separately in each republic, which enabled political parties and movements to stand for elections in one of the republics only. This option proved to be attractive to many. In June 1990, at the first free parliamentary elections after 41 years of one-party rule, only 11 out of 22 participating parties, movements and coalitions were standing in all Czechoslovakia, while five parties sought election in the Czech Republic only and six solely in Slovakia. Of the 11 federally contending parties only the Communist Party of Czechoslovakia won seats in both republics, while a Hungarian coalition was alone among the remaining ten to pass the 5 per cent threshold in one of these (Slovakia). By contrast, three of five contenders standing in the Czech Republic only and three of six from Slovakia gained access to the Federal Assembly, winning 248 of the Assembly's 300 seats. Regionally restricted campaigning was to be expected from the Movement for Self-Governing Democracy – Association for Moravia and Silesia, which called for greater autonomy for these two historical "lands" within the Czech republic (the third, and dominant, being Bohemia), and from the Slovak National Party demanding full Slovak independence, but even "pro-Czechoslovak" parties with similar political programmes chose to organize and contest the seats separately. This was the case of the Christian Democrats and of the democratic umbrella organizations that led the "velvet revolution" of 1989, the Civic Forum in the Czech Republic and the Public Against Violence in Slovakia, the two great winners of the June 1990 elections.

The trend was even more explicit at the parliamentary elections on June 5–6, 1992. Of the 21 contending parties in the Czech Republic and 22 in Slovakia only seven were found in both republics, and none of these managed to appeal to the voters in both. The Association for the Republic – the Republican Party of Czechoslovakia (henceforth the Republicans) won 14 Czech seats in the Federal Assembly, but found support among less than 0.4 per cent of the Slovak voters, and a Hungarian coalition won 12 seats in Slovakia (as in 1990) while getting less than 0.1 per cent of the votes in the Czech Republic. None of the other five parties got more than 1.5 per cent in any one half of the Federal Assembly's two chambers. Some 274 seats in the Federal Assembly thus went to parties representing only one of the halves of Czechoslovakia, and between 1990 and 1992 even two parties with a strong tradition of centralism and political "Czechoslovakism", the Communists and the Social Democrats, had split along national lines. Irrespective of their attitude to the preservation of Czechoslovakia, all parties were thus confronted with a very strong drive towards the emergence of two autonomous party systems, and the formation of a Czech multi-party system after 1989 (though of course not political developments in Czechoslovakia) may thus be analysed as by and large a self-contained process.

Czech party formation began in the 1860s when constitutional rule was introduced in Habsburg Austria. The loose "National Party" of patriotic notables split in 1874 into a conservative faction, the "Old Czechs", and the liberal "Young Czechs", who dominated Czech politics in the 1890s. In 1878 a Czech Social Democracy was founded within the Austrian labour movement, and around 1900 a Czech multi-party system emerged, whose basic features survived until 1938. Its five leading members were the Young Czechs (from 1919 the National Democratic Party), the Social Democrats, the Agrarians and the National Socialists (who must not be confused with the German National Socialists). The party was a strong defender of Czechoslovak democracy after 1918, and Edvard Beneš, long-time Foreign Minister and later President, was a party member. Finally, Czech political Catholicism took shape, united from 1919 in the People's Party.

Well-established within Austria, most Czech parties simply continued work in the new Czechoslovak Republic while extending their activities to Slovakia, where Hungarian repression until 1918 had stopped all feeble attempts at Slovak national politics. The Constitution of 1920 claimed that Czechs and Slovaks formed one Czechoslovak nation (though with two branches), and most Czech parties adhered to this philosophy, but as a rule these "Czechoslovakist" parties achieved less than 50 per cent of the Slovak vote, a proof to the limited validity of the one nation doctrine. The German and Hungarian minorities had their own parties, and the only truly "trans-ethnic" party in inter-war Czechoslovakia was the Communist Party, founded in 1921.

The Republic's proportional electoral system and national heterogeneity resulted in a great proliferation of parties and in corresponding limits to the their size. From 1920 to 1938 there were always at least 14 parties in Parliament, and except for the Czechoslovak Social Democrats, who in 1920 (before the Communists broke out) obtained 25.7 per cent, no party ever gained more than 15.7 per cent of the vote. Coalition governments were therefore required, and to bolster party stability a law prescribed that a seat in Parliament belonged to the party, not to the elected deputy. This contributed to weakening the Parliament *vis-à-vis* the party leaders. Czechoslovakia was unique in inter-war Central Europe in offering ministerial offices to a national minority (there were German ministers in all Cabinets from 1926 to 1938) and in not forbidding communist or fascist parties, but essentially the country was governed by the same Czech(-oslovakist) parties for two decades. This made the Czechoslovak inter-war political system very stable, but also highly inflexible, which may account for the lack of veneration for it after the Munich crisis of September 1938.

The "second republic", created in what was left of Czechoslovakia after the German seizure of the "Sudetengerman" borderlands, made a swift and radical break with the parliamentary multi-party system of before. All pre-Munich Czech parties were replaced by two new ones, a National Unity Party containing the "non-socialist" parties and a National Labour Party of Social Democrats and National Socialists. The Communist Party was forbidden and in Slovakia, which obtained full autonomy, a fascist one-party system emerged. The National Labour Party served as a loyal opposition to the National Unity Party in an arrangement of "authoritarian democracy" which met with little popular protest. The interests of the state and the nation were to take precedence over "party egoism", and a cautious strategy of partial compliance with German norms was adopted.

Yet Hitler chose to create a "Protectorate of Bohemia-Moravia" on March 15, 1939, while letting the Slovaks establish their own state. The two Czech parties were dissolved, and an association called National Solidarity formed to administer what little autonomy was left. Eventually, German repression wiped out all resistance rooted in the first republic, and only President Beneš's exile government in London implied some continuity of pre-Munich Czechoslovakia. But nor here (or among the Czechoslovak Communists in Moscow) was there any wish to restore the pre-Munich party system. Beneš wanted a reduction of the number of parties to two or three —a leftist, a rightist, and perhaps a centrist — and in

December 1943 he and Communist leader Klement Gottwald agreed upon a scheme for post-war Czechoslovakia that forbade all right-wing parties (including the Agrarians, the largest Czechoslovak pre-war party) and united the rest in a "National Front", exempted from outside control or challenges. In much, the "rightist authoritarianism" of the second republic was thus replaced by an equally uncontrolled "leftist authoritarianism", and it is exaggerated to talk of a restoration of Czechoslovak democracy in 1945.

From May 1945 the new regime was installed. Czechoslovakia was restored within its pre-Munich borders except for the Soviet annexation of Ruthenia, but a massive expulsion of Germans began and similar plans were made (though not realized) for the Slovak Hungarians. The National Front consisted of four Czech and two Slovak parties, but only the Communists, who had cleverly established an autonomous Slovak party beside the Czechoslovak mother party, could operate in all Czechoslovakia (this asymmetric arrangement, in which no Czech Communist Party existed next to the Slovak, was preserved until 1990). From 1945 to 1948 the government was *de facto* responsible to the National Front rather than to the weak parliament, but the elections to the Constituent National Assembly on May 26, 1946, were important as a test of party strength within the National Front, and if one neglects the ban on opposition parties (two minute Slovak parties supporting the National Front were permitted), and the suspended franchise of real or alleged collaborators (which affected about 250,000 people), Hungarians and Germans, they may be characterized as free. The results are displayed in Table 1.

The Communists were content with a Czechoslovak average of 38 per cent, but the strength of the newly founded Democratic Party in Slovakia caused them to initiate a fierce campaign to undermine the party's position and to curb Slovak autonomy, in which they efficiently exploited continued Czech mistrust in the Slovaks at a time of rising tension between the Communists and the other parties in the National Front. The resignation of 12 non-communist ministers in a clumsy attempt to provoke the government's fall gave the Communist seizure of power on February 25, 1948, an air of constitutional legitimacy, but the following persecution of all political opponents ruthlessly infringed all principles of a constitutional state. At the elections to the National Assembly on May 30, 1948, the "renewed" National Front presented only one joint candidate in each constituency, 70 per cent of whom were Communists. The electorate could protest only by returning a so-called "white paper" (see Table 2).

The figures tell of some continued opposition, and even at the elections in November 1954 2.11 per cent of the voters used the white papers, which were then abolished. From 1960 the candidates of the National Front obtained at least 99.7 per cent of the votes. The National Front thus continued to exist, as did four of its member parties, the Communists, the National Socialists (since 1948 the Czechoslovak Socialist Party), the People's Party, and the Freedom Party, while the Social Democracy in June 1948 was forced to merge with the Communists, and the Democratic Party was replaced by a Party of Slovak Renewal. In reality, all institutions were subjugated to the Communists, as also expressed in the Constitution of 1960. It declared (Art. 4) that the Communist Party was "the leading force in state and society", including the National Front, of which now also trade unions, youth and women's unions, etc, were members (Art. 6). Its main tasks were to nominate candidates for elections and to serve as a "transmission belt" for Communist policies, and

Table 1: Elections to the Constituent National Assembly, May 26, 1946

	% Votes	Seats
The Czech Lands		
Communist Party of Czechoslovakia	40.17	93
Czechoslovak National Socialist Party	23.66	55
Czechoslovak People's Party	20.24	46
Czechoslovak Social Democracy	15.58	37
Blank voting papers	0.35	
TOTAL	100.00	231
Slovakia		
Democratic Party	62.00	43
Communist Party of Slovakia	30.37	21
Freedom Party	3.73	3
Labour Party	3.11	2
Blank voting papers	0.79	
TOTAL	100.00	69

Source: Československé dějiny v datech (Prague 1986), p. 632–33.

Table 2: Elections to the National Assembly, May 30, 1948

	The Czech Lands % Votes	Slovakia % Votes
For the list of the National Front	87.12	84.91
White papers	9.32	13.98
Invalid votes	3.56	1.11
TOTAL	100.00	100.00

Source: Československé dějiny v datech (Prague 1986), p. 633.

the strictly controlled non-Communist parties had narrow limits to their membership and social role.

The "Prague Spring" in 1968 did not challenge the Communist monopoly of power although there was talk about introducing some political pluralism. The non-Communist parties were activated, plans were made to renew the Social Democracy and a "Club of Committed Non-Party Members" sought official recognition. The Communist Party itself envisaged in its "Action Programme" of April 1968 only a growth in inner-party democracy and a revitalization of the National Front in a model that would have kept parliament in a role as rubber-stamp for decisions made elsewhere, and all reform plans were abandoned after the Soviet-led invasion of Czechoslovakia on Aug. 21, 1968.

Thoroughly purged in 1969 and 1970, Czechoslovak society sank into a lethargy that was only disturbed in January 1977 with the publication of the Charter 77 manifesto. The Charter 77 carefully stressed that it was not a political party nor in opposition to the regime, and the manifesto did not include the lack of freedom of association on its long list of violations of human rights in Czechoslovakia. In spite of this "non-political" approach, the initial 242 signatories and those who joined them were met with harassment and persecution. Even so, Charter 77 survived as a forum for co-operation and free debate among people of very different persuasions and it came to form the nexus of the democratic alternative that emerged in November 1989. Yet it was Gorbachev's *perestroika* policy in the Soviet Union that eventually destabilized a regime incapable of reform, and from the autumn of 1988 the Czechoslovak public began to engage in greater numbers in opposition activities. A petition called *"A few sentences"*, published in June 1989, was far more explicit than the Charter 77 in its call for political pluralism and economic reform, and within a few months it was signed by about 37,000 people. As Communist regimes all over eastern Europe crumbled, culminating with the fall of the Berlin Wall on Nov. 9, 1989, the time was ripe for explosive change in Czechoslovakia, and an occasion came on Nov. 17 when the police broke up a student demonstration in Prague.

On Nov. 19 the Civic Forum was founded in Prague as an umbrella organization to co-ordinate the democratic opposition to the regime, and the following day a similar organization, the Public Against Violence (PAV), was founded in Bratislava. Mass protests spread all over the country and within a week the authorities were forced to negotiate. On Dec. 10, before resigning, President Husák swore in a "Government of National Understanding", led by the Slovak Communist Marián Čalfa who later joined the PAV and with a non-Communist majority, and on Dec. 29, 1989, the Federal Assembly — still largely Communist — unanimously elected Civic Forum leader Václav Havel president. Many Communists withdrew or were expelled from the Federal Assembly, which on Jan. 23, 1990, passed a law allowing for their replacement by deputies appointed by the Civic Forum or the PAV. Similar changes took place in the National Councils, and so the Communists lost their parliamentary majority months before the elections on June 8–9, 1990.

On Jan. 23, a Law on Political Parties recognized the five parties existing prior to Nov. 17, 1989, and the Civic Forum and the PAV as political parties, and established rules for the formation of new parties (or movements with a similar status). To obtain registration with the Ministry of the Interior a party was to present its statutes and aims, which had to be in conformity with the law, and a list of at least 1,000 supporters. By mid-1990 over 100 parties and movements had registered with the ministry, of which 22 were able to present a list of 10,000 members or supporters, as demanded for participation at the elections to the Federal Assembly in the Electoral Law of Feb. 27, 1990. The elections, in which an impressive 96 per cent of the electorate took part, created the results shown in table 3.

Five Slovak parties obtained representation in the Federal Assembly, their number of seats in the House of the People/House of the Nations in brackets: Public Against Violence (19/33), Christian Democratic Movement (11/14), Communist Party of Czechoslovakia (8/12), Slovak National Party (6/9) Coexistence — Hungarian Christian Democratic Movement (5/7).

Table 3: Elections to The Federal Assembly of the Czech and Slovak Federative Republic, June 8–9, 1990 (Czech results only)

	% Votes	Seats
House of the People		
Czech Republic		
Civic Forum	53.2	68
Communist Party of Czechoslovakia	13.5	15
Christian and Democratic Union	8.7	9
Association for Moravia and Silesia	7.9	9
Social Democracy	3.8	
Alliance of Farmers and the Countryside	3.8	
Green Party	3.1	
Others (parties with less than 3% of the vote)	6.0	
TOTAL	100.0	101
House of the Nations		
Czech Republic		
Civic Forum	50.0	50
Communist Party of Czechoslovakia	13.8	12
Association for Moravia and Silesia	9.1	7
Christian and Democratic Union	8.8	6
Social Democracy	4.2	
Alliance of Farmers and the Countryside	4.0	
Green Party	3.4	
Others (parties with less than 3% of the vote)	6.7	
TOTAL	100.0	75

Source: Statistická ročenka ČSFR 1991 (Prague 1991), p. 629–30.

With 127 of the 200 seats (49.5 per cent of the vote), the Civic Forum won the absolute majority in the Czech National Council, while the Communists came second with 32 seats (13.2 per cent), the Association for Moravia and Silesia third with 22 (10.0 per cent), and the Christian and Democratic Union with 19 seats (8.4 per cent of the vote) was the fourth and last party to gain representation.

The present Czech party system has developed in three phases, separated by the elections in 1990 and 1992. In the first seven months after the "velvet revolution", a multitude of political initiatives emerged beside the Civic Forum and the three "established" parties, most of them small and amorphous, so it was difficult for the public to distinguish between them. At the first free elections virtually all contenders had similar programmes, as all (including the Communists!) declared their wish to break with the past and seek a pluralistic, democratic, prosperous Czechoslovakia. The second phase was marked by disagreement within the ruling Civic Forum, which led to its division into three relatively solid parties, and by a gradual "sorting out" among the other parties, as their political profile and resources became more discernible. There was, inevitably, ample scope for populism, but in June 1992 the electorate had a chance to know "who was who". The third phase, lasting until the present, is characterized by greater coherence among the members of the Czech coalition government, while the opposition has been less stable. For over a year opinion polls have shown only modest fluctuations in electoral sympathies, and few of the parties not represented in Parliament may today be considered serious applicants to political influence.

A typical feature has been the high number of parties. A survey from March 1991 included 111 political parties and movements in Czechoslovakia, 47 in both republics, 26 in the Czech Republic, and 38 in Slovakia. Three years later, in March 1994, 52 political parties and 26 movements were registered in the Czech Republic. The political scene has been accordingly volatile. Parties have made coalitions, fused, split or vanished and very often changed their name. Also, there was among voters and activists alike and especially shortly after 1989 great scepticism about parties, as an institution and a concept. This accounts for the many initiatives that — though not dissimilar to traditional parties in structure or goals — prefer to be labelled movements. Eventually, however, the trend clearly points towards the consolidation of a multi-party system organized, in the main, along a left-right axis. So the Moravian regionalists have changed their name into the Bohemian-Moravian Centre Party, and for demographic reasons "ethnic" parties have little political scope: Romany (Gypsy) associations may play a local role, but the Gypsy population is too small to bring any such party to parliament, and the 300,000 Slovaks who have stayed in the Czech Republic (the biggest minority in the country), have typically also chosen Czech citizenship without forming their own parties. Of the "one cause parties", only the Greens have some position, while the Friends of Beer Party, the Independent Erotic Initiative, and the like are mere curiosities.

One may discern five modes of party formation after 1989. One is the continuation or "revival" of the parties permitted within the post-1948 National Front. These parties have had the advantage of having good party headquarters and other assets (much, but not all property of the Communist Party was surrendered to the state), including well-established party newspapers, although the former Communist daily *Rudé Právo* is now independent of the party and supports (according to the Communists) the Social Democrats. Their main concern has been — especially in the case of the People's Party and the Czechoslovak Socialist Party — how to distance themselves from their role before 1989 and get rid of their discredited "old structures". The Communists have not — unlike their sister party in Slovakia or in nearly every other ex-socialist state — felt any urge to change their name or denounce their past.

Secondly, some previously forbidden parties have reappeared, like the Social Democrats and the Club of Committed Non-Party Members. There is no such continuity from the Agrarians of the first republic to the present Agrarian Party, which has been seen as a lobbyist for the co-operative farms, and which in March 1994 decided to integrate in the Liberal Social Union. Thirdly, parties have emerged from the Civic Forum as it disintegrated in 1991. Some of these, including the Civic Democratic Alliance, were political factions within the Civic Forum before the split, but the main heirs to the organization were the Civic Movement of Jiří Dienstbier and Václav Klaus's Civic Democratic Party. These parties all had the advantage of being well represented in parliament and government and of inheriting the Civic Forum's assets. Fourthly, new parties have been formed outside the Civic Forum umbrella. They have all started without the capital of the previously mentioned and although in the majority, few have succeeded. Today, three such parties, the Republicans, the Bohemian-Moravian Centre Party and the Christian Democratic Party, are represented in parliament. Finally, parties have been formed by dissenting members of established parties. From 1992, such divisions have affected all opposition parties in the Czech parliament except the Social Democrats so that the number of party clubs has grown from nine to twelve.

For all parties with a pre-1948 record, the renting-out of parts of their attractive Prague headquarters buildings has been a valuable source of income although a system of financial support for political parties was introduced in October 1991 (each vote for a party with more than 2 per cent of the vote released an annual sum of 15 crowns). On 29 April, 1994, an amendment to the Law on Political Parties substantially changed this system: now all parties that at the 1992 elections obtained at least 3 per cent of the vote obtain an annual sum of three to five million crows, depending on their share of the vote. Also, all parties represented in parliament receive an additional annual 500,000 crowns for each seat in parliament. In consequence, state support of the parties has grown from 70 million crowns to approximately 160 million.

In June 1990, the Federal Assembly was elected for two years only, since it was recognized that a complete political spectrum has not yet taken shape. Its main task was to prepare a new Czechoslovak Constitution and to continue the political and economic transformation of society. A federal coalition government was formed by the Civic Forum, the PAV, and the Slovak Christian Democratic Movement. Marián Čalfa remained Prime Minister, Jiří Dienstbier Minister of Foreign Affairs and Václav Klaus Minister of Finance, while Alexander Dubček was Speaker of the Federal Assembly. Petr Pithart of the Civic Forum became Czech Prime Minister and Vladimír Mečiar his Slovak counterpart. The federal government was quite successful in the economic sphere, although uneven developments in the Czech Republic and Slovakia caused increasing tensions, but it proved unable to solve the task of writing a Constitution. The split within the Civic Forum in March 1991 did not affect the movement's work in the government, while a crisis in the PAV had more serious consequences. Mečiar broke with the PAV in March 1991 to form his own party and was replaced as Slovak Prime Minister by Ján Čarnogurský of the Christian Democrats. Both Čarnogurský and the increasingly radicalized Mečiar demanded a degree of independence for Slovakia within the federation that was unacceptable to nearly all Czech parties, and the elections in June 1992 took place in an atmosphere of national and political polarization. They brought the results shown in table 4.

The victory of Václav Klaus's Civic Democratic Party (and its small coalition partner, the Christian Democratic Party) was clear and in Slovakia Vladimír Mečiar's Movement for a Democratic Slovakia won equally convincingly with 33.5 per cent of the vote for the House of the People and 33.9 for the House of the Nations. In the Czech half of parliament there was a majority of the right (the Civic Democratic Party and the two Christian Democratic parties), favouring a continuation of the economic reforms and opposed to a weakening of the Czechoslovak federation, while no liberal party was elected from Slovakia. Also, all major Slovak parties demanded more Slovak autonomy, if not full independence. Neither the economic, nor the national programmes of the Czech and the Slovak majorities were compatible, so the two winning parties (supported by the Czech Christian Democrats) decided to form a federal government with the task to prepare a peaceful division of Czechoslovakia. The Czech Jan Stráský became federal Prime Minister and the Slovak

Table 4: **Elections to the Federal Assembly of the Czech and Slovak Federative Republic, June 5–6, 1992 (Czech results only)**

	% Votes	Seats
House of the People		
Czech Republic		
Civic Democratic Party + Christian Democratic Party	33.9	48
Left Bloc	14.3	19
Czechoslovak Social Democracy	7.7	10
Association for the Republic — the Republican Party of Czechoslovakia	6.5	8
Christian and Democratic Union — Czechoslovak People's Party	6.0	7
Liberal Social Union	5.8	7
Civic Democratic Alliance	5.0 (4.98!)	
Civic Movement	4.4	
Association for Moravia and Silesia	4.2	
Movement of Pensioners for Life Securities	3.3	
Others (parties with less than 3% of the vote)	9.9	
TOTAL	100.0	99
House of the Nations		
Czech Republic		
Civic Democratic Party + Christian Democratic Party	33.4	37
Left Bloc	14.5	15
Czechoslovak Social Democracy	6.8	6
Association for the Republic — the Republican Party of Czechoslovakia	6.4	6
Christian and Democratic Union — Czechoslovak People's Party	6.1	6
Liberal Social Union	6.1	5
Association for Moravia and Silesia	4.9	
Civic Movement	4.7	
Civic Democratic Alliance	4.1	
Movement of Pensioners for Life Securities	3.4	
Others (parties with less than 3% of the vote)	9.6	
TOTAL	100.0	75

Source: Lidové noviny, June 10 and 12, 1992

Table 5: Elections to the Czech National Council, June 5–6, 1992

Party	% Votes	Seats
Civic Democratic Party + Christian Democratic Party	29.7	76
		(66 + 10)
Left Bloc	14.1	35
Czechoslovak Social Democracy	6.5	16
Liberal Social Union	6.5	16
Christian and Democratic Union —		
Czechoslovak People's Party	6.3	15
Association for the Republic —		
the Republican Party of Czechoslovakia	6.0	14
Civic Democratic Alliance	5.9	14
Association for Moravia and Silesia	5.9	14
Civic Movement	4.6	
Movement of Pensioners for Life Securities	3.8	
Party of Czechoslovak Entrepreneurs, Tradesmen		
and Farmers	3.2	
Club of Committed Non-Party Members	2.7	
Others	4.8	
TOTAL	100.0	200

Source: Lidové noviny, June 10 and 12, 1992

Jozef Moravčík Foreign Minister, while the two "strong men" in Czechoslovak politics, Klaus and Mečiar, became Czech and Slovak prime ministers.

One consequence of this decision, to which no viable alternative was formulated, was that the Federal Assembly's only function became to make itself superfluous and to prepare the legislative framework for the division. As a result, the centre of gravity in Czech and Slovak politics moved to the National Councils, which (to the dissatisfaction of many deputies of the Federal Assembly) simply decided to take over responsibility as national parliaments of the two emerging states. The elections to the Czech National Council, which had also taken place on June 5–6, 1992, therefore came to determine the political profile of the new state (see Table 5).

As in the Federal Assembly the elections brought a liberal and conservative victory. While the Communists (as members of the Left Bloc with a minor socialist party) again did well and the Social Democrats crossed the 5 per cent threshold (as probably the best-established Social Democratic party in the post-communist countries), the political centre was weakly represented. The Liberal Social Union was a heterogenous coalition of three very different parties (technically appearing as one party to avoid the 7 per cent coalition threshold) that fell apart shortly after the elections, and in spite of its strong representation in the Federal and the Czech governments the Civic Movement, one of the heirs to the Civic Forum, did not succeed at all. Led as it was by former Charter 77 activists, the defeat of the Civic Movement has been called the end of dissident influence in Czech politics which, although exaggerated, does not entirely miss the point. The bad result may, however, also be ascribed to the party's neglect of organizational matters (while the Civic Democratic Party quickly built an efficient party apparatus), and for its seeming compliance towards Slovakia when in office. The Republicans, by contrast, who surprised most observers in getting 6 per cent of the votes, represent an aggressive populism with racist overtones in radical opposition to everybody else in Czech politics.

It had great political significance that the Civic Democratic Alliance (which has the profile of a conservative élite party and has been seen as the "intellectual" right-wing alternative to the Civic Democratic Party) passed the 5 per cent threshold in the Czech National Council. Together, the Civic Democratic Party, the Civic Democratic Alliance, the Christian Democratic Party and the People's Party had 105 seats in parliament, which enabled them to form the majority coalition government still in office. In the last months of 1992 the Czech National Council prepared a Constitution of the Czech Republic which was eventually passed with a great majority on Dec. 16, 1992. Only the Republicans and four Moravian autonomists voted against.

According to the Constitution the Czech Parliament is bicameral with a Chamber of Deputies (into which the Czech National Council transformed itself) of 200 members, elected for a period of four years and with a proportional system, and a Senate of 81 members, elected for six years by majority vote and with new elections of one-third of the senators every second year. The president is elected by both chambers of the parliament for a period of five years and may only be re-elected once. The Senate may delay, but not reject legislative measures passed in the Chamber of Deputies, and its other competences are few. The institution has therefore been sharply criticized by the opposition and even some government members favour a unicameral system. There has also been disagreement over how to occupy the seats in the Senate (both a French and a British model are being considered), so as a result the Senate still exists only on paper. Due to internal strife in the coalition government and massive resistance from the opposition a Law on elections to the Senate was rejected in Parliament on June 2, 1994, and the future of the Senate is now highly uncertain. New elections for the Chamber of Deputies are to take place in 1996, so the first elections in the new state will be the total elections to be held on Nov. 18–19, 1994. It may be expected that their outcome will again provoke new mergers or alliances, especially among the smaller parties.

Directory of Parties

Agrarian Party
Zemědělská Strana (ZS)

Address. Křižova 60, 16000 Praha 6.

Telephone. (02) 530186.

Foundation. Jan. 12, 1990.

Leadership. Jiří Vačkář (ch.)

History and affiliations. After an unsuccessful campaign at the 1990 elections, then party chairman František Trnka led the Agrarians into the Liberal Social Union (LSU), an electoral union with the Green Party and the Czechoslovak Socialist Party, through which the Agrarians obtained representation in the Czech parliament. Trnka eventually became chairman of the LSU, while Jiří Vačkář replaced him as Agrarian Party leader. On March 12, 1994, a conference of the Agrarian Party decided with to fuse with the LSU, while Jiří Vačkář, who opposed the decision, gave up his functions and left the conference. It remains to be seen if he will seek to establish a new, independent Agrarian Party.

Association for the Republic – the Republican Party of Czechoslovakia
Sdružení pro republiku – republikánská strana Českoslovennska (SPR-RSČ)

Address. Bělohorská 74, 16900 Praha 6.

Telephone. (02) 354833.

Foundation. February 1990.

Leadership. Miroslav Sládek (ch.), Jan Vik.

Membership. 70,000.

History. A populist party of the extreme right, the Republicans seek to win adherents through radical agitation at street meetings, demonstrations, etc. At the June 1992 elections the party won 14 seats in the Czech parliament. Support for the Republicans was greatest in Northern Bohemia, an area with many social problems and tension between Czechs and Gypsies, and as a rule the Republicans and the Communists had their stronghold in the same electoral districts. Party politics and agitation is dominated by the leader, Miroslav Sládek, and personal controversies have led to a split in the Republican Club in parliament, which has today only seven members. Membership figures stem from the party and have been challenged by other sources, which claim that 10,000 is a more realistic number.

Programme. The Republicans present themselves as a right-wing party with a strong social programme. The party favours economic protectionism, a halt to Czech support of the UN, the IMF and similar organizations, military neutrality, measures against "inadaptable ethnic groups" such as Gypsies, law and order and the reintroduction of capital punishment, drastic cuts in the state bureaucracy and the number of ministries, reductions in the salaries of deputies and civic servants, an abolition of the Senate and the introduction of a law allowing for deputies to be recalled by their voters if they do not live up to their electoral programme. The Republicans also call for a renewal of Czechoslovakia within the borders of the first republic, i.e. including Slovakia and Ruthenia.

Bohemian-Moravian Centre Party
Českomoravská strana středu (ČMSS)

Address. Františkánská 1-3, 60200 Brno.

Telephone. (05) 42215279.

Fax. (05) 42215276.

Foundation. April 1990.

Leadership. Jan Kryčer.

Membership. 5,000.

History. The Movement for Self-Governing Democracy – the Association for Moravia and Silesia was founded in April 1990. Its goal was to give the historical province (or "land") of Moravia-Silesia the same political status as Bohemia and Slovakia. Strong Moravian support secured the movement's election to the Federal Assembly and the Czech National Council in June 1990, and though doing less well in June 1992, it again crossed the threshold to the Czech National Council. In January 1993, after a conflict between a liberal faction emphasizing parliamentary work and a radical wing, the movement changed its name into the Movement for Moravian and Silesian Self-Governing Democracy. As a result the Movement's parliamentary club split in two. In January 1994 the movement turned itself into a political party, the Bohemian-Moravian Centre Party and decided to extend party activities to Bohemia.

Programme. The Bohemian-Moravian Centre Party demands a political and administrative division of the Czech Republic that respects the historical autonomy of Bohemia and Moravia-Silesia. As a novelty, the party suggests giving the city of Prague the status of a "land". Such a political regionalism is seen as the only effective defence against centralism and is not supposed to represent any "Moravian nationalism". The party sees no purpose of a bicameral system unless the Senate represents the different "lands" as defined above. The party supports the ongoing economic transformation, but wants to preserve some social achievements of the Communist regime, primarily state support of health, education, culture and sports. Political partners are selected according to their views on decentralization.

Christian Democratic Party
Křestánskodemokratická strana (KDS)

Address. Revoluční 28, 11000 Praha 1.

Telephone. (02) 2310345.

Foundation. Dec. 3, 1989.

Leadership. Ivan Pilip (ch.)

Membership. 2,200.

History. The Christian Democratic Party was initially a member of the Civic Forum, but left the movement in March 1990 to form a coalition with the Czechoslovak People's Party and the Christian Democratic Movement — the Christian and Democratic Union — which was elected to the Federal Assembly and the Czech National Council at the June 1990 elections. The Christian Democratic Party had two ministers in the Czech government. As the party's conservative political profile became more pronounced, it left the coalition and formed an electoral alliance with the Civic Democratic Party in November 1991 that helped the party to win ten seats in the Czech parliament and two ministerial offices

(Education and Environment). At a congress in December 1993 the party chairman since 1989, Václav Benda, was replaced by the younger Ivan Pilip.

Programme. The party presents itself as a non-denominational party based on Christian Democratic moral principles, including the protection of the family and support of mothers who stay at home to raise their children, restrictions on the access to divorce and a ban on abortions. Charitable organizations are to play a greater role in the social sector. The party supports a rapid conclusion of the economic transformation initiated in 1990, market economy and Czech membership of the EU, and favours strong local self-government in support of villages and other small communities.

Affiliations. The Christian Democratic Party has a "partnership agreement" with the Club of Committed Non-Party Members (KAN), which includes regular consultations and participation at each others' meetings. A fusion of the two is, however, not likely for the time being.

Christian and Democratic Union
Křestănská a demokratická unie (KDU)
see **Christian Democratic Party**

Christian Democratic Union – Czechoslovak People's Party (KDU-ČSL)
Křestănskodemokratická unie – Československá strana lidová

Address. Revoluční 5, 11015 Praha 1.

Telephone. (02) 24810794, (02) 24812114.

Foundation. Oct. 21, 1918.

Leadership. Josef Lux (ch.), Jan Kasal, Jindřich Kabát, Tomáš Rubáček.

Membership. 75,000.

History. Founded in 1918, the Czechoslovak People's Party was represented in nearly all Czechoslovak governments from 1918 to 1938 and again from 1945 to 1948 as a member of the National Front. Since November 1989 the party has fought to free itself from the heritage of a collaborating "satellite" during Communist rule. After some confusion the party has stabilized its position as a right-of-centre, non-denominational, yet predominantly Catholic party with its stronghold in Moravia and southern Bohemia. The party obtained its present name in April 1992, when the Czechoslovak People's Party fused with the smaller Christian Democratic Union. It has been represented in Parliament since 1990, first as a member of a coalition with the Christian Democratic Party, and since 1992 on its own. The People's Party is a member of the Czech coalition government and has three ministers in the government (Agriculture, Defence and Economic Competition).

Programme. The party describes itself as a conservative party, founded on Christian humanism. It supports the ongoing economic transformation and favours Czech membership of the EU and NATO. The party's 1992 electoral programme demanded a re-establishment of Moravian autonomy, and although the party has abandoned the idea after the division of Czechoslovakia, its sympathy for it is reflected in its organizational structure with two regional sections, one for Bohemia and one for Moravia and Silesia.

Civic Democratic Alliance
Občanská demokratická aliance (ODA)

Address. Rytířská 10, 11000 Praha 1.

Telephone. (02) 24214134, (02) 24223629.

Foundation. Dec. 17, 1989.

Leadership. Jan Kalvoda (ch.), Vladimír Dlouhý, Pavel Bratinka.

Membership. 2,000.

History. The Civic Democratic Alliance was active within the Civic Forum until the movement's dissolution in March 1991 when it became a fully independent party. Its adherents were strongly represented in the Federal and the Czech governments and the very popular Vladimír Dlouhý (Czech Minister of Industry and Trade since June 1992) and Tomáš Ježek (former Czech Minister of Privatization) belong with Václav Klaus as the main architects of the economic reform programme. At the June 1992 elections the party won 14 seats in the Czech parliament and it has four ministers in the present coalition government. It is probable that personal matters and a party structure favouring élite rather than mass membership have contributed more to prevent a fusion with the Civic Democratic Party than the rather small programmatic differences.

Programme. The Civic Democratic Alliance defines itself as an adherent of conservative values in politics and liberal values in the economy. The party is an unconditional adherent of a bicameral system with a Senate. The Civic Democratic Alliance supports a further reduction of the role of the state in all spheres of society and seeks a greater degree of regional self-government than the Civic Democratic Party.

Civic Democratic Party
Občanská demokratická strana (ODS)

Address. Sněmovní 3, 11800 Praha 1.

Telephone. (02) 3114809, (02) 3114800.

Foundation. April 20–21, 1991.

Leadership. Václav Klaus (ch.), Petr Čermák, Jan Stráský, Jiří Vlach, Josef Zielenec.

Membership. 24,500.

History. The Civic Democratic Party was founded in April 1991 by Václav Klaus and his followers in the Civic Forum after unsuccessful attempts since October 1990 to transform the movement into a right-of-centre political party. During 1991 the Civic Democratic Party built a strong party apparatus, and in November it formed an electoral alliance with the Christian Democratic Party. In December, the Civic Democratic Party also decided to extend its activities to Slovakia, and in March 1992 the Slovak branch of the party formed an alliance with the Democratic Party. However, while the Civic Democratic Party won a convincing victory in the Czech Republic at the June 1992 elections, the Slovak coalition registered a poor result with only about 3.5 per cent of the votes. As the Civic Democratic Party decided to co-operate with Vladimír Mečiar's Movement for a Democratic Slovakia in dividing Czechoslovakia, party activities were again restricted to the Czech Republic, where the Civic Democratic Party has a dominant position. Ten out of 19 ministers in the present Czech government represent the Civic Democratic Party, and the Fourth Party Congress in December 1993 confirmed Václav Klaus's position as the party's undisputed leader.

Programme. The Civic Democratic Party is one of the main advocates of, and architects behind the Czech (formerly Czechoslovak) economic reform programme, which aims at massive privatizations in industry and trade, the creation of a market economy, low inflation and a balanced state budget, balance in foreign trade and, in the longer term, a fully convertible currency, so far with a fair amount of success. The Civic Democratic Party has often been more radical in its neo-liberal rhetoric than in its political practice, for which it has been criticized by other right-wing parties. Also, the party shows little enthusiasm for the Senate and prefers only a slow and limited introduction of regional self-government. The party seeks Czech integration in western economic, political and military structures, and it has downplayed the "Visegrad co-operation" with Poland, Hungary and Slovakia favoured by President Havel in an attempt to exploit a Czech lead in political stability and economic achievements.

Affiliations. The 1992 electoral alliance with the Christian Democratic Party is not likely to be renewed.

Civic Movement
Občanské hnutí
see **Free Democrats (Civic Movement)**

Club of Committed Non-Party Members (KAN)
Klub angažovaných nestraníků

Address. Štefánikova 17, 15000 Praha 5.

Telephone. (02) 543445.

Foundation. March 31, 1990.

Leadership. Emil Dejmek (ch.)

Membership. 1,300.

History. Originally founded in 1968, the Club of Committed Non-Party Members (KAN) was banned shortly after the Warsaw Pact invasion of Czechoslovakia on Aug. 21 that year. The movement was re-established in March 1990 and participated in the June 1990 parliamentary elections as part of the Civic Forum. It competed without success at the 1992 elections, obtaining about 2 per cent of the votes.

Programme. KAN describes itself as more to the right than the Civic Democratic Party. It demands a decisive break with the Communist past, including a strict implementation of the "lustration" legislation (which excludes former security police members, Communist militia members and Communist top functionaries from jobs in the higher civil service), and the expulsion of judges with a Communist past from the judicial system. Restitution of property confiscated from emigrants from Communist Czechoslovakia is also called for. Though not formally a party, KAN functions as one. It recognizes only individual membership, and has a very non-centralistic organization as all local clubs are legally, politically and financially independent. Joint congresses of the local clubs are held each year. KAN co-operates very closely with the Christian Democratic Party, with which it has a partnership agreement.

Communist Party of Bohemia and Moravia
Komunistická strana Čech a Moravy (KSČM)

Address. Politických vězňů 9, 11100 Praha 1.

Telephone. (02) 24210172.

Foundation. March 1990 (May 1921).

Leadership. Miroslav Grebeníček (ch.)

Membership. 200,000. Pensioners make up for much of the membership.

History. The Communist Party of Bohemia and Moravia (KSČM) was founded in March 1990 as a territorial organization of the Communist Party of Czechoslovakia and became an independent party in October 1990. The KSČM was the dominant force in the Left Bloc coalition at the 1992 elections. Throughout 1993 the party experienced much internal strife about the name and political line of the party, which eventually, at the party congress in June 1993, led to the departure of a reform faction that joined the Democratic Left. In the autumn, another group of dissatisfied members, strongly represented in Parliament, continued to challenge the party leadership and in December they founded the Left Bloc Party. A majority of Communist delegates has thus left the party during 1993, but the exodus of ordinary party members to the two splinter parties has been modest. The former Communist daily *Rudé Právo* is no longer controlled by the party, which instead publishes its own *Haló Noviny*.

Programme. The Programme of the KSČM from December 1992 holds socialism as the party's ultimate goal, defined as a "society of free and equal citizens, a democratic, self-governing society with political and economic pluralism, wealth and social justice" in accordance with the humanitarian message and theoretical achievements of Marx and Engels, cleansed of later deformations. A socialist market economy based on economic democracy and favouring co-operatives, workers' collective ownership or shareholding without forbidding private enterprise is seen as the way to social justice. The programme also advocates political decentralization and self-government. The party is against all attempts to criminalize the activities of representatives of the former regime. With strong national accents the Communists warn against Czech dependence on the "German sphere of influence" and oppose Czech membership of NATO while accepting the perspective of joining the EU.

Czech Social Democratic Party
Česká strana sociálně demokratická (ČSSD)

Address. Lidový dům, Hybernská 7, 11100 Praha 1.

Telephone. (02) 24223778, (02) 24226222.

Foundation. 1878.

Leadership. Miloš Zeman (ch.), Pavel Novák, Petra Buzková.

Membership. 11,000. Approximately 20 per cent of all party-members were also in the party before February 1948.

History. Founded in 1878 as an autonomous part of the Austrian labour movement the Czech Social Democracy became fully independent of the Austrian mother party in 1911. From 1921, after the exodus of the Communists from the party, the Czechoslovak Social Democrats were strong supporters of the inter-war Czechoslovak political system, and mostly in the government. In 1945 the party was renewed only in the Czech part of the country, and after the Communist seizure of power in 1948 it was forced to merge with the Communists. A party organization therefore existed only in exile. Preparations for the renewal of the party began in November 1989, and in March 1990 the Social Democracy was officially re-established. The party received its present name at the 26th Congress of the Czechoslovak Social Democracy in February 1993 after the division of Czechoslovakia. Also, Miloš Zeman replaced the more moderate Jiří Horák as chairman.

Programme. Under the leadership of Miloš Zeman the Social Democracy has made a turn to the left, seeking a profile in sharp opposition to the government, and especially to Václav Klaus. The Social Democrats call for employee participation in management and co-ownership to the means of production, a defence against "economic mafias" and the sale of national property to foreigners, increased state investment in education, health, the environment and infrastructure, and improvements in the social security system. The party favours a constitutional change abolishing the Senate. The party programme rejects all co-operation with the Communists, but Miloš Zeman has recently expressed willingness to accept ex-Communists with an unstained past in the party.

Affiliations. The Czech Social Democracy is a member of the Socialist International.

Czechoslovak Socialist Party
Československá strana socialistiká (ČSS)
see **Liberal National Social Party**

Democratic Left of the Czech Republic
Demokratická levice České republiky (DL)

Address. Mariánské náměstí 2, 60200 Brno.

Telephone. (05) 42211677.

Leadership. Lotar Indruch (ch.)

History and affiliations. The Democratic Left ran at the 1992 elections as part of the Left Bloc. In June 1993 a faction of the Communist Party joined the Democratic Left, which was then transformed into the Democratic Left Party, a decision not accepted by Lotar Indruch.

Democratic Left Party
Strana demokraticé levice (SDL)

Address. Žitná 49, Praha 2.

Telephone. (02) 24221313.

Leadership. Josef Mečl (ch.)

Membership. 10,000.

History and programme. The party was founded in June 1993 by reform Communists, who fused with most of the Democratic Left. The party describes itself as non-Communist in the sense that it does not demand a complete change of the political and social system of the Czech Republic, but by no means as anti-Communist. Its goal is a wealthy, democratic and socially just Czech state. The Democratic Left Party seeks a revival of socialist ideas in a modern interpretation and wants to facilitate the co-operation and unity of all leftist forces in the Czech Republic. The party co-operates closely with the Left Bloc Party and the Communists.

Democratic Union
Demokratická unie (DEU)

Address. Kotlaska 5/64, 18000 Praha 8.

Telephone. (02) 684 76 55.

Leadership. Alena Hromádková, Milan Hulík, Ratibor Majzlík.

History. The party was registered with the Ministry of Interior in March 1994 and it has announced its first congress to be held by the end of May 1994. Its emergence and activities have been strongly promoted by Josef Kudláček, the publisher of the daily *Český deník*.

Programme. The Democratic Union criticizes the present government, and especially the Civic Democratic Party, for caring only about economic reform, while neglecting morality and justice. Law and order is a main theme of the Democratic Union's declarations, especially the struggle against corruption and the cleansing of all judicial organs (including the Faculties of Law) of people connected with the former regime. The party demands a complete restitution of property confiscated by the former regime. It appeals to small and middle businessmen and entrepreneurs and hopes to unite the right wing in Czech politics. The Civic Democratic Party and the Civic Democratic Alliance are described as centrist parties.

Free Democrats (Civic Movement)
Svobodní demokraté (Občanské hnutí (SD)

Address. Jungmannovo nám. 9, 11000 Praha 1.

Telephone. (02) 24222316, (02) 24226528.

Foundation. April 27, 1991.

Leadership. Jiří Dienstbier (ch.), Tomáš Sokol.

Membership. 2,000.

History. In December 1990 a Civic Forum Liberal Club was founded in opposition to Václav Klaus's efforts to turn the Civic Forum into a right-of-centre political party. As the division of the Civic Forum could not be prevented, members of the Liberal Club constituted the Civic Movement in April 1991. The new party sought to preserve the open structure of the Civic Forum, which prevented it from attracting a broad nationwide base outside the dominant circles of mostly Prague intellectuals. In spite of its many prominent members, and the great popularity of party chairman Jiří Dienstbier, the Civic Movement thus failed at the 1992 elections. The lack of public support and low level of activism led in the autumn of 1993 a so-called "radical" faction to demand that the Civic Movement be transformed into a traditional party while changing its name into the Free Democrats. Most of the radical platform became official party policy at the fourth congress of the Civic Movement in October 1993.

Programme. The Congress resolutions present the Free Democrats as a liberal alternative to both conservatives and socialists. They emphasize the party's commitment to human rights and demand a politics combining a high degree of ecological and social consideration with respect for the free market. The party also wants a legal and financial strengthening of local self-government and asks for legislative and other measures against corruption and crime. The Free Democrats seek Czech integration in the EU and NATO.

Green Party
Strana zelených (SZ)

Address. Jandova 2, 19000 Praha 9.

Telephone. (02) 824267.

Foundation. Feb. 3, 1990.

Leadership. Jaroslav Vlček (ch.), Miloslav Kejval, Roman Haken.

Membership. 3,000.

History. Founded shortly after the "velvet revolution", the Greens had a lot of initial support in the electorate without eventually passing the 5 per cent threshold at the June 1990 parliamentary elections. Before the June 1992 elections the party therefore joined the Liberal Social Union (LSU), which obtained representation in the Czech parliament. Soon there was tension in the union, and as the LSU decided to transform itself into a party, the Greens officially left the union in November 1993.

Programme. Apart from the overriding ecological concerns, which determine the party's approach to all spheres of the economy, the Greens favour a decentralized democracy with extensive regional and local autonomy. Social concerns are also emphasized. The party is against all military blocs and advocates wide-ranging disarmament.

Left Bloc
Levý Blok

Foundation and history. A coalition of the Communist Party of Bohemia and Moravia and the Democratic Left, formed before the 1992 elections at which it obtained 35 seats in the Czech parliament.

Left Bloc Party
Strana Levého Bloku (sLB)

Address. Parlament České republiky, Sněmovní 4, 11826 Praha 1.

Telephone. (02) 530347.

Leadership. Marie Stiborová (ch.), Jaroslav Ortman.

Membership. c.2,000.

History and programme. The party was founded on Dec. 18, 1993 after long-time factional strife within the Communist Party of Bohemia and Moravia. The Left Block Party claims to be more loyal to the original election programme of the Left Bloc than the Communist Party, and more pragmatic in practical politics. The foundation of the Left Bloc Party led in January 1994 to a split in the parliamentary club of the Left Bloc, founded after the 1992 elections. The new Left Block club has 24 members and the Communist Club has ten.

Liberal Social Union
Liberálně sociální unie (LSU)

Address. Práčká 1881, 10600 Praha 10.

Telephone. (02) 756549.

Leadership. František Trnka (ch.), Jan Tomášek.

Foundation. May 1991.

Membership. 5,000 (if the fusion of the Agrarian Party and the Liberal Social Union is confirmed, 1,000 without it).

History. Founded as a political movement with collective membership, consisting of three parties, the Czechoslovak Socialist Party, the Agrarian Party and the Green Party, the Liberal Social Union won 16 seats in the Czech parliament at the 1992 elections, but due to internal tensions the union soon ceased to function as a single political body. Led by František Trnka, former chairman of the Agrarian Party, the Liberal Social Union has gradually transformed itself into a political party with individual membership taking with it some of the deputies and party members of the original three parties, a decision officially confirmed on Jan. 27, 1994. In March 1994 the Liberal Social Union's parliamentary club had 12 members.

Programme. The party demands an ecologically and socially responsible market economy with great emphasis on local self-government.

Liberal National Social Party
Liberální národně sociální (LSNS)

Address. náměstí Republiky 7, 11149 Praha 1.

Telephone. (02) 24225406.

Foundation. 1897.

Leadership. Pavel Hirš (ch.)

Membership. 12,000.

History. Formerly the Czechoslovak National Socialist Party and from 1948 the Czechoslovak Socialist Party. The party failed at the June 1990 elections and then joined the Liberal Social Union, through which it became represented in the Czech Parliament at the June 1992 elections. Since November 1989 the party has sought to rid itself of its image as a long-time subordinate ally of the Communist Party within the National Front, and as an outcome of this protracted process the party changed is name to its present form at a congress in June 1993. The congress also resulted in a move to the right, and the party now seeks to stress its liberal profile. The change led to a split in the party's parliamentary group: one member joined the Social Democrats, two have opted for the Liberal Social Union, and five still represent the Liberal National Social Party.

Programme. The party claims to be the sole representative of the political centre in parliament and it blames the Liberal Social Union for having moved too far to the left. It seeks the support of the "middle strata" of society and refers a lot to its democratic past and central role in the first Czechoslovak Republic. The party seeks partners in the liberal centre of the political spectrum, but has also declared its willingness to co-operate with the government. The party is a strong adherent of a bicameral system with a Senate elected by majority vote.

Moravian National Party
Moravská národní strana (MNS)

Address. Křenová 61, Brno, PO Box 394.

Telephone. (05) 43212406.

Foundation. September 1990.

Leadership. Ivan Dřímal.

Programme. A small nationalist party, which insists that Moravians form a nation of their own, independently of the Bohemian Czechs. The party seeks autonomy, if not full political independence for Moravia.

Movement for Self-Governing Democracy – Association for Moravia and Silesia
Hnutí za samosprávnou demokracii – Společnost pro Moravu a Slezsko (HSD-SMS)
see **Bohemian-Moravian Centre Party (ČMSS)**

Movement for Moravian and Silesian Self-Governing Democracy
Hnutí za samosprávnou demokracii Moravy a Slezska (HSDMS)
see **Bohemian-Moravian Centre Party (ČMSS)**

Movement of Pensioners for Life Securities
Hnutí důchodců za životní jistoty
see **Pensioners for Life Securities**

Party of Entrepreneurs, Tradesmen and Farmers of the Czech Republic
Strana podnikatelů a rolníků České republiky (SPŽR)

Address. Rašínovo nábřeží 54, 12801 Praha 2.

Telephone. (02) 24912782, (02) 204485.

Foundation. Feb. 23, 1992.

Leadership. Rudolf Baránek (ch.)

Membership. 2,500.

History. Founded in February 1992, the party claims to follow the political heritage of two parties from inter-war Czechoslovakia: the Agrarian Party and its close ally the Tradesmen's Party. It obtained 3.2 per cent of the votes for the Czech National Council at the 1992 elections.

Programme. The party's main ambition is to facilitate, by legislative and other means, the emergence of a strong estate of small and medium businessmen and farmers in the Czech Republic, and to co-operate in these efforts with colleagues in Slovakia and among Czechs abroad. It demands a minimum of state intervention in private enterprise, better conditions for small private businessmen, and a more efficient use of the state budget for well-defined social projects. Private sponsoring in education, culture and sports is to be stimulated. The party describes itself as a right-of-centre party.

Pensioners for Life Securities
Důchodci za životní jistoty

Address. Sudoměřská 32, 13000 Praha 3.

Telephone. (02) 6276645.

Foundation. December 1989.

Leadership. Josef Koníček.

Membership. 30,000.

History and programme. The Movement of Pensioners for Life Securities did not participate in the June 1990 elections, but in 1992 the party obtained 3.8 per cent of the votes for the Czech National Council. The movement claims to have trebled its following between 1992 and 1994, and on April 7, 1994, it decided to become a political party. Its overriding concern is, now as before, to secure better living conditions for pensioners in the Czech Republic, and the party will co-operate with all forces contributing to this. Politically it describes itself, with some hesitation, as slightly left-of-centre.

All information on membership numbers stems from the respective parties themselves and may at times be optimistic.

ESTONIA

Ole Nørgaard
Lars Johannsen
Anette Pedersen

For an analysis of the evolution and working of political parties in Estonia see chapter entitled "The Baltic Republics Estonia, Latvia and Lithuania: the Development of Multi-party Systems" on pages 47–65.

Directory of Parties

Entrepreneurs' Party
Eesti Ettevotjate Erakond

Address. Tallinn EE0001, Sakala 14, "TEA".

Telephone. (372) 6 31 80 87.

Foundation. March 2, 1990.

Leadership. Tiit Made.

Membership. 260.

Estonian Citizens' Union
Eesti Kodanike Liit

Address. Tallinn EE0100, Rahukohtu 1–24.

Telephone. (372) 2 44 21 73; 31 66 60.

Foundation. Nov. 28, 1992.

Leadership. Jüri Toomepuu.

Membership. 1,000.

Programme. To change three fundamental laws: the election law, the constitution law and the law of citizenship.

Estonian Coalition Party
Eesti Koonderakond

Address. Tallinn EE0104, Kuhlbarei 1-335; EE0100 Rahukohtu 1–9.

Telephone. (372) 2 43 15 51.

Foundation. Dec. 9, 1991.

Leadership. Tiit Vähi.

Membership. 200–300.

History. The party contested the 1992 parliamentary elections as part of the Secure Home (*Kindel Kodu*) coalition.

Estonian National Independence Party (ENIP)
Eesti Rahvusliku Soltumatuse Partei (ERSP)

Address. Tallinn EE0001, PK 3533, Piinkopi 2.

Telephone. (372) 2 44 54 21.

Foundation. Aug. 20, 1988.

Leadership. Vello Salum (acting head).

Membership. 1,260.

Affiliation. Part of a government coalition.

Estonian Rural Union
Eesti Maaliit

Address. Tallinn Lai 39–41; Rahukohtu 1–9.

Telephone. (372) 6 31 66 90; 31 66 91.

Foundation. March 23, 1991.

Leadership. Arvo Sirendi.

Membership. 400.

History. The party contested the 1992 parliamentary elections as part of the Secure Home (*Kindel Kodu*) electoral coalition.

Estonian Rural Centre Party
Eesti Maa-keskerakond

Address. EE00100 Tallinn, Rahukohtu 1–15.

Telephone. (372) 2 44 68 15.

Foundation. April 7, 1990.

Leadership. Ivar Raig.

Membership. 300–400.

Affiliation. The Rural Centre Party is part of the government coalition, having contested the 1992 parliamentary elections as part of the Moderates electoral coalition.

Estonian Social Democratic Party
Eesti Sotsiaaldemokraatlik Partei

Address. EE0090 Tallinn, Postimaja PK 3437, büroo Tatari 7 II k.

Telephone. (372) 2 44 30 38.

Foundation. Sept. 9, 1990.

Leadership. Marju Lauristin.

Membership. 220–270.

Affiliation. The Social Democratic Party is part of the government coalition, having contested the 1992 elections as part of the Moderates electoral coalition.

Green Party
Erakond "Eesti Rohelised"

Address. Tartu EE2400, PK 318; Küütri 2–5.

Telephone. (372) 2 23 90 01; 34 32 986.

Foundation. December 1991.

Leadership. Jüri Liim.

Membership. 200.

Moderates
Moodukad

See Estonian Rural Centre Party, Estonian Social Democratic Party

Popular Front of Estonia/Estonian Centre Party
Eestimaa Rahvarinne/Eesti Keskerakond

Address. Tallinn EE0090, Viru 6; PK 3737.

Telephone. (372) 2 44 52 52; 44 06 20.

Foundation. October 1988.

Leadership. Edgar Savisaar.

Membership. 500.

History. Having worked as an umbrella organization for many different types of political groupings for some time, the Popular Front gradually split into several political parties. In October 1991 the remainder of the Popular Front transformed themselves into the Centre Party. At the first elections after independence in September 1992 the Centre Party chose to run under the name of the Popular Front, probably in order to benefit from the reputation and popularity of the Popular Front. It is unclear whether this has had any significance for the party, but shortly after the Centre Party chose to resume the name, the Centre Party, probably realizing that the epoch of the Popular Front had now become a closed chapter in Estonian politics.

Pro Patria National Coalition Party
Rahvuslik Koonderakond Isamaa

Address. EE0109 Tallinn, Mustamäe tee 10.

Telephone. (372) 2 59 53 96.

Leadership. Mart Laar (ch.).

Membership. 900–1,000.

History. Before the election Pro Patria was a coalition consisting of four mainly conservative parties: the Republican Coalition Party, Conservative Peoples' Party, Christian Democratic Union and Christian Democratic Party. After the election in September 1992 the coalition turned into a political party.

Affiliation. Pro Patria is part of the government coalition.

Royalists
Solumatud Kunningriiklased

Address. Tartu EE2400, PK 300; Tallinn EE0100, Lossi plats 1A-266.

Telephone. (372) 34 31 466.

Foundation. Sept. 27, 1989.

Leadership. Kalle Kulbok.

Membership. 140–300.

Programme. The party seeks to establish a monarchy in Estonia.

Secure Home
Kindel Kodu

See Estonian Coalition Party, Estonian Rural Union

GEORGIA

Tamara Dragadze

The political developments and the emerging political structures in Georgia have not been that different to other parts of the former Soviet Union except that they often happened earlier than elsewhere and in a more dramatic way. The convulsions that in Georgia have accompanied the collapse of the Soviet Union have been the outcome of particular characteristics in the body politic of the former communist state, but simply in more dramatic form than those experienced elsewhere. Volatile political leaders, violent attempts to overthrow regimes, rife ineptitude and corruption in the government as it struggled to replace the *troika* of 1 CP Central Committee, 2 Council of Ministers and 3 Supreme Soviet with something else, usually an executive presidency, are all typical of the post-Soviet aftermath. Likewise, the proliferation of political parties, identified by their leader rather than by specific policy programmes, and all unable to work together, are present in Georgia as they are everywhere else in the former Soviet Union.

The most distinguishing feature of the Georgian experience was the early decision in Georgia to turn the *perestroika* process into a struggle for independence. Concerns such as those over the military training grounds of the Soviet Army being too close to buildings of historic architectural importance or the ecological effects of improving transport links across the High Caucasian Range from Russia into Georgia were all used as examples of reasons why Georgia could only flourish as an independent state outside the Soviet Union. This was nothing new. In 1956, when Georgians had protested against Krushchev's "secret speech" to the 20th CPSU congress denouncing Stalin, their demonstrations had a "sub-text" which claimed their right to independence. Again, in 1978, the Georgians were the first, when 12 of the 15 Soviet republics had already agreed, to denounce the clause in Brezhnev's new constitution making Russian the state language of all republics. The sentiment expressed in the demonstrations was so strong that the then First Party Secretary of Georgia, Eduard Shevardnadze, had to put his own career on the line by imploring Brezhnev's administration in Moscow to drop the clause. Thanks to this, Armenia was also subsequently allowed to drop the clause and the language question in the constitution was generally revised. Nationalist dissidents in the early 1970s in Georgia, however, joined the ranks of Ukrainian and other nationalist dissidents in the prison camps at the time, the Georgians being members of the "Initiative Group for the Defence of Human Rights" whose position was strengthened by the Helsinki Declaration of 1975. One of them, Zviad Gamsakhurdia, broke ranks by publicly repenting on Soviet television and was thus allowed to return to Tbilisi in 1979. This incident was to be the first of many in the political career of the maverick Gamsakhurdia which was to single him out as the catalyst in Georgian politics who has been the most difficult to comprehend and analyse.

By 1987 the "Ilia Chavchavadze Society" had been formed, deriving its name from a 19th–early 20th century aristocrat who had fought for a national movement in the Russian Tsarist period. This Society purported to create a movement to promote Georgian nationhood but at the time it avoided calling for the direct overthrow of the Soviet Empire, although this was its hidden agenda.[1] Another society, which tried to act as a less provocative organization to the Soviet establishment and to be less embarrassing for the Communist Party in Georgia, which contained sympathisers for the nationalist cause, was the Rustaveli Society founded in 1988.[2]

Around this time, however, various rival organizations were also set up that centred around the personal difficulties which various emerging political figures had in working with each other. It is also in this period that the foundations were laid for the dominant political tendencies and formations in Georgia which have created its present body politic. For example, the Ilia Chavchavadze Society split because some members would not accept Gamsakhurdia's membership which one of its founders, Merab Kostava, had demanded. This group was called the "Fourth Group" of the "Ilia Chavchavadze Society", once again reminiscent of 19th-century Georgian nationalist politics when a movement called the "Third Group" had been the precursor of the Georgian Social Democratic Party which had eventually led the country to its short-lived independence in 1918. Yet another Society member, Giorgi Chanturia, founded the National Democratic Party and another, Irakli Tsereteli, founded the National Independence Party. Even so, Tsereteli joined forces with Gamsakhurdia to found another society, that of Saint Ilia the Righteous, since by now there was a demand that Prince Ilia Chavchavadze be canonized by the Georgian Orthodox Church. In the summer of 1988, emulating the Baltic States, a Georgian Popular Front was set up, with Nodar Natadze as chairman, but it was unable to become the umbrella organization it had wished for, once again because of Gamsakhurdia's refusal to join it and because it could not neutralize the divisions between its radicals and its more cautious members. Although they were united in their goal to achieve independence ultimately, they were divided over tactics and, above all, between extreme nationalist rhetoric and the distaste it provoked in the more moderate members who disliked any display of intolerance or xenophobia towards people of non-Georgian nationality, whatever the reason. As the groups multiplied, so did the rallies and demonstrations which had begun timidly but which gathered momentum.

There was no doubt in any politician's mind, whether within the Communist Party, now with Jumber Patiashvili at its head since Shevardnadze's departure to become Foreign Minister, or outside it, that the Moscow-led Soviet government was going to take great displeasure at the political activity in Georgia aimed at independence. There were two ways, however, in which the Soviet government could take comfort: resentments between the Osset and Abkhaz minorities against the Georgian majority were there to be exploited and secondly, the use of force could be resorted to since Georgians would have no weapons of their own to defend themselves.

In April 1989 a massacre of unarmed civilians took place, where most of the victims targeted and killed were young women, carried out by Soviet Army troops armed with sharpened shovels. The troops were also accused of using chemical gases against the other demonstrators. This event so traumatized the Georgian public, both urban and rural, that from then on any compromise on independence from the Soviet Union became increasingly remote. From then on, too, the Soviet structures were viewed as Russian in character, not politically Soviet. In turn, the verbally most uncompromising political leader,

Zviad Gamsakhurdia, gathered strength because he was seen to be the only politician fanatically single-minded enough to stand up to Soviet Russia's great might. Many members of the Georgian intelligentsia had grave doubts about his ethno-nationalist principles and his unstable personality, but their reservations were branded as unpatriotic by their rivals. Although by October 1990, when elections took place to the Georgian Supreme Soviet, around 35 parties had been created, including moderate ones such as the Green Party, and a rival group of parties who had refused to take part in Soviet elections at all and had set up a rival "Congress", the radicals led by Gamsakhurdia won a majority of seats. The following May of 1991 he was elected president, again with a strong majority.

The other arm of Soviet policy towards Georgia, however, had also been gathering strength throughout the whole period. The Abkhaz and the Ossets, who form 2 per cent and 3 per cent of the total population of Georgia respectively, had had the advantage of "autonomous" administrations under the Soviet system. This had not only allowed them a certain amount of national independence but had given them direct access, in their own right, to the corridors of power in Moscow over many decades. Their distaste for the ethno-nationalist rhetoric of some of the Georgian radicals could be totally justified according to any political or ethical criteria, but their disproportionately abundant access to former Soviet weaponry from the Russian Federation has created the most destabilizing factor in Georgian politics up to the present day. In both autonomies, the separatist movements included leading members of the Communist Party. Although they had first asked for attachment to the Russian Federation, the Abkhaz in particular began to ask for a fully independent republican status. The problem that arose from this, which was that they constituted only 17 per cent of the total population of the autonomous republic, was countered by the argument that the original majority of Abkhaz had been systematically eroded by the forced settlement of Georgians in the region. The Lykhni Declaration of March 18, 1989, was a focal point in the Abkhaz movement calling for Moscow to recognize Abkhazia as a full Union Republic. This consolidated the political profile of Abkhazia: an Abkhazian Popular Forum (*Aidgylara*) which the Abkhazian Communist Party did not register till June 1990 but which eventually created the bedrock of Abkhaz popular support in the ensuing years; other elements which eventually led to the creation of the Abkhaz Salvation Front that was more conciliatory to the Georgian central government, and then all the Georgian parties within Abkhazia. The ensuing attempts by the Abkhaz leadership at conciliation with the Georgian government came to nothing since the Georgian radicals would not countenance major constitutional changes which the Abkhaz needed to make to create a genuinely separate and Abkhaz-led government. Neither did the Georgian liberals nor the Abkhaz leaders have the backing of the Soviet government in Moscow to reach any agreement, without which nothing practical could be decided.

The Ossets wanted their autonomous region to be separated from Georgia and attached to the Russian Federation in order to create one governmental unit with the autonomous republic of North Ossetia. To this end the "Popular Shrine" (*Adaemon Nykhas*) was created in January 1989. Georgians were more united in their negative reaction to the Ossetian claims than to those of the Abkhaz over which they had been more divided. Yet tactics on how to contain the escalating violence in the region could not be agreed on.

Within months of Gamsakhurdia having been elected President of Georgia, he and his government began to lose popularity, because he was less of a necessity since the failure of the attempted coup in Moscow had resulted in a loosening of the hold and lessening of the threat of the central Soviet government on Georgia. Political groups opposed his increasingly idiosyncratic ways and the growing economic deterioration due to his failure to reach an agreement with Russia which provided electricity and fuel to Georgia. Some spectacular fighting between presidential and opposition forces in the main avenue of Tbilisi at the end of 1991 resulted in the flight of President Gamsakhurdia into exile in Chechnia. A few months later, former Soviet Foreign Minister Eduard Shevardnadze returned to Tbilisi, visiting the Patriarch of the Georgian Church on the way from the airport, who abolished the position of president in order to conform to the original constitution of the independent Georgia of 1918–21. As head of state Shevardnadze instituted elections both for himself to be confirmed in this position and for a new parliament.

The result of these most recent elections have led to a result which many Georgians believe has vindicated the claim that Georgia is a "democratic" country: there were 37 parties presented at the elections, 35 of which gained representation in the parliament. There is a mixture of political personalities who range from supporters of the former late President Gamsakhurdia to former first Communist Party secretary, Jumber Patiashvili. The parliament is rumbustuous and chaotic at times. The main debates have been on the economy and on relations with Russia. In September 1993 the Georgian National Army was defeated and driven out of Abkhazia, as were all ethnic Georgians (around a quarter of a million of them). This setback was followed by the return into the north-west region of the former President Gamsakhurdia. Recognizing that the source of weapons for both Abkhazian rebels and Gamsakhurdia and for the Georgian government was in all cases of Russian provenance, Shevardnadze went to Moscow to ask for intervention in Georgia to stem the fighting in return for Georgia joining the CIS and eventually allowing Russian peacekeeping troops into Abkhazia and the enlargement of the now diminished Russian bases on Georgian soil.

To date, no attempt at curbing the highly fissiparous nature of party politics has succeeded. Eduard Shevardnadze launched the Georgian Citizens Union into which he hoped like-minded politicians with their parties would enter but some of the most intense personal criticism against him has sometimes come from the ranks of the Union itself. For the local governments of the Abkhaz and the Ossets, the end of hostilities will allow their peoples to rebuild their lives although no permanent solution to their political arrangements has yet been found. Some comfort can be derived from the fact that the region of Adjara where the majority of Georgians are muslim and the Marneuli district, where ethnic Azerbaijanis dominate, have maintained stability. The death of Gamsakhurdia and the slow return to tranquility in the Mengrelian region, which was shaken to the core during the battles with his supporters, have also given some encouragement to the Georgian government. Crime rates in Tbilisi have also diminished somewhat. Freedom of the press and media is dependent on the supply of paper and electricity more than it is on particular government policy. There is official nervousness about the holding of vast political meetings, yet they do take place, although nothing is to be seen as lively and argumentative as within the parliament itself.

Nevertheless, at the time of writing, the loss by the Georgian administration of territory to the Abkhaz and Ossets and the dire economic conditions throughout Georgia have moderated the political will of citizens everywhere either to curb the return of Russian influence or to make new political arrangements for their multi-party system.

Directory of Parties

This section is divided into two sections. The first section deals with parties linked to the "Union of Citizens of Georgia", the second lists parties that are currently outside of the Union of Citizens of Georgia.

Parties linked to the "Union of Citizens of Georgia"

Republican Party

Address. Parliament of the Republic of Georgia, Rustaveli Avenue, Tbilisi, Republic of Georgia.

Leadership. Vakhtang Jabiradze (ch.)

Programme. Occasionally the Republican Party has united with the Popular Front led by Mr. N. Natadze and "Charter 91" led by Tedo Paatashvili to form the "United Republican Party". At present they are an important faction in their own right in the umbrella group of the Union of Citizens of Georgia.

Green Party
Also known as the "Georgia Greeens"

Address. Parliament of the Republic of Georgia, Rustaveli Avenue, Tbilisi, Republic of Georgia.

Leadership. Zurab Mjvania (ch.)

Social Democratic Party

Address. Parliament of the Republic of Georgia, Rustaveli Avenue, Tbilisi, Republic of Georgia.

Leadership. Guram Muchaidze (ch.)

Parties currently outside of the "Union of Citizens of Georgia"

National Democratic Party

Address. Parliament of the Republic of Georgia, Rustaveli Avenue, Tbilisi, Republic of Georgia.

Leadership. Giorgi Chanturia (ch.)

Monarchist Party
Also known as the "Monarchist–Conservative Party"

Address. Parliament of the Republic of Georgia, Rustaveli Avenue, Tbilisi, Republic of Georgia.

Leadership. Teimur Jorjoliani (ch.)

Traditionalist Party
Also known as the "Union of Georgian Traditionalists"

Address. Parliament of the Republic of Georgia, Rustaveli Avenue, Tbilisi, Republic of Georgia.

Leadership. Akaki Asatiani (ch.)

The following are a selection, based on general accessibility, of the names of further Georgian parties: **Afghan Veterans' Party, Agrarian Party, Christian-Democratic Party, Christian-Liberal Party, Constitutional-Democratic Party, Georgian Communist Party, Ilia Chavchavadze Society, Liberal-Democratic Party, Merab Kostava Society, National Independence Party, Reformers Union, Round Table, and Workers' Communist Party.**

Notes
1 This view is also that of R. Parsons "Informal Organisations in Georgia", May 1989.
2 The "neutralising effect" of the Rustaveli Society which recruited local establishment figures as well as intellectuals who at one time or another had been repressed in the Soviet period, has been commented on also by J. Aves "Paths to National Independence in Georgia, 1987–1990" University of London 1991 SSEES Occasional Paper 15.

HUNGARY

Mark Pittaway and Nigel Swain

In the years that followed the 1956 uprising against Stalinism, Hungary gained a reputation as the crucible of reform in Eastern Europe. Living standards improved steadily and, after János Kádár (who came to power with the Soviet tanks) had consolidated his personal power in the early 1960s, the stage was set for a series of reforms which culminated in the market socialist New Economic Mechanism of 1968. In the two and a half decades between 1963 and 1988 Kádár successfully achieved a dual compromise with the Soviet Union on the one hand and the Hungarian population on the other. The essence of the Soviet compromise was that Kádár would remain loyal in foreign policy — to the extent of joining the invasion of Czechoslovakia in 1968 — in return for leeway in domestic and especially economic reform. The essence of Kádár's "social compact" with the Hungarian people was that the regime should provide constantly improving living standards in a relaxed ideological climate in return for acceptance of the legitimacy of the regime of the Hungarian Socialist Workers' Party (HSWP). Although in the wake of the Czechoslovakia invasion neither the economic nor the political reforms were as radical as originally conceived, the consumerist compromise continued, and with it Kádár's popularity.

By the mid-1980s, however, both compromises were breaking down. With the advent of Gorbachev, a fine line no longer had to be trod between what was acceptable to the Soviet Union and what was not. More importantly, living standards had stopped rising at the end of the 1970s, and the population was tiring of promises that recovery would begin the following year. Public opinion surveys revealed significant increases in the numbers of people who felt that the government was unable to resolve the country's economic problems; economists advised more radical reform including changes in property relations; dissident groups increased in self-confidence; and Kádár proved incapable of going beyond the parameters of his original compromises. From 1985 onwards, when the 13th HSWP Congress promised a return to economic growth inconsistent with the realities of Hungary's parlous economic situation, this questioning of government confidence escalated, slowly at first, into a legitimation and, finally, political crisis.

Central moments in the burgeoning crisis were the following. In 1985, at a two-and-a-half day political gathering at Monor in 1985, the "populist" and "urban" (the self-styled "democratic opposition") groupings within the dissident movement came together for the first time. In 1987, four significant events took place. First, radical economists published a document, written the previous year, entitled *Turnabout and Reform*, which, for the first time, brought into the public domain the parlous state of the economy and radical proposals to deal with it. Second, in the summer of 1987 the "urban", "democratic opposition", which had been producing samizdat material since the mid-1970s (and on a regular basis since

1980), produced a special issue of its magazine *Beszélő* entitled the *Social Contract*, calling for political pluralism and a free press. Third, on Sept. 27, the Hungarian Democratic Forum (HDF) was founded in the village of Lakitelek, at a gathering attended by writers and critics of the "populist" persuasion and by reformist communists such as Imre Pozsgay, with whom many of the former had close links. Finally, the HSWP announced that a special Party Conference would be held in May 1988 to consider how to handle the situation it was reluctant to call a crisis.

In 1988, the pace of political events accelerated. In the first half of the year a series of dissident meetings was held at the Jurta Theatre which, as a Small Co-operative, was independent of government control. In March, the "democratic opposition" and other groups established the Network of Free Initiatives, while a younger generation of opposition members founded the Alliance of Young Democrats (FIDESZ). In April, four prominent reform-minded intellectuals were expelled from the party for attending the Jurta and similar meetings; but at the HSWP special Party Conference in May, it was the hardliners who were defeated. Kádár was replaced as First Secretary, and a new generation of cadres, who had lived their adult lives under actually existing socialism, came into the leadership.

After a quiet summer, opposition activity began again in the autumn of 1988. The HDF held a second meeting in Lakitelek in September and the Alliance of Free Democrats (AFD) was established as a party in November out of most of the organizations in the Network of Free Initiatives. The Independent Smallholder Party (ISP) re-founded itself, also in November, and Hungary's Social Democrat Party (HSDP) followed suit in January 1989. By February 1989, the HSWP had accepted that Hungary would become a multi-party democracy; in March the opposition groups and parties established an Opposition Round Table and the Christian Democratic People's Party (CDPP) was founded; and in June, as its reformist wing gained in strength, the HSWP agreed to negotiations with the Opposition Round Table on the transformation of the political system. While these talks were under way, on Sept. 11, the government made its historic decision to allow East German "tourists" to cross the border into Austria, so triggering the fall of the Berlin Wall and the other Eastern European regimes.

On Sept. 18, 1989, the talks concluded with an agreement on certain "cardinal laws", such as amending the constitution, establishing a Constitutional Court, and introducing an electoral law to clarify the status of political parties. The AFD and FIDESZ refused to sign the agreement, however, because they rejected the proposal that the direct election of a new president by popular ballot should precede parliamentary elections, and because they were unhappy that the HSWP had not committed itself to disbanding the workers' militia, withdrawing from work-places and rendering an account of its property. While the HSWP held an extraordinary 14th Party Congress in October, at which the reformists won the day and the party's name was changed to the Hungarian Socialist Party (HSP), the AFD and FIDESZ collected sufficient signatures to force a referendum on the disputed elements in the September agreement.

Although many viewed the referendum as a distraction since, in the interim (on Oct. 23, 1989) Hungary had become a Republic (as opposed to a People's Republic) and all reference to the "leading role" of the HSWP had been removed from the Constitution, it served the purpose of highlighting, at an early date, the differences of opinion within the opposition. While the two new liberal parties (the AFD and FIDESZ), together with the re-founded ISP and HSDP opposed the government, the new nationalist-Christian HDF advised its members to abstain. To the HDF's chagrin, however, turnout for the

Table 1: Support for Major Parties 1989–90 (% of those who stated which party they would vote for, not of those asked)

Party	Date of Public Opinion Survey												
	Jan	Mar	May	Jun	Jul	Aug	Sep	Oct	Oct–Nov	Nov	Dec	Jan	Mar
HDF	11	17	13	13	14	18	24	20	27	22	23	21	21
AFD	7	12	6	5	3	6	6	9	8	14	18	20	
ISP	10	10	12	6	11	9	7	6	5	9	12	16	16
HSP	–	–	–	–	–	–	–	35	25	16	16	11	10
HSWP	23	34	32	29	37	32	23	–	6	7	5	4	–
AYD	11	9	16	9	7	7	11	10	8	13	8	7	7
CDPP	–	–	–	5	2	4	4	3	5	4	3	3	5
HSDP	6	11	12	12	10	8	8	6	4	8	6	5	6
HPP*	1	8	5	5	4	3	3	4	2	3	4	2	–

*Péter Veres Association in January 1989.
Source: HangSúly, Vol 1, No. 1, p. 19; No. 4, p. 19, No. 5, p. 18; No. 6–7, p. 35; No. 8–9, p. 35; No. 10, p. 20; Magyar Nemzet, 22/11/89, 17/2/90, 14/3/90.

referendum on Nov. 26 exceeded 50 per cent, and the anti-government view narrowly won the day.

Following the referendum, the political situation changed radically. The AFD gained mass popular support, something it had not thought possible a year earlier. The HDF momentarily lost prestige and accepted that it would have radically to distance itself from the HSP, despite the fact that until then an HDF-dominated parliament and a reform HSP socialist president in the person of Imre Pozsgay had seemed the most probable political outcome. The HSP went into decline, despite a short-term increase in popularity immediately after its change of name. The referendum had proved that it could be defeated; and, when socialist regimes were collapsing around it, its justifiable claim to be truly reformist cut little ice. These radical changes in support for the old and the new parties can be seen from Table 1.

Parliamentary elections finally took place in two rounds in March and April, 1990. As indicated in Table 2, no party gained an absolute majority, but the HDF had most seats and, after a month of negotiating, it formed a coalition government with the two other parties of a nationalist-Christian orientation, the ISP and CDPP. The elections, furthermore, indicated the nature of the ideological divisions within the Hungarian electorate. The major political actors could be assigned to three ideological groupings: the victorious national-Christian grouping, a liberal grouping consisting of the AFD and FIDESZ, and a social democratic or left-wing group, represented in parliament only by the HSP. In 1990 the social democratic grouping was both the smallest and the most divided of the tendencies and it seemed then that the liberal parties would be the most likely beneficiaries from future government unpopularity.

The six parties that entered parliament in 1990 can be split into three broad ideological groups: the nationalist-Christian persuasion, represented by the coalition government of the HDF, with its origins in the "populist" dissidents, the ISP and the CDPP, both re-founded

Table 2: Parliamentary Elections March–April 1990

Share of Vote on Regional List (per cent) and Number of Seats Won

Party	Regional List	Seats
Hungarian Democratic Forum (HDF)	24.73	165
Alliance of Free Democrats (AFD)	21.39	91
Independent Smallholders (ISP)	11.73	44
Hungarian Socialist Party (HSP)	10.89	32
Alliance of Young Democrats (AYD)	8.95	22
Christian Democratic People's Party (CDPP)	6.46	21
Hungarian Socialist Workers Party (HSWP)	3.68	
Hungary's Social Democratic Party (HSDP)	3.55	
Agrarian Alliance	3.13	1
Entrepreneurs' Party	1.89	
Patriotic Electoral Coalition	1.87	
Hungarian People's Party (HPP)	0.75	
Hungary's Green Party	0.36	
National Smallholders Party	0.20	
Somogy Christian Coalition	0.12	
Hungary's Co-operative and Agrarian Party	0.10	
Independent Hungarian Democratic Party	0.06	
Freedom Party	0.06	
Hungarian Independence Party	0.04	
Alliance for the Village and Countryside		1
Independent		6
Jointly sponsored		3

Source: Magyar Közlöny (Hungary's official gazette), 1990, No. 25.

parties active in the 1940s; the liberal, social-liberal persuasion of the AFD and FIDESZ; and social democracy, represented by the HSP. All six parties support a variant of the "social market economy", and all favour increasing the profile of the Hungarian cultural heritage. They disagree only on the degree of emphasis to accord to that heritage, on priorities in social policy, on the pace of privatization, and on the desirable degree of state intervention in the economy. Most important, they differ on the relative importance given to individual liberties versus collective obligations to family, church and nation. Although the fortunes of the six parliamentary parties varied over the four-year parliamentary term, this three-way orientation of Hungarian politics remained constant.

The newly elected government's first task was further to amend the constitution, and in order to facilitate this the AFD and HDF entered into a pact by which the former would not vote against key measures requiring a two-thirds majority, provided the latter acceded to having the president appointed by parliament and supporting Árpád Göncz — a member of the AFD — as candidate. Constitutional changes in the summer of 1990 abolished the office of the President of the Council of Ministers, replacing it with a Prime Minister with

Table 3: Local Authority Elections in 2,926 settlements of less than 10,000 (per cent)

	Mayors	*'Small list'*
Independent	82.9	71.2
ISP	3.7	6.2
HDF	2.3	4.3
AFD	1.9	4.0
CDPP	1.8	2.8
Agrarian Alliance	–	1.3
HSP	–	1.1

Source: Magyar Közlöny (Hungary's official gazette), 1990, No. 44.

increased powers, and removed reference in the Constitution to "the realization of the values of democratic socialism". Having the president appointed by parliament also required a constitutional amendment, and this was delayed by a last ditch referendum sponsored by supporters of a directly elected president. Göncz was finally appointed President of the Republic on Aug. 3, 1990.

Despite commitments to rapid privatization, the government's first 100 days achieved little, other than establishing a framework for local elections, and causing a furore by appearing to give churches a free hand for religious education in schools. Elections to the new local authorities took place in two rounds in September and October. Turnout was lower than in the parliamentary elections of the spring: 40.18 per cent in the first round, 28.94 per cent in the second. Forty-two of the 65 registered parties ran candidates, as did 647 social organizations and 12 national minorities; and there were also many more jointly sponsored candidates. The coalition government was severely punished for its inertia in the summer, as Tables 3–5 indicate. In the smaller villages, the winners were the independents, many of whom had previously held office in the HSWP-dominated local government-party structure. In the larger communities, the coalition parties won a majority of seats in only one Budapest district and in only five of Hungary's 19 counties. They fared even worse in the county towns. Only in Kecskemét did the government parties win a clear victory. The local elections consituted a defeat for two of the three coalition parties (the HDF and the ISP — the CDPP maintained its share of the vote). On the other hand, they represented a considerable victory for FIDESZ who had, in Viktor Orbán, a leader of charisma. The behaviour of FIDESZ after the election, however, led some to suspicions that popularity and power, rather than the implementation of a political programme, were the party's overriding goals. Despite entering the elections in many towns, including Budapest, in an apparent coalition with the AFD, after the elections, in Budapest and some other towns, FIDESZ refused to participate in government.

In October 1990, the strength of the political institutions created during the "peaceful revolution" was put to the test by the direct action of a group of workers who, although neither numerous nor particularly underprivileged, manifestly enjoyed popular support. After months of postponing petrol price increases, the government announced an average 65 per cent rise from midnight on Thursday, Oct. 25. Spontaneously, throughout the

Table 4: Local Authority Elections in 141 Settlements of over 10,000 (per cent)

	Individual Candidates	List
AFD	17.1	20.7
AFD-AYD joint	17.0	5.0
Independent	14.9	–
HDF	12.0	18.3
AYD	8.4	15.2
ISP	6.0	7.7
CDPP	5.7	8.0
HSP	2.6	10.1
HDF-CDPP joint	2.5	2.5
HDF-ISP-CDPP joint	2.4	2.2
HDF-ISP joint	2.1	–
HSWP	–	1.3

Source: Magyar Közlöny (Hungary's official gazette), 1990, No. 44.

Table 5: Election for Budapest Assembly

Party	share of vote (%)
AFD	34.68
HDF	27.35
AYD	18.16
HSP	7.25
CDPP	4.95
HSWP	3.61
ISP	2.30
Alliance*	0.72
Hungary's Social Democratic Party	0.56
National Alliance**	0.41

*Alliance of Town Defence and Citizen Organizations.
**National Alliance of Small Industrialists.
Source: Magyar Közlöny (Hungary's official gazette), 1990, No. 44.

country, communicating by means of short-wave radio, lorry and taxi drivers blockaded towns, bridges, and border crossings during the course of the Thursday–Friday night.

The blockade lasted until the following Sunday evening. At first, the government stood firm, but the situation soon turned to stalemate as the Budapest police chief made it clear he would not use force against the crowds, and the barricades did not come down despite apparent agreement on the Saturday night. Negotiations on the Sunday, broadcast in their entirety live on television, were successful however: the government gave in, withdrawing

Table 6: Answers to the question: "To what extent do you think the current Hungarian government is directing the country in the right direction?" (per cent)

	November 1990	November 1989
"Completely"	6	8
"Mostly"	19	29
"A little"	54	52
"Not at all"	15	7

Source: Adapted from Sándor Kurtán et al., *Magyarország Poltikai Évkönyve, 1991,* Budapest, 1991, pp. 639–40.

the price rise until such time as petrol prices were fully liberalized and hence outside the political domain.

Public opinion surveys taken immediately after the negotiations revealed high levels of support for the drivers and criticism of the government, especially for the ministers who had taken the initial tough line. The regime's dramatic decline in popularity after its first six months is further reflected in a public opinion survey taken in November 1990, as indicated in Table 6. After only six months in office, the first democratically elected government in 40 years inspired rather less confidence than the previous undemocratic government that had led Hungary to political crisis and the highest per capita foreign debt in Eastern Europe.

In 1991, the coalition came increasingly under strain as the ISP insisted on the direct restitution of those who had lost property, especially land, under the previous regime. A compromise solution, already passed by parliament, was ruled unconstitutional in May on the grounds that it treated land and other forms of property differently. Voices from the ISP subsequently called for full compensation for all, while the HDF, mindful of the needs to attract foreign investors and manage an already sizeable national debt, insisted that this was economically acceptable. Though a compromise was found in June 1991 it did not satisfy the radicals within the ISP or the party's new president, József Torgyán, who came from within their ranks. Torgyán threatened to leave the coalition if a more radical compensation package compensation package were not adopted. He finally did so in February 1992 after failing to reach an agreement with the HDF, but this decision was only taken at the cost of splitting his own party, most ISP deputies remained within the coalition and were expelled from the party.

The ISP was not the only party to experience serious internal tensions in 1991 and 1992. The AFD was also split between the veteran dissident faction within the party and the party's professional politicians, when the former lost control of the leadership in November 1991. After a year's interregnum under the more populist Tölgyessy, Iván Pető became the new AFD leader, someone who better bridged the veteran dissident–professional politican divide.

During 1991 concern was increasingly expressed at the growing authoritarianism of the government, focused by the leak in September of a secret document to *Magyar Hirlap*, written by the HDF parliamentary leader Imre Kónya, in which he argued the HDF should take control of the media. Concern was also being expressed at the rise of the extreme right. These twin developments had already led to the formation of the Democratic Charter in summer 1991. Founded by the author and former dissident, György Konrád, its founding statement warned of the dangers to Hungary's young democracy. The Charter subsequently served as a rallying point for the liberals and the left when campaigning against both the influence of extreme-right and government authoritarianism.

Throughout 1992, with unemployment on the rise and the government intervening increasingly in economic life, dissatisfaction with the centre-right coalition government also grew. This was expressed by the public at large in the huge opinion poll leads which FIDESZ enjoyed throughout the year. Within the HDF, the right-wing populists also became more active. In August István Csurka, the leader of the party's populist wing, wrote an article in the *Magyar Fórum* newspaper, in which he attributed the growth in social tension, in part, to the continued presence in positions of influence of former communists, whom he linked to liberals and Jews. To advance his ideas Csurka formed the *Magyar Út (Hungarian Way)* movement, which gained considerable support within the HDF. Over the next year the HDF was rocked by internal strife, initially between the party's populist and liberal wings, but later specifically between Antall and Csurka. The dissent was only quelled by the expulsion of Csurka and his allies in summer 1993, who formed the Hungarian Justice and Life Party. Interestingly, support did not grow for the new political parties which aimed to occupy the social democratic terrain, Pozsgay's National Democratic Alliance and Király's rejuvenated Social Democratic Party.

During 1993, FIDESZ, the leader in the opinion polls for most of the parliament, underwent radical changes. It distanced itself from its past as a youth movement and attempted to become more of a conventional political party. In addition, it began to move noticeably towards the centre-right, much to the unease of the party's social liberal minority. In the autumn of 1993, the main figure in the social-liberal wing, Gábor Fodor, contested the election for the post of chair of the party's national committee, losing to an Orbán loyalist. He subsequently left the party with three of his allies, and ran on the AFD list in the 1994 elections.

During 1993 the standing of the HSP rose steadily in the opinion polls, in part due to falling living standards and increasing unemployment and in part due to the party's reputation among the electorate for economic competence. It had gradually become accepted by the AFD as a democratic, rather than former communist party, largely due to its unequivocal opposition to the far right and the participation of many HSP members in the Democratic Charter. By the end of 1993, it was the HSP and not FIDESZ that led in the opinion polls.

Throughout the summer and autumn of 1993 the health of József Antall gradually worsened. He was increasingly absent from government while undergoing treatment for cancer and the Interior Minister, Péter Boross, assumed more and more of his responsibilities. In December, after Antall's death, Boross replaced him as Prime Minister. A further change of personnel in 1993 was the emergence in September of the hitherto unknown Gábor Kuncze as the AFD's nominee for Prime Minister. As a man from the provinces with no dissident past, his nomination was designed to counter the claim that the AFD was dominated by urban, Jewish intellectuals.

Politics in early 1994 was dominated by the parties' preparations for the May parliamentary elections and the media question. Opinion polls suggested in April 1994 that the HSP would become the largest party in parliament. Commentators agreed that, as in the 1990 elections, the period between the two rounds would be decisive, and that a centre-left coalition between the HSP and the AFD seemed most likely. The media issue was a running sore of Hungary's first post-socialist government. The April 1990 government–opposition pact had included a new law on the media as one that required a two-thirds majority. This could never be achieved and, in the absence of a law, government, president and the heads of the radio and television services sniped at one another for four years, culminating in March 1994 with the sacking on the grounds of cost cutting of 129 radio journalists involved in a programme often critical of the government. As was the case four years earlier, the parties differed far more on presentation and ideological orientation than on concrete issues of economic and social policy.

The electoral campaign was negative in tone, largely due to an aggressive assault by the HDF, waged through the state television, on the HSP's communist past and that of its leader, Gyula Horn. This was only interrupted by Horn's involvement in a road accident returning from a campaign rally three days before polling began. The first round of the elections held on May 8, 1994, demonstrated the HSP's strength. The Socialists polled just under a third of all votes cast, followed by the AFD. The HDF with only 11.73 per cent of the vote was as utterly defeated as the HSP had been four years earlier. The HSP led in every county and in 160 of the 176 individual constituencies. Against the expectations of many commentators, though not the opinion polls, this strength was demonstrated again in the second round of the elections held on May 29. The HSP won 209 seats, a clear absolute majority, and won 149 of 176 individual constituencies, defeating (in their individual constituencies but not necessarily on the lists) many prominent personalities from the other parties, including the HDF Finance Minister, Iván Szabó, the AFD president, Iván Pető and campaign manager Bálint Magyar, and the FIDESZ president, Viktor Orbán. Despite its absolute majority, the HSP set about forging a coalition government with the AFD, a coalition in which, against the historic precedent of the 1940s, it concentrated on the economic rather than the security ministries.

The 1994 elections were conducted under a modified version of the electoral system which had emerged from the Opposition Round Table negotiations in 1989 and the subsequent electoral law. It is an amalgam of first-past-the-post and proportional representation systems and contains five hurdles to prevent minor parties entering parliament. First, parties have to be registered at the Court of Registration. Second, candidates have to be supported by the signatures of 750 voters within the constituency. Third, in order to figure on any regional (county or Budapest) list (the first proportional representation element in the electoral system), the party has to have candidates in 25 per cent, or at least two, of the constituencies of the region. Fourth, in order to qualify the candidates on the national list (the second proportional representation element in the electoral system), parties have to have candidates on at least seven of the 20 (19 county and Budapest) regional lists. Fifth, candidates elected on either of the lists can only enter parliament if the party's share of the total list vote exceeds 5 per cent (the increase from 4 per cent to 5 per cent was the result of an amendment to the electoral law in February 1994). Thus, minor parties can get popular local candidates elected as one of the 176 individually elected constituency members, but they are unable to supplement them with any of the 152 proportionally allocated list seats unless the 5 per cent barrier is crossed. This electoral system is likely to be modified further in the future. The nomination system was severely criticized at the beginning of the 1994 election campaign, and alleged abuses had resulted in criminal investigations in Salgótarján and Veszprém.

Table 7: Changes in party preferences from January 1991 to March 1994 (per cent)

Party	Jan–March 1991	Apr–Jun 1991	Jul–Sep 1991	Oct–Dec 1991	Jan–Mar 1992	Apr–Jun 1992	Jul–Sep 1992	Oct–Dec 1992	Jan–Mar 1993	Apr–Jun 1993	Jul–Sep 1993	Oct–Dec 1993	Jan–Mar 1994
HDF	11	12	11	9	11	8	8	8	8	7	7	6	7
AFD	15	11	10	11	8	7	7	9	7	8	7	8	9
ISP	7	8	6	6	6	6	4	5	5	5	5	4	4
HSP	6	4	4	6	6	7	7	6	10	11	14	17	18
AYD	20	20	20	21	29	27	29	30	25	26	23	18	11
CDPP	4	4	4	3	5	4	4	4	5	4	5	5	44
Others	3	4	3	3	2	7	6	5	8	7	8	7	7
Don't know/ won't vote	34	40	41	39	35	35	36	35	34	31	32	35	38

Source: Adapted from *Népszabadság*, April 15, 1994.

Table 8: Changes in the composition of parliamentary fractions, May 2, 1990–April 7, 1994

| | May 2, 1990 | | April 7, 1994 | |
	total	%	total	%
HDF	165	42.75	136	35.23
AFD	94	24.35	83	21.50
ISP	44	11.40	9	2.33
Anti-Torgyán				
Smallholder			36	9.33
HSP	33	8.55	33	8.57
FIDESZ	22	5.70	26	6.73
CDPP	21	5.44	23	5.95
HJLP			12	3.11
Indep.	7	1.81	28	7.25

Source: Adapted from *Változások az Országgyűlés összetételében*, Budapest, 1994.

Table 9: By-elections in the 1990–94 parliament

Constit. and date	Outgoing member and party	Victor and party
Budapest 9 (22.04.91)	Dr Gábor Demsky (AFD)	Pál Filló (HSP)
Borsod-Abaúj- (30.09.91)	Miklós Németh (independent)	Dr Mihály Kupa (HDF)
Békés 5 (08.06.92)	Zoltán Szokolay (HDF)	Dr Éva Lukovics (AFD)
Komárom-Esztergom 3 (31.08.92)	Sándor Deák (AFD)	György Keleti (HSP)
Bács-Kiskun 4 (03.05.93)	József Faddi (ISP)	Tamás Nagy (AA)

Source: Adapted from *Változások az Országgyűlés összetételében*, Budapest, 1994.

Table 10: May 1994 parliamentary election results. Share of the vote (regional list) and number of seats won

Party	Regional List (%)	Seats
Hungarian Socialist Party (HSP)	32.96	209
Alliance of Free Democrats (AFD)	19.76	70
Hungarian Democratic Forum (HDF)	11.73	37
Independent Smallholders Party (ISP)	8.85	26
Christian Democratic Peoples Party (CDPP)	7.06	22
Alliance of Young Democrats (FIDESZ)	7.00	20
Workers' Party	3.18	0
Republic Party	2.53	0
Agrarian Alliance	2.11	1
Hungarian Justice and Life Party	1.58	0
Hungarian Social Democratic Party (HSDP)	0.95	0
United Smallholders Party (USP)	0.82	0
Entrepreneurs Party (EP-LBA)	0.62	1
National Democratic Alliance (NDA)	0.52	0
Hungary's Green Party	0.16	0
Reconciled Smallholders Party	0.11	0
Conservative Party	0.04	0
Green Alternative	0.02	0
Market Party	0.01	0

Sources: Népszava, May 10, 1994; *Magyar Hírlap*, May 30, 1994.

Directory of Parties

Active Party (AP)
Aktiv Párt (AP)

Address. Budapest VIII, Karácsony Sándor u. 2/b, 11;23.

Telephone. (1) 141 4637.

Leadership. József Szecsi (pres.); Ildikó Czomor, Géza Güdenüs (vice-pres.)

Membership. 121 (April 1994).

History. The party was formed on June 30, 1992, when the local organization of Hungary's Green Party in Budapest's VII district decided to leave. The party calls for social problems to be solved only with moral and cultural realities in mind. Its programme calls for an end Hungary's nuclear power programme, a programme of energy conservation and the non-intervention of the state in the cultural sphere. In the 1994 elections the party's president did attempt to obtain sufficient nominations to become a candidate for the Budapest 9 parliamentary constituency yet failed in his bid to appear on the ballot.

HUNGARYAgrarian Alliance (AA)
Agrárszövetség (ASZ)

Address. Budapest V, Arany János utca 10.

Telephone. (1) 131 0953, 131 0954.

Fax. (1) 111 2663.

Foundation. Dec. 3, 1989.

Leadership. Tamás Nagy (pres.); Lajos Buzassy (party national manager); György Fábri (campaign manager); post of general secretary vacant.

History. The Alliance was formed out of a merger between the Agrarian Reform Circles Movement (established May 2, 1989) and the Association of Agrarian Reform Circles (established May 16, 1989) which emerged within the HSWP after it acknowledged the right to form party factions in February 1989.

Although the Alliance did not receive sufficient votes to cross the 4 per cent threshold on the proportional representation part of the parliamentary elections, it figured on the regional and national lists and gained two seats, one in association with the Alliance for the Village and the Countryside. This joint candidate (Dr Ferenc Wekler) subsequently joined the AFD, leaving the other, Dr Ildikó Piros Vargáné, as the party's only representative in parliament for just under three years.

The party was far from discouraged by its failure to surmount the 4 per cent barrier in the 1990 elections, attributing this, at least partly, to its failure to campaign in Budapest. It maintained a relatively strong organization in its areas of strength in rural east and south-west Hungary. This organizational strength was highlighted in April and May 1993 when the party president, Tamás Nagy, with the support of the Republic Party of János Palotás, won a parliamentary by-election in the constituency covering the town of Kunszentmiklós in south-eastern Hungary, caused by the death of the previous ISP member of parliament (*see* Table 9). In the summer of 1993, former deputy president Tibor Nagy-Husszein left office, apparently in disagreement over the more liberal orientation the party was adopting.

The party received 27.1 million forints in state subsidy in 1993, though no further information on the party's financial situation appears to be available, except that it was allocated 7.18 million forints in state subsidies in order to contest the 1994 elections and planned to spend 100 million forints from its own resources on the election campaign. In the 1994 elections, the party received sufficient nominations to place its candidates on the ballot in 131 individual constituencies, including 14 of the 32 Budapest seats. It also was able to stand candidates on every county and the national list. The party ran as part of the four-party liberal block alongside the AFD, FIDESZ and the EP. In early April the party came to an agreement with the Green Alternative, who then advised their supporters that where their candidates did not stand they should cast their votes for the Agrarian Alliance. The first round of the 1994 elections proved to be a major disappointment for the party as it failed to overcome the 5 per cent barrier to gain seats allocated through the party lists and lost votes compared to its 1990 performance across the country, polling only 2.11 per cent. The second round also proved disappointing. The party leader, Tamás Nagy, was defeated narrowly by the HSP in his own constituency and continued representation in parliament was only ensured by an unexpected victory in the Tolna 3 parliamentary constituency.

Programme. The Alliance focuses on agricultural policy. It argues that, for some time to come, Hungarian agriculture will have to be based on the co-existence of different forms of property ownership. It calls for government intervention to promote the development of the agriculture sector, calling for the creation of new kinds of agricultural co-operatives for the marketing of agricultural products. It also encourages foreign investment in agriculture and advocates the formation of an Agrarian Bank.

Alliance of Free Democrats (AFD), Free Democrats
Szabad Demokraták Szövetsége (SZDSZ), Szabad Demokraták

Address. Budapest V, Mérleg u. 6, H-1051.

Telephone. (1) 117 6911.

Fax. 118 7944.

Foundation. Nov. 13, 1988.

Leadership. Iván Pető (pres.); spokespersons: Gabriella Beki, Dr Peter Hack, Dr Bálint Magyar, Imre Mécs, Károly Attila Soós, Dr István Szent-Iványi, Marton Tárdos, Péter Tölgyessy, Ferenc Wekler; National Council Leadership: Gáspár Miklós Tamás (pres.); Tamás Bauer, László Rajk, Domokos Szász, Dr István Szigethly (members); Party Director: Ferenc Wekler; Leader in parliament: Gábor Kuncze.

Membership. 32,763 (early 1993).

History. Founded on Nov. 13, 1988, out of the majority of the organization which had established the Network of Free Initiatives the previous March. It represents an offshoot of the "urban" rather than "populist" strand in opposition thought (the "democratic opposition"), many of them lapsed marxists, who produced samizdat material over the preceding one-and-a-half decades and established the unofficial Poor Support Fund. It was the first party to produce an elaborated programme, which is not surprising given the high proportion of economists, sociologists and lawyers in its membership. Indeed, in its first year, it thought of itself as a small party of intellectuals.

By the time of the parliamentary elections, however, as a result of the November 1989 referendum and the party's unearthing of the "Danube-gate" scandal (the continued tapping by the security services of the telephones of opposition party leaders) it had transformed itself into a party with mass support. It fielded 169 candidates in the parliamentary elections in 1990 and ended up with 91 members of parliament, becoming the largest opposition party.

In late 1991 a major internal dispute arose between the party's intellectual founders and its membership, most of which had joined the party in late 1989. The dispute was precipitated by the resignation of János Kis as party president in October. Partially as a reaction to the dissident old guard, the party elected as president Péter Tölgyessy, who had only become active in the party at the time of the Round Table talks. In response several of the AFD's founders, Gáspár Miklós Tamás, Miklós Vásárhelyi, László Rajk, Miklós Haraszti and Ferenc Köszeg, left the party's executive, whilst Iván Pető resigned as parliamentary group leader accusing the party membership of trying to take over the party. During 1992 the party was wracked by internal dispute which was only resolved in 1992 when Pető defeated Tölgyessy and replaced him as party president.

Since Iván Pető's election the dispute has largely disappeared and the influence of the intellectuals over the direction of the party has gradually diminished. This can be seen in the decisions of Gáspár Miklós Tamás (though still remaining chairman of the party's national council) and Miklós Haraszti not to seek re-election to parliament in 1994. It can also be seen in the appointment of Gábor Kuncze, the parliamentary group leader who was virtually unknown before 1993, as the party's candidate for Prime Minister in September 1993. Opinion polls placed the party in either third or second place during the first months of 1994, though all polls indicated that it would lose votes in comparison to its 1990 electoral performance. In the first round of the 1994 elections it polled more votes than most opinion polls had predicted taking 19.76 per cent of the vote. Although, with 70 seats, the AFD emerged as the second largest party in the new parliament, results from the second round of voting proved disappointing. First, they failed to prevent the HSP winning an absolute majority, and second, almost all of the party's leadership were defeated in their own constituencies, the losers including Iván Pető, Bálint Mágyar, Ferenc Köszeg, Alajos Dornbách and László Rajk.

The party received 188 million forints in state subsidy in 1993 and was due to receive a further 8.04 million forints in state support for the 1994 elections. No further information on the party's finances was available, except that it planned to spend 170 million forints from its own resources during the election campaign. It established its own company — Liberty Ltd — in 1990 and is closely associated with the Foundation for a European Hungary and AB-Beszélőkft.

Organization. A Delegate Assembly of delegates from local organizations elects an 80-member National Council and an Executive Body made up of the spokespersons listed above.

Programme. The party is on the liberal wing of Hungarian politics, and encompasses two major and one minor strands of opinion. The latter is a small liberal-conservative tendency, represented by the philosopher and writer for the *Spectator*, Gáspár Miklós Tamás. The two major strands of opinion within the party are the liberal and social-liberal, bordering on social-democratic views. The latter were somewhat marginalized in 1990 but seem to have become more influential in the past year, perhaps as a result of the changes within the party leadership and perhaps in reaction to rising unemployment and associated social tensions.

The AFD was the first party with a programme for the "change of system" in 1989. In it the party put forward a liberal variant of the "social market economy", minimal state intervention, low taxes, an independent central bank, religious freedom, and a health service provided in the main by private companies. The 1994 election programme was marked by a significant change of emphasis. In the economic field the party still called for more foreign investment and lower taxes but also argued for more state intervention in the economy to create jobs. To this end it has advocated the creation of a fund to finance infrastructural projects and tax incentives for businesses which take on new workers. The party called for cuts in unnecessary government expenditure, targeting both bureaucracy and government plans to move the seat of government to Budapest's castle district, in order to finance an expanded welfare state. It called for the transformation of maternity benefits and pensions into citizens' rights, the creation of an adequate social minimum, special subsidies to poor families with children of school age and universal health insurance. Furthermore, it argued that more power should be given to local government and that the mayors of major cities should be directly elected.

Affiliations. The AFD was finally granted membership of the Liberal International in September 1993 after three years of confusion over whether it was a liberal or a social democratic party. It claims links with the socialist parties of Austria, France and Germany.

Alliance of Nature and Society Conservers (AHSC)
Természet és Társadalomvédők Szövetsége (TTSZ)

Address. Budapest V, Belgrád rkp. 24, H-1056.

Leadership. Sámuel Kántor (pres.).

History. Founded on Jan. 6, 1990, with Dr Tibor Ganti as president of its Co-ordinating Body. It received two million forints state support in 1990 but has not filed accounts for the year. It managed to get two candidates onto the ballot, but none was elected, and one in Szabolcs-Szatmár-Bereg county received only 206 votes. The party was apparently still in existence in January 1994, listing its president as Sámuel Kántor and based at the same address as the ISP. Nothing further is known about its structure and activities.

Alliance of the Poor and Defenceless (APD)
Szegények és Kiszolgáltatottak Szövetsége (SZKSZ)

Address. Budapest VIII, Szentkirály u. 22, H-1088.

History. The Alliance was registered as a party on Feb. 8, 1990, and was still reported to be in existence in January 1994. Its programme called for concrete improvements in the quality of life for all citizens, particularly pinpointing improvements in housing conditions, and argued for a vigorous defence of the level of workers' real wages and the building of a strongly independent civil society as means of achieving this goal.

Beer Party
Sörpárt

Address. Budapest V, Váci u. 17, H-1052.

Foundation. March 30, 1992.

Leadership. Szabolcs Imredi (pres.); Zsolt Ujjady (vice-pres.).

Membership. 500–600 members (April 1994).

History. The party was founded in 1992 and was partly inspired by the success of the Polish Beer Party in obtaining seats in the *Sejm* in the 1991 parliamentary elections. Its programme calls for the protection of beer drinkers and in addition to its 500–600 members claims to have organizations in 11 counties. The party did not manage to get any of its candidates onto the ballot for the 1994 elections.

Catholic People's Party (CPP)
Katolikus Néppárt (KNP)

Address. Budapest II, Hidegkúti út. 332, H-1028.

Leadership. Dr Endre Varga (pres.).

History. Founded on Dec. 21, 1989, it claims to be a continuation of the party of the same name established in 1895. Its president is listed as Dr Endre Varga. Its structure and subsequent activities are unknown, although it was reported to be still in existence in January 1994.

Christian Democratic People's Party (CDPP)
Kereszténydemokrata Néppárt (KDNP)

Address. Budapest XII, Nagy Jenő u. 5, H-1126.

Telephone. (1) 175 0333, 155 3658.

Fax. (1) 155 5772.

Foundation. March 17, 1989.

Leadership. László Surján (pres.); Dr László Varga (dep. ch.); Dr Miklós Palos, Dr Miklós Hasznos (vice-pres.); Dr Terézia Császár Szilágyiné (vice-pres., sec. of nat. organization); Dr János Birkás, Béla Csepe (leader in parliament); Dr György Katona, Dr Kálmán Kovács, Dr Gyula Mézáros, Miklós Rusznák, János Úrsprung (national executive members); Dr György Rubovsky (g. s.); István Eszes (campaign manager).

Membership. 20,409, early 1993.

History. The party is a continuation of the more progressive Barankovics branch of the Democratic People's Party, founded in October 1944 but not permitted by the Allies to operate as a political party until Sept. 25, 1945. In the 1947 election it achieved 16.4 per cent of the vote, the second highest share. The party leaders were forced into emigration in 1949. The immediate predecessor of the re-founded party was the Áron Márton Society, formed on Dec. 10, 1988. The CDPP was the last of the six parties in parliament to be established, but made up the deficit and ran 105 candidates, winning 21 seats. It received 4 million forints (approximately £29,000) state support in 1989, a similar figure in 1990 plus 7.1 millions for the elections. In the 1990 local elections it was the only member of governing coalition not to lose votes. During the next three years the party consolidated its organization and expanded its membership, aided by the popularity of its president, László Surján, Minister of Social Welfare. The party has generally been regarded as the most quiescent member of the governing coalition, though during summer 1993 the CDPP briefly adopted a more independent stance in relation to the HDF. The party called for an expansion of social policy and launched a "buy Hungarian" campaign to combat unemployment.

As the 1994 election approached it was regarded as a potential coalition partner for either the liberal parties or the HSP. Partly in response to this it stressed its close ideological links to the HDF. Its improved organizational position can be illustrated by the fact that significantly more of its candidates managed to secure more places on the ballot in the 1994 elections than in 1990. In May its candidates appeared on the ballot in 163 individual constituencies, on every county list and the national list. Despite its improved organizational strength it only won 7.06 per cent of the vote and 22 seats in parliament. Exit polls showed that the party was largely supported by the old (it polled 12 per cent among people between 60 and 70, and 18 per cent among people over 70), and women, who made up 62 per cent of its voters. Its voters also had a lower level of education than the average and lived predominantly in rural areas. It received 99.8 million forints in state subsidy in 1993 and was due to receive 7.85 million forints for the 1994 elections in addition to the 60 million forints it planned to spend from its own resources on the election campaign. Like the other major parties, it has a foundation and limited liability company closely associated with it — the Barankovics Foundation and Hunniapack Ltd.

Organization. A National Committee with representatives from local organizations appoints a 31-member Executive Committee and the Presidium listed above.

Programme. The CDPP sees itself as an ideological, but not denominational, party, representing the values of the Judeo-Christian world view. It regards moral values as more important than policies, and uses the designation "people's" party to show that it does not see itself as representing the interests of a single class. The party contains several different tendencies, ranging from right-wing nationalist to Christian socialist, although the moderate right form the majority within the party. Its economic programme advocates the creation of a Christian democratic variant of the social market economy, that is, an economy based on private property but underpinned by strong social guarantees. It also favours the family wage, family taxation, and the defence of motherhood. It also advocates the creation of more part-time employment opportunities for women, a Christian environmental policy, and allowing churches to establish church schools.

Affiliations. The party claims to have links with the Christian democratic parties of Austria and the Netherlands.

Conservative Party, Farmers and Citizens Alliance
Konzervativ Párt, Gazdák és Polgárok Szövetség

Address. Budapest I, Batthyány u. 10, 1 em., H-1015.

Telephone/Fax. (1) 201 1886.

Foundation. Sept. 24, 1993.

Leadership. László Csizmadia (pres.); Dr Ágnes Paszti, Dr Emese Ugrin, Gyula Lehoczky (vice-pres).

Membership. 4,000 members claimed (April 1994).

History. The party is the successor to the Conservative Smallholders and Bourgeois Party, a failed attempt by Béla Németh and 17 others in March 1993 to unite the 36 strong anti-Torgyán fraction in the HISP. The Conservative Party, which was formed in September 1993, has something of the character of a rump party given that most of the members of its predecessor joined the USP in late 1993. Despite this the party began to consolidate itself in early 1994, publishing its own periodical, the *Konservativ Szemle* (Conservative Review). Indeed, at the time of the dissolution of parliament in April 1994, its only parliamentary deputy was one of the party's vice-presidents: the maverick right-winger Dr Emese Ugrin. Ugrin had been originally elected on the CDPP's national list and defected, joining the Torgyán-led ISP in August 1991. There Ugrin became leader of the ISP parliamentary group before leaving the party in 1992. In the 1994 parliamentary elections the party managed to gain sufficient nominations to appear on four county lists and stand in 13 individual constituencies, but only succeeded in winning 0.04 per cent and no seats in parliament.

Organization and programme. Nothing is known about the party's structure or organization, whilst the programme does not differ significantly from any of the other Smallholders parties.

Democratic Coalition (DC)
Demokrata Koalició

Address. Budapest XVI, Hunyadvár u. 52, H-1165.

Telephone. (1) 251 2362, 251 9317.

Foundation. Aug. 4, 1990.

Leadership. József Mráv (exec. pres.).

Membership. 4,000 claimed (January 1994).

History. The party was formed on Aug. 4, 1990, when the Patriotic Electoral Coalition decided to relaunch itself as the Democratic Coalition. In early 1994 its leadership was confident that in the forthcoming elections it would be able to field candidates on seven county lists and on the national list. Despite this it failed to gain sufficient nominations to appear on any county list and only managed to get candidates onto the ballot in four individual constituencies. It failed to proceed to the second round in any of them.

Programme. The party describes itself as a nationalist party of Hungarian patriots. Despite this it differentiates itself from other small right-wing nationalist parties by claiming to have nothing to do with anti-Semitism.

Democratic Party (DP)
Demokrata Párt

Address. Budapest II, Forint u. 12, H-1024.

Telephone. (1) 115 5909, 268 5630.

Fax. (1) 268 5954.

Leadership. Vilmos Bereczki (pres.).

History. The party was founded in October 1993 as a breakaway from the Democratic Smallholders and Bourgeois Party. Its president, Vilmos Bereczki, was a parliamentary deputy originally elected on the ISP's national list in 1990 who left the party in November 1992. Sitting as an independent he became associated with the Democratic Smallholders and Bourgeois Party in February 1993 and became the leader of the Democratic Party in October 1993. In the 1994 parliamentary elections the party gained sufficient nominations to stand candidates in four constituencies but none of its candidates gained sufficient votes to proceed to the second round. Nothing is known of its structure, organization or programme.

Democratic Party of the Unemployed (DPU)
Demokratikus Munkanélküliek Pártja (DMP)

Address. 3200 Gyöngyös, Orallo u. 6.

Telephone. (37) 312 8444.

Leadership. Ferenc Mikola, Márton Szalai (co-pres).

History. The party was founded on Dec. 16, 1993, and is not registered with the authorities. Other than the information listed above nothing is known about its history, structure, activities or programme.

Democratic Smallholders and Citizens' Party (DSP)
Demokratikus Kisgazda és Polgári Párt (DKPP)

Address. Budapest IV, Nádasy Kálmán u. 30. 111.8, H-1046.

Telephone. (1) 180 9632.

Fax. (1) 268 5954.

Leadership. Gyula Venczel (pres.).

History. The party was formed in February 1993 as a result of a split within the ISP and considers itself the heir of the party's radical faction. It briefly attracted the support of Vilmos Bereczki, a parliamentary deputy, who left the ISP in November 1992 to sit as an independent. He was, however, later to leave the party to found and lead the Democratic Party in October 1993. The party claims a membership of 3,000 though nothing further is known of the party's current activities.

Electoral Alliance for Hungarians
Magyarságért Választási Szövetség

Address. Budapest XI, Köbölkút út. 35, H-1118.

Leadership. Béla Benedek (pres.); Tibor Pokorny (campaign manager).

History. The party is not registered with the authorities but is associated with the anti-Semitic writer, Béla Benedek, who is the alliance's president. Beyond the information given above nothing is known about its structure, activities or programme.

Electoral Alliance for the Nation
Nemzetért Választási Szövetség

Leadership. Izabella B. Király (exec. pres.).

History. The Electoral Alliance for the Nation is closely associated with the name of Izabella B. Király, a right-wing parliamentary deputy who was expelled from the HDF in June 1993 for her extreme right-wing views. Király went on to form the Hungarian Interests Party in October 1993 (*see* below), which entered the 1994 parliamentary elections in its own right. The relationship between the Hungarian Interests Party and the Electoral Alliance for the Nation is somewhat unclear.

Entrepreneurs Party (EP), Liberal Bourgeois Alliance (LBA)
Vállalkozók Pártja (VP), Liberális Polgári Szövetség (LPSZ)

Address. Budapest XVI, Hunyadvár u. 52, H-1165.

Telephone/Fax. (1) 251 4732, 252 0954.

Foundation. Oct. 22, 1989.

Leadership. Ferenc Cs. Kiss (honorary pres.), Péter Zwack (pres.); vice-presidents: Csaba Csikós (exec. vice-pres.), Zoltán Kresz (campaign director), Dr Lajos Kupcsok (general).

History. Founded in Debrecen as an amalgamation of the Debrecen Democratic Club and the Kapuvár Union of Private Entrepreneurs, the Entrepreneurs Party participated in the draw for party political broadcast radio and TV slots and received 10 million forints state support in 1990, together with a further 4.3 million forints for the elections. Prior to the 1990 elections it stated that it hoped to win seven or eight seats, but in this it failed. Nevertheless, it got 63 candidates onto the ballot, sufficient to figure on most regional and the national lists, although it achieved only 1.89 per cent of the total vote. This qualified it for a further 9.8 million forint tranche of state support. At its second congress in June 1990 it voted to change its name to the Liberal Bourgeois Alliance and move its headquarters to Kecskemét.

It has since moved back to Budapest and has elected Péter Zwack, the owner of company making the *Unicum* liqueur and former Hungarian ambassador to the United States, as its president. In January 1994 it joined the liberal electoral pact together with the AFD, AYD and the AA. For the 1994 elections it managed to gain sufficient nominations to contest 67 individual constituencies, to put forward a list in 14 of the 20 counties and to appear on the national list, but won only 0.62 per cent. Zwack himself, standing as a candidate supported by all four liberal parties, won a constituency in Kecskemét. It was decided that the party should receive 4.62 million forints in state subsidies to contest the elections and planned to spend between 20 and 40 million forints of its own resources on the campaign, two to four times as much as it had spent in 1990.

Programme. As the name suggests, it is a party of businessmen. It gives first priority to the economy and calls for a stabilization of the economic environment in which businesses must operate, much faster privatization and a more thoroughgoing restructuring of Hungarian industry. This, it argues, is the only way in which Hungary will be able to compete in the world market thus laying the ground for dynamic growth and an eventual improvement in the standard of living

Europe Party
Európa Párt

Address. Budapest XII, Lejtő u. 12, H-1121.

Leadership. Pál Szente (pres.).

History. The party is not registered with the authorities. Its programme calls for a pan-European politics to be developed, for state ownership in the economy to be reduced by 10 per cent, agriculture to be developed through the revival of peasant traditions and for the promotion of employee share-ownership.

FIDESZ, Alliance of Young Democrats
FIDESZ, Fiatal Demokratak Szovetsege

Address. Budapest VI, Lendvay utca. 28, H-1062.

Telephone. (1) 269 5353.

Fax. (1) 269 5343.

Foundation. March 30, 1988.

Leadership. Committee: Dr Viktor Orbán (pres.); Dr János Ader (exec. vice-pres. campaign director); Tamás Deutsch, Balázs Medgyesy, Zsolt Németh, Zoltán Rockenbauer, Gabriella Selmeczi, Tamás Tirts, Zoltán Trombitás (vice-pres); Dr László Kövér (leader in parliament); József Szajer (national committee chair).

Membership. 13,254 (January 1993).

History. One of the first opposition parties to be formed, the HSWP initially disdained to invite FIDESZ to the Opposition Round Table negotiations, although it did subsequently participate and, like the AFD, refused to sign the final agreement. It played a prominent role in 1989, and its spokespersons made virulently anti-Soviet statements in its campaigns for the withdrawal of Soviet troops and at the ceremonial re-burial of Imre Nagy in June 1989.

It received 4 million forints of state support in 1989, 7 million in 1990, plus a further 7.3 million for the elections. For a party aimed at a specific group — young people — it performed well electorally, forwarding 85 candidates of whom 22 were elected.

The party's popularity increased during the summer of 1990 as a result of the parliamentary performance of Viktor Orbán and the party's stand against all displays of nationalism and against all forms of reprivatization. It was even more successful electorally in the local authorities (beating the HSP); but this revealed something of a weakness in depth. In some local authorities it could only field recent school-leavers as committee members.

The party led in the opinion polls from 1991 until the end of 1993. Despite this lead, however, it failed to win any of the five by-elections held during the 1990–94 parliament. This left the impression that the party's popularity was more of a protest against the ruling HDF and a sign of disillusion with the other opposition parties which could not easily be converted into votes in a general election. Because of the origins of the party in a broadly based anti-Communist youth movement, two different tendencies emerged in the party after 1990; a majority centre-right tendency associated with the parliamentary leader Viktor Orbán and a social-liberal tendency associated with parliamentary deputies Gábor Fodor, István Hegedűs, Péter Molnár and Klára Ungár.

It was against this background that major reforms to the party's constitution were passed at its conference in Debrecen in April 1993 with a view to making the party fit for government. The age limit of 35 was scrapped and the structure of the party was overhauled with the creation of the post of party president. Orbán was unanimously elected to the latter post, but only after Fodor, who was known to be uneasy about the changes, stepped down as a candidate at the last moment.

During the summer Orbán began to reshape FIDESZ into a distinctively centre-right party, leading Fodor to announce that he would stand for the newly created post of chairman of the party's national council against Orbán's preferred candidate, Dr József Szajer. After a bitter campaign Fodor was defeated, prompting him to leave the party in November 1993 along with two of his supporters, Péter Molnár and Klára Ungár.

At the time Fodor was the second most popular politician in the country after President Göncz and his departure seriously damaged FIDESZ's electoral prospects. In December 1993 the party fell behind the HSP in the opinion polls and seemed to be in free fall throughout the spring of 1994. In the 1994 elections, however, the party managed to place its candidates on the ballot in 172 constituencies, on all county lists and the national list as well but performed disastrously, winning 7.00 per cent of the vote and 20 seats. Despite Orbán's efforts to broaden the party's support it remained strong only among the youngest voters, polling 26 per cent among first time voters and 19 per cent among voters in their 20s.

The party received 107.7 million forints in state subsidy for 1993 and had been allocated 8.02 million forints for the 1994 elections. In addition the party planned to spend 170 million forints from its own resources on the campaign.

Programme. Prior to 1993 FIDESZ was clearly at the liberal end of the political spectrum, with a commitment to radicalism. Since then the party has moved distinctly to the right and its leaders prefer to speak of harmonizing "individual freedom and national values". Its programme calls for faster privatization, more spending on infrastructure and lower taxes for business in order to stimulate the economy. It calls for a minimum welfare state, sufficient to maintain social peace, and also calls for a contract between welfare recipients and the state, through which welfare recipients will agree to enter training schemes in exchange for their benefits. It advocates rapid integration into both NATO and the EU, and calls for the creation of a fund to facilitate the rapid return of church property.

Organization. Prior to the April 1993 Debrecen conference an (at least) annual congress of delegates from local organizations appoints a 46-member National Committee. After April 1993 the annual conference elects an 11-member leadership committee of which the party president, the parliamentary group leader and the chairman of the national committee are members.

Affiliations. The party is a full member of the Liberal International whose conference it hosted in Budapest in autumn 1993.

For a Historical Hungary Party
Történelmi Magyarországért Párt

Address. Budapest XXII, Mézesfehér u. 5, H-1222.

Telephone. (1) 227 0020.

Leadership. Ernő Diószegi (pres.).

History. The party was founded in 1992 and subsequently registered with the authorities. In the 1994 elections it gained sufficient nominations to contest one individual constituency and stand on one county list. Nothing more is known about the party's structure, programme or activities.

For a Provincial Hungary Party (FPHP)
Vidéki Magyarországért Párt (VMP)

Address. Tiszaersz, Felszabadulás u. 20, H-5243.

Telephone. (59) 355 351.

Fax. (59) 355 351.

Leadership. Dr Kornelia Safar (pres.).

History. Founded on Nov. 20, 1989, in Tiszadersz, nothing is known of the party's activities except that in 1990 it succeeded in getting Dr Dezső Herédy onto the ballot in Jász-Nagykun-Szolnok county's eighth district. He received 690 votes, 60 fewer than the number needed to get him onto the ballot in the first place. The party was reported to be still in existence in January 1994.

Freedom Party (FP)
Szabadságpárt (SZP)

History. Founded in Hungary on July 12, 1989, following its re-foundation in New Brunswick, USA on May 28, 1989, the party was originally founded by Dezső Sulyok in 1946 after he had been excluded from the ISP (under pressure from the Communist dominated Left Wing Block) for his right-wing views. The party lists two presidents — Ernő Hoka in the USA and Gyula Gueth in Hungary. It participated in the draw for party political broadcast slots in January 1990, received 2 million forints state support in 1990, with a further 300,000 forints specifically for the elections, and forwarded five candidates (including its Hungarian president), sufficient to make the regional list in Somogy and Zala counties. It achieved only 0.06 per cent of the total vote, however, failing to qualify for state support in 1991, and closed 1990 with a surplus of 500 forints (less than £4), having spent most of the state money on three issues of its paper *Hungarian Tomorrow* (*Magyar Holnap*). It is at the nationalist Christian end of the political spectrum. In November 1992 Torgyán announced that it had merged with the ISP.

Future Party
A Jövő Pártja

Address. Budapest XIII, Kresz G. u. 8, H-1132.

Telephone. (1) 131 0071.

Leadership. András Pollák (pres.).

History. The party was not registered with the authorities. The party's programme calls for a minimum of 12 classes of elementary education for children, an expansion in summer camps for children, the provision of agricultural machinery to peasants to revive agriculture and the sale of enterprises to those who work there.

General Party (GeP)
Általános Párt (AP)

Address. Budapest XIII, Katona J. u. 2/E, H-1137.

Leadership. Béla Lukácsi (pres.); János Zelki (spokesman).

History. The party was registered with the authorities in 1990 and was reported to still be in existence in January 1994. Nothing further is known about its structure, organization, programme or activities.

Green Alternative
Zöld Alternatíva

Address. Budapest II, Margit körút 29/a, H-1024.

Telephone. (1) 116 8554.

Leadership. György Droppa, Erzsébet Schmuck (co-chairs).

History. The party was formed as a result of a split within Hungary's Green Party in 1993 after its president, Tibor Enekes, moved the party drastically to the right. It contains many of the major activists in the conservation movement and has a very decentralized structure, resembling that of the German and British Greens. Whilst calling for an ecologically sustainable society its programme concentrates on concrete environmental concerns, giving the highest priority to clean air, clean water, removing hazardous waste and to agricultural issues, particularly soil erosion. In the 1994 elections its candidates only gained sufficient nominations to stand in five individual constituencies and on the county list in Nógrád county polling 0.02 per cent of the total vote and not winning any seats in parliament. Due to its weakness it advised its supporters to cast their votes for the Agrarian Alliance in those constituencies it failed to contest.

Happiness Party (HP)
Boldogság Párt (BP)

Address. Budapest XXII, Tanító u. 9, H-1221.

Telephone/Fax. (1) 226 2723.

Leadership. Gyula Hernádi (pres.); Miklós Jancsó (vice-pres.); György Kassa (g. s.).

History. Founded in the spring of 1991, its aim is reported to be that of freeing society from dry, day-to-day politics. The party was still reported to be active in January 1994 and formed part of the National Strength Movement which successfully managed to place a candidate on the ballot in one individual constituency for the 1994 elections, though he failed to gain sufficient votes to proceed to the second round.

Historic Independent Smallholders Party (HISP)
Történelmi Független Kisgazdapárt (TFKP)

Address. Budapest XII, Logodi u. 60, H-1012.

Foundation. November 1992.

Leadership. Tivadar Pártay (pres.); István Haeffler (spokesman).

History. The party is one of the three Smallholders' parties in the 36 strong Smallholder parliamentary fraction which refused to accept the authority of the ISP president József Torgyán. It is grouped around Tivadar Partay, the former honorary president of the ISP and a veteran of the pre-Communist Smallholders party, who left the ISP in July 1991 following Torgyán's election as party president. The party was originally formed as an attempt to unite the various tendencies in the 36-strong fraction into a single party in November 1992. The attempt failed in spring 1993 when 17 deputies left and was further frustrated in December 1993 when another attempt to unify the 36-strong fraction by creating the USP depleted ranks still further, leaving it with only five parliamentary deputies. In the 1994 elections, however, the party failed to gain sufficient nominations to appear on either the national or the county lists and only managed to contest two individual constituencies. It failed to win sufficient votes to proceed to the second round.

Programme. The party's ideology and policies do not differ significantly from those of the other Smallholders parties. It claims, however, to be the true heir of the Independent Smallholders Party which existed prior to 1948.

Homeland and Entrepreneurship Party
Haza és Vállalkozás Párt

Address. Budapest XII, Zugligeti út 50/B, 11/8, H-1121.

Foundation. May 7, 1989.

Leadership. Dr István Utasi (pres.).

History. The party is the successor to the Homeland Party which soon after its foundation put forward a presidential candidate in October 1989 when it seemed likely that a presidential election would precede the parliamentary ones. In January 1990 it took part in the draw for party political broadcast time-slots, but ran no candidates in the 1990 parliamentary elections. It registered its change of name in 1990 soon after the elections, but its subsequent activities are unknown.

Programme. The party's primary long-term aim is given as preventing the Hungarian nation from dying out. In the shorter term it advocates improving the material and spiritual condition of the individual, the family, and the nation; creating a state based on national traditions, the principles of Christian morality and on western European values. It also supports military neutrality, reducing taxes, a convertible forint, and cancelling existing foreign debts. More controversially, it advocates peacefully re-examining the historical injustices Hungary has suffered over the past 70 years.

Hungarian Christian Movement
Magyar Keresztény Mozgalom

Address. Hódmezővásárhely, Rudnay Gy. u. 2/b, H-6800.

Telephone. (62) 342 959.

Leadership. Dr Antal Endrey (pres.).

History. The party is not registered with the authorities. Other than the information given above nothing is known about the party's structure, organization, programme or activities.

Hungarian Democratic Christian Party (HDCP)
Magyar Demokrata Keresztény Párt (MDKP)

Address. Miskolc, Szabó Lajos u. 63, H-3501.

Leadership. Pál Vörös (pres.).

History. The party was registered in Miskolc on Jan. 15, 1990, having been established in October 1989 out of the Christian wing of the HDF. Its president is listed as Pal Vörös, and the party received 2 million forints (approximately £14,500) state support in 1990. It followed the HDF in advocating a boycott of the November 1989 referendum. It was reported to be still in existence in January 1994 though its current activities are unknown.

Hungarian Democratic Forum (HDF), Democratic Forum
Magyar Demokrata Fórum (MDF), Demokrata Fórum

Address. Budapest II, Bem József ter 3, H-1027.

Telephone. (1) 212 4601, 212 4603, 212 4604, 212 4605.

Fax. (1) 156 8522.

Foundation. Sept. 27, 1987.

Leadership. Dr Lajos Für (pres.); Sándor Lezsák (exec. pres.); Dr Péter Boross, Gabriella Farkas, Dr Imre Kónya, Dr Ferenc Kulin (leader in parliament), Péter Nahimi, Dr Tamás Szabó (deputy pres); National Executive members — Dr István Balsai, Dr Zoltán Bogárdi, Dr Krisztina Dobos, Dr Gyula Fekete, Dr Géza Jeszenszky, Dr Tamás Katona, Dr László Medgyásszay, Dr László Salomon, László Sárossy, Dr György Schámschula, Dr György Szabad, Dr Iván Szabó, Dr Zsolt Zétényi; András Rubovsky (party dir.).

Membership. 31,000 (January 1993).

History. The first Lakitelep meeting at which the party was founded was a meeting of populist writers (five of its nine founding members were writers or poets) and reform communists. By the spring of 1989 its support base had broadened and Christian democratic and liberal elements could also be found under its umbrella. Having started life as a "movement" many members were reluctant to transform it into a party. When this change took place, the balance within the party also changed. The "populist" tradition, which emphasized the uniqueness of Hungary's past and postulated the possibility of a "Third Way" of neither capitalism nor socialism, was marginalized. The party found itself a new guard of economic experts, many of them associated with the planning office, but also including Gábor Széles, president of one of Hungary's most dynamic private companies.

By February 1990, József Antall, who was appointed party president at the Second National Conference (after he had turned down leading roles in the CDPP and ISP) publicly rejected "Third Way"-ism. Having marginalized the populists (using only their nationalism verging on anti-Semitism to bolster their popular appeal), in its electoral campaign it sought to distance itself from the reform communists by vying with the AFD to prove its anti-Communist credentials. The party received 15 million forints worth of state support in 1989, a further 15 million in 1990 in addition to 9.6 million specifically for the elections. It fielded 174 candidates and attained a total of 165 seats. An independent *Forum Foundation* was established with the aim of supporting the party's electoral campaign, and leading party figures established *Forum plc* in June 1989, with an initial capital of 31.5 million forints (approximately £230,000).

Since the elections, the HDF's nationalist-Christian orientation has been confirmed and both populist and liberal strands continue to be isolated. At the Third Congress in June 1990, the populist wing was particularly upset by the pact with the AFD and capitulation on the issue of a directly elected president. In power the party also revealed a predilection for authoritarianism. Antall placed his representatives in every ministry, and ISP leaders complained bitterly of his intervention into their affairs. When Kiss of the liberal wing of the party resigned from the leadership at the Fourth Congress in December 1990, he cited the excessively presidentialist running of the party as a reason. In addition, it placed the State Property Agency under government rather than parliamentary control, introducing Republican Representatives (the equivalent of the French *préfet*) into each county. In society as a whole this style of government has been most dramatically highlighted in the so-called "media war", the attempt by the HDF to exercise control over the news output of both state radio and television which was a recurring theme during the first post-socialist government. The party leadership also behaved autocratically on occasions to silence criticism from outside, such as when Antall prosecuted the independent political analyst László Lengyel for slander in the summer of 1993 after he alleged that corruption within the government was widespread.

The HDF-led government was unpopular for most of its parliamentary term and in late 1992 and early 1993 the party was racked by serious internal dissent between the party's populist wing and the more moderate majority. This dissent was sparked in August 1992 by an article written by the party's then vice-president, István Csurka, who was also the leading figure on the party's populist wing, which appeared in the *Magyar Fórum* newspaper. In it Csurka argued that social tensions were being exacerbated because of the continued influence of former Communists in the country. Csurka attributed this continued power to an international conspiracy organized by liberals and former communists orchestrated in Paris, New York and Tel Aviv. He called for the purging of former communists from the state and for a government based on a more thorough application of Christian-national principles. In order to advance his cause Csurka founded the *Magyar Út*, a movement dedicated to promoting his ideas which attracted significant support from HDP members, though his initiative provoked strong criticism from István Elek and József Debreczeni on the party's liberal wing. At the HDF's conference in January 1993 Csurka's supporters gained five of the 20 places on the national executive.

After the conference, the leadership began to distance itself from Csurka. In March, Antall openly attacked Csurka in a newspaper interview arguing that he intended to seize power. Spring 1993 was marked by severe internal conflict between the party's populist and liberal wings which led the acting president, Lajos Für, to resign in exasperation in May. The dispute was finally settled in June with a wave of expulsions. In June 1993, István Csurka was expelled from the HDF parliamentary fraction along with three other right-wing deputies, Emil Bogdán, László Bognár and Lukács Szabó, and two liberals István Elek and József Debreczeni. A further wave of defections and expulsions, as well as the creation of the HJLP in July 1993 caused the size of the HDF parliamentary fraction to drop to just 136 members, 29 less than in May 1990. As a result, the government's parliamentary majority evaporated.

213

The situation stabilized in the autumn as concern about József Antall's health (he was seriously ill with cancer) grew. His death in December 1993 led to leadership changes in the HDF, but these seemed unlikely to lead to any change in the party's direction, at least before the May 1994 elections. Antall was replaced as Prime Minister by the Interior Minister, Péter Boross, who had deputised for Antall during his illness. Sándor Lezsák, assumed by most observers to be the main power-broker in the party, took over the position of executive president. At the party's conference in February 1994, Lajos Für, a representative of the conservative, national-Christian majority within the HDF, was elected as party president. The HDF approached the 1994 elections behind the HSP, the AYD and FIDESZ in opinion polls. It managed to gain sufficient nominations to stand candidates in 174 individual constituencies and on all the county lists, polling 11.73 per cent of the vote and winning 37 seats in parliament. Their strongest performances came from predominantly middle-class urban constituencies: the four individual constituency seats which they won were all in the relatively wealthy districts in western Budapest. Their votes came disproportionately from older voters.

The party received 255.5 million forints in state subsidies in 1993 and was allocated 8.06 million forints in subsidies for the 1994 elections. It planned to spend 231 million forints of its own resources on the campaign; more than any other party.

Programme. In its 1994 election manifesto, the HDF called for an economic recovery based on foreign investment and calls for improvements in infrastructure and more help for small businesses. It advocated a speedy end to the restitution process and more privatization, with the pharmaceutical industry high on its list. In social policy it regarded the family as the cornerstone of society and argues that mothers with four or more children should be given sufficient state support to make motherhood a full-time career. It favoured speedy integration into both NATO and the EU. It also believed that the church should be given a major role in education and, reflecting its role in the "media war", called for the media to serve the public interest and advocated the creation of a school to train unbiased journalists.

Organization. Delegates from local organizations meet at least annually in a National Assembly to appoint an 88-member Greater National Committee and the National Executive listed above. A Smaller National Committee is made up of the executive bodies of the county party organizations, its work being co-ordinated by a six-person executive committee from the National Executive.

Affiliations. It claims links with the European Democratic Union, the European Democratic Union, and the Centre Group of the Nordic Council (CENTERN), together with most conservative and Christian democratic parties of Europe.

Hungarian Employees' Party
Magyar Munkavállalók Pártja

Address. Budapest XX, Tájkép u. 23, H-1209.

Leadership. Márton Palásti (representative); Péter Antal (spokesman).

History. The party was founded in 1991 by several workers' council activists in order to promote the representation of employees in politics. Besides the information given above nothing is known about the party's structure, organization, programme or activities.

Hungarian Freedom Party
Magyar Szabadságpárt

Address. Budapest VII, Péterffy S. u. 42, H-1076.

Leadership. Sándor Bozsó (g. s. and exec. dep. leader).

History. The party registered on Dec. 14, 1989, as a Hungarian continuation of the Hungarian Freedom Party (*Magyar Szabadságpárt*) which had been formed on April 10, 1946, but which had not been a major force in politics and which had gone into emigration in the United States. It received 2 million forints state support in 1990 and participated in the draw for party political radio and television slots. No candidates reached the ballot in 1990 under its banner. It was still reported to be in existence in January 1994. The relationship with the Freedom Party, since merged with the ISP, is unclear.

Hungarian Gypsies Peace Party
Magyar Cigányok Béke Pártja

Address. Budapest VII, Dembinszky u. 2, H-1071.

Leadership. Albert Horváth (pres.)

Membership. 5,000 (April 1994).

History. The party is not registered with the authorities. It appears, however, to be a successor of the New Hungarians Justice, Gypsy party which was founded on Oct. 18, 1989, as a successor to the Party of Hungarian Gypsies, which the party's current president, Albert Horváth, also led. It received 7 million forints (approximately £51,000) state support in 1990. It fielded no candidates, however. It sees itself as a party of "new Hungarians" rather than gypsies and sees itself as representing the Hungarian majority within the gypsy community and differentiates itself from the Vlach minority. In the 1994 elections it managed to secure sufficient nominations to place a candidate onto the ballot in one individual constituency, but its candidate failed to gain sufficient votes to reach the second round.

Hungarian Health Party (HHP)
Magyar Egészség Párt (MEP)

Address. Budapest XI, Rimaszombati út. 3/b, H-1118.

Telephone. (1) 165 8748.

Leadership. Dr István Kajtár (pres.); Dr Edit Bereczki (organizational sec.).

History. The party was founded on Aug. 24, 1989, out of the Temperate Life Health and Family Protection National Alliance. The original president was Mihály Gergely, who in 1990 was part of the provisional leadership which also included Dr Lászlóz Berzsenyi, Ilona Bognár, Tibor Dezse, János Attila Eötvös, Dr Frigyes Funk and László Róbert. The party was originally based in Törökbálint, a village near Budapest, with its headquarters in a member's house. At some point Istvan Kajtár became the new president; and by the spring of 1991 the party had an address in Budapest (Budapest VI, Andrássy ut. 124) which it did not occupy, although someone occasionally came to collect the mail. Since 1991 the party has moved again to occupy the address given above. The party was sufficiently active in early 1990 to take part in the draw for party political broadcast radio and television slots, but did not get any candidates onto the ballot. In January 1994 the party was still reported to be active but failed to get any candidates onto the ballot for the May elections.

Programme. The party's programme emphasized the moral as well as political crisis occasioned by socialism, and placed great stress on the role of good health, social security, and the defence of the environment in this process.

Hungarian Humanists Party (HHUMP)
Magyar Humanisták Pártja (MHP)

Address. Kaposvár, Arany János utca 97, H-7400.

Telephone/Fax: (82) 416 000.

Leadership. László Landek (pres.); István Stier.

History. Founded in December 1989 in Kaposvár out of the Association of Hungarian Humanists, itself formed in June 1988. It received 2 million forints of state support in 1990, and closed the year with most of it (1.7 million, approximately £12,000) intact. Its activities since the election are unknown, and letters to its office are returned to sender. Despite this it was reported to be still in existence in January 1994.

Hungarian Independence Party (HIP)
Magyar Függetlenségi Párt (MFP)

Address. Budapest XIV, Kolumbusz u. 11, H-1145.

Telephone. (1) 183 6179, (1) 183 6706.

Foundation. January 1989.

Leadership. Gyula Szőnyi (pres.).

History. The party claims continuity with the party of the same name founded in August 1947 (which won 13.4 per cent of the vote in the 1947 elections) and briefly re-founded in 1956. In October 1989 it announced the republication of its paper *Ellenzék*, which was still being published in January 1990, but has since folded. It received 4 million forints of state support in 1989, and a further 4 million in 1990, in addition to 200,000 for the elections, which it entered as part of the National Alliance of Parties of the Centre. It ran four candidates and gained the least support of all the parties that got onto the regional list, a mere 0.04 per cent of the total vote, all recorded in Tolna county. The president abolished the party at the end of 1990, but other members of the National Committee excluded him from the party and in May 1991 were reported to have appealed to the Budapest courts to have the process to abolish the party set aside. They appear to have succeeded as the party was reported to be still in existence in January 1994, though it was run from the flat of the party's president (the address given above).

Programme. The party is on the nationalist-Christian end of the Hungarian political spectrum, propounding Christian values and stoutly defending the Hungarian minority in Transylvania. It is stronger on rhetoric — punctuating documents with slogans calling for God, Homeland, Freedom — and criticizing the former regime than on propounding new policies. In addition to calling for re-establishing private property and the abolition of monopolies, it advocated returning property to the basis of Oct. 6, 1944 when "foreign armies" first entered Hungary. This must refer to Soviet troops, since German troops occupied Hungary in March 1944. But this policy is then contradicted in the discussion of agricultural policy which implies returning land to the holding structure effective after the 1945 land reform. In health care it advocated a voucher system, and in education the introduction of optional religious education. It favoured military neutrality and the peaceful settlement of all disputes with its neighbours.

Hungarian Industrial Unity Party (HIUP)
Magyar Ipari Egység Párt (MIEP)

Address. Budapest X, Gyömröl út. 117, H-1108.

History. Registered on Feb. 12, 1990, with Tibor Novák as president. Nothing more is known about its activities or structure, though it was still reported to be in existence in January 1994.

Hungarian Interests Party
A Magyar Érdek Pártja

Address. (headquarters) Abony, Újszászi út. 18 fszt. 1, H-2740; (Budapest office) Budapest XIII, Széchényi rkp. 19, room 306.

Telephone. (1) 268 5554, 268 5564, 268 5989.

Fax. (1) 268 5989.

Foundation. October 1993, registered December 1993.

Leadership. Izabella B. Király (national pres.); Zsolt Alkay, István Sasvári, Sándor Tömöri (national vice-pres).

History. The party has its roots in the far-right wing of the HDF. The party's founder and national president, Izabella Király, had been elected as a HDF deputy on the Pest county list in 1990. She gained notoriety for her extreme right-wing views after claiming to be the spiritual mother of all Hungarian skinheads, whom she prefers to call "short-haired young men", and calling for the expulsion of gypsies from Hungary and the creation of a homeland for them in the Danube delta. She was expelled from the HDF in late June 1993 for her views and sat as an independent until she founded the Hungarian Interests Party in October. She claimed that the party was founded by former members of the HDF, the various Smallholders parties and "four short-haired young men" (skinheads). In the 1994 elections the party only gained sufficient nominations to contest a single constituency, at

Nagykörös in Pest county, where Király stood as the party's candidate and came in last place in the first round.

Programme. The party is on the ultra-nationalist extreme right of Hungarian politics. It calls for the revision of "Hungary's historical role here and abroad based on ancient history and historical facts".

Hungarian Jeans Party
Magyar Farmer Párt

History. The party was founded in March 1992 by 42 people in a factory at Csetény in Veszprém county in order to protect the interests of Hungarian jeans producers. It was subsequently registered with the authorities in May 1993. Nothing more is known about the party's organization, structure, activities or programme.

Hungarian Justice and Life Party (HJLP)
Magyar Igazság és Élet Pártja (MIÉP)

Address. Budapest V, Akadémia u. 3, H-1054.

Telephone. (1) 112 2822.

Fax. (1) 112 2822.

Leadership. Lajos Horváth (exec. pres.); István Csurka (co-pres.); János Kurucz Tóth (party dir.); National Executive members: Emil Bogdán, László Bognár (campaign dir.), Zoltán Deme, Pál Péter Marsi, Géza Polgárdi, Miklós Réti, Lukács Szabó; spokesman: Béla Győri.

History. The party was founded by István Csurka following his expulsion from the ruling HDF in July 1993 and thus has its roots in right-wing populism. At the time of the party's foundation Csurka was joined in the new party by the three former HDF parliamentary deputies who had been expelled with him, Emil Bogdán, László Bognár and Lukács Szabó, and further eight HDF deputies. In the 1994 parliamentary elections the party obtained sufficient nominations for its candidates to appear on the ballot in 66 individual constituencies, 11 of the 20 county lists and the national list, but only polled 1.58 per cent of the total vote and gained no seats in parliament. The party was awarded 4.68 million forints in state subsidy for the 1994 elections, and planned to spend a total of 15 million forints on the campaign.

Programme. The party's programme reflects its origins in the radical-populist wing of the HDF. It argues strongly for a national-Christian Hungary and calls for vigorous action to combat foreign influences. It advocates a thorough purge of all those who collaborated with the old regime and what it calls a real "change of system". It further calls for education to be conducted according to national and Christian values, tough restrictions to be placed on non-Hungarians owning property, greater social justice and measures to prevent the decline in living standards.

Affiliations. The party is believed to have close links with Hungarian emigré groups in the United States.

Hungarian Liberal People's Party (HLPP)
Magyar Liberális Néppárt (MLNP)

Address. Budapest VI, Dózsa György u. 80, H-1065.

History. The party was founded at the end of June 1989 with Sándor Sz. Nagy as president. It received 2 million forints state support in 1989 and 4 million in 1990. Despite taking part in the draw for party political broadcast radio and television slots, it failed to field any candidates in the parliamentary elections and nothing is known of its activities since then, although it was still reported to be in existence in January 1994.

Hungarian Market Party
Magyar Piacpárt

Address. Budapest XIII, Széchényi rkp. 19.V.500.

Telephone. (1) 268 5399.

Fax. (1) 268 5985.

Leadership. Dr István Balás (pres.).

History. The party has its origins in the spate of defections and expulsions from the right of the HDF in Summer 1993. The party was founded in September 1993 by four right-wing, former HDF parliamentary deputies, István Balás, István Halász, György Szilassy and Gyula Zacsek. Soon after its formation, the Hungarian Market Party's leadership came to an agreement with the Torgyán-led ISP by which their four deputies would join with Torgyán's eight deputies so they would gain the required number together to constitute a parliamentary fraction. In the 1994 elections the party gained sufficient nominations to appear on the ballot in eight individual constituencies and on the Fejér county list, but won only 0.01 per cent of the total vote and won no individual constituencies.

Programme. The party's programme reflects its origins in the right-wing of the HDF. It calls for a government guided by national-Christian values and calls for privatization to be conducted only according to national interests.

Hungarian Mothers National Party
Magyar Anyák Nemzeti Pártja

Address. Pápa, Kalvária u. 3. 11.2, H-8500.

Telephone. (89) 324 460.

Leadership. Ágnes Tell Sokorayné (pres.); Anna Tóth (sec.-gen.).

History. The party was founded in the provincial town of Pápa in 1992 by a group of young mothers who believed that, despite the promises of the major parties to support motherhood as an institution, they had done nothing. The party's programme stresses the need for an expansion of social policy which will create the conditions to make full-time motherhood a realistic option for women. Furthermore, they argue that government policy should be geared to restoring the prestige and responsibility of fathers as family heads. In the 1994 elections the party only gained sufficient nominations to contest one individual constituency but failed to gain sufficient votes to proceed to the second round.

Hungarian National Bourgeois Party
Magyar Nemzeti Polgári Párt

Address. Postfach 40, Budapest, H-1241.

Telephone. (1) 129 6453.

Leadership. Zoltán Hegyvári (pres.).

History. The party was registered in 1993 and listed Zoltán Hegyvári as its president. Nothing further is known about its structure, activities, organization or programme.

Hungarian National Party (HNP)
Magyar Nemzeti Párt (MNEMP)

Address. Budapest X, Népliget ut 4-Jurta Színház, H-1101.

Telephone. (1) 113 1280.

Leadership. István Balázs (pres.).

History. The party received 2 million forints state support for 1990 and figured in the draw for party political broadcast radio and television slots. It entered the 1990 elections as part of the Christian National Union which, soon after he gave an infamous anti-Semitic radio address, called for István Csurka to be brought into government. It failed, however, to get any candidates on the ballot. The address and telephone number above are those of the Jurta Theatre. In 1992 on the 73rd anniversary of the signing of the Trianon peace treaty the party organized a protest demonstration at Heroes Square in Budapest. The party was reported to be still in existence in January 1994.

Programme. The party is hard to track down as a physical entity, but it lets its name be associated with extreme right-wing positions. The views presented in *Szent Korona* (Holy Crown), a newspaper published by László Romhányi, president of the Jurta Theatre, which prints the party's name underneath the title, reject every aspect of the former system and accuse other parties of having fifth columnists from the communist party in their ranks, a line continued even after the elections, with crypto-communists being unearthed in all areas of life. In the early spring of 1991 the paper called for signatories to a petition demanding new elections. It describes the mainstream press as "liberal bolshevik". In a television interview, Romhanyi publicly identified himself with statements suggesting that the Jews were responsible for communism and for the Trianon treaty.

Hungarian October Party (HOP)
Magyar Október Párt (MOP)

Address. Budapest III, Juhász Gyula u. 14.IV. em. 13, H-1039.

Telephone. (1) 180 0253.

Foundation. June 27, 1989.

Leadership. Endre Csukás, Miklós Kónya, Alfred Scheidt, Pál Szegedy (committee members).

History. The party is very much associated with one man (György Krassó), a student leader in 1956, who figured prominently in all its activities. Nevertheless, it survived Krassó's death in March 1991. The party finally accepted 2 million forints state support in 1990, took part in the draw for party political broadcast radio and television slots, but received no additional support for the elections which it entered as the only member of the Christian National Centre (*Keresztény Nemzeti Centrum*). The party was very critical of the hurdles that had to be overcome to get candidates onto the ballot. Although four of its 21 prospective candidates received sufficient nominations to have qualified for the ballot, as a gesture of opposition to what they saw as an unfair system, the party burned the papers and returned their ashes instead to the electoral authorities. Since Krassó's death the party has been a shadow of its former self and is today run by a four-member leadership committee.

Programme. The party considers itself the only truly revolutionary party and the party of the streets. Its primary aim is to realize, by means of the will of the people, with the weapon of telling the truth against its enemies (violence, misery and falsehood), the aims (as it saw them) of the 1956 revolution: true people's power, freedom, prosperity, neutrality. It opposed the Opposition Round Table negotiations because it did not recognize the legitimacy of the HSWP. Immediately after the parliamentary elections it erected a tent on the grass in front of the parliament buildings, planning to remain there for four years as a further protest against the electoral law. It also organized a petition to bring the criminals of 1956 to justice; appointed George Bush an honorary party member; organized soup kitchens for the poor; and was a primary mover in campaigns to get street names with communist associations changed back to their original form. The most unusual of the party's early demands was that Hungarians living in the West should share equal rights with Hungarians living in Hungary, and hence not be subject to visa regulations. The party's prospective candidate for the presidential elections, which did not take place, was Sándor Rácz, leader of the Greater Budapest Workers' Council in 1956.

Hungarian People's Party (HPP), Hungarian People's Party – National Peasant Party Magyar Néppárt (MNP), Magyar Néppárt – Nemzeti Parasztpárt

Address. Budapest VIII, Baross utca 61, H-1082.

Telephone. (1) 113 4651, (1) 113 9092.

Foundation. March 8, 1989.

Leadership. Ferenc S. Szabó (hon. life pres.); Dr János Márton (pres.); Dr Károly Dobszay (g. s.); Dr Bálint Balogh (chief exec.).

Membership. No figures released in 1991, 30,000 were claimed in August 1989.

History. The party sees itself as a continuation of the National Peasant Party, established in December 1944 following its initial formation in 1939, which operated under the name Petőfi Party in 1956. Its immediate predecessor was the Péter Veres Association.

The party was significant enough in the spring of 1989 to be invited to take part in the Opposition Round Table negotiations. It interpreted the November 1989 referendum as an attack on the Opposition Round Table, however, and adhered to the government line. It received 10 million forints (approximately £73,000) in 1989, a further 10 million in 1990, with an additional 4.8 million for the elections. It ran only 45 candidates, despite claims in May 1989 to have organizations in every town and village in Hungary. Although this was sufficient for the party to figure on most regional lists and the national list, its total share of the vote (0.75 per cent) fell well below the 4 per cent barrier for entry into parliament. It still continues to exist, however, and in early 1994 it claimed between 3,000 and 5,000 members. It failed to get any candidates onto the ballot for the 1994 elections.

Programme. It was one of the few parties to keep a reference to the "Third Way" and Hungary's own way in its manifesto for 1990, which focused on agricultural and rural issues such as local government reform and a new land law. It sees itself as the party that understands the provincial "silent majority", and openly calls for a return to the situation at the beginning of the decade when agriculture was supported by the government.

The party's decline was the result of two factors. First, since the summer of 1989, when the HDF abandoned the notion, there was much less discussion nationally of the "Third Way". As a result, the HPP was left holding an idea whose time had passed. Second, the growth of the Agrarian Alliance and Hungary's Co-operative and Agrarian Party siphoned off some of the collective farm, village establishment constituency.

Organization. A Greater Council of 100 members made up of representatives from local organizations appoints an 18-member National Executive.

Hungarian Radical Party (HRP)
Magyar Radikális Párt (MRP)

Address. Budapest VII, Dózsa György u. 80/a, fsz 5, H-1071.

Leadership. Mihály Rózsa (honorary life pres.); Magnusz Tibor Tóth Vásáry (vice-pres.).; János Makovics (spokesman).

History. Founded on March 3, 1989, as a continuation of the party of the same name which was established in December 1944 but which received tiny shares of the popular vote in the 1945 and 1947 elections (0.2 per cent and 1.7 per cent respectively). The party received 1.3 million forints state support in 1989, 6.8 million in 1990, but none specifically for the elections, despite its participation in the draw for party political broadcast slots on radio and television. It failed to get any candidates onto the ballot, although it announced that it was entering the elections as part of the National Alliance of Parties of the Centre. Its programme called for "economic self-regulating pluralism", a social policy which prevented all from falling below the subsistence minimum, neutrality, and family-centred policies to help large families. Its activities since the 1990 elections are unknown. It was reported to be still in existence in January 1994.

Hungarian Realist Movement (HRM)
Magyar Realista Mozgalom (MRM)

Address. Budapest XVI, Döböce u. 38, H-1163.

History. Registered as a party on February 19, 1990. Nothing further is known about its structure or activities, though it was reported to be still in existence in January 1994.

Hungarian Republican Party
Magyar Republikánus Párt

Address. Budapest II, Buday László u. 5/c, H-1024.

Telephone/Fax. (1) 115 1018.

Leadership. Gergely Walcz (pres.).

History. It was registered as a party in 1990. In the same year the organization is listed as having received two million forints state support. For the 1994 elections it joined with Gyula Hernádi's Happiness Party to form the National Strength Movement, an electoral alliance, which gained sufficient nominations to put György Klutsik onto the ballot in the Budapest 27 constituency, but in the May election Klutsik failed to receive sufficient votes even to proceed to the second round.

Hungarian Royalist Party (HROP)
Magyar Legitimista Párt (MLP)

Address. Budapest XI, Élőpatak u. 29, H-1118.

Telephone. (1) 186 4135.

Leadership. László Pálos (pres.).

History. Founded on January 11, 1990, with László Pálos as president. It participated in the January 1990 draw for party political broadcast radio and TV slots. The party was still active in January 1994 and Pálos claimed that the party had 200 members. It advocates the restoration of the monarchy and argues that the House of Habsburg should return to take the Hungarian throne.

Hungarian Socialist Party (HSP)
Magyar Szocialista Párt (MSP)

Address. Budapest VIII, Köztársaság tér 26, H-1081.

Telephone. (1) 210 0046, 210 0011, 210 0078.

Fax. (1) 113 0817, 210 0011.

Foundation. October 7, 1989.

Leadership. Dr Gyula Horn (pres.); Imre Szekeres (exec. deputy pres., economic policy, campaign director); Ferenc Baja (deputy pres.); Dr György Jánosi (deputy pres., education and science policy); spokespersons — Sándor Csintalan (interest group policy), Gábor Kiss Gellért (cultural policy), László Kovács (foreign policy), Dr Mihály Kökény (social policy), Sándor Orosz (agricultural and village policy), András Tóth (party organization, internal party affairs); Zoltán Gál (leader in parliament).

Membership. 40,000 (January 1993).

History. The party is the direct descendant of the Hungarian Communist Party, which went through a number of guises during the war, merged with the HSDP in 1948 to form the Hungarian Workers Party and, following the revolution of 1956, rechristened itself the Hungarian Socialist Workers Party. Its history is virtually synonymous with post-1949 Hungarian history until the 14th Party Congress in October 1989 when it changed its name and accepted that it would relinquish its privileged "leading role".

Gyula Horn, a former Foreign Minister, took over from "father of economic reform", Rezső Nyers, as party president in May 1990. State support for the party was 19.6 million forints in 1989, 15 million in 1990 with an additional 9.5 million for the elections. It fielded 172 candidates and won a total of 33 seats. It adapted well to the role of an opposition party and the popularity of its president, Gyula Horn, exceeded that of the party for the whole of the parliament.

Despite the fact that it remained well behind the other major parties in the opinion polls until 1993, it performed well in by-elections, winning two of the five held between 1990 and 1994. This was more than any other party. Other than the defection of Imre Pozsgay in Autumn 1993 to form the NDA, there were no splits in the HSP, and the party's by-election performance ensured that when parliament was dissolved in April 1994 it had the same number of deputies as in May 1990. The party's standing in the opinion polls rose throughout 1993, overtaking FIDESZ and becoming the leading party in the polls by December. In early 1994 the party began to prepare for the election by concluding a series of electoral alliances with various social groups. The HSP promised leading figures in these groups a place on the party lists in exchange for their electoral support. To this end, in January 1994, the HSP signed an agreement with the National Association of Hungarian Pensioners and, most controversially, in February, it signed a pact with MSZOSZ, the former Communist trade union federation. This occasioned accusations from FIDESZ that the HSP was trying to create a left-wing block.

Throughout the spring of 1994 the HSP consolidated its opinion poll lead and its strength at the grassroots level is reflected in the fact that it was the only party with sufficient nominations to contest every seat in the country in the May 1994 elections. These confirmed its position as the country's strongest political force. It won 32.96 per cent of the votes cast and 209, or 54 per cent, of the seats in the new parliament. It won relative majorities in every county in the country, though was stronger in crisis ridden industrial areas like the steel town of Dunaújváros, where it won 49.7 per cent of the vote. Exit polls showed that it gained votes from across the social scale, though it performed relatively poorly among both the very young and very old. In 1993 it received 138.6 million forints in state support and was allocated a further 8.1 million forints to contest the elections. In addition the party planned to spend 200 million forints, the second highest figure for any party, on the campaign.

Programme. Since the change of name at the October 1989 Party Congress, the party has adopted social democratic policies and a commitment to mixed forms of property and the social market economy. It has inherited a number of private companies and foundations as a result of its past involvement in all aspects of Hungarian life.

The party contains a number of different tendencies which are organized into a variety of different party platforms. Among these are the Association of Socialist Believers, the Liberal Socialists, the Alliance for a Social Democratic HSP and the Left-Unity group. One key difference within the party, over economic policy, is reported to have come to a head in early 1994. This was between those closely associated with the former Finance Minister, László Békesi, who favoured a liberal economic policy, and the party president, Gyula Horn, an advocate of greater state intervention. Commentators attached much significance to the fact that, when the national list was drawn up for the elections, Békesi appeared in third place and not in the expected second place, and attributed this to the dispute.

The party's 1994 election manifesto, approved at a special conference in February 1994, affirmed its social democratic direction. Its economic policy called for a steady devaluation of the forint to re-establish Hungarian competitiveness, reduction in corporate and income taxes to be paid for by an increased capital gains tax, reduction of waste in the state budget, the re-establishment of parliamentary control over the State Property Agency and allowing local authorities to levy taxes. It advocated the development of environmentally friendly technology and calls for a threefold increase in conservation spending in order to cut air and water pollution. In social policy it argued for the maintenance of the value of the family allowance and called for increases in pensions. In foreign policy, it called for more co-operation between Hungary and its neighbours and for eventual EU membership.

Organization. At the local level the party consists of party communities, party organizations and regional associations. Delegates from the party organizations attend a congress which appoints a National Committee with 73 members. The latter appoints the National Executive listed above.

Affiliations. The party was given observer status by the Socialist International in 1992 and links are claimed with most socialist parties of Europe, the Socialist Group of the European Parliament, and the Confederation of the Socialist Party of the European Community.

Hungarian Socialist Workers Party, (HSWP)
Magyar Szocialista Munkáspárt, (MSZMP)

Address. Budapest XIV, Thököly út 126.11.3, H-1146.

Leadership. László Fazekas (sec.); Elémer Csaba, József Forizs (vice-secs).

History. The party was registered in 1993. It has its origins in a split within the Workers' Party, and was formed by a group of hardliners unhappy with the failure of the Workers' Party leadership to oppose what they saw as "the war against the working class" conducted by the national-Christian government. Nothing further is known about the party's structure or activities, except that in the 1994 elections one of its candidates gained sufficient nominations to contest an individual constituency.

Hungarian Unemployed Persons Party
Magyar Munkanélküliek Pártja

Address. Dunaújváros, Kohász u. 6.111/2, H-2400.

History. The party was founded in 1993 and subsequently registered with the authorities. In the 1994 elections it only received sufficient nominations to contest one individual constituency, though this candidate failed to receive sufficient votes to reach the second round. Nothing more is known about the party's structure or activities.

Hungarian Workers' Democratic Centre Party (HWDCP)
Magyar Dolgozók Demokratikus Centrum Párt (MDDCP)

Address. Tápiószele, Zoltán u. 1, H-2766.

History. The party was registered on Feb. 14, 1990, but nothing is known about its policies, history or leadership. It ran one candidate in the parliamentary elections (Tibor Majoros in Pest county) who received under 1,000 votes. It was still listed as existing in January 1994.

Hungary's Communists' Party (HCP)
Magyarországi Kommunisták Pártja (MKP)

Address. Budapest VIII, Práter u. 49, H-1083.

History. Founded on Dec. 8, 1989, with István Salga as provisional president, claiming to be a left-wing party "from below". Nothing is known of its structure and activities. It was still reported to be existing in January 1994.

Hungary's Green Party (HGP)
Magyarországi Zöld Párt (MZP)

Address. Budapest III, Kiskorona utca 3.

Telephone. (1) 168 8800.

Foundation. Nov. 8, 1989.

Leadership. Zoltán Medvecziki (pres.); Tibor Elekes (sec.).

Membership. 1,500 (May 1991).

History. The party emerged out of the large number of environmental groups (such as the Danube Circle, the Tisza Circle, the Green Circle, the Hungarian Nature Conservancy Alliance) which were instrumental in the political collapse of the old regime. Some of the regional branches are separately registered, and the Debrecen branch claims parentage in a Hungary's Regional Green Party (*Magyarországi Regionális Zöld Párt*). Many of the prominent figures of the environmental movement joined the AFD or FIDESZ when it came to expressing party allegiance. At the time of the parliamentary elections in 1990 it considered entering an alliance with the Hungarian Health Party and Voks Humana. It ran 14 candidates, figured on a number of regional lists, but not the national one. It received 0.36 per cent of the total vote, concentrated in four counties. The party fielded more candidates than expected for the local elections, but was no more successful in them.

Controversy erupted in the party in the summer of 1993, when the party's new president, Tibor Elekes, shifted the party dramatically to the right. He began to develop close contact with István Csurka's HJLP and the *Magyar Út* movement. As a result, many prominent environmentalists left the party to found the Green Alternatives. For the 1994 elections the party gained sufficient nominations to stand candidates in 19 individual constituencies, on seven county lists and on the national list, but polled only 0.16 per cent of the total vote. It was also allocated 1.61 million forints in state subsidy to contest the 1994 election.

Programme. The party favours a society based on ecological principles and local level democracy, a non-violent society in which all minority rights are guaranteed. More specifically, it advocates environmental taxation and supports animal rights. The element in its programme which distinguishes it from other European Green parties is its new commitment to right-wing nationalism. It argues, specifically, that international, and particularly Jewish, capitalism, is buying up Eastern Europe promoting environmental destruction and endemic over-consumption.

Organization. A congress of delegates from local organizations elects a 40-member Green Representation which elects an executive.

Affiliations. The shift to the right appears to have severely damaged the party's relations with other European Green parties.

Hungary's Indebted Citizen's Party
Magyarországi Adós Polgárok Pártja

Address. Budapest VIII, Práter u. 56, H-1083.

Leadership. József Gyurcsok (pres.); Zoltán Bíró (sec.).

History. The party is not registered with the authorities. Except for the information given above nothing is known about the party's structure, organization, activities or programme.

Hungary's Party of Curers of Nature and Reformers of Life
Magyarországi Természetgyógyászok és Életreformerek Pártja

Address. 1465 Budapest, Postfach 1751.

Leadership. József Andirkó (co-pres.).

History. The party was founded in Debrecen on Dec. 9, 1993, and listed its goal as making nature conservation a major political issue in Hungary. All that is known about the party, besides the information given above, is that in the 1994 elections it gained sufficient nominations to contest two individual constituencies, though both of these candidates failed to gain sufficient votes to proceed to the second round.

Hungary's Party of Transylvanian Hungarians (HPTH)
Érdely Magyarok Magyarországi Pártja (EMMP)

Address. Miskolc, Rákóczi út. 14, H-3525.

History. The party was registered on Jan. 15, 1990, in the provincial town of Miskolc and founded in either late November or early December 1989. Its president is registered as

Vilmos Kakuszi, but further details about its structure and activities are unknown. It was reported to be still in existence in January 1994.

Hungary's Social Democratic (Centre) Party
Magyarországi Szociáldemokrata (Centrum) Párt

Address. 1384 Budapest, 62, Postfach 61.

History. This party is not registered with the authorities. The only information which can be found is that its leadership consists of a four-member committee.

Hungary's Social Democratic Party (HSDP)
Magyarországi Sociáldemokrata Párt (MSZDP)

Address. Budapest VII, Dohány u. 76, H-1074.

Telephone. (1) 121 5400, 142 2385.

Fax. (1) 121 4442.

Foundation. January 9, 1989.

Membership. 23,000 (May 1991).

Leadership. Andor Bölcsföldi (hon. pres.); Zoltán Király (pres.); Dr Endre Borbely (dep. pres.); István Podkoniczky (g. s.).

History. Hungary's Social Democratic Party (HSDP) was first formed Dec. 7, 1890, was reorganized on Dec. 21, 1944, merged with the Communists on June 12, 1948, existed briefly again as an independent party in 1956 and re-founded finally on Jan. 9, 1989. The party has been plagued with internal conflicts around personalities rather than policies. Despite spending the summer and autumn of 1989 papering over the cracks, it finally split at its conference on Nov. 6, 1989, when the Independent Social Democratic Party and the Social Democratic Party were formed. Attempts to resurrect the party's paper, *Sociáldemokrata Népszava*, were unsuccessful, although some trial issues appeared. The party received active encouragement from Europe's social democratic parties, and figured on most regional lists together with the national one. It fielded 76 candidates, but none was elected. Following the party's poor electoral showing, there were rumours that Petrasovits, its then rather controversial woman leader, had attempted suicide.

Throughout 1991, 1992 and 1993 the party continued to suffer from serious internal problems. These were solved, at least temporarily, in October 1993 when the HSDP merged with both the Independent Social Democratic Party and Social Democratic Peoples Party, but not the Social Democratic Party (SDP), under the leadership of Zoltán Király. Király, who had been an independent member of parliament in the socialist years, had originally been elected to parliament as an independent with HDF support for a Szeged constituency in 1990. He subsequently formed the Social Democratic People's Party. The new social democratic unity seemed fragile, however, when members of the Social Democratic old guard began to organize the "Anna Kethly" platform in early 1994. In the 1994 elections the party gained sufficient nominations to contest 53 individual constituencies, 15 of the 20 counties and the national list. The party suffered a crushing defeat, however, polling only 0.95 per cent of the vote, whilst the party leader, Zoltán Király polled just over 7 per cent of the vote in his own Szeged constituency. Given the fragile unity of the party it seems that in the near future the party will be severely shaken by further internal convulsions. The party was allocated 4.48 million forints in state support to contest the elections and planned to spend 15 million forints from its own resources on the campaign.

Programme. The new party president, Zoltán Király claims that the party is to the left of the HSP. The party's programme advocates the traditional social democratic notions of a mixed economy, but with social provision provided on a non-market basis. Party programme statements are rarely more detailed than reiterating the principles of social democracy.

Organization. A congress of delegates from local organizations appoints a committee with 101 members and a 27-member National Leadership.

Affiliations. Links are claimed with the Socialist International and socialist parties of Europe and the rest of the world, though largely due to the HSDP's disarray these parties have increasingly concentrated their attention on the HSP.

Independent "Ferenc Deak" Electoral Alliance
Függetlenek "Deák Ferenc" Választási Szövetsége

Address. Budapest, Király u. 93.

Telephone. (1) 142 7537, 269 7991.

Fax. (1) 269 7991.

Leadership. Dr Mihály Tarcsai (pres. and spokesman).

History. This organization is not registered as a political party with the authorities. Apart from the information provided above nothing is known about the party's structure, organization, activities or programme.

Independent Hungarian Democratic Party (IHDP)
Független Magyar Demokrata Párt (FMDP)

Address. Budapest V, Nádor u. 36, H-1051.

Telephone. (1) 131 7550/1319.

Fax. (1) 153 0042.

Foundation. May 5, 1989.

Leadership. Gyula Kövár (pres.); Dr Korosi Imre (deputy pres.); János Dolmány, Attila Földváry, József Németh, László Neveri (national executive committee members).

History. The party is a re-foundation of the party of the same name led by Father Balogh that operated between June 1947 and 1951. In the November 1989 referendum it supported the anti-government line. It entered the elections in association with the National Alliance of Parties of the Centre. It ran three candidates, but received only 0.06 per cent of the vote (all votes coming in Komáron-Estergom county where it figured on the regional list), so excluding it from parliament and from further state funding. Its activities since the elections are unknown. At its height, it was publishing a Sunday paper entitled *Hungarian Sunday (Magyar Vasárnap)*, edited by Sándor Ambrus; but by the spring of 1991 the newspaper had folded. The party is rumoured to have had connections at various times with the HDF-led government, the ISP and the Workers' Party and to have had close links with the former HDF deputy Imre Korosi. In the 1994 elections, however, it managed to gain sufficient nominations to field candidates in three individual constituencies in its own right, though it did not appear on any of the county lists. None of these candidates received sufficient votes to proceed to the second round.

Programme. Agriculture figured prominently in its 1990 programme, with calls for a market in land, agrarian banks, the disbanding of bureaucratic bodies associated with collectivized agriculture, higher pensions and an improved infrastructure. More generally it called for tax concessions for investors, an ending to technical backwardness, new property relations, an independent banking system, democratic education free from party interference, and freedom of religion.

Independent Liberal Party
Független Liberális Párt (FLP)

Address. Budapest VI, Paulay Endre u. 16, H-1061.

Telephone/Fax. (1) 122 7908.

Leadership. Sándor Sz. Nagy (pres.).

History. The party was founded in 1991 and is registered. The party is known to have contact with both the Hungarian Peoples Party and the ex-smallholder Conservative Party, and has attempted to establish links with the liberal parties in parliament. Apart from the information given above nothing is known about the party's structure, organization, activities or programme.

Independent Smallholder, Land Labourer and Citizens' Party (ISP), Smallholders' Party
Független Kisgazda-, Földmunkás és Polgári Párt (FKgP), Kisgazda Párt

Address. Budapest V, Belgrád Rakpárt 24, H-1056.

Telephone. (1) 118 2855, 118 1824, 118 1434.

Foundation. October 1930, Oct. 28, 1956, Nov. 12, 1988 in Szentendre, Nov. 18, 1988 in Budapest.

Leadership. Dr József Torgyán (pres); Géza Gyimóthy (sec.-gen.); Dr Sándor Kavassy (first vice-pres.); István Bakos, Ágnes Maczó, Dr Sándor Győriványi, József István, Sándor Szabó, Dr Ferenc Virág (vice-pres).

Membership. 50,000 (January 1993).

History. The party has suffered from much schism and factional fighting. In February 1989 it expelled four members, in March it allowed them back in again, and in April it declared itself whole again, but just before the elections the National Smallholders' Party split away. For the 1990 election the party fielded 163 candidates and won a total of 44 seats. Like the other major parties, it has a foundation and public limited company closely associated with members of the leadership — the ISP Electoral Foundation and Hangya plc.

Factionalism continued after the parliamentary elections. The summer of 1990 was spent persuading the government to introduce the party's central policy goal: the return of land to its owners of 1947 or their heirs. Over the remainder of 1990, however, and during the first half of 1991, it became clear that restitution would not take the form of the direct return of agricultural land. The Smallholders had been outmanoeuvred by appeals to the Constitutional Court. Meanwhile, József Torgyán, demagogic leader of the party in parliament until the spring of 1991, caused a furore by getting himself elected (at a possibly inquorate meeting) joint president of the party. The leadership crisis this occasioned was resolved at a special Committee meeting on June 29, 1991, when Torgyán was elected sole president.

Previously, former president Ferenc József Nagy had stated that Torgyán's confirmation as president would split the party. His election succeeded both in doing just that and in causing major strains within the governing coalition. Almost as soon as he had been confirmed president, Torgyán began to oppose the compromise Restitution Bill strongly, although it was eventually passed by parliament in June 1991 with the backing of ISP members of the government. He also began to attack the position of former communists in the privatization process. During autumn 1991 a feud developed between the majority in the ISP parliamentary faction and Torgyán as he threatened to withdraw the ISP's support for the government. At this time the Hajdú Bihar county organization took the unprecedented step of disassociating itself from the party leadership, a step which would eventually lead to the formation of the Reconciled Smallholders' Party in October 1993. At the same time the ISP veteran Tivadar Pártay denounced Torgyán as "paranoid megalomaniac".

By the end of 1991 it was clear that the ISP had almost ceased to function as a party: the largest group in parliament, with 33 deputies, opposed Torgyán. In February 1992 Torgyán formally announced the withdrawal of the ISP from the coalition and the 33 deputies who remained loyal to it were expelled from the party. By August 1992 the ISP parliamentary fraction fell below 10 members, due to defections and deaths, and so lost its right to constitute a fraction in parliament. It only managed to recover its earlier position in the autumn of 1993 through an alliance with the right-wing Hungarian Market Party.

By summer 1993 Torgyán found himself in competition with five other Smallholders' parties. As a result he attempted to found the Torgyán Party in early autumn 1993 in an attempt to help obtain the largest number of votes for the party in the 1994 elections. When the party was refused registration on the grounds that it was illegal to name a party after a living individual, Torgyán complained arguing that his civil rights had been infringed. He did, however, manage to register the party successfully as the Torgyanist Hungarian Future Party. Torgyán also attempted a number of strategies to broaden the electoral base of the ISP, unifying with the Freedom Party in November 1992, concluding an alliance with the 1956 League led by Sándor Rácz in 1993 and, to emphasize his nationalist credentials, holding a joint rally with István Csurka in the Budapest Sportcsarnok in February 1994.

In the 1994 elections the party gained sufficient nominations to stand candidates in 156 individual constituencies, in all 20 counties and on the national list. The party won 8.85 per cent of the votes cast and 26 seats in the new parliament. The party attracted substantial support from older voters, those with only elementary education, and men, who made up 64 per cent of the party's electorate. The party received 144.4 million forints in state subsidies in 1993 and was allocated 7.72 million forints for the 1994 elections.

Programme. The party continues to reject the now virtually completed restitution process in favour of the reprivatization of land on the basis of 1947. It also advocates rapid privatization, although with barriers against foreign ownership, low taxation to encourage entrepreneurship, negotiations to ease the burden of foreign debt, and the recreation of moral values with compulsory religious education in schools. A policy which strikes a particular chord with the disadvantaged is its call for the "calling to account" of all those who benefited under privatization. Former apparatchiks who converted political power into economic capital should be deprived of their gains. The party also demands constitutional reform, preferring a bicameral legislature and, more important, members of parliament and local councillors subject to recall.

Organization. A National Committee, made up of delegates from the local organizations, appoints a Political Committee of 20 members plus the leadership listed above as *ex officio* members.

Left Wing Revision Party (LWRP)
Baloldali Revízió Pártja (BRP)

Address. Budapest IX, Napfény u. 6, földszint, H-1098.

Foundation. Beginning January 1991.

Leadership. Dr István Punyi (rep.).

History. With a membership of 13 in 1991, the party was never going to be a force in Hungarian politics. However, it was prominent enough in January 1990 to participate in the draw for television and radio slots for party political broadcasts. Nothing is known of the party's current activities but it was reported to be still in existence in January 1994.

National 1956 Revolutionary Political Youth Party
Országos 1956-os Forradalmi Politkai Ifúsági Párt

History. Nothing is known about this party except that its president was listed as Bernát Holczinger Jr. in January 1994.

National Alliance of Hungarian Families, Family Alliance
Magyar Családok Országos Szövetsége, Családi Szövetség

Address. Szigetszentmiklos, Bercsenyi út. 14, H-2310.

Leadership. József Szabó Urbán (pres.); Ádám Eliás (nat. sec.).

History. The party was founded on July 2, 1993, in Sziget Szentmiklós. In the 1994 elections the party's candidates received sufficient nominations to contest five individual constituencies, though none gained sufficient nominations to proceed to the second round. Nothing more is known about the party's structure, organization, activities or programme.

National Alliance of Smallholders, Small Industrialists, Small Businessmen and the Intelligentsia
Kisgazdák – Kisiparosok – Kiskereskedó/k – Értelmiségiek Nemzeti Szövetsége

Address. Budapest VI, Vörösmarty u. 44/a, H-1064.

Telephone. (1) 112 6781.

Leadership. Ferenc Bajczi (pres.).

History. The party was registered in September 1993. Apart from the information given above nothing is known about its organization, structure, activities or programme.

National Democratic Alliance (NDA)
Nemzeti Demokrata Szövetség (NDSZ)

Address. Budapest VIII, Irányi u. 17, H-1056.

Telephone/Fax. (1) 118 0182, 118 0338.

Leadership. Imre Pozsgay (pres.); Zoltán Bíró (co-pres.).

History. The party was formed in late 1990 following the taxi drivers' blockade by Imre Poszgay, formerly a leading figure in the HSP and the most prominent reformer in the HSWP in the late 1980s, and Zoltán Bíró, the first president of the HDF, who left the party in protest against its shift to the right. Its stated objective was to provide a home for the large number of disillusioned Hungarians (believed by many commentators to be social democratic in orientation) who had failed to vote in the local elections. The party, however, failed to become a major force and by 1993, Pozsgay, though still a member of parliament, had taken a teaching job at the Lajos Kossuth university in Debrecen. In the 1994 parliamentary elections the party received sufficient nominations to contest 58 individual constituencies, to stand candidates on 12 out of the 20 county lists and to appear on the national list, but polled only 0.52 per cent of the vote and failed to win any seats in parliament. It was due to receive 4.03 million forints in state support for the 1994 elections, but only planned to spend 1 million forints of its own resources on the campaign.

Programme. The party positions itself firmly on the centre-left of Hungarian politics arguing for a parliamentary democracy and a mixed economy with a strong social welfare component. The party's distinctive feature is that it argues that a healthy commitment to national values is not incompatible with a commitment to democratic left-wing ideals.

National Movement against Impoverishment
Elszegényedésellenes Nemzeti Mozgalom (EL-NEMO)

Address. Óföldeák, Széchényi u. 38, H-6923.

Founder. József Gulyás.

History. This party was founded on March 10, 1992. Apart from the information given above nothing is known about the party's organization, structure, programme or activities.

National Party of Pensioners in an Unfavourable Situation
Hátrányos Helyzetű Nyugdíjasok Országos Pártja (HANYOP)

Address. Budapest, Pf. 773, H-1462.

History. This party is not registered with the authorities. Apart from the information provided above no information is available on the structure, organization, programme or activities of this party.

National Radical Unity
Nemzeti Radikális Egység

Address. Debrecen, Varga u. 34, H-4024.

Leadership. László Bakó (pres.); János Makar (g. s.).

History. This party is not registered with the authorities. Apart from the information given above nothing is known about the party's structure, organization, programme or activities.

National Reconstruction Party (NRP)
Nemzeti Újjáépítés Pártja (NUP)

Address. Budapest I, Iskola u. 38–42, H-1011.

Leadership. Dr Bertalan Tóth (g. s.).

History. Nothing is known of this party other than that it was registered on Feb. 20, 1990, and that it was still reported to be in existence in January 1994.

National Smallholder and Bourgeois Party (NSBP)
Nemzeti Kisgazda és Polgári Párt (NKgPP)

Address. (headquarters) Szeged, Lechner tér. 13, H-6721; (Budapest office) Budapest XXII, Kossuth Lajos u. 60, H-1221.

Telephone. (headquarters) (62) 12 370, 12 844; (Budapest office) (1) 226 6140.

Leadership. Dr István Szeghő (pres.); Dr Pál Ádám, Dr György Pálos (vice-pres); Dr Imre Boross (g. s.).

History. Established in Szeged on Dec. 29, 1989, resulting from a split within the ISP. The split was not ideologically inspired, although the new party was accused of being "left wing". It participated in the ballot for party political broadcast radio and television slots, received 4 million forints state support in 1990, with a further 700,000 forints specifically for the elections. It entered the elections as a member of the National Electoral Alliance, fielded 13 candidates, sufficient to get onto the regional list in Heves, Csongrád and Nógrád counties, but achieved only 0.2 per cent of the vote. It claimed, in January 1991, to be going on the offensive, despite newspaper reports that its office address was being used by a local painter to run a sexual services business.

During the period following Torgyán's election as president of the ISP and the subsequent political turmoil within the Smallholder movement the party frequently figured in plans to unify the anti-Torgyán Smallholder parties, although in November 1992 Torgyán was announcing that plans to unify his official party with the National Smallholders were under way. In December 1993, moves by the party leadership led by the general secretary to unify with the anti-Torgyán parliamentary fraction in the USP provoked serious internal conflict within the party, leading to the, at least temporary, suspension of moves toward the unification of the party organization. Despite this, some of the party's leaders stood on the USP ticket in the 1994 elections; the party's president Dr István Szeghő headed the USP county list in Csongrád county. In early 1994 there was rumoured to be a steady stream of members leaving the party for the Agrarian Alliance. The party's programme follows the mainstream ISP line on most issues.

National Strength Movement (NSM party)
Nemzeti Erők Mozgalom (NEM part)

Address. Budapest II, Buday L. u. 5/c, H-1024.

Telephone/Fax. (1) 115 1018.

Leadership. György Kassa (pres.); Gyula Hernádi, Imre Oláh (co-pres.).

History. This organization is an electoral alliance between the Happiness Party of Gyula Hernádi and the Hungarian Republican Party designed to contest the 1994 elections. Only one of its candidates, György Klutsik, managed to receive sufficient nominations to contest an individual constituency (Budapest 27), although Klutsik failed to win sufficient votes to proceed to the second round.

Party for the Defence of the Family and Children
Család és Gyermekvédők Pártja

Address. Budapest VII, Osvát u. 3, H-1073.

Leadership. József Povisel (pres.).

History. The party was founded in 1993 and subsequently registered with the authorities. The party declares that its aims are similar to those expressed in the European Social Charter and the United Nations' declaration of children's rights. Its programme calls for the strengthening of the child protection law and the amendment of the family code in order to give higher priority to the balanced development of children.

Party of Hungarian Unity
Magyar Egység Pártja

Address. Budapest XIV, Hungaria körút 157/b, H-1146.

Telephone. (1) 121 7225.

Leadership. Dr János Lenkei (representative).

History. The party was registered on Sept. 3, 1993. Apart from the information listed above nothing is known about its structure, organization, programme or activities.

Party of Republican Youth (PRY)
Republikánus Fiatalok Pártja (RFP)

Address. Budapest III, Kiscelli ut. 4, H-1032.

History. Nothing is known about this party other than that it was registered on Feb. 20, 1990, as party representing young people. It was reported to be still in existence in January 1994.

Party of Small Entrepreneurs, Bourgeois Alliance
Kisvállalkozók Pártja, Polgári Szövetség

Address. Fot, Németh Kálmán u. 50/b, H-2151.

Leadership. József Habina (pres.).

History. The party was founded in 1992 and subsequently registered with the authorities. None of its candidates received sufficient nominations to get onto the ballot, however, in the 1994 elections. Nothing more is known about the party's structure and activities.

Party of Solidarity with Hungarian Gypsies
Cigányok Magyarországi Szolidaritási Pártja

Address. Budapest VIII, Tavaszmező u. 6, H-1084.

Telephone. (1) 134 0560.

Leadership. Béla Osztojkán (pres.).

History. The party is not registered with the authorities. In the 1994 elections, however, four of its candidates gained sufficient nominations to contest individual constituencies. Nothing more is known about the party's structure or activities.

Party of the Hungarian Republican Poor
Magyar Republikánus Szegények Pártja

Address. Győr, Árpád u. 2.11/203, H-9021.

Telephone. (96) 313 364.

Leadership. János Horváth (pres.); Éva Lakatos (vice-pres.); László Sarmaság (g. s.).

History. The party was registered with the authorities in 1990. Apart from the information listed above nothing is known about its structure, organization, programme or activities.

Party of Transylvanian Hungarians in Hungary
Érdelyi Magyarok Magyarországi Pártja

Address. Miskolc, Rákóczi u. 14, H-3530.

History. The party was founded in 1990 and was subsequently registered with the authorities. It was still reported to be active in January 1994 though none of its candidates gained sufficient nominations to appear on the ballot in the 1994 elections.

Pensioners' Party
Nyugdíjasok Pártja

Address. Budapest XIII, Kresz G. u. 6, H-1132.

Telephone. (1) 111 1971.

Leadership. Dr Vilmos Michaletzky (pres.); Dr Gyula Pinter (vice-pres.).

History. The party was founded in 1990 and subsequently registered with the authorities as a party representing the interests of pensioners. The party claims 5,000 members and calls for the representation of old people's national, Christian and social interests. Its programme calls for the inflation indexing of pensions and the speedy completion of the restitution process for the old. In the 1994 elections one of its candidates gained sufficient nominations to contest an individual constituency, though insufficient votes to proceed to the second round.

People of the East Party Christian Democrats (PEPCD)
Kelet Népe Párt Kereszténydemokraták (KNPKD)

Address. Budapest VII, Péterffy Sándor utca 42, H-1076.

Telephone. (1) 141 5437.

Leadership. Frigyes Szent-Tamási (pres.); Dr László Vertessy (deputy pres.); Dr János K. Bartha, László Bogdányi (vice-pres); János Csuport (g. s.).

Membership. 10,000 claimed (implausibly) May 1991.

History. Although the party received 4 million forints (approximately £29,000) state support in 1990, it received no funds for the elections and successfully fielded only one candidate (István Bukovics) who received votes from less than half the number of people who had nominated him. The party was reported to be still in existence in January 1994 though fielded no candidates for the election. Its current activities are unknown.

Programme. The party is at the nationalist end of the spectrum, with specific policies for Transylvania. It advocates: an independent and free Hungary which achieves a moderately democratic bourgeois democracy, a bi-cameral constitutional monarchy, an independent Transylvania built on the union of the three nations, autonomy for areas inhabited by Hungarians which were formerly parts of Hungary, a national economy based on radical property relations, a 35-hour week, and education in the spirit of Christian and Hungarian values. No foreign or domestic affiliations are listed.

People's Will Party (PWP)
NépAkarat (sic) Párt (NAP)

Address. Dunaharazti, Klapka u. 20, H-2330.

Leadership. János Maczó (pres.).

History. The party was registered in 1990 though nothing is known of its activities or structure, other than that the president's name is János Maczó. Its programme calls for the increasing use of referenda in public life. Nevertheless, it filed accounts for 1990 showing a deficit of 46,173 forints (approximately £340) on the basis of a total income, mainly from membership fees, of 5,900 forints (approximately £43). The party was reported to be still in existence in January 1994.

Private Entrepreneurs Party
Magánvállalkozók Pártja

Address. Budapest IX, Lónyay u. 54/b, H-1093.

Telephone. (1) 218 7077/113, 123.

Leadership. Lajos Tuli (pres.); János Gyovai, László Oláh, Erzsébet Demeter Servokkné (vice-pres).

History. The party was founded in 1993 and was subsequently registered with the authorities. It fielded no candidates in the 1994 elections and nothing is known about its current activities or programme.

Reconciled Independent Smallholders Party (RISP)
Kiegyezés Független Kisgazdapárt (KFKP)

Address. Budapest XIII, Hegedűs Gyula u. 45-7, H-1136.

Telephone. (1) 149 0973, 149 7792.

Foundation. October 1993.

Leadership. Sándor Cseh (pres.); Sándor Szabó (g. s.).

History. The origins of the party lie in autumn 1991 when the Hajdú-Bihar county organization of the ISP disassociated itself from both the party's controversial president,

József Torgyán, and the parliamentary fraction claiming that both of them were bringing the party into disrepute. The party was founded two years later in October 1993 by Sándor Cseh, president of the ISP in Hajdú-Bihar county and a former vice-president of the national organization. In the 1994 elections it gained sufficient nominations to appear on two county lists and to stand candidates in seven constituencies, achieving 0.11 per cent of the total vote though winning no seats in parliament.

Programme. The party's president, Sándor Cseh, claims that the party is part of the broader Smallholder movement. He states that no major ideological or policy differences, only style of leadership, separate it from the other Smallholders parties.

Red-White-Greens Party
Piros-Fehér-Zöldek Partja

History. The party was registered with the authorities in 1993. It was formed as a result of a split within Hungary's Green Party in Summer 1993. The new party claims to link the Green Alternatives, the Hungarian Health Party and the national anti-smoking campaign. It states that in its name the red stands for a strong democracy, the white for its purity and the green for health. These are also the colours of the Hungarian flag.

Republic Party
Köztársaság Párt

Address. Budapest VIII, Szentkirály u. 8, H-1088.

Telephone. (1) 138 3744/141.

Fax. (1) 138 4642.

Leadership. János Palotás (pres.); Dr András Veer (exec. pres.); Dr Péter Barandy, Dr László Fodor (vice-pres.); László Takács (party dir.).

History. The party is very much a personal creation of the party's president, János Palotás, one of the most colourful and popular figures in Hungarian politics. Palotás, a successful businessman, was elected to parliament as an independent with the support of the HDF in the 1990 elections. He very quickly became alienated from the HDF, criticizing both its economic policy and its ideological anti-Communism. Palotás left the HDF fraction in March 1992 and together with Mihály Mozes, who left the AFD in June, founded the Republic Party in November 1992. In early 1993 Palotás rose in the opinion polls to become the most popular politician in the country, but by the end of the year this popularity seemed to have worn off. During early 1994 opinion polls suggested his party was close to, but just below, the new 5 per cent barrier required to obtain seats in the proportionally elected section of parliament. In the 1994 elections the party obtained sufficient nominations for 84 of its candidates to appear on the ballot in individual constituencies, to enter lists in 17 of the 20 counties and appear on the national list. However, it polled only 2.53 per cent of the vote and its leader, Palotás, was defeated in his own constituency in the second round by the HSP candidate. The party was allocated 5.81 million forints in state subsidy to contest the 1994 elections.

Programme. The party is on the liberal centre-left end of the political spectrum. The party president, János Palotás, has made no secret of his admiration for the HSP president, Gyula Horn, though in the second round of the May 1994 some local branches backed the local AFD candidates. The party advocates policies to promote business such as lower taxes, privatization and the continued restructuring of industry. It also calls for reform of government to reduce corruption and to introduce an Anglo-American notion of public service into the bureaucracy.

Organization. The party is governed by a leadership committee consisting of the president, executive president, the two vice-presidents and the party general secretary.

Republican National Party (RNP)
Republikánus Nemzeti Párt (RNP)

Address. Budapest VII, Dembinszky u. 41, H-1071.

Leadership. Dr Tamás Banovics.

History. Founded on Oct. 21, 1989, with Dr József Banovics as president. Nothing more is known about the party, other than a newspaper report that it opposed government measures in November 1989 to introduce foreign currency controls. It was reported to be still in existence in January 1994.

Romany Parliament Electoral Alliance (RP)
Roma Parlament Választási Szövetség (RP)

Address. Budapest VIII, Tavaszmező/ utca 6, Hungary.

Telephone. (1) 113 1887.

Leadership. Aladár Horváth (pres.); János Bogdán, Tibor Oláh (vice-pres); Jenő Zsigó (spokesman).

History. Although not registered as a political party, this body was reportedly created out of a number of smaller gypsy parties and interest groups. Its president, Aladár Horváth, was elected to parliament in 1990 on the AFD's national list and has constantly drawn attention to the difficulties faced by gypsies in the light of the rise of the far-right and police racism. It sees its role as co-operating with the liberal and centre-left opposition in parliament. In the 1994 elections it stood no candidates in its own right but sought to persuade other parties to attempt to increase gypsy representation in parliament.

Small Pensioners' Party (SPP)
Kisnyugdíjasok Pártja (KNYP)

Address. Budapest VIII, Rákóczi ter. 2, H-1084.

History. The party was registered on Feb. 1, 1990, with Dr József Buzas as president. Its structure and activities are unknown, though it was reported as still being in existence in January 1994.

Social Democratic Party (SDP)
Szociáldemokrata Párt (SZDP)

Address. Budapest VIII, Baross utca 61, Hungary.

Telephone. (1) 133 7983.

Leadership. Imre Takács (pres. and spokesperson).

History. The party was originally founded in Diosd on Nov. 6, 1989, as a break-away from Hungary's Social Democratic Party. It received 7 million forints state support in 1990, but none for the parliamentary elections and none subsequently. It entered the elections as part of the National Alliance of Centre Parties and participated in the draw for party political broadcast radio and TV slots, but did not succeed in getting any candidates onto the ballot. It was not included in the merger which relaunched the HSDP in October 1993 and in the 1994 elections its candidates appeared on the ballot in three individual constituencies.

Organization. A Committee of local organizations appoints a 15-member National Leadership.

Social Democratic Party of Hungary's Gypsies (SDPHG)
Magyarországi Cigányok Szociáldemokrata Pártja (MCSZDP)

Address. Budapest VII, Dohány u. 76, H-1077.

Telephone. (1) 112 8161.

Leadership. Pál Farkas (pres.).

History. Founded on Oct. 1, 1989, with Pál Farkas as president as an off-shoot from Hungary's Social Democratic party, it received 10 million forints state aid in 1990. It got one candidate onto the ballot for the parliamentary election (Csemer Elemér in Nográd county) who received fewer votes than the number of signatures necessary to nominate him. The party was a signatory to a petition to the German ambassador in Hungary in November 1990, but by the spring of 1991 it was believed to have merged into the Romany Parliament. Despite this there were reports that the party was still separate in January 1994.

Torgyanist Hungarian Future Party
Torgyáni Magyar Jövő Párt

History. This party is the successor to the Torgyán Party which was founded in the autumn of 1993. The party was created by the controversial ISP president, József Torgyán, as a way of differentiating the ISP from the other Smallholders. The idea was that the Torgyán Party should stand alongside the ISP in every constituency and so pull in the maximum number of votes. Torgyán appointed his wife president of the party and his face became its symbol. In September, however, the Budapest courts refused to register the Torgyán Party on the grounds that a party which used the proper name of a living person in its title could not be legally registered. A furious Torgyán accused the court of violating his civil rights, but later re-submitted its application under the new name of the Torgyánist Hungarian Future Party. This name change was accepted. Despite this, the party ran no candidates in the 1994 elections.

United Smallholders' Party (USP)
Egyesült Kisgazdapárt (EKgP)

Address. Budapest VI, Jókai u. 34, H-1065.

Telephone. (1) 132 2900, 131 2742.

Foundation. Nov. 16, 1993, registered March 1994.

Leadership. János Szabó (pres.); István Boroczs (exec. deputy pres.); Lásló Horváth, Gyula Kiss, Zsolt Rajkai (deputy pres); Antal Bélafi (g. s.).

History. The party was the largest of the Smallholder parties represented in Hungary's first post-socialist parliament. It had its origins in the internal disputes in the ISP during late 1991 and early 1992 when initially 33 deputies refused to follow the József Torgyán led ISP into opposition. The group, which had grown to 36 by summer 1992, earned the collective name, "the thirty-six" (*harminc hatos*) and tried to unify several times into one party. The first unsuccessful attempt was in November 1992 when the Historical Independent Smallholders' Party was formed. This attempt failed in March 1993 when 17 parliamentary deputies left to form the Conservative Smallholders' and Bourgeois Party. The United Smallholders' Party was the product of a further attempt to unify the Smallholders parliamentary fraction so that it would be able to contest the 1994 elections as a united force. The party, which is the product of a union between the majorities of the Conservative Smallholders' and Bourgeois Party and the Historical Independent Smallholders' Party in parliament and a stalled union with the National Smallholders' Party outside parliament, was founded in November 1993. It attracted the support of 28 of the 36 strong anti-Torgyán parliamentary fraction, including all the Smallholder ministers in the government, notably János Szabó, Minister of Agriculture, who became the new party's president. The party, despite its parliamentary strength, is relatively weak compared to the Torgyán-led ISP. In the 1994 elections it managed to obtain sufficient nominations to contest only 54 individual constituencies, to stand on 14 of the 20 county lists and on the national list. However, it polled only 0.82 per cent of the total vote and none of its candidates were elected. For the 1994 elections the party received 4.05 million forints in state subsidy.

Programme. The party's 1994 election manifesto calls for government to pay more attention to the rural provinces. The need to halt the crisis in agriculture is, not surprisingly, the party's top priority and it calls for a speedy end to the restitution process and more positive support for agriculture.

Organization. Because of the party's recent origins and the ambiguous status of the National Smallholders and Bourgeois Party within it, nothing is known about the party's structure or organization.

Voks Humana, Voks Humana Movement, Biosphere Party (VH)
Voks Humana Mozgalom, Bioszféra Párt (VH)

Address. Budapest VIII, Köztarsaság tér 26, H-1081.

Telephone. (1) 133 5390 extension 170.

Leadership. Péter Czajlik (pres.); József Agocs (vice-pres.); Imre Gyulai (sec.).

History. The party claimed in 1990 to be more radical than the environmentalists and to transcend their technocratic principles. It called for "Life's right to life". Its concrete aim was "the construction of a Hungarian and international living space network by which the living world can survive us as an environment". It received 2 million forints (approximately £14,000) state support in 1990. It was still reported to be in existence in January 1994.

Workers Party, Hungarian Socialist Workers' Party
Munkáspárt, Magyar Szocialista Munkáspárt

Address. Budapest VIII, Baross u. 61, H-1082.

Telephone. (1) 134 2721, 134 1509.

Fax. (1) 113 5423.

Foundation. Dec. 17, 1989.

Leadership. Gyula Thürmer (pres.); Sándor Nyiró (vice-pres.).

History. The party consists of the rump of the former HSWP which refused to go along with the party's change of name to the Hungarian Socialist Party in October 1989 and its metamorphosis into a social democratic party. At its founding congress (which it viewed as a continuation of the 14th) Gyula Thürmer, foreign policy advisor to the former leader, Károly Grósz, was appointed president. The Central Committee retained many prominent hard-liners such as János Berecz and the publicity-seeking Stalinist Róbert Ribanszki. In the 1990 elections it fielded 96 candidates and, with 3.68 per cent of the vote, came top of the list of parties which failed to cross the 4 per cent threshold. In the local elections it fared slightly worse. It bitterly criticized the HSP for "taking our assets and leaving us Marx". The party was optimistic that as the economic crisis bit its popularity would grow, though by 1994 there was little sign of this happening. Opinion polls showed that it had a small, but solid base of support. By January 1991, it had adopted the name Workers Party (*Munkáspárt*). In June 1991 it published its programme for the third millenium.

It retained its organization and continued to maintain an active presence, organizing demonstrations for the next four years. In the 1994 elections its strong organization was demonstrated when it gained sufficient nominations to contest 156 individual constituencies, to stand on every county list and to appear on the national list. The party polled 3.18 per cent, failed a second time to enter parliament, and lost votes compared to its 1990 performance. Its losses were far from even, however, and it managed to gain votes in industrial towns like Ózd, Salgótarján and Komló. The dimension of its performance suggests that it could in the future realistically hope to exploit working-class discontent with the new left-of-centre government in Budapest. It was earmarked 7.68 million forints in state subsidy to contest the 1994 elections and planned to spend 20 million forints from its own resources on the campaign.

Programme. Despite being made up of the old guard of the party, its programme would have been considered radical and reformist under the old regime, encapsulated in the statement: "This HSWP is not that HSWP." It is committed to Kádárist reformism, and wants to carry it further in areas such as restoring national traditions. It does not oppose privatization and the introduction of foreign capital; and mention is even made of the "social market economy", although public (not state) ownership is advocated in preference to private, and it is vociferous concerning the dangers that will accompany capitalist restoration. It also advocates political neutrality for Hungary. It remains explicitly a party primarily of the working class, based on the intellectual foundation of Marx. The party criticized moves to restore church property and reprivatize agricultural land. As part of a left-wing movement, it feels it must build itself from below and seek co-operation with the trade unions, the HSP and the Agrarian Alliance. It explicitly embraces struggle using constitutional means to further its goals, and declares that it does not want to force its ideology on anyone.

Organization. A congress of delegates from local organizations appoints a 89-member Central Committee.

Affiliations. Links are maintained exclusively with communist parties of Eastern and Western Europe.

World Alliance of Hungarian Patriots
Magyarok Hazafias Világszövetsége

Address. Debrecen, Simonyi út. 40, H-4028.

Telephone. (52) 315 393.

Leadership. János Albert (Hungarian pres.); Gyula Náday, Sándor Tóth (vice-pres.).

History. The party was founded in 1990 and subsequently registered with the authorities. Nothing further is known, however, about its organization, structure, programme or activities.

World National People's Rule Party
Világnemzeti Népuralmista Párt

Address. Budapest VII, Péterffy S. u. 42, H-1076.

Leadership. Albert Szabó (pres.).

History. Though not formally registered as a party it gained considerable notoriety in early 1994 when it organized rallies commemorating Ferenc Szálasi, the leader of Hungary's Nazi Arrow Cross Party in the 1940s who briefly led a Nazi-style dictatorship in Hungary following the German invasion in 1944. Following this incident, there were legal moves to wind the party up because it allegedly sought to deprive individuals of their basic rights, but the outcome of these proceedings was unclear in April 1994. The party's president, Albert Szabó, an Australian of Hungarian origin, defended his party claiming that Szálasi was a patriot and that his party merely sought to introduce a socialism which respected national values in Hungary. The party's address is the same as that of the People of the East Party Christian Democrats and the Hungarian Freedom Party, and "People of the East Party" figures more prominently on its door.

KAZAKHSTAN

Zhanylzhan Dzhunusova
Rustem Sartaev

Since its formal declaration of independence on Dec. 16, 1991, the Republic of Kazakhstan has been moving from a totalitarian state towards a market-oriented democracy. This transition demands dramatically different political institutions from those prevalent in the Soviet era. Yet the new political system was beginning to take shape even before the old system was officially dismantled. The first indications of this can be traced back to mid-1988 with the emergence of groups presenting themselves as informal alternatives to the CPSU. Most of the hundred or so organizations that declared themselves at that time had insignificant followings — groups were formed and reformed haphazardly and some ceased to operate within a few days. Others, whose slogans proved effective in attracting and retaining supporters, have gradually been transformed into political parties and movements.

The current multi-party system derives from these early informal movements: the Civil Movement *Azat* (Freedom); *Edynstvo* (Unity), the inter-ethnic movement; the Social Democratic Party of Kazakhstan; and the *Alash* Party. Characteristically, all these groups had pretensions of attracting a mass membership and made clear appeals to particular ethnic groups — in spite of their names: for example, the "unity party" *Edynstvo*, had a predominantly Russian membership.

Of major importance for the move towards real democracy were the parliamentary (Supreme Soviet) elections of March 1990. For the first time in the history of the Kazakh legislature, three-quarters of the deputies' seats to be decided by the people were subject to a real contest between opposing parties. A third of all deputies, however, gained their seats in the Supreme Soviet in accordance with the old party model: 90 seats were given to the representatives of socialist organizations, including 17 seats given to the CPSU. The institution of the presidency was established shortly afterwards. The first Kazakhstan president, Nursultan Nazerbaev, was elected by parliament on 24 April, 1990. He was re-elected in nationwide referendum on Dec. 1, 1991.

New, democratic ideas on the division of power, the parliamentary system and the development of a legalistic state with a market economy were incorporated in the Declaration of State Sovereignty of October 1990 and in the Constitutional Law on State Independence of the Republic of Kazakhstan in December 1991. In addition to the creation of a judicial basis for reforms, however, there was also a need to change the old legal system and this required a new constitution. The constitutional document of 1978, adopted under the Soviet leader, Leonid Brezhnev, had been amended hundreds of times in the previous few years and

247

was completely out of date. The first constitution in the history of the young independent state was adopted on Jan. 28, 1993.

Part of the new constitution concerns itself with the development of the Kazakhstan multi-party system: Chapter 10 "Public Associations"; Article 16 of Chapter 4 "Political Rights and Freedoms"; Article 117 of Chapter 18 "Elections". Article 16, for example, runs as follows: "The citizens of the Republic have the right to create public associations on the basis of free will and interests in common for the realization of their rights and freedoms." "Public associations" are defined in Article 53 as political parties, mass movements, professional and creative units, religious and other associations of citizens. Article 117 fixes that registered political parties, equally with other public associations, are guaranteed the freedom to promote candidates at elections, detailed discussion and the freedom to campaign.

The law defines precisely (in Article 54) that interference of state institutions and officials with the activities of public associations is illegal as is interference by public associations with the activity of the state and its officials. Article 55 proscribes those public associations whose foundation and activity proclaim and promote racial, national, social or religious intolerance, or call for the violent overthrow of the constitutional order, or encroach on the territorial integrity of the Republic. It also bans the formation of militarized associations and clandestine associations and unions.

All these constitutional articles confirm the democratic course on which Kazakhstan should proceed. This move to democracy, however, is compromised and inconsistent. For instance: the constitution interprets the position and role of political parties very narrowly; there is no mention of the principle of political pluralism; the constitutional status of parties is not provided for; and parties have no rights in initiating legislation or in the formation of government. Moreover, Chapter 18 on elections is not predicated on a multi-party system and the forthcoming law on political parties is not included in the list of constitutional laws. In addition, Article 58 prohibits the foundation of religious parties because of fears of provoking a religious split or promoting Islamic fundamentalism.

At present in Kazakhstan there are dozens of small political parties and movements, but they have little popular support. They have no influence on the legislature or the executive, although they try to overcome this by initiating and promoting draft laws on political parties, on the Supreme Soviet and on the elections of deputies. Foremost among the registered parties are the Socialist Party of Kazakhstan, the People's Congress of Kazakhstan, the Union of People's Unity and the Republican Party of Kazakhstan. They are all headed by famous writers and well-known public figures.

Political parties in any pluralistic society reflect and are a natural product of its evolution: they are different expressions of the will of the people. Thus, the programmes of the Kazakh nationalist parties — *Azat, Zheltoksan* and *Alash* — express the idea of the "return" of the Kazakh ethnic identity, resurfacing in spite of past attempts by Russia and the USSR to abolish it. The orthodox ideals of the recent past, on the other hand, are visible in the programme offered by the Communist Party. The Socialist Party follows a Marxist ideology. The People's Congress and the Union of People's Unity each have similar goals: peace, inter-ethnic concord and the economic welfare of the state; these, as well as their adherence to a centrist ideology have led to repeated combining of their political efforts.

The change in the position of Russian and Slavic communities in Kazakhstan, as regards state sovereignty and the elevation of the Kazakh language to the state language, has led to the discomfort of Russian speakers generally and ethnic Russians in particular. Unlike other minority groups such as Koreans, Uighurs and Germans, Russians were pre-eminent in the power structures of the old regime. In response to economic hardship and to the challenges to their privileged status under the Soviet system they have recently begun to mobilize and are evolving into a potent political force.

The Russian nationalist movement includes political unions such as *Edynstvo*, the Party of Democratic Progress, the Slavic movement *Lad* and the Russian communities. It also embraces cultural groups, veterans associations, pensioners, trade unionists and even Cossacks, despite these diverse groups historically having little in common. Their programmes concur, however, albeit to varying degrees, in areas such as the need for the increased protection of economic, political and cultural rights of Russian speakers. The intensity of these demands is strongest in the Russian-dominated north and east of the country.

As the Kazakhstan multi-party system is in the making it is too premature to talk about a developed and stable party system or to identify easily the boundaries of political difference. The majority of parties and movements have difficulties in forming distinct ideological images and the differences between platforms are more quantitative than qualitative. There is an absence of developed communications between parties and society at large. That parties are small as a rule, unknown and have not captured the public's interest reflects the uncompleted processes of transition: stratification, the differentiation of groups within society and the realization of distinctive group interests have not yet materialized fully. Thus, the parties themselves have no clear policies on the protection of group interests and base their programmes predominantly on ideological values. In addition, and rather bewilderingly, the concrete actions of parties are sometimes distinct from their stated programmes.

Table 1: Results of parliamentary elections, March 7, 1994

Party	Seats
Union of People's Unity of Kazakhstan	33
Federation of Trade Unions of Kazakhstan	11
The People's Congress of Kazakhstan	9
Socialist Party of Kazakhstan	8
Agrarian Union of the Republic of Kazakhstan	4
Republican Public Movement *Lad*	4
Veterans Organization of Kazakhstan	1
Youth Union of Kazakhstan	1
Democratic Committee for Human Rights	1
Association of the Lawyers of Kazakhstan	1
International Public Committee	1
Aral – Asia – Kazakhstan	1
Congress of Entrepreneurs of Kazakhstan	1
Deputies of the 12th Supreme Soviet of Kazakhstan	40

Source: *Kazakhstanskaya Pravda*, March 17, 1994

Thus, while there exist numerous organizations that identify themselves as political parties or public movements, none presents a serious challenge to the authorities. And yet the foundation of a multi-party system is a natural and irreversible process and is an index of real movement towards democracy and a state governed by the rule of law.

Directory of Parties

Alash
Partiya Natsionalynoi Svobody Alash

Foundation. April 1990

Leadership. Aron Atabek, Rashid Nutushev.

History. Alash is named after a legendary founder of the Kazakh nation. Party leaders refute any link with the nationalist party of the 1920s and 1930s of the same name. *Alash* considers itself to be an unofficial people's opposition with no need to be registered.

In 1989, Aron Atabek created the cultural-ethnographic society *Zheruyik*. After the discovery of financial irregularities he avoided investigation and moved to Moscow, where he began to publish the Islamic political newspaper *Hakh* (People). *Hakh* (1992, issue 3) published excerpts of Karishal Asanov's book which violated the honour and dignity of President Nazerbaev. Atabek was due to return to Kazakhstan to take part in a hearing of the case, but he requested political asylum in Azerbaijan where he is currently living.

The leadership of *Alash* has been subject to the most harrassment from the authorities. Seven leaders were arrested in December 1991 in connection with the assault on Mufti Nysanbaev. Three of the leaders were held for over six months.

Programme. Alash advocates the real independence of Kazakhstan and counterbalances Eurocentric ideas by putting forward ideas of Turkic unity. It presses for a nationalist revival of Kazakhstan as the nucleus of a future state of "Great Turkestan". It is intolerant of colonial expansion by the superpowers and calls for non-violent, constitutional methods of political struggle and solutions to inter-ethnic problems. Recently *Alash* strongly criticized the communists although now it actively supports their demands for the suspension of privatization, their outcry against private ownership of land and against the invasion of foreign capital into the republic's economy.

Civil Movement *Azat* (Freedom)
Grazhdanskoye Dvizhenie Kazakhstana Azat (GDK AZAT)

Foundation. June 1, 1990.

Membership. 90,000.

Leadership. Hasen Kozhakhmetov.

History. Initially, this party was set up as the Civil Movement of Kazakhstan at the constituent conference in Alma-Ata. The Declaration of Fundamental Goals and Principles was adopted and the movement soon embraced all national groups. By mid-1993 the party's position had weakened: the republic's independence had caused some of *Azat's* slogans to become redundant and there were internal divisions. The latter reason was denied, however, by the party's leadership.

In order to strengthen the various national-democratic movements the idea was floated of a merger between *Azat*, The Republican Party of Kazakhstan and *Zheltoksan*. After initial problems the Unifying Congress took place on Oct. 11, 1992. It decided to consolidate the three national-democratic groups into one party: the Republican Party *Azat*. Academician Kamal Ormantaev became its head and its first deputy was Hasen Kozakhnetov. The party was short lived, however, because of further internal dissension.

Programme. Azat seeks a completely politically and economically independent Kazakhstan. Its desire to create a civil and democratic society depends upon "mutual understanding" between the disparate ethnic components of the republic's population. The movement implies a need for an equalization of the rights of the indigenous population who have long been repressed by Moscow and its politics.

Highlighting the gap between urban and rural standards of living, the demographic disbalance between numbers of urban versus rural residents and the corresponding lack of possibilities available to Kazakh villagers, the movement stresses the importance of abolishing the disparities between ethnic groups.

The complete primacy of the Kazakh language is a fundamental issue for *Azat*.

Publication. Azat (currently not published because of financial difficulties).

Communist Party of Kazakhstan
Kommunisticheskaya Partiya Kazakhstana (KPK)

Foundation. Autumn 1991. Registered on March 16, 1994.

Membership. 55,000.

Leadership. Leonid Korolykov.

History. After the Extraordinary Congress of the Communist Party of Kazakhstan some of its members, opposed to the renaming of the party and its legal transformation into the Socialist Party, held the 19th Congress of the Communist Party in autumn 1991. The movement for the revival of the Communist Party began from below. There are no former representatives of the *nomenklatura* among the top party leaders. The KPK has been denied official registration several times, on the grounds that the revival of the restored KPK contradicts the law on The Organisation of Public Associations (1991). On March 16, 1994, however, the Communist Party was finally registered with the Ministry of Justice.

Programme. The KPK's main demands are the restoration of the former USSR economic sphere, state regulation of the economy but in flexible conjunction with market mechanisms, diverse forms of property with state ownership at the forefront. The KPK advocates social equality, protection from market forces, access to the state education system and the health service, freedom of culture and of consciousness. It calls for the strengthening of international ties between peoples and is against discrimination on ethnic or linguistic grounds. Prospectively, a rather strong alliance between communists and socialists could be created if mutual distrust, particularly evident on the socialists' side, could be overcome.

Co-ordinating Committee of Public Associations "The Republic"
Koordinatsionnyi Sovet Obshestvennyih Obyedinenyi "Respublika" (KS)

Foundation. March 24, 1994.

Membership. Socialist Party, *Azat*, Communist Party, *Lad*, Federation of Trade Unions of Kazakhstan, Ecological Party *Tabigat* (The Nature), Democratic Committee on Human Rights, etc.

Leadership. Serikbolsyn Abdildin.

History. The Co-ordinating Council of Public Associations (KS) was created by the representatives of different parties and movements. There is past experience of the foundation of such a union in Kazakhstan, for example, the Coalition for Social Protection; The Round Table. The initiator of the emergence of the KS was the Socialist Party despite its relative success in the 1994 parliamentary election.

The KS leader is Serikbolsin Abdildin, an experienced politician, head of the previous Supreme Soviet and a member of the Socialist Party. He declared in an interview "First of all we are going to work up an alternative programme of the country's survival and its economic revival, even if it is not acceptable to the current government. We will do it jointly, because declarations by individual parties are either not given attention or they are drowned in the bureaucratic apparat's bosom. We do not affirm that we will jointly pressure the government but we are obliged to restrain it from destructive decisions" (*Panorama* no. 14, 1994).

Programme. The primary goals of KS are: the creation of a real constructive opposition to the politics of the government; the foundation in the Supreme Soviet and the *Maslikhats* (*Oblast* councils) of deputies' factions and the co-ordination of their activity; to give objective information about the country's problems and to increase public political activity.

A KS memorandum concerning the work of parliament accentuates protection from violations to the constitution and laws by the executive; a widening of the control functions of the Supreme Soviet; and preservation of a one-chamber professional parliament. The memorandum expresses solidarity with the CSCE experts concerning their estimates of the March 1994 parliamentary elections.

The difficulty for KS lies in its mixed structure. Political parties, movements and unions are united not on an ethnic basis but in wanting to solve common social and economic problems. It is difficult to forecast how long this coalition will last.

Edynstvo (Unity) Movement
Dvizheniye "Edynstvo"

Foundation. Mid-1990.

History. The *Edynstvo* movement was founded as a result of the Russians' anxiety about their status within Kazakhstan. The predominantly Russian group advocates measures against the violent acts of Russian-speakers, as well as the increasing political power of the Kazakhs.

Programme. The party supports greater protection of the economic, political and cultural rights of Russian-speakers. The intensity of these demands is strongest in the Russian-dominated north.

Human rights are generally discussed only in terms of the loss of Russian rights (e.g. changes in the language laws, the introduction of Kazakhs into the Russian-dominated industrial complexes, etc).

They aspire to the exchange of opinions with other associations and unions, which was realized in co-operation with the latter on some problems.

The National Democratic Party of Kazakhstan
Natsionalyno-Demokraticheskaya Partiya Kazakhstana (NDPK)

Foundation. Oct. 5, 1993.

Leadership. Kamal Ormantayev.

History. The NDPK also emerged out of the *Azat* movement. It gives priority, however, to ethnic Kazakhs who inhabit the ecologically unfavourable territories.

Party of Democratic Progress of Kazakhstan
Partiya Demokraticheskogo Progressa Kazakhstana (PDPK)

Foundation. Nov. 24, 1991.

Membership. Over 1,000, including 200 members in Alma-ata.

Leadership. Alexandra Dokuchaeva.

History. The party emerged as a counter-balance to the national-democratic parties and movements of *Azat, Alash* and *Zheltoksan.* Composed primarily of former members of the inter-ethnic *Edynstvo* movement, the PDPK is not registered with the Ministry of Justice.

Programme. A parliamentary-style party, its main purpose is to build a civil society with a focus on the primacy of human rights, economic freedom, a legalistic state and equal opportunities for all citizens irrespective of nationality. It believes in the maintenance of different forms of property, free enterprise and ecological security. It also advocates close economic and political integration within the CIS, particularly between Kazakhstan and the Russian Federation. Currently, PDPK is not well known and its policies are vague. With the election of Alexandra Dokuchaeva as the leader of *Lad*, it is possible to foresee that the party will disappear from the political scene before it has had time to organize itself.

The People's Congress of Kazakhstan
Narodnyi Kongress Kazakhstana (NKK)

Foundation. Oct. 5, 1991.

Membership. 50,000.

Leadership. Olzhas Suleimenov.

History. This party emerged out of Kazakhstan's largest and most successful popular movement, the Nevada-Semipalatinsk Anti-nuclear Movement. Under the leadership of the famous Kazakh poet, Olzhas Suleimenov, the movement succeeded in 1990 in shutting down the nuclear test site near the city of Semipalatinsk.

Programme. The NKK's programme is very similar to that of SNEK (*see* below). Olzhas Suleimenov has said that to debate SNEK's programme is to argue about their own. However, the leaders' repeated declarations of possible co-operation and even a merger remain only as statements. Not all members of NKK are overjoyed with this idea. Politically, NKK advocates the creation of a democratic society, an independent and law-governed state and the development of an underlying ecological perspective in state politics.

The Congress's economic programme advocates multi-structured growth through small business development and repudiates bureaucratic interference; it also advocates equality of different forms of property.

Although the leadership sees the present period as one of rising national consciousness, it also believes that the quantitative balance between Russians and Kazakhs produces a very positive stalemate to ethnic violence. It seeks to portray itself as an international party.

Publications. newspapers: *Halyk Kongresi* (in Kazakh), *Narodny Kongress* (in Russian)

Republican Party of Kazakhstan
Respublicanskaya Partiya Kazakhstana (RPK)

Foundation. Nov. 22, 1992 (registered Dec. 26, 1992).

Membership. 17,000.

Leadership. Sabetkazy Akataev.

History. The RPK was born out of the *Azat* movement's inner split which centred primarily on the different estimates of the political and economic course of the government but was also linked with the personal ambitions of the *Azat* leaders.

Programme. In general, the RPK supports the foreign policy and the reformist programme of the Kazakhstan government. One of the slogans of the RPK political platform was that "the mutual understanding of the Kazakh and Russian populations is the foundation for harmony and peace in the Republic".

Republican Public Slavic Movement *Lad*
Respubliukanskoye Obshestvennoye Slavyanskoye Dvizhenie Lad

Foundation. Summer 1993.

Membership. 17 organizations.

Leadership. Alexandra Dokuchaeva.

History. Lad is the largest Russian national movement, based in Alma-ata. It is an umbrella organization that encompasses several groups in Kazakhstan and it maintains contacts with others outside through a network of Slavic movements that extends throughout the former Soviet Union.

The extension of the deadline for choosing citizenship for Russian-speakers to March 1995 was in part due to the work of *Lad.*

Programme. Lad espouses economic and political protection for all citizens of Kazakhstan, although it places emphasis on the rights of the Slavic population. Its appeal reaches to members of diverse Russian-speaking groups, including Koreans, Germans, Tatars and some Kazakhs.

In anticipation of the March 1994 elections, *Lad* adopted a platform that included the establishment of a joint army and open borders with Russia, a return to the ruble zone and the legalization of dual citizenship for the Russians of Kazakhstan.

Publication. "*Lad*", newspaper.

Social Democratic Party of Kazakhstan
Sotsial-Demokraticheskaya Partiya Kazakhstana (SDPK)

Foundation. May 26–27, 1990 (not registered).

Membership. Two-tier membership. Activists (nearly 1,000) take part in party meetings, pay fees, are engaged in the party's activities. Supporters cannot participate in the activities of the party and do not pay fees. They are sympathisers.

Leadership. Dos Kushimov.

History. Calling itself the oldest party in the republic, this organization has no official membership and enforces no party discipline. Since its inception, the party has refused on principle to register with the Ministry of Justice. Party leaders assert that the registration requirements violate democratic standards and norms.

Programme. The SDPK's fundamental principles are freedom, solidarity and justice, but not equality. They are against the violent revolutionary transformation of society.

They are against any form of dictatorship, except the dictatorship of common sense. They are opponents of divisions in society on social, class or corporative grounds. The most important task is the social protection of citizens.

The party leaders are committed to a democratic path that includes vast economic reforms. They advocate the introduction of private ownership of land.

Socialist Party of Kazakhstan
Sotsialisticheskaya Partiya Kazakhstana (SPK)

Foundation. Sept. 7, 1991.

Membership. 47,000 (1,586 primary organizations).

Leadership. Peter Svoik, Gaziz Aldamzharov.

History. The Socialist Party of Kazakhstan is the legal successor of the outlawed Communist Party of Kazakhstan, renamed at the Sept. 7, 1991, Congress of the Communist Party. The famous Kazakh writer Anuar Alimzhanov was the first elected head of the SPK. From a position of initial support for the republican reforms, the SPK has evolved into the loyal opposition, coming out against the economic course of the current government.

Programme. The party's platform is based on the democratization of society; the foundation of a law-governed state with the division of powers; political pluralism; the development of democratic institutions; equality of nations and the freedom of consciousness.

In economics it favours changes in the structure of state expenditure and a reduction in the unprofitable funding of enterprises; hard finance politics; adoption of laws on tax reform; free prices; the abolition of indirect taxes. In the social sphere it advocates greater social protection of pensioners, invalids and other vulnerable groups; anticipation of unemployment. Its approach to domestic politics is based on inter-ethnic concord, equality of all Kazakhstanis, the introduction of both Kazakh and Russian languages as languages of the state and a "norm" of postponed citizenship. Its foreign policy proposes the transformation of Kazakhstan into a factor for international peace and stability.

Publication. Respublika (The Republic), newspaper.

Union of People's Unity of Kazakhstan
Soyuz "Narodnoye Edinstvo Kazakhstana" (SNEK)

Foundation. Feb. 6, 1993.

Membership. Nearly 50,000.

Leadership. Kuanysh Sultanov.

History. SNEK is famous as "the party of President Nazarbaev", who is its unofficial leader. SNEK's leadership and membership consists primarily of middle-level and high-ranking former Communist Party officials. SNEK has members throughout the country and is organized on the national level as well as at local levels. It surpasses all its competitors in organization.

Programme. The SNEK platform advocates most of the points manifested in the People's Congress and Socialist platforms, such as inter-ethnic harmony, the construction of democracy, and the primacy of the individual. However, SNEK boasts its staunch support for Nazarbaev and his reform programmes in its plaform, and further positions itself as a "centrist" organization.

In the political sphere SNEK advocates a strong presidency, a division of powers and a professional parliament. Its economic platform espouses gradual economic reform and favours moderately-paced privatization supported by foreign investment, where privatization is based on initial equality of opportunity and the social protection of the population. SNEK propounds a state regulated economy but without undue interference in entrepreneurial activity. In the social sphere it proposes the social protection of indigents, the security of citizens and a revival of morality. There should be inter-ethnic stability as a guarantee of economic modernization. The party espouses close but egalitarian ties with the Russian Federation and firmly opposes both dual citizenship and dual languages of the state.

Publication. "*Vremya*" (The Time).

Zheltoksan (December)
Zheltoksan

Foundation. Mid-1989.

Leadership. Hasen Kozhakhmetov.

History. Commemorating the December 1986 riots in Alma-Ata, *Zheltoksan* was founded in 1989. A direct spur to its emergence was a disagreement with the official assessment of the events surrounding the riots. In May 1990, some public associations (*Adilet, Akikat, Zheruiyk, Forum*) called the constituent congress where the founding of the party, based on the public committee *Zheltoksan*, was proclaimed.

The *Zheltoksan* leader, Hasen Kozhakmetov, a composer by profession, enjoys authority not only because of his long dissident record (he was first sentented in 1977) but also for his personal participation in the December 1986 riots and his ensuing imprisonment. He was proposed as a candidate in the 1991 presidential elections but was not registered.

In September 1992 some of *Zheltoksan's* members separated from the parent party and declared the emergence of the *Zheltoksan* public movement led by A. Nalibaev. Currently the party has been renamed the *Zheltoksan* Committee for Human Rights.

Programme. The party's platform calls for the total political and economic independence of the republic and the unequivocal adoption of Kazakh as the state language; it also presses for the rehabilitation of victims of the oppression following the December riots and calls for close relations with compatriots living outside Kazakhstan.

Zheltoksan wants to heighten the role of Islam in the life of the Muslim population. It is against any form of unity with Moscow and the sale of natural resources or their development by foreign concerns. It aims to promote economic ties with Turkey and Iran and to raise the overall living conditions of workers. It sees the necessity of redressing the current inequities between the rural living conditions of the majority of ethnic Kazakhs with that of the urban population, dominated by Russians.

The organization has been denied official registration.

KYRGYZSTAN

Bogdan Szajkowski

After the establishment of the Bolshevik regime in Russia and its extension to the regions of Central Asia, Kyrgyzstan was incorporated into the Turkestan Autonomous Soviet Socialist Republic within the Russian Soviet Federative Socialist Republic (RSFSR) in 1918. In 1924 it became the Kara-Kirghis Autonomous *Oblast* within the RSFSR. In 1925 it was renamed the Kirghis Autonomous *Oblast* and in February 1926 it became the Kirghis Autonomous Soviet Socialist Republic. Finally, on Dec. 5, 1936, the Kirghis Soviet Socialist Republic was established as a constituent republic within the USSR.

During the communist period, Kyrgyzstan was ruled by one of the most conservative and hardline of élites. Mikhail Gorbachev's policies of *glasnost* and *perestroika* made only a minimal impact on the republic. By the late 1980s there was, however, slightly greater openness in the press, particularly in the newspaper of the Writers' Union, *Literaturny Kirghistan*. Between 1989 and 1990 two unofficial political groups, the *Ashar* and the *Osh Aymaghi* emerged. Both were concerned with the acute housing crisis and the land issue in the republic, and were partially tolerated by the authorities.

However, the event that gave a substantial impetus in the direction of change in Kyrgyzstan was the creation of an unofficial Democratic Movement in the middle of 1990. The Movement, comprising some 22 unofficial opposition groups, emerged in the aftermath of ethnic riots between Uzbeks and Kyrgyz in Osh (the republic's second largest city, heavily populated by Uzbeks), in June 1990. According to official figures, some 212 Kyrgyz and Uzbeks were killed. Independent reports, however, claim the death toll was over a thousand. Following the riots young demonstrators besieged the headquarters of the Communist Party in Bishkek (formerly called Frunze) blaming the communists for mismanaging the crisis and causing needless bloodshed. Mass demonstrations, hunger strikes and protest campaigns organized by the Democratic Movement demanding the resignation of the hardline communist leader, Absamat Masaliyev, eventually forced the regime to hold elections for the post of the chairman of the Supreme Soviet (president). At the Supreme Soviet session held on Oct. 28, 1990, reformed-minded deputies and some communists narrowly managed to defeat Masaliyev and elected, again by a narrow margin, the President of Kyrgyz Academy of Sciences, Askar Akayev, as the president of the republic.

In his first major policy statement Akayev promised the democratization of political life, far-reaching economic reforms, and greater autonomy. Kyrgyzstan declared its sovereignty within the Soviet Union on Oct. 30, 1990, with Kyrgyz laws taking precedence over Soviet-federal laws and regulations. On Dec. 12 of the same year it dropped both "Soviet" and "Socialist" from its title and adopted the name Republic of Kyrgyzstan (changed to the

Kyrgyz Republic in 1993). The name of the capital was also subsequently changed from Frunze to the original Bishkek.

During the Moscow *coup* in August 1991 Kyrgyz communist hardliners attempted to stage their own *coup*. Local KGB officials came to arrest Akayev, while a commander of the Central Asian military district attempted to deploy tanks in the streets of Bishkek. The Communist Party of Kyrgyzstan declared its support for the *coup* leaders. After the crushing of the *coup* Akayev banned the Communist Party, removed its state support, and forbade the publication of its newspapers. In less than a week after the victory of democratic forces in Moscow, Kyrgyzstan declared its independence from the USSR on Aug. 31, 1991.

Since independence the country has embarked slowly and cautiously on the process of social, political and economic change towards democracy and a free market economy. Kyrgyzstan became the first newly independent republic to hold free national presidential elections, on Oct. 12, 1991. The elections aimed both at bringing over four million of the country's electorate into the democratic process and at giving the president a popular mandate. However, somewhat embarrassingly for Askar Akayev, no one was willing to run against him. In a turnout of 90 per cent he gained 95 per cent of the votes.

In December 1992 the unicameral Supreme Soviet, elected under the old Soviet rule on Feb. 25, 1990, in which the communists controlled 310 of the 350 seats voted to change its name to *Zhogorku Keneshom*, thus assuming a Kyrgyz name.

A major step in the consolidation of change was the adoption on May 5, 1993, of a new constitution. The document was approved after several months of wrangling, during which the legislature, elected in 1990 when the republic was tightly controlled by one of most conservative communist party leaderships in Central Asia, put almost every phrase of the text to a vote. The *Zhogorku Keneshom* rejected a large part of the President's programme which was designed to encourage private enterprise and permit private ownership of land (albeit under certain conditions). The deputies also voted to limit many of the presidential powers. Ironically, the constitutional battle also saw a confrontation between the President and the parliament in which Kyrgyz nationalist forces, convinced that Akayev was not giving priority to Kyrgyz national interests as defined by themselves, made alliances with the reconstituted communists — the Party of Communists of Kyrgyzstan. The adoption of the constitution, after an appeal from Akayev, has provided the country and its political leadership with a firmer framework for continuing the changes.

The constitution guarantees basic human rights and stipulates that the Kyrgyz Republic is a law-governed, secular, unitary and democratic state. It provides for a parliamentary system of government with a 105-seat legislature. The parliament, which is in permanent session, is elected by universal adult suffrage for a maximum term of five years. (The current 350-seat parliament is to continue until general elections are held.) The document stipulates the separation of powers between the executive, legislature and an independent judiciary. According to the constitution, the President of the Republic is elected by direct universal adult suffrage for a term of five years. He has to have a fluent command of the Kyrgyz language which is the state language. At the same time, however, the constitution grants the Russian language equality with Kyrgyz. It allows for the use of Russian as a language of inter-ethnic communication. The Prime Minister, who is appointed by the President, is chosen from amongst the largest political party — he has to command the majority support of the *Zhogorku Keneshom*. The document also provides for a Constitutional Court as a guarantor of the provisions and the basic rights granted by the constitution.

The operation of political parties in Kyrgyzstan is governed by a Law on Public Organizations under which organizations wanting to operate publicly have to be registered by the Ministry of Justice. It allows for the creation and operation of ethnic or religious-based parties. Although most organizations have in fact been granted registration, in marked contrast to other Central Asian countries, the law permits the government to refuse registration of any group that it considers "extreme".

At the beginning of 1993 several political parties and organizations attempted to create a Bloc of Democratic Forces. However, a congress of representatives of ten groups and organizations convened on Feb. 27 in Bishkek, failed to form an umbrella organization due to serious differences among its participants.[1]

Kyrgyzstan is considered by most observers to have gone the furthest in implementing political reforms than any of the other Central Asian republics. Democratic transformation has, by and large, been the product of few men directing change from the top. The central figure in this process has been President Askar Akayev. A physicist by training, he became a member of the Central Committee of the Soviet Communist Party in July 1990. However, it is reputed that his involvement with the CPSU was insignificant. Akayev is recognisably the most committed of all the leaders of the Central Asian republics to the rapid transition to working democracy and a market economy — he has spoken of making Kyrgyzstan the "Switzerland of Central Asia". However, he faces many formidable obstacles which have slowed down the process of change.

The communist-dominated parliament has on several occasions watered down and vetoed more radical presidential proposals. The sharp differences between Kyrgyzstan's parliament and the president became particularly apparent during the prolonged debate of the country's post-communist constitution. The president appealed on several occasions for the passage of the constitution. When the parliament still continued to block the approval of the document he used veiled threats stating that unless the document was approved he would call a constitutional convention and thus by-pass the assembly, and/or call a new election.

In the absence of other suitably qualified people the old communist *nomenklatura* still plays a major role in the running of the institutions of the central and local government and the economy. A Mission of the Conference on Security and Co-operation in Europe which visited Kyrgyzstan in April 1994 reported that although "the reform programme . . . pursued by the President and his closest collaborators appears to be supported by state and government institutions, opponents of the reforms are to be found in lower echelons of government and administration as well as among members of the old *nomenklatura* in the provinces".[2] This has evidently limited the room for manoeuvre for President Akayev and his supporters in the government, eager to speed the process of political, economic and social reforms. The extent to which the President has to be conciliatory to the former communists, in order to facilitate his reform programme, can only be guessed at.[3] What is, however, apparent is that the residue of the communist system in terms of personnel has clearly slowed down the transformation process.

The complex ethnic mix of the country (Kyrgyz 52.4 per cent, Russians 21.5 per cent, Uzbeks 12.9 per cent, Ukrainians 2.5 per cent, Germans 2.4 per cent, Tatars 2 per cent, others including Kazakhs, Dungans, Uighurs, Turks, and Koreans 6.3 per cent) has brought to the surface ethnic tensions, which although successfully contained since the declaration of independence, have served as a division for increased politicization between the Kyrgyz, Uzbeks and the Slavs in particular. This has brought about the creation of several political organizations along ethnic lines and some loss of support for Akayev's policies. Thus, for example, the President's attempts to preserve ethnic harmony, by insisting on the rights of all inhabitants of the country, rather than just the Kyrgyz, was one of the main reasons for the withdrawal of support for Akayev's policies by the Kyrgyz Democratic Movement (which originally endorsed him). The Movement has subsequently opposed the President on a number of issues, including the policy of allowing all ethnic groups an equal right to land ownership. Despite criticism Akayev has pursued his balanced policies towards the Slav minority. These resulted in the creation in 1993 of a Slavonic university, the Kyrgyz-Russian University in Bishkek. In February 1994 the President agreed to support the idea of dual citizenship for ethnic Russians in Kyrgyzstan.

Another significant obstacle are the fierce rivalries that lie just beneath the surface between the northern and southern clans. These have the potential for major destabilization of the country and their careful management involves compromises in the progressive developmental process.

The government also has to respond to the increasing demands from Kyrgyz nationalists. Kyrgyz nationalist parties have become increasingly assertive: the change of the country's name to the Kyrgyz Republic from the more ethnically neutral Republic of Kyrgyzstan used in the immediate post-independence period was indicative of their growing strength. Akayev and his administration have been increasingly accused by the nationalists of betraying the interests of the Kyrgyz population and in particular of giving in to the demands of the Uzbeks and the Slavs.

Another major obstacle to speedy change in Kyrgyzstan has been the emigration of well-qualified people, mostly ethnic Russians. In an effort to stop the out-migration of a large number of Russian-speakers, many of whom occupy key positions in the economy and industry, Akayev signed a decree on June 14, 1994, making Russian an official language in predominantly Russian-speaking areas. The decree also guarantees representation of minorities in state institutions.[4] Akayev's actions earned him considerable criticism and distrust from the Kyrgyz nationalists.

While Kyrgyzstan is probably the most democratic Central Asian republic in principle, its people are the least politicized. The CSCE Mission reported that although the draft of the constitution was made public it met with little response. "There are no political philosophies of the kind that characterize political parties in the West, i.e. conservatism, liberalism, social democracy, for this pre-supposes socio-political structures that have not yet evolved. Political movements meet with more acclaim as they are free of any legacy of the past".[5]

Kyrgyzstan's democratic structures are inherently fragile and largely the result of the personal leadership of President Akayev.[6] While President Akayev's and the Kyrgyz government's commitment to democratic reforms is generally not seriously questioned, during 1993 democratic opposition groups did voice serious objections to the slow progress of political and economic reforms. Thus, for example, in January 1993 the President was severely criticized by the leader of the *Erkin Kyrgyzstan* party for introducing the institution of *akim* (a local governor appointed by the President) and its consequence on the process of democratization in the country. When this post was created, local council (soviets) were abolished giving the *akims* quasi-dictatorial powers.[7] He also came in for a share of criticism from a gathering of several opposition groups in February 1993, when he and his team were accused of wrecking the economy. Nevertheless, despite these criticisms Akayev received a renewed mandate in referendum on Jan. 30, 1994, when in a turnout of 95.6 per cent of the electorate, 96.2 per cent supported the President and his policies. The referendum was seen as nationwide vote of confidence in the President and his policies. There have, however, been some indications that besieged by Kyrgyz nationalists, undermined by the old communist *nomenklatura* and frustrated by the still communist-dominated parliament, Akayev may have to resort to other means in order to promote his political and economic programme. On June 13, 1994, he told a meeting of local government officials that, while he himself favours democracy, strong state power was needed because "the people are not prepared for democracy"; reality had shown that democratic methods are ineffective during a difficult reform period.[8] Kyrgyzstan's young democracy faces the danger that its people will not be able to keep up, and that the absence of development could increase disillusionment and political discontent.

Directory of Parties

Agrarian Party of Kyrgyzstan

Foundation. 1993.

Leadership. A. Aliyev (ch.).

Programme. The party aims to represent the interests of farmers and rural communities.

Alta-Mekel (Fatherland)

Foundation. Nov. 7, 1992.

Leadership. Omurbek Tekebayev (pres.)

History. The party emerged from the Democratic Party *"Erkin Kyrgyzstan"* (Free Kyrgyzstan) in November 1992.

Programme. The party claims to favour a reasonable compromise between various groups in society, and constructive co-operation with the government.

Ashar (Mutual Aid or Help) Movement

Foundation. December 1990.

History. The movement emerged in 1990 in response to the acute housing crisis in Kyrgyzstan. It was partially tolerated by the authorities before it developed wider political role.

Programme. The movement, whose membership comprises almost exclusively of ethnic Kyrgyz, is primarily concerned with the advancement of this section of the country's population. It has supported Kyrgyz land rights by physically seizing land for building and has articulated demands for compensation of the Kyrgyz victims of the Osh riots in June 1990.

Affiliation. The group is affiliated with the Kyrgyz Democratic Movement.

Aqigat (Truth)

The main student political organization located in Bishkek. *Aqigat* is affiliated with the Kyrgyz Democratic Movement.

Civic Accord

A coalition representing non-native minority groups.

Erkin Kyrgyzstan (Free Kyrgyzstan)

Foundation. October 1991.

Leadership. Topchubek Turganaliyev (ch.).

History. Also known as *Erk* Party ("Will" or "Freedom") or *Erkin* (Free) Kyrgyzstan Democratic Party, it emerged from the Democratic Movement "Kyrgyzstan" (*see* Kyrgyz Democratic Movement). It began as a party of businessmen, farmers and intelligentsia concerned with economic reforms. In November 1992 a split within Erkin Kyrgyzstan gave rise to the *Alta-Mekel* (Fatherland) party.

Programme. The party rejects nationalism, chauvinism, fascism and racism. It is opposed to Islamic fundamentalism, though it is in favour of maintaining the positive features of Islam. It seeks to restore and raise the rights of the indigenous population to the necessary level without jeopardizing the rights of all the people of Kyrgyzstan.

Affiliation. Leading opposition party. It has two deputies in the parliament.

Kyrgyz Democratic Wing

Founded in 1990 in Osh, the organization works for greater religious tolerance and the construction of mosques and religious schools.

Kyrgyz Democratic Movement

Foundation. May 1990. Registered November 1990.

Leadership. Qazat Akmakov (pres.).

History. Also known as the Democratic Movement of Kyrgyzstan, the organization originally grew as coalition of several different groups supporting the independence of Kyrgyzstan, the removal of the Communist Party of Kirghizia from power and democratic reforms in the country. Many of the groups within the movement split along national lines, and some eventually broke away to form separate political parties.

National Revival Asaba (Banner) Party

Foundation. December 1991.

Leadership. Asan Ormushev (ch.); Abjalbek Anarbekov, Asylbek Cholponbayev.

History. The party originally formed a part of the Kyrgyz Democratic Movement. It left the movement in November 1990, apparently in protest of the lack of its organization and a sufficiently strong nationalist orientation.

Programme. "The defence of the economic, social and political interests of the Kyrgyz people who are at long last coming out from under the colonial yoke".

Affiliation. Nationalist party. It has no deputies in the Kyrgyz parliament.

National Unity Democratic Movement

Founded in 1991 in Bishkek, this moderate democratic party aims to unite different ethnic groups within Kyrgyzstan.

Osh Aymaghi (Osh Region)

Located in Osh, the organization is primarily concerned with the allocation of land in the Osh region. Founded in 1990 it was one of the earliest independent political organizations in Kyrgyzstan. The group is affiliated with the Kyrgyz Democratic Movement.

Party of Communists of Kyrgyzstan

Foundation. June 22, 1992. (re-founded).

Leadership. Dzhumgalbek Amanbayev (first sec.).

Membership. 10,000.

History. The party is a successor to the Communist Party of Kirghizia which was disbanded immediately after the August 1991 Moscow *coup*. A criminal investigation for supporting the Moscow *coup* leaders continued until January 1992 when the charges were dismissed. On June 22, 1992, a constituent congress of the Party of Communists of Kyrgyzstan took place. It was attended by 250 delegates (many of whom were said to be young people). The congress was chaired by Absamat Masaliyev (former first secretary of the Communist Party of Kirghizia, dismissed from his party post in April 1991). The party was registered on Sept. 18, 1992.

Republican Popular Party of Kyrgyzstan

The party was founded in Bishkek in 1993 by prominent scientists and academics as a centrist organization.

Slavic Fund

Foundation. June 1990 (founding congress), October 1991 (registered).

Leadership. Anatoly Sorokin (pres.); Anatoly Bulgakov (vice-pres.).

Membership. Several thousands.

History. The Fund, also known as the Slavic Association, is an organization of the Russian-speaking population. It was organized originally in the middle of 1990 as a non-political group concerned with literature and culture. However, after the independence of Kyrgyzstan the group became quickly politicized in defence of the interests of the Russian population in the republic. It enjoys the support of some 70 members of the Kyrgyz parliament.

Programme. It aims to defend the rights of the non-Kyrgyz in Kyrgyzstan.

Social Democratic Party

The party's membership consist largely of Russians living in Kyrgyzstan. Its initial application for registration was refused by the Ministry of Justice on the basis that its programme contained "extreme" statements.

Uzbek Adalet (Uzbek Justice)

Foundation. 1989.

Membership. 400,000 (claims).

History. Uzbek Adalet was established in Kyrgyzstan's second largest city Osh — the administrative capital of the Osh region in the Fergana valley on the border with Uzbekistan. The overwhelming majority of the region's inhabitance are ethnic Uzbeks. Osh had been incorporated into Kyrgyzstan in 1924 and the Uzbeks are demanding the establishment of an Uzbek autonomous region.

Programme. Autonomy for the Uzbeks in the Osh region of Kyrgyzstan and the use of Uzbek as a state language in the region.

Notes

1 *RFE-RL News Briefs*, vol. 2. no. 11, 1993. pp. 7–8.
2 "Report of the CSCE Rapporteur Mission to Kazakhstan and Kyrgyzstan". Secretariat of the Conference on Security and Co-operation in Europe, Prague. CSCE Communication no. 149. Prague, April 24, 1992. p. 2.
3 *Human Rights and Democratization in the Newly Independent States of the Former Soviet Union.* Compiled by the Staff of the Commission on Security and Co-operation in Europe, Washington, DC. January 1993. p. 174.
4 *RFE-RL News Briefs*, vol. 3. no. 25, 1994. p. 8.
5 "Report of the CSCE Rapporteur Mission to Kazakhstan and Kyrgyzstan". *op. cit.* p. 2.
6 Conference of Security and Co-operation in Europe. "Report by the Chairman-in-Office on Her Visit to the Participating States of Central Asia". Ministry for Foreign Affairs, Stockholm, May 21, 1993.
7 *RFE-RL News Briefs*, vol. 2. no. 6, 1993. p. 7.
8 *RFE-RL News Briefs*, vol. 3. no. 25, 1994. p. 8.

LATVIA

Ole Nørgaard
Lars Johannsen
Anette Pederson

For an analysis of the evolution and working of political parties in Latvia see chapter entitled "The Baltic Republics Estonia, Latvia and Lithuania: the Development of Multi-party Systems" on pages 47–65.

Democratic Centre Party
Demokratiska Centra Partija (DCP)

Address. Valnu iela 9, Riga.

Telephone. (371) 2 21 67 54.

Foundation. Oct. 17, 1992.

Leadership. Juris Celmins (ch.)

Membership. 500.

History. The DCP is a new small party with roots back to the pre-occupation years of Latvian independence. J. Cakste, Latvia's first State President, founded the DCP with fellow deputies. The DCP was politically active up until the coup of May 15, 1934, after which all political parties were banned. The new party founded Oct. 17, 1992, was set up by centrist democratic politicians not as a literal renewal of the old party, but a new organization with new statutes and goals. The majority of the founding members were members of the governing body of the Latvian Popular Front movement during its first years of existence. The name of the party was changed on Sept. 20, 1993, to the Democratic Party.

Democratic Party
(*see* Democratic Centre Party)

Equal Rights
Lidztiesiba

Address. Ranka dambis 9, Riga.

Telephone. (371) 2 61 41 07.

Foundation. Feb. 27, 1993.

Leadership. Sergejs Diamanis (ch.)

Membership. Approx. 1,500.

History. The founders of the Equal Rights movement in Latvia were mainly deputies from the Supreme Council's "Equal Rights" faction. The Latvian Russian Association (chairman O. Kapranov) endorsed "Equal Rights" for the parliamentary elections. Alfreds Rubiks, the former leader of the Communist Party in Latvia, currently in prison awaiting trial for treason, was not allowed to vote, but under Latvia's constitution was allowed to stand as a candidate in the elections. He duly stood as an Equal Rights candidate and was elected to the Parliament (*Saeima*). However, the first session of the parliament, held on July 6, 1993, voted to withold his mandate pending a final court ruling.

Programme. Equal Rights believes that Latvia should be recognized as a new republic (not a continuation or renewal), founded upon the principles of a united, multinational state.

Farmers' Union
Latvijas Zemnieku Savieniba

Address. Republikas laukums 2 (12. stavs), Riga.

Telephone. (371) 2 32 71 63; 22 53 81.

Foundation. 1917.

Leadership. Andris Rozentals.

Membership. Approx. 2,000.

History. The second oldest political party in Latvia, founded in 1917 in Valka, and instrumental in founding the first parliament of the Republic of Latvia. During the inter-war years of independence, the Farmers' Union participated in 12 of the 14 coalition governments. During this time, notable Farmers' Union deputies were K. Ulmanis (Minister President, Foreign Minister and State President), Z. Meierovics (Minister President and Foreign Minister) and A. Kviesis (State President). The party, along with other political parties, was banned after the coup of May 15, 1934, but on Feb. 28, 1991, the Farmers' Congress in Riga renewed the political party. The statutes and goals of the Farmers' Union are based on those of the earlier party. In the elections for the parliament, the Farmers' Federation (chairman A. Rozentals) and the Federation of the Politically Repressed (chairman G. Resnais) united to contest the elections. The Farmers' Union also received endorsements from several military organizations including the Latvians Riflemens' Association, the Latvian National "Daugavas Vanagu" Welfare Fund and the Latvian Army Officers' Association.

Affiliation. The party is the second party in the governing coalition.

For Fatherland and Freedom
Tevzeme un Brivibai

Address. Jckaba 16, room 310, 311, Riga.

Telephone. (371) 2 32 50 41.

Foundation. Feb. 17, 1993.

Leadership. Maris Grinblats (ch.); J. Jakobsons (sec.)

Membership. 200

History. The coalition was formed in early 1993 as an electoral federation between the following groups: the Latvian National Federation "Fatherland", founded on Dec. 12, 1992 (chairman R. Milbergs); the 18th of November Union (chairman J. Straume); Latvia's National Independence Movement, the break-away group from the LNNK; the Radical Federation, a break-away group from the Latvian Popular Front movement founded on Jan. 12, 1992 (chairman E. Blumnieks); the Latvian National Partisan Federation; the Anti-Communist Federation; the World Latvian Businessmen's Union, and other minor organizations.

Programme. The three D's: de-occupation, de-Bolshevization and decolonization.

Harmony for Latvia
Saskana Latvijai–Atdzimsana Tautsaimniecibai (SLAT)

Address. Elizabetes iela 2a, 414–416 Riga.

Telephone. (371) 2 32 33 29; 32 08 80.

Foundation. March 15, 1993.

Leadership. Janis Jurkans (ch.).

History. Harmony for Latvia is a federation consisting of Latvia's Support Fund, founded in November 1992 (chairman J. Jurkins, former Foreign Minister); the Latvian Youth Progress Union (chairman A. Ameriks); the Peasants' Union (chairman V. Bresis); the Fishermens' Union (chair M. Pese); and the League for the Economy (chairman J. Lucans). The SLAT draws much of its electoral support from Latvian citizens who are not ethnically Latvian and hence also derives support from Moscow.

Programme. The party's programme is based upon the idea that the Latvian nation can only achieve its goals by supporting other nationalities, offering them voluntary integration into Latvia.

Latvian Christian Democratic Union
Latvijas Kristigo Demokratu Savieniba (KDS)

Address. Lacplesa iela 24–4, Riga.

Telephone. (371) 2 32 35 34.

Foundation. March 9, 1991.

Leadership. Paulis Kalvins (chn.)

Membership. 500.

History. During Latvia's pre-World War II years of independence there were several Christian democratic parties and in the parliamentary elections of 1931 they won a total of 24 seats. The KDS was refounded in Latvia in 1991. The party has branches not only in Latvia (Riga, Jekabpils, Rezekne, Cesis, Sigulda), but also in emigré communities throughout the world (Toronto, Boston, New York, Germany, Belgium and Australia). The KDS has established good relations with other Christian democratic movements in the world and receives financial support from its overseas branches.

Latvian National Independence Movement
Latvijas Nacionala Neatkaribas Kustiba (LNNK)

Address. Elizabetes iela 23, Riga.

Telephone. (371) 2 23 37 30.

Foundation. July 10, 1988.

Leadership. Aristids Lambergs.

History. The LNNK has existed for five years and during the struggle for independence had a very high membership. In May 1992, at its fifth congress, the party adopted a new programme defining the future direction of LNNK activities. It was agreed then that the party should not become a party, but technically remain a "movement". However, individuals who are members of other political parties cannot join the LNNK. The LNNK has always had strong links with the Latvian emigré community, and several members of that community have been elected to parliament as LNNK deputies. A splinter group of the LNNK, also using the movement's name, under the chairmanship of O. Dzenitis, broke away from the main LNNK on Nov. 17, 1992. On June 18, 1994, the seventh annual congress of the movement decided to transform the organization into a highly structured national conservative party. The American-Latvian Aristids Lambergs was elected chairman of the new party. At the same time a new party programme and statutes were adopted.

Programme. The party believes in the strengthening of Latvia as a national state; the defence of the interests of Latvians and Livs, membership of the Council of Europe and the European Union; and the creation of an economy corresponding to market principles and Latvia's national interest.

Latvia's Way
Latvijas Cels

Address. Terbatas 4–9, Riga.

Telephone. (371) 2 22 41 62; 28 76 10.

Foundation. Feb. 28, 1993.

Leadership. A. Pantelejevs; Valdis Birkavs.

Membership. About 700.

History. Latvia's Way did not become a real political party until after the election in June 1993 largely for tactical reasons. The grouping was established in February because a dominant political centrist force was missing in Latvian political life. The World Federation of Free Latvians (WFFL) was the economic sponsor and Club 21 was the political donor. The WFFL was for decades an umbrella organization for the principal associations of Latvians in exile campaigning for the restoration of the Republic of Latvia. After the independence the WFFL committed itself to helping shape the restored Latvian Republic into a democratic and economically prosperous state. Club 21 has existed since the winter of 1991 as a lodge-like organization and is considered to be the most influential organization in Latvia. Its members all belong to the élites in different branches of society, politics, business and culture. Rumours claimed that Club 21 itself would become a political party, but this failed too. Instead, Latvia's Way was created, but with strong personal connections to Club 21.

Organization. Latvia's Way is still an élite organization. There is a youth department at the University of Riga.

Affiliation. The party is the largest party in the two-party government coalition.

LITHUANIA

Ole Nørgaard
Lars Johannsen
Anette Pedersen

For an analysis of the evolution and working of political parties in Lithuania see chapter entitled "The Baltic Republics Estonia, Latvia and Lithuania: the Development of Multi-party Systems" on pages 47–65.

Directory of Parties

Alliance of the Christian Democratic Union of Lithuanian National Youth "Young Lithuania" for a United Lithuania
Krikscioniu demokratu ir Lietuviu tautinio jaunimo "Jaunoji Lietuva" sajungu susivienijamas "Us vieninga Lietuva"

Address. Nepriklausomybes 5, 3000 Kaunas.

Telephone. (307) 20 60 54; 77 08 52.

Foundation. Statute registered July 11, 1992. (Founded Oct. 8, 1927.)

Leadership. S. Buskevicius (dir.).

Programme. The goal of the Union is an independent, free and Lithuanian Lithuania, as well as a united nation with its own national culture and strong personality.

The Citizen's Charter of the Republic of Lithuania

Address. Jadsto St. 9-204, 2001 Vilnius.

Telephone. (307) 62 61 71.

Foundation. Statute registered July 24, 1992.

Leadership. Vytautas Kubilius (ch.).

Programme. The aim of the Charter is to foster democratic civic society and to establish the rule of law. The Charter desires that the population of Lithuania and the world should be given full and objective information on the political situation in Lithuania; that issues of political and social concern be addressed publicly; that state and public projects and decisions be prepared with competence and professional skills.

Independence Party
Nepriklausomybes Partija

Address. Pylimo st. 38/1, 2001 Vilnius.

Telephone. (370) 61 47 21; 62 67 53.

Foundation. Oct. 20–23, 1990.

Leadership. Kestutis Jurgelenas (ch.).

Membership. 512.

Organization. 11 sections, the strongest in Vilnius, Panevezys and Klaipeda.

Affiliation. The election programme envisages the party's independent participation in elections, but also allows it to join coalitions. The party contested the 1992 election in coalition with The National Union, under the name Lithuanian National Union.

Publication. KOVO 11 (weekly newspaper).

Lithuanian Centre Movement
Lietuvos Centro Judejimas

Address. Gedimino Ave. 53, 2026 Vilnius.

Telephone. (370) 61 36 55; 47 65 94.

Foundation. Date of statute registration Aug. 11, 1992.

Leadership. Prof. Romualdas Ozolas (ch.).

Programme. The aim of the movement is to build a democratic civil society; to defend the constitutional rights and freedoms of citizens. The movement supports private ownership; fair competition; the promotion of small and medium-sized businesses; a radical reform of property rights; an economic system based on an effective market; economic freedom; private initiatives, and decentralization of economic management.

Lithuanian Christian Democratic Party
Lietuvos Krikscioniu Demokratu Partijos

Address. Sv. Ignoto sst. 14–6, 2001 Vilnius.

Telephone. (370) 61 81 15.

Fax. (370) 61 81 15.

Foundation. Jan. 27–28, 1990. (Revival of the original party, established in 1904.)

Leadership. Povilas Katilius (ch.); Algirdas Saudargas (dep. ch.).

Membership. 5,251.

Organization. Sections in most Lithuanian cities, towns and districts, the strongest being those in Zemaitija and Kaunas.

Publication. Apzvalga (weekly).

Lithuanian Democratic Labour Party (LDLP)
Lietuvos Demokratine Darbo Partija (LDDP)

Address. Barboros Radvilaites 1, 2600 Vilnius.

Telephone. (370) 61 39 07; 61 26 56.

Foundation. Dec. 8–9, 1990.

Leadership. Algirdas Mykolas Brazauskas (ch.).

Membership. 15,000.

Programme. The LDLP is a parliamentary political organization with a social-democratic orientation. Its main goal is the establishment of a civil democratic society in the Republic of Lithuania in which humanistic values such as individual liberty, work, welfare, morality, social justice and civil harmony would be fostered. The LDLP co-operates with all political parties, public organizations and movements in strengthening democracy in independent Lithuania. The primary orientation of its socio-economic policy is to protect the interests of the working class and of those in the most vulnerable social strata. LDLP policy is based on the priority of consistent reforms and social progress in the development of society.

Organization. Sections in every city, town and district, the largest being those in Vilnius and Kaunas.

Affiliation. LDLP is the ruling party and comprises the majority government.

Publication. TIESA (daily newspaper).

Lithuanian Democratic Party (LDP)
Lietuvos Demokratu Partijos Jungtinis Saras

Address. Gedimino Ave. 34–9, 2001 Vilnius.

Telephone. (370) 62 60 33; 62 87 08.

Fax. (370) 47 92 75.

Foundation. Feb. 5, 1989. (Revival of the original party founded in 1902.)

Leadership. Saulius Peceliunas (ch.).

Membership. Approx. 1,000.

History. Many members are former members of *Sajudis* who re-established the original party because they realized that *Sajudis* could no longer exist efficiently as a movement.

Programme. The principal goal of the LDP is to consolidate a free, independent and democratic Lithuanian state governed by law in which power would belong to its citizens and would be exercised democratically. The main task of the LDP is to achieve the application of democratic principles in political, legal, economics, education, health care, social guardianship and public activities of the state.

Organization. Has 20 sections in Lithuanian cities, towns and districts. The strongest sections are in Vilnius, Kaunas, Klaipeda, Alytus and Kelme.

Affiliation. Ran for election 1992 in coalition with Christian Democratic Party and Union of Political Prisoners and Deportees. At present part of the opposition.

Publication. Vasario 16 (February 16).

Lithuanian Social Democratic Party
Lietuvos Socialdemokratu Partija

Address. Jono Basanaviciaus st. 16/5, 2009 Vilnius.

Telephone. (370) 65 23 80; 65 23 11.

Fax. (370) 65 21 57.

Foundation. Aug. 12, 1989. (Revival of the original party, established in 1896.)

Leadership. Prof. Aloyzas Sakalas (ch.).

Membership. 550.

Organization. Has 21 groups and 12 sections, the strongest being those in Vilnius, Kaunas, Marijampole and Klaipeda.

Publication. Lietuvos Zinios.

National Union of Lithuania
Lietuviu Tautiniku Sajunga

Address. Gedimino Ave. 22, 2600 Vilnius.

Telephone. (370) 62 49 35.

Fax. (370) 61 73 10.

Foundation. April 11, 1989. (Revival of the original party, established in 1924.)

Leadership. Rimantas Smetona.

Membership. Approx. 800.

Organization. 33 sections, the strongest being in Vilnius, Kaunas and Siauliai.

Affiliation. Based on preliminary information, the party will not join a political coalition, but will participate in elections independently. Ran for election 1992 in coalition with the Independence Party.

Publication. Viltis (weekly).

Sajudis/Homeland Union (Conservatives of Lithuania)
Sajudis/Tevynes Sajunga (Lietuvos konservatoriai)

Foundation. As a popular front *Sajudis* was founded during the summer of 1988. The successor in shape of a political party (Homeland Union) was established at a founding conference on May 1, 1993. (The remains of *Sajudis* exist as a social movement since December 1993.)

Leadership. Vytautus Landsbergis (ch.).

Membership. Approx. 10,000.

History. For the history of *Sajudis* see pages 47–65. Brazauskas's victory in the presidential elections seemed to have convinced *Sajudis* of the need to change its structure. On February 27, 1993, a session of the *Sajudis* faction (the parliamentary part of *Sajudis*) decided that the organization should become a political party with the provisional name of Union for the Rebirth of the Homeland (*Tevynes Atgimimo Sajunga*) and appointed a seven-member committee, headed by Vytautus Landsbergis, to draft guidelines for the new political party. On May 1, 1993, at a founding conference in Vilnius, it was decided to adopt the name Homeland Union (Conservatives of Lithuania).

Programme. The creation of the Homeland Union is engendered by the needs of political reality, the necessity to defend freedom and democracy, the inherent and civil rights of the people of Lithuania, to resist the restoration of the Soviet order. The Homeland Union will foster the ideas and make decisions close to the principles of the European neo-conservatives, and will seek their implementation in the political reality of Lithuania.

Union of Lithuanian Political Prisoners

Address. Pylimo st. 38/1, 2001 Vilnius.

Telephone. (370) 61 77 72; 61 49 73.

Foundation. Statute registered Feb. 26, 1991.

Leadership. A. Stasiskis (ch.).

Programme. The Union seeks to unite political prisoners, present and former citizens of Lithuania.

Affiliation. Ran for election in 1992 as part of the *Sajudis* coalition.

Union of Poles of Lithuania
Lietuvos Lenku Sajunga

Address. Didzioji st. 40, a/d 901, 2001 Vilnius.

Telephone. (370) 22 33 88.

Foundation. Statute registered August 1992.

Leadership. Jan Mincewicz (ch.).

Programme. The aim of the Union is the national rebirth of the Poles of Lithuania; the promotion of Polish education at all levels; contribution to the public, economic and cultural development of Vilnija as an integral part of the Republic of Lithuania.

Publication. Nasza Gazeta.

Union of Political Prisoners and Deportees of Lithuania
Lietuvos Politiniu Kaliniu ir Tremtiniu Sajungas

Address. Donelaicio st. 70 b, 3000 Kaunas.

Telephone. (370) 20 67 35.

Foundation. Statute registered June 26, 1991.

History. The Union originated in 1988 as the Club of Deportees under the aegis of *Sajudis* and the Cultural Fund.

Programme. The Union unites former political prisoners and deportees, aims at their complete rehabilitation, and seeks to ensure they obtain assistance and support.

MACEDONIA

John B. Allcock

For analysis of the developments prior to the declaration of the Republic of Macedonia, see chapter entitled "Yugoslavia (The Socialist Federal Republic of Yugoslavia)" on pages 615–632.

Macedonia was only freed from Turkish rule in 1913 following the Balkan Wars when it was divided between Serbia, Greece and Bulgaria. The Macedonian territories included in Serbia were brought into the Kingdom of Serbs, Croats and Slovenes in 1918 (renamed Yugoslavia in 1929). Upon partition under Axis occupation in 1941, Yugoslav Macedonia was occupied principally by the Bulgarians, with the western part allocated to the Italian client state of Albania. Following liberation in 1945 a Macedonian republic was created within the Yugoslav federation. With a surface area of 25,713 sq km the Republic of Macedonia was the fourth largest of the six republics of Yugoslavia (10 per cent of the total).

When the disintegration of Yugoslavia became an active possibility after 1989, Macedonian opinion was initially strongly in favour of the maintenance of the federation. Leading Macedonian politicians (especially Kiro Gligorov and Vasil Tupurkovski) were actively engaged until the last minute in negotiations which might have prevented its disintegration. A Macedonian state owed its existence to Yugoslavia; and the collapse of the federation only held out the prospect that this small country of 2,147,090 people (census of 1991) would be exposed to irredentist claims by its neighbours. Consequently it was not until Sept. 8, 1991, that a referendum was held, seeking popular approval for independence. This was secured with a 95 per cent majority (on a 75 per cent turnout). It is worth noting that the terms of the referendum motion mentioned that Macedonia retained "the right to join an alliance of independent states" — implicitly some revived future version of Yugoslavia. On Sept. 18 the Assembly declared the independence of the Republic from Yugoslavia. A new constitution was adopted.

The withdrawal of the Yugoslav National Army from Macedonia was quickly agreed, and accomplished without difficulty by the end of March 1992. International recognition of the new state was a more problematic matter, however, largely as a consequence of the implacable hostility of Greece, which regarded the existence of a state bearing the name "Macedonia" as constituting a *de facto* claim upon Greek territory. In December 1991 the Macedonians filed a claim, along with other republics of former Yugoslavia, for recognition by the European Community, and that claim was referred (with others) to the commission of arbitration headed by Robert Badinter. In reporting on the matter, Badinter recommended recognition, but it was agreed that the Macedonians would make minor constitutional changes making it plain that they had no territorial claims against

Table 1: The Elections of December 1990 for the Macedonian Assembly

Parties in the Assembly	(120 seats)	
	Dec. 1990	Adjustments to June 1994
Internal Macedonian Revolutionary Organization–		
Democratic Party for Macedonian National Unity	38	33
Party of Democratic Change (LCM — later SDAM)	31	28
Party for Democratic Prosperity	17	19
Liberal Party	—	19
Alliance of Reformed Forces of Macedonia/		
Young Democratic Progressive Party*	6	—
Party for Democratic Prosperity/		
National Democratic Party*	5	3
Socialist Party of Macedonia	4	4
Democratic Party	—	3
Party of Yugoslavs in Macedonia	2	2
IMRO–DP	—	1
IMRO–Fatherland	—	1
National Democratic Party	1	1
Socialist Party of Macedonia/Alliance of Reform Forces of		
Macedonia/Young Democratic Progressive Party*	1	1
Socialist Party of Macedonia/Party for the Full		
Emancipation of Romanies*	1	1
Independents	3	4

Source: Secretariat for Information, Republic of Macedonia
Notes: *Joint candidates

Greece. Accordingly, two amendments to the Constitution were approved by the Assembly on Jan. 6, 1992, repudiating "territorial pretensions towards any neighbouring state", and interference in the sovereign rights of such states. Even so, Greece continued to fight a strenuous rearguard action against international recognition, and admission to the United Nations was only secured on April 13, when the Skopje Assembly accepted the compromise title of the "Former Yugoslav Republic of Macedonia" (FYROM). In spite of their effective international isolation, the Greeks continued to make life difficult for the new state, taking advantage of international sanctions against Serbia and Montenegro to obstruct trade with Macedonia, and also instituting exceptional border controls.

The changing international context of the republic has had a very direct bearing upon the development of parliamentary politics. The first multi-party elections were conducted in three rounds, on Nov. 9 and 25 and Dec. 9, 1990. These returned the candidate of the former communist Party of Democratic Change, Kiro Gligorov, as the state President, and an Assembly (*Sobranie*) of 120 seats, the composition of which is described in Table 1. No single party was able to form a majority within the Assembly; and the largest single party (IMRO–DPMNU, with 38 seats) was invited to form a government. The government, which relied heavily upon ministers recruited from outside the parties themselves, came to be known as the "government of experts". This was not the expression of some constitutional principle, but rather the reflection of the fact that the largely working-class and populist IMRO was unable to provide nominees of appropriate experience and qualification from within its own ranks.

The failure to achieve international recognition for the republic was one of the primary reasons why this government was faced with a vote of no-confidence in the *Sobranie* on July 16, 1992. In any case it was hard to reconcile in the Assembly the politics of a moderately nationalist and anti-communist IMRO with the need to create effective coalitions either with the Albanian Party of Democratic Prosperity (PDP), or with the former League of Communists (LC). A period of uncertainty ensued, in which Petar Gošev of the former LC (which had by now changed the title of the party yet again, to the Social Democratic Alliance of Macedonia — SDAM) was first asked to form a government, and then declined. It was not until Aug. 13 that a viable new coalition was put together, headed by Branko Crvenkovski, combining the SDAM, the PDP, the Liberals and the Socialist Party.

The composition of the new government is significant in particular because of its success in drawing the principal Albanian party firmly into the governmental process. As with all of the republics of former Yugoslavia, ethnicity is an important factor in electoral politics. The most numerous ethnic group in the republic are Macedonian Slavs, with 64.8 per cent of the population (census of 1991), followed by Albanians, with 21.5 per cent. (This latter figure is generally regarded as an underestimate, as many Albanians boycotted the census, and the figure had to be projected on the basis of natality and mortality figures, thus leaving the influence of migration largely to guesswork.) There are also small but locally significant minorities of Muslims, Roma, Serbs and Turks. (Numbers of Serbs are believed to have been much reduced by the withdrawal of federal military, business and administrative personnel.) The majority of Albanians are concentrated in a triangular area in the north-west of the republic and adjacent to the border with Albania, although the capital, Skopje, also has a substantial Albanian minority.

Although relations between Macedonians and Albanians have never reached the low ebb which characterizes ethnic relations in Kosovo, there is a long tradition of communal suspicion and even hostility. Albanians typically share a historical sense of the injustice of the Albanian border, but this is strengthened by a growing feeling of their own disadvantaged position within Macedonia. In the post-independence period there has been a marked tendency to define Macedonia as the republic of Macedonians, in which by implication other minorities have a second-class position. The closure of Albanian language facilities at Priština University has meant that it has become impossible to obtain a university-level education anywhere in former Yugoslavia through the medium of the Albanian language. Kosovo also provided a centre for Albanian cultural expression in a much more general sense in Yugoslavia, and the curtailing of publishing and other activities there has left Albanians without a cultural focus. Pressure has thus fallen upon republican authorities within Macedonia to meet these needs at least on behalf of Macedonian Albanians.

The coalition government has attempted to address these concerns directly, and to some extent the inclusion of an Albanian party in the governing coalition is an affirmation of the recognition of the seriousness of the problem. Albanian leaders continue to emphasize the inadequacy of action with respect to provision for Albanian education and public communication. At the time of writing a central point of political controversy in Skopje is the conduct of the planned census, which Albanians believe will confirm the weight of their claims for a greater share in public life and social provision.

Coalition has involved a delicate balancing act, in the attempt to make a serious response to Albanian demands, without giving Macedonian nationalist opinion the impression that national interest is being set aside in order to appease Albanians.

New elections are projected for the autumn of 1994, and at the time of writing it is expected that these will take place under a new electoral law, which will add to the 120 territorially-based seats in the Assembly a number of seats still to be determined (an additional 20 is widely canvassed) which will be allocated on a proportional basis, and which will help to ensure greater sensitivity to the ethnic balance of representation in political life. The combination of the effect of the census, new elections and the extremely fragile international situation within which Macedonia continues to operate makes for a highly unpredictable future for the republic and for parliamentary politics within it.

Any assessment of the future direction of party politics within Macedonia is rendered difficult by the instability of both these organizations and of their support among the electorate. The first edition of this volume recorded around 25 registered political parties/associations within the republic. This number had expanded by mid-1994 to nearly 60. This process is fuelled in part by the fission of earlier groups — so that the original IMRO, for example, has spawned at least three smaller offspring by the secession of dissidents. Political conditions have changed, and the agenda of politics is markedly different in independent Macedonia than within Communist Yugoslavia. The umbrella organization of the former League of Communists has disintegrated, and around the SDAM circles a Saturnian ring of political fragments, reflecting the wider crisis of the left after the collapse of the Soviet Union. The rise of what might be called "ideological politics" has produced (in Macedonia as elsewhere) local versions of current European ideological trends, with a rising Liberal Party, Greens and (improbably in a predominantly Orthodox country) Christian Democrats.

The single factor which probably accounts more than any other for this proliferation of parties is nothing new at all — the persisting liveliness of the old Balkan tradition of personal patronage. Gošev's newly formed Democratic Party and Menduh Tači's impact upon Albanian ethnic politics are only the most prominent of a wide range of what might be called "followings" rather than parties. The continuing electoral success of independents, as well as their numbers, attests to the importance of this factor. Countervailing processes of fusion, exemplified both in the Liberal and Democratic Parties, have done little to offset this picture of extreme fragmentation.

Political activists and commentators within the republic accept the view supported by polls of public opinion, that the electorate to date has very fragile loyalties in relation to parties. The measure of recorded support changes constantly, and the proportion of "undecideds" is invariably very high. (See also the discussion of this issue in the section on Croatia, p. 135–148.) The outstanding importance for the development of *internal* party politics of events in Macedonia's immediate *external* environment also has a decided effect upon the perception of parties among the voters. Prediction about the future development of party life, and the future of parties, would be rash indeed. Some features of the scene do appear to be reasonably stable in a general sense, however, at least for as long as Macedonia is not embroiled in war.

The struggle for office will take place within and between three "blocks": the inheritors of the mantle of the LC (probably including here Gošev's Democrats as well as the SDAM and other socialist fractions); non-Communist and nominally ethnically "neutral" modernizers (primarily the Liberals); and ethnic or nationalist parties (including here IMRO, as well as the representatives of non-Slav minorities, such as Albanians or Turks).

Changes in public support for parties between elections in Macedonia will become easier to follow as regular polling becomes established. The Gallup organization now co-operates with the Skopje-based company BRIMA to conduct opinion surveys within the republic. These have been commissioned and published by the Skopje daily *Nova Makedonija*.

Directory of Parties

Democratic Party (DP)
Demokratska Partija (DP)

Address. Partizanski odredi 89, 91000, Skopje, Macedonia.

Telephone. 91 363-099; 363-101

Fax. 91 222-710.

Foundation. June 27, 1993.

Leadership. Petar Gošev (pres.); Ǵorǵi Marjanovik.

History. Gošev made his career as a senior member of the League of Communists in Macedonia (where he was for a time a member of the Federal Presidency), and later the SDAM (of which he was President). With the fall of the IMRO-led "government of experts" he refused to head an alternative coalition government, and after a year in the political wilderness withdrew to set up his own party. His support was drawn partly from within the SDAM, but four smaller parties also dissolved and united with the DP.

Organization. Has branches in all 34 communes of the republic, and the establishment of neighbourhood units is in progress. The DP is setting up its own youth organization. The strength of this organization is as yet untested in an electoral contest. In many respects the organization and activity of the DP are characterized by charismatic centralism around the figure of Gošev.

Programme. During his period with the LCM Gošev was associated with the extension of civil liberties, especially the removal of the law on "verbal delicts", and to some extent this concern for personal freedom still figures largely in party material. It describes itself as a party of the centre, offering a non-sectarian and cross-national platform. (In the event, its support is almost entirely Macedonian-Slav.) The DP takes a vigorous line on privatization and economic reform, and it is hard to distinguish its policy statements (on paper) from those of the LP. External commentators differentiate late the two on the basis of political *style*, with the DP having a strongly populist and personalist approach.

Affiliations. None, although the DP was refused observer status in the Liberal International!

Publication. Demokratskǐ forum.

Democratic Party of Serbs (DPS)
Demokratska Partija na Srbite (DPS)
Demokratska Partija Srba (DPS)

Address. Partizanski odredi 20, 91000, Skopje, Macedonia.

Leadership. Dragiša Miletić (pres.)

Programme. The party was founded after the secession of the republic from Yugoslavia, and claims to represent the interests of the Serb minority. Since the size of this is believed to have been greatly reduced following the break-up of the federation, and the withdrawal of many federal military, governmental and business officials from Skopje, and the party has yet to contest an election, its influence is far from clear. It underwent an internal coup in early 1994, when the founder (Boris Ristić) was replaced as president, with a take-over by a faction clearly allied to President Slobodan Milošević of Serbia, and it can now be regarded as the voice and arm of the Serbian government in Macedonia.

Internal Macedonian Revolutionary Organization–Democratic Party for Macedonian National Unity (IMRO–DPMNU)
Vnatrešna Makedonska Revolucionerna Organizacija–Demokratska Partija za Makedonsko Nacionalno Edinstvo (VMRO–DPMNE)

Address. Petar Drapšin 36, 91000, Skopje, Macedonia.

Telephone. 91 211-586; 227-627.

Fax. 91 111-441.

Foundation. June 17, 1990.

Membership. Claimed at one time 100,000, but certainly fewer.

Leadership. Prof. Ljupčo Georgievski (pres.); Dosta Dimovska (vice-pres.); Tome Stefkovski (co-ordinator of group in Assembly).

History. The name of IMRO can be traced back to the revolutionary organization which fought for independence from the Turks at the end of the nineteenth century, founded by Goce Delčev in 1893. There is no direct link with the present party. It was refounded in Skopje, after a split within MAAK, and then merged with the DPMNU, which was founded by Macedonian migrant workers in Sweden. Emerging as the largest party in the Assembly after the 1990 elections, IMRO–DPMNU formed the core of the first elected government, participating in the short-lived and unsuccessful "Government of Experts". After a year this was replaced by a new coalition, and the party is now in opposition.

Organization. The party has branches in all municipalities. With 33 seats in the republican Assembly it is the largest parliamentary party in Macedonia. (IMRO–DPMNU won 38 seats in the elections, but has since undergone several splits and defections.) It is distinguished by the solid base of its support among the manual working class.

Programme. The party sought the creation of an independent Macedonian state even before the secession of the republic from the Yugoslav federation. It aspires to the unification of Macedonia, but rejects the use of force to that end, and its manifesto stresses Balkan co-operation. The party thinks that Macedonian cultural identity should be affirmed more strongly, and it sets great store by the building of close links with the Macedonian diaspora. Expresses concern about the Albanian "demographic explosion". Calling itself a party of the "democratic centre", IMRO–DPMNU recognizes the need for a market economy and for the stimulation of foreign private investment, although economic issues feature in a relatively subordinate place in its literature, and without concrete detail. Overall, its stance is fairly staunchly anti-communist and firmly nationalist.

Publication. Glas.

Liberal Party of Macedonia (LP)
Liberalnata Partija na Makedonija (LP)

Address. Ilindenska bb., 91000, Skopje, Macedonia.

Telephone. 91 233-944.

Fax. 91 228-004.

Foundation. July 3, 1993.

Membership. 7–8,000, claiming strength among the better educated, and especially the new private sector middle class.

Leadership. Stojan Andov (pres.); the LP holds five posts in the coalition government: Petruš Stefanov (Economy), Stevo Crvenkovski (Foreign Relations), Jovan Tofovski (Health) Risto Ivanov, and Gordana Siljanovska (without portfolio).

History. The Liberal Party of Macedonia is a relatively new creation in its present form, as it began life within Yugoslavia as the Alliance of Reform Forces of Macedonia — the Macedonian section of the federation-wide group led by the former Prime Minister, Ante Marković. After the secession of Macedonia from the Federation it began the process of self-redefinition, although there are very substantial continuities of policy.

Organization. The LP has a complete territorial coverage of constituencies in the republic. It also has a youth organization, the Liberal Union of Youth. It has 18 members in the Assembly, seven of these were originally elected on the ARF ticket, and others have joined by transfer from other parties. The LP does not have its own paper, but purchases a monthly two-page supplement in the Skopje daily *Nova Makedonija*.

Programme. The LP describes itself as a "party of the centre". It wishes to push ahead more rapidly with the process of privatization, and has pushed several proposals creating for greater public accountability. A great deal of attention is given in party publicity material to economic affairs, and the modernization of the economy. The party has contributed to the coalition programme proposals for the reform of the Ministry of the Interior: they take a strong stand on individual and civil rights. They insist that the LP is concerned to promote the "spiritual" and not the "territorial" unification of Macedonians.

Affiliations. The LP is proud of its acceptance as an associate member of the Liberal International, and it has active links with the British and other European Liberal Parties.

Movement for Pan-Macedonian Action (MAAK)
Dviženje za Semakedonska Akcija (MAAK)

Address. Maksim Gorki 18/III, 91000, Skopje, Macedonia.

Telephone. 91 226-363; 116-540.

Foundation. March 11, 1990.

Leadership. Ante Popovski (pres.)

History. Founded originally under the leadership of the poet, Gane Todorovski, who was later replaced after the disastrous showing of the movement in the election. Although the party began as a spectacular national movement, its exclusively intellectual leadership was out of touch with popular responses, and it was soon overtaken by IMRO as the principal vehicle for popular nationalism. The party is now largely in eclipse.

Organization. Branches in most communes in the republic.

Programme. MAAK seeks the creation of a democratic political order based upon the "inviolable sovereignty of the people". Although its programme does touch briefly upon economic issues, including the "radical transformation" of agriculture, by far the greater part of its concerns have to do with "the Macedonian question" — the cultural heritage and prestige of the Macedonian people, and the question of the relationship between the republic and neighbouring states in which Macedonians are resident. The most concrete implications of this are seen to lie in the improvement of transport links and in problems of population policy.

National Democratic Party (NDP)
Partis Demokratis Populore (PDP)

Address. Gorna Čaršija bb., 94000, Tetovo, Macedonia.

Foundation. July 23, 1990.

Leadership. Ilijaz Halili (pres.)

Organization. Active in six communes with large Albanian populations. Secured election of one representative to the republican Assembly.

Programme. Somewhat more explicitly nationalist in its stance than the rather more accommodationist PDP. It is unclear without an electoral test how its fortunes will be affected by the split in the PDP, in which process it has clearly been implicated.

Party for Complete Emancipation of the Roma (PCER)
Partija za Celosna Emancipacija na Romite (PCER)

Address. Orizari bb., 91000, Skopje, Macedonia.

Telephone. 91 612-726; 115-539.

Leadership. Abdi Faik (pres.)

Programme. The PCER is, as its name suggests, principally concerned to defend the civil rights of the estimated 57,000 Roma who live within the republic. This concern is extended to cover a range of issues concerned with social justice, toleration and equality. With the collaboration of the SDAM (with which it works amicably in the Assembly) PCER secured one seat in the elections of 1990.

Party for Democratic Prosperity in Macedonia (PDP)
Partia per Prosperitet Demokratik (PPD)
Partija za Demokratski Prosperitet vo Makedonija (PDP)

Address. Serava bb, 91000, Skopje; Karaorman 62, 94000, Tetovo, Macedonia.

Telephone. 91 265-070; 111-892; 94 32-267 or 25-709.

Foundation. April 15, 1989.

Membership. 100,000.

Leadership. Dželadin Murati (pres); Sami Ibraimi (vice-pres.); Mohamed Halili (co-ordinator of group in the Assembly). The party holds five posts in the coalition government: Dževdet Hajredini (Finance), Ilijaz Sabiru (Labour and Social Policy), Aslan Selmani (Science), Bekir Žuta and Servet Avziju (without portfolio).

History. The party was founded by Nevzet Halili, and before the secession of Macedonia was one of the few trans-republican parties in Yugoslavia, with branches in other republics. It subsequently merged with another smaller Albanian group, the National Democratic Party. After a period in opposition, during the IMRO-led "government of experts" the PDP joined the new governing coalition.

Organization. Although this is made explicit neither in its name nor even its programme, the party is in effect the principal political vehicle for Albanian opinion within Macedonia. It operates only in those communes with large Albanian populations. In the elections of 1990 it secured 17 seats, and as a result of merger and transfer of allegience now has 19 seats in the Assembly. In the spring of 1994 the PDP underwent a split during its Congress in Tetovo, with a more radical faction seceding under the leadership of Menduh Tači. This group, recruiting support particularly from the Gostivar constituency, is not officially registered as a distinct organization at the time of writing.

Programme. The party's programme (as does its title) specifically denies its attachment to a specific ethnic group. It demands the depoliticization of the judiciary and the military, and a state which is specifically not associated with the interests of any ethnic group. In economic affairs it is in favour of a radical programme of the privatization of social property and the expansion of private investment, both indigenous and foreign. The

PDP repeatedly emphasizes the disadvantage under which it claims that Albanians live in Macedonia, demanding positive action to rectify this situation, especially in the fields of education and communication. Even so, it has been prepared to co-operate with other groups in the governing coalition. Indeed, its accommodationist stance led to the secession of more radical members.

Party of Yugoslavs in the Republic of Macedonia (PYRM)
Stranka na Jugosloveni vo Republika Makedonija (SJRM)

Address. Ženevska 6/2-6, 91000, Skopje, Macedonia.

Telephone. 91 220-711.

Foundation. June 26, 1990.

Leadership. Voislav Karastojanovski (pres.)

Organization. Branches in nine larger towns in the republic. Has two representatives in the republican Assembly.

Programme. The PYRM aspires to represent all those who consider themselves to be of Yugoslav nationality. It seeks the protection and enhancement of human and civil rights, mentioning those of women and minors as well as ethnic minorities, the freedom of the press and an independent judiciary. It describes itself as a "centre-left" party, and co-operates generally with the government coalition.

Affiliations. Loosely linked to similar organizations in other republics of former Yugoslavia.

Social Democratic Alliance of Macedonia (SDAM)
Socijaldemokratski Sojuz na Makedonija (SDSM)
(formerly the League of Communists of Macedonia–Party of Democratic Change (LCM–PDC); Sojuz na Komunistite na Makedonija–Partija za Demokratska Preobrazba (SKM–PDP))
NB Not to be confused with the Social Democratic Party of Macedonia.

Address. Bihačka 8, 91000, Skopje, Macedonia.

Telephone. 91 231-371; 233-610.

Fax. 91 221-071.

Foundation. The title SDAM was adopted in April 1991.

Leadership. Branko Crvenkovski (pres.) Prime Minister of the Republic; Nikola Popovski (vice-pres.); Kiro Gligorov, President of the Republic. The party is the principal partner in the governing coalition, and has nine ministers: Ljubomir Frčkovski (Interior), Vlado Popovski (Defence), Tuše Gošev (Justice), Eftim Ančev (Agriculture), Guner Ismail (Culture), Sofija Todorova (Development), Dimitar Bajaldžiev (Education), and two ministries without portfolio.

History. The Communist Party of Macedonia was founded in 1943. The reformed party (LCM–PDC) was set up in 1989, after the collapse of the LCY. Following the first freely contested elections in 1990 it was forced into opposition to the IMRO-led government, but took power in August 1992. The SDAM was weakened somewhat by the defection of its former leader, Petar Gošev, who refused to head a coalition government, and left at that time to found the Democratic Party (DP).

Organization. The party has inherited the organization and some of the physical resources of the former LC, and is therefore operationally and materially well-endowed. With 28 representatives it is the second largest party in the Assembly.

Programme. In its reformed state the party now describes itself as standing in the "European democratic tradition". It is in favour of economic reform, an "effective" market economy and the "transformation" of property relations (although progress towards privatization has been slow), democratic socialism, social freedoms, rights and solidarity. The SDAM is specifically *non*-national, and indeed two ethnic Turks hold ministerial posts. It has been highly preoccupied with the negotiation of international recognition of the republic, and its position here is tied closely to its need to tread a delicate path between a moderately nationalistic stance abroad and its position of ethnic neutrality at home.

Affiliations. The nature and extent of links between former LCs is unknown.

Publication. Demokratija.

Socialist Party of Macedonia (SPM)
Socijalistička Partija na Makedonija (SPM)
(formerly Socijalistički Sojuz–Socijalistička Partija na Makedonija (SS–SPM))

Address. Ilindenska bb., 91000, Skopje, Macedonia.

Telephone. 91 118-022; 228-015.

Foundation. Sept. 28, 1990.

Leadership. Kiro Popovski (sec.)

History. The party grew out of the former "Socialist Alliance" within the republic.

Organization. Represented in many communes within the republic, although there are reports that its organization has been damaged by the emergence of the Democratic Party. Four representatives in the republican Assembly.

Programme. The SPM identifies itself specifically with the socialist traditions of "Macedonia, Yugoslavia and Europe", and looks for the creation of a "politically free, economically effective, ecologically responsible and socially just state". The key to this project it sees the creation of a parliamentary democracy, the organs of which will control institutions, in place of "the bureaucracy". Several specific projects are mentioned, including fiscal reform, the need to improve the social security situation of the agricultural population and the improvement of water supplies.

Social Democratic Party of Macedonia (SDPM)
Socijaldemokratska Partija na Makedonija (SDPM)

Address. J.H. Konstantinov 20, 91000, Skopje, Macedonia.

Telephone. 91 334-207.

Foundation. March 18, 1990.

Leadership. Tihomir Jovanovski (pres.)

History. The party was founded by Prof. Slavko Milosavljevski, one of the principal figures in the history of post-war dissent in Macedonia, who was dismissed from the League of Communists in 1972 for his liberalism.

Programme. The party is distinguished by its openly non-nationalistic stance — "the Republic of Macedonia is the common fatherland and state of all of the people who live in it". It seeks a secular, modern state with a depoliticized administration and judiciary, and the expansion of civic freedoms — including that of free trade union organization. In the "tradition of western European social democracy" it aspires to combine "economic democracy" with a market economy. It expresses particular concern for the development of small enterprises, and for the economic development of the more mountainous areas of the republic. As with other Macedonian parties, attention is given to the situation of Macedonia in relation to its Balkan neighbours.

The following minor parties either contested the elections of 1990 or have appeared since then. Information has been obtained from the Macedonian Secretariat for Information, although some of these groups no longer exist, having been assimilated into more successful parties. Some of them declare themselves to be "political associations" rather than parties, although the difference is by no means always clear. All have their headquarters registered in Skopje, unless stated otherwise. Titles in Macedonian or other local languages are given only where these have been confirmed.

Albanian Democratic Alliance–Liberal Party (ADA–LP). Alexander the Great Society (AGS): (full title is "Alexander the Great Society–Association for Protection and Spreading of the Truth about Alexander the Great.") **Association of Egyptians in Macedonia (AEM).** Registered in Ohrid. **Association of Serbs and Montenegrins in Macedonia (ASMM). Balkan Federation–Balkans without Frontiers (BF–BWF). Christian Democratic Party of Macedonia (CDPM)** *Demohrščanska Partija na Makedonija* (DPM). Registered in Ohrid. **Civil-Liberal Party in Macedonia–Party for Economic Action (C-LPM–PEA). Democratic Alliance–Party of Cultivators of Macedonia (DA–PCM)** *Demokratski Sojuz–Zemjodelska Partija na Makedonija* (*DS–ZPM*). (Interesting particularly as a rare example of a party explicitly oriented towards small business as well as simply farmers.) **Democratic Communist Party (DCP). Democratic League of Turks in Macedonia (DLTM)** *Demokratski Sojuz na Turcite vo Makedonija.* (Turkish title unknown. Specifically defines itself as a "league for political action" rather than a party; but the significance of the distinction is unclear.) **Democratic Macedonian Workers' Association (DMWA)** *Demokratsko Makedonsko Rabotničko Obedinuvanje* (DMRO). Registered in Prilep. (Apparently based upon the tobacco industry there.) **Democratic Movement of Macedonia (DMM).** Registered in Struga. **Democratic Party of Educational and Cultural Workers of Macedonia (DPECWM).**

Democratic Party of Macedonia–Justice (DPM–J). Democratic Progressive Party of Roma (DPPR). Dignity. (The full title is: "Dignity–Association for Protection of Human Rights of those Discriminated against by the Republic of Greece". The Association is led by a prominent academic, Prof. Dimitar Dimitrov.) **Forum for Human Rights in Macedonia (FHRM).** There are several minor parties all laying claim to the title and inheritance of IMRO, usually having broken away from the parent body. **IMRO–Democratic Party (IMRO-DP)** *VMRO-Demokratska Partija.* **IMRO–Fatherland (IMRO–F)** *VMRO-Tatkovinska* (VMRO-T). **IMRO–Goce Delčev (IMRO–GD)** *VMRO–Goce Delčev.* **League of Communists of Macedonia–Movement for Yugoslavia (LCM–LJ)** *Savez Komunista Makedonije–Pokret za Jugoslaviju (SKM–PJ).* (Branch of a Serbian-based organization dedicated to the restoration of Communist Yugoslavia.) **League for Democracy (LD)** *Liga za Demokratija* (LD). (The Macedonian branch of the major Kosovo Albanian party.) **Macedonian Council for the European Movement (MCEM).** (Clearly not a "party" in the conventional sense, but primarily an educational movement and pressure group.) **Macedonian Democratic Party (MDP)** *Makedonska Demokratska Partija* (MDP). **Macedonian Party for Peace and Independence (MPPI).** Registered in Kičevo. **Multinational People's Party (MPP).** Registered in Prilep. **Party for Democratic Macedonian Workers' Unity (PDMWU).** Registered in Prilep. **Party for Democratic Action (PDA).** Registered in Tetovo. (Macedonian branch of the Bosnian-based party of Muslims. Not to be confused with the following.) **Party for Direct Action (PDA). Party for Democratic Action in Macedonia (PDAM).** (Not to be confused with previous entries.) **Party of Greens in Macedonia (PGM). Party of Human Rights of Macedonia (PHRM)** *Partija Ljudskih Prava Makedonije* (PLPM). (Possibly an ethnic minority group.) Registered in Strumica. **Party of Prosperity (Marxist) (PP(M)). Party of United Macedonians (PUM). People's Party of Macedonia (PPM)** *Narodna Partija na Makedonija* (NPM). **Political Party of the Unemployed of Macedonia (PPUM)** *Politička Partija Nezaposlenih Makedonije* (PPNM) (Macedonian title not known.) Registered in Prilep. **Republican Party of Macedonia (RPM). Workers' Cultivators' Party (WCP), Workers' Party (WP)** *Rabotnička Partija* (RP). **Workers' Party of Macedonia (WPM)** *Rabotnička Partija na Makedonija* (RPM). **Young European Federalists of Macedonia (YEFM).** (A "political association" rather than a "party".)

291

MOLDOVA

Charles King

Prior to the abolition of the leading role of the Communist party in March 1990, the party system in Moldova (anglicized Russian "Moldavia") largely mirrored that of the other 14 Soviet republics. The Communist Party of Moldova (*Partidul Comunist al Moldovei*, PCM), the local affiliate of the Communist Party of the Soviet Union (CPSU), was established in 1940, when much of the present Republic of Moldova was annexed from Romania. The eastern Romanian province of Bessarabia was invaded by Soviet troops on June 28, 1940, with portions in the north and the south of the province apportioned to the Ukrainian Soviet Socialist Republic (along with the northern part of the province of Bucovina) and the remainder incorporated into a newly created Moldovan Soviet Socialist Republic (MSSR). Well over a decade earlier, on Oct. 12, 1924, a smaller Moldovan Autonomous Soviet Socialist Republic (MASSR) had been created inside Ukraine on the east bank of the Dnestr river (a region known in Romanian as Transnistria and in Russian as Pridnestrov'e). The MASSR, although subordinated to Ukraine, was meant to serve as a bridgehead of Communist influence in Romanian-held Bessarabia. The Soviets argued that the inhabitants of Bessarabia and the MASSR — mainly Romanian-speaking Moldovans — formed an ethnic group separate from Romanians and that, therefore, Bessarabia should be "liberated" from the Romanian kingdom and all Moldovans united into a single Soviet nation-state. On Aug. 2, 1940, the "unification" of Moldova was proclaimed when the city of Tiraspol' and six *raions* from the MASSR were combined with the city of Chişinău (Kishinev) and six districts of the truncated Bessarabia to form the new MSSR, the second-smallest republic of the Soviet Union. The MASSR's party structure had previously been linked to the Communist Party (Bolshevik) of Ukraine, with a special Moldovan oblast' committee serving as the highest party organ inside the MASSR. On Aug. 14, 1940, however, the PCM was created for the new MSSR and its first congress held on Feb. 6–8, 1941.

After the annexation of Besssarabia, the Soviet government attempted to shore up its hold on the former Romanian territory by continuing to argue that Romanians and Moldovans represented two separate nations. The Moldovan "language" was declared a completely independent east-Romance tongue (even though Romanian and the Moldovan "language" were mutually intelligible) and the Cyrillic script introduced for written "Moldovan" on Feb. 10, 1941 (even though the MASSR had used the Latin alphabet from 1932 to 1938). Similar policies were followed in other academic disciplines, with ethnographers, historians, literary critics and other scholars obliged to underscore the differences between Moldovans and Romanians in their respective fields. Soviet cultural policy was buttressed by even harsher methods of social engineering. Forced deportations of ethnic Moldovan/Romanian families in 1940–41, 1944–48 and 1949, as well as the famine of 1946–47 which resulted from collectivization in the newly acquired Bessarabian districts, further reduced the Moldovan/Romanian component of the MSSR's population. Further "voluntary" migrations took place in the 1950s and 1960s, when thousands of Romanians/Moldovans were relocated to Central Asia and, in exchange, large numbers of ethnic Ukrainians and Russians were resettled in the MSSR.

Throughout the Soviet period, the MSSR remained a bone of contention between Moscow and Bucharest. Especially after the early 1960s, when the Romanian Communist Party under Gheorghe Gheorghiu-Dej and his successor, Nicolae Ceauşescu, began to distance itself from Moscow's control, the outstanding territorial dispute over the annexed Bessarabian territory increasingly came to the fore. Indeed, as late as November 1989, Ceauşescu raised the territorial question by calling for the liquidation of all the consequences of the Second World War, including presumably the incorporation of Bessarabia into the Soviet Union. Thus, because of the MSSR's sensitive international position, the republic remained largely untouched by the liberalizing reforms initiated by Mikhail Gorbachev after 1985. Several of Gorbachev's predecessors had had first-hand experience with Moldova, both before and after the 1940 annexation, and were thus well-acquainted with the thorny Bessarabian question. Nikita Khrushchev, as a party functionary in Ukraine in the 1920s then as Ukrainian first secretary after January 1938, had been involved with the work of the MASSR oblast' committee. Leonid Brezhnev had served as first secretary of the PCM from July 1950 to October 1952, while Konstantin Chernenko had headed the PCM Central Committee's agitprop department from 1948 to 1956 and had also served as a deputy to the MSSR Supreme Soviet from 1955 to 1959. Moreover, since any political instability in the MSSR would have aggravated the dispute between Ceauşescu and the Kremlin, the CPSU leadership was especially eager to promote "stability of cadres" in the MSSR. Whereas the PCM had at least five different first secretaries from 1940 to 1961, the top leadership post was changed only once from 1961 to 1989. Ivan Ivanovich Bodiul, who served as PCM first secretary from May 1961 to December 1980, was thus the last republican party leader to be replaced under Brezhnev, and his successor, Semion Kuzmich Grossu (served December 1980 to November 1989), was likewise the last to be dismissed under Gorbachev.

Not surprisingly, the dispute over the ethno-linguistic identity of the MSSR's titular nationality proved to be the key factor in galvanizing political opposition in the republic and hastening the demise of the PCM. In the summer of 1988, two informal social organizations, the Moldovan Movement in Support of Restructuring (MMSR) and the Alexei Mateevici Literary-Musical Circle (CLMAM), were formed with the goal of promoting Gorbachev's reforms inside the MSSR. While a range of political demands were originally articulated by the two groups (including an anti-corruption drive, greater environmental protection and human rights guarantees), the MMSR and CLMAM gradually began to focus on the issue of the Moldovan language. By the autumn of 1988, both groups had begun to issue calls for a return to the Latin script and an official recognition of the unity of the Romanian and Moldovan languages. In response, the Moldovan Supreme Soviet formed a special inter-departmental commission to investigate the demands. The commission's final report, issued on Dec. 28, 1988, supported the transition to the Latin script, and the Supreme Soviet further empowered the commission to prepare draft legislation that would incorporate the change into a new republican language law.

The PCM leadership, under first secretary Grossu, proved incapable of dealing effectively with the MMSR and the CLMAM. In an attempt to pre-empt the groups' demands, on Nov. 11, 1988, the PCM issued its own draft theses, "Let Us Affirm Restructuring through Concrete Actions", which merely reiterated the standard Soviet line on Moldovan-Romanian separateness. By December, however, the wave of popular demonstrations which followed the theses' publication forced Grossu to concede gradual Latinization. More importantly, the lead taken by the MSSR Supreme Soviet on the language issue shifted attention away from party structures and enhanced the role of the Supreme Soviet as a genuine legislative body.

As the Supreme Soviet's inter-departmental commission continued to debate the draft legislation, the MMSR and the CLMAM combined forces to press the language issue. Along with the Democratic League of Students, the Society of Historians, representatives of the republic's ethnic minorities and other smaller informal organizations, on May 20, 1989, the MMSR and the CLMAM established the Popular Front of Moldova (*Frontul Popular al Moldovei*, FPM), a mass socio-political movement modelled on similar organizations in the Baltic republics. By staging demonstrations in Chişinău, developing a vast grassroots network in the countryside, and portraying itself as a movement of all the MMSR's ethnic groups, the FPM was able to present a serious challenge to Grossu and the PCM.

The election of Mircea Snegur as president of the MSSR Supreme Soviet on July 29, 1989, was a major turning point in the evolution of the language question. Although Snegur was a member of the PCM Politburo and had made his career in the state and party agricultural administration, he proved to be far more politically astute than first secretary Grossu. Snegur embraced the demands of the FPM, spoke at FPM rallies and quickly became the movement's key supporter within the Moldovan political élite. Under Snegur's leadership, on Aug. 31, 1989, the Supreme Soviet adopted new legislation returning the Moldovan language to the Latin script, making it the official language of the republic and implicitly acknowledging its unity with the Romanian language. Outside the Supreme Soviet building, the FPM staged a "Grand National Assembly" (*Marea Adunare Naţională*), a mass demonstration at which some 500,000 participants sanctioned the new legislation, unfurled the Romanian tricolour, and proclaimed the rebirth of Romanian culture in the MSSR.

The adoption of the new language laws and the rise of Snegur represented the beginning of the end for the PCM. Because of his complete failure to deal with the FPM and control the situation in the republic, Grossu was replaced as PCM first secretary on Nov. 16, 1989. His successor, the younger and more reform-minded Petru Lucinschi, had spent much of his career in party posts outside the MSSR. As second secretary in Tajikistan after 1986, and then as first secretary in Moldova after 1989, Lucinschi was one of the beneficiaries of Gorbachev's house cleaning of older party cadres in the republics. His political acumen and links with Gorbachev, however, could not halt the PCM's decline; its inability to control both the flow of events in the republic as well as the mass defections from its own ranks challenged its putative "leading role" in Moldovan society. By the time of its 17th Congress in 1990 (its last), the party could merely affirm its support for Moldovan sovereignty and the establishment of an independent Moldovan Communist Party outside the CPSU. By contrast, Mircea Snegur, who had earlier used his position in the Supreme Soviet as a lever against Grossu, increasingly portrayed himself as a non-party statesman committed to the rebirth of Moldovan culture while virtually ignoring party structures, a stance which further undermined Lucinschi's attempts to revitalize the PCM.

The elections for the USSR Congress of People's Deputies in March 1989 and to the MSSR Supreme Soviet in February 1990 sealed the PCM's fate as an organized political force. Representatives of the FPM soundly defeated PCM candidates for seats in the new congress and gave some of the organization's most articulate members an all-Union platform from which to issue calls for Moldovan sovereignty and cultural renaissance.

Likewise, while the PCM was still the only party permitted in the 1990 Supreme Soviet elections, multiple independent candidates were allowed to stand in several constituencies, and, as a result, FPM supporters took 140 of the Supreme Soviet's 380 seats in the first round of voting. With strong FPM backing, Snegur led the new Supreme Soviet in changing the republic's name (from the Moldovan Soviet Socialist Republic to the Soviet Socialist Republic of Moldova on June 5, 1990, and then again to the Republic of Moldova on May 23, 1991), adopting the Romanian tricolour as the new state flag and the traditional Moldovan bull's-head as the state seal in April and November 1990, and declaring sovereignty within the USSR on June 23, 1990. Petru Lucinschi's elevation to the CPSU Central Committee on Feb. 4, 1991, and his replacement by Grigore Eremei as PCM first secretary marked the final stage in the demise of Communist power in the MSSR. Shortly after the August coup, the Moldovan parliament declared the creation of an independent Republic of Moldova on Aug. 27, 1991, suspended the PCM's activities and confiscated all party assets.

In the wake of these triumphs, the FPM quickly became a victim of its own success. Once its goals had been reached — engineering a rebirth of Romanian culture, eradicating the notion of an independent Moldovan identity and pulling Moldova out of the Soviet Union — serious questions about the FPM's future naturally arose. For the radical pan-Romanianists within the FPM's leadership, an independent Moldova was only the first step towards eventual unification with Romania; the logical culmination of the FPM's activities was therefore to be not only the destruction of a separate Moldovan identity, but the destruction of a separate Moldovan state as well. For more moderate figures, the organization's aim was to encourage increased cultural and economic links with Romania while proceeding more slowly on the question of political union.

These internal disagreements between radicals and moderates were exacerbated by the FPM's brief experience in government. Following the FPM's strong showing in the 1990 republican elections, Snegur appointed one of its leaders, Mircea Druc, as prime minister. Druc used his position to press the issue of Moldovan–Romanian unification, sparking fears among the MSSR's ethnic minorities that the future would see their forced "romanianization" and incorporation into "Greater Romania". Disputes had been brewing since 1989 with the Gagauzi (Orthodox Christian Turks) in southern Moldova and with the Ukrainian and Russian populations in the strip of land on the east bank of the Dnestr river (the Transnistria or Pridnestrov'e region which had formed part of the MASSR before 1940). In opposition to the language laws, the Transnistrians staged strikes, blocked railway lines leading to central Moldova and declared the new laws void in the east-bank region. By early 1990, several Transnistrian cities had held referenda on secession from the MSSR, and in August and September, Gagauz and Transnistrian separatists declared independent "Soviet Socialist Republics" in southern Moldova and on the east bank of the Dnestr. In response, Prime Minister Druc issued a call to arms to defend the integrity of the Moldovan state, and Moldovan volunteer forces engaged in sporadic fighting with the nascent Gagauz army in the autumn of 1990. While the Moldovans rightly maintained that the disputes were less about ethnicity and more about the separatists' desire to resurrect the old Soviet Union, the pan-Romanian nationalism of the Druc government was largely to blame for the escalation of the conflict to open warfare. Disputes with the separatists continued even after Druc's dismissal in 1991, and by the summer of 1992 pitched battles had erupted along the Dnestr river between Moldovan and Transnistrian forces. A cease-fire brokered by Boris Yeltsin on July 21, 1992, halted the fighting and paved the way for the deployment of Russian peace-keeping troops along the river, but no final agreement with either the Transnistrians or the Gagauzi has yet been reached.

Druc's replacement by Valeriu Muravschi in May 1991 ended the "Frontist" period of Moldovan politics and further radicalized the FPM leadership. At its October 1991 conference, the FPM declared itself in opposition to President Snegur and called for a boycott of the Moldovan presidential elections in December. After Snegur emerged from the elections as Moldova's first popularly elected president, the FPM proclaimed that the national movement had been usurped by the former Communist *nomenklatura*, added a formal commitment to Moldovan–Romanian union to its political programme, and transformed itself into a political party, the Christian-Democratic Popular Front of Moldova (FPCD) at its 3rd congress in February 1992. The transformation from mass movement to political party aggravated tensions within the Frontist leadership. The period after 1990 had seen increasing defections from FPM ranks; especially after May 1990, when the Moldovan constitution was amended to allow non-Communist political parties the opportunity to participate in government, the FPM's role as the chief challenger to the PCM became far less significant.

The first two years of Moldovan independence saw the continued fall from grace of the pan-Romanianists and the further fragmentation of the FPM's main successor, the FPCD. The "national consensus" government of Andrei Sangheli, appointed to replace Valeriu Muravschi as prime minister in July 1992, contained no FPCD supporters. The last remaining pan-Romanianist in high office fell in January 1993, when the Moldovan parliament forced the resignation of its speaker, Alexandru Moşanu, along with the first deputy speaker and two members of the presidium. Petru Lucinschi was re-called from Moscow, where he had been serving as Moldova's first ambassador to the Russian Federation, and elected to the post of parliamentary speaker. With the fall of Moşanu, the country's three top political posts — president, prime minister and parliamentary speaker — were occupied by persons firmly opposed to the agenda of the FPCD, a sea-change from the situation under the Druc government. The FPCD's strength was further weakened in April 1993, when Moşanu and several former FPCD leaders established the Congress of the Intelligentsia (CI), a moderate unionist organization hoping to rescue the ideal of pan-Romanianism from its monopolization by radical unionists in the FPCD. The CI, which includes some of Moldova's leading intellectuals, has articulated a programme of gradual cultural and economic rapprochement with Romania without setting a time-table for political union.

Despite the fragmentation of the old FPM and the purge of pan-Romanianists from the government, the questions of Moldovan identity and the republic's relationship to Romania have continued to be the main issues in Moldovan politics. A number of new political parties have all attempted to turn public attention away from the contentious issue of Moldovan–Romanian union and towards such other pressing problems as economic reform, territorial separatism and relations with the other former Soviet republics. The results of the February 1994 parliamentary elections, however, illustrate that Moldova's population continues to be sharply divided between pan-Romanian and pro-independence camps. Before the February 1994 elections, the 380-member Moldovan Parliament (a renamed version of the Supreme Soviet elected in 1990) had become an unwieldy relic from the Soviet period. Since the PCM had been the only party allowed in the 1990 elections, the parliament no longer reflected Moldova's post-Soviet political landscape, and with no binding party mandates, deputies often moved erratically from one parliamentary faction to another. Moreover, with a permanent boycott by all but one of the deputies from Transnistria and frequent walk-outs by Gagauz and other deputies, the dominant parliamentary faction — the "Agrarian Club" of deputies — was often unable to muster enough votes to pass important legislation. Most spectacularly, in August 1993, the small group of deputies still loyal to the FPCD successfully blocked the parliament's ratification of the founding document of the Commonwealth of Independent States (CIS). Although President Snegur had signed the Alma Ata accords on the establishment of the CIS in December 1991, the documents had not yet been ratified by the Moldovan parliament, and the Russian Federation began to place increasing pressure on Moldova to ratify its membership or face harsh trade sanctions as a non-member state. Snegur publicly supported the republic's membership of the CIS, arguing that Moldova's economic situation necessitated continued participation in the trade and energy structures of the former Soviet Union; the FPCD, along with other anti-CIS factions in parliament, denounced the commonwealth as a continuation of the Soviet Union under another name. While the vote failed on a procedural technicality (because of the boycotts, the pro-CIS deputies were unable to garner the two-thirds majority of all registered parliamentarians needed to pass the bill), its failure was a personal embarrassment to Snegur and a victory for the anti-CIS FPCD and its allies.

In response to the vote, the Russian Federation placed heavy tariffs on goods imported from Moldova, thus effectively cutting off the republic's chief market for its agricultural and other goods. Despite the vote, the parliamentary presidium, chaired by Lucinschi, continued to act as a mini-parliament after the full assembly agreed to an "indefinite recess" in October. At the end of the month, the presidium voted to ratify the Alma Ata accords, thus completely ignoring the parliamentary vote, and the Russian Federation dropped its punitive tariffs. The presidium further voted to ratify the CIS economic treaty, which President Snegur had signed on Sept. 24, and to hold Moldova's first post-Soviet parliamentary elections on Feb. 27, 1994.

The revised electoral law, promulgated on Oct. 14, established a voting age of 18 and a 4 per cent threshold for parliamentary representation. The new scaled-down unicameral parliament — with 104 members as opposed to the previous 380 — was to have been elected through a closed party-list voting system (although independent candidates could also stand) in multi-candidate districts. However, since the establishment of the new electoral districts was dependent on the still-unadopted law on territorial administration, the presidium decreed on Oct. 19 that the entire republic would be considered a single electoral district. This temporary change in the electoral law, while an objective necessity, had the further advantage of implicitly including the separatist regions in the vote. Since the new deputies were elected on a national party-list system in one large electoral district (the whole republic), they are considered *de jure* representatives of all Moldovan citizens, rather than the delegates of particular territorial constituencies. The Moldovan government can thus argue that the new parliament is in fact representative of the entire republic, even though the Transnistrians banned the elections in the east-bank region. Of course, such arguments carry little weight with the separatists, but from a legal point of view, the electoral law avoided the problem of legitimizing territorial separatism by creating new electoral districts in only those regions still under the control of the central Moldovan authorities. Under a special agreement, the Transnistrian leadership allowed persons resident in the east-bank region to cross the Dnestr in order to vote, while Snegur decreed that such persons could register their votes up to six days before the elections. Only about 6,000 Moldovan citizens actually took advantage of this provision. No such special provisions were made for persons living in the self-proclaimed Gagauz Republic since the Gagauz leadership agreed to allow polling stations to operate unhindered.

A week after the elections, on March 6, President Snegur organised a "popular consultation", a legally non-binding referendum which asked the question "Do you want Moldova to develop as an independent and unified state in the borders recognized by the United Nations, to implement a policy of neutrality, to support mutually advantageous economic relations with any country and to guarantee all citizens equal rights in accordance with the norms of international law?" The referendum confirmed the results of the parliamentary elections: in February, over 40 per cent of voters cast ballots for the Agrarian Democratic Party (PDA), the successor to the "Agrarian Club" in the old Supreme Soviet and the chief voice in favour of independence and membership in the CIS, and likewise, over 90 per cent of participants in the referendum voted "Yes" to the consolidation of an independent Moldovan state. By contrast, the pan-Romanianists — divided between the FPCD and the "Bloc of Peasants and Intellectuals" (essentially the CI) — received collectively less than 20 per cent of the vote. Despite a large number of ballots (just over 93,000) ruled invalid for technical reasons, the elections were nevertheless deemed fair by international observers.

The new parliament, while having significantly diminished the power of the pan-Romanian unionist minority which had paralysed its predecessor, nevertheless contains a potentially troublesome bifurcation. The PDA, the chief power base of President Snegur, Prime Minister Sangheli and other key political figures, has an absolute majority of seats (56 of 104) and has thus been able to form a new single-party government. On certain issues, it will no doubt also enjoy the support of the second-largest group, the conservative coalition composed of the Socialist Party and the Edinstvo Movement (28 seats). Both the Agrarians and the Socialist–Edinstvo bloc are committed to maintaining an independent Moldovan state, granting wide-ranging local powers to the two separatist regions and strengthening economic ties with the former Soviet republics. Their general political philosophies — based on a go-slow approach to economic reform, avoidance of economic restructuring that would lead to social unrest and cultivation of a separate Moldovan ethno-national identity — are likewise highly compatible. At the same time, however, the PDA is far less sanguine about closer relations with Russia than are the Socialist–Edinstvo deputies. The status of the Russian 14th Army (former Soviet forces still stationed in Transnistria), will undoubtedly be a bone of contention between the two largest parliamentary camps. While the Socialist-Edinstvo bloc sees the 14th Army as a welcome source of stability, the PDA views its presence as an encouragement to the separatists and as an effort by the Russian Federation to undermine Moldovan independence. As President Snegur has argued repeatedly, no state can be truly independent so long as a portion of its territory is occupied by the military forces of a foreign power.

The most important result of the elections and the March referendum was the popular rejection of immediate Moldovan–Romanian union, and indeed, of the fundamental tenet of pan-Romanianism – that the Moldovans and Romanians form part of the same historical nation which should, through increasing cultural and economic ties, move closer towards integration in a single nation-state. However, the poor showing by the pan-Romanianists in the elections and referendum does not indicate their ultimate defeat. Although the unionists' political power began to wane with the fall of the Druc government in 1991, the lasting legacy of the FPM's brief period of political ascendancy is the continued control of education, publishing, language planning, scholarly research and the arts by persons committed to Moldovan–Romanian unification. While the process is certainly a long one, the power of educators and other professionals to reshape ethno-national identity should not be underestimated. Dedicated to awakening the Romanian spirit in the Moldovan population, the pan-Romaniaists will continue to be an important force on the margins of Moldovan politics and, with time, are likely to re-enter the mainstream.

The current parliament's mandate extends to 1998. In the interim, three parties which failed to pass the 4 per cent threshold — the Social Democratic Party, the Democratic Labour Party and the Party of Reform — will be the parties to watch. All three have been termed "asphalt parties": appealing mainly to non-unionist urban intellectuals, bureaucrats, industrial managers and the new class of upwardly mobile Moldovan businessmen, they have so far been unable to extend their message to the Moldovan countryside, the home of some 53 per cent of the republic's population. Now that the pan-Romanian issue has been laid to rest, at least for the time being, these three parties can concentrate on pressing the issues of economic reform and privatization, areas in which the PDA and the Socialist-Edinstvo coalition are unlikely to make significant progress. By criticizing the leading parties on these key issues, as well as by establishing stronger ties with the countryside, they may be able to gain considerable support in the next elections.

In the months following the February parliamentary elections, two important changes took place within the Moldovan party system. First, the sizeable opposition press which flourished during the electoral campaign disappeared by mid-March 1994. The few non-governmental newspapers which did remain curtailed their output, both in terms of frequency of publication and number of pages per issue. By the summer of 1994, no non-governmental daily newspaper existed in Moldova. Only a handful of important weeklies or monthlies (*Literatură şi Artă, Glasul Naţiunii, Spravedlivost'/Dreptate, Pămînt şi Oameni/Zemlia i Liudi, Mesagerul, Moldovanul*) had managed to survive, and many of these were the official organs of the PDA, the Socialist-Edinstvo alliance or the fellow-traveller Republican Party. While the continuing government monopoly on printing services and scarce paper supplies no doubt contributed to the virtual disappearance of an independent press, the opposition parties themselves were also partly to blame. Moldova's two most professional papers — *Observatorul de Chişinău* and *Dnevnoi Ekspress*, both sponsored by the Party of Reform — quickly lost the backing of their chief financial supporters after the party failed to win any parliamentary seats in the February elections. Clearly, the growth of democracy in Moldova will depend as much on the commitment of political parties and their supporters to continue their work even after an electoral loss as on equal access to printing resources.

A second important development involved the merger of several parties and socio-political organizations into larger political groupings. In late June 1994, the Congress of the Intelligentsia, Democratic Party and Christian Democratic Party joined to form the new United Democratic Congress (*Congresul Democrat Unit* — CDU). Although its name is new, the CDU retains the CI's old statute, which calls for, among other things, the realization of the country's "national ideal", i.e., closer integration with Romania. In the summer of 1994, a similar merger of the Party of Reform with like-minded reformist, non-unionist forces was also expected. The upcoming local elections — although not yet formally scheduled as of July 1994 — will represent the first trial of these new political formations and will test their ability to unseat the representatives of the PDA in *raion*-level political institutions.

300

Table 1: Moldovan Parliamentary Elections, Feb. 27, 1994

Party	Total votes	%	Deputies in Parliament
Agrarian Democratic Party	766,589	43.2	56
Socialist Party/Edinstvo Bloc	390,584	22.0	28
Bloc of Peasants and Intellectuals	163,513	9.2	11
Christian Democratic Popular Front Bloc	133,606	7.5	9
Social Democratic Bloc	65,028	3.7	—
Association of Women	50,243	2.8	—
Democratic Labour Party	49,210	2.8	—
Party of Reform	41,980	2.4	—
Democratic Party	23,368	1.3	—
Association of Victims of the Totalitarian Communist Regime	16,672	0.9	—
Republican Party	16,529	0.9	—
Ecological Party "Green Alliance"	7,025	0.4	—
National Christian Party	5,878	0.3	—

*Out of a total of 2,356,614 registered voters, 1,869,090 (79.3 per cent) participated. An additional 152,754 persons were added to the lists on the day of voting after presenting the required documents. A total of 1,775,377 valid ballots were cast, with another 93,116 ruled invalid. Twenty independent candidates also stood in the elections, but none received even 1 per cent of the total votes.

Source: Electorala 94: documente și cifre (Chişinău: Ediţie a Comisiei Electorale Centrale, 1994), p. 136.

Table 2: Composition of Moldovan Parliament elected in February 1994

	FPCD Bloc	CI Bloc	PDA*	PS-UE Bloc*
Total current deputies	9	11	54	27
of which, number who served in previous Parliament	4	6	9	6
Average age	36	48	48	50
Self-reported nationality				
Romanian	9	8	1	—
Moldovan	—	3	45	9
Russian	—	—	2	10
Ukrainian	—	—	2	5
Bulgarian	—	—	2	1
Gagauz	—	—	2	2
Self-reported profession				
Lawyer	1	1	9	3
Economist	2	—	6	—
Journalist	3	1	3	—
Historian	—	2	4	2
Engineer/technician	1	2	8	8
Teacher	1	—	1	7
Philologist	1	—	1	—
Physician	—	—	—	1
Agronomist/livestock expert	—	2	19	3
Other	—	3	3	3

Source: Valeriu Opincă, Moldovan Academy of Sciences; and *Electorala 94: documente şi cifre* (Chişinău: Ediţie a Comisiei Electorale Centrale, 1994), pp. 137–147.
*Changes in PDA and PS-UE representation were made after the adoption of the new constitution in July 1994.

Directory of Parties

Note: Foundation dates indicate the dates on which parties were officially registered with the Ministry of Justice.

Agrarian Democratic Party
Partidul Democrat Agrar (PDA)

Address. Bdul Ştefan cel Mare 162, et. 4, Chişinău.

Telephone. 24.61.44, 24.86.50, 24.88.59, 26.66.67.

Foundation. Nov. 21, 1991.

Leadership. Dumitru Moţpan (ch.), Zosim Bodiu.

Membership. 8,928

History. The PDA has been President Mircea Snegur's main base of support since its formation in 1991 out of the "Agrarian Club" in the former Supreme Soviet. Andrei Sangheli, Petru Lucinschi, two deputy prime ministers, several members of the government and numerous local administrators and agro-industrial bosses were all included on the PDA's list of candidates in the 1994 elections. The party's grassroots support comes from Moldova's agricultural *nomenklatura* — collective farm presidents, managers of agro-industrial enterprises and other persons who (like President Snegur himself) all graduated from the Chişinău Agricultural Institute or made their careers in Moldova's large agricultural sector. While the party's political programme emphasizes Moldovan independence and co-operation with the other former Soviet republics, support for the PDA is based primarily on personal loyalties to local agrarian élites. As a result, the party emerged with an absolute majority in the new parliament (56 or 104 seats) and formed a single-party government.

Programme. The party supports the maintenance of a law-governed, fully independent Moldovan state; the creation of "a market economy with a social orientation"; equality of all citizens regardless of ethnicity, language, religion or social class; transformation of collective farms into peasant joint-stock associations on the *kibbutz* model; and participation in economic but not political or military structures of Commonwealth of Independent States.

Publication. Pămînt şi Oameni/Zemlia i Liudi (Land and People).

Association of Victims of the Totalitarian Communist Regime
Asociaţia Victimelor Regimului Totalitar Comunist (AVRTC)

Address. Str. Mihai Cogălniceanu 52, Chişinău.

Telephone. 22.51.21, 24.46.19.

Foundation. Dec. 31, 1992.

Leadership. Mihail Moroşanu (ch.)

Membership. 413.

History. Having its roots in the early Popular Front of Moldova, the AVRTC is composed of older pan-Romanian unionists united in their opposition to Russia and the CIS. The association is not represented in parliament, although the interests of its members are articulated by both the FPCD and the CI.

Programme. The party supports economic and cultural integration with Romania and the European Union; reparations payments from Russia for Moldovan famines in 1930s and 1940s, as well as for Moldovan lives lost in Soviet invasions of Hungary, Czechoslovakia and Afghanistan; restitution of property nationalized by Communists.

Association of Women
Asociaţia Femeilor (AF)

Address. Str. Alexei Mateevici 109/1, Chişinău.

Telephone. 23.33.23.

Fax. 22.64.07.

Foundation. Feb. 19, 1992.

Leadership. Liudmila Scalnîi (ch.)

Membership. 10,000

History. The AF is the direct descendant of the former Moldovan Women's Union which effectively collapsed at the same time as the Communist Party of Moldova. Although it did not pass the 4 per cent threshold necessary for parliamentary representation in the 1994 elections, its comparatively strong showing indicated that the social demands articulated in the AF's programme are of concern to a considerable portion of the Moldovan population.

Programme. Promotes a "harmonious policy" which would eliminate the polarization between rich and poor; cultivate the same "equilibrium" in society found in the family; use "female intuition" to resolve the problems of the transition period; strengthen Moldovan independence; and introduce special protection for children, pensioners and single mothers.

Christian-Democratic Popular Front
Frontul Popular Creştin-Democrat (FPCD)

Address. Str. Nicolae Iorga 5, Chişinău.

Telephone. 23.45.47; 24.44.27.

Fax. 23.44.80.

Foundation. March 11, 1992.

Leadership. Iurie Roşca (ch.)

Membership. 18,000.

History. The FPCD represents the more radical pan-Romanian unionist wing of the old Popular Front of Moldova, the mother of all Moldovan political parties. Hoping to stem the tide of defections to the various other political movements which arose after 1990, the Front's leadership transformed itself into a political party, added "Christian Democratic" to its name and inserted an overt commitment to Moldovan–Romanian union in its political programme at its 3rd congress in February 1992. Along with the PNC and other smaller unionist formations, in October 1992 the FPCD set up an umbrella organization (the Christian Alliance for the Reintegration of Romania, ACRR) in order to press the issue of Moldovan–Romanian union. The ACRR has since become defunct, as the failure of the PNC to participate in the FPCD electoral bloc indicates. Although the FPCD toned down its unionist rhetoric for the election campaign, it continues to see an independent Moldova (which members call Bessarabia) as merely the first step towards reunion with Romania. The time-table for union, however, remains unclear. All other political and social dimensions of the FPCD's programme are subordinated to this goal, and the party's leaders see any concessions to political pragmatism as a betrayal of the "sacred cause" of pan-Romanian integration.

Programme. Rejection of membership in the Commonwealth of Independent States; realization of the "sacred cause" of national integration with Romania; promotion of Orthodox Christianity as the "principal guide" for the Romanian nation.

Affiliation. Stood in electoral block with OTCD and MV in February 1994 parliamentary elections.

Publication. Ţara (The Country).

Congress of the Intelligentsia
Congresul Intelectualităţii (CI)

Address. Str. Mitr. Dosoftei 68, et. 7, Chişinău.

Telephone. 22.27.82, 22.85.38, 22.83.30, 24.87.62.

Foundation. June 18, 1993.

Leadership. Alexandru Moşanu (ch.), Vasile Nedelciuc.

Membership. 349.

History. The CI is the more moderate face of pan-Romanianism in Moldova. Composed of many of the Popular Front's former leading lights (including several eminent academics, writers, and the former chair of the Moldovan parliament), the CI was originally formed in April 1993 in opposition to the abrasive unionist rhetoric of the FPCD. The electoral alliance with the ATL allowed the CI to include the word "peasant" in the name of its electoral bloc, although most of the members of the ATL are in fact functionaries in the state agricultural administration rather than genuine peasants.

Publication. Mesagerul (The Messenger) and *Literatură şi Artă* (Literature and Art, officially the organ of the Moldovan Writers' Union).

Programme. The party favours increased economic contacts with Romania and the West; special administrative districts in separatist regions; strengthening of Romanian identity within a genuinely independent Moldovan state; and gradual economic and "spiritual" integration with Romania.

Affiliation. Stood in "Bloc of Peasants and Intellectuals" electoral alliance with the LCDF, PCD, PNL and ATL in February 1994 parliamentary elections.

Democratic Party
Partidul Democrat (PD)

Address. Str. Bucureşti 68, Chişinău.

Telephone. 23.70.53.

Foundation. March 26, 1992.

Leadership. Gheorghe Ghimpu (ch.)

Membership. 315.

History. Originally founded in December 1990, the PD was composed of early defectors from the FPCD led by the former dissident Gheorghe Ghimpu. Although the PD rarely co-operated with other political factions in the outgoing parliament, for the 1994 elections it concluded an electoral alliance with the PPG, the small mainly Gagauz party opposed to the actions of the separatists in southern Moldova.

Programme. The PD wants to strengthen the "genuine independence and territorial integrity" of Moldova. It also wants a bicameral parliament, with lower house elected by party-list system and upper house elected by first-past-the-post system in single-member districts; self-administration for separatist regions.

Affiliation. Stood in electoral bloc with PPG in February 1994 parliamentary elections.

Publication. Clopotul Renaşterii (The Bell of Rebirth).

Democratic Labour Party
Partidul Democrat al Muncii (PDM)

Address. Str. Dosoftei 112, Chişinău.

Telephone. 22.45.55, 22.85.76, 22.46.25, 22.33.26.

Foundation. April 28, 1993.

Leadership. Alexandru Arseni (ch.)

Membership. 367.

History. The PDM, which held its constitutive congress in March 1993, is a pro-independence party composed mainly of ethnic Moldovan/Romanian directors of state enterprises. The PDM bloc in the outgoing parliament supported the pan-Romanian unionists during the vote on CIS membership in August 1993, largely as a reaction against Russian attempts to force Moldova into the commonwealth. The PDM's supporters are primarily industrial managers who stand to gain from large-scale privatization but who fear that the current privatization programme will benefit only the state bureaucracy. The PDM is strongly supported by the "Moldovahidromaş" industrial concern, whose director-general was placed first on the list of PDM candidates in the 1994 elections.

Programme. Flexible, pragmatic foreign policy; integration of Moldovan economy with countries inside and outside the Commonwealth of Independent States; gradual transition to market economy; re-working of privatization programme to ensure that entire population shares the benefits.

Publication. Plus-Minus (Plus-Minus).

Ecological Party "Green Alliance"
Partidul Ecologist "Alianţa Verde" (AV)

Address. Str. Puşkin 24, cam. 59, Chişinău.

Telephone. 57.04.66.

Foundation. April 9, 1992.

Leadership. Mircea Ciuhrii (ch.)

Membership. 790.

History. The largest of Moldova's ecological organizations, the AV has generally supported the political aims of the CI.

Programme. Creation of "ecological police" to enforce anti-pollution legislation; economic and cultural integration with Romania; participation of United Nations and other international organizations in resolving problems with separatist regions; "ecologization" of all areas of economic activity.

Edinstvo Movement
Mişcarea "Unitatea-Edinstvo" (UE)

Address. Str. Hînceşti 35, cam. 12, Chişinău.

Telephone. 73.12.96, 26.00.48.

Foundation. April 9, 1992.

Leadership. Petr Shornikov (ch.), Vladimir Solonari.

Membership. 340.

History. Originally set up as part of the all-Union "Interdvizhenie" organization in 1989, the UE opposed the new language laws and initially supported the demands of the Transnistrian separatists. Its leader, Petr Shornikov, was not allowed to stand in the 1994 elections since it was alleged that he had aided the Transnistrian separatists.

Affiliation. Stood in electoral bloc with PS in February 1994 parliamentary elections.

307

National Christian Party
Partidul Naţional Creştin (PNC)

Address. Str. Nicolae Iorga 5, Chişinău.

Telephone. 77.40.01, 57.40.11.

Foundation. March 11, 1992.

Leadership. Vladimir Nicu (ch.)

Membership. 3,450.

History. Originally established in 1990 by a few of the most radical members of the Popular Front, the PNC is the only political party calling for immediate Moldovan–Romanian union. The PNC's main base of support lies among historians, philologists, teachers and other members of the ethnic Romanian cultural élite in Chişinău. The PNC received fewer votes than any other party in the 1994 elections.

Programme. The party demands immediate Moldovan–Romanian political union; the cultivation of Orthodox Christian values; wide-ranging agricultural import substitution; and reconquest of separatist regions.

Party of Reform
Partidul Reformei (PRef)

Address. B-dul Ştefan cel Mare 4, Chişinău.

Telephone. 22.95.56, 22.64.06, 26.60.52, 26.60.85.

Foundation. Sept. 28, 1993.

Leadership. Anatol Şalaru (ch.)

Membership. 470.

History. The PRef is one of the youngest and most well-financed parties in Moldova, as evidenced by its ability to support two newspapers during the electoral campaign, both of extremely high quality. Its support comes from ethnic Moldovan/Romanian economists and businessmen sceptical of the government's voucher privatization programme, which the PRef sees as detrimental to the growth of new business and foreign investment.

Programme. Growth of private sector in economy; low taxes to stimulate foreign investment; reorientation of scientific research to address the needs of the economy; self-administration for separatist regions; strengthening of unitary, independent Moldovan state.

Publication. Dnevnoi Ekspress (Daily Express) and Observatorul de Chişinău (The Chişinău Observer).

Republican Party
Partidul Republican (PR)

Address. Str. Melestiu 7, Chişinău.

Telephone. 25.20.47, 21.39.77.

Foundation. Feb. 18, 1993.

Leadership. Victor Puşcaş (ch.), Gheorghe Mazilu.

Membership. 337.

History. Led by the deputy speaker of the outgoing parliament, the PF's goals and constituency differ little from those of the PDA.

Programme. Strengthening of unitary, fully independent state; reduction of state bureaucracy by half; transformation of Moldova into demilitarized zone based on collective security agreements; criminal prosecution for "anti-state agitation" in state institutions; adoption of new, non-Romanian state symbols.

Publication. Moldovanul (The Moldovan).

Social Democratic Party
Partidul Social Democrat (PSD)

Address. Str. Mihai Cogălniceanu 11, Chişinău.

Telephone. 26.45.30, 26.42.15, 22.33.25, 22.66.18.

Foundation. April 9, 1992.

Leadership. Oazu Nantoi (ch.), Viorel Ciubotaru, Victor Josu.

Membership. 300.

History. The PSD, originally set up on May 13, 1990, is composed mainly of pro-independence intellectuals and bureaucrats opposed to both the radical "moldovanism" of the Snegur-Sangheli government and the pan-Romanianism of the FPCD and CI. Some of Moldova's brightest young technocrats have joined the PSD, and its electoral list included the Moldovan ambassador to the Russian Federation, the director of the state department for privatization, the president's chief advisor, the interim foreign minister and other prominent political figures. Although the PSD can claim to have the most broad-based support of any party in Moldova (in terms of ethnic group and social status), it nevertheless failed to reach the 4 per cent threshold needed for parliamentary representation.

Programme. Growth of civil society not based on ethnicity; independent Moldovan state; special legal status for separatist regions; privatization based solely on egalitarian voucher system; depoliticization of educational and cultural institutions; reduction of state bureaucracy; strengthening of general European, humanitarian values.

Affiliation. Stood in "Social Democratic Bloc" in February 1994 parliamentary elections with UTM, LNT and MDD.

Publication. Respublica (The Republic).

Socialist Party
Partidul Socialist (PS)

Address. Str. Cosmonauţilor 6, cam. 408, Chişinău.

Telephone. 72.32.37, 22.38.97, 53.03.69.

Foundation. Aug. 11, 1992.

Leadership. Valeriu Senic (ch.)

Membership. 310.

History. The PS is the most direct descendant of the Communist Party of Moldova, which was suspended indefinitely in August 1991. Its large base of support, which allowed it to gain 22 per cent of the vote in the 1994 elections, lies among mainly Russian urban workers and pensioners outside the separatist regions. The PS–UE bloc won five of Moldova's seven urban centres in the February vote.

Programme. Membership in all structures of Commonwealth of Independent States; independent, multi-ethnic Moldovan state; government regulation of most important areas of economy; gradual privatization through voucher system; maintenance of independent, non-Romanian linguistic and ethnic identity; creation of independent Moldovan Orthodox Church.

Affiliation. Stood in electoral bloc with UE in February 1994 parliamentary elections.

Publication. Spravedlivost'Dreptate (Justice).

Smaller parties and socio-political organizations

Christian Democratic Youth Organization (*Organizaţia Tineretului Creştin-Democrat —* OTCD, Sept. 2, 1992), the youth wing of the FPCD.

Movement of Volunteers (*Mişcarea Voluntarilor* — MV, Dec. 25, 1992), an organization of persons who participated in battles with the Gagauz and Transnistrian separatists (1990 and 1992); allied with the FPCD.

Union of Youth (*Uniunea Tineretului* — UT, Nov. 21, 1991), the successor to the former Moldovan Union of Communist Youth (Komsomol) but now allied with the PSD.

National Youth League (*Liga Naţională a Tineretului* — LNT, Oct. 18, 1991), allied with the PSD.

Left-Bank Democratic Movement "Dignity" (*Mişcarea Democratică din Stînga Nistrului 'Demnitatea'* — MDD, March 11, 1992), composed of persons from the Transnistrian district of Slobozia who are opposed to the actions of the separatists; allied with the PSD.

Christian Democratic Women's League *(Liga Creştin-Democrată a Femeilor* — LCDF, March, 26, 1992), originally the women's organization of the FPCD but since 1993 allied with the CI.

Christian Democratic Party (*Partidul Creştin Democrat* — PCD, March 26, 1992), an early defector from the FPM, the PCD did not support the boycott of the 1991 presidential elections and, despite its name, is not linked with the FPCD; allied with the CI.

National Liberal Party (*Partidul Naţional Liberal* — PNL, Sept. 10, 1993), allied with the CI.

Alliance of Free Peasants (*Alianţa Ţăranilor Liberi* — ATL, Sept. 10, 1993), composed mainly of bureaucrats in the central agricultural administration, rather than peasants themselves; allied with the CI.

Gagauz People's Party (*Partidul Popular Gagauz/Gagauz Halk Partisi* — PPG, Sept. 10, 1993), composed of ethnic Gagauzi opposed to the actions of the separatists in southern Moldova; allied with the PD.

Association of Former Political Prisoners (*Asociaţia Foştilor Deţinuţi Politici* — AFDP, Feb. 19, 1992), similar in aims to the AVRTC but allied with the FPCD.

POLAND

Frances Millard

The process of incipient party development in post-communist Poland depended in its initial stages on some highly distinctive and specific features of Poland's post-war history. It was Poland that in 1989 became the first East European country to install a non-communist prime minister and by so doing test the validity of Mikahil Gorbachev's new "Sinatra Doctrine" that the East Europeans could at long last do things "their way", without fear of external interference from the Soviet Union.

The events of 1989 came about largely because of the chronic weakness of Poland's ruling communist party, the PZPR (Polish United Workers' Party, *Polska Zjednoczona Partia Robotnicza*), in the face of a society which had asserted itself in protest against its leaders with grim regularity — in 1956, 1968, 1970, 1976, 1980 and 1988. The formation of the independent trade union Solidarity in 1980 was a triumphant watershed, as Solidarity developed into a vast social movement mobilizing the various strands of opposition to the regime, as well as embracing numerous ordinary members of the PZPR itself. Solidarity survived as an alternative focus of political loyalty throughout the 1980s, despite General Jaruzelski's desperate imposition of a period of martial law (December 1981–July 1983) and the regime's pursuit, though neither consistently nor successfully, of economic and political reform policies later in that decade. Solidarity survived as a small underground movement that maintained the loyalty of a substantial element of the population. By the end of the decade the contradictions and irrationalities of the centrally planned economic system were becoming increasingly evident in shortages and dislocations, a growing burden of foreign debt, and a failure to provide the welfare services which people had come to expect. When a new wave of strikes swept the country in the spring and summer of 1988, the bankrupt regime sought to incorporate the opposition into the political process through a negotiated settlement.

The prospect of negotiations caused tension and resistance, as conservatives within the PZPR and Solidarity's radical wing opposed the concept of the Round Table. However, by the turn of the year the Solidarity leader, Lech Wałęsa, and the PZPR party leader, Wojciech Jaruzelski, had each gained sufficient support for discussions to proceed. The Round Table convened in February 1989. It should be stressed at this point, however, that the Communists did not expect to relinquish power. They fully expected the arrangement to benefit them, and expected to continue to control the state even while relinquishing some of their previous mechanisms of rule. Solidarity expected this too, but while the Communists saw a deal as presenting the possibility of peaceful transformation *within* the system, Solidarity saw it as the first phase of the transmutation *of* the system. Solidarity was correct because it understood the depths of anti-communist sentiment and the regime did not: indeed the party leaders thought that the government of the reformist Mieczysław Rakowski was gaining in popularity in 1989. The PZPR's general strategic miscalculation was also accompanied by a number of tactical errors, as well as some uncomfortable behaviour by its own allies.

Following the Round Table accord or "contract" of spring 1989, freedom of association was dramatically extended to permit not only the trade union pluralism which had been a key demand of underground Solidarity, but also the organization of political parties. A number of small parties emerged from clandestine activity, notably the Confederation for Independent Poland (*Konfederacja Polski Niepodległej* — KPN), which had an opposition pedigree dating back to 1979. The ruling PZPR encouraged this (albeit ambivalently), for it counted on a divided opposition to deprive Solidarity of seats in the Round Table election in June. In that election 35 per cent of deputies to the lower house or *Sejm* were to be elected by competing elements outside the official establishment. Just over 7 per cent (35 deputies) were to be elected on an uncontested "National List", with the remaining 57 per cent to be elected by competing candidates from the official ruling parties, i.e. the PZPR and its satellites: the United Peasant Party (*Zjednoczone Stronnictwo Ludowe* — ZSL), the Democratic Party (*Stronnictwo Demokratyczne* — SD) and a few pro-regime religious groupings. The Communists would have a majority in the *Sejm*, but only with the support of their allies. The newly established Senate was elected on a fully competitive basis.

In the event the PZPR's tactics failed. Solidarity won all 35 per cent of the *Sejm*'s opposition seats and all but one in the Senate. No non-Solidarity anti-establishment "party" made any impact. The election dealt a mortal blow to the PZPR. Firstly, all but two members of the National List were defeated; the electorate voted against them by deleting their names from the ballot paper. This meant the absence from Parliament of all the leaders of the hitherto ruling coalition parties. Secondly, the Party was shocked by the sheer scale of Solidarity's success. In addition, Solidarity had influenced the character of the deputies elected for the establishment parties by identifying and supporting the reformist elements among competing candidates. This intensified the divisions between the new deputies and their party bureaucracies; among other things it undermined the traditional party discipline that was a major strength of the old Leninist-style Communist parties. It also served to break the links between the PZPR and its erstwhile satellites, the ZSL and SD, which promptly entered into negotiations with Solidarity over the shape of the new government. The PZPR still nominally controlled 38 per cent of deputies but could not count on their cohesion or obedience. In accordance with implicit understandings of the Round Table the new parliament elected General Jaruzelski as President, but by a margin of only one vote.

In September 1989, after complex negotiations, Solidarity took charge of a Grand Coalition of ministers drawn from Solidarity itself, the PZPR, the United Peasant Party and the Democratic Party under the premiership of one of its leading Catholic intellectuals, Tadeusz Mazowiecki. Solidarity's leader Wałęsa remained outside parliament as leader of the trade union wing, centred in Gdańsk. Solidarity was functioning as a quasi-party with a trade union element, the local and regional citizens' committees which had provided its election machine, and the OKP, the Citizens' Parliamentary Club in Parliament.

The situation was further complicated because Solidarity, formally disavowing the party label for itself, permitted dual membership; thus some nascent parties had put forward candidates in the Round Table election under the Solidarity imprimatur. The OKP included members of the Liberal Democratic Congress (KLD), the Solidarity Peasant Party (PSL-S), the Polish Socialist Party (PPS) and the Christian Democratic Labour Party (ChDSP);

POLAND

the founding of the Christian National Union (ZChN) in September 1989 added another handful of deputies claiming allegiance both to Solidarity and to a "political party". They began working to extend their incipient organization within the country at large.

The PZPR, beset by internal conflicts, a moribund party bureaucracy, and a haemorrhage of its membership, was in the last throes of decline. Yet Solidarity still perceived it as a potential danger because of anxieties about the position of Moscow, the party's control of the key ministries of Defence and the Interior, and because its appointees still occupied key posts in central and local government administration. In fact, these fears proved groundless, and in January 1990 the PZPR dissolved itself, generating two successor parties rejecting the last vestiges of Marxism-Leninism and declaring their conversion to social democracy. Of these, Social Democracy of the Polish Republic (*Socjaldemokracja Rzeczpospolitej Polski — SdRP*) persisted as a significant political force.

The United Peasant Party (ZSL) remained strong in terms of both organization and membership, and it moved quickly to break with the past by removing its leader; changing its name to the more traditional Polish Peasant Party (PSL) and merging with a new, smaller PSL (Wilanów); asserting its commitment to Christian teachings, and speaking out vigorously on behalf of its rural constituents. The Democratic Party by contrast failed to establish a new identity and faded rapidly.

Outside government and parliament a flourishing universe of small clusters of "couch parties" developed, so-called because their members were said to be able to fit onto a single settee. Some, like the National Party (SN), represented attempts to reconstruct historic parties of the inter-war period. A small Green Party (highly prone to splits) had existed since late 1988. The ultra-liberals of the Union of Political Realism and the xenophobes of the Polish Union of the National Commonwealth provide further examples. These groups laid claim to the status of political party. All were organized outside the capital, albeit often through isolated individual contact persons; they were virtually unknown to the general population. They aimed to contest elections and offered more or less coherent sets of policies. In this respect they were distinguishable from the myriad of political clubs and economic lobbies which also contributed to political debate. However, only one of the extra-parliamentary "parties" would genuinely seem to warrant that label, namely the KPN, led since 1979 by Leszek Moczulski. The KPN was a radical, uncompromising, anti-communist party with an extensive organization, a core of disciplined young activists and a knack for attracting publicity through demonstrations and protests.

The major political actors, from 1989 to October 1991 (the date of the first fully competitive parliamentary elections), however, were those represented in parliament. Solidarity had provided Poland with a counter-élite able to take control in a process of peaceful transformation. The Communists presented little obstacle to the Mazowiecki government and there was a broad parliamentary consensus regarding the need for fundamental change. The government embarked on a programme of vetting and replacement of personnel, especially in the Interior and Justice ministries. Constitutional amendments removed all reference to the socialist order, changed the country's name to the Polish Republic, and restored the national symbol of the crowned eagle. The rule of law, democratic pluralism and social justice became the main operating principles of the amended constitution, while Parliament began work on drafting a new one. After the PZPR's dissolution in January 1990, many of the Old Guard retired from politics. Its former members in parliament broadly supported the economic strategy of the radical Balcerowicz programme, with the dismantling of the planning system, preparations for

315

privatization, wage limitations, currency convertibility, and the reduction of subsidies. The results shook the new social consensus, with dramatic price increases, a rapid fall in output, a profound decline in real wages, and rising unemployment. New tensions arose, and in the absence of a common communist enemy and with communist regimes falling rapidly throughout Eastern Europe, Solidarity began to split apart.

By April 1990 simmering tensions with Solidarity emerged into open conflict. The trigger was Lech Wałęsa's determination to replace former Communist Party leader Jaruzelski as President of Poland. Wałęsa argued that the dissolution of the PZPR rendered the Round Table contract an anachronism and demanded an early presidential election. The ensuing "war at the top" generated two broad camps within Solidarity, one favouring Wałęsa's presidential candidacy, the other supporting Mazowiecki. Solidarity's unity became increasingly strained, creating inexorable pressure to bring forward the date of the presidential elections.

In May 1990 Jarosław Kaczyński formally inaugurated the Centre Democratic Accord (*Porozumienie Demokratyczne Centrum* — PC) as a broad coalition supporting Wałęsa and the "acceleration" of change. Kaczyński by his own admission sought to cleave Solidarity in two. The PC attracted a group of Solidarity's parliamentary representatives, large numbers of the local citizens' committees, trade union branches, and individual members of many small right and centre "parties". Kaczyński presented the PC as a group of like-minded people determined to prevent the so-called Solidarity "Left" from turning Solidarity into a left-wing party which would rule Poland as a new monolith. However, the PC did not succeed as the unifying vehicle for Wałęsa's candidacy. Many other groups supporting Wałęsa remained outside it, and Wałęsa kept himself aloof, despite his increasingly close association with Kaczyński and his twin brother.

Two organizations formed to support Mazowiecki's presidential candidacy: the Democratic Right Forum, with a strong Christian Democratic and liberal emphasis; and ROAD, the Citizens' Movement for Democratic Action, which presented itself as the embodiment of Solidarity's quintessential values and ideals. The Forum was closely associated with a group of Krakow intellectuals around Jerzy Turowicz. Aleksander Hall was another prominent member, formerly associated with the Gdańsk "Young Poland Movement". ROAD contained many of Solidarity's intellectual luminaries, including Bronisław Geremek, leader of the OKP; Jacek Kuroń, Mazowiecki's Minister of Labour; Adam Michnik, parliamentary deputy and editor of *Gazeta Wyborcza* (Election Gazette), the Solidarity daily founded as its vehicle for the 1989 election. It also embraced former underground Solidarity leaders such as Zbigniew Bujak and Władysław Frasyniuk. The two groupings formed an electoral alliance as the Democratic Union, favouring a continuation of the policies of the Mazowiecki government. Following the presidential election they united into a single political party of that name (*Unia Demokratyczna* — UD).

By September, with the formal declaration of his candidacy, Wałęsa was the clear favourite. Most of the Solidarity trade union movement supported him; so did most of Rural Solidarity, the Solidarity Peasant Party, and the local citizens' committees. He had the support of the PC, the Liberal Democratic Congress, the Christian National Union, the Christian Democratic Labour Party, the Union of Political Realism and elements of the Green Party.

Four other candidates also stood in the presidential election. Of these, the expatriate Polish-Canadian businessman Stan Tymiński — who proved to be the dark horse of the race — at that time had no political party, nor indeed a political base of any kind. Włodzimierz

Table 1: Presidential election 1990

	Votes	%
First ballot, 25 November (turnout: 61 per cent)		
Lech Wałęsa (PC + others)	6,569,889	39.96
Stan Tymiński (Ind.)	3,797,605	23.10
Tadeusz Mazowiecki (UD)	2,973,264	18.08
Włodzimierz Cimoszewica (Left)	1,514,025	9.21
Roman Bartoszcze (Peas.)	1,176,175	7.15
Leszek Moczulski (KPN)	411,516	2.50
Second ballot, 9 December (turnout: 54 per cent)		
Lech Wałęsa	10,622,698	74.75
Stan Tymiński	3,683,098	25.25

Cimoszewicz stood as the candidate of the united Left, in effect an alliance of the SdRP with the former communist-organized (but quasi-independent) trade union movement, the OPZZ. Roman Bartoszcze was the candidate (and at that time leader) of the reconstituted former Communist satellite peasant party, now the PSL. Leszek Moczulski stood for his party, the KPN. The campaign was lacklustre, but it did give the virtually unknown non-Solidarity candidates the opportunity for public exposure and they gained ground as the campaign progressed.

The victory of Wałęsa was expected, but the surprise of the election was the strong performance of Tymiński, who pushed Mazowiecki into third place on the first ballot. The second ballot provided overwhelming support for Wałęsa, as many supporters of losing candidates voted for Wałęsa on the principle of the lesser evil. Thus Lech Wałęsa won the presidency on the basis of a disparate coalition. A high proportion of the population took no part in the election or expressed its alienation through support for Tymiński. The old party system had broken up, but there was as yet nothing to take its place.

President Wałęsa appointed Jan Krzysztof Bielecki (leader of the KLD) as prime minister of a new minority government in January 1991. The Bielecki government was seen as a temporary one in the light of expected parliamentary elections. It largely continued Mazowiecki's political and economic strategy, although its relations with the *Sejm* were far more difficult. Although the election timetable was gradually extended, not least because of controversy surrounding the electoral system, political parties prepared for the coming election. New parties mushroomed, while others split or merged. On the eve of the October 1991 election, there were well over 100 registered "parties". Most were tiny cadre parties or "para-parties" without social roots or public recognition; only a few could be regarded as serious contenders. These could be roughly divided into Solidarity "pro-reform" parties wishing to continue the current economic policies; Solidarity "anti-reform parties" arguing broadly for increased economic interventionism; the old regime's successor parties; and a heterogeneous group of small, mainly new parties testing their electoral appeal. Moczulski's KPN was distinctive: it was not linked to Solidarity, it had developed an effective organization and it bore no responsibility for policies pursued since 1989. Neither ideological nor class divisions were clear cut; most parties appealed to a diffuse "national interest".

The 1991 election was the first fully competitive parliamentary election and thus the first real test of strength for the political parties. However, with few exceptions the public remained largely ignorant of the nature of the parties they were being invited to support. Those who had held important offices enjoyed some public recognition, as did some who had been highly visible in the *Sejm*'s televised sessions. Some prominent dissidents of the communist period were still known and some previous pro-regime activists also. Individuals were more easily recognized than their parties. This was one reason why, despite presidential opposition, the electoral system gave voters the opportunity to choose a named individual.

The electoral system was quite complex, not least because it was the product of a series of compromises. Of the 460 deputies to the *Sejm*, 391 were elected in 37 constituencies based mainly on existing provincial boundaries and ranging in size from five seven-member constituencies to the 17-member constituencies of Warsaw City and part of Katowice province. These deputies were elected on the basis of the list system of proportional representation; voters chose one individual candidate from his/her party list. The number of seats was calculated using the Hare-Niemeyer system.

The 69 deputies elected from the all-Polish party lists were determined by the votes cast in the constituencies. Committees registering lists in at least five constituencies could submit a national list, chosen from among candidates on their constituency lists. To be eligible for all-Polish seats a party (or "election committee") needed to win seats in at least five constituencies or receive at least 5 per cent of the total vote. Committees registering an electoral alliance between lists had their vote aggregated and treated as a single list. The total sum of the valid votes cast for a list would be divided successively by 1.4, 3, 5, 7 and subsequent odd numbers until the number of quotients matched the number of seats to be allocated (the Sainte Lague method). The parties would then receive seats in descending order, from the highest quotient in the lowest.

The system used for electing the Senate was far simpler: all but two provinces had two seats (Warsaw and Katowice had three) and voters could choose two candidates. Those two (or three) with the highest vote won. However, the Senate was less powerful than the *Sejm*. Although it had the ability to obstruct the *Sejm*, the prime minister was responsible to the lower house.

The system for electing the *Sejm* was widely interpreted as providing a good opportunity for small groupings to obtain representation. In this respect it provided a means of escape from the bewildering confusion of party competition. Ethnic minorities, pressure groups (including the Solidarity trade union) and numerous local organizations fielded candidates, sometimes gathering around a popular figure reluctant to adopt a party affiliation. In all, 36 election committees registered lists in two or more constituencies; 19 registered in 30 or more; nine registered in all 37. A total of 6,980 candidates contested 391 seats.

On Oct. 27, 1991, fewer than half the electorate voted. The national average turnout was 43.2 per cent, with a high of 53 per cent in Warsaw city. As expected, the result produced a polarized and fragmented parliament. Some 29 different electoral committees gained representation in the *Sejm*. Leaving aside local alliances and KPN satellite parties, there remained 14 parties/party alliances, two trades unions, two minority groups and a motley

Table 2: Election to the *Sejm*, October 1991

Party	% of vote	Seats won
Democratic Union (Unia Demokratyczna)	12.31	62
Alliance of the Democratic Left (SLD)	11.98	60
Catholic Election Action (WAK)	8.73	49
Centre Democratic Accord (Centrum)	8.71	44
Peasant Party–Programmatic Alliance (PSL)	8.67	48
Confederation for Independent Poland (KPN)	7.50	46
Liberal Democratic Congress (KLD)	7.48	37
Peasant Accord (PL)	5.46	28
Solidarity	5.05	27
Polish Friends of Beer (PPPP)	3.27	16
German Minority (Mniejszość Niemiecka)	1.17	7
Christian Democracy (DC)	2.36	5
Polish Western Union (PZZ)*	0.23	4
Party of Christian Democrats (PCD)	1.11	4
Labour Solidarity (Solidarność Pracy)	2.05	4
Union of Political Realism (UPR)	2.25	3
Party X	0.47	3
Movement for Silesian Autonomy	0.35	2
Democratic Party (SD)	1.41	1
Democratic-Social Movement (RDS)	0.46	1
Union of Great Poles		1
Peasant Unity (PL and PSL)		1
Great Poland and Poland		1
Solidarity 80		1
Piast Peasant Election Alliance (PL and PSL)		1
Electoral Committee of Orthodox Believers		1
Krakow Coalition of Solidarity with the President		1
Union of Podhale		1
Alliance of Women against Life's Hardships*		1
TOTAL		460

*KPN ally

collection of "others". Eighteen clubs took shape in the new parliament, giving a rough indication of the distinct groups in the *Sejm* at the end of 1991.

What was not foreseen, however, was the evenness of the distribution of *Sejm* seats. Opinion polls had led most observers to expect that the Democratic Union would provide a large number of deputies and the nucleus of a future government coalition. Yet the UD failed even to retain Mazowiecki's supporters from the presidential campaign. The top seven parties received between 7 and just over 12 per cent of the vote, with the first-place Democratic Union gaining 12.3 per cent and the seventh-place Liberal Democratic Congress (KLD) 7.5 per cent. Solidarity's weak performance was also unexpected. However, both the second-place SLD (the alliance of the SdRP, successor to the PZPR, with the trade union OPZZ) and the third-place Catholic WAK (hiding the ZChN) did far better than any opinion poll had suggested.

The top ten were all national parties or groupings, followed generally by regional parties with a concentrated vote (and thus a low national average) and local committees. The German Minority and the Silesian autonomists were regionally based, for example. Stan Tymiński's Party X was a regional party by default, having been disqualified in all but four constituencies for alleged irregularities in nominating its candidates.

The results of the elections to the Senate were somewhat less fragmented and, with minor exceptions, only the Solidarity-generated parties and the two successor parties achieved representation in the upper house.

Despite its fragmentation, parliament did ultimately prove capable of generating coalition government. The first, a minority coalition led by Jan Olszewski of the Centre Accord, lasted from December 1991 until June 1992, when it fell on a vote of no confidence. Waldemar Pawlak of the Polish Peasant Party (PSL) succeeded Olszewski as prime minister but failed to form a government. In July, Hanna Suchocka of the Democratic Union became prime minister of a new coalition, which maintained its parliamentary majority into the spring of 1993. After a vote of no confidence in her government in May, President Wałęsa dissolved parliament and announced a premature election for September.

Intra-party tensions emerged immediately following the October election. The eccentric Friends of Beer split, with the larger element forming Big Beer or the Polish Economic Programme (PPG), another liberal grouping. By the end of the year the Solidarity peasant parties, which had campaigned jointly, had also split again. More important was the gradual decline of the Centre Accord (PC), which had occupied key positions in Wałęsa's

Table 3: Composition of the Senate by Party

Party	No. of seats	Origin
Democratic Union (UD)	21	Solidarity
Solidarity (trade union)	12	Solidarity
Centre Alliance (PC)	9	Solidarity
Catholic Action (mainly ZChN)	9	Solidarity
Peasant Party (PSL)	8	successor
Peasant Accord (PL)	7	Solidarity
Liberal Democratic Congress (KLD)	6	Solidarity
Confederation for Independent Poland (KPN)	4	clandestine
Democratic Left Alliance (SLD)	4	successor
Party of Christian Democrats	3	Solidarity
Christian Democracy	1	mixed
German Minority	1	ethnic
Nationalist	1	historic revival
Independents/Regional	14	
TOTAL	100	

presidential office. The President made wholesale changes to his staff early in 1992, and PC leader Jarosław Kaczyński departed with most of his party colleagues. Conflicts between President Wałęsa and Prime Minister Olszewski also took their toll on the PC, which proved unable to capitalize on its holding of the premiership. Wałęsa also battled with Defence Minister Jan Parys over control of the armed forces. When Parys resigned he formed a new political movement called the Third Republic Movement (RTR), based primarily on the view that Wałęsa was the spearhead of a new communist resurgence. Public denunciations of Wałęsa by his former associates came to exceed the bitterness expressed during the earlier "war at the top" between Wałęsa and Mazowiecki.

When Olszewski fell in June 1992 on a vote of no confidence for mishandling the sensitive issue of screening public figures by using suspect security files from the communist period, the PC seemed effectively finished. It had lost members to the liberal KLD and to Olszewski's new formation, the Movement for the Republic (RdR). It was excluded from the new Suchocka coalition and it appeared obsessed with the President.

Suchocka's government was originally a coalition of seven parties — the UD, the Liberals, and the Polish Economic Programme (the main opposition to Olszewski); three parties of the former government, (the ZChN, the Peasant Accord (PL), and the Peasant Christian Alliance); and the tiny Party of Christian Democrats. Solidarity and some others promised their support, giving the government a clear majority. The governing parties also agreed to avoid matters of conscience, which would be left to parliament. The coalition would provide a "government of ideological peace", and it held together reasonably well until early 1993. Then the Peasant Alliance left the coalition after disagreements over agricultural policy, while Solidarity withdrew its support and organized a series of strikes by health and education workers, embittered over low pay and poor conditions. Indeed, it was a motion of no confidence brought by Solidarity which defeated the Suchocka government in May. Wałęsa, however, dissolved parliament rather than trying to form a new government. Suchocka remained in a caretaker capacity until the September election, while Wałęsa himself sought to inspire a new presidential party (or anti-party), the BBWR, the Non-Party Reform Bloc (*Bezpartyjny Blok Wspierania Reform*).

Just as the government fell, parliament endorsed an amended electoral law. This was explicitly designed to favour larger parties, thus avoiding the extreme fragmentation of the 1991–93 parliament. The size of the *Sejm* remained at 460 members, with 391 deputies to be elected from territorial constituencies and a further 69 to be allocated to parties from their national lists in accordance with their vote. Voters would again cast their vote for an individual name, rather than simply for a party list. The main difference lay in the introduction of a 5 per cent threshold for individual parties or electoral committees and 8 per cent for coalitions; 7 per cent was now necessary for seats from a party's national list. The number of electoral districts increased from 37 to 52, while the method of calculating votes into seats shifted from Hare to d'Hondt.

The new thresholds did reduce the number of groups contesting the 1993 election. In 1991 over 100 election committees registered candidates in at least one district; in 1993 the figure was 35. The serious contenders were the 15 committees registered in all or nearly all constituencies. However, although the new system encouraged mergers or alliances, few of the smaller parties managed to agree to submerge their identities in a wider grouping. The Democratic Union, the Liberal Democratic Congress, the KPN, the PSL, the Union of Labour, the tiny PL peasant party, the radical extra-parliamentary peasant movement Self-Defence, and Solidarity all chose to stand alone, though Solidarity lost supporters to the BBWR and the PL's and Liberals' positions were seen as particularly fraught. The Social Democrats (SdRP) retained their Democratic Left Alliance of the 1991 election with the OPZZ trade union movement, along with a number of other pressure groups.

Spurred on by changes in the electoral system, numerous smaller groupings did seek electoral alliances, but in most cases they failed. First off the mark were the parties of the self-styled "centre-right". Olszewski's Movement for the Republic (RdR) and Kaczyński's Centre Accord (PC), along with several other smaller groupings, called for a Christian-Patriotic bloc. This was the latest stage in a year-long attempt to unite the pro-lustration forces of the Olszewski government. However, the alliance foundered, largely on personal rather than programmatic differences, which were minimal. Several groupings, none of significance, decided to stand under the banner of the PC: they included Parys's Third Republic Movement, the Christian Democratic Labour Party, the Party of Fidelity to the Republic, and Christian Democracy. Olszewski himself finally formed the Coalition for the Republic (KdR) with two other tiny groupings. In the midst of all the arguments the peasant PL changed partners on several occasions before deciding to stand alone.

A third right-wing alliance did generate a coalition, brokered by the Archbishop of Gdańsk. The Catholic Election Committee "Fatherland" (*Oyczyzna*) brought together the ZChN and Hall's Conservative Party with two very small parties of the Suchocka coalition, the Party of Christian Democracy and the Christian-Peasant Party. They were uneasy bedfellows. Hall had consistently criticized the excessive clericalism of the ZChN, which in turn was more sympathetic to state economic intervention than Hall's Conservatives. However, Hall had left the UD in autumn 1992, giving his new party little time to establish its identity, while the ZChN found itself worryingly low in the opinion polls. As its name suggests, the *Ojczyzna* group hoped to appeal especially to the religious devotees of the electorate.

The parties' bickering did not help their image with the electorate, and the anti-communist fervour of elements of the right wing seemed increasingly remote from the concerns of everyday life. Increasingly, disillusion with successive governments' perceived failure to alleviate the social consequences of liberal economic reforms favoured parties of centre-left or social democratic persuasion in the eyes of urban voters. Even a new economic dynamism, spearheaded by a burgeoning private sector, did not alleviate the deep pessimism felt by large sections of the population. The peasants, mainly holders of small private plots, had proved vociferous opponents of the reforms since their onset, though in 1991 their votes had been divided among various peasant parties of Solidarity provenance and the larger PSL. As the election approached, the only doubts concerned the scale of the victory of the SLD and PSL, the two successors to the old regime. Indeed, both the Democratic Left Alliance (SLD) and the PSL performed well, and they reaped the benefits of a divided opposition. Only six parties, plus representatives of ethnic Germans, secured parliamentary representation.

The SLD had increased its vote from 12 per cent to 20.4 per cent and the PSL from 8.7 per cent to 15.4 per cent in comparison with 1991. The Union of Labour's result was even more impressive, given its very small membership, its recent identity and the paucity of its resources. In 1991 the combined vote of the two groups which had later merged to form the UP (Labour Solidarity and the Democratic-Social Movement) was 2.5 per cent, while in 1993 the UP won 7.3 per cent of the vote. Because the electoral system magnified the success of the larger parties, the SLD and PSL together received just under two-thirds of parliamentary seats on the basis of 36 per cent of the vote. The Democratic Union (UD) and

Table 4: 1993 Election Results: the *Sejm*

	% of vote	Seats	% of seats
Left Democratic Alliance (SLD)	20.4	171	37.2
Polish Peasant Party (PSL)	15.4	132	28.7
Democratic Union (UD)	10.6	74	16.0
Union of Labour (UP)	7.3	41	8.9
Confed. for Indep. Poland (KPN)	5.8	22	4.8
Non-Party Reform Bloc (BBWR)	5.4	16	3.5
German Minority*		4	0.9

*the 5 per cent threshold did not apply to minorities

Table 5: Better-known Parties failing to win *Sejm* seats in 1993

Party/coalition	Vote (%)
Ojczyzna [Christian Nats(ZChN) plus Conservative (KP)]	6.37
Solidarity (trade union)	4.90
Centre Accord (PC)	4.42
Liberal Democratic Congress (KLD)	3.99
Union of Political Realism (UPR)	3.18
Coalition for the Republic (KdR)	2.70
Peasant Accord (PL)	2.37
Party X	2.79
Self-Defence*	2.78
TOTAL	33.50

*not previously represented in the *Sejm*

the Union of Labour (UP) also benefited from the new system. The KPN and the BBWR, by contrast, passed the threshold for parliamentary representation but not the higher threshold for allocations of seats from their national lists. Furthermore, over one-third of voters had voted for parties which failed to cross the threshold.

The Senate, despite a somewhat composition from the *Sejm*, also emerged transformed, with the SLD and PSL even more strongly placed. Although more parties achieved representation in the Senate, none made a significant impact and a single Senate seat was not a promising base for continuing political relevance. Indeed, the September election proved a disaster for most political parties.

The 1993 election marked the end of the initial period of post-communist political development and the defeat of Solidarity in its now multifarious manifestations. It also clarified the party system in reducing the numbers of parliamentary actors. The new electoral

Table 6:   Senate after the 1993 election

Party	Seats
SLD	37
PSL	36
Solidarity	9
Independent	5
UD	4
BBWR	2
UP	2
German Minority	1
Rural Solidarity	1
KLD	1
PL	1
Centrum	1
TOTAL	100

system performed its task only too well, but it left the party system in considerable confusion because of the skewed nature of parliamentary representation, leaving most of the right-wing outside parliament and with some obvious "interests" unrepresented: the absence of a strong coherent conservative or Christian Democratic party was particularly glaring. However, the election also improved the prospects for a period of stable majority government.

The main victors — the SdRP, the main component of the SLD, and the Polish Peasant Party — agreed after tense negotiations to form a coalition under the premiership of the PSL leader, Waldemar Pawlak. Aleksander Kwaśniewski, leader of the SdRP, did not enter the government, but he was regarded as "premier without portfolio" because as leader of the SLD parliamentary club, neither strategic decisions nor personnel changes were to be made without his agreement.

The new government provided the promise, if not the guarantee of political stability. It had a sizeable majority, considerable programmatic consensus, and it came to power in circumstances of economic upturn. Aware that both at home and abroad many remained suspicious of their democratic credentials and their economic intentions, the coalition partners needed to move cautiously and to work hard to maintain a united front. However, within a short time visible tensions had emerged between the two and it was clear that the relationship would not be smooth nor particularly amicable.

Sources of future tension between and within the coalition partners lay in matters of both style and substance. Pawlak was seen as determined to concentrate as much power as possible in his own hands, and his apparently cold character and secretive style were the focus of much media attention. Personnel issues were controversial from the start, and the SdRP found one of its most prominent ministers resigning the finance portfolio almost before he had begun. It was the liberal wing of the SdRP which took initial control of key economic ministries, and controversy over issues of budget determination and privatization revealed important divisions between the two partners. Pressure from the PSL for greater assistance to the peasantry also raised the spectre of the resurrection of divisions between town and countryside. In addition, the PSL was more sympathetic to the Church than was the Left Alliance; and the Catholic Church, with its most ardent advocates roundly defeated, hastened to build new bridges to the PSL.

The parties which had arisen from Solidarity, as well as the Solidarity trade union, now unrecognizable as the movement begun in 1980, obviously needed a period of stocktaking and adjustment to their new position following the September election. Unlike the successor parties few new political parties had displayed much concern with developing strong local and regional structures; indeed, the election results showed the price they paid for ignoring party development. After the 1993 election only the Democratic Union and the Union of Labour had a significant parliamentary base from which to work. The Democratic Union had great difficulty in adjusting to its new role in opposition, although it showed its willingness to accept structural adjustment by rapidly opening discussions with the Liberal Democratic Congress with a view to merger. The two parties agreed a process for unification for spring 1994. The BBWR, inspired by President Wałęsa, had a few seats; but it seemed destined to eventual oblivion, for it lacked a coherent identity, an effective leadership, ideological direction and any secure nucleus of electoral support on which to build.

The election's most obvious losers were those parties of the right which had failed to achieve representation. The Liberals had an enthusiastic partner in the UD, with whom they had always enjoyed good relations. However, most of the others moved immediately in two contradictory directions, one of new divisions and defections, the other of seeking alliances and mergers. The first resulted primarily from the need to apportion blame for the fiasco of defeat. This led to tensions within the Centre Accord (PC), where one group wanted both to call the leadership to account and to repair the damage wrought by open warfare against the president. Divisions within the Movement for the Republic (RdR) led to the replacement of Olszewski as leader by the eccentric Romuald Szeremietiew and the former's subsequent withdrawal. Olszewski's followers continued to claim irregularities in the party's leadership election; this led to the existence of two competing Movements for the Republic in spring 1994. Elements of the so-called "fundamentalist" wing of the Christian National Union accused some of its leaders of having moved too close to the Democratic Union during their period in the Suchocka coalition. The ZChN's erstwhile ally, Aleksander Hall's Conservative Party, suffered greater loss when that party also split over allegations that Hall was too close to the UD and the Liberals and over the question of potential partners for the future.

At the same time, almost before the final votes were counted, leaders of these parties began to embark on discussions and negotiations with a view to the development of a coherent right-wing political party. Initially it appeared that two blocs would form, a more radical one organised by Jarosław Kaczyński of the PC and a conservative, Christian democratic one under Hall. In November 1993 the PC, Christian National Union, and Peasant Accord (PL) issued a declaration of co-operation. By April 1994 they had been joined by one of the two then-competing RdRs and by the Conservative Coalition, a splinter group from Hall's Conservatives. Hall had also reached agreement in November with the extreme laissez-faire Union of Political Realism (UPR), the Christian Peasant Alliance (SLCh), and the Party of Christian Democracy (PChD); in February 1994 the small, nationalist National Democratic Party joined the alliance. However, the situation remained fluid. There was as yet little indication that the respective parties could overcome their personal and political antagonisms to agree a common programme, structure, or strategy.

We can see then, that the development of political parties in Poland has been closely linked to parliamentary and electoral processes. Although between 1990 and 1994 several hundred "political parties" registered their existence in accordance with the 1990 law on political parties, most proved either ephemeral or irrelevant or both. The "genuine" political parties were those with a degree of public recognition and a least a minimum measure of coherent structure and organizational linkage between members and leaders. The new parties possessed few resources with which to spread their message to an electorate little versed in democratic practices, so parliamentary representation was the most effective way to gain the media exposure which is now the stuff of modern political campaigning. The successful parties were those with deputies in parliament, and their bureaux and resources aided, but could not guarantee, party development. Indeed, in the first four years following the communists' loss of power, no successful party was organized from the bottom up, i.e. as an extra-parliamentary force, with the partial exception of the BBWR, launched by the president and achieving publicity because of that (tenuous) link. However, even parliamentary representation could not guarantee success. The 1993 election represented a defeat for the Solidarity-generated parties and for many other small groupings which had achieved a single seat. The victors were the two successor parties with continuity of structures and a bedrock of support. The election led to a considerable reduction in the number of parties and offered some hope for, though no guarantee of, a future consolidation of the party system. The obvious gap in the political spectrum lay in the absence of a strong conservative or Christian democratic force. Immediate prospects in the spring of 1994 did not appear very favourable to such a development, while longer term developments would depend not only on the ability of parties to put down roots in society but also on future institutional relationships and a greater stability of the class forces and social cleavages still being shaped by the process of socio-economic transformation.

Directory of Major Parties

Centre Accord
Porozumienie Centrum (PC)

Address. 02-58 Warsaw, ul. Puławska 41 m. 1.

Telephone. 49-82-34, 48-37-55.

Foundation. May 12, 1990; formal registration as a political party on March 2, 1991.

Leadership. Jarosław Kaczyński remained the acknowledged leader of the PC from its inception. At the first congress in March 1991, Jacek Maziarski became chair of the Executive, with Adam Glapiński, Przemysław Hniedziewicz, and Marcin Przybyłowicz as his deputies. Of the initial leadership team, only Kaczyński and Glapiński remained members of the PC in 1994, when the other vice-chairmen of the party were Ludwik Dorn, Krzysztof Tchórzewski, Antoni Tokarczuk and Adam Lipiński.

Membership. Estimated 35,000 (1990), 15,000 (1993); but these are certainly over-estimates of paid-up members.

History. The PC was formed to spearhead a broad Solidarity alliance supporting Lech Wałęsa's candidacy in an early presidential election and, according to its founders, to prevent the so-called "left laity" from transforming Solidarity into a new mono-party system. It gained the support of most regional Solidarity Citizens' Committees, and it also attracted members from right and centrist elements of other small parties. Wałęsa easily won the presidential election of November–December 1990 but the PC did not gain as much political capital as expected. Prominent members, including leader Senator Jarosław Kaczyński and deputies Sławomir Siwek and Teresa Liszcz, dominated the presidential staff for a time, while three members of the PC also gained posts in the minority Bielecki government of January 1991. Despite the presence of its ministers, the PC was critical of Bielecki, but its political venom was directed mainly towards the so-called "contract *Sejm*" of the Round Table agreement and delay in holding fully competitive parliamentary elections.

When the election was finally called for October 1991 the PC was disappointed by the Solidarity trade union's decision to field its own candidates. However, the PC was still expected to do well, and in the event (with a few small allies) it performed reasonably, winning 8.71 per cent of the vote and 44 seats in the *Sejm* and nine seats in the Senate. However, it lost the confidence of the president, who replaced most of the presidential staff associated with the PC. Although the new prime minister, Jan Olszewski (December 1991), was formally a member of the PC, in practice the party exerted little influence over the Olszewski government. It did, however, support the premier in his increasingly acrimonious battle with Wałęsa; this was partly an institutional struggle for power and partly a product of difficult personal relations. By spring 1992 the PC was firmly in the anti-presidential camp and it continued to express its bitter criticisms of the president, but at some cost to party unity.

The divisions within the PC came to a head with the events of May–June 1992 over the lustration affair. Kaczyński himself appeared firmly in the anti-Wałęsa camp; but at the same time he was schizophrenic about the government, which he now frequently criticized and whose coalition he favoured extending. The PC did not support the vote of no confidence in Olszewski's government. However, after his defeat, Olszewski himself left the PC to found the Movement for the Republic (RdR), taking with him important elements of the Christian democratic faction of the party, notably the PC's "organization man", Przemysław Hniedziewicz.

Kaczyński, despite earlier hostility to the Democratic Union, had strongly favoured its inclusion in a broadened Olszewski coalition; yet the PC set too high a price for participation in the new coalition formed by Hanna Suchocka of the UD in July 1992. The PC's exclusion left it largely isolated, and its strident anti-presidential and anti-communist rhetoric struck a diminishing chord with the population in 1992–93. Attempts to reunite with Olszewski's group failed, provoking yet another loss of members, and the PC entered the September 1993 election in association with several tiny groups; these did little to bolster electoral support. The results were disappointing, for with 4.42 per cent, the PC came close to the 5 per cent threshold.

After their exclusion from parliament, the PC further divided over demands to call the leadership to account and to repair relations with the president. The PC issued a declaration of co-operation with the Christian National Union (ZChN) and Peasant Accord (PL) in November 1993. In March 1994 this group was joined by one of the two then-competing RdRs and by the Conservative Coalition, a breakaway group from the Conservative Party.

At the time of writing in April 1994, continuing disagreements over matters of organization and strategy rendered the prospects of a full merger unlikely.

Programme. In its early stages the PC appeared as a broadly pro-capitalist Christian Democratic party advocating the "acceleration" of the reform process and strong measures of decommunization. Increasingly, anti-communism and lustration became the main rallying cries of the PC, which became closely associated with the discredited notion that President Wałęsa himself had operated as a communist collaborator. In its 1993 electoral programme the PC supported greater state economic intervention, including a year's freeze on energy prices and greater social provision (e.g. higher pensions, longer entitlement to unemployment benefit). It continued to stress the importance of decommunization and renewal of the state apparatus to combat the evils emanating from the government, the (presidential) Belvedere Palace, and the *Sejm*. Its slogans were "Poland! Time for Change! ... Poland is badly governed!"

Organization. By September 1990 the PC claimed to have branches in 35 of the 49 provinces. The first congress assembled on March 2, 1991, and elected its 100-member Supreme Political Council and a smaller executive committee. Its parliamentary contingent then numbered some 38 deputies and senators. After the 1991 election the PC had 44 deputies, but this number dwindled to about 25. The Second Congress was held on June 14, 1992. Kaczyński was re-elected leader and given additional powers in that capacity. Many provincial party structures opposed the concentration of power, however, while others crumbled when prominent individuals associated with particular constituencies left the party. In 1994 the PC was deeply in debt and its local and regional structures were extremely weak even in areas of previous strength, for example along the "eastern wall".

Christian National Union
Zjednoczenie Chrześcijańsko-Narodowe (ZChN)

Address. 00-853 Warsaw, ul. Twarda 28 m. 8.

Telephone. 20-18-00.

Foundation. Sept. 21, 1989.

Leadership. The leader of the ZChN from its inception was Professor Wiesław Chrzanowski of the Catholic University of Lublin. In 1994 its Deputy Chairs were Ryszard Czarnecki and Tomasz Szyszka, its Secretary-General was Mirosław Jakubowski, and Marek Jurek chaired its Supreme Council.

Membership. Claimed membership of 4,000 in 1990; 5,000–6,000 in early 1994.

History. The ZChN arose from the linking of a number of regional Catholic groupings, including those centred around the journal *Głos* (Voice) associated with Antoni Macierewicz; the Poznań group Order and Freedom (*Ład i Wolność*) centred around Marek Jurek, and a group in Łódź associated with Stefan Niesiołowski. In the first ("contract") *Sejm* its three deputies (the "holy trinity") were visible and vocal advocates on behalf of the Catholic Church. The ZChN supported Wałęsa in the 1990 presidential election. In the 1991 election it stood under the banner of WAK, the Catholic Electoral Committee, in which it played the major role; and with the support of the Church achieved an unexpectedly high vote of 8.73 per cent, leading to 49 seats in the *Sejm*.

The ZChN participated in the governments of Jan Krzysztof Bielecki, Jan Olszewski and Hanna Suchocka, although its role in these varied coalitions generated tensions within the party. The ZChN was the major advocate of the restrictive anti-abortion legislation passed in 1993, the restoration of Church property, and the requirement that the media "respect Christian values". Its then deputy leader, Antoni Macierewicz, played the key part, as Minister of the Interior, in the lustration crisis of June 1992, when Chrzanowski, the party's respected leader and Marshal of the *Sejm*, found himself on the dubious list of secret communist collaborators circulated by Macierewicz, himself subsequently expelled from the party.

As the population increasingly came to perceive the Catholic Church as too heavily involved in politics, the ZChN lost support. In September 1993 it stood with Hall's Conservative Party and the Christian Peasant Alliance as the Fatherland Catholic Electoral Committee, a coalition brokered by the Archbishop of Gdańsk. They narrowly failed to reach the 8 per cent threshold required for coalitions, and after September functioned as an extra-parliamentary force seeing new allies in a new right-wing Christian-oriented political movement.

Programme. In domestic policy the ZChN stressed the need to reconstruct the system imposed by "really existing socialism" on the basis of Catholic thought and national traditions. It stressed private property and the defence of the family and family life, including prohibition of abortion and contraception. Initially, the ZChN was rather interventionist, urging the maintenance of a strong welfare state and a cushion of security against the ravages of economic transformation. During its period in the Suchocka coalition, however, the ZChN became more obviously pro-capitalist. It stressed that the majority nation must defend its identity, while also in theory acknowledging equal rights for national minorities. In the 1993 election it advocated controls on immigrants from abroad, with the introduction of visas for eastern visitors. It wished to guard jealously Poland's new-found independence and sovereignty.

Organization. In 1990 the ZChN already claimed incipient organization in 22 provinces, but with certain exceptions the party's structures remained rather weakly developed, with its main support in Białystok in the north-east and in the south around Tarnów and Nowy Sącz. It gained strong support in Łódź, where it played a major role in local government after 1990. At the 1992 congress limitations were imposed on the central leadership's domination of the provincial bureaux, but the party's centre of gravity remained in Warsaw. In 1994 the Executive Bureau, dealing with current operations, was firmly under the control of leader Wiesław Chrzanowski, while the Supreme Council, concerned with strategy, was chaired by Marek Jurek, of the so-called "fundamentalist" wing of the party.

Christian Peasant Alliance
Sojusz Ludowo-Chrześcijański (SLCh)

Address. Warsaw, ul. Radzymińska 52 m. 9.

Foundation. May 1992.

Leadership. Józef Slisz is the leader. Artur Balazs is another prominent figure.

Membership. Dubious claims of some 20,000 members (early 1994).

History. Originally the Polish Peasant Party-Solidarity (PSL-S), an offshoot of Rural Solidarity; then an element of the Peasant Accord (PSL-PL), then once again PSL-S. The party then changed its name again to the present one at its second extraordinary Congress held in May 1992. It aimed to transform itself from a class party to a national centre-right grouping based on the traditions of the peasant movement and the social teachings of the Church. The SLCh participated in the Olszewski coalition, but by spring 1992 it was effectively opposing the government and voted against it in the no-confidence vote in June. It entered the 1993 elections as an element of the Fatherland (*Ojczyzna*), coalition with the ZChN, Hall's Conservative Party, and the Party of Christian Democracy (PChD), but the grouping failed to pass the coalition-threshold of 8 per cent and the SLCh appeared effectively moribund compared with the massive peasant support shown for the PSL.

Programme. This was the most right-wing of the parties springing from the countryside. It was pro-market (unlike the protectionist views of most peasant parties) and pro-Europe, with emphasis on the role of the Catholic Church and the importance of "Christian values".

Confederation for Independent Poland
Konfederacja Polski Niepodległej (KPN)

Address. 00-373 Warsaw, Nowy Świat 18/20.

Telephone. 26-10-43.

Foundation. Sept. 1, 1979.

Leadership. The KPN is dominated by its leader, Leszek Moczulski, the party's founder. Other important members of the party's Political Council are Krzysztof Król, Adam Słomka, Dariusz Wójcik and Andrzej Ostoja-Owsiany.

History. The KPN began as the first significant clandestine political party in communist Poland, with a strongly nationalist anti-communist and anti-Soviet stance and claiming to draw inspiration from the Polish inter-war leader, Marshal Józef Piłsudski. The KPN rejected the Round Table but stood unsuccessfully in the 1989 elections. In the 1990 presidential election Moczulski received 2.5 per cent of the vote. In 1991 the KPN campaigned strongly on an anti-liberal economic platform of massive government spending. It attracted 7.5 per cent of the vote and, with a number of satellite groups, won about 51 seats in the *Sejm*. Although involved in successive coalition negotiations, the KPN always set too high a price for its participation and it remained permanently excluded from office. It strongly favoured lustration, but fell out with the right-wing parties of Olszewski's government when Moczulski's name appeared on the notorious (and unreliable) list of collaborators, though it had much in common with the interventionist parties of the populist right. It displayed a marked inclination to direct action and street demonstrations. It supported numerous strikes, and it persistently wooed workers in areas of the industrial heartland, also setting up its own trade union movement, *Kontra*, in summer 1992. Most observers expected the KPN to perform well in September 1993, but its support proved extremely volatile; in the event the KPN won just 5.8 per cent of the vote, yielding 22 seats.

Programme. The KPN was consistently interventionist in its economic policies, advocating open-ended budget deficits and slower privatization by means of non-cash credit issued to permit the population to purchase economic assets (housing, shares) and opposing significant reprivatization. It favoured a mixed economy of public and private ownership and far greater expenditure on social services. Although favourable to "Europe" and NATO, the KPN favoured an activist eastern policy to prevent the re-establishment of Russian hegemony.

Conservative Party
Partia Konserwatywna (PK)

Address. 00-585 Warsaw, Bagatela 14.

Telephone/fax. 628-87-92.

Foundation. September 1992.

Leadership. Aleksander Hall.

Membership. Before the 1994 split, membership was about 1,500.

History. The Conservative Party arose from the departure from the Democratic Union of a group of its right-wing fraction in autumn 1992. Many, including the leader, Aleksander Hall, had been associated with the Democratic Right Forum established in spring 1990 to support the candidacy of Tadeusz Mazowiecki, later leader of the UD. Hall wished to establish a "civilized" Christian Democratic party in opposition to the ZChN and PC; but the timing of the 1993 election gave him little opportunity to establish the group's identity, and the PK in fact entered an electoral alliance (*Ojczyzna*) with the ZChN and the Christian-Peasant Alliance, but the coalition failed to cross the 8 per cent threshold. The tiny party then split in January 1994, when the Conservative Coalition under Kazimierz Michał Ujazdowski opted for a close association with the Centre Accord, Peasant Accord, Movement for the Republic and Christian National Union in contrast to Hall's preference for agreement with the Union of Political Realism, the Christian Peasant Alliance and the Party of Christian Democrats. The splinter group included three vice-chairs and claimed half the local structures of the PK.

Programme. The PK stressed laissez-faire economic policies, with an anti-trade union bias; Christian values embodied in strong hostility to abortion and strong endorsement of religious education in schools; and a pro-Western foreign policy orientation.

Democratic Union
Unia Demokratyczna (UD)

Foundation. May 1991.

Membership. c. 15–20,000 (February 1994).

Leadership. Tadeusz Mazowiecki was elected leader in May 1991. The UD was replete with luminaries from the old Solidarity opposition, including Bronisław Geremek, Jacek Kuroń, Andrzej Wielowieyski, Zofia Kuratowska and Władysław Frasyniuk. One prominent leader, Aleksander Hall, withdrew from the UD in September 1992 to found the Conservative Party.

History. The UD was a product of the merger of the two major groups formed to support the presidential candidacy of Tadeusz Mazowiecki (Mazowiecki was Solidarity's first non-communist prime minister) against that of Lech Wałęsa in 1990, namely ROAD, the Citizens' Committee for Democratic Action, and the Forum of the Democratic Right. Their decision to form a political party followed Mazowiecki's defeat. The two groups held their unity congress on May 11, 1991, but the new party acknowledged its internal differences by formally recognizing its fractions, the centre-left Liberal-Social fraction led by Zofia Kuratowska, the centre-right Democratic Right fraction led by Aleksander Hall (who withdrew in September 1992 to found the Conservative Party), and a small Green fraction led by Radosław Gawlik.

The UD saw itself as the quintessential embodiment of the ideas of Solidarity and the direct heir of the intellectual traditions of 1980 (in practice, they failed to continue Solidarity's particular stress on workers' self-management), with unconditional support for principles of democratic tolerance, including minority rights. The UD (along with the Liberals) became the party most closely associated with the "shock therapy" of the liberal economic reforms of Finance Minister Leszek Balcerowicz (1989–91), though the various elements of the UD differed in the extent of their demands for greater social protection to cushion the impact of reform. The party also remained divided over the abortion issue, with its secular element opposing the Christian democratic wing. The UD was formally in opposition during the Bielecki government's tenure in 1991, but in practice frequently supported that government, which continued many of the reforms first inaugurated by Mazowiecki.

The Democratic Union appealed mainly to the urban intelligentsia and the limits of its support were demonstrated in the first fully competitive elections of October 1991, when it polled just over 12 per cent of the vote, though its 62 deputies constituted the largest party in the *Sejm*. Following the 1991 elections President Wałęsa invited Bronisław Geremek to form a government, but Geremek failed, largely due to considerable hostility to the UD from other elements of the former Solidarity movement. During the brief term in office of Jan Olszewski's minority government the UD formed the main opposition force, allied with the Liberals and the Polish Economic Programme ("Big Beer", now defunct) in the so-called "small coalition". When the lustration affair led President Wałęsa to throw his support behind the small coalition's motion of no confidence in May 1992, Olszewski's government fell. After an interim period when Waldemar Pawlak of the PSL tried unsuccessfully to form a new government, the UD again took office in July 1992 at the head of a seven-party coalition under the premiership of the UD's Hanna Suchocka. Suchocka's government brought together disparate parties and failed to maintain a clear sense of direction. Its main achievement was the passage of the "Little Constitution", which clarified some institutional relationships, especially between president and parliament. After a series of protests and strikes by public sector workers in spring 1993 and the loss of its majority after the withdrawal of the small Solidarity peasant party PL, the government fell on May 28 on a vote of no confidence. President Wałęsa, however, saw little chance of forming a new coalition from the highly fragmented *Sejm* and dissolved parliament, called new elections, leaving Suchocka in a caretaker capacity until September.

The UD was the party most experienced in government between 1989 and 1993, but proved itself unable to capitalize on the popularity of Suchocka, and ran a lacklustre election campaign in 1993. Its share of the vote fell to 10.6 per cent, yielding 74 seats. It remained the largest (and in some sense the only) post-Solidarity party in the new *Sejm*, but had difficulty adjusting to its new role in opposition. The UD bitterly regretted its failure to conclude an electoral alliance with the Liberal KLD, and the two parties immediately began negotiations with a view to merger. Joint commissions set to work to prepare the unification congress of April 1994, when the UD merged with the KLD in the new Union of Freedom (*Unia Wolności*).

Programme. The UD was strongly pro-market and favoured privatization, but also had an active social democratic wing; and was fervently pro-European and pro-NATO. In the 1993 election its campaign leaflets offered little in the way of specific policies other than the introduction of the Pact for Industry (a set of agreements with the trade union movement) and the realization of the mass privatization programme. It promised a state based on the rule of law, the establishment of "genuine" banks and new markets, defence of consumers and strengthening of local government.

Liberal Democratic Congress
Kongres Liberalno-Demokratyczny (KLD)

Address. Warsaw, ul. Krucza 26, room 222a/Gdańsk, ul. Grunwaldzka 8.

Telephone. (Warsaw) 27-48-07, 27-49-25.

Foundation. Feb. 15, 1990.

Leadership. Donald Tusk, Jan Krzysztof Bielecki, Janusz Lewandowski, Jacek Merkel.

History. The Congress was established as a result of the Congress of Liberals (KL) held in Gdańsk in December 1988. The KL in turn had developed around a group associated with the journal *Przegląd Polski* (Polish Review) and several clubs of self-styled liberals and entrepreneurs operating in the Gdańsk area in the 1980s. It evolved into a typical liberal party, ardently pro-capitalist (indeed, Bielecki styled himself a "Thatcherite" after British prime minister Margaret Thatcher) but also strongly in favour of safeguards for individual civil liberties and strong local democracy. The then tiny KLD supported Wałęsa's presidential candidacy in 1990, but gained enormously in recognition and respect after Wałęsa nominated its leader, Jan Krzysztof Bielecki, for the premiership following Mazowiecki's resignation. Bielecki served from January to October 1991, largely continuing the policies of his predecessor. In the October elections the KLD received 7.5 per cent of the vote and 37 seats in the *Sejm*. The KLD remained in opposition to Olszewski, forming an element of the "small coalition" with the UD and the Polish Economic Programme, the latter later incorporated in large measure into the KLD. In July 1992 the KLD joined the Suchocka coalition and Lewandowski once more resumed the privatization portfolio, with Bielecki serving as minister for liaison with the European Community. In the public mind, however, the Liberals became the party most closely associated with economic shock therapy, with privatization, and with the many corruption scandals accompanying the process of economic transformation. The KLD paid for its decision to stand alone in 1993, when it secured only 3.99 per cent of the vote and thus failed to achieve parliamentary representation. Immediately following the election the leadership moved towards merger with the stronger Democratic Union, resulting in spring 1994 in the new Union of Freedom.

Programme. Strongly secular, pro-European (a Europe "of regions"), pro-capitalist and entrepreneurial, receptive to foreign capital, and widely associated with the country's rising unemployment, the KLD generated some surprise with its 1993 campaign slogan "One million new jobs", to be generated through lower taxes and export-promotion. The party also favoured limiting social provision to those "most in need".

Movement for the Republic
Ruch dla Rzeczpospolitej (RdR)

Address. 00-567-Warsaw, Pałacyk Sobańskich, Aleje Ujazdowskie 13.

Telephone. 694 16 07; 694 10 50.

Fax. 211 524.

Foundation. July 1992.

Leadership. Jan Olszewski was the first leader, but Romuald Szeremietiew replaced him at the Second Congress in December 1993. A dissident alternative Extraordinary Congress in March 1994 elected Stanisław Węgłowski leader, with Jan Olszewski as honorary leader in acknowledgement of his past activities.

Membership. After the split in December 1993, each group claimed a preponderance of members. Szeremietiew loyalists claimed 5,000 members, with only 150 defectors to the counter-RdR. Węgłowski's supporters claimed that the dissidents retained 3,500 of a total of 4,000 members.

History. After the lustration debacle and the fall of his government, Jan Olszewski withdrew from the Centre Accord (PC) along with other members of its Christian democratic faction and over the summer of 1992 he established the RdR, which was also joined by the tiny Polish Independence Party of Romuald Szeremietiew. Subsequently, the party's development centred closely on its leadership's protracted negotiations and alliances with and disaffections from other right-wing groupings (or self-styled "centre-right"), notably Kacyński's PC and a number of small, insignificant groupings such as the Christian-Democratic Labour Party (ChDSP), and Partys' Movement of the Third Republic (RTR). In September 1993, however, the RdR finally stood with Macierewicz's Polish Action (AP) and Kornel Morawiecki's Freedom Party (formerly Fighting Solidarity), neither of which added to Olszewski's electoral appeal, as the Coalition for the Republic (KdR). It achieved 2.7 per cent of the vote and subsequently split after the controversial election of Romuald Szeremietiew, Olszewski's erstwhile defence minister, as the new party leader. Both the Olszewski wing and the Szeremietiew wing joined other unsuccessful parties in discussions over a new, united right-wing formation.

Programme. The RdR regarded itself as a Polish, Christian party seeking to unite honest "patriotic and pro-independence forces" against the continuing communist threat. It was associated primarily with demands for lustration and fundamental decommunization, as well as immediate accession to NATO in order to safeguard Poland's sovereignty against a resurgent Russia. It was economically interventionist, opposing the methods of ("corrupt") privatization adopted by previous liberal governments and it stressed the need to protect the weak from the ravages of privatization through enhanced social provision.

Non-Party Bloc for the Support of Reform
Bezpartyjny Blok Wspierania Reform (BBWR)

Foundation. June 1993.

Leadership. The acknowledged, unofficial leader of the BBWR was Andrzej Olechowski. Jacek Lipiński succeeded Olechowski after the latter became Minister of Foreign Affairs in the Pawlak government.

History. After failing to persuade the parties of the Suchocka coalition to enter an electoral alliance, President Wałęsa announced his patronage (but not membership) of a new political formation, the BBWR, which sought to appeal to "four legs" of the new order: Solidarity, the business community, the peasantry and local government bodies. However, he encountered considerable reluctance in all four groupings. Save its *de facto* leader Andrzej Olechowski, BBWR candidates were little known. Still, the political parties feared that the president's authority would itself suffice to paper over the uncertain response and the undoubted contradictions among the "four legs". In the event, the BBWR performed badly in the 1993 election, only gaining 5.4 per cent of the vote, 16 seats in the *Sejm* and two in the Senate. Its erstwhile unofficial leader Olechowski was the president's nominee for the Foreign Affairs portfolio, regarded as one of the "presidential positions" in the government. The BBWR in parliament, however, was devoid of influence and lacked coherence, while many of its local organizing committees disintegrated in the aftermath of the election, making its future appear at best uncertain.

Programme. Generally pro-market in orientation, the most notable element of the party's 1993 electoral manifesto was the promise of 300 million zloties' credit for all. The programme also included a strong emphasis on the strengthening of the president's role, law and order, a Charter of Human Rights, and increased powers for local government.

Party X
Partia X

Address. Warsaw, Nowy Swiat 25 m.35.

Leader. Stan Tymiński, Józef Kossecki.

History. Stan Tymiński, an eccentric expatriate businessman from Canada and Peru, formed Party X after Tymiński's stunning second place position on the first ballot in the 1990 presidential election. Tymiński, previously totally unknown, played on his self-proclaimed success in business and campaigned effectively on a platform promising a speedy and painless transition to affluent capitalism. His entourage attracted much negative publicity on the grounds that it included individuals previously associated with the communist security services. Party X failed to make an impact, however. It was beset by internal tensions and splits, and it was effectively barred from the 1991 elections in most areas by a controversial decision claiming irregularities in the collection of signatures for nominating candidates. In the event the party gained three seats in the *Sejm* (all three deputies were later expelled). It remained a fringe grouping, stressing the negative role of international financial institutions and the "theft" constituted by privatization. Party X won 2.79 per cent of the vote in 1993.

Peasant Accord
Porozumienie Ludowe (PSL–PL)

Address. 00-682 Warsaw, ul. Hoża 66/68.

Foundation. July 31, 1991.

Leadership. Gabriel Janowski; others included Henryk Bąk and Feliks Klimczak.

Membership. In 1994 dubious claims of 20,000.

History. The Solidarity Polish Peasant Party (PSL-S) and the peasant union Rural Solidarity contested the October 1991 election jointly as the Peasant Accord. Shortly after the election, however, one element of PSL-S withdrew from the PL parliamentary club (later becoming the SLCh), leaving PSL-PL, still largely composed of activisits from Rural Solidarity. The PL participated in the coalitions of Jan Olszewski and Hanna Suchocka but bitterly opposed the attempts of PSL leader Pawlak to form a government in June 1993. Its leader Janowski served as Suchocka's agriculture minister until his withdrawal in spring 1993 in opposition to the government's lack of support for agriculture. The party strongly stressed its anti-communism (with strong support for lustration) and adherence to "national" and "Christian" values. Most of its deputies voted for the anti-abortion law and the law requiring "respect for Christian values" in the media. It accused successive governments of the wanton destruction of small family farms. After the debacle of the September 1993 elections, when the PL received 2.37 per cent of the vote, it began discussions with other right-wing parties and in November jointly issued a declaration of co-operation with the Centre Accord and the Christian National Union.

Programme. Protectionism, cheap credit, and a price support system for agriculture and improved pensions and welfare benefits for farm workers; "honest" privatization and destruction of the "financial mafia", support for health and education; pro-Church.

Polish Peasant Party
Polska Stronnictwo Ludowe (PSL)

Address. Warsaw, ul. Grzybowska 4.

Telephone. 20-60-20, 20-60-25, 20-02-51.

Foundation. May 5, 1990.

Leadership. Roman Bartoszcze became leader at the party's founding congress. Waldemar Pawlak replaced him in June 1991. In 1994 Pawlak combined his party leadership with the posts of prime minister and leader of the PSL's parliamentary club. Other prominent individuals are Aleksander Łuczak and Józef Zych.

Membership. Estimated 185,000 in July 1991; c. 200,000 members in September 1993. It was consistently the largest party in Poland after 1989.

Organization. The PSL is the most highly developed party, with roots in almost every commune throughout the country. It is also highly centralized.

History. Although formally founded in May 1990, the PSL is rightly regarded as the successor party to the satellite party of the communist period, the United Peasant Party (ZSL). The May Congress united the ZSL's direct successor, the Reborn Polish Peasant Party [PSL(O)] with the smaller PSL (Wilanów). The PSL-W stressed its links with the 1945 PSL established by Stanisław Mikołajczyk. The new party aimed to establish itself as a "third force" in Polish politics.

In September 1990 the PSL withdrew its support from the Mazowiecki coalition; this was partly a reflection of continuing hostility to the government's agricultural policies and partly due to the party's loss of the Ministry of Agriculture in the government reshuffle. The recurrence of sporadic peasant protests also played a role. PSL leader Bartoszcze stood in the 1990 presidential election, when he won 7.2 per cent of the vote. The PSL then underwent a process of "verification" and exchange of membership cards designed to weed out the *nomenklatura* from its ranks. This was also a period when village and commune structures weakened considerably. Tensions within the PSL increased in the spring of 1991, mainly over the issue of alliances in the forthcoming parliamentary election. Bartoszcze's leadership was suspended, and he was replaced in June by the young, little-known Waldemar Pawlak, who worked hard to defuse the party's tensions and consolidate its structures.

The PSL Parliamentary Club, led by Józef Zych, had 69 deputies as a result of the Round Table election of 1989. In October 1991 the PSL won 8.67 per cent of the vote and 48 seats. This was a creditable performance, given the splitting of the rural vote by the Solidarity peasant parties. The PSL broadly supported the Olszewski government and was on the verge of entering the coalition when the lustration affair of June 1992 brought the government down. However, the PSL did not favour lustration and supported the vote of no confidence in Olszewski and then naturally strongly endorsed its leader Pawlak, nominated by President Wałęsa as the new prime minister. Pawlak failed to form a government, but he gained enormous credibility from his 33 days in office. At the same time the Solidarity peasant parties, which had effectively controlled the agriculture portfolio in successive governments, had delivered little to the increasingly frustrated peasantry. In September 1993 the PSL won some 46 per cent of the peasant vote, a historically high proportion; its average share of the vote, 15.4 per cent, had almost doubled since 1991, yielding 132 seats and making the PSL the second largest party in the *Sejm*.

In October 1993 Waldemar Pawlak took charge of a PSL–SdRP coalition government, marking the end of the initial domination of post-communist politics by Solidarity-inspired parties and the signal that the "successor" label was no longer an automatic bar to political success. The new coalition displayed tensions almost from the outset, notably over personnel decisions. Pawlak, known as "the ice man" because of his unflappable composure, was regarded by many as having an autocratic leadership style, but electoral victory made the party increasingly attractive and alone of Polish political parties, its membership continued to rise.

Programme. The PSL argued vigorously against the shock therapy of the first post-communist governments under Finance Minister Balcerowicz and proposed greater government support for agriculture. In 1993 it also favoured cheap credit for agriculture and a degree of protectionism, with a broad "anti-recessionist" policy for the economy as a whole, including a larger budget deficit. It opposed reprivatization and regarded liberal privatization strategies as excessively "ideological". It also opposed lustration and specific measures of "decommunization". It favoured a strong parliamentary system of government with a unicameral parliament. The PSL endorsed the aspiration of Poland's membership of the European Union, but only after a process of greater economic restructuring had been achieved, especially in agriculture. On religious issues the party was disunited, with both religious and anti-clerical tendencies apparent. However, its strategy included a clear rapprochement with the Catholic Church.

Self-Defence
Samo-Obrona

Foundation. June 1992.

Leader. Andrzej Lepper.

Membership. Inflated claims of 300,000 (autumn 1992).

History. Self-Defence first emerged as a new radical peasant trade union organization, formed in January 1992 as a consequence of earlier demonstrations and hunger strikes outside parliament in October–November on behalf of peasant debtors struggling with repayment. It continued to attract attention through its use of direct action, with occupation of the Ministry of Agriculture in April and frequent road blockades in June and July. In June Self Defence extended its ambit with the formation of a new political "party of working people, of the impoverished, of the injured (*skrzywdzonych*)". It attracted considerable interest and apparent support, including disaffected members of the Green Party, including Janusz Bryczkowski, and reportedly certain paramilitary organizations. Its leader Andrzej Lepper became known as the "peasant Tymiński". He blamed the banks, Leszek Balcerowicz and the American economist Jeffrey Sachs, the IMF and Western governments for dumping cheap produce on the Polish market, and all of those, plus the president, for the difficult situation of the peasantry. In the September 1993 elections Self Defence received 2.78 per cent of the vote.

Social Democracy of the Republic of Poland
Socjademokracja Rzeczpospolitej Polskiej (SdRP)

Address. Warsaw, Rozbrat 44a.

Telephone. 21-03-41.

Foundation. Jan. 28, 1990.

Leadership. Aleksander Kwaśniewski led the party after 1990, with Leszek Miller as its Secretary-General, succeeded in 1993 by Jerzy Szmajdziński, when Miller, Józef Oleksy and Izabella Sierakowska became Kwaśniewski's deputies. Its main organs are the Presidium and the 150-member Supreme Council.

Membership. 47,000 (March 1990); *c.* 65,000 (February 1994).

History. The SdRP arose as a direct result of the dissolution of the former ruling Communist Party, the PZPR, in January 1990. It fully acknowledged its successor status

338

and laid claim to the assets of the PZPR (many of them later confiscated by government on grounds of suspect legal title), while rejecting the principles of Marxist-Leninist ideology and organization in favour of pluralism and European social democracy. The SdRP supported Mazowiecki's government but went into opposition following the 1990 presidential election and worked to rebuild a social democratic consensus on the basis of the hardships, insecurity and increasing inequalities of the transformation to capitalism.

It adopted a consistent electoral strategy based on standing as an element of a broad centre-left alliance, joined in 1991 by the trade union movement OPZZ, a quasi-autonomous body in the communist period which remained subsequently the largest workers' organization. It also retained considerable resources, experience, organizational skills and the daily newspaper *Trybuna* (formerly *Trybuna Ludu*). In 1990 its presidential candidate was Włodzimierz Cimoszewicz, who polled 9.2 per cent in the first round. In 1991 the Solidarity parties were shocked when the Democratic Left Alliance (SLD) emerged from the election as the second largest grouping in the *Sejm* (and later, after a split in the Democratic Union, the largest), with 12 per cent of the vote and 60 seats. It faced considerable hostility and a degree of ostracism within parliament, but its image improved rapidly in the country as a whole, not least because of the quality of the party's leader, Kwaśniewski, and the SLD leader Cimoszewicz. In the 1993 election the SLD was extended to include elements of the small Polish Socialist Party (PPS) and some 20 other organizations. It capitalized on society's widespread insecurity, increasing attachment to welfare-state values, and growing secularism, as well as benefiting from the fragmentation of the right-wing parties. Its strong electoral showing, with 20.4 per cent of the vote, was magnified by the electoral system, giving it 37.2 per cent of the seats in the new *Sejm*. The SdRP entered a majority coalition with the PSL as the more economically liberal of the two partners and highly conscious of its need to confirm its democratic credentials. In a speech to the *Sejm* in November 1993 Kwaśniewski broke formally with the party's past by apologizing to all who had suffered ill-treatment and degradation at the hands of the communist regime.

Programme. In 1993 the party stood for continuing reform to achieve a "genuine social market economy". It advocated greater social protection, more expenditure on social services such as health and education, and a more active policy to reduce unemployment. It had supported the Suchocka government's mass privatization legislation after winning certain amendments, but it opposed reprivatization and was favourable to the retention of a measure of state ownership and a greater voice for trade unions. It favoured a strong parlimentary system with a unicameral parliament, provision for referenda, and constitutional guarantees of civil, social and national minority rights. Its deputies voted solidly against the anti-abortion legislation and it endorsed a secular state, neutral in matters of religious faith. In foreign policy it favoured European integration and membership of NATO alongside the cultivation of good relations with eastern neighbours.

Solidarity
NSZZ "Solidarność"

Leadership. Marian Krzaklewski led the trade union. Prominent figures in 1994 included Alojzy Pietrzyk, Andrzej Smirnow and Maciej Jankowski (leader of the Warsaw region).

History. The recent history of Solidarity dates from Lech Wałęsa's resignation in 1990 as leader of the national trade union movement. Wałęsa failed to secure the election of his favoured candidate Leszek Kaczyński and did not enjoy close relations with the new leader Krzaklewski. Under Krzaklewski Solidarity decided to contest the parliamentary elections of October 1991, when it achieved an unexpectedly low 5.05 per cent of the vote and 27 seats in the *Sejm*. Increasingly, tensions emerged between the union and its parliamentary representatives, who included prominent individuals such as Bogdan Borusewicz and Jan Rulewski. The trade union became both more right-wing, reflected in its support for lustration and decommunization and its readiness to detect a resurgence of communist forces, and more radical, with increasing propensity to industrial action and hostility to privatization policies. Significant elements of Solidarity also displayed animosity to its former leader, President Wałęsa, manifested at the Solidarity Congress following the fall of the Olszewski government and in subsequent demonstrations supporting the unsubstantiated notion that Wałęsa had acted as a communist collaborator.

However, Solidarity deputies proved instrumental in the negotiations leading to the formation of Hanna Suchocka's seven-party coalition in July 1992 and, although the union did not enter the coalition, it undertook to support it. Widespread strikes in the summer and autumn of 1992 appeared to threaten this agreement, but positive signs of a union–government accord then emerged, including negotiations (also undertaken with numerous other trade unions) for a corporatist-style package of legislation known as the Pact for Industry. Further strikes in the mining industry in December and a wave of strikes in the public sector in spring 1993 then brought relations to breaking point. The parliamentary group had by then divided, with some Solidarity deputies continuing to support the government, while others voted against it on the budget, public sector pay and pensions. It was Solidarity which tabled the successful vote of no confidence in Suchocka's government in May 1993, although it appeared that the union did not expect the motion actually to pass. As a result, a number of prominent parliamentarians withdrew (or were withdrawn) from political activity on Solidarity's behalf.

Few elements of Solidarity proved receptive to Wałęsa's call for a new Non-Party Reform Block (BBWR) in June 1993 and Wałęsa clearly dissociated himself from the trade union, which retained a vocal anti-Wałęsa element. Some erstwhile deputies stood on the Democratic Union's list, but Solidarity again stood under its own banner in the 1993 election. It received 4.9 per cent of the vote. It was profoundly weakened by the end of 1993, both as a direct political force and as a trade union.

Union of Labour
Unia Pracy (UP)

Address. Warsaw, ul. Grójecka 17.

Foundation. June 1992.

Leadership. Ryszard Bugaj led the party from its inception. Other prominent figures included Zbigniew Bujak, Aleksander Małachowski, Wiesława Ziółkowska and Wojciech Lamentowicz.

History. The Union of Labour was a product of the unification of two small parliamentary groupings of Solidarity provenance: Labour Solidarity and the Democratic-Social Movement

(RDS), with elements of the equally small Polish Socialist Party (PPS) and the Great-Poland Social Democratic Union. Labour Solidarity had been closely associated with the 1989 Solidarity (OKP) fraction in parliament, the Group for the Defence of Workers' Interests, from which it emanated; while the RDS was basically a one-man band, formed when former underground Solidarity leader Bujak withdrew from ROAD, the precursor of the Democratic Union. Professor Bugaj proved one of the most articulate and respected critics of the liberal economic policies of Finance Minister Balcerowicz from 1989 to 1991. In the 1991 elections, the combined vote of Labour Solidarity and the RDS was 2.5 per cent. Given the paucity of its resources the UP performed well in the 1993 elections, gaining 7.3 per cent of the vote and 41 seats in the *Sejm*. Although it portrayed itself as the "modern left", neither communist nor Solidarity successor, it was regarded as a Solidarity-inspired alternative to the SdRP. In the new parliament it rapidly assumed the mantle of left opposition to the Pawlak government.

Programme. The UP was often hard to distinguish in policies and outlook from the SdRP, though its economic policies could be regarded as somewhat more interventionist. It attacked the transformation to capitalism as "too rapid" and too insensitive to the needs and interests of the population. It favoured a mixed economy with a measure of protection for Polish industry, a strong welfare state and a halt to the "degradation and commercialization of health and education". It advocated separation of church and state; a parliamentary system with a unicameral parliament and limited presidential powers; safeguards for civic and social rights; and rapid integration into the European Union and NATO.

Union of Political Realism
Unia Polityké Realnej (UPR)

Address. Warsaw, Nowy Świat 41.

Telephone. 26-46-42, 26-74-77.

Foundation. November 1987, registered April 1989.

Leadership. Janusz Korwin-Mikke led the party from its inception. Close associates included Stanisław Michalkiewicz and Lech Pruchno-Wróblewski.

Membership. c. 4,000.

History. The Union was established by a group of self-styled "conservative liberals", including the late highly respected publicist Stefan Kisielewski and the eccentric Janusz Korwin-Mikke. Korwin-Mikke failed to win election in his 1989 campaign for the Senate and similarly failed to secure nomination for the presidential election, in which the UPR then supported Wałęsa. The party won 2.25 per cent of the vote in 1991, yielding three parliamentary seats. It had little influence, though Korwin-Mikke will be remembered as the man who introduced into parliament the infamous lustration resolution of June 1992. The UPR improved its performance to 3.18 per cent in 1993 but failed to cross the threshold for parliamentary representation. After the election it entered discussions with the Conservative Party, the Christian Peasant Alliance and the Party of Christian Democrats. The four agreed a statement favouring a presidential–parliamentary system of institutions; emphasizing Christian traditions and the necessity of co-operation between Church and state; favouring limits on trade unions and on state intervention in the economy, the reduction of taxes, thoroughgoing reprivatization and the rapid privatization of the public sector.

Programme. The UPR was the most radical laissez-faire party of all, advocating wholesale privatization of the economy and social services, with a dramatic reduction of the state apparatus to the minimum needed to support a strong police force and a professional army. It based its election campaign largely on the promise of lower taxes. It was authoritarian by inclination, favouring a strong presidency and patriarchy within the family. It endorsed Christian and "family" values, but without taking a position on the relation between church and state. It was the only nationally known party to endorse the principle of capital punishment.

ROMANIA

Rasmus Bing
Bogdan Szajkowski

In Romania the elimination of multi-party politics in the post-war period took place between 1944 and 1948 through the familiar Soviet process used for the purposes of establishing a Leninist system. Under the watchful eye of the Soviet military, which remained in Romania after the Second World War, this process involved the communists gaining control of key ministries; the penetration, internal splitting and eventual incorporation of rival parties and other mass organizations; and the extensive use of terror and annihilation of the opposition. In August 1947 two out of three major parties in the political life between the wars, the National Peasants' Party and the National Liberal Party, were respectively banned or had dissolved itself in order not to expose rank-and-file party members to persecution. The process of creation of a communist party was completed in February 1948 with the merger of the Communists and the Social Democratic Party. The disappearance of the third "historical" party, the Social Democratic Party of Romania, established the communist monopoly of power.

Although for the next two decades Romania followed closely the Soviet pattern of social, political and economical development under the leadership of Gheorghe Gheorhiu-Dej, towards the end of his rule an increasing emphasis was placed on the merger of Romanian nationalism and communism. This "re-Romanization" campaign stressed the separateness of the political processes in the country from that of the Soviet Union and became a centrepiece of the policy of Nicolae Ceauşescu, who succeeded Gheorhiu-Dej as Secretary-General of the Romanian Communist Party — RCP in 1965, and as President in 1974. Initially regarded as a reformer, because of his opposition to the Warsaw Pact invasion of Czechoslovakia in 1968, Ceauşescu in fact headed an increasingly authoritarian and despotic regime. Throughout his 24 years' rule Ceauşescu managed successfully to present his policies to the world as anti-Soviet and little attention was paid to his bizarre version of nationalism and his use of extensive terror in order to emasculate even the slightest manifestation of dissent and opposition. After his trip to China and North Korea in 1971, apparently impressed by social engineering in both countries, Ceauşescu embarked on a similar process in Romania. The stated aim of the so-called "systematization" policy was the elimination of differences between towns and the countryside. It involved the reduction of the number of 13,000 villages by half through the forcible re-location of people into new concrete housing blocks and the destruction of old dwellings. More precisely, however, this process was an attempt to increase further the state's control over the population. Closer scrutiny over individuals and families could be exercised more effectively in a communal environment.

The "systematization" policy formed a part of a larger process of homogenization of social and political life which has been the hallmark of Ceauşescu's rule. The extensive use of the secret police, the Securitate, and the placement of his and his wife Elena's family members in important government and party positions also became a characteristic of the Ceauşescu regime over the years.

The Romanian dictator was very much aware of the changes taking place in the Soviet Union and the rest of Central and Eastern Europe, but did not approve them. In the summer of 1989 he even suggested that the other Warsaw Pact countries should invade Poland in order to prevent the Solidarity-led government from taking office.

The eventual fall of the Ceauşescu regime was precipitated by mass protests in the Transylvanian town of Timişoara. On Dec. 17, 1989, the security forces fired on demonstrators from Romania's ethnic Hungarian community protesting against attempts to remove from the town an outspoken Lutheran pastor, Lászlo Tökes. As news of the actions in Timişoara spread to Bucharest, Romanians joined the demonstrations, which grew into a popular uprising against the dictatorship. Ceauşescu, to demonstrate that he was firmly in control, staged a mass rally in Bucharest on Dec. 21, but although several hundred thousand people gathered in the centre of Bucharest the crowd turned against him. Ceauşescu and his wife had to flee by helicopter from the roof of the Palace of the Republic, as crowds began to attack the building. The rally in support of the regime turned into an anti-Ceauşescu demonstration. The fate of the regime was sealed during the night of Dec. 21–22 when the army changed sides and joined the uprising. Nicolae and Elena Ceauşescu were captured, brought before a hastily convened court, sentenced to death, and executed by a firing squad on Dec. 25. The shooting of the Ceauşescus weakened the resistance of the Securitate, who attempted to mount resistance to the revolution by staging indiscriminate attacks on civilians and army units. Many of the events of December 1989, i.e. the role of the Securitate and the extent of pre-planning by disaffected RCP members, are still unclear.

Within hours of the flight of the Ceauşescus, the so-called National Salvation Front (NSF) announced that it had taken power as a provisional government. In the list of the original members of the NSF Council released on Dec. 22, 1989, appeared a number of former communists, such as Ion Iliescu, Petre Roman and Silviu Brucan, among others. Other members included intellectuals known for their opposition to the Ceauşescu regime, army officers and students who joined the anti-communist revolt. On the same date the NSF issued a 10-point programme stipulating among other things the introduction of a democratic, pluralistic form of government, the abolition of the leading role of a single party, and the elimination of centralized economic management. However, the interim government, formed until elections could be held, was largely composed of former officials who had fallen into disgrace during the previous regime.

Within days the membership of the NSF Council was increased to 145 persons to include writers, artists and academics, but the real power remained in the hands of the initial core members, headed by Ion Iliescu as Chairman of the Council and interim President, and Petre Roman as Prime Minister of an interim government. The Council quickly consolidated its position by setting up committees of the NSF in workplaces and on all state-levels, asking these bodies to "function as bodies of state power".

Following the Council's decision to outlaw the leading role of one single party, several political organizations soon emerged. For instance, the three "historical" parties founded before the Second World War: the National Liberal Party, the National Peasants' Party and the Social Democratic Party of Romania.

During the first weeks after the revolution the NSF still maintained that it was not a political party, but as it continued to increase its hold on power, the NSF Council began to advocate that the Front should nominate its own candidates for the forthcoming elections. The Front's increased control and the fact that the inner core of the NSF Council was dominated by former communists made the opposition parties argue that the revolution was being taken over by an anti-Ceauşescu, but not anti-communist group. The past associations of the prominent leaders of the NSF infuriated students and intellectuals, who made up the majority of supporters of the main opposition parties, but did little to disturb the blue-collar workers who formed the bulk of supporters of the Front. Reconciling the desire for multi-party democracy and the realization that, in many sectors, former communists held the key, is and will remain for some years one of the most delicate matters in Romanian politics and daily life. The links of many members of the NSF with the previous regime prompted a number of violent demonstrations during the first months of 1990, raising fears that Romania was heading for a period of instability. But the NSF interim government quickly reversed some of Ceauşescu's most unpopular policies, i.e. removed restrictions on domestic consumption of energy, stopped food exports, relaxed measures to enforce labour discipline, which assured the support from the majority of Romanians.

On Jan. 23 the NSF Council declared that it would take part in the elections, scheduled for April 1990, due "to pressure from the bottom", as Ion Iliescu explained. The opposition protested, charging the Front with overt intentions of consolidating its grip further and prolonging it beyond the elections. The three "historical" parties maintained that the Front had lost its capacity of provisional administrator of power and demanded a new provisory government consisting of representatives of the active political parties and prominent personalities.

Under mounting pressure the Front's Council agreed to hold round table negotiations with all 30 political parties registered at that time. The negotiations resulted in a compromise under which the NSF Council was reconstructed as a Provisional Council of National Unity, to operate as a legislative body until the elections, and included three representatives of each of the political parties present at the talks. The agreement also stipulated that the NSF should become a "political formation", eligible to take part in the forthcoming elections set for May 20.

According to the electoral law, until the adoption of a new constitution, legislative power should be vested in a bicameral Parliament comprised of a Assembly of Deputies (387 members) and a Senate (119 senators). The Law also stipulated that organizations representing national minorities registered until March 14 that did not receive the required number of votes for a seat in the Assembly would be entitled to a seat *ex officio*. The Assembly of Deputies and the Senate formed *de jure* the Constituent Assembly which was to adopt the new constitution within 18 months. The Law also defined the procedures of electing the president, by absolute majority in the first ballot, or simple majority, if the election had to go to a second round. It prohibited the president from being member of any political party or group.

Controversy dogged the election campaign from the start with the opposition parties alleging violence and intimidation by the supporters of the NSF, but some 400 observers monitoring the election around the country reported that although the electoral process had its flaws, they found no indications of systematic fraud. Apart from the NSF, virtually all other political parties consisted at that time of only small initiative committees, having

Table 1: Parliamentary Election Results, May 1990

	% of total	Total vote	Seats
Lower House of Parliament (Chamber of Deputies)			
National Salvation Front	66.3	9,089,659	263
Hungarian Democratic Union of Romania	7.2	991,601	29
National Liberal Party	6.4	879,290	29
Romanian Ecological Movement	2.6	358,864	12
National Peasants Party – Christian Democrat	2.6	351,357	12
Alliance for the Unity of Romanians	2.1	290,875	9
Romanian Ecologist Party	1.7	232,212	8
Romanian Socialist Democratic Party	1.1	143,393	5
Romanian Social Democratic Party	0.5	73,014	1
Other votes split among 60 parties			(19)
Upper House of Parliament (Senate)			
National Salvation Front	67.0	9,353,006	91
Hungarian Democratic Union of Romania	7.2	1,004,353	12
National Liberal Party	7.1	985,094	10
National Peasants' Party – Christian Democrat	2.5	348,687	1
Romanian Ecological Movement	2.5	341,478	1
Alliance for the Unity of Romanians	2.2	300,473	2
Romanian Ecologist Party	1.4	192,574	1
Other votes split among 52 parties			(1)

Source: *Partide Politice 1993*, Burcur-Ioan Mica (ed.), Rompres.

an inconsequential membership and presenting a barely improvised declaration of political intentions. Some 75 parties and organizations took part in the elections.

The NSF won a convincing victory in both the Assembly and the Senate with 66 per cent of the vote. The NSF presidential candidate, Ion Iliescu, also surpassed by a wide margin the opposition candidates with 85 per cent of the popular vote. The NSF message, based on promises of stability, ample social provision and gradual reform, appealed to an electorate wary of abrupt changes. The disunited opposition advocated a fast transition to capitalism and a reckoning with all those tainted by association with the old regime — these proposals were unpopular. The new Parliament contained representatives of more than 20 political parties, but due to the NSF majority Ion Iliescu, who as President had the power to appoint the Prime Minister, asked Petre Roman to form a government.

Despite the election results, anti-Front demonstrations continued demanding the removal of Iliescu and all former communists from power. In mid-June 1990 Iliescu appealed to the population, claiming that the Front's opponents were attempting to stage a "fascist coup". Miners from the Jiu Valley came to Bucharest to break-up demonstrations. Six people were killed and several hundred injured. The episode shocked the outside world and several countries suspended aid to Romania, which made Prime Minister Petre

Roman give assurances that the Romanian government would continue to consolidate the democratization process and fully observe human rights. The miners' rampage has, however, never been properly explained.

The government proceeded with an impressive legislative programme and presented a draft of a new constitution to the parliament in February 1991. In March, however, five main opposition parties, the National Liberal Party, the National Peasants' Party, the Social Democratic Party, the Romanian Ecologist Party and the Hungarian Democratic Union issued a message presenting an alternative political and economic programme. It also called for the replacement of the NSF government. During the period December 1990 to June 1991 there were a number of contacts and negotiations between the NSF and the opposition parties about the formation of a national unity or coalition government, but the discussions broke down in June 1991 when the NSF refused to concede the main opposition demand for Roman to be replaced by a "neutral" Prime Minister. The NSF managed, however, to gather support for a "Charter for Reform and Democracy", signed in July by the NSF, the Romanian Ecological Movement, the Agrarian Democratic Party and the National Liberal Party–Youth Wing.

By mid-1991 many industrial workers had become disaffected with the NSF and its increasingly reformist economist policies and as anti-government demonstrations and strikes swept the country and organized labour became more militant two factions developed within the NSF. Throughout 1990 the dominant faction was the conservative one, centred around President Iliescu, which successfully acted as a drag on the reform. By early 1991, however, the pro-reform faction, led by Prime Minister, Petre Roman, had managed to win support for the second stage of its reform programme, having his pro-reform programme adopted by a majority at the first national convention of the NSF, despite a divisive debate.

Nevertheless, Petre Roman was forced to resign in September 1991 as striking miners rampaged through the streets of Bucharest. They protested against inflation, cuts in their living standards and, more generally, demanding the resignation of Roman and of President Ion Iliescu. The official version was that President Iliescu apparently was shaken by the demonstrations and, together with the conservative faction of the party, was concerned about the NSF's loss of support.

Following Roman's resignation (or the handing in of his mandate, as he put it) the miners began to withdraw from Bucharest. On Oct. 1 it was announced that the President had given Theodor Stolojan, formerly Finance Minister, the responsibility of forming a new broad-based coalition government. Most opposition parties refused to co-operate with the NSF. The new government was, therefore, mainly made up of members, or associates, of the NSF, but also representatives from the National Liberal Party, the Romanian Ecological Movement and the Agrarian Democratic Party were represented in the government.

The economic situation was deteriorating rapidly and the country was in the throes of a year-long wave of strikes and protests against the government's measures to introduce a more free-market economic system.

In November 1991, the Parliament, meeting as the Constituent Assembly, endorsed a new constitution guaranteeing pluralism, human rights, and a free market. The constitution was confirmed in a national referendum in December, the "yes" recorded as 77.3 per cent, with a turnout of about two-thirds of all eligible voters. The new constitution was, however, criticized by opposition parties as according too much power to the President. The constitution places executive power in the hands of a directly elected President (if no single candidate wins an overall majority then a run-off contest is held between the two who secure

347

most votes) who appoints a Prime Minister and a Cabinet who in turn are accountable to the legislature. The Chamber of Deputies (the lower house) consists of 341 elected members and 13 representatives of the country's national minorities, while the Senate (the upper house) has 143 seats. (The distribution of the number of seats in each of Romania's 42 counties is subject to changes in the population. The numbers mentioned were valid in the 1992 general elections.)

The first signal of political change came in the beginning of January 1992 when the Charter for Reform and Democracy ended its existence. The last junior member, the Agrarian Democratic Party, left the Alliance following the example of the National Liberal Party–Youth Wing and the Ecological Movement. This created a problem for the NSF, which had set up the alliance to counter-balance the growing popularity of the democratic opposition. The next signal came in the February and March local elections which resulted in a significant loss of support for the ruling NSF, compared with the parliamentary elections held in May 1990, while the Democratic Convention, a new centre-right alliance of 14 opposition parties, gained substantial support.

The pressure from conservative NSF members, including President Iliescu, was further fuelled by the poor showing at the local elections, which also became a significant issue at the NSF National Convention in April 1992. However, the pro-reform wing managed to re-elect Petre Roman as leader of the party and his free-market reform programme was approved by 802 out of 1,268 votes. Due to these political divergences and as a result of a personality clash between Iliescu and Roman, President Iliescu's faction split from the NSF forming its own party, known initially as the NSF–December 22, but subsequently renamed the Democratic National Salvation Front (DNSF).

Another name change took place in April. The Democratic Convention was renamed Democratic Convention of Romania following the departure of the National Liberal Party from the alliance.

The second general election and presidential election since the overthrow of Ceauşescu was held on Sept. 27, 1992, the main issues in the elections being the qualities and personalities of the presidential candidates, the nature of reform, and the position of the national minorities. The effect of the split within the NSF became apparent when the DNSF won the largest number of seats in the parliamentary elections, calling for a slowing down of market-oriented economic reforms. The Democratic Convention of Romania, now a 18-party convention, performed well in urban areas, while in rural areas there was a strong support for the incumbent President, Ion Iliescu, and the DNSF, which nominated him. The NSF, led by Petre Roman, took third place.

This configuration meant that the political map of the country had been radically changed. The opposition now had a much stronger presence in the parliament, which also was the case for the extremist parties RNUP, GRP and the SPL.

Some changes to the electoral law had re-defined numbers of seats in each of Romania's 42 counties according to population. There were 328 (rather than 387) elected seats in the Chamber of Deputies, plus seats reserved for the smaller minorities, not able to pass the 3 per cent threshold (i.e. other than the Hungarians). There were 143 (rather than 199) seats in the new Senate. Election was by proportional representation and on party lists. A 3 per cent threshold was in force, but alliances had to gain an additional 1 per cent for each constituent party, with a maximum threshold necessary being 8 per cent.

In the presidential elections no presidential candidate received an overall majority, but the run-off between Iliescu and the DCR presidential candidate, Emil Constantinescu, was

Table 2: Parliamentary Election Results, September 1992

	% of total	Total vote	Seats
Lower House of Parliament (Chamber of Deputies)			
Democratic National Salvation Front	27.7	3,015,708	117
Democratic Convention	20.0	2,177,144	82
National Salvation Front	10.2	1,108,500	43
Romanian National Unity Party	7.7	839,586	30
Hungarian Democratic Union of Romania	7.5	811,290	27
Greater Romania Party	3.9	424,061	16
Socialist Party of Labour	3.0	330,378	13
Other votes split among 72 parties	20.0		13
Upper House of Parliament (Senate)			
Democratic National Salvation Front	28.3	3,102,201	49
Democratic Convention	20.2	2,210,722	34
National Salvation Front	10.4	1,139,033	18
Romanian National Unity Party	8.1	890,410	14
Hungarian Democratic Union of Romania	7.6	831,469	12
Greater Romania Party	3.9	422,545	6
Agrarian Democratic Party of Romania	3.3	362,427	5
Socialist Party of Labour	3.2	349,470	5
Other votes split among 57 parties	15.0		

Source: *Partide Politice 1993*, Burcur-Ioan Mica (ed.), Rompres

won by Iliescu, albeit with a much lower share of the vote than he gained in 1990. (For comments on the candidates, see their respective party entries below.)

The DCR called for the annulment of the election on ground of fraud. Foreign observers, however, described the elections as generally free and fair, although reports of some intimidation and violence were confirmed.

After the elections Iliescu opened talks with party leaders on the formation of a new government to succeed the administration of Theodor Stolojan. After a period of uncertainty and failed attempts to form a government, Ion Iliescu appointed Nicolae Vacaroiu, a 49-year-old economist without party political affiliation Prime Minister on Nov. 4. The list of Cabinet members submitted by Vacaroiu was dominated by members of the DNSF and also included several non-party independents, forming a minority government based on DNSF, surviving through a tacit support in parliament by the far-left Socialist Labour Party, the far-right Greater Romania Party and the nationalist Romanian National Unity Party. The Agrarian Democratic Party of Romania has also supported the PSDR on crucial occasions. The fact that the SPL and the GRP has set up a joint faction, called National Unity Bloc, in the parliament has also strengthened their influence.

Nicolae Vacaroiu promised that the continuation of reform was his "absolute priority", but the government would "assure special care for the social costs of this process". This was widely interpreted by the opposition parties as indicating a switch to economic conservatism.

The government's reliance on the nationalist and neo-communist parties has reinforced the government's own gradualist tendency, as far as reform is concerned. However, Romania's acute dependence on international financial aid — as well as the leadership's fear of international isolation — have kept the government on a broadly reformist course although the government has been accused of continuously delaying reforms. The government's foreign policy, however, has resulted in a series of successes: i.e. Romania has been accepted as the 32nd member of the Council of Europe, has signed an association agreement with the European Union and has regained the most-favoured nation trading status.

On the party political scene the two years since the general elections in 1992 have been dominated by changes of names and a number of mergers, which, however, still leaves an extremely large number of parties in Romania's political life, as the directory below shows.

The two most important changes of names are the DNSF calling itself the Social Democracy Party of Romania after its national Convention in July 1993 and the opposition NSF calling itself Democratic Party (NSF) after the Party merged with the Democratic Party in May 1993. Both parties, however, claiming to be social democratic. The rest of the opposition in the Parliament is organized within the Democratic Convention of Romania.

In the spring of 1993 the extreme nationalists, GRP, SPL and the PRNU, threatened to leave the DNSF short of a parliamentary majority and withdraw the tacit support it had hitherto enjoyed. The threats were shown, however, to lack credibility in the short term, but remain a reality in the country's political life.

The autumn of 1993 and the spring of 1994 were dominated by the fact that the government was fighting for its survival against an increasing minority in the Parliament. Several no-confidence votes brought against its economic reform programme by the centrist opposition parties have revealed diminishing support for the government. In December 1993 the Vacaroiu government survived a parliamentary vote of confidence by only 13 votes, supported only by the GRP, SPL and the RNUP. The latter is determined to make its future support for the government conditional on formal membership of a ruling coalition.

In the meantime the government has carried out negotiations in order to find out the possibilities of making a broader-based coalition government (or, perhaps, to gain time for the DNSF-government to continue). First, with its supporters within the GRP, RNUP and the SPL. However, that did not become a reality, to a large extent due to the widespread perception that such a government might seriously damage Romania's image abroad. Then the SDPR held talks with the opposition DP(NSF) and DCR, but they also came to an end, as the SDPR could not comply with the conditions set by the DCR and the DP(NSF) that the extremist parties should be excluded and that it implements a genuine reform. All negotiations until the summer of 1994 did not bear fruit and the tactics of the government seemed to be to retain its backing from the extremist parties while preserving its reformist contours. However, in the summer of 1994 the RNUP received seats in the government as members of the party took posts in the Communications Ministry and Ministry of Agriculture.

According to the constitution the next elections must be held before September 1996 and many mergers are expected within the huge number of political parties. In the following Directory all parties registered with the Municipal Court of Bucharest, showing a sign of life, are listed, the list being updated up to and including June 1994. The Directory includes, as well, political alliances and major ethnic unions having political influence.

Directory of Parties

The following directory is based on research carried out by Rasmus Bing.

Agrarian Democratic Party
See Agrarian Democratic Party of Romania

Agrarian Democratic Party of Romania (ADPR)
Partidul Democrat Agrar din România (PDAR)

Address. Sector 1, 71273 Bucharest, Aleea Alexandru 45.

Telephone. 633.66.72; 633.77.76

Fax. 312.87.63.

Foundation. Jan. 29, 1990 (registration date).

Leadership. Victor Surdu (exec. pres.)

Membership. 169,000.

History. Participated in the Council of Ministers led by Prime Minister Theodor Stolojan October 1991–September 1992. The Party obtained 8.04 per cent in the local elections in 1992. Obtained five seats in the Senate after the September 1992 general elections. Belongs to the so-called "Pentagon" and has supported the SDPR government in several no-confidence votes. Joined the PRNU-faction in the Senate in November 1993 and formed the National Unity Bloc, which strengthened the extremist profile in Parliament. Did, however, join the other junior members of the Pentagon in criticising the SDPR during the spring of 1994.

Programme. The party states that it is a centre-party and that its activity is based on an agrarian doctrine, i.e. to put agriculture in the centre of the economical development to promote the interest of the peasants and future farmers, and to fight for the development of modern agriculture in Romania.

Agrarian National Party
Partidul Naţional Agrar (PNA)

Address. Bucharest, Allea Fuiorului 7, bloc H 17, scare C, et.4, ap.59, sector 3.

Telephone. 674.31.98.

Foundation. March 2, 1992 (registration date).

Leadership. Gheorghe Scrieciu (hon.pres.)

Programme. The party states that it is against any kind of dictatorship, for a presidential republic, supports the market economy and considers itself based in the centre of the political spectre.

Alliance for Democracy Party
Partidul Alianţa Pentru Democraţie

History. The party was registered on Feb. 13, 1990. On May 23, 1991, the party merged with other parties and formed the Democratic Party.

Alliance for National Dignity
Alianţa pentru Demnitate Naţională (A.D.N.)

Address. Sector 2, Bucharest, Şos. Pantelimon 245 (Address of the prime vice-pres.Emil Monceanu).

Telephone. 628.24.37.

Foundation. July 31, 1992 (registration date).

Leadership. Ion Marin Uţă (pres.)

History. The Alliance was created as an electoral alliance for the general elections in September 1992 in which the Alliance obtained 63,000 votes. It contains 20 different parties among which the following: Progressive Democratic Party, National Progressist Party and Romanian Revolution Party. Held its first national conference on Sept. 18, 1992. In the summer of 1994 the members of the Alliance discussed its future.

Programme. The Alliance works for national reconciliation, practising the idea of political and ideological tolerance, and new methods of political debates. Tries to enforce the centrist political spirit.

Anti-Monarchial League "Pro Romanian Republic"
Liga Antimonarhică "Pro Republica România"

Address. Bucharest, str. Valea Buzăului, bloc. G 31, scara A, et. 2, apart 57, sector 3.

Telephone. 673.55.31.

Foundation. Feb. 4, 1991 (registration date).

Leadership. Eugenia Bărbulescu (pres.)

Bratianu Liberal Union
Uniunea Liberală "Brătianu" (ULB)

Address. Bucharest, Calea Victoriei 85, etaj 1, sector 1.

Telephone. 659.30.26; 611.97.77.

Foundation. April 4, 1990 (registration date).

Leadership. Ion I. Bratianu (pres.)

History. The Union emerged as a result of a split with the National Liberal Party. The split followed personal differences between Ion I. Bratianu and the leader of the NLP, Radu Campeanu, each accusing the other of "personal ambitions".

Programme. Claims to have a neo-liberal platform. Wants to find a liberal and responsible solution to the problems confronting the state and society.

Publication. *Viitorul Liberal* (Liberal Future).

Centre-Left (Social Democratic) Alliance
Alianţa de centru-stânge (social-democrate)

History. Formed in June 1990 by the following organizations: Alliance for Democracy Party, Co-operative Party, Democratic Labour Party, Romanian New Society Party, and the Socialist Justice Party. Not very active on the political scene. The alliance is maintained by the Democratic Labour Party and the Independent Social Democratic Party (the successor of the Socialist Party of Justice).

Centrist Democratic Group
Gruparea Democrate Centrist

History. An electoral alliance formed for the general elections in 1990 by the following parties: National Democratic Party, National Progressist Party and the Romanian Democratic Front of Timişoara. Obtained two members of Parliament. No longer exists.

Charter for Reform and Democracy

A group formed in July 1991 including the National Salvation Front, the Agrarian Democratic Party, the National Liberal Party-Youth Wing and the Ecological Movement of Romania, designed to pave the way for a future coalition government.

Christian Democratic National Party
Partidul Naţional Democrat Creştin (PNDC)

Address. 70668 Bucharest, str. Antim Ivireanu 8, sector 5.

Telephone. 631.47.30; 631.47.74.

Foundation. Sept. 6, 1990 (registration date).

Leadership. Ion Puiu (pres.)

Programme. The party considers itself within the general frame of European Christian democracy. Belongs to the peasant Christian democratic doctrine and fights for the borders from 1939. Supported Mircea Druc at the presidential elections in 1992.

Christian Democratic National Peasants' Party
(*See* National Peasants' Party–Christian Democrat)

Christian Democratic Party of Romanian Romanis
Partidul Democrat Creştin al Romilor din România

Address. Cluj-Napoca, str. Calea Dorobanţilor 14–16, jud. Cluj.

Leadership. Gheorghe Loghin (pres.)

Christian Democratic Revolution Party
Partidul Revolutjei Creştin Democrat (PRCD)

History. At the moment there are two political parties which claim to have the right to bear the name. They are contesting this in court.

1: Address. Bucharest, str. Podul Giurgiului 3, bloc 11, apart 3, sector 5.

Telephone. 686.68.74.

Foundation. June 7, 1990 (registration date).

Leadership. Ştefan Săceanu (hon. pres.)

Programme. Centre-right.

2: Address. Bucharest, str. Olari 9, sector 2.

Telephone. 635.73.79.

Foundation. June 7, 1990 (registration date).

Leadership. Ion Flueraş (pres.)

Affiliations. Member of the National Union for the Victory of the Revolution. The party claims to be affiliated to the "International Christian Democratic of Germany" (the party's spelling).

Christian Democratic Union (CDU)
(*See* Christian Democratic Union Party)

Christian Democratic Union Party
Partidul Uniunea Democrat Creştina (UDC)

Address. Bucharest, Piata Amzei 13, sector 1.

Telephone. 650.24.10; 650.23.96

Fax. 659.74.66.

Foundation. Jan. 5, 1990 (registration date).

Leadership. Mihai Grama (pres.)

History. The party was set up by exiled Romanians in West Germany in late 1989 and later registered in Romania. Even though the party is a member of the Democratic Convention of Romania, some of its founding members have a clear past in the inter-war Legionary Movement. During 1990 a splinter-group left the party, calling themselves Christian Democratic Union–Sibiu Convention.

Affiliations. Member of the Democratic Convention of Romania. Also in alliance with the Ecological Federation of Romania.

Christian Democratic Union Party of Romania
Partidul Uniunea Creştin Democrată din România

Address. Municipiul Timişoara, N. Titulescu 2, judeţul Timiş.

Telephone. (561) 15170.

Leadership. Prof. Tiberiu Stoian (pres.)

Christian Democratic Union–Sibiu Convention

This formation was a splinter-group which left the Christian Democratic Union Party in 1990 under the leadership of Marcel Petrisor. It was never registered as a party and has not been very active on the political scene during 1994, but its members took part in a 1993 campaign aimed at rehabilitating the Iron Guard, placing the party among the extreme right parties, pledging for a "radical return" (*see* Movement for Romania). The leader, Marcel Petrisor, has left the formation in favour of the New Christian Romania Party.

Christian Human Rights and Freedom Party
Partidul Creştin al Libertăţi şi Drepturilor Omului

History. The party was registered on March 26, 1990, but transformed itself into a humanist-religious movement in the end of 1991.

355

Christian Party of Justice
Partidul Creştin şi al Dreptăţii (PCD)

Address. Bucharest, str. Ioviţă 10, bloc AP 13, et. 1, apart. 4–7, sector 5.

Telephone. 631.35.54; 620.80.16.

Foundation. April 20, 1990 (registration date).

Leadership. Petre Duşmanu (pres.)

Affiliations. National Union for the Victory of the Revolution, Homeland Assembly and Coalition of Democratic Forces.

Christian Republican Party
(*See* Christian Republican Party of Romania)

Christian Republican Party of Romania
Partidul Republican Creştin din România (PRCR)

History. Two political parties exist under this name, having identical constitutions and aims, but the leaderships are contesting each other, also in the court. In the following both groups will be represented.

1: Address. Sector 1, Bucharest, B-dul Carol 100.

Telephone. 635.02.51

Fax. 311.03.11

Foundation. Jan. 15, 1990 (registration date).

Leadership. Gheorghe Popilean (pres.)

History. The party president is currently under charge of fraud and has left Romania.

2: Address. 70781 Bucharest, str. Berzei 46, sector 1.

Telephone. 638.32.15; 638.52.00.

Leadership. Nicolae Garvăn.

History. This section was registered on July 18, 1990, in protest against the accusations of fraud brought against Gheorghe Popilean and his actions proved by the police.

Affiliations. National Alliance of Social Democracy and National Union for the Victory of the Revolution.

Publication. Republica (Republic).

Christian Union Party of Romania
Partidul Uniunii Creştine din România

Address. Cluj-Napoca, str. Dorobanţilor 5, jud. Cluj.

Telephone. (064) 118.53.

Fax.(064) 160.69.

Leadership. Mihai Pop (pres.)

History. The party consists mainly of Catholic Greeks.

Civic Alliance Party
Partidul Aliantei Civice (PAC)

Address. Bucharest, Bd. Natiunile Unite 5, bloc 110, sector 5.

Telephone. 615.21.63; 615.31.01.

Fax. 312.50.35.

Foundation. Aug. 1, 1991 (registration date).

Leadership. Nicolae Manolescu (pres.)

Membership. 11,200.

History. Civic Alliance started as a coalition of extra-parliamentary opposition groups and played a major role in the anti-government strikes in 1990–91. In July 1991 Civic Alliance decided to found a political party, but there is no longer a connection between the party and the Civic Alliance coalition, due to personal disagreement. The party obtained seven seats in the Chamber of Deputies after the September 1992 general elections as a member of the Democratic Convention of Romania. On July 3, 1993, the so-called Liberal Civic Group from the Civic Alliance Party merged with the Liberal Party-1993.

Programme. The party defines itself as a neo-liberal party, the ideology being based on the values of democracy, moral and citizenship. It wants to promote the fundamental human rights and develop the civil institutions of the Romanian society.

Affiliations. Affiliated to the Democratic Convention of Romania.

Civil Forum–Free Organization for Democracy
Forumul Cetăţenesc–Organizaţie Liberă Pentru Democraţie

Address. Mun. Cluj-Napoca, str. Moţilor 18, jud. Cluj.

Telephone. (64) 122.18.

Leadership. Nicolae Ruja (pres.)

History. At present the party is not active.

357

Civil–Liberal Alliance

Address/Telephone. See the entries for the founding parties.

Foundation. July 21, 1994.

Leadership. Nicolae Manolescu and Mircea Ionescu Quintus.

History. The Civil–Liberal Alliance is a political alliance formed by the National Liberal Party and the Civic Alliance Party with the aim to pave the way for the National Liberal Party to be accepted as a member of the Democratic Convention of Romania.

Programme. To strengthen the liberal doctrine.

Cluj-Napoca Civic Forum
(*See* Civil Forum–Free Organization for Democracy)

Coalition of Democratic Forces
Coalitja Fortelor Democratjce

The coalition was founded for the local elections in February 1992, including Civic Radical Union, Radical Democratic Party, National Democratic Party of Romania for Justice, Conservative Christian Democratic Romanian Party, Romanian House of Democratic Europe, Christian Party of Justice. The coalition is not active on the political scene.

Conservative Christian Democratic Romanian Party
Partidul Conservator Creştin Democrat Român (PCCDR)

Address. 73284 Bucharest, str. Vasile Cristescu 14, sector 2.

Telephone. 622.11.38.

Foundation. May 15, 1990 (registration date).

Leadership. Alexandru Naniu (pres. gen.)

Programme. The party considers itself a centre-right, Christian democratic, conservative and monarchist party.

Affiliations. The party used to be a member of National Union for the Victory of the Revolution, but has since left it. Member of Coalition of Democratic Forces and Homeland Assembly.

Conservative Humanist Party
Partidul Umanist Conservator (PUC)

Address. 1500 Drobeta-Turnu Severin, str. Traian 48, jud. Mehedinţi.

Foundation. April 23, 1990 (registration date).

Leadership. Puiu Păunescu (pres.)

Constitutional and Monarchical Union of Romania
Uniunea Monarchică Constituțională din România

Address. Bucharest, str. Doamna Chiajna 6, sector 3.

Leadership. Gheorghe Vişan (pres.)

Convention of Social Solidarity
Conventia Solidaritatii Sociale (CSS)

The party was founded with the assistance of the trade union Fratia on April 9, 1992 (registration date), with the purpose of taking part in the general elections of 1992. The party obtained 30,000 votes. When the two trade union confederations CNSLR and Fratia merged in the summer of 1993, the party under the leadership of Tudor Florescu enjoyed close links with the new confederation. In July 1994 a new party was founded by leading Fratia officials having the same headquarters as the Convention of Social Solidarity (see Party of Social Solidarity).

Co-operative Party
Partidul Cooperatist

History. Initially registered with the above mentioned name, later the party changed name to Democratic Co-operatist Party. On June 30 the party merged with the FDSN, then renamed SDPR.

Democratic Agrarian Party of Romania
(*See* Agrarian Democratic Party of Romania)

Democratic Agricultural, Industrial and Intellectual Workers' Party
Partidul Democrat al Muncii Agricole, Industriale şi Intelectuale

History. The party was registered with the above mentioned name on April 11, 1990, but merged later with the ADPR.

Democratic Alliance Party of Romani of Romania
Partidul Alianța Democrată a Romilor din România (PADRR)

Address. Ramnicu Vâlcea, cartier Goranu 889, cod 1000, jud. Vâlcea.

Telephone. (507) 19012.

Foundation. March 2, 1990 (registration date).

Leadership. Octavian Stoica (pres.)

History. The party was registered on March 2, 1990, under the name United Democratic Party of the Romani, Fiddlers and Woodworkers of Romania. On Feb. 5, 1992, the name was changed to the above.

Programme. The party wants to help the integration of the Romani into the society and to protect the rights of the Romani.

Affiliation. To the International Organization of Romanis, "Romani Union".

Democratic Constitutional Party of Romania
Partidul Democrat Constituţional din România

History. The party was registered on Feb. 6, 1990, but has not appeared in public since the May 1990 general elections.

Democratic Convention
(*See* Democratic Convention of Romania)

Democratic Convention of Romania (DCR)
Conventja Democratică din România (CDR)

Address. 70001 Bucharest, Splaiul Funirii 5, sector 3.

Telephone/fax. 312.40.14; 312.40.41.

Leader. Emil Constantinescu (pres.)

History. The Convention was formed for the February 1992 local elections and named Democratic Convention, containing 14 opposition parties. The parties in the Convention put up joint lists at elections, distributing the candidates according to the relevant strength of the parties in the area. The individual parties preserve their own programme and political independence. In the 1992 local elections the Convention gained substantial support, winning the mayoralities of all six sectors of Bucharest and 24.3 per cent of the total seats in the country councils.

The Convention was renamed Democratic Convention of Romania following the departure of the National Liberal Party from the alliance in April 1992. The party was opposed to thoughts about changing the Convention into a permanent political alliance. This change of names was necessary, as the electoral law forbade coalitions to use the name under which they had run in previous elections unless all former members of the coalition agreed to it — and the National Liberal Party did not.

The Convention had a common candidate for the September 1992 presidential elections, Emil Constantinescu, the rector of Bucharest University, who had only been named as a compromise choice at the July 27 Democratic Convention of Romania congress. He came second in the first round and obtained more than 37 per cent in the second round.

In the general elections the Democratic Convention of Romania, now a 18-party coalition, performed well in urban areas, obtaining more than 20 per cent of the votes. Since the elections the Convention has been in opposition in the Parliament.

The Convention contains the following 18 parties: Civil Alliance Party, Romanian Ecological Party, Liberal Party–1993, National Liberal Party–Democratic Convention, National Peasant Party–Christian Democrat, Romanian Social Democratic Party, Democratic Unity Party, Party Christian Democratic Union Party, Hungarian Democratic Union of Romania, Civic Alliance Party, Association of Former Political Detainees of Romania, Association "21st of December", Ecologist Federation of Romania, Movement for Romania in the Future, Workers' and Peasants' Brotherhood Political Trade Union of Romania, Universitary Solidarity, The Global Union of Free Romanians, National Union of Unemployed of Romania.

Programme. The Democratic Convention of Romania has elaborated a political, economical and social programme containing solutions for all the main problems. This Programme is the Democratic Convention of Romania's base for governing. The Convention is situated in the centre-right of the political spectre.

Democratic Co-operatist Party
Partidul Democrat Cooperatist
(*See* Co-operative Party).

Democratic Ecological Party
Partidul Democrat Ecologist

Address. Tirgumures, str. Magurei 30, jud. Mures.

Telephone. (095) 435.94.

Leadership. Gheorghe Ispas (pres.)

Democratic and Free Union of Romanis of Romania
Uniunea Liberă Democratică a Romilor din România (ULDRR)

Address. 3400 Cluj-Napoca, str. Tipografiei 28, jud. Cluj.

Telephone. (064) 17615.

Fax. (064)116.37.

Foundation. May 19, 1990 (registration date).

Leadership. Ilie Gerebenes (pres.)

Democratic Front of Romania
Frontul Democrat din România

Address. Bucharest, B-dul Aviatorilor 5, sector 1.

Telephone. 618.00.65.

Foundation. 1990 (registration date).

Leadership. Vladut Misipeanu.

History. In 1992 the Party initialed a merger with the Democratic National Salvation Front, but the merger is as yet not completed.

Democratic Future of the Homeland Party
Partidul Viitorul Democrat al Patriei (PVDP)

Address. Bucharest, Bd. 1 Mai 333, etaj 3, apart. 13, sector 1.

Telephone. 666.54.06; 635.48.60.

Foundation. 27 March, 1990 (registration date).

Leadership. Eugeniu-Dragoş Petria (pres.)

Programme. The party is associated with the two nationalist groupings, Vatra Românescă and Association "Pro-Bessarabia og Bucovina". The party states that it wants to bring back lost territory to Romania.

Democratic Labour Party
Partidul Democrat al Muncii (P.D.M.)

Address. Bucharest, str. Radu Beller 26, sector 1.

Telephone. 633.28.63; 665.55.09.

Fax. 312.97.76.

Foundation. Feb. 26, 1990 (registration date).

Leadership. George Şerban (pres.)

Programme. The party fights for the right to private property and the development of a market economy.

Affiliations. Centre-Left (Social Democratic) Alliance and Social Democratic Convention.

Democratic National Salvation Front (DNSF)
(*See* Social Democracy Party of Romania)

Democratic Opposition Party
Partidul Opozitja Democrată

Address. Bucharest, Caleea Victorei 26, sector 1.

Foundation. Jan. 20, 1992 (registration date).

Leadership. Dumitru Dincă.

Democratic Party
Partidul Democrat

History. In the 1991 edition of this book a party with this name was mentioned. This party was the so-called Democratic Party of Cluj (Partidul Democrat din Cluj) registered Jan. 15, 1990. In September 1990 the Party decided to merge with the National Liberal Party–Youth Wing.

Democratic Party
Partidul Democrat

Foundation. June 1991 (registration date).

History. This party was created by the Alliance for Democracy Party, the Romanian Christian Social Democratic Party, People's Party of Romania and the Bucharest branch of the Romanian Popular Front. In December 1991 a group from the former Alliance for Democracy split from the Democratic Party and formed the Independent Democratic Party. In May 1993 the Democratic Party merged with the party of Petre Roman, NSF.

Democratic Party
(Often used for the Democratic Party–National Salvation Front).

Democratic Party of Free Romanis
Partidul Democrat al Romilor Liberi

Address. 4000 Sfântu Gheorghe, Str. Varide Iosif 177 and Garoafei 2, judeţul Covasna.

Telephone. (067) 12260.

Leadership. Daniel Dima (pres.)

Democratic Party–National Salvation Front (DP–NSF)
Partidul Democrat (F.S.N.) (usually abbreviated PD)

Address. Allea Modrogan 1, sector 1.

Telephone. 679.36.18/633.72.32.

Fax. 633.53.32; 679.54.97.

Foundation. The official name of the party was adopted on May 28–29, 1993.

Leadership. Petre Roman (ch.)

History. The National Salvation Front (*Frontul Salvarii Nationale*) — NSF, was registered as a party on Feb. 5, 1990, and held its First National Convention on April 7–8, 1990 (for previous period see first part of this chapter). The Convention elected Ion Iliescu as President. Iliescu was also the party's candidate for president. In the 1990 general elections the NSF won 66 per cent of the votes and Iliescu obtained 85 per cent of the presidential votes. On March 14–15, 1991, the NSF held its second National Convention. A reform programme presented by Prime Minister, Petre Roman, spoke about establishing a social democratic party committed to market economy. Despite a divisive debate, Roman's programme was adopted by a large majority. Roman was endorsed as party leader and Ion Aurel Stoica elected executive chairman. During the congress a "conservative" faction criticized the programme and after the congress nine NSF deputies withdrew from the parliamentary group.

The local elections in February 1992 demonstrated a significant loss of support for the ruling NSF, compared with the parliamentary elections held in May 1990.

Due to the election losses, growing personal animosity between Iliescu and Roman, and not least ideological differences between the "conservatives" siding with Iliescu and more "reformist" minded members siding with Roman — in recent months Roman's leadership had come under pressure from NSF members including President Ion Iliescu. On March 30, 1992, the NSF held a National Conference and a number of delegates left the Conference. On April 7, 1992, these delegates and at least seven parliamentary members withdrew from the NSF parliamentary group to form a "NSF-22 December Group", accusing Roman of introducing "tension and a non-democratic and élitist spirit" into the NSF, and blamed the Party's recent election losses on this (*see* NSF-22 December Group).

However, at the NSF National Convention held on April 27–29, 1992, Petre Roman was confirmed as party president, and his free-market reform programme, entitled "The future — today", was approved by 802 out of 1,268 votes, marking what he described as a "true, clean and clear-cut break with the past". On the same day the pro-Iliescu faction, which had split from the NSF, registered as the Democratic National Salvation Front on the basis of the NSF-22 December.

In the September 1992 general elections the NSF won 43 seats in the Chamber of Deputies and 18 in the Senate, gaining about 10 per cent of the votes. The party's candidate for the September 1992 presidential elections was Caius Dragomir. He was chosen as candidate on July 25 when Petre Roman, former Prime Minister and leader of NSF, had refused to stand for the presidency.

On May 28–29, 1993, the NSF merged with the small extra-parliamentary Democratic Party and changed its name to Democratic Party–National Salvation Front, in daily life calling itself the Democratic Party. By this merger, the NSF tried to rid itself of the association with the more conservative DNSF while keeping the legitimizing label of the days of revolution.

Programme. The April 1992 convention is considered the starting point of transforming NSF into a modern social democratic party. The party considers itself a centre-left social democratic party in favour of political pluralism, representative democracy, private property, social protection and a market economy in which the state shall be the guarantor of equal opportunity. The role of the state shall be to interfere to protect national security, and the consumers. The party finds that it is necessary to accellerate the privatization of state property, to reduce budget expenses and subsidies for state enterprises and to ensure local autonomy in the financial field. The party supports a social protection policy for reducing the social costs of transition.

Publications. AZI (Today), daily, independent, but often reflects the opinion of the DP-NSF.

Democratic Party of Romania
Partidul Democrat din România

History. The party was registered on Jan. 16, 1990. On April 28, 1992, this party merged with the Social Democratic–National Salvation Front, which afterwards took the name Social Democratic Unity Party.

Democratic Solidarity Party of Romania
Partidul Solidarităţi Democratice din România

Address. 70700 Bucharest, Bd. G. Coşbuc 1, Bl. P5B, sc. 2, et. 4, ap. 36, sector 4, c.p.1-888.

Telephone. 780.64.81.

Fax. 780.64.81.

Foundation. April 20, 1990 (registration date).

Leadership. Ion Antonescu (pres.)

History. Until the beginning of 1993 the party was called the Party to Honour the Revolution's Heroes and for National Salvation (*Partidul pentru Cinstirea Eroilor Revoluţiei si Salvare Naţională* — PCERSN).

Affiliations. In April 1994 the party created the Democratic Solidarity of Romania together with the Smallholder's and Free Initiative Party and the Movement of Agricultural Producers for Human Rights.

Democratic Solidarity of Romania
Solidaritătea Democratica din România

History. An alliance set up in April 1994 by the Smallholder's and Free Initiative Party, the Movement of Agricultural Producers for Human Rights and the Democratic Solidarity Party of Romania.

Democratic Union
Uniunea Democratică

Foundation. July 17, 1990 (registration date).

Organization. The Union was an umbrella organization for eight political parties: Democratic Unity Party, Liberal Socialist Party, Democratic Party of Cluj, Progressive Democratic Party, the Romanians' Union Republican Party, Christian Socialist Democratic Party, Free Democratic Party, and the Party to Honour the Revolution's Heroes and for National Salvation. The Union cannot be considered active on the political scene.

365

Democratic Unity Party (DUP)
Partidul Unităţi Democratice (PUD)

Address. 71261 Bucharest, Piaţa Aviatorilor 3. Correspondence: B-dl Dacia 5, sector 1.

Telephone. 611.14.86.

Foundation. Jan. 6, 1990 (registration date).

Affiliation. Member of Democratic Convention of Romania, the Democratic Union and initiated in 1991 The National Union for the Victory of the Revolution.

Leadership. Nicu Stancescu (pres.)

Publications. *Mesager* (Messenger), periodically.

Democratic Unity Party of Moldova
Partidul Unităţi Democratice din Moldova

Address. 6600 Iasi, Bd. Stefan cel Mare 15, judetul Iasi.

Telephone. (032) 350 60.

Leadership. Dumitru Maftei (pres.)

Ecologist Federation of Romania
Federaţja Ecologistă din România (FER)

Address. 73226 Bucharest, str. Matei Voievod 102.

Telephone. 635.27.43.

Foundation. July 19, 1990 (registration date).

Leadership. Alexandru Ionescu (pres.)

History. The party was founded by a group of members from the Romanian Ecologist Movement in the belief that the Movement was too close to the new communist way of thinking.

Programme. The party states that it tries to include the ecological mentality in all the social and economical sectors.

Affiliation. Affiliated to Democratic Convention of Romania.

Federation of the Jewish Communities of Romania
Federaţja Comunitătilor Evreieşti din România

Address. Sector 1, 70478 Bucharest, Str. Sf. Vineri 9–11.

Telephone. 613.25.38

Fax. 312.08.69

Telex. 10798.

Leadership. Nicolae Cajal (pres.)

Free Change Party
Partidul Liber Schimbist (PLS)

Address. 70778 Bucharest, Str. Transilvaniei 12.

Telephone. 613.62.94.

Foundation. May 1, 1990 (registration date).

Leadership. Vasile Groza (s.g.). The former president and founder, Stefan Kazimir, left the party and joined the SDPR.

Free Democratic Party
Partidul Liber Democrat (PLD)

Address. Sector 5, 70629 Bucharest, Bd. Mihai Kogalniceanu 25.

Telephone. 614.12.35; 312.43.15.

Fax. 312.33.37.

Foundation. Jan. 19, 1990 (registration date).

Leadership. Nica Leon (pres.)

Programme. Centre-right.

Affiliations. Member of Democratic Union.

Free Democratic Social Justice Party
(*See* Social Justice Party of Romania)

Free Democratic Youth Party
Partidul Tineretului Liber Democrat

History. Registered on Feb. 1, 1990, with the above mentioned name, but merged with the Republican Party on Feb. 13, 1992.

Free Republican Party
Partidul Liber Republican (PLR)

Address. Bucharest, str. Foişorului 16, bloc. F11C, ap. 30, scara 1, sector 3.

Telephone. 321.38.24.

Foundation. Aug. 2, 1990 (registration date).

Leadership. Florin Mihai Nahorniac (pres.)

Publication. *Stefan cel Mare* (Stefan the Great).

Programme. The party considers that the only way of developing Romania is the socialist way, but under other forms than those practised before 1989.

Freedom and Romanian Democracy Party
Partidul Libertăţi şi Democratjei Române (PLDR)

History. The party was registered on Jan. 29, 1990, and merged in September 1990 with the Democratic Party of Romania. The new party was called Romanian Democratic Party.

German Democratic Forum of Romania
Forumul Democrat al Germanilor din România (FDGR)

Address. 2400 Sibiu, str. General G. Mageru 1–3.

Telephone. (092) 41.81.45.

Fax. (092) 41.54.17.

Leadership. Paul Philippi (pres.)

Greater Romania Party (GRP)
Partidul România Mare (P.R.M.)

Address. Sector 1, Bucharest, Calea Victoriei nr. 39A, etaj 3.

Telephone. 613.97.96.

Fax. 615.02.29.

Foundation. June 20, 1991 (registration date).

Leadership. Corneliu Vadim Tudor (ch.)

History. The party first obtained a parliamentary foothold in the 1992 general elections, supported by almost 4 per cent of the vote. This entitled the party to 16 seats in the Chamber of Deputies and six in the Senate. Since the elections, the party has been a part of the so-called Pentagon, giving the SDPR minority government external support, and set up a joined faction with the SPL and the ADPR in the Parliament after the elections to strengthen its influence.

Programme. The GRP is clearly chauvinistic, authoritarian and anti-Semitic, and belongs to what one can define as the far right parties of "radical continuity" (*see* PRNU). All the more, the party is the chief promoter of the rehabilitation of Romania's wartime dictator, Marshal Ion Antonescu.

The party declares itself to be a party of the centre-left, but at the same time hails the "achievements" of the former regime. In a speech delivered to the congress, Tudor urged that there should be a crack down on the activities of HDUR, accusing it of planning a Yugoslavia-style division of Romania. It praises former Romanian dictator Nicolae Ceauşescu as a patriot, describing the revolt which overthrew him in 1989 as an "armed attack" against Romania by the former Soviet Union and Hungary.

Publications. Romania Mare (Greater Romania), weekly, *Politica*, weekly.

Homeland Assembly
Sfatul Tării

The Forum was founded on Dec. 21, 1991, by a number of groups including the Romanian Revolution Party, Democratic Party, Civic Radical Union, Radical Democratic Party, Romanian House of Democratic Europe Party, League of Detainees for Justice, National Democratic Party of Romania for Justice, Conservative Christian Democratic Party of Romania, Christian Party of Justice, National Progressist Party, Romanian League of War Veterans, Convention of Cernauti, Association of Romanian Victims of the Stalinist Repression of Bessarabia and Bucovina and "Golgota"-Association of the Repressed and the Association of the Victims and the Repressed of Moldavia.

Humanist-Ecological Party founded in Arad
Partidul Ecologist-Umanist fondat la Arad (PE-U)

Address. 2900 Arad, Bd. Revolutiei 73.

Telephone. (057) 35.975.

Foundation. Jan. 20, 1990 (registration date).

Leadership. Petru Barbu (pres.)

Programme. In the centre of the political spectrum.

Publication. Viaţa (Life), periodically.

Humanist Party of Romania
Partidul Umanist din România (PUR)

Address. Bucharest, Calea Victoriei 118, etaj 5 cam. 501–502.

Telephone. 659.22.35; 659.68.30.

Fax. 659.70.50.

Foundation. Dec. 18, 1991 (registration date).

Membership. 6,000.

Leadership. Gavrilă Vasilescu (dir.)

Affiliations. The party is consultative member of the European Humanist Federation.

Humanitarian Peace Party
Partidul Umanitar al Păcii

Address. 75100 Bucharest, B-dul G. Coşbuc 1, bloc P5B, scara 2, etaj 4, apart. 34–36.

Telephone. 781.38.39.

Foundation. Feb. 20, 1990 (registration date).

Leadership. Teodor Tipa (pres.)

Hungarian Christian Democratic Party of Romania (*)
Partidul Creştin Democrat Maghiar din România

Address. Municipiul Tg. Mureş, str. Bolyai 10, jud. Mureş.

Telephone. (065) 20237.

Leadership. Vargo Laszlo (pres.)

Affiliations. The party is associated to the HDUR.

Hungarian Democratic Union of Romania (HDUR)
Uniunea Democrată Maghiară din România (UDMR)

Address. 71297 Bucharest, str. Herăstrău 13, Of. Postal 63, C.P. 27 and 3400 Cluj-Napoca, str. Pavlov 21, C.P. 1093 or str. Donath 68.

Telephone. (Bucharest). 633.35.69.

Fax. (Bucharest). 679.66.75.

Fax. (Cluj-Napoca). (641) 18.79.38.

Foundation. Jan. 28, 1990 (registration date).

Leadership. Béla Markó (pres.)

History. The HDUR is the political party representing the majority of the Magyar population, getting a stable 7 plus per cent in the general elections. In September 1992 the party received 27 seats in the Chamber of Deputies and 12 in the Senate. It is a member of the DCR, but runs for elections on a separate list as the only DCR-member.

Programme. The HDUR aims to contribute to the construction of a free democratic Romania, where all citizens alike can enjoy the same rights, without having to show consideration for nationality, political persuasions, race, creed or sex. The HDUR Congress in January 1993 called on the Romanian government to help the Hungarian minority preserve its identity, culture, religion and education, but adopted a moderate tone on demands for Hungarian autonomous areas, calling for regional self-administration rather than territorial autonomy. The HDUR, which had recommended that the European Council delay Romanian membership pending guarantees on ethnic rights, nevertheless welcomed the decision to allow Romania to join. The HDUR expects a political fight between a pragmatic and a radical wing of the party in the future.

Affiliations. Member of the Democratic Convention of Romania.

Hungarian Free Democratic Party of Romania
Partidul Liber Democrat Maghiar din România

Address. Mun. Tg. Mureş, str. Bolai 30, jud. Mureş.

Telephone. (065) 274.20.

Foundation. Feb. 8, 1990 (registration date).

Leadership. Kiss Kalman (pres.)

History. The party initially registered under the name of Hungarian Independent Party, but on May 12, 1992, the name was changed to Hungarian Free Democratic Party of Romania.

Programme. Considers the HDUR as the only political force of all the Hungarians of Romania.

Hungarian Independent Party
(*See* Hungarian Free Democratic Party of Romania)

Hungarian Smallholders' Party in Romania
Partidul Gospodarilor Maghiari din România

Address. 4100 Miercurea Ciuc, str. Timişoarei 15, jud. Harghita.

Telephone. (066) 142.80.

Foundation. Feb. 22, 1990 (registration date).

Leadership. Kiraly Karoly (hon. pres.), Buzas Laszlo (ex. pres.)

Affiliations. The party is among the allied organizations of the Hungarian Democratic Union of Romania.

Independent Democratic Party
Partidul Democrat Independent (PDI)

After the creation of the Democratic Party in June 1991, one of the founders of the Alliance for Democracy Party withdrew and registered the Independent Democratic Party on Dec. 19, 1991. In the local and general elections of 1992 the party supported the Republican Party of Ion Manzatu. In December 1993 the party transformed itself into the Republican Popular Party. The party was affiliated to National Alliance of Social Democracy.

Independent National Christian Party
Partidul Naţjonal Creştin Independent (PNCI)

Address. 73986 Bucharest, str. Popa Sapcă 19, comuna Voluntari, SAI.

Telephone. 655.46.95.

Foundation. April 11, 1990 (registration date).

Leadership. Eugen Ioachim Tudor (pres.)

Independent National Peasants' Party-Christian Democrat
Partidul Naţional Ţărănesc Creştin şi Democrat Independent (PNŢCDI)

Address. Craiova, str. 13 Septembrie 11, jud. Dolj.

Telephone. (051) 18.635.

Foundation. June 22, 1990 (registration date).

Leadership. Victor Ionică (pres.)

History. The members of the party split from the National Peasants' Party–Christian Democrat on generational and personal grounds. The party participated in the local elections in 1992 within the United Democratic Opposition. Part of the National Union for the Victory of Revolution.

Independent Social Democratic Party
Partidul Social Democrat Independent (PSDI)

Address. Sector 1, Bucharest, Calea Victoriei 151.

Telephone. 659.68.00; 659.48.69.

Fax. 312.96.65.

Foundation. Dec. 23, 1989. (registration date).

Leadership. Alexandru Dan Popescu (pres.)

History. The party held congresses in 1990, 1991 and 1992. It believes it is the successor to the historical social democratic party from the inter-war years.

Programme. The party adopted a new programme at its congress in November 1992 in accord of a social democratic, centre-left doctrine.

Affiliations. Centre-Left (Social Democratic) Alliance. Established the Social Democratic Convention together with the Democratic Labour Party on Oct. 11, 1992. Member of Forum for Democracy.

Independent Socialist Party for Justice

This was the name of the Independent Social Democratic Party until the elections in 1990.

Justice and Social Democracy Party of Romania
Partidul Dreptăţii şi Social-Democratjei din România (PDS–DR)

Address. Bacău, str. Alexandru cel Bun, bloc 1, scara A, ap. 3.

Telephone. (034) 482.36.

Foundation. Aug. 8, 1991 (registration date).

Leadership. Eugen Panianopol (pres.)

Labour Party
Partidul Muncii

History. Merged in May 1991 with the Traditional Social Democratic Party.

Labour and Social Justice Party of Romania
Partidul Muncii şi Dreptăţi Sociale din România

History. Merged on Sept. 1, 1993, with the ADPR.

Liberal Alliance

History. Created by the National Liberal Party–Democratic Convention and the National Liberal Party–Youth Wing in order to prepare for the September 1992 general elections under the Democratic Convention, which both parties were members of.

Liberal Monarchist Party of Romania
Partidul Liberal Monarchist din România (PLMR)

Address. 70336 Bucharest, str. Caimatei 10, et. 1, sector 2.

Telephone. 613.21.41; 613.49.40.

Foundation. Jan. 19, 1990 (registration date).

Leadership. Emil Munteanu (vice-pres.)

History. The party was first registered on Jan. 19, 1990, under the name of Liberal Party of Freedom of Romania. The party adopted its present name on Jan. 30, 1992.

Publication. CUGET (Believe).

Liberal Party

The National Liberal Party–Youth Wing changed its name to the Liberal Party in October 1991, without changing the registered name. *See* Liberal Party 1993.

Liberal Party 1993
Partidul Liberal 1993 (PL–1993)

Address. Bucharest, Calea Victoriei 133–135, et. 1, sector 1.

Telephone. 650.79.58; 659.50.95.

Foundation. 25 May, 1993 (registration date).

Leadership. Horia Rusu (exec. pres.)

History. Following factional splits within the National Liberal Party, expelled members of the Party formed the NLP–YW on July 23, 1990. Two candidates elected on the National Liberal Party ticket joined the new party. At first, in July 1991, the party joined the Charter for Reform and Democracy, led by the NSF, but then in September it withdrew. In June 1992 the party joined the opposition Democratic Convention of Romania in the event that the NLP would quit it, co-operating with the National Liberal Party–Democratic Convention within the Convention in an alliance created in May 1992 between the two, called the Liberal Alliance. Participating in the general elections on the Democratic Convention of Romania list, the Youth Wing obtained 11 seats in the Chamber of Deputies and one in the Senate after the September 1992 general elections.

In February 1993 a splinter group from the Youth Wing, registered as the New Liberal Party since July 1992, joined the NLP. On Feb. 19–20, 1993, at the so-called "Liberal Unification" congress — the National Liberal Party–Youth Wing and the Group of Moral and Political Reform of the National Liberal Party merged in order to create a strong liberal party. They were joined by a group from the NLP–CD, led by Vintilă Brătianu, and the party was called the Liberal Party. On May 25, 1993, the party registered as the Liberal Party–1993. On July 3, 1993, the PL-93 merged with the Liberal Civic group from the Civic Alliance Party. PL-93 has 25 deputies and seven senators in the Romanian Parliament. The party is a part of the DCR-opposition in Parliament and often plays an active role in opposition.

Programme. The party is a liberal party, advocating a fast and effective economic reform based on liberalist ideas. It is in favour of a thorough privatization of all parts of Romanian economical life. The party states that it wants to eliminate the dictatorship of the state upon the human being, to fight against bureaucracy, to stimulate the individual initiative and to create a new generation of investors.

Affiliations. To the Democratic Convention of Romania.

Liberal Socialist Party
Partidul Socialist Liberal

History. The party registered with the above mentioned name on Jan. 23, 1990. On Oct. 18, 1990, the party led by Nicolae Cerveni merged with the National Liberal Party. In April 1992 some of the members of the former Liberal Socialist Party withdrew from the National Liberal Party and established the National Liberal Party-Democratic Convention.

Merchants' and Businessmens' Union of Romania
Uniunea Negustorilor și Oamenilor de Afaceri din România (UNOAR)

Address. Bucharest, str. Turda 25, bloc 3, scara 3, et. 1, apart. 95.

Telephone. 666.19.19; 618.06.73.

Foundation. May 6, 1992 (registration date).

Leadership. Ion Alexandru Mischie (pres.)

Programme. The party is based on a centre, liberal and non-violent doctrine aiming at protecting the interests of the businessmen and merchants. The party, which supports the SDPR, works for perfect social and loyal harmony.

Modern Democracy Movement
Mişcarea Democraţja Modernă

Address. Craiova, str. N. Titulescu 7, jud. Dolj.

Telephone. (511) 181.16./140.49.

Leadership. Paul Şt Petre Popa (pres.)

Movement of Agricultural Producers for Human Rights (*)
Mişcarea Producătorilor Agricoli pentru Drepturile Omului

Address. Făgăraş, str. Trandafirilor 43, jud. Braşov.

Foundation. Aug. 28, 1990 (registration date).

Leadership. Ion Scarlat (pres.)

Affiliations. Democratic Solidarity of Romania.

Movement for European Integration
Mişcarea pentru Integrare Europeană (MIE)

Address. Bucharest, Bdul Republicii 214, bloc 1, scara 1, ap. 16, sector 3.

Telephone. 685.08.11.

Fax. 685.32.27.

Foundation. May 8, 1990 (registration date).

Leadership. Radu Coca (pres.)

Programme. Fights for bringing back Romania to the civilized countries of the Continent and to facilitate the integration of Romania in the common European house and to rebuild the image of Romania in the world. From August 1992 member of the Democratic Convention of Romania.

Movement for Romania
Mişcarea pentru România (MPR)

Address. 78158 Bucharest, str. Scărlătescu 14, sector 1.

Telephone. 659.45.72.

Fax. 312.41.15.

Foundation. Dec. 23, 1991 (registration date).

Leadership. Marian Munteanu (chief of movement).

History. In the general elections of 1992 the party garnered less than 0.1 per cent of the votes and is not represented in the parliament. Many reports indicates that MPR is gaining support especially among the younger generation.

Programme. The party belongs to the extremist groups of "radical return", advocating a revival of what they regard as genuine Romanian nationalism, unspoiled by the national-communist distortion of nationalistic thought. The embodiment of this genuine nationalism is considered to be the inter-war Iron Guard, also known as the League of the Archangel Michael or the Legionary Movement. The MPR is considered the main exponent of the parties of "radical return". Looks on democracy "as means, rather than an end in itself", and finds that "sectoral militarization" of the economy is the solution to the crisis of the country.

Publication. Mişcarea (Movement), twice-monthly.

Muslim Turkish Tartars Democratic Union of Romania
Uniunea Democrată a Tătarilor Turco-musulmani din România (UDTTMR)

Address. Constanta, str. Revolutiei din Decembrie 1989 6, jud. Constanta.

Telephone. (041) 61.66.43.

Leadership. Ekrem Menlibay (pres.)

National Alliance of Social Democracy
Alianţa Naţională a Social Democratjei (ANSD)

Address. Bucharest, str. Ion Câmpineanu 4.

Telephone. 614.34.24; 614.34.84

Fax. 312.50.50.

Foundation. July 26, 1993 (registration date).

Leadership. Mircea Istru Stănescu (pres.)

History. The alliance is a coalition of parties based on social democratic political doctrine: Social Democratic Party "Constantin Titel Petrescu", Independent Democratic Party, Romanian Labour Party, New Democracy Party, National Democratic Party, Christian Republican Party of Romania and the Social Democrat Unity Party.

National Christian Democratic Peasants' Party
(*See* National Peasants' Party-Christian Democrat)

National Convention for Democracy
(*See* Democratic Convention of Romania)

National Convention for the Establishment of Democracy

Created in May 1991 by opposition forces.

National Convention of the Extra-parliamentary Opposition

Set up by opposition forces in February 1991.

National Democratic Party (NDP)
Partidul Naţjonal Democrat

Address. 70208 Bucharest, str. Aaron Florian 1, sector 2.

Telephone. 746.64.72.

Foundation. Jan. 18, 1990 (registration date).

Leadership. Liviu Enică.

Affiliation. Member of the Centrist Democratic Group. Member of the National Alliance of Social Democracy.

National Democratic Party of Romania for Justice
Partidul Naţjonal Democrat pentru Dreptate din România (PNDD)

Address. Bucharest, Bd. George Cosbuç 112B, Of.P. nr. 42, C.P. 42–89.

Telephonelfax. 623.40.09.

Foundation. July 8, 1991 (registration date).

Leadership. Gheorhe Răileanu (hon. pres.), Mihai Isbăsoiu (pres.)

Programme. It considers itself a centre-party.

Affiliation. The party is a part of the National Union for the Victory of the Revolution. The party took part in the foundation of the United Democratic Opposition. A member of Coalition of Democratic Forces and Homeland Assembly.

National Legionary Party

Foundation. Sept. 22, 1992 (registration date).

Leadership. Ionica Catanescu.

History. Set up shortly before the general elections in 1992 by a former graduate of a Securitate school advocating the thoughts of "radical continuity" (*see* Movement for Romania). Nothing has been heard of the party since the elections.

National Liberal Party
Partidul Naţional Liberal (PNL)

Address. 70112 Bucharest, Bd. Nicolae Bălcescu 21, sector 1.

Telephone. 614.32.35.

Fax. 615.76.38.

Foundation. 1864, re-registered on Jan. 7, 1990.

Leadership. Mircea Ionescu Quintus and Radu Câmpeanu are contesting the title of president.

History. The party has been established as such since 1875, when several liberal groups set up a common organization, some of these groups originally founded in 1864. In 1947 the party decided to suspend operations in order not to expose rank-and-file members to persecution from the communists. The party was re-established by returned émigres and local liberal veterans in early January 1990, electing the prominent exile liberal, Radu Câmpeanu, as president. In the May 1990 elections the party came third with about 7 per cent of the votes, Câmpeanu getting over 10 per cent as the party's presidential candidate. This relative success encouraged Câmpeanu to seek compromises with the NSF government from 1990 to 1992, joining the Stolojan government in October 1991. Paradoxically, the party remained a member of the opposition National Convention for the Establishment of Democracy and joined the newly created Democratic Convention in November 1991, thereby being in power and in opposition at the same time. However, in April 1992 the party left the Convention, a fact which marked the beginning of the party's decline, as did Câmpeanu's decision to propose Romania's former king as the party's candidate for the 1992 presidential elections. These events contributed to fact that the party did not pass the 3 per cent threshold in the 1992 general elections. This led to Câmpeanu's removal at the party's nationwide conference in February 1993 and the election of Mircea Ionescu Quintus as the new president. The congress also approved the merger with the so-called New Liberal Party. In February 1994 Câmpeanu managed to convene an extraordinary congress of the party, which re-elected him as president. A court case between Quintus and Câmpeanu on the legal manoeuvres behind the two congresses is in summer 1994 taking place in the Supreme Court, the Municipal Court of Bucharest having ruled in favour of Câmpeanu.

As early as during 1990 several fractures occured within the PNL. The first split of March 26, 1990, gave rise to the Brătianu Liberal Union. In July 1990 a Youth Wing was created and formed a party, the National Liberal Party–Youth Wing, criticizing the party's leadership. On Oct. 18, 1990, the Liberal Socialist Party led by Nicolae Cerveni merged with the National Liberal Party until May 1992, when Cerveni and some of the members withdrew from the party and established the National Liberal Party–Democratic Convention, protesting against the Câmpeanu party's withdrawal from the Democratic Convention (for further details see the respective new parties).

Programme. The party is based on a liberal doctrine, working for guarantees of individual freedom, the separation of powers in the state, the establishment of democracy, freedom of expression and dissemination of opinion, the freedom of the press and all religious denominations, the abolition of collectivization and nationalization in agriculture and the creation of propitious conditions for agricultural property to go to those willing to have it, the gradual privatization of enterprises and their restructuring according to principles of profitability, as part of a market economy.

Publications. Viitorul (The Future), daily. *Liberalul* (The Liberal), weekly.

National Liberal Party – Democratic Convention
Partidul Naţional Liberal – Convenţia Democratică (PNL–CD)

Address. Bucharest, Calea Victoriei 176, sector 1.

Telephone. 650.47.19.

Foundation. Jan. 23, 1990, as the Liberal Socialist Party (registration date).

Leadership. Nicolae Cerveni (pres.)

History. On Oct. 18, 1990, the Liberal Socialist Party, led by Nicolae Cerveni, merged with the National Liberal Party until April 1992, when Cerveni and some of the members withdrew from the party and established the National Liberal Party–Democratic Convention, in protest at the National Liberal Party's withdrawal from the Democratic Convention. The party elected Vintilă Brătianu as its president and formed the Liberal Alliance with the National Liberal Party–Youth Wing in order to prepare for the general elections under the Democratic Convention, which both parties were members of. The PNL-CD obtained two seats in the Chamber of Deputies after the September 1992 general elections. In February 1993 a group led by Vintilă Brătianu merged with the Youth Wing, under the name of the Liberal Party. Cerveni, however, did not join the merger.

Programme. The party states that it is based on a liberal platform.

Affiliations. Member of the Democratic Convention of Romania.

National Liberal Party-Youth Wing
Partidul National Liberal-Aripa Tanara
(*See* Liberal Party-1993).

National Movement "The Homelands Shield"
Mişcarea Natinală "Scutul Patriei"

Address. Bucharest, str. Laborator 234, bloc S22, scara a, et. 7, ap. 37, sector 3.

Foundation. Aug. 27, 1992 (registration date).

Leadership. Ioniţă Borşan (pres.)

National Party of Free Producers of Romania
Partidul Naţional al Producâtorilor Liberi din România (PNPL)

Address. 70122 Bucharest, B-dul N. Balcescu 23A, sc. B, et. 8, apart. 48, sector 1.

Telephone. 614.83.23.

Foundation. Aug. 21, 1991 (registration date).

Leadership. Constantin Ungureanu (pres.)

Membership. 3,000.

Programme. It considers itself as a national, centre-party against the DP(NSF) and the SDPR. They are for a mixed market economy and the republic.

National Peasants' Party

(This name is used for both the National Peasants' Party and the National Peasants' Party-Christian Democrat)

National Peasants' Party
Partidul Naţional Ţărănesc (PNŢ)

Address. Bucharest, str. Italiana 1, sector 2.

Telephone. 772.70.52.

Foundation. Oct. 16, 1990 (registration date).

Leadership. Virgil Lambru (pres.)

History. The party fights with the National Peasants' Party-Christian Democrat for the right to call itself the successor of the historic inter-war National Peasants' Party.

Programme. The party considers its politics based on a centre, Christian Democratic doctrine.

Publication. Dreptatea Nouă (New Justice), weekly.

National Peasants' Party–Christian Democrat (NPP–CD)
Partidul Naţional Ţărănesc–Creştin Democrat (P.N.T.C.D)

Address. Bucharest, Bd. Carol I, nr. 34, sector 3.

Telephone. 615.41.53.

Fax. 312.13.03; 614.32.77.

Foundation. 1869, re-founded on Dec. 26, 1989.

Leadership. Corneliu Coposu (pres.), Ion Diaconescu (first vice-pres.), Valentin Gabrielescu (s.g.).

History. The NPP–CD is the successor of the historical National Peasants' Party, originally founded in 1869, then re-founded in 1895. During the inter-war period it was one of the strongest parties in the country, but was banned by the communist regime and all its property confiscated in 1947. The party was the first party legally established after the December 1989 revolution. The party explains that it changed its name to make its political position more clear.

In the 1990 general elections, the party obtained 2.5 per cent for the Parliament and the party's presidential candidate, Ion Ratiu, obtained 4 per cent of the votes. After the 1992 general elections the party was the second biggest party in the parliament, with 14 per cent of the mandate, obtaining 42 seats in the Chamber of Deputies and 21 in the Senate. The party supported the Democratic Convention of Romania candidate for presidency, Emil Constantinescu.

Programme. The party declares itself to have a centre-right orientation, representing the Christian democratic doctrine within Romania. The party's aims are pluralist democracy, a state *de jure* with the strict observance of laws, a return to the market economy and the restoration of peasant property, the re-organization of education, the national rebirth in the spirit of Christian morals, the separation of state powers, equality of all nationalities and religious beliefs. It is the largest pro-monarchist party in the country.

Affiliations. Member of the Democratic Convention of Romania. Affiliated to the European Union Christian Democrat (EUCD) and the International Christian Democrat (ICD).

Publications. Dreptatea (Justice), weekly.

National Progressist Party
Partidul Naţional Progressist (P.N.P.)

Address (provisional). Bucharest, Sos. Pantelimon 245, bloc 51, sector 2.

Telephone. 628.24.37.

Foundation. March 19, 1990 (registration date).

Leadership. Emil Monceanu (pres.)

Membership. 5,000.

History. The party has the same president as the Alliance for National Dignity. On Jan. 15, 1991, the party initiated the formation of the "Ethnic Alliance", joined by the Romanian International League, The League for Protecting Human Rights and Environmental Protection and the Christian Party of Justice.

Programme. Strongly nationalist, advocating a return to traditional cultural and religious values of Romanian society.

Affiliations. Centrist Democratic Group, Homeland Assembly and Alliance for National Dignity.

National Reconstruction Party
(*See* Party for National Reconstruction and Democracy)

National Reconstruction Party of Romania
Partidul Reconstructjei Natjonale din România

History. This former Bucharest-based party merged with the ADPR on Sept. 1, 1992.

National Republican Party
Partidul Natjonal Republican

History. Merged with the Republican Party on Sept. 1, 1991.

National Resurrection Unity Party
Partidul Unitatęa Renaşterii Nationalê

Address. Brasov, str. G. Baritiu 1.

Foundation. Dec. 10, 1993 (registration date).

Leadership. Nicolae Amaristei.

National Reunification Party
Partidul Natjonal al Reîntregirii (PNR)

Address. 70601 Bucharest, Bd. M. Kogălniceanu 19, sector 5.

Telephone. 614.09.59.

Foundation. Dec. 28, 1992 (registration date).

Leadership. Mircea Druc (pres.)

Membership. 4,800.

History. On Nov. 4, 1992, Mircea Druc was elected leader of the National Reunification Party, registered at Court on Dec. 28, 1992. Mircea Druc is former Prime Minister of

Moldova and stood in the presidential elections in September 1992 as an independent candidate campaigning for the unification of Romania, Bessarabia (now Moldova and parts of Ukraine) and Bukovina (also part of Ukraine).

Programme. The party considers Bessarabia, north of Bucovina and Hertei as Romanian territories and its main aim is to work for the re-integration of these territories into Romania in one single national state. The party states that it supports political pluralism and the right of private property.

National Royalist Party
Partidul Naţional Regalist (PNR)

Address. 73331 Bucharest, str. Sachelarie Visarion 14, bloc 117C, scara B, et. 5, apart. 65, sector 2.

Telephone. 653.38.42.

Foundation. Aug. 19, 1992 (registration date).

Leadership. Mihai Zamfir (pres.)

History. The party has tried to become a member of the Democratic Convention of Romania, but has not yet been allowed to join.

Programme. Considers itself as the only party trying to restore the monarchy without conditions, not representing the interests of King Michael I, but of the Romanian people.

National Salvation Front (NSF)
Frontul Salvării Nationale (FSN)

(*See* Democratic Party–National Salvation Front)

National Salvation Front – "20th of May"
Frontul Salvării Naţionale – "20 Mai"

Registered on Jan. 24, 1992, but merged in August 1992 with the Social Democratic Unity Party.

National Salvation Front-22 December group

History. See Democratic Party–National Salvation Front. The formation of the NSF-22 December group (supporting Ion Iliescu) in March 1992 marked the split in the ruling National Salvation Front. The group held its founding conference on April 7, electing as its leadership a 25-strong provisional national council and adopting a programme which described the NSF-22 December group as a "social-democratic" party, the name referring to the date of Ceauşescu's overthrow in 1989.

National Union for the Victory of the Revolution
Uniunea Naţională pentru Victoria Revolutjei (UNVR)

Address. Bucharest, Piata Aviatorilor 3, sector 1. Correspondence: Bucharest, Bdul Dacia 5, sector 5.

Telephone. 611.14.86; 615.32.94.

Foundation. Nov. 28, 1990 (registration date).

Leadership. The job of leader is on a rotation basis among the parties in the Union, each party having the leadership for a period of one month. Nicu Stăncescu is honorary president.

History. The Union was registered on Nov. 28, 1990, by the following parties: Romanian House of Democratic Europe Party, "Jilava"-organization, Progressive Democratic Party, National Democratic Party of Romania for Justice, Independent National Peasants Party–Christian Democratic, Christian Republican Party of Romania, Democratic Unity Party, Confederation of Alliances for Justice and Truth, Democratic League for Justice, Christian Democratic Revolution Party, League for Professional Integration of the Unemployed, the Christian Party of Justice.

Programme. The Union considers itself a centre-right movement with the aim to restore real democracy in Romania. The Union holds weekly meetings to co-ordinate its politics, which usually are against the SDPR government.

National Unity Bloc

History. Formed in November 1993 when the Agrarian Democratic Party joined the RNUP faction in the Senate. The SPL is also a part of this bloc.

National Unity and Democracy Forum of Romania
Forumul Democratjei şi Unitatji Naţionale din România (FDUNR)

Address. Bucharest, str. Desişului 12, bloc. 27, et. 4, ap. 58, sector 6.

Telephone. 772.44.97.

Foundation. Jan. 15, 1990 (registration date).

Leadership. Gheorghe Pârgaru (pres.)

National Unity Party

(*See* Romanian National Unity Party)

Neo-liberal Movement
Mişcarea Neoliberală

Address. Bucharest, Aleea Slatioara 7, bloc 12, scara A, et. 4.

Telephone. 685.20.50.

Foundation. June 8, 1990 (registration date).

Leadership. Mihai Piscoci.

New Christian Romanian Party
Partidul Noua Românie Creştină (PNRC)

Address. The party does not have a central office.

Telephone. 635.14.74; 642.45.48.

Foundation. May 18, 1991 (registration date).

Leadership. Nicolae Goga (pres.)

Programme. The party claims to be a national, Christian democratic party which fights for the restoration of the borders recognized by the Trianon Treaty from 1920. The party belongs to the extreme right parties, pledging for a "radical return" (*see* Movement for Romania). Not very active on the political scene. Announced to be dissolved in April 1994.

New Democracy Party
Partidul Noua Democraţje

Address. Bucharest, B-dul Muncii 110, bloc L8, scara A, et. 6, apart 16, sector 2.

Foundation. June 22, 1990 (registration date).

Leadership. Eugen Gălăteanu.

Affiliations. Member of National Alliance of Social Democracy.

New Democracy Social Justice Party of the North-West of Romania
Partidul Dreptăţi Sociale (Noua Democratie) de Nord-Vest din România

Address. Oradea, str. Independenţei 20, jud. Bihor.

Telephone. (059) 62419.

Foundation. Feb. 27, 1990 (registration date).

Leadership. Dumitri Mircea Matula (pres.)

New Democracy Social Justice Party
(*See* New Democracy Social Justice Party of the North-West of Romania)

New Generation Group
Gruparea Noua Generaţje (GNG)

Address. 77386 Bucharest, str. Poiana Muntelui 2, bloc. OD3, scara 3, ap. 97, sector 6.

Telephone. 745.04.39.

Foundation. May 12, 1993 (registration date).

Leadership. Mihael Crivăţ, (pres.)

New Liberal Party

History. In July 1992 a splinter group from the National Liberal Party–Youth Wing registered a party under the above mentioned name. This party merged with the National Liberal Party on Feb. 26, 1993.

Orphans and War-prisoners Party
Partidul Orfanilor şi Prizonierilor de Război (POPR)

Address. Satul Pescari 132, communa Gurahonţ cod 2841, jud. Arad.

Foundation. July 25, 1991 (registration date).

Leadership. Pavel Măruşteri (national leader)

History. The party has written the following: "the party has no material possibilities, no headquarters, no political alliances, no funds, no subsidies from the state, no relations with the rest of the country — therefore, the party has not proposed any candidates for the elections, they do not wish to take over the power, but they will fight to ensure the future of the Romanian people"!

Party for the Fatherland
Partidul Pentru Patrie

Leadership. Nistor Chioreanu (leader).

History. The party was founded before World War II as a fascist party, but was outlawed by the Communists. The party was set up again in June 1993, originally asking to be registered under the name of the Legionary Movement's political arm in the years 1935–38.

Programme. The Party belongs to the extreme right, pledging for a "radical return" (*see* Movement for Romania).

Party for National Reconstruction and Democracy
Partidul pentru Reconstructja Naţională şi Democratică

History. Merged in August 1992 with the Democratic National Salvation Front, later the Social Democracy Party of Romania.

Party of the National Right
Partidul Dreptei Naţjonale

Address. Bucharest, str. Boteanum no. 3B.

Foundation. April 20, 1992 (registration date).

Leadership. Radu Sorescu.

History. Set up in April 1992. Its performance in the general elections a few months later was very bad, but there are numerous reports that the party's popularity is growing among the younger generation.

Programme. The party belongs to the extreme right. It is second in importance of the "radical return" parties (*see* Movement for Romania). The party is in favour of an "ethnocratic state" and rejects democracy. Has set up a paramilitary organization called the Civic Guards.

Publications. *Noua Dreapta* (New Justice), *Dreapta Nationale* (National Justice)

Party for National-Democratic Solidarity
Partidul Solidaritatea Naţjonal-Democrata

Telephone. 615.12.66.

Foundation. May 6, 1992 (registration date).

Leadership. Constantin Cojocaru (pres.).

Party of Nomadic and Cobblersmith Romanis of Romania
Partidul Romilor Nomazi şi Căldărari din România

Address. str. Strehaia, Jud. Mehedinti.

Foundation. June 20, 1990 (registration date).

Leadership. Mihai Gheorghe (Mitae).

History. The party's initial president, Ion Cioaba, was crowned King of Romanis, and withdrew. His position as president was taken over by Iulian Radulescu, who was elected "Emperor of the Romanies of the World". The party leadership then elected Ilarie Mihai and afterwards Mihai Gheorghe.

Party of Romanian National Resurrection
Partidul Renaşterii Natjunii Române (PRNR)

Address. Bucharest, str. Pictor Iosif Iser 13, sector 1.

Telephone. 666.61.63; 658.38.24.

Foundation. June 17, 1991 (registration date).

Leadership. Lucian Vasilescu (founder).

History. The party is reported to consist of mainly orthodox, religious members, hailing the achievement of ex-dictator Ceauşescu.

Programme. The party considers itself to be in the centre-left of the political spectrum, fighting for the state of law and is against corruption.

Publication. Renasterea (Resurrection).

Party of Romanian National Unity
(*See* Romanian National Unity Party)

Party of Romanians' Resurrection and Independence
Partidul "Renaşterea şi Independenţa României"

Address. Petrosani, str. 1 December 90.

Foundation. June 26, 1991. Re-registered on Aug. 5, 1993.

Leadership. Sebestyen Augustin.

Party of Social Solidarity

Address. Bucharest, Splaiul Independentiei 202 A, sector 6.

Telephone. 613.41.79.

Fax. 638.23.13; 312.36.17.

Foundation. July 28–30, 1994 (founding congress).

Leadership. Miron Mitrea (ch.)

History. The party is founded on the basis of the Convention of Social Solidarity (*see* CSS). The party is expected to receive strong support from some of the trade unions as the chairman of the party is president of the trade union Fratia. (Fratia merged with the trade union CNSLR in the summer of 1993, and Miron Mitrea became one of two presidents in the new CNSLR–FRATIA trade union. The two confederations might split again during the autumn of 1994.)

Programme. The party states that it is a social democratic party.

Party to Honour the Revolution's Heroes and for National Salvation
(*See* Democratic Solidarity Party)

Pentagon

Term used to refer to the tacit alliance since the general elections in 1992 between the SDPR, GRP, SPL, RNUP and ADPR.

People's Party of Romania
Partidul Poporului din România

History. This party merged with three other parties to form the Democratic Party, later renamed Romanian Democratic Party.

Political Trade Union "Brotherhood"
Sindicatul Politic "Fraternitatea"

(*See* Workers' and Peasants' Brotherhood Political Trade Union of Romania)

Progressive Democratic Party
Partidul Democrat Progresist (PDP)

Address. 70401 Bucharest, Splaiul Independenţiei 2J, ap. 1, sector 3, Of.P. nr. 1.

Telephone. 615.32.94; 615.32.07.

Foundation. Dec. 26, 1989 (registration date).

Leadership. Ion Martin Uţă (pres.)

Affiliations. In 1990 it was announced that the party was a member of the Centre-Left (Social Democratic) Alliance. Later it left in favour of the National Union of the Victory of the Revolution, which the party later split from. A member of the Democratic Union and the Alliance for National Dignity.

Publications. Quo Vadis (ceased publication in March 1993).

Republican Party
Partidul Republican

Foundation. Jan. 30, 1990 (registration date).

History. On Nov. 16, 1991, the RP merged with the Social-Liberal Party–20th May to form a new grouping retaining the name Republican Party.

The party's candidate for the September 1992 election, and leader of the party, was Ion Manzatu, a professor and founder of the party. He was formerly connected with the Ceauşescu leadership. On May 26, 1993, the party merged with the DNSF, later named the SDPR. On July 17, 1993, the representatives of 15 district-organizations of the Republican Party established an Executive Directorate, as they did not accept the merger (*see* Republican Party of Timişoara).

Republican Party of Timişoara
Partidul Republican din Timişoara

Address. Timişoara, str. Iuliu Maniu 11.

Foundation. Sept. 29, 1993 (registration date).

Leadership. Lorin Fortună.

History. On May 26, 1993, the Republican Party merged with the DNSF, later named SDPR. On July 17, 1993, the representatives of 15 district-organizations of the Republican Party established an Executive Directorate, as they did not accept the merger. They later formed the Republican Party of Timişoara.

Republican Peasants' Party
Partidul Tărănesc Republican

History. The party was first registered on Jan. 24, 1990, under the name Romanian Peasants' Party, before the name was changed to the above mentioned. On June 26, 1992, the party merged — through absorption — with the National Liberal Party.

Republican Popular Party
Partidul Popular Republican

Address. Bucharest, Bd. Dacia 97, sector 2.

Telephone. 210.47.22; 611.51.26.

Foundation. Dec. 8, 1993 (registration date).

Leadership. Radu Theodoru.

History. The party was founded through a transformation of the Independent Democratic Party.

Republican Tribune Party
Partidul Tribuna Republicană (TR)

Address. 2400 Sibiu, str. Vasile Cârlova 11, jud. Sibiu.

Foundation. May 3, 1990 (registration date).

Leadership. Doru Herţoiu (pres.)

Programme. The party is reported to be a apocalyptic, religious sect. Considers itself a right-wing party based on the ideas of Woodrow Wilson.

Republican Union Party
Partidul Uniunea Republicană (PUR)

Address. Bucharest, str. Sirenilor 53, sector 5.

Telephone. 781.32.90; 781.28.65.

Foundation Feb. 13, 1990 (registration date).

Leadership. Mihai Nițu (pres.)

Programme. Centre-left.

Republican Unity Party of Romania
Partidul Republican de Unitate a Românilor

History. Registered on March 20, 1990, but registered on Sept. 23, 1992, under the name of Industry Party (*Partidul Industriei*). Since the 1992 electoral campaign it has not played a role on the political scene.

Romani of Romania Party
Partidul Țiganilor din România

Address. 2400 Sibiu, str. Uzinei, bloc 1, apart 1, jud. Sibiu.

Foundation. March 5, 1990 (registration date).

Leadership. Ilie Mihai (pres.)

Romania Mare
(*see* Greater Romania Party)

Romanian Christian Social Democratic Party
Partidul Social Democrat Creștin Român

History. Registered on Jan. 25, 1990. Founded with other political parties the Democratic Party on May 23, 1991 (*see* Democratic Party.)

Romanian Communist Party (RCP)
Partidul Communist Român

History. On Jan. 12, 1990, the Executive Bureau of the National Salvation Front issued a decree outlawing the RCP. This decree was the subject of a national referendum on Jan. 28. However, the decree was annulled by the Council of the NSF on Jan. 17, 1990, on the ground that outlawing any party is an anti-democratic measure. On the same date the assets of the RCP were transferred to state ownership, the total value of the assets being 43,825.2 million lei.

An attempt to register the party in Craiova resulted in a court case in the Municipal Court of Bucharest. The court granted the party permission to register. However, this initiated a debate among certain members of Parliament who appealed to the Supreme Court. The Supreme Court reversed the decision of the Municipal Court and prohibited the party's registration.

Romanian Democratic Front of Timişoara
Frontul Democrat Român din Timişoara

Address. Timişoara, str. Mihai Eminescu 5, etaj. 2, ap. 24.

Telephone. (561) 580.50; 368.44.

Foundation. Feb. 9, 1990 (registration date).

Leadership. Petrişor Morar (pres.)

History. In the elections of 1990 the party won one seat in the Chamber of Deputies as member of the Centrist Democratic Group. The party's president continued as member of the lower chamber after the 1992 elections.

Romanian Democratic Party
Partidul Democrat Român (PDR)

Address. Bucharest, Allea Emil Botta 4, bloc M104, scara 2, ap. 55, sector 3.

Telephone. 321.25.56.

Foundation. Dec. 28, 1989 (registration date).

Leadership. Stelian Cinca (pres.)

History. The PDR is the successor of the Freedom and Romanian Democracy Party which was founded in Craiova on Dec. 28, 1989. In September 1990, the Freedom and Romanian Democracy Party merged with the Democratic Party of Romania. The new party was unofficially called Romanian Democratic Party. On Jan. 25, 1993, it registered the new name and moved its headquarters to Bucharest.

Programme. The party is in the centre of the political spectrum. Its strategic aim is to structure a modern democratic society through the encouragement of the middle class.

Romanian Democratic Popular Realistic Revolutionary Party
Partidul Român Democrat Popular Realist şi Revoluţionar

Address. Com. Bragadiru, str. Alexandriei, SAI.

Foundation. Oct. 3, 1991 (registration date).

Leadership. Constantin Vicenţiu (pres.)

Romanian Ecological Movement
Mişcarea Ecologistă din România (MER)

Address. 70259 Bucharest, Alexandu Philippide 11, sector 2.

Telephone. 611.29.43; 611.03.77.

Fax. 610.48.58.

Foundation. Jan. 11, 1990 (registration date).

Leadership. Eduard-Victor Gugui (pres.)

History. Participated in the Council of Ministers led by Prime Minister Theodor Stolojan from October 1991 to September 1992. Obtained 2.88 per cent in the 1992 elections but did not win any seats. Absorbed the National Ecologist Party in June 1993.

Programme. The party states that it works on the political, economical, social and spiritual plane in conformity with the ecologist doctrine. It is against communist and extremist doctrines.

Romanian Ecologist Party
Partidul Ecologist Român (P.E.R.)

Address. Bucharest, Stelea Spataru 10 A, sector 3.

Telephone. 615.82.85.

Foundation. Jan. 16, 1990 (registration date).

Leadership. Otto Weber (pres.)

Membership. 12,500.

History. Obtained four seats in the Chamber of Deputies after the September 1992 general elections. In permanent contact with the National Peasants' Party–Christian Democrat.

Programme. The party considers itself a centre-right party.

Affiliations. Member of the Democratic Convention of Romania.

Romanian Ecology Party
(*See* Romanian Ecological Party)

Romanian Home of Democratic Europe
(*See* Romanian House of Democratic Europe Party)

Romanian House of Democratic Europe Party
Partidul Casa Româna a Europei Democrate (CRED)

Address. Bucharest, Bd. Alexandru Obregia 2 bis, bloc 2-A, et. 1, apart. 10, sector 4.

Telephone. 684.80.51; 789.59.45.

Foundation. Feb. 7, 1990 (registration date).

Leadership. Mihail Candea Muscel (pres.)

Programme. The party states the following: "the people are the real owners of the power, and people have to be involved in all spheres of society. Will restore the Romanian civil society as a European democratic society."

Affiliations. National Union for the Victory of the Revolution and Coalition of Democratic Forces.

Romanian Labour Party
Partidul Laburist Român

Address. Iaşi, str. Vasila Contra 9, jud. Iaşi.

Telephone. (032)13.113; 15.117.

Leadership. Tudor Ghideanu (pres.)

Affiliations. Member of the National Alliance of Social Democracy.

Romanian National Party
Partidul Naţjonal Român (PNR)

Address. Bucharest, Calea Victoriei 103-105, scara C, etaj 2, apart. 63.

Telephone. 650.76.13; 653.28.92.

Foundation. Jan. 20, 1990 (registration date).

Leadership. Ion Di Cezare (pres.)

History. The party considers itself as the successor of the historical Romanian National Party, which fought and achieved the great re-unification of Romanians of Dec. 1, 1918.

Programme. The party considers itself centre-right.

Romanian National Unity Party (RNUP)
Partidul Unitatji Naţjonale Române (PUNR)

Address. Bucharest, Piaţa Amzei 13, etaj 1, sector 1.

Telephone. 659.52.56.

Foundation. March 15, 1990 (registration date).

Leadership. Gheorghe Funar (pres.)

Membership. 49,000.

History. The RNUP was founded in Transylvania after the ethnical clashes in March 1990 when the ultra-nationalistic *Vatra Românească* (Romanian Hearth) openly defended the Romanians' rights in Transylvania.

The party writes: "the party is the result of the events in Tirgu Moures in March 1990, which was the first attempt to destroy a modern Romania after the disaster of the communist occupation". After the general elections of 1992 the RNUP gained a relative strong representation in the Parliament, obtaining about 8 per cent of the vote. Since then, the party has held a central position in the parliament supporting the minority ruling party, the PSDR, as a part of the so-called Pentagon. The RNUP has tried to coerce the PSDR into accepting it as a full-fledged coalition partner. Since the elections, the party at first gained strength in the polls, but in the summer months of 1994 it received less than in the 1992 elections. Its strength in the parliament increased, however, when the Agrarian Democratic Party joined the RNUP-faction in the Senate in November 1993, forming the National Unity Bloc. In the summer of 1994 the RNUP received seats in the government when members of the party took posts in the Communications Ministry and the Ministry of Agriculture.

The executive of the RNUP elected Gheorghe Funar as party leader in succession to Radu Ceontea on Oct. 3, 1992. Funar had been the party's presidential candidate in the September 1992 presidential elections. He was also Mayor of the Transylvanian Capital of Cluj, where he was known for his anti-Hungarian measures. Funar set about transforming the RNUP from a regional into a national party.

Programme. The RNUP belongs to the group of extremist parties, which advocate continuation and stepping up of the policy of "radical continuity", i.e. the continuation of the "national communism" from the pre-1989 years. It tries to project the image of defenders of a "national interest" besieged by international plots against the country, thus placing the "enemy image" as a central ideological factor.

The RNUP has advocated an "iron-fist" or military government as the solution to Romania's problems, and Funar is on record as supporting anti-Semitic views.

The party considers itself a political organization of the Romanian citizen, not taking in view ethnic, religious and others divergences. Its aims are the noble ideas of freedom, democracy, national unity and prosperity. The party defines its economical doctrine as based on Romanian classical neo-liberalism.

Publications. Unitatea Nationale, daily since December 1993.

Romanian New Society Party
Partidul Român Pentru Noua Societate (PRNS)

Address. Bucharest, Calea Victoriei 39/A, etaj 2, sector 1.

Telephone. 615.82.31.

Foundation. April 6, 1990 (registration date).

Leadership. Victor Voichiţă (pres.)

Affiliations. Centre-Left (Social Democratic) Alliance.

Romanian Party of Humanity
Partidul Român al Humanitaţi

Address. Bucharest, B-dul Unirii 14, bloc 6, scara 2, etaj. 2, apart 32, sector 4.

Telephone. 631.64.88.

Foundation. April 1, 1991 (registration date).

Leadership. Christina Ciontu (exec. pres.)

Romanian Peasants' Party
(*See* Republican Peasants' Party)

Romanian Peasant-Workers' Party
Partidul Muncitoresc Tăranesc Român

Address. Târgu Jiu, str. A.I. Cuza 13, parter.

Foundation. Oct. 13, 1993 (registration date).

Leadership. Dumitru Calotă.

Romanian Popular Front
Frontul Popular Român

History. The party was founded in February 1990, but in August 1990, the Front — with the exception of the Bucharest branch— merged with the RNUP. On May 23, 1991, the Bucharest Branch participated in the establishment of the Democratic Party together with other political parties.

Romanian Popular Party
Partidul Popular Roman

Address. Bucharest, str. S. Gheorghiu 8, ap. 2.

Foundation. Feb. 3, 1994 (registration date).

Leadership. Velicu Radina.

Romanian Revolution Party
Partidul Revolutjei Române (PRR)

Address. Bucharest, Calea Victoriei 133–135, et. 7, sector 1.

Telephone. 659.53.76; 659.48.95.

Foundation. April 23, 1990 (registration date).

Leadership. Mihai Voicu (pres.)

History. In the local elections in 1992 the party took part within the Coalition of Democratic Forces, but withdrew from the coalition before the general elections.

Programme. The party considers itself to be in the centre.

Affiliations. The party initiated the following coalitions: Coalition of Democratic Forces, Homeland Assembly and Alliance for National Dignity.

Romanian Social Democratic Party (RSDP)
Partidul Social Democrat Român (P.S.D.R.)

Address. 70119, Sector 1, Bucharest, Dem. I. Dobrescu 9.

Telephone. 616.41.10; 616.47.21

Fax. 614.60.89/312.28.97.

Foundation. 1893, reactivated Dec. 24, 1989.

Leadership. Sergiu Cunescu (pres.), Adrian Dimitriu (hon.pres.)

History. The party was re-established as a continuation of the Social Democratic Party of Romania's Workers existing prior to 1947 headed by Constantin Titel Petrescu, thereby being one of Romania's three historical parties. The party was forced to merge with the RCP in February 1948. After the December 1989 revolution a number of parties have claimed to be the successor of the historical party, but a court has decided that the RSDP is the only party entitled to look upon itself as a continuation of the historical party and to call itself Romanian Social Democratic Party. It obtained 10 seats in the Chamber of Deputies and one in the Senate after the September 1992 general elections.

Programme. The party bases its politics on the modern social democratic principles, taking in consideration the specificity of former communist countries.

Affiliations. Member of the Democratic Convention of Romania, member of the Socialist International.

Romanian Socialist Democratic Party
Partidul Socialist Democratic Român

History. The party held its first national congress on April 9, 1990, during which it identified itself fully with the policy of the National Salvation Front. The party was in the years to come often referred to as the Front's (later the DNSF/SDPR) satellite. At the elections in 1990 the party obtained five seats on the basis of 143,000 votes and supported Iliescu for president. The party was unsuccessful at the 1992 parliament elections. Satellite or not — on July 9–10, 1993, the party merged with the DNSF, then renamed the SDPR. The party chairman, Cornel Nica, became one of a number vice-presidents in the new party.

Romanian Socialist Party
Partidul Socialist Român

Address. Bucharest, str. Episcop Radu 3i, sector 2.

Telephone. 665.78.55.

Foundation. Aug. 18, 1992 (registration date).

Leadership. Florian Petrescu.

Russian Lippovans Community of Romania
Communitatea Ruşilor Lipoveni din România (CRLR)

Address. 70421 Bucharest, str. Lipscani 18, et. 1, cam. 3.

Leadership. Feodor Petuhov (pres.)

Serbian and Carasovens Democratic Union of Romania
Uniunea Democratică a Sărbilor şi Caraşovenilor din România (UDSCR)

Address. Timişoara, Şoseaua Victor Babeş 18, jud. Timis.

Telephone. (056) 111.947.

Leadership. Borislav Krstici.

Smallholders' and Free Initiative Party
Partidul Micilor Proprietari şi al Liberei Initjative (PMPLI)

Address. Bistrita, Piata Centrala 1, et. 1, jud. Bistriţa-Năsăud.

Telephone. (063) 243.00.

Foundation. May 28, 1990 (registration date).

Leadership. Marian Florin (pres.)

Programme. Supports the Democratic Convention of Romania, fights for fast privatization and for bringing foreign investments to Romania.

Affiliations. Democratic Solidarity of Romania.

Smallholders' Union of Romania
Partidul Uniunea Micilor Proprietari din România

Address. Brasov, B-dul Gării 38, bloc 227, scara A, ap. 23.

Foundation. May 6, 1992 (registration date).

Leadership. Gheorghe Tinca (pres.)

Social Democracy Party of Romania (SDPR)
Partidul Democratjei Sociale din România (P.D.S.R.)

Address. 71271 Bucharest, str. Atena 11, sector 1.

Telephone. 212.06.95.

Fax. 312.46.55.

Foundation. April 28, 1992 (registration date).

Leadership. Oliviu Gherman (pres.), Adrian Nastase (exec.pres.)

History. The SDPR was founded by a group which split from the National Salvation Front and formally constituted itself as a separate party at its National Convention June 28–29, 1992, calling itself the Democratic National Salvation Front.

In the September 1992 general elections DNSF became the largest party in the Parliament and formed a single-party minority government. It had called for a slowing down of the reform. At the national conference of the DNSF, held on July 9–10, 1993, the party merged with the Republican Party, Socialist Democratic Party of Romania, Democratic Co-operatist Party and changed the name of the party to the Social Democracy Party of Romania.

Programme. By its policies and ideology the party defines itself as a social democratic, popular, national, centre-left party. It supports the Vacaroiu government and wants to continue the social and economical reform, to stop the decrease in industrial and agricultural production, to reduce inflation, to increase the economic activity by using own resources and attracting foreign capital.

Publications. The daily *Dimineata* (Morning) is independent, but often reflects the opinion of the SDPR.

Social Democratic Alliance
Alianţa Social Democrată (ASD)

Address. Sector 1, Bucharest, Aleea Modrogan 1.

Telephone. 679.36.18/633.72.32.

Fax. 633.53.32/679.54.97

Foundation. July 1, 1993 (registration date).

Leadership. Victor Babiuc (pres.)

History. The alliance contains the following parties: Democratic Party (National Salvation Front) and the Traditional Social Democratic Party.

Programme. The aim of the Alliance is to unify the social democratic movement of Romania, to strengthen the collaboration between — and in the end to merge — all the parties which accept the social democratic doctrine. The Alliance affirms its option for modern social democracy close to the centre of political spectrum and wants to promote the Euro-Atlantic spirit.

Social Democratic Convention

History. Established by the Independent Social Democratic Party and the Democratic Labour Party on Oct. 11, 1992.

Social Democratic National Salvation Front
Frontul Salvării Naţionale — Social Democrat

Foundation. April 30, 1991. (registration date).

History. The Front emerged from the NSF in the aftermath of its first National Convention held in March 1991. The Front claimed that its creation was the result of a dissent from within the NSF over the government's economic programme. It maintained that the NSF had shifted from social democratic leanings to a liberal right-wing position. Changed name to Social Democratic Unity Party on May 27, 1992.

Social Democratic Party
(*See* Romanian Social Democratic Party)

Social Democratic Party-"Constantin Titel Petrescu"
Partidul Social Democrat-"Constantin Titel Petrescu" (PSD "CTP")

Address. Bucharest, str. Eroilor Sanitarii 12, sector 5.

Telephone. 637.70.36.

Foundation. Dec. 6, 1991 (registration date).

Leadership. Mircea Istru Stănescu (pres.)

History. The party claims to be the real successor of the historical social democratic party of Romania, and looks upon the Traditional Social Democratic Party and the Social Democratic Party of Romania as only working for the ambitions of their leaders.

Programme. The party wants to transform Romania into a real social democratic country based on pluralism and liberty of conscience.

Affiliation. National Alliance of Social Democracy.

Social Democratic Party of Romanies
Partidul Romilor Social Democrat

Address. Bucharest, str. Anton Pann 24.

Foundation. April 29, 1992 (registration date).

Leadership. Gheorghe Răducanu (pres.)

Social Democratic Unity Party
Partidul Unităţji Social Democrate (PUSD)

Address. Bucharest, str. Ion Câmpineanu 5, et. 1, sector 1.

Telephone. 614.34.24.

Fax. 312.50.50.

Foundation. April 30, 1991 (registration date).

Affiliations. National Alliance of Social Democracy.

Leadership. Serghei Mesaroş (pres.)

History. The party partly consists of people who left NSF in February 1991, calling the party the "Social Democratic National Salvation Front". On April 28, 1992, the party merged with the Democratic Party of Romania, renaming itself the Social Democratic Unity Party. In September 1992 the party absorbed the so-called National Salvation Front "20th of May 1990".

Programme. The party claims to be a centre-left, social democratic party.

Publications. *Voice of Romania*, twice monthly.

Social Justice Party of Romania
Partidul Dreptatji Sociale din România (PDS)

Address. 70518 Bucharest, Calea Şerban Vodă 70, sector 4.

Telephone. 623.34.50

Foundation. Feb. 10, 1990 (registration date).

Leadership. Pompiliu Mateescu (pres.)

History. The party was registered on Feb. 10, 1990, under the name Free Democratic Social Justice Party, but later changed its name to Social Justice Party of Romania. In October 1993 the party decided to change its name to Christian and Democratic Social Justice Party of Romania. On April 18, 1990 the party initiated together with six other parties the Central Group (New Romania).

Programme. The party considers itself as a centre-party and underlines that it was against the anti-national politics of the Roman government.

Social Liberal Party–20th May
Partidul Social Liberal–20 Mai

Originally the party used the name National Salvation Front–20th of May, but registered under the above mentioned name. The party merged on Nov. 16, 1991, with the Republican Party to form a new grouping retaining the name Republican Party.

Social National Party
Partidul Social Natjonal

Address. Municipiul Iaşi, str. 9 Mai.

Telephone. (032) 43030.

Foundation. Registered on July 25, 1990, under the name Organization for Social Support and Security. Adopted the new name in August 1992.

Leadership. Eugen Petre Voicu (pres.)

Socialist Justice Party – Independent
(*See* Independent Socialist Party for Justice)

Socialist Party of Labour (SPL)
Partidul Socialist al Muncii (P.S.M.)

Address. Sector 3, Bucharest, Str. Neugustori nr. 3.

Telephone. 312.03.23; 312.04.06.

Foundation. Nov. 16, 1990 (registration date).

Leadership. Ilie Verdeţ (pres.)

History. The formation of the SPL followed a merger of groups from the Democratic Labour Party, the Socialist Party and remnants of the Communist Party. The creation of the party has been seen as a continuation of the Romanian Communist Party. The party held its first congress on Aug. 11, 1991, during which the party elected a former Prime Minister under Ceauşescu, Ilie Verdet, as president. He is also Nicolae Ceauşescu's brother-in-law. In the general elections in 1992 the SPL obtained parliamentary foothold, obtaining 3.04 per cent for the Chamber of Deputies and 3.19 per cent for the Senate and forming a joint faction with GRP and ADPR, called the National Unity Bloc.

During the parliamentary debates after the September 1992 parliament elections it became clear that the government would be able to count on external support from the SPL on the far left, which made the party a member of the five-party tacit alliance, called the Pentagon.

The party did, however, suspend the coalition talks with SDPR in February 1994, following the example of GRP.

Programme. The party belongs to what can be defined as the parties of "radical continuity", combining nationalistic, anti-Semitic and xenophobic views with communistic traditions of ensuring the progressive traditions of the working class, socialist and democratic movement of Romania. The party considers itself as a leftist, democratic successor of the democratic, socialist workers' movement and it is trying to establish a society of labour, liberty and justice, dignity and welfare in Romania. It defines its doctrine as socialist, humanist progressist and in favour of a mixed social-market economy.

Affiliations. Created in 1991 the so-called Left Democratic Union.

Publications. Socialistul (The Socialist), monthly, *Totusi Iuburea* and *Vremea*.

Sportsmen and Supporters Party of Romania
Partidul Sportivilor şi Sustĵnătorilor din România

Address. Iasi, str. Chişinău 17.

Foundation. Oct. 21, 1993 (registration date).

Leadership. M. Ungureanu.

Ţara Oaşului Democratic Union
Uniunea Democratică "Ţara Oaşului"

Address. Oraşul Negresti-Oaş str. Victoriei 95, jud. Satu Mare.

Telephone. (061) 511.13; 509.30.

Foundation. March 27, 1990 (registration date).

Leadership. Mihai Pop (hon. pres.), Mihai Nistor (pres.)

Traditional Social Democratic Party of Romania
Partidul Social Democrat Tradiţjonal din România (P.S.D.T.)

Address. Bucharest, str, Aron Florian 1, sector 2.

Telephone. 611.04.79; 611.38.15.

Foundation. May 8, 1991 (registration date).

Leadership. Eugen Brânzan (pres.)

History. The party was established by former members of the Social Democratic Party of Romania, led by a French businessman of Romanian origin, Lucian Cornescu. In 1993 the party divided in two, the two groups both claiming to be the Traditional Social Democratic Party of Romania. A court case ruled in favour of the group led by Eugen Brânzan at the expense of the other group led by Cornescu.

Programme. The party considers itself a modern social democratic party to the centre-left and states, that it promotes European social democratic ideas, social protection and solidarity. It wants to focus its appeal on the middle class.

Affiliation. Social Democratic Alliance.

Union of Armenians of Romania
Uniunea Armenilor din România (UAR)

Address. 70334 Bucharest, str. Armenească 13, sector 2.

Telephone. 613.84.59.

Fax. 311.14.15.

Leadership. Varujan Vosganian (pres.)

United Democratic Party of Romani, Fiddlers and Woodworkers of Romania
(*See* Democratic Alliance Party of Romani of Romania)

Vatra Românească Union (VR)
Uniunea Vatra Românească

Address. Bucharest, str. Moliere 13–15.

Telephone 212.02.26/212.06.30.

Foundation. Feb. 1, 1990 (registration date).

Leadership. Zeno Opris.

History. Vatra Românească (Romanian Hearth) was formed against the background of the growth of importance of the Hungarian minority in Transylvania. After the overthrow of Ceauşescu, the NSF decided in January 1990 to restore Hungarian language radio broadcasts and to reorganize primary and secondary schools guaranteeing the minorities education in their native languages. Also the Hungarian Bolai University in Cluj, closed by the communist regime in 1958 was reopened. The efficiency and speed with which the Hungarian minority rights were asserted aroused suspicion and resentment among Romanians in Transylvania. They feared that granting concessions to the Hungarians would encourage the two million Hungarians in Transylvania to seek greater autonomy and closer association with Hungary. Since its formation the VR has been accused of forming organized riots and individual attacks on Hungarians in Transylvania. VR's history is linked with the Romanian National Unity Party, the political branch of *Vatra Românească*.

Programme. Vatra Românească describes itself as an organization of the Romanian spirituality of Transylvania and the expression of the identity of all those who feel and speak Romanian in that part of the country. The union is against any manifestation of separatism, chauvinism and nationalism. It protests against attempts at harming state unity and the culture of Romanian people, opposes the creation of administrative-territorial and cultural enclaves, asking that the historic rights of the Romanian population that has been living in Transylvania from time immemorial be observed. It demands the use of the Romanian language as the only official language throughout the country's territory.

Workers' and Peasants' Brotherhood Political Trade Union of Romania
Sindicatul Politic "Fraternitatea al Muncitorilor" şi Tăranilor din România

Address. Timişoara, str. Cermena 10, jud. Timiş.

Telephone. (561) 39.469.

Foundation. Feb. 5, 1990 (registration date).

Leadership. Traian Florea (pres.)

Affiliations. Member of the Democratic Convention of Romania.

Workers' and Peasants' Party of Romania
Partidul Muncitorilor şi Tăranilor din România

Address. Arad, str. Eminescu 2, ap. 6.

Foundation. Jan. 19, 1994 (registration date).

Leadership. Gheorghe Sava.

Young Democracy Party
Partidul Tânăra Democratje (PTD)

Address. 71300 Bucharest, str. Serdarului 13, bloc 48, apart. 27, sector 1.

Telephone. 617.76.46.

Foundation. April 17, 1990 (registration date).

Leadership. Florea Preda (pres.)

History. Supported the SDPR in the general elections of 1992. Considers itself left-democratic.

RUSSIAN FEDERATION

Martin McCauley
Domitilla Sagramoso

After the defeat of the attempted coup in August 1991, political parties and movements were slow to develop in Russia. Over 100 parties and movements had been founded in the Russian Federation under communism but they were held back by the fact that parliamentary elections were not held in Russia until December 1993. The major party before August 1991 was, of course, the Communist Party of the Soviet Union (CPSU). The banning of the CPSU after the attempted coup left two other main groups to take over the high ground of political organization. These were nationalist and patriotic groups, and the Democratic Russia bloc and its supporters.

It has surprised many observers that President Boris Yeltsin has never attempted to establish a presidential party. This was largely because he did not place the renewal of the deputies of the Russian Supreme Soviet very high on his agenda. A new constitution for a new Russia was also not forthcoming. Yeltsin's reluctance to proceed to constitutional and institutional reform was linked to his belief that his authority and legitimacy would be higher if he remained above party politics, as a father figure who represented all citizens of the Russian Federation. His reluctance to become involved in party politics may also have been connected with his traumatic experience in October 1987 when he was dismissed as first party secretary of Moscow and forced into grovelling submission. President Gorbachev abandoned one of his staunchest supporters and the two men thereafter became political foes. President Yeltsin's failure to enact a new constitution and a new parliament was of seminal importance for the evolution of political parties and movements in Russia. Russian politics continued along the communist path and remained personalized politics. Personal networks were more important than political parties and power and privilege were not linked to membership of any political party.

One of the consequences of the above was the appearance of highly fragmented political parties with narrow support bases and fractious leaderships. This produced another striking phenomenon, the transitory nature of political parties, coalitions and alliances. A prime example of this is the Democratic Russia bloc. It was established in October 1990 by nine political parties, including the Social Democratic Party of Russia (Aleksandr Obolensky, Oleg Rumyantsev and Pavel Kudyukin), the Republican Party of Russia (Vladimir Lysenko, Vyacheslav Shostakovsky and Stepan Sulakshin), the Democratic Party of Russia (Nikolai Travkin), the Free Democratic Party, the Russian Christian Democratic Movement (Viktor Aksyuchits and Gleb Anishchenko) and the Constitutional Democratic Party (Viktor Astafev), and 18 social movements. The bloc fractured in November 1991 over whether it should support the break-up of the Soviet Union or not. The DPR, for instance, opposed the formation of the Commonwealth of Independent States. The Russian Christian Democratic Movement, the Democratic Party of Russia and the Constitutional Democrats left to form the Popular Accord group. These defections revealed that the Democratic Russia bloc was incapable of developing into a national, democratic party. In February 1992 Aksyuchits convened the Congress of Civic and Patriotic Forces in Moscow which set up the Russian People's Assembly (RPA) with Aksyuchits as chair of the board. The RPA laid great stress on democracy and patriotism but this began to drift towards nationalism. The congress was attended by the Russian Christian Democratic Movement, the Constitutional Democratic Party, the Russian People's Union (Sergei Baburin), the National Republican Party (Aleksandr Lysenko), the Smena (Change) faction in the Russian Supreme Soviet and the Union of Cossacks. A major reason for disillusionment with formal democracy was the uncertain status of Russians in many parts of the country. Aksyuchits spoke of the pro-Yeltsin democrats favouring an "anarchic utopia" and regarded them as anti-Russian and anti-state. The RPA wished to promote a strong Russia which would gather in the territories of the former Soviet Union. Hence they placed the interests of the state above those of the individual. Those who shared these views became known as *gosudarstvenniki*, advocates of a strong, united Russian state. Aksyuchits accepted a tactical alliance with the communists — even though he rejected communist ideology — in order to oppose the "anti-national" and "anti-state" policies of the Yeltsin administration. This gave birth to a communist-nationalist-patriotic opposition.

The onset of economic shock therapy on Jan. 2, 1992, began to stiffen resistance to reform policies. By the time of the Sixth Congress of Russian People's deputies, held in April 1992, both communists and conservatives had recovered their nerve and organizational ability. The prospects of privatization and exposure to the market were not welcomed by many enterprise managers. The Russian Union of Industrialists and Entrepreneurs (RUIE), headed by Arkady Volsky, became the backbone of the industrial lobby. Industrialists regretted the demise of the Soviet Union and favoured a strong Russian state that would be dominant in the space occupied by the former Soviet Union. In June 1992 Volsky set up the All-Russian Union for Renewal (*Obnovlenie*) with the aim of transforming it into a political party to represent economic interests. Vice-President Aleksandr Rutskoi and his party, People's Party for a Free Russia, gradually sided with the *gosudarstvenniki*. Nikolai Travkin's Democratic Party of Russia also shared these views. In June 1992 all three came together and founded Civic Union. The political landscape had changed. Civic Union saw itself as a constructive opposition and as a tactical alliance to apply pressure on the President to reduce the impact of stabilization. Some Civic Union nominees entered government in June 1992. With opposition to the President consolidating and democratic support fragmenting, over 40 groups, including the Democratic Russia bloc, the Republican Party and the Russian Democratic Reform Movement (Gavriil Popov), convened in July 1992 in Moscow to set up the Democratic Choice bloc to support the President and the government, even though the Russian Democratic Reform Movement did not agree to join. This new bloc regarded the nationalist-communist alliance as the major danger and hoped to reach some agreement with Civic Union.

The Democratic Russia bloc splintered again in July 1992 with the radical pro-market reformers around Marina Sale leaving. They now opposed the Gaidar government because they regarded the cabinet changes of June 1992 as a betrayal and accused the President of caving in to the "threat of the dictatorship of the military-industrial complex". Sale and her supporters set up the Russian Constituent Union advocating land reform and popular privatization. The Democratic Russia bloc, led by Lev Ponomarev, Ilya Zaslavsky and Gleb Yakunin, continued to support the President but were a waning force. In July 1992 the Russian Unity group, formed by communists and nationalists in the Russian Supreme Soviet in April 1992, called on the government to resign. Battle lines were being drawn. Henceforth Russian Unity would constitute the core of the implacable opposition to President Yeltsin and his administration in parliament. In October 1992 the National Salvation Front (NSF) was established by nationalists and communists to oppose the economic policies of the government and its foreign policy. Based on Russian Unity, the NSF was the most extreme manifestation of national patriotic opposition yet to appear. It took exception to the break-up of the military-industrial complex and the failure of Russian foreign policy to defend Russia's national interests, especially *vis-à-vis* the United States. President Yeltsin reacted swiftly and banned the NSF at the end of October 1992, the first political movement to be declared unconstitutional since the attempted coup. The President's ban was challenged and the Constitutional Court lifted the ban in February 1993.

At the Seventh Congress of Russian People's Deputies, in December 1992, President Yeltsin's confrontational policies failed and the congress gradually whittled away the extraordinary powers granted to him in 1991. The legislature, ably marshalled by Ruslan Khasbulatov, its speaker and a former Yeltsin ally, gradually began to sense that it could block, perhaps even defeat, the President. The tactic adopted was to erode presidential control over the government step by step. In an attempt to circumvent opposition in parliament, the President announced a referendum on a new constitution for April 11, 1993.

The Eighth Congress of Russian People's Deputies, on March 10, 1993, began with a blistering attack on President Yeltsin by Ruslan Khasbulatov who accused the President of acting unconstitutionally. The congress voted to amend the constitution, strip the President of many of his powers and cancel the scheduled April referendum. The President stalked out of the congress. Vladimir Shumeiko, deputy Prime Minister, declared that the referendum would go ahead but on April 25. On March 16 the President signed a decree conferring ministerial rank on Viktor Gerashchenko, chairman of the Central Bank, and three other officials; this was in accordance with the decision of the congress but the new ministers were to be subordinate to parliament and not the government.

On March 20 President Yeltsin in a TV address announced that he was going to impose a "special regime". He bitterly attacked parliamentary deputies, accusing of them of attempting to restore the old communist order. Vice-President Aleksandr Rutskoi condemned the President's actions and Valery Zorkin, chairman of the Constitutional Court, declared the move unconstitutional. The President did not impose the special regime.

The Ninth Congress of Russian People's Deputies opened on March 26, 1993, with a vitriolic attack on the President by Ruslan Khasbulatov. An attempt was made to impeach the President but it failed by 72 votes to muster the two-thirds majority necessary. Khasbulatov then attempted to make a deal with Yeltsin which included the abandonment of the April 25 memorandum and the calling of simultaneous elections for President and parliament in November 1993. However, congress turned on him and one-third of the deputies voted for his sacking. The referendum would go ahead but congress ruled that in order to win, the President needed 50 per cent of the votes of the whole electorate, not 50 per cent of the turnout on the day. The Constitutional Court supported the President and ruled that in order to win he needed the support of 50 per cent of those who voted on the first two questions (confidence in the President, and his economic and social policies) but 50 per cent of the whole electorate to call new presidential and parliamentary elections. The President's gamble paid off and he obtained a simple majority in favour of his own record and his economic and social policies. However, he lacked a constitutional mechanism to take advantage of his victory and introduce a new constitution which in turn would have allowed him to move towards the election of a new parliament.

In order to circumvent parliament President Yeltsin convened a constitutional assembly in June. A draft constitution was adopted in July which envisaged a bicameral legislature and the dissolution of the existing Congress of People's Deputies. The Supreme Soviet, the standing parliament, immediately rejected the draft and declared that the Congress of People's Deputies was the supreme lawmaking body and hence would decide on the new constitution. Parliament was very active in July and passed numerous decrees on economic policy contradicting governmental policy, and initiated proceedings against key advisers of the President, accusing them of corruption.

The President launched his offensive on Sept. 1 when he temporarily suspended Vice-President Aleksandr Rutskoi while accusations of certain irregularities were checked. Two weeks later the President offered early presidential elections providing parliament called early parliamentary elections. Parliament turned a deaf ear and Egor Gaidar was brought back into the government as deputy Prime Minister and Minister for the Economy. The Supreme Soviet refused to endorse this appointment. On Sept. 21, the President issued a decree dissolving the Congress of People's Deputies and the Supreme Soviet and set a date of Dec. 11–12 for elections to a new bicameral legislature — the State Duma and the Council of the Federation. The Supreme Soviet acted instantly and during an all-night session declared the presidential decree null and void, elected Aleksandr Rutskoi President, dismissed the ministers of defence, security and interior and appointed its own nominees. Russia now had two Presidents, two ministers of defence, security and interior. This was dual power in earnest.

The political impasse developed into an armed conflict during the afternoon of Oct. 3 when Moscow police failed to control a demonstration near the White House. Demonstrators made for Ostankino TV centre and Khasbulatov called for the storming of the Kremlin. The military were initially very reluctant to accede to the President's call for help but eventually various units intervened, shelling the White House on Oct. 4 resulting in loss of life and a burnt-out parliamentary building. Rutskoi and Khasbulatov stayed to the bitter end. The President banned many political parties and newspapers which had supported parliament and forced the resignation of Valery Zorkin, chairman of the Constitutional Court. Most regions and heads of administration (appointed by Yeltsin) had opposed him during the crisis. This led to changes in the draft constitution which withdrew many of the concessions to the regions. In November the President introduced his new draft constitution, to be put to a referendum on Dec. 12, 1993. It was a presidential constitution, reminiscent of the French constitution, and conferred extensive powers on the presidency. The lower house of the legislature, the State Duma, was only to sit for two years. Half of the 450 deputies were to be elected on federal lists, or by proportional representation, and half directly from single-member constituencies. This was the German system and was used to encourage the formation of pan-Russian parties and movements. Only those parties and movements which collected 100,000 signatures by a certain date would be allowed to participate in the elections. The President could also ban parties and movements from participating.

This gave a new emphasis to party formation and 21 parties and blocs garnered the necessary 100,000 signatures. Of these, eight, including the Constitutional Democratic Party – Party of People's Freedom (Mikhail Astafev) and the Russian National People's Union (Sergei Baburin), were disqualified.

Russia's Choice, led by Egor Gaidar, was committed to support of Yeltsin, but at its founding congress he failed to turn up to make a keynote speech. He appeared incapable of committing himself to one political party. Opinion polls gave the impression that Russia's Choice might obtain one-third of the votes and become the leading party. Russia's Choice and the other 12 parties and blocs which contested the election are analysed in the directory below. Some of the parties which did not contest the election are also included.

The election results were a terrible shock for the President, the government and the democrats. For the first time since August 1991 a clear majority of the population had rejected the President and his policies. The victors were the nationalists (Liberal Democratic Party) and communists (Communist Party of the Russian Federation and the Agrarian Party of Russia). Nevertheless the President did manage to obtain a majority in favour of the new constitution.

Besides pan-Russian parties and blocs analyses of parties and movements in some of the constituent republics of Russia are also provided within this chapter. This provides a flavour of local politics and underlines the inter-ethnic conflicts which are an ever-present reality inside Russia. Russia has yet to develop political parties along Western lines where a few major parties, coalitions of various interest groups, dominate parliament. In mid-1994 it is clear that regional economic groupings are becoming more and more significant. Eventually they will produce their own political leaderships. Will these become parts of a pan-Russian political party system?

Directory of Parties

Agrarian Party of Russia
Agrarnaya Partiya Rossii

Address.

Telephone.

Foundation. Feb.26, 1992.

Leadership. Mikhail Lapshin (ch.), director of the Zavety Ilicha *sovkhoz*, Moscow *oblast* (most of it is a joint stock company); Aleksandr Zaveryukha, Deputy Russian Prime Minister for agriculture; Magomedtagir Abdulbasirov, ch. of the state committee for the food industry; Aleksandr Davydov, ch. of the central committee of the trade unions of workers in the agro-industrial complex; Vasily Vershinin, ch. of the Peasants' Democratic Party of Russia; Ivan Rybkin, dep. ch. of the Central Executive Council, Communist Party of the Russian Federation, and leader of the Russian Supreme Soviet faction, Communists of Russia; Vladimir Isakov, former ch., Council of the Republic, lawyer; Igor Klochkov, former ch. of the Federation of Independent Trade Unions of Russia; Academician Valentin Koptyug.

Membership. 55 regional organizations (Nov. 1993).

History. The decision to set up the APR was taken in early 1992 at the All-Russian Congress of Kolkhozniks. An organizational committee was elected and began drafting a programme and statute. The founding members of the APR were the Agrarian Union, the Russian Supreme Soviet faction, the Agrarian Union of Russia (which has about 28,000 farms as members and is headed by Vasily Starodubtsev), the Russian Federation Committee for the Food and Processing Industry, regional agro-industrial structures and the Trade Union of Workers in the Agro-Industrial Complex (which has about 15 million members). The constituent congress took place in Moscow on Feb. 26, 1992. It was attended by 219 delegates from 47 regions. The congress elected an 80-member Central Council (Soviet), adopted a resolution, programme and statute. Mikhail Lapshin was elected chairman of the Central Council. The congress took place two weeks after the founding congress of the Communist Party of the Russian Federation (CPRF). Lapshin had been the head of the agrarian faction, the largest faction, in the Russian Supreme Soviet. He was also a member of the founding committee for the congress of the CPRF and was elected one of the party's six vice-chairmen.

The Second Extraordinary Congress met in Moscow on Oct. 16, 1993, with 91 delegates from over 40 regions attending. The congress was convened to adopt the party's election programme and approve candidates for election to the State Duma and the Council of the Federation. Mikhail Lapshin said that the party should take part in the elections as an independent electoral association. The elections would not be restricted to the Federal Assembly and the party would attempt to win deputy mandates at all levels of local executive power, relying on the rural population, the rural intelligentsia, and townspeople engaged in agriculture and related industries. Vasily Starodubtsev, a member of the Extraordinary Committee during the attempted August 1991 coup, said that the elections were the last opportunity to save Russia. . . The changes under way in Russia were not reforms but a programme developed by the West, the goal of which was to turn Russia into its source of raw materials.

The party's draft election programme called for a major review of agricultural policy and all agrarian practices in Russia, together with the forms and methods of land use and ownership. The programme claimed that the present situation in the country was the result of the general overall crisis and that the party seeks economic stabilization, upholding farmers' interests in agricultural reform. It advocated the handing-over of land to farmers free of charge, with a simultaneous right to inherit it but opposed free land sales as well as the irresponsible privatization vouchers. The party favoured the allocation of free plots of land for town dwellers and supported Cossacks in their attempts to restore their original lifestyle. The APR claimed it was struggling for the restoration of people's rule, first of all for the majority of working people and its peasant component in particular as the group having the fewest rights in society; for the salvation and strengthening of Russia's spirituality and culture; and for patriotism, love of native land, language, traditions and culture. A central plank of the election platform was to combat the unimpeded buying and selling of land which leads to land speculation. . . The party considers it necessary to maintain the provision of credits on easy terms for domestic goods producers, to abolish all subsidies on imported agricultural products, to move to a uniform land tax and to guarantee the budgetary financing of agro-industrial research. The APR supported

Table 1: Election results of the Agrarian Party of Russia

Before the election the party gained 500,000 signatures.

State Duma

Total number of seats: 47
Seats obtained on party lists: 21 (7.9 per cent of the vote)
Seats obtained in single member constituencies: 26 [2]

State Duma faction: 55

State Duma Committees headed by the APR:
— Legislative and Judicial Reform (Vladimir Isakov)
— Agrarian Affairs (Aleksandr Nazarchuk)

Speaker of the State Duma: Ivan Rybkin

Council of the Federation
Seats: 2 (Vladimir Sidorenko; Vasily Starodubtsev)

Russia's integrity as a state and political, economic and cultural equality of all subjects of the Russian Federation.

Among those who were to appear on the election list were Aleksandr Zaveryukha, Deputy Prime Minister, and Valery Zorkin, former chairman of the Constitutional Court. There was a heated debate about Zaveryukha's nomination and attempts to include Aleksandr Rutskoi on the list were unsuccessful.[1] Later a spokesman for the Constitutional Court stated that Zorkin remained a member of the Constitutional Court and as such could not engage in political activity. Lapshin said that since the party was concerned about self-preservation, Vasily Starodubtsev would not be included among those standing for the State Duma but would be a candidate for the Council of the Federation in Tula *oblast*. His brother Dmitry would be a candidate in Yaroslavl *oblast*. Lapshin was concerned not to identify allies, referring to them as patriotic forces, and not to be seen co-operating with the communists in the countryside. There are 34 million voters living in rural areas and another 9 million working in the agro-industrial complex (including the processing industry). That comes to 43 million or about one-third of the electorate. Lapshin expected almost all votes in the countryside to go to the APR and the CPRF.

The results of the APR in the elections are summarized in Table 1.

Programme. The APR is keen to dispel the idea that it is the rural branch of the CPRF. As Mikhail Lapshin has commented: "We do not consider ourselves a branch of any other group, and we have decided to go into the elections independently, without forming a bloc with anyone. Those who share our position — that Russia's revival is only possible through the revival of the countryside — will be close to us. This category may include Zhirinovsky or Gaidar, the Communists or Civic Union. We would like to be a healthy nucleus in parliament around which others gather."[3]

Aleksandr Zaveryukha has also spelt out the party's beliefs. He has made it clear that the APR does not claim to represent the President, nor the opposition, nor the government. "Today the Agrarian Party bloc could be a basis for uniting in the future parliament all healthy forces concerned for the future of the fatherland." The party is concerned that correct budgetary, credit, tax and price policies are adopted by the new parliament. "It is a matter of importance to us who will be tackling these issues on the agrarians' behalf and what understanding all the deputies in the State Duma have in general of the problems of the agro-industrial complex.[4] We are the party without political ambitions, without extremism, but we are the party of action. One of the most important concerns of the party is the territorial integrity of Russia, the avoidance of ethnic and national conflicts."

Zaveryukha has conceded that the APR is not popular enough: "The Agrarian Party does not yet enjoy special influence, but united with agricultural trade unions and other organizations, it will occupy a worthy place in the State Duma. . . and will exert influence on the formation of agrarian policy in Russia. . . Private farmers currently do not produce the necessary amount of food, but they, as competitors, made state and collective farms work better. I am sure that the countryside will strengthen thanks to that and various forms of property should not be counterposed. . . Private farming should be widely supported."

Although the party regards the decisions on land ownership to be incorrect (it opposes a market in land) it regards the constitution as a basis that can be adopted. It underlines that the provision for the national ownership of land must not be deleted.

In economic policy it stresses concerns to the agrarian community. It is necessary to ensure that meat and milk production is profitable. The party recognizes private ownership of land but with reservations. The Agrarian Party wants land to pass from peasant to peasant and farmland to be used for its proper purpose, not for the building of houses and dachas.[5]

The APR favours a sensible destatization of the means of production, the implementation of a truly popular privatization and the adoption of a state programme for the protection of domestic goods producers, first of all agricultural producers. It supports the free allocation of land with ownership rights to all urban and rural residents who wish to conduct personal farming, till orchard and garden plots and build family homes in rural areas, but are against turning land into an object of thoughtless and reckless buying and selling, into a means for laundering dishonestly gained capital. The Agrarian Party advocates a state regulated change-over to market relations and the creation of a civilized, socially oriented market.[6] The state should control the land and agricultural land should be leased to farmers and entrepreneurs, not sold. The party will also look after the interests of hunters and fishermen, for whom these activities are sometimes the only way of adequately feeding their families. As agricultural workers cannot afford to use strikes as a political weapon, due to the nature of their work, so it believes they should have a political organization to defend their interests. Only real professionals should be involved in managing the economy and agriculture needs to be restored as the backbone of the economy.

The Agrarian Party is constantly advocating reforms based on the understanding that the market is not the final goal but a means of increasing the effectiveness of production and improving the living standards of the Russian people. The Agrarian bloc advocates the development of all forms of ownership in rural areas, including reasonable privatization of enterprises in the food and food processing industries.[7]

The Agrarian Party wants prime necessities (bread, milk and meat) to be accessible to all strata of the population. To that end it proposes to subsidize the commodity producer and assist the needy sections of the population without limits since pension supplements will not resolve the problem.

Notes

1 SWB, SU/1823, 19 Oct. 1993, pp. B/2 and B/3; *Current Digest of the Post-Soviet Press*, Vol. xlv, no. 46, Dec. 15, 1993, p. 5, from *Megapolis–Express*, Nov. 17, 1993.
2 16, plus 12 who stood as independents but who are members or supporters of the party (Vladimir Pribylovsky and Grigory Tochkin, *Russkaya Mysl*, 6–12 Jan. 1994.
3 Mikhail Lapshin, *Current Digest of the Post-Soviet Press*, Vol. xlv, no. 48, Dec. 29, 1993, from *Izvestiya*, Nov. 27, 1993.
4 SWB, SU/1869, 11 December 1993, p. B/5 from Russia TV, 9 Dec. 1993.
5 FBIS-SOV-93-218, 15 Nov. 1993, from *Rossiiskie Vesti*, 12 Nov. 1993.
6 Mikhail Lapshin, *Current Digest of the Post-Soviet Press*, Vol. xlv, no. 48, Dec. 29, 1993, from *Izvestiya*, Nov. 27, 1993.
7 FBIS-SOV-93-232, 6 Dec. 1993, from *ITAR-TASS*, 3 Dec. 1993.

Civic Union for Stability, Justice and Progress
Grazhdansky Soyuz "Vo Imya Stabilnosti, Spravedlivosti i Progressa"

Address.

Telephone.

Foundation. June 21, 1992.

Leadership. Arkady Volsky.

History. The Sixth Russian Congress of People's Deputies, in April 1992, saw a fierce struggle between parliament and government over the issue of President Yeltsin's personal powers. It took a great deal of behind-the-scenes lobbying by Yeltsin and his ministers to convince congress to abandon its demands that President Yeltsin relinquish his additional powers by July 1992, and halt radical economic reform. Vice-President Rutskoi managed to strengthen his personal position at the top and widen his base of popular support, and he even brokered a promising centre-right coalition by aligning his People's Party for a Free Russia with the Democratic Party of Russia, led by Nikolai Travkin.[1] "A political party of *gosudarstvenniki* (supporters of a strong Russian state) is now being set up by Rutskoi and Travkin. The latter is known to have been an advocate of a renewed, 'democratized' Soviet Union and to have resisted the collapse of the USSR. The Rutskoi-Travkin alliance was not cemented earlier because Travkin, an anti-Communist, disliked Rutskoi's plea for reforming the Communist Party of the Soviet Union. After Rutskoi had distanced from Marxist dogma, however, the two populist leaders joined forces and agreed to develop a strategy for strengthening Russian statehood."[2]

"The backbone of the industrialists" lobby is the RUIE, headed by Arkady Volsky, who was the chief economic adviser to several general-secretaries of the CPSU. This body also has a suborganization to represent the interests of production managers — the All-Russian Renewal Union, which is also led by Volsky. Apart from gaining direct access to the country's decision-making through the inclusion of some of its leading representatives in the government, the All-Russian Renewal Union strengthened its socio-political base and sought greater influence by forming an alliance with two of the strongest political parties in Russia: the DPR, the PPFR. It was these three forces that organized themselves into the major political bloc called Civic Union.

It favours a less painful and more socially oriented economic reform and an isolationist approach toward foreign policy. A coalition of liberals and Civic Union could, theoretically, consolidate the broadest spectrum of forces in Russian society. Travkin's DPR is known to count on blue-collar workers for support, Rutskoi's PPFR on reformist elements in the armed forces, and Volsky's unions on the military-industrial complex and scientists. The aims of Civic Union are to preserve the integrity of the Russian Federation, stabilize the economy, and eliminate social tension. It rejected calls for the abolition of the then parliament, since it had more deputies in it than any other parliamentary faction.

Rutskoi stated that Civic Union would work out its own economic reform programme as an alternative to Gaidar's. However, like other leaders of Civic Union, he stressed that he did not want to see Gaidar replaced and that Civic Union would support the government and defend it against attacks from the far Right.'[3]

On June 21, 1992, representatives of three influential Russian political parties gathered in Moscow for the first formal meeting of a new centrist bloc, Civic Union. An article in *Literaturnaya gazeta* (June 24, 1992) stated that Nikolai Travkin (DPR) could call on "wide democratic public support"; Arkady Volsky was backed by "industrialists, enterprise directors, the military-industrial complex, and administrators"; Rutskoi commanded "real levers of power and loyalty of moderate, soberminded statists and patriots"; and the New Generation-New Policy parliamentary faction was influential in the Russian Parliament.

Civic Union presented a sort of ultimatum to the government: the Gaidar team, Civic Union declared, should make radical changes to soften the impact and slow the pace of its reform. If the government refused to modify its programme the bloc would use its parliamentary muscle to call a vote of no confidence in the government and to replace it with a cabinet made up of its own representatives.

Civic Union stood ready "not only to put forward proposals aimed at achieving political and economic stability in Russia but also to carry them out." (However there were clear nuances between Civic Union's member organizations.) All the bloc's members professed total loyalty to President Yeltsin. At first, this was a source of some confusion. A compromise was eventually found whereby Civic Union's members stressed that they were a 'loyal' or 'constructive', opposition. What they opposed, according to Civic Union was not the aims but the methods of the Gaidar government; they themselves were not seeking power for its own sake. If Gaidar and his colleagues heeded Civic Union's warnings and modified the means by which they were carrying out their policies, they could stay in office.

In May, the industrial lobby forced three of its representatives into the cabinet (Vladimir Shumeiko, Georgy Khizha and Viktor Chernomyrdin); and formed its own party, Renewal, which in turn became one of the founders of Civic Union. Using these institutions, the industrialists began to speak into President Yeltsin's other ear, warning him that the industrial disruption and social upheaval accompanying macro-economic stabilization could spark uncontrollable unrest. According to Nikolai Vishnevsky in *Rossiiskie Vesti*, June 9, 1992, Volsky started from the assumption that even hyperinflation pales into insignificance compared with the really important thing: rescuing enterprises from bankruptcy.

While professing loyalty to President Yeltsin, the new bloc expressed open opposition to the government President Yeltsin appointed. Civic Union brought together in one bloc the two parties with the largest membership in Russia at that time (the DPR with 50,000 members and the PPFR with 100,000) and was the first party in Russia to try to form around an economic interest group (Renewal, representing the interests of state enterprise directors). At Civic Union's forum on June 21, representatives adopted a political declaration laying down priorities for collective action. Pride of place went to "the preservation of Russia's integrity as a strong, multinational, democratic state.". Next Civic Union agreed that President Yeltsin should keep the extraordinary presidential powers he had been granted by the Russian parliament at the end of 1991; but it stated strong opposition to President Yeltsin's plans to dissolve the legally elected legislature. Civic Union called for the declaration of a moratorium, until the end of 1992, on the holding of elections and referenda in Russia (in order to prevent President Yeltsin from holding a referendum in order to muster public support for the dissolution of parliament).

Furthermore, Civic Union recommended that constitutional reform be postponed until after the achievement of a stable economic and social situation. This would prevent President Yeltsin from introducing a new constitution giving the presidency increased powers *vis-à-vis* parliament. Finally, Civic Union called for modifications to be made to the government's economic reforms. In particular it demanded increased state subsidies to industry in order to halt the fall in production and stimulate economic growth. Speakers at the forum were especially critical of President Yeltsin's edict (June 14, 1992) which opened the way for the first time to enterprise bankruptcies. Speakers also said that the massive privatization of state property being planned by Deputy Prime Minister Anatoly Chubais would be accompanied by the disbanding of the present "corps of industrial managers" and would totally destroy Russian industry. They called instead for state-owned enterprises to be given to their employees free of charge.[4]

Members of Civic Union

The People's Party of Free Russia: Founded on Aug. 2–3, 1991 (only a few weeks before the attempted coup) by a group of reformist communists in the Russian parliament, the new party set out to become an alternative to the hardline Communist Party of the RSFSR and to attract reform communists to its ranks. Initially it described itself as an organization operating "within the CPSU" (but on Aug. 6 the leaders of the new party — Rutskoi and Lipitsky — were expelled from the Communist Party of the RSFSR, apparently because the creation of such a party was an infringement of the ban on the formation of factions within the CPSU. Nevertheless the CPSU's Democratic Platform already existed. During the attempted August coup Rutskoi and Lipitsky sided with President Yeltsin and, when in the aftermath of the coup, President Yeltsin suspended the activities of the CPSU and the CP of the RSFSR on Russian territory and confiscated the two parties' property, Rutskoi's party declared that it would make no claim to be the CPSU's successor or to its property. At its Congress in October 1991, the party declared that it was abandoning its adherence to socialism and would in future advocate market reforms, albeit buttressed by strong social guarantees. It described itself as an organization with a "left-democratic orientation" and an emphasis on "social justice and mixed forms of ownership of the means of production." In July the PPFR claimed around 100,000 members. It was well-organized and has developed regional structures spanning the Russian Federation.[5]

Democratic Party of Russia (see separate entry)

The All-Russian Renewal Union: It held its founding conference on May 30, 1992, and was set up on the initiative of the RUIE, which represents the interests of Russian businessmen (primarily but not exclusively directors of state-owned enterprises, many of them in the defence sector). Renewal co-chairman Aleksandr Vladislavlev argued that if state enterprises were removed from the hands of managers with experience in running them, they would be mismanaged and Russia's economy would go to wrack and ruin; and secondly, that Russia's state enterprise directors had already invested so much energy in their companies over the years that they had acquired some kind of ownership rights to at least a share of them. Vladislavlev insists that Renewal supports market reforms but that these must be carried out under strict state supervision and must not be permitted to impoverish the population. In general, Renewal states that its aim is the construction in Russia of a socially oriented, regulated market economy. In addition to the industrialists' lobby, Renewal's founding conference was attended by heads of administration (local government officials) and representatives from 52 Russian republics and *oblasts*.[6]

New Generation–New Policy (*Smena*): This parliamentary faction was set up in 1990. Its members are predominantly young (30 and 40 years old). Originally the group comprised members of the "democratic camp" such as Sergei Shakhrai, as well as supporters of the opposite nationalist camp, such as Sergei Baburin. Since then, however the faction has split. The more extreme members, both left-wing and right-wing, have left the group, leaving a centrist core with "patriotic" leanings. Although its political programme was vague and its membership not large, *Smena* has quite often found itself holding the balance of power when the Russian parliament was split between the pro-democracy and pro-communist groups. Since the attempted August coup, *Smena* attacked President Yeltsin's leadership on several occasions accusing him of authoritarian and undemocratic tendencies. At the beginning of 1992, *Smena* was calculated to have 10 per cent of the votes in the standing Russian parliament, the Supreme Soviet.

The Industrialists were now (August 1992) on the offensive, attacking a weakened and demoralized government on several fronts at once. On July 24, Volsky addressed a press conference and said that "Power belongs to the those who have property and money" ... "At present," he said, "it is not the government but the industrial managers who have both." In May 1992 they also acquired their own mass-circulation newspaper: RUIE became the co-publisher of *Rabochaya Tribuna*, together with the Federation of Independent Trade Unions of Russia (FITUR).[7]

Civic Union lost no time in announcing that it was drawing up its own economic reform programme and in presenting the government with an ultimatum: if the Gaidar team did not modify its reform programme in accordance with Civic Union's, the alliance would use its parliamentary muscle to call for a vote of no confidence in the government and to replace it with a cabinet made up of its own representatives. But the new programme announced by Gaidar (the Yasin-Vasilev programme) seemed not to be enough for the industrialists. Vladislavlev dismissed the government's programme on the grounds that it would lead to the "Kuwaitization of Russia" — this meant that it would destroy Russia's industrial base and reduce the country to the status of an exporter of energy to rich Western-nations. Vladislavlev's statement was seen as a clear sign that the industrial lobby was determined to force President Yeltsin to abandon Gaidar, his team, and his reforms. On July 16 Civic

Union's Political Consultative Council met for the first time. At the top of its agenda was a document entitled "Economic Policy Alternatives."[8]

At the meeting on July 16, Civic Union's leaders called on President Yeltsin to make 'energetic corrections' to the reform programme and assured him that Civic Union was ready to provide not only an economic programme but also the cabinet ministers to carry it out. By cultivating new partners — firstly the official trade unions, secondly the members of Civic Union — the industrial lobby acquired extremely useful allies. Through the unions, it gained access to the labour force. By allying itself with the parties of Rutskoi and Travkin, it established contact with a wide network of grassroots political organizations. Through its connections with these parties and with the New Generation–New Policy group of deputies, the industrial lobby acquired the parliamentary muscle it had previously lacked. Its third and latest alliance brings together Russia's "old" entrepreneurs into partnership with the country's "new" private businessmen represented by the Party of Economic Freedom (led by the millionaire Konstantin Borovoi). The alliance was announced on July 24. This party represents Russia's new business class working in stock markets, private banks and commercial agencies. Borovoi made his fortune through the Moscow Commodities Exchange, which he himself founded in October 1990. Announcing their new alliance, Volsky and Borovoi made it clear that they had been brought together by shared hostility to the plan for the privatization of state property announced at the beginning of July by Russian Deputy Prime Minister Anatoly Chubais.[9]

Recent developments suggest that Russia's industrial managers may be less capable of acting as a coherent political lobby than they had appeared to be in the spring and early summer of 1992. Arkady Volsky's RUIE has in the recent past given the impression of a mighty and growing political force, pressing almost irresistibly for more conservative economic policies and latterly an alliance with other groups in Civic Union. In mid-August 1992, however, it became clear that there were a great many serious divisions among the industrialists themselves (RUIE and the Industrial Union caucus of the Russian Parliament led by parliamentary deputy Yury Gekht). This was shown by strong disagreements expressed by participants at an All-Russian Conference of Manufacturers held in Moscow on Aug. 13–14, as well as by the publication of a draft programme for Civic Union that was disowned by Volsky himself and others among his Civic Union partners. It seems that some industrial managers are in favour of more radical reform than Volsky has espoused, while another contingent is opting for a more reactionary line which Volsky cannot easily embrace if he is to maintain his credibility as a "centrist".[10]

The best-organized political force in Russia in mid-1992 was Civic Union. The core of the union consisted of officials who under communism wore the label of "technocrat" (sought to introduce into the system some elements of the market economy) in contrast to that of the "ideologists". Some analysts believed that Russia was in the midst of a constitutional coup, albeit a gradual one, by means of which these former technocrats of the communist era were gaining power. The shift of power in the Soviet Union from the ideologists to the technocrats began under Yury Andropov. Some argue that Volsky, not Gorbachev, was the true heir to Andropov. Volsky although he still denied his intention of seeking the prime ministership, appeared to have come under increasing pressure from his own ranks to try for that office.

It seemed that major political decisions in the Kremlin were being made not by President Yeltsin but largely by Civic Union. It had demanded greater participation in the governmental affairs of Russia. Volsky and Rutskoi wanted to replace the government's reform programme with that of Civic Union, which was aimed at saving the Russian industrial sector from collapse by re-establishing, in effect, partial government control over the economy. The stimulation of production through decentralization and privatization was foreseen only at a later stage.

At the Sixth Congress of People's Deputies, in April 1992, the "industrial lobby" complained that President Yeltsin had formed a government of young reformist academics, without taking into account representatives of the industrialists. That powerful lobby forced President Yeltsin to change the composition of the government at the Sixth Congress: he appointed representatives of the lobby to top positions in the government, receiving in return a promise from the industrialists that they would not oppose but would fully support the government's radical reform course. In the summer of 1992 Civic Union's pressure on acting Prime Minister Egor Gaidar's team to replace the economic shock therapy with a more socially oriented programme became so strong that Gaidar was forced to yield and make one compromise after another to Volsky and Rutskoi.

Gaidar, realizing that only the West could save his radical reform course, continued to base his polices on support from the International Monetary Fund and the World Bank. But internal support for him and his radical reform programme was significantly waning in Russia; not only such advocates of a strong centre as Volsky, Rutskoi or Khasbulatov and Shumeiko, but more liberal politicians such as Popov, Filatov, Sobchak and Rumyantsev have openly questioned the need for foreign economic help and called for the adoption of a different plan that would take account of Russia's unique situation. Popov believed that Gaidar had already abandoned his own initial reform programme and was now adopting ideas advocated by Volsky. Gaidar admitted that he could not govern without the support of Civic Union and the conservative head of the Russian Central Bank, Viktor Gerashchenko (who seems to be allied with Civic Union); but at the same time he emphasized that he wanted to return to the "shock therapy" programme that he had been forced to abandon in April 1992.[11]

Now, however, more and more representatives of Civic Union began clamouring to join the government; a group of Civic Union members even compiled its own list of ministers and presented it to President Yeltsin. The President, who needed Civic Union as a centrist force in parliament to counter the far right, agreed to some of Civic Union's more constructive proposals but resisted any pressure to make personnel changes. However, with the aim of enlisting Civic Union's support at the forthcoming Congress, he gave in to its demands and removed some of the most outspoken reformist politicians.[12]

Civic Union, which had appeared to be a major force in Russian politics before the events of October 3–4, 1993, has now lost almost all its influence in Moscow, although it has maintained its position in the republics and regions. Its most prominent leader, former Vice-President Aleksandr Rutskoi, spent several months in jail, and his party, once the backbone of Civic Union, was briefly banned by President Yeltsin, then permitted to register again, and has now split. Civic Union, renamed Civic Union for Stability, Justice and Progress after the October uprising, now consists almost entirely of state enterprises and military-industrial directors. Civic Union continues to advocate the ending of radical economic reform and a partial return to central state planning.[13]

Immediately after the October crisis, Vasily Lipitsky, leader of the centrist Civic Union bloc, which unites the People's Party of Free Russia of which the former Russian Vice-President was the honorary chairman, tried to distance himself from the arrested Aleksandr Rutskoi, his former ally. Lipitsky told a press conference on Tuesday that

Civic Union urged Rutskoi and former parliament chairman Ruslan Khasbulatov to adopt the "zero option" (which envisaged the cancellation of the presidential decree dissolving parliament and of all other documents adopted by the conflicting sides). "Civic Union revised its position and then categorically denounced calls for violence coming from the White House", Lipitsky said: "We roundly denounce the actions by Aleksandr Rutskoi; we denounce the actions of the White House leaders, who got themselves under the thumb of the leaders of "Working Moscow", Anpilovites, and other fascist elements".[14]

Civic Union bloc joined the election campaign in order to have a channel for the "parliamentary lobbying" of the interests of domestic industrialists and entrepreneurs, said Volsky at a congress of the Russian Union of Industrialists and Entrepreneurs (RUIE).[15] The bloc's list was headed by Arkady Volsky — leader of the Russian Union of Industrialists and Entrepreneurs. Among the candidates were (second on the list) Nikolai Bekh, general director of the Kamaz Automotive Plant; Gonchar, former head of the Moscow City Soviet, Aleksandr Tsipko, the political scientist and former communist intellectual (director of the Gorbachev Foundation's research programme); Academician Stanislav Shatalin; and Admiral Kasatonov. Aleksandr Vladislavlev was listed as a public figure, without any indication that he was the leader of the Renewal League; Vasily Lipitsky was named not as being from the People's Party of Free Russia, but as a citizen. Also on the list as individuals were Oleg Rumyantsev (former Executive Secretary of the Supreme Soviet Constitutional Commission, [who had long harboured ambitions of co-operating with Civic Union] — his Social Democratic Centre was a co-founder of the bloc), Iosif Kobzon, Aleksandr Tsipko, Fedor Burlatsky (president of the Foundation for Humanitarian Cooperation), Konstantin Lubenchenko, Ruslan Aushev, Aleksandr Dzasokhov. The list also included a number of industrialists, such as Petr Semenenko, director of the Kirov Plant, St Petersburg, and Vladimir Piskunov, vice-president of the Almazy Yakutii-Sakha (Yakutia-Sakha Diamonds) concern and[16] Sergei Rogov, deputy director of the Institute of the USA and Canada (the Arbatov Institute) and also includes Vladimir Ispravnikov, defender of Khasbulatov's line in the Supreme Soviet.[17]

The strong points of bloc were: the financial possibilities and the support of old, experienced economic-management cadres at the local level. The weak spots were its modest social base, as well as its low popularity with voters. (According to Academician Boris Koval, Civic Union was going through a crisis now that Rutskoi's party had been banned. The only two real forces now left in the bloc were the Union of Renewal, led by Arkady Volsky and Aleksandr Vladislavlev, and the Russian Union of Industrialists and Entrepreneurs.)[18]

Civic Union list of candidates abounded with the names of managers of major Russian enterprises: the Kamaz joint-stock society, the "Russia-Saha Diamonds" joint-stock company, the Kirov plant, the "Russian Weapons" corporation, etc. The bloc's 270 candidates include 78 directors, 38 civil servants, 35 entrepreneurs, 32 scientists, 29 heads of unions of industrialists and businessmen and 15 trade union leaders.[19]

Civic Union includes the All-Russia Renewal League (All-Russian Union for Renewal), the Russian Union of Industrialists and Entrepreneurs, the Social Democratic Centre (Oleg Rumyantsev) and the Russian Youth League. (The trade unions for timber industry workers and construction workers were also bloc founders.) One should not discount the trade unions, wrested from the once orderly ranks of the now-collapsing Federation of Independent Trade Unions of Russia. They will be able to lobby the bloc through their own channels. It cannot be ruled out that the "workers" representation will improve the image of the "directors' bloc".[20]

Table 2: Election results of Civic Union

Signatures collected for the elections: 150,000 (total number of candidates: 184)[27]

State Duma
Total number of seats: 18[28]
Seats obtained on party lists: none (the party obtained 1.92 per cent of the vote and hence failed to surmount the 5 per cent barrier)
Seats obtained in single-member constituencies: 18

The PPFR, whose activities were temporarily suspended, intended to go into the elections as part of Civic Union bloc. Vasily Lipitsky emphasized that the PPFR, while definitively reinterpreting its role, will maintain continuity in its basic political principles, which according to him, are social democratic. Its chief principles are a market with social guarantees and the idea of Russian statehood based on the equality of regions, with centralization for a number of questions.[21] The PPFR leadership has been dispirited by the "forced absence" of Aleksandr Rutskoi and the continual "shutdowns" and "reopenings" of the party. Civic Union can only rely on the regional structure of the party. In addition, no PPFR functionaries hold top roles in the current Civic Union, because of their dubious "Rutskoi-ist past". The party was not even among the founders of the bloc.[22]

On Oct. 8, 1993, the activities of the PPFR together with the Communist Party of the Russian Federation (CPRF) (Gennady Zyuganov – Central Executive Committee chairman) were suspended.[23] On Oct. 20, the Ministry of Justice announced that the PPFR and the CPRF had the right to prepare the necessary documents for taking part in the elections and to put forward their candidates. Vasily Lipitsky, a member of the board of the PPFR, stated that the party would nominate its candidates only from the party lists of Civic Union bloc and a new bloc which has provisionally been called Russia's Future–New Names.

Civic Union's failure in the December 1993 elections to the State Duma to surmount the 5 per cent barrier came as a shock to the leadership. It underlined the weakness of centrist factions in the State Duma. However, observers have estimated that some 60 deputies in the Council of the Federation, the 178-member upper house, either support Prime Minister Viktor Chernomyrdin or are close to the concepts of Civic Union. The new Russian government contains many with centrist tendencies similar to those propounded by Civic Union and the DPR. In May 1994 Nikolai Travkin was appointed a Minister without portfolio by President Yeltsin.

Civic Union and the DPR are the only groups in the State Duma which may properly be termed centrist. The Women of Russia group, which obtained 8.1 per cent of the party lists vote (and 21 seats) and another four in single member constituencies, adopts policies which are in many ways similar to Civic Union and the DPR. The Russia's Future-New Names bloc, which obtained one seat in single member constituencies, has faded from view. The Party of Russian Unity and Accord (Yabloko bloc) is often classified as centrist by Russian commentators, and offer a more moderate approach to market reform than Russia's Choice, but its members and policies differ from those of Civic Union and the DPR. Many of the independent deputies in the State Duma have joined the New Regional Policy faction and may be centrist in economic orientation.

Although Civic Union performed poorly in the elections, Pavel Bunich, an advisor of President Yeltsin and a deputy for Russia's Choice, was quoted as saying that Civic Union had lost the elections but had won the government (*Los Angeles Times*, Jan. 24, 1994) due to the departure of Egor Gaidar and Boris Fedorov as Minister of Finance. Volsky, it was reported, was offered a government post which he refused.[25] Under the new constitution the State Duma has limited influence over the economy, while the Council of the Federation is more powerful. It would seem in spring 1994 that the Yeltsin administration has responsibility for foreign and security policy and the government for the economy.[26] This heralds greater influence for the industrial lobbies and regional economic associations and consequently Civic Union may again assume a high profile.

Programme. Civic Union spoke out against the draft constitution, advising its voters to vote against the text in the referendum. The Union believes that the very concept of a "Constitution" has been discredited. The Constitution can be put into effect by presidential decree by a victorious President.[29]

On economic policy, the Union is a strong critic of government policy. At the Fifth Congress of the Russian Union of Industrialists and Entrepreneurs on Nov. 16, 1993, its leader Aleksandr Volsky sharply criticized the Russian government, though his target was not the entire cabinet but individual members of it from the "monetarist school", above all first Deputy Prime Minister Gaidar. Volsky blamed him for the fall in Russia's GDP from January to September 1993 of 13 per cent (compared to 17 per cent for same period in 1992). Volsky said that the result of monetary stabilization is a catastrophic drop in industrial production "comparable to the periods of the Civil and Great Patriotic Wars" and the mass impoverishment of the population.[30] RUIE see its main task as overcoming the slump as quickly as possible and attaining steady growth for industrial production (how this goal is to be reached remains unknown).

Its programme calls for strengthening state regulation of the economy, increasing investment in the basic branches of the economy and in the processing industry, creating holding companies and financial-industrial groups, bringing about joint ownership by means of an exchange of stock among industrial enterprises, and setting up cartel-type agreements on prices and the population's income. "We must do everything we can to keep the economy from finally collapsing and to prevent its key sector — industry — from winding up on the sidelines of civilized development". At the Fifth Congress Viktor Gerashchenko, head of the Central Bank, said that, in his opinion, money in Russia had never performed the function of a measure of value. Therefore he believes that parity prices for basic types of raw materials and output must be established by directives, rather than trying to do this through the market. He is convinced inflation in Russia can be overcome not by a tough-credit and monetary policy but by investment activity.

RUIE's leaders are confident that the former socialist economy has already been through the stage of structural reorganization and is ready to make efficient use of financial resources. All that has to be done is to give the command from above, which is what the directors' establishment will expect from the new government to be formed after the elections.[31] (According to another article in *Segodnya*, Nov. 18, the economic provisions confirmed by the RUIE congress are not much different from the Union's previous programmes.)

Volsky supports socially-oriented free market reforms, sustaining business, the need for unity in the government — as expressed by the President — Burlatsky, said that the bloc approves reasonable, moderate reforms, is against revolutionary leaps and shock therapy and in favour of a gradual transition to a market-oriented democracy.[32] Volsky said that Egor Gaidar wants to use Western economic models which are not suitable for Russia.

Market transformation must be carried out in the interests of citizens and not a handful of crooks. Taxes on superfluous goods must be raised and taxes for the producers of goods and services must be lowered, while for under-privileged citizens, veterans, and invalids they must be abolished altogether. State subsidies for prime necessities must be targeted on consumers, not producers.[33]

Volsky stressed that his party was not calling for the revival of Gosplan (State Planning Commission) or Gossnab (State Committee for Material and Technical Supply), but he was not renouncing the idea of state regulation of the economy "if it is sensible". Andrei Neshchadin, chief RUIE economic analyst said that "the time for radical reform ended (with the coming of the edict on land.) Painstaking work is now beginning whose core will not be monetary methods but structural reform. Financial stabilization is of course achievable, but who needs it in an economic graveyard?". He focused on the need for state investments (credits and subsidies) for "Russia's commodity producers regardless of forms of ownership".

The bloc considers the introduction of the private ownership of land both necessary and timely and will strive to ensure that the tax system and other levers of state management encourage the efficient use of agricultural land by land owners.[34]

RUIE stands for the need to preserve benefits and guarantees for needy strata of the population, including the introduction of "poverty cards", the holders of which would be eligible for low rates in paying for housing and purchasing food. Civic Union wants priority to be given to housing construction, the subsidizing of which will revive the whole economy, resolve social problems, and give the citizens a free choice: either to buy his own home or rent it anywhere in Russia[35]

The leaders of Civic Union regret the demise of the Soviet Union, but they do not advocate reunification by military force.[36] Political philosopher Aleksandr Tsipko has described the CIS as a "fiction" and the Minsk agreement (establishing the CIS) as "Russia's death sentence". In his view, the "leaders of the Russian Federation do not understand that, without Ukraine, there can be no Russia, in the old real sense of the word".[37] Civic Union's main foreign policy goal is, therefore, the restoration of the former Soviet Union by peaceful means, including, if necessary, economic pressure on the former Soviet republics. In September 1992, the Political Council of Civic Union advocated the setting up of movements within the parliaments and governments of the countries of the CIS aimed at reestablishing a closer union among the states. It also recommended the establishment of a joint body to be responsible for conducting a unitary economic, scientific and cultural policy throughout the CIS.[38]

Civic Union favours good relations with the West, so long as they do not jeopardize Russia's role as an independent, great power with its own "sphere of influence".[39] It regards close relations between Russia and the US as a "stabilizing force in world politics" but wants the Washington to acknowledge Russia's status as a world power.[40] In 1993 Civic Union adopted its foreign policy programme on the basis of a project prepared by the USA and Canada Institute and led by Sergei Rogov. The project criticized President Yeltsin's foreign policy for relying too much on good relations with the West and for disregarding Russia's relations with the countries of the former Soviet Union. According to Rogov, Yeltsin's policy failed to integrate the country into a "new system of international relations".[41] In his view, Russia lacks allies in both the economic and military spheres. The project proposes that Russian foreign policy should aim at finding a political solution to the problem of the Russian-speaking population in the near abroad, preserving Russia's defence capacities in the wake of the dissolution of the unified Soviet Army and preserving the ruble zone on the territory of the former Soviet Union.[42] Civic Union supports the idea of an Economic Union among the states of the former USSR and regards Russia as a bridge between the North Atlantic and Asia-Pacific markets. The bloc, which includes quite a few prominent specialists in the military-industrial complex and production leaders, also advocates a solicitous, state attitude to the defence industry and its scientific and technical potential.[43]

Notes

1 *ITAR-PRESS*, 15 March, 1992.
2 *RFE/RL Research Report*, Vol. 1, no. 18, 1 May 1992.
3 *RFE/RL Research Report*, Vol. 1, no. 29, 17 July 1992.
4 *RFE/RL Research Report*, Vol. 1, no. 30, 24 July 1992.
5 *Ibid.*
6 *Ibid.*
7 *Trud*, July 18, 1992.
8 *RFE/RL Research Report*, Vol. 1, no. 32, 14 Aug. 1992, 38, 25 Sept. 1992.
9 *RFE/RL Research Report*, Vol. 1, no. 32, 14 Aug. 1992.
10 *RFE/RL Research Report*, Vol. 1, no. 35, 4 Sept. 1992.
11 *Financial Times*, 24 Sept. 1992.
12 *RFE/RL Research Report*, Vol. 1, no. 48, 4 Dec. 1992.
13 *RFE/RL Research Report*, Vol. 2, no. 47, 26 Nov. 1993.
14 *FBIS-SOV-93-192S*, 6 Oct. 1993, from *Nezavisimaya Gazeta*, 5 Oct. 1993.
15 *FBIS-SOV-93-219*, 16 Nov. 1993, from *ITAR-TASS*, 16 Nov. 1993.
16 *Current Digest of the Post-Soviet Press*, Vol xlv, no. 43, Nov. 24, 1993, from *Segodnya*, 28 Oct. 1993.
17 *Izvestiya*, 30 Oct. 1993.
18 *SWB, SU*, 20 Oct. 1993, p. B/2.
19 *FBIS-SOV-93-212*, 4 Nov. 1993, from *Interfax*, 3 Nov. 1993.
20 *Current Digest of the Post-Soviet Press*, Vol. xlv, no. 43, Nov. 24, 1993, from *Segodnya*, 28 Oct. 1993.
21 *Izvestiya*, 26 Oct. 1993.
22 *Segodnya*, 28 Oct. 1993.
23 *Izvestiya*, 9 Oct. 1993.
24 *Russkaya Mysl*, 6–12 Jan. 1994.
25 *ITAR-TASS*, 19 Jan. 1994.
26 *Novoe Vremya*, no. 9, March 1994.
27 *Segodnya*, 11 Nov. 1993.
28 Vladimir Pribylovsky, *Russkaya Mysl*, 6–12 Jan. 1994, states that 7 Civic Union candidates were elected in single member constituencies but that another 14 regarded themselves as supporters of Civic Union.
29 *Segodnya*, 27 Nov. 1993.
30 *Current Digest of the Post-Soviet Press*, Vol. xlv, no. 46.
31 *Segodnya*, 18 Nov. 1993.
32 *FBIS-SOV-93-212*, 4 Nov. 1993, from *Interfax*, 3 Nov. 1993.
33 *Rossiiskie Vesti*, 12 Nov. 1993.
34 *Rossiiskie Vesti*, 12 Nov. 1993.
35 *FBIS-SOV-93-218*, 15 Nov. 1993, from *Rossiiskie Vesti*, 12 Nov. 1993.
36 Alexei Arbatov, 'Russia's Foreign Policy Alternatives', *International Security*, Vol. 18, no. 2 (Fall 1993), p. 13.
37 *Komsomolskaya Pravda*, Jan. 14, 1992.
38 Alexander Rahr, 'Upcoming Congress will Test Yeltsin's Loyalty to Democrats', *RFE/RL Research Report*, Vol. 1, no. 38, 25 Sept. 1992, p. 8.
39 Arbatov, *op. cit.* p. 13.
40 Alexander Rahr, 'Russia: The Struggle for Power Continues', *RFE/RL Research Report*, Vol 2, no. 6, 5 Feb. 1993, p. 4.
41 *Ibid.* p. 3.
42 *Ibidem.*
43 *Krasnaya Zvezda*, 2 Dec. 1993.

Communist Party of the Russian Federation (CPRF)
Kommunisticheskaya Partiya Rossiiskogo Federatsii

Foundation. Feb. 13–14, 1992 (registered March 24, 1993).

Leadership. Gennady Zyuganov, first sec. (In January 1992 he was elected chairman of the Council of the People's Patriotic Forces of Russia. In June 1992 he was also elected co-chairman of the Duma of the Russian National Assembly (Sterligov's party). In October 1992 he actively participated in the formation of the National Salvation Front and became one of its co-chairmen.) Valentin Kuptsov; Viktor Ilyukhin, also co-ch. of the Front for National Salvation and "general procurator" of the Russian opposition; Valentin Seleznev (editor-in-chief, *Sovetskaya Rossiya*); Gennady Seleznev (former editor-in-chief, *Pravda*); Yury Leonov (former leader of the Marxist Workers' Party–Party of the Dictatorship of the Proletariat MRP–PDP); Omar Begov (chairman of the Stalin society); Yury Belov; Svetlana Goryacheva; Mikhail Lapshin; Ivan Rybkin; Viktor Zorkaltsev.

Membership. About 600,000 members.[1]

History. On Dec. 3, 1992, three days after the Constitutional Court had ruled that President Yeltsin's decree banning the activities of communist parties partially contravened the constitution and activity by communist party cells was now legal, Valentin Kuptsov, the last first secretary of the Communist Party of the RSFSR (he had succeeded Ivan Polozkov on Aug. 6, 1991), called on all the communist parties which had formed after the banning of the CPSU, to convene a congress of Russian communists. The congress took place on Feb. 13–14, 1992, at Klyazm, outside Moscow. It was called the Second Extraordinary Revival-Unification Congress of the Communist Party of the Russian Federation (CPRF). The legality of the congress was questioned by the Russian government and the Constitutional Court. The congress was attended by 650 delegates, representing about 500,000 members who had registered, from local party organizations from all parts of the Russian Federation. Local party conferences had been held in most parts of the country beforehand, except in regions with aspirations towards autonomy, such as Maritime *krai*, Tatarstan, Chechnia and Ingushetia. The delegates were mostly from the older generation with modest qualifications. Roi Medvedev, leader of the Socialist Party of the Working People, complained that the creative intelligentsia was hardly represented at the party conference of the Moscow branch. Other parties which attended included the Russian Party of Communists and the Union of Communists. The Russian Communist Workers' Party (RCWP) and the All-Union Communist Party of Bolsheviks refused to participate and Viktor Anpilov, leader of the RCWP, attempted to persuade delegates to join his party instead. The RCWP held a rival congress on the same day and it declared the RCWP to be the "sole, legal successor of the Communist Party of the RSFSR" and expelled all the organizers of the CPRF from the CP of the RSFSR.

The CPRF Congress elected an 89-member Central Executive Committee (CEC), among whom were Anatoly Lukyanov and Oleg Shenin. They had been accused of involvement in the attempted coup of August 1991. At the first meeting of the CEC, Gennady Zyuganov was elected chairman of the CEC. [He was proposed by General Albert Makashov.] Yury Belov, Svetlana Goryacheva, Valentin Kuptsov, Mikhail Lapshin, Ivan Rybkin and Viktor Zorkaltsev were elected deputy chairpersons.

The election of Zyuganov clearly identified the CPRF with nationalist and patriotic forces. He is a co-chairman of the National Salvation Front, formed in October 1992 by communists and nationalists. It had been banned by President Yeltsin but had been relegalized by the Constitutional Court on Feb. 12, 1993, the day before the Congress convened. The CPRF considered itself the legal successor of the CPSU and laid claim to all CPSU property in the Russian Federation.

There was a debate about whether precedence should be afforded the refounding of the republican-based communist parties or the CPSU, but it soon became obvious that republican parties would come first. The CPRF continued the Leninist tradition of banning factions and gave all members who were also members of other parties until Nov. 6, 1993 (the date of the next Congress) to decide which party they wished to belong to. Like the Bolsheviks the CPRF demanded total loyalty. Its support base was the working class.[2] The CPRF was registered in the Ministry of Justice of the Russian Federation on March 24, 1993. Its stated membership is 500,000.

On Sept. 18, 1993, the Central Executive Committee, CPRF, adopted a decision drawing the attention of communists and all Russian citizens to the impending danger of the ruling anti-people regime's destroying the foundations of the country's statehood. The preservation and strengthening of the state's constitutional institutions which serve as an obstacle to the establishment of a monopoly of power of capital and to the collapse of Russia as a unified multinational power was proclaimed as one immediate task for the party.[3]

The party's activities were suspended on Oct. 8, 1993, by the Ministry of Justice. However, the presidential decree of Oct. 19, banning certain parties from taking part in the elections did not include the CPRF and the party received permission to participate in the elections from Yury Kalmykov, Minister of Justice and Nikolai Ryabov, chairman of the Central Electoral Commission, since the party had come out against political extremism and in favour of early elections as a way out of the crisis that had developed in the country. With the end of the state of emergency, the period of the party's underground existence also expired.[4]

Before the elections, Zyuganov declared that Yeltsin's regime had suffered a complete moral and political collapse, and that "Shakhrai ... will surely seek and alliance with the CPRF." In addition to him, the Communist Party hoped to co-operate with Baburin's Russian National Union and with the Agrarian Party. Zyuganov claimed that the "Federal Assembly is illegitimate both in its origin and in its election procedures and the only thing it has a right to do is to institute criminal proceedings against the organizers of the coup [President Yeltsin and his administration]". The CPRF hoped to win about 28 seats in the State Duma, but in the event performed much better than had at first been expected (see Table 3).

Radicals accuse Zyuganov of social democracy, the signs of which are a retreat from communist positions and compromise with the authorities. In order to preserve the unity of the oppositionist electorate, Zyuganov proclaimed his willingness to enter into talks with the ultra-communists and patch up all differences, and also to continue consultations with the national patriotic organizations that failed to succeed in collecting 100,000 signatures to back them (first of all, Sergei Baburin's Russian Union of All the People, Viktor Aksyuchits's Russian Christian Democratic Movement and Mikhail Astafev's Constitutional Democratic Party/Party of People's Freedom) with the hope of co-ordinating action in single seat election districts.[5]

A number of extreme left organizations called for a boycott of the elections. It took the leadership of the CPRF nearly a week to conduct informational and explanatory work in

Table 3: Election results of the Communist Party of the Russian Federation

---

Number of signatures collected: 187,000 from 78 regions of Russia (one third of these are young people and over 50 per cent are not party members)

State Duma

Total number of seats: 65[8],[9]
Seats obtained on party lists: 32 (the party polled 12.35 per cent)
Seats obtained in single-member constituencies: 33[10]

This makes it the third largest party in the State Duma, after Russia's Choice and the LDPR. (Among those elected were Gennady Zyuganov, who is also co-chairman of the Front for National Liberation; Viktor Ilyukhin, also co-chairman of the Front for National Salvation and 'general procurator' of the Russian opposition; Valentin, editor-in-chief, *Sovetskaya Rossiya*; Gennady Seleznev, former editor-in-chief, *Pravda*; Yury Leonov, (former leader of the Marxist Workers' Party–Party of the Dictatorship of the Proletariat (MRP-PDP); Omar Begov, chairman of the Stalin society; Vitaly Sevastyanov, cosmonaut)

Head of Committees in State Duma:
— Security (Viktor Ilyukhin)
— Public Associations and Religious Organizations (Viktor Zorkaltsev)

Council of the Federation
Seats: 11; most well-known is Yury Lodkin, former head of administration (*gubernator*) of Bryansk *oblast*, elected in April 1993 but in late September sacked for opposing the presidential decree on constitutional reform; Aleksandr Epimakhov; Pavel Gorbunov; Leonid Ivanchenko; Lyudmila Ivanova; Sergei Korepanov; Leonid Korotkov; Vyacheslav Lyubimov; Lidia Nimaeva; Leonid Sablin; Pavel Shtein. Also Viktor Stepanov, chairman of the Supreme Soviet of Karelia declared his allegiance to the Union of Communists of Karelia which is part of the CPRF and the Communist Party CPSU (SKP–KPSS); there are also others who are officially non-party who were communist activists in the dissolved Russian Supreme Soviet: Aman Tuleev (member of the political council of the Front of National Salvation); Maiya Ettyryntyn; and also Egor Stroev, former first Party secretary and since April 1993 elected head of administration, Orlov *oblast*; and Aleksei Ponomarev, former Party first secretary, Belgorod *oblast*.

---

the regions and prepare for a party conference, at which, through the efforts of delegates from the provinces, it was decided to participate in the elections after all.[6]

In an interview, Gennady Zyuganov stated that the elections were illegal but that since 85 of the CPRF's 89 organizations insisted on participating in them the party had joined the struggle for seats. "We hope, through participating in the work of the future parliament, to try to restore legality, and at the same time to broaden the range of our allies and test the effectiveness of our party cells".[7]

As he further elaborated: "I once tried to explain to Gorbachev, albeit unsuccessfully, that any state machine has its own regulatory mechanism which functions irrespective of any political convictions, ideological direction, and so on that people might have. If you break the rudder, the braking system, the undercarriage, or the control mechanisms, you cannot help having an accident. Our party does not intend to share the CPSU's fate. It is only one of many parties. It is obliged to prove its advantages by persuasion. We have already published a whole series of documents setting out our programme, one of which proclaims, among other things, early elections to both branches of power provide a peaceful way out of the political crisis. We stand for broad state and democratic priorities.

The state should meet five great spiritual needs: the need to procreate, the need to work, the need to learn, the need to communicate and the need for beauty."

Programme. The party aims to adopt extraordinary measures to combat crime, speculation and corruption and stop further plunder of the country's natural, technological and intellectual resources. The party bases its activities on the spiritual culture of the peoples of Russia, on Marxist-Leninist scholarship, adapted to take into account the lessons of history and the present-day world. It rejects the total commercialization and Americanization of the spiritual sphere.

In economic policy the party favours the abandonment of shock therapy, the introduction of state regulation, taking emergency measures to combat crime and ensuring the social and economic rights of the working people, which are: free education and medical care, low cost housing and state run transport, and social security.[11]

It recognizes that the denationalization (destatization) of property is a necessary process, but that reverse collectivization cannot be conducted. The monopoly-based economy cannot be eliminated overnight without bringing down the entire system of production and management at the same time. Democracy cannot be established by shutting down opposition newspapers. There can be no talk of the nation's rebirth when its historic values and national shrines are being trampled on. "Today we communists have learned several important things: first, reforms must proceed on the basis of reality; the diversity of life is much richer than any theoretical constructs; second, the broken link between eras must be restored; third, Russia cannot exist without the idea of social justice and it is impossible to deceive the Russian conscience with any kind of vouchers. Russian national distinctiveness has existed, exists today and will continue to exist."[12]

It claims that the present poverty, the declining national birth rate and poor health and the loss of superpower status are the result of economic reforms which have only benefited a small group of "corrupt dealers and speculators" and the achievements of socialist rule, housing, health care and education, have been lost. The party would reintroduce social security, ban the selling of land and reintroduce planning alongside the market economy. Short-term goals are a guaranteed supply of food and medicines, the indexation of benefits and the prevention of mass unemployment.

It proposes that links all types of links and primarily economic links, be restored with former republics, and as a minimum with Ukraine, Belarus and Kazakhstan. The results of what it calls the "Belovezhe plot" (foundation of CIS) must be denounced as illegal and contrary to the nationwide referendum.

The right relationship must be found among the proportions of ownership; state ownership — the state should be primarily concerned with the sphere of power engineering, the defence complex, communications, transport, and so on; collective ownership; and private ownership, which is most applicable to the service sphere, municipal services, commerce, and so on.[13]

The party sees the "so-called" parliament as a cover for dictatorship and to legitimize its unconstitutional actions. The goal of the state-patriotic opposition is to prevent the dictatorship from being legalized. The party's "programme for restoring civil peace and legality and returning the country to a civilized course of development" involves, first of all, the restoration of the activity of the three branches of power on a legitimate basis. To that end, it is necessary, through the new parliament, to declare Yeltsin's decree on stage by stage constitutional reform invalid, to call to account the participants in the *coup d'état* (the President and his administration) and to schedule, together with the soviets, elections for a constitutional assembly that will form a transitional government of national accord.[14] "The representative power must be able to supervise the executive power. Otherwise we will not have any guarantee against a repetition of the bloody and dramatic October events. And the President in this case should also be under the supervision of the representative power. What is now set out in the constitution provides for no supervision at all. This means that the President, and, as a rule, his immediate entourage are in a position to manipulate the whole of the country's life."[15]

The party stresses that Russia should defend fellow Russians in the "near abroad". The party regards the question of dual citizenship as very real and legitimate, but states that violence should be avoided. The guarantee of Russia's security is the speediest conclusion of an interstate treaty on an economic, diplomatic and defence alliance of countries, the former republics of the USSR. Communists regard the current military reform as the "destruction of defence", particularly with regard to manpower acquisition. The social problems of the army and navy are being resolved extremely slowly. It believes that the residue principle for supplying the armed forces with everything they need is simply inadmissible.[16]

Notes

1 *Current Digest of the Post-Soviet Press*, Vol xlv, no. 46, December 15, 1993, from *Megapolis-Express*, Nov. 17, 1993.

2 Wendy Slater, 'Russian Communists Seek Salvation in Nationalist Alliance', *RFE/RL Research Report*, Vol. 2 no 13, 26 March 1993, pp. 8–13.

3 *FBIS-SOV-93-226*, 26 Nov. 1993, from *Izvestiya*, 19 Nov. 1993.

4 *Current Digest of the Post-Soviet Press*, Vol. xlv, no. 43 Nov. 24, 1993, from *Segodnya*, Oct. 28, 1993.

5 *Current Digest of the Post-Soviet Press*, Vol. xlv, no. 46, Dec. 15, 1993, from *Segodnya*, Nov. 13, 1993.

6 *Current Digest of the Post-Soviet Press*, Vol. xlv, no. 46, December 15, 1993, from *Megapolis-Express*, Nov. 17, 1993.

7 *Current Digest of the Post-Soviet Press*, Vol. xlv, no. 48, Dec. 29, 1993, from *Izvestiya*, Nov. 19, 1993.

8 62–67 according to Vladimir Pribylovsky and Grigory Tochkin, *Russkaya Mysl*, 6–12 Jan. 1994.

9 45 registered as a State Duma faction, *FBIS-SOV-94-010*, 14 Jan. 1994, from *Interfax*, 13 Jan. 1994.

10 10 deputies were elected as official CPRF candidates and another 20–25 deputies elected as independents but are members of the CPRF; Prybylovsky and Tochkin, *op. cit.*

11 *The Current Digest of the Post-Soviet Press*, Vol. xlv, no. 46, Dec. 15, 1993, from *Megapolis-Express*, Nov. 17, 1993.

12 *Current Digest of the Post-Soviet Press*, Vol. xlv, no. 48, Dec. 29, 1993, from *Izvestiya*, Nov. 19, 1993.

13 *FBIS-SOV-93-234*, 8 Dec. 1993, from Ostankino TV.

14 *Current Digest of the Post-Soviet Press*, Vol. xlv, no. 46, Dec. 15, 1993, from *Megapolis-Express*, Nov. 17, 1993.

15 *Current Digest of the Post-Soviet Press*, Vol. xlv, no. 48, December 29, 1993, from *Izvestiya*, Nov. 19, 1993.

16 *FBIS-SOV-93-230*, 2 Dec. 1993, from *Krasnaya Zvezda*, 2 Dec. 1993.

Democratic Party of Russia (DPR)
Demokraticheskaya Partiya Rossii

Foundation. May 26–27, 1990.

Leadership. Nikolai Travkin (ch.); Valery Khomyakov (ch. of Board); Evgeny Malkin (sec.); Ilya Roitman (ideology sec.).

Membership. 40,000 (1993).

History. The Democratic Party of Russia (DPR), led by Nikolai Travkin, the charismatic construction engineer, was set up in 1990 and was initially part of the broader Democratic Russia movement. But unlike the liberal-oriented Democratic Russia, Travkin's party spoke out against the break-up of the Soviet Union, and this led to the departure of Travkin's party from the movement in 1991. Travkin's coalition with the Christian Democrats and Kadets (Constitutional Democrats) lasted only a few months. The DPR resisted the latter's move to the far right. In 1992 Travkin's party became a co-founder of Civic Union (*see* above). The DPR is said to have the strongest regional network of all current parties (with the exception of the Communist Party of the Russian Federation — CPRF). It has experienced several internal splits and lost a number of prominent members who have criticized Travkin's authoritarian leadership, but the fact that it has nevertheless survived as a political force means that it may have the potential to play a stronger role — for example in future elections.[1]

The idea of setting up a large democratic party that would challenge the authority of the CPSU, first emerged in December 1989 among leaders of the radical wing of the Leningrad People's Front, including Marina Sale and Ilya Konstantinov. After the elections of 1990 (to the Russian Congress of People's Deputies and regional and local soviets) the project received the support of the leadership of the Moscow Association of Voters (Vera Krieger and Lev Ponomarev, members of its co-ordinating council), part of the CPSU Democratic Platform (Igor Chubais, Nikolai Travkin, Gennady Burbulis and Georgy Khatsenkov), and part of the Interregional Group of Deputies Group (Arkady Murashev). World chess champion Gary Kasparov also supported the project. (The organizing conference, chaired by Nikolai Travkin, took place between April 21 and May 3, 1990. On May 12–13, 1990, RSFSR People's Deputy Marina Sale and Ilya Konstantinov, and Mikhail Tolstoi organized a preparatory conference for the Leningrad branch of the DPR.)

The DPR founding conference, held in Moscow on May 26–27, 1990, was attended by delegates from 99 cities and 85 regions of the RSFSR. The party declared as its primary aim, the "creation of Russian statehood in the form of a democratic Republic". Its programme called for the "creation of a multi-party law-governed state with the separation of legislative, executive and judicial power", and decentralization of the state. The economic section called for the destatification and demonopolization of the economy, market relations and equal opportunities and the economic independence of the worker.[2]

At this early state, however, the party broke up into quarrelling groups, following the general trend to division among most of the democratic formations of the *perestroika* period. Nikolai Travkin intended from the start to create a centralized, disciplined party, capable of beating the CPSU, and led by a chairman. But the Leningrad section (led by Marina Sale) of the DPR opposed Travkin's centralization, and favoured a number of co-chairpersons as it feared the emergence of a popular dictatorship in the person of Travkin. The Leningrad section left the newly created DPR party and established a separate Free Democratic Party of Russia led by Marina Sale and Ilya Konstantinov. Travkin managed to impose his single chairmanship with the support of the majority of the delegates. Arkady Murashev and Gary Kasparov decided to stay in the party, but formed a "free democratic faction".

During 1990, the DPR extended its network throughout the Russian Federation. Several branches were created and members of local organizations joined the party (for example, members of the Kazan Initiative Centre of the Tatar People's Front, activists from the Stavropol People's Front, and a section of the Yaroslavl People's Front).

On Dec. 1–2, 1990, the First Congress of the DPR convened in Moscow. It adopted a party charter, a political programme that had been approved at the founding conference, and elected Travkin as chairman. The congress also rejected the formation of ethnic/national factions within the DPR, and those members who refused to accept this were expelled from the party. The Free Democratic faction had virtually ceased to exist by the time of the congress, and was succeeded by the Liberal faction, led by Arkady Murashev. (In October 1990, the Democratic Russia movement held its founding congress. It was attended by regional organizations of the DPR and in several regions the organizations of the DPR formed the core of Democratic Russia's local branches. Originally, however, Travkin was strongly critical of the DR, but in January 1991, he revised his position and the DPR joined Democratic Russia. Democratic Russia was being organized among others by Murashev, board member of the DPR, and Travkin, Gasparov and Khomyakov finally became members of the movement's council of representatives.)

By its Second Congress in April 1991, dominated by Nikolai Travkin, the DPR was the largest party in Russia, apart from the Communist Party of the RSFSR, claiming 50,000 members. At the Congress, held in Moscow on April 26–28, 1991, the party programme was approved and the DPR joined the Russian Christian Democratic Movement (RCDM) and the Constitutional Democratic Party–Party of People's Freedom (CDP-PPF) and created the People's Accord bloc. Opposed to Democratic Russia, the People's Accord bloc rejected the disintegration of the Soviet Union and advocated the creation of a united democratic state to replace the USSR. In the all-Union referendum of March 17, 1991, it supported the preservation of a "renewed Union". Disagreements over party programmes forced Murashev and Kasparov to withdraw from the party.

Opposed to the leadership of Democratic Russia, the DPR from the very beginning spoke out against the policies of the Georgian President Zviad Gamsakhurdia in the South Ossetian conflict, supported the Transdniester republic in Moldova against Chisinau (Moldova) and sharply criticized the "discriminatory" nationality laws in Latvia and Estonia. In June 1991 Travkin attempted, together with Stanislav Shatalin, Aleksei Repnikov, A. Krichevsky, Nikolai Bogaenko (the last three were members of the Republican Party of the Russian Federation) and leaders of democratic parties in Central Asia to set up a Union-wide democratic party — the United Democratic Party — but the founding congress never took place due to the attempted August 1991 coup. The basic aim of new party, an interrepublican party on a confederate state basis, was to participate in presidential and parliamentary elections. The group supported the Novo–Ogarevo project for a Union Treaty and advocated the preservation of a single federal state.

Together with the RCDM and the CDP–PPF, Nikolai Travkin's DPR eventually withdrew from Democratic Russia in November 1991 due to disagreements regarding the disintegration of the USSR. Democratic Russia opposed the Union Treaty and this was interpreted as a policy favouring the disintegration of the USSR.

At the Third Congress of the DPR, on Dec. 7–8, 1991, the withdrawal of the party from Democratic Russia was confirmed. However, some of the regional organizations of the DPR (especially those that occupied a key position in the local organizations of Democratic Russia) opposed this decision. The Novosibirsk organization of the DPR separated from the party and created the Independent Democratic Party. (The St Petersburg Organization of the DPR revived the liberal fraction of the party.)

By early 1992, Travkin's allies in the People's Accord (RCDM and CDP–PPF) invited his party to participate in a congress of civic (*grazhdansky*) and patriotic forces of Russia, where the Russian People's Assembly was created. The DPR did not accept this invitation after it discovered the possible attendance of "red" and "brown" groups (neo-communists and national-patriots). The creation of the Russian All-People's Union signified the move of the RCDM and the CDP–PPF to the national-patriotic camp, which meant that the previous People's Accord alliance was no longer viable. Travkin began looking for new allies, those who would support the "forces of a democratic multi-ethnic state". On March 15, 1992, the DPR formed an alliance with Aleksandr Rutskoi's People's Party of Free Russia (PPFR) and on June 21, 1992, together with Arkady Volsky's Renewal Union — an industrial lobby founded in May 1992 — the three groups formed a coalition bloc, named Civic Union. It opposed President Boris Yeltsin's economic policies and the dissolution of parliament and called for the stabilization of Russia's economy and the preservation of its territorial integrity. They were joined by many other organizations of a centrist orientation — i.e. between Egor Gaidar's radicals and the communist-patriotic opposition; the All-Russian Renewal Union, the Smena parliamentary faction, and the Russian Youth Union, formerly the Komsomol.

On Dec. 18, 1992, the Fourth Congress of the DPR took place and amendments to the party charter were approved. On Aug. 24, 1993, the press service of the Democratic Party of Russia announced the party's withdrawal from Civic Union in connection with a sharp disagreement over Vice-President Aleksandr Rutskoi's political stance. The Smolensk branch of the party had protested officially about a speech by Rutskoi during the latter's visit to Smolensk on Aug. 10–11, calling it the "cheapest populism in the spirit of the Natioal Salvation Front". The DPR had decided to contest the elections independently.[3]

On Oct. 15, 1993, the Democratic Party of Russia, which had split from Civic Union, held its Fifth Congress in Moscow. In one afternoon, about 170 delegates observed the pre-election formalities — they confirmed the party's Federation-wide list for the elections to the State Duma and a programme, a pre-election platform. The DPR had already turned into an eclectic party. Its party list proved to be eclectic too: Travkin offered places to Govorukhin and former ministers Titkin and Nikolai Fedorov.[4]

Delivering the main report, party leader Nikolai Travkin stated that the DPR's political goals coincided with the goals proclaimed by Russia's Choice; however, the DPR could not adopt a revolutionary path to attain those goals but would take an evolutionary path. At the same time, Travkin believed, the main yardstick for the effectiveness of the policy being pursued should be the people's standard of living. "There is no democracy on an empty stomach. A hungry person is an angry person. If the policy pursued by the present government continues, a very angry society awaits us," he emphasized.[5] He continued: "the Democratic Party of Russia is working for the creation of strong democratic power in Russia, of a market-oriented economy and civic society which would guarantee security, the observance of human rights and freedoms, law and order."[6] Travkin described DPR members as "healthy pragmatists", for whom the main criterion is the "people's quality

Table 4: Election results of the Democratic Party of Russia

The party collected a total of 109,000 signatures.

State Duma:
Total number of seats: 21
Seats obtained on party list: 14 (these included the leaders of local branches of the party in, for example, Ekaterinburg (German Karelin), Primorsky *krai* (Yury Yakovlev), Nizhny Novgorod (Irina Zubkevich, the only women elected) and Samara (Aleksei Leushkin).
Seats obtained in single-member constituencies: 7 (in April 1994 down to 6)

State Duma faction: 15 members

State Duma Committees headed by the DPR:
— Economic Policy: Sergei Glazev, formerly Russian Minister of Foreign Economic Relations
— International Affairs: Oleg Bogomolev is deputy chairman

Council of the Federation
Seats:

Members in government
— Nikolai Travkin was appointed minister without portfolio in May 1994

of life, not the degree of democratization," since "there is no democracy on an empty stomach."[7]

Since regional branches of the DPR were not as subordinate as the leader would have liked (some still remained part of the local branch of Democratic Russia) measures were taken at the DPR's Sixth Congress on Feb. 19–20, 1994, to correct this by allowing the party's central office to dissolve regional branches for breaking party rules or acting in a manner detrimental to the party.[8] However the formation of alliances among anti-communist parties at local level may prove very attractive to local activists and they may ignore the wishes of the centre. Travkin continues to pursue his goal of a disciplined political party.

Programme. On the constitution the DPR spoke out against President Boris Yeltsin's Basic Law (constitution). Its members urged the electorate to vote against the draft Constitution of the Russian Federation. The party maintains that "Yeltsin's Constitution is bloody." It establishes a presidential dictatorship. In Travkin's view, it is necessary to discuss each of the Constitution's constituent parts.

At a press conference on Oct. 8, 1993 Travkin stated: "We are at present living under the system of autocratic power and are still far away from honest democratic elections. But the Democratic Party of Russia will nevertheless be taking part in these elections."[9] Travkin challenged President Yeltsin's claim that any rejection or criticism of the constitution was tantamount to a refusal to contest the elections, saying that he was running for a seat in a legislative body, and the legitimacy of his claims would be determined by the number of votes cast for his party. He talked about a "revised democratic campaign and revised *glasnost*", because contestants in the elections were told not to criticize each other; speakers were told not to criticize the authorities; and not to criticize the constitution.[10]

The text of the party's pre-election platform called the current economic reforms "foreign" and "imposed". The platform proclaimed "healthy down-to-earth actions, priority for the agricultural sector through sensible state financing of its needs, the provision of incentives for the self-employment of citizens in economic endeavours, through an ad hoc registration procedure", and the "need to reform the federal structure while ensuring the country's integrity."[11] In the economic sphere, top priority should be given to the agricultural sector by the state giving it reasonable financial support and there should be favourable taxation, credit and legal conditions for entrepreneurs producing consumer goods.[12] Agriculture should receive financial support from the state, credit incentives and a fair exchange between the agricultural sector and industry.[13]

Travkin, at a press conference on Oct. 8, 1993, said he would give priority in the economy to small-scale privatization, development of a system of tax allowances and agricultural reforms.[14]

Travkin stated that his party relied on people realizing the necessity of building a civic society and believing that the price of the reforms of President Boris Yeltsin and Egor Gaidar was too high for the country. He also said his party also supports reform, but disagrees with the government policy of liberal radicalism and the sequence of steps taken in the name of reform.[15]

The DPR advocates a market economy in which consumers' rights and interests and freedom of competition would be protected and the energy of entrepreneurs channelled primarily into the development of production. In this regard the DPR acknowledges the need for state intervention in the economy "in addition to the interplay of market forces". To overcome the structural crisis, the DPR proposes encouraging activity in areas of future economic growth, developing competitive sectors and production units, and implementing conversion projects aimed at assimilating new high-technology output for civilian purposes. Enterprises' costs incurred in the development of production should be exempt from taxation.

The DPR intended to promote the adoption of a package of new laws to guarantee the observance of the principle of fair competition and the protection of consumers' rights and the economic rights and freedoms of citizens and to endow local organs of power with sufficient powers for the development of the regional production and social infrastructure.

On fiscal policy and budgetary policy Travkin consistently "campaigned for each *raion* or city to have the right to its own legitimate internal reserves. . . . Or take extra budgetary funds. . . . My proposal is this, make extra budgetary funds free from taxation. Give us the right to introduce local taxes. . . . [But] the authorities embarked first of all on the privatization of large-scale industry. However, I think, that large-scale industry should have waited until we had sorted out the countryside."[15]

On agrarian policy the DPR has always advocated the introduction of private land ownership. "We consider the President's latest edict on land a definite step forward. We do however realize that the mechanical introduction of private ownership will by no means solve the problem of increasing productivity in agriculture. Additional measures are needed. In particular, reasonable state financial support on the principle of money from the budget is not to be shared by everyone equally, it will only go to those working efficiently; credit incentives for the reformation of state and collective farms and joint-stock companies into smaller structures based on departments, private farms, construction bases, and individual peasant farms, which turn the peasant into the real master of the land; equal support from the state for the countryside and cities in the social sphere."[16]

"We are unambiguously for reforms. Yes all (forms of ownership) have the right to exist — collective farms, joint stock companies which have appeared from the collective farm, and the private farm; but the state must assign the priorities here. I would assign the priorities this way so that the last ruble should not go to all equally, but to the one that works effectively. Second, the state pursues a protectionist policy towards the countryside (it imports expensive goods from the West, potatoes from Poland and does not favour exports or consumption of domestic products)."[17]

The DPR believes that peasants should be granted extensive opportunities to choose for themselves the forms of organization of their own production activity based on different types of ownership. In Travkin's opinion, many contentious issues remain which need urgent solution. The *kolkhozes* and *sovkhozes* have been transformed into joint-stock companies. Although each shareholder has the right to take his share, the board can keep a tight rein on it because it is in the board's power how to assess the value of that share. It is necessary to elaborate a mechanism whereby the shareholder can leave the farm. He is convinced that the centre of gravity of reform should be switched to the local self-management level.[18]

The basis for social policy is to increase the purchasing power of a broad spectrum of the population and a network of boards of guardians [*popichitelsky sovet*] are to provide social support for the population.[19] The DPR's position in social policy is based not only on who should be helped but also on where to find the resources. They propose the following measures: Firstly, selective social support through the creation of a network of boards of guardians in village, settlement, and *raion* administrations. Tax exemptions for sums received by boards of guardians. Secondly, tax exemption for resources from non-budgetary funds of local authorities which are channelled into solving social questions. Thirdly, the development of a municipal ownership sector as a source of meeting a territory's social expenditure. Fourthly, local authorities should be given the right to introduce socially targeted local taxes and there should be compulsory public accountability to the population for the use of these resources. Fifthly, a state social protection programme for people working in education, culture, and health care, and finally, restraining housing prices in real terms through market mechanisms, above all by restricting the use of housing for speculative transactions and introducing a tax on the purchase of apartments by legal entities. "Strategically we are proposing a profound reform of the entire social welfare system. The present system, based on the redistribution of the state's budget's current income according to the residuary principle, not only fails to guarantee a normal level of social welfare but also generates inflation, as well as saddling production with additional taxes. What is needed is a very rapid transition to a market democratic social welfare system based on stimulating citizens' personal savings for the purposes of social insurance and their effective utilization in funds: pension, medical insurance, and social protection funds. Of course, the state must guarantee every citizen a minimum standard of social welfare, but everyone must also have the opportunity automatically to choose the forms and methods of his pension and medical provisions, and to determine the amount he will put by from his current income for these purposes."

Creating a system of private pensions and medical insurance funds which is protected against the risk of incompetent administration will make it possible to ensure an increase in the accumulation ratio in the national income and will facilitate the formation of a capital market, an increase in investment activity, a reduction in the taxation level for current economic activity, and a reduction in budget expenditure. Unconditional priority must be given to selective support for the most needy strata of the population, primarily children, single mothers, families with several children, and temporarily unemployed people who have been dismissed because of a reduction in production or a change in production specialization. Expenditure on education and professional training for young people must be sharply increased. Pensioners and invalids must be guaranteed a decent standard of living.[20]

During 1991, the DPR opposed the disintegration of the Soviet Union and advocated the creation of a united democratic state to replace it. It favoured the Novo-Ogarevo process (the negotiation of a Union Treaty by Presidents Mikhail Gorbachev, Boris Yeltsin and the heads of eight other republics at Novo-Ogarevo, Gorbachev's summer dacha near Moscow) and during the All-Union referendum of March 17, 1991, supported the preservation of a "renewed union". The DPR also believed that the autonomous republics and regions of the Russian Federation should not be allowed to leave its jurisdiction. Disagreements over these issues finally led to the withdrawal of the DPR from Democratic Russia in November 1991.[21]

In June 1991 Travkin, together with Stanislav Shatalin, Aleksei Repnikov, A. Krichevsky, Nikolai Bogaenko, and the leaders of democratic parties in Central Asia to set up a Union-wide democratic party — the United Democratic Party — but the founding congress never took place. The basic aim of the new formation — and inter-republican party on a confederate state basis — was to prepare for the presidential and parliamentary elections. The group supported the draft Novo-Ogarevo Union Treaty and advocated the preservation of a single federal state.

After the attempted August 1991 coup, Travkin criticized president Yeltsin's moves aimed at the disintegration of the Soviet Union. An opponent of the CIS, Travkin insisted on the overriding importance of preserving a strong Russian state and maintaining close institutional links between the former Soviet republics.[22] In his view, the CIS, created solely to suit Ukraine, would increase the centrifugal tendencies among Russia's autonomous formations and regions and lead to the final break-up of Russia itself.[23] During 1992 the DPR supported the Transdniester republic in Moldova and sharply criticized the "discriminatory" nationality laws of Latvia and Estonia. Travkin, at a press conference on Oct. 8, 1993, stated that national interests should form the basis of foreign policy, which in his opinion, would mean, *inter alia*, that Russia "should no longer rely on foreign aid and move towards partnership-type relations with the USA and the G7 countries."[24]

The text of the pre-election platform proclaims the need to reform the federal structure while ensuring the country's integrity. Addressing the charge that the DPR is a party of statists, Nikolai Travkin underlined that the division of power between the tsar and the regional boyars is the path to confederation.[25]

In Nikolai Federov's view, because the President has long been persuaded to abandon the constitution and the formal bounds of law, since they have fallen behind the times, lawlessness has soared. (There has been no mechanism to fight crime.) "And this situation, the problem of the scale of crime, has become extremely acute after the events of Oct. 3–4, 1993. Having abandoned the formal bounds of the law we have thus entered an area outside the law and the constitution, where law is replaced by the fist, by force, by the stick, by a corporal, a master, a tsar . . . The net of law in Russia always caught small fish and let large fish escape. Criminological analysis shows that crime on such scale can only exist if there is a state infrastructure that supports it along the entire line of the state system, the infrastructure that informs and backs the criminal underworld. Otherwise crime cannot exist. This means we have to look closely at who is doing what, along the entire line of presidential and government authority, in the centre, in the provinces, and in the republics of the Russian Federation. But nothing has changed in the fight against crime since the Supreme Soviet was disbanded."

"Why has it not changed? . . . because there is no political will. . . . The Interior Ministry and the minister himself seem to believe that their main task is to inform society about the scale of crime and frighten everyone." The DPR proposes instead to change the law to protect witnesses from persecution by criminals by introducing anonymity during the investigation and in court. It also proposes to enhance the role of the street policeman.

Travkin and Fedorov say that the money spent on fighting crime and the money that state or non-state enterprises are prepared to spend on this, has to be exempt from taxes. Travkin believes that local bodies must retain taxes to organize the fight against crime. If they manage to find some extra money outside the budget for this purpose, this money should be exempt from taxation. Fedorov states that the draft constitution envisages an increase in the number of militia generals, rather than enhancing the role of the local militia. In contrast, the DPR puts the emphasis on an effective professional militia and responsibility on local authorities equipped with necessary powers and incentives.

Fedorov maintains that if you want to fight crime, the main principle is inevitability of punishment, and that means supremacy of the law and the judiciary. But the draft constitution says the President, not the independent judiciary, is the guarantor of the constitution and of the rights of the individuals. The DPR also proposes changing economic policy in order to prevent crime from flourishing. Fedorov believes that Western loans generate bureaucracy and corruption and set a bad example for the population.

The DPR proposes that the local bodies of power should take part in the creation of technical back-up for the militia, in the *raions* and towns. There is an opportunity also for the entrepreneurial structures that today are forced to appeal to racketeers for protection. to take part in the creation of this back-up.

Notes

1 *RFE/RL Research Report*, Vol. 2, no. 20, May 14, 1993.
2 Geoffrey A. Hosking, Jonathan Aves and Peter J. S. Duncan, *The Road to Post Communism. Independent Political Movements in the Soviet Union 1985–1991* (London, Pinter 1992), p. 100.
3 *FBIS-SOV-93-197*, 14 Oct. 1993, from *Izvestiya*, 14 Oct. 1993.
4 *Current Digest of the Post-Soviet Press*, Vol. xlv, no. 42, Nov. 17, 1993, from *Metropolis-Express*, no. 42, 27 Oct. 1993.
5 *Current Digest of the Post-Soviet Press*, Vol. xlv, no. 42, Nov. 17, 1993, from *Segodnya*, 16 Oct. 1993.
6 *FBIS-SOV-93-199*, 18 Oct. 1993, from *ITAR-TASS*, 15 Oct. 1993.
7 Ibid.
8 *Kommersant Daily*, Feb. 22, 1994.
9 SWB SU, 16 Oct. 1993, p. B/3.
10 *FBIS-SOV-93-228*, 30 Nov. 1993, from *Interfax*, 29 Nov. 1993.
11 *Current Digest of the Post-Soviet Press*, Vol xlv, no. 42, November 17, 1993, from *Segodnya*, 16 October 1993.
12 SWB SU, 19 Oct. 1993, p. B/2.
13 *FBIS-SOV-93-199*, 18 Oct. 1993, from *ITAR-TASS*, 15 oct. 1993.

14 SWB SU, 16 Oct. 1993, p. B/3.
15 *FBIS-SOV-93–226*, 26 Nov. 1993, from *Izvestiya*, 24 Nov. 1993.
16 *FBIS-SOV-93-223*, 22 Nov. 1993, from *Rossiiskie Vesti*, 17 Nov. 1993.
17 *FBIS-SOV-93-226*, 26 Nov. 1993, from *Izvestiya*, 24 Nov. 1993.
18 Ibid.
19 The electoral platform is in SWB SU, 19 Oct. 1993, p. B/2; *FBIS-SOV-93-223*, 22 Nov. 1993, from *Rossiiskie Vesti*, 17 Nov. 1993.
20 *FBIS-SOV-93-223*, 22 Nov. 1993, from *Rossiiskie Vesti*, 17 Nov. 1993.
21 Democratic Russia regarded the disintegration of the Soviet Union as inevitable and opposed any attempt to preserve it by force. Vladimir Pribylovsky, *Slovar novykh politicheskikh partii I organizatsii Rossii*, Panorama, Moscow, December 1992.
22 Vera Tolz and Elizabeth Teague, 'Russian Intellecutals Adjust to Loss of Empire', *RFE/RF Research Report*, Vol. 1 no. 8, 21 Feb. 1992, p. 5.
23 *Izvestiya*, 19 Dec. 1991.
24 SWB SU, 16 Oct. 1993, p. B/3.
25 *Segognya*, 16 Oct. 1993.

Dignity and Charity Bloc (DCB)
Blok Dostoinstvo I Miloserdie

Leadership. Konstantin V. Frolov (co-ch., vice-pres. of the Russian Academy of Sciences); Aleksandr Lomakin, co.-ch.).

History. The bloc was founded by the All-Russia Organization of War, Labour, Armed Forces and Law-Enforcement Organ Veterans, the All-Russia Invalids Society, and the Chernobyl Union of Russia. "Behind these organizations are more than 30 million Russian citizens — the most vulnerable and unprotected socially. It will be strange if these people do not have people in parliament to represent their interests."[1]

Programme. On the proposed constitution, the bloc found some aspects are objectionable; for example, the first draft spoke clearly of provision of pensions, stating that pensions should be above subsistence level. The second draft says blandly that pensions will be fixed by law and nothing more. The constitution has to work for everyone.[3] The movement's social demands are not reflected in the draft. There has been too little time given for discussion.[4]

On cultural policy the movement states that "Only recently we took rightful pride in our science, education and enlightenment, and the world treated us with the greatest respect. Now, alas, we are losing much ground. Suffice it to say that the share of spending on scientific research in the expenditure part of the budget has fallen by almost one third this year. The average monthly wage in science stands at half the wage in industry. A number of institutions and scientific centres are in a critical state. This is precisely why, in enshrining in our election platform the need to renounce the residual principle for funding the social sphere, we gave a special mention to science and education. When defining the priorities here, it is necessary to give preference to investment in people, not iron."[5]

On economic policy "We are convinced that the purchase and sale of land can only be carried out by taking local conditions, opportunities and traditions into account. We need to prepare and adopt a new law on the basic principles of land use and land ownership in Russia.[6]

"Our association is in favour of reforms but what kind – that is the question. We advocate reforms for people, not at their expense. This is the essence of our election platform . . . its contents may be defined as follows: There is a need to halt a further slump in production

Table 5:   Election results of the Dignity and Charity Bloc

Before registration the bloc collected 130,000 signatures

State Duma
Seats obtained on party lists: none (failed to overcome 5 per cent barrier)
Seats obtained in single member constituencies: 3, including Aleksandr Zhukov with the support of Russia's Choice[2]

State Duma Committees headed by DCB: none

Council of the Federation
Seats: none

---

and end the slide towards hyperinflation which casts more and more new masses of people into the abyss of poverty and degrades human dignity. A kind of limit has already been reached here and cannot be crossed.

The elaboration of a credit and tax system which will ensure that all kinds of production activity are encouraged must be one priority measure. There is no such mechanism at present . . . By last year 500 veteran co-operatives had been set up in Russia but now 100 of them have already collapsed. Why? Not only because they did not receive the necessary support with premises and materials at the first stage. Fourteen kinds of taxes were levied on them! Can you imagine? This prevented a good initiative from getting off the ground. People wishing to provide themselves with worthy, honest labour found themselves deprived of that opportunity.[7]

The question of compensation for Savings Bank deposits embezzled from the population, particularly from people of the older generation. This is, after all, a debt of the state. Maybe it is worth suggesting adopting, without delay, a law on the status of veterans and on the veterans' movement, for which there has long been a need, and a law on intellectual property — in order to protect the interests of every author of a scientific or artistic work."[8]

The movement will try to ensure that the government presents society with a clear and universally comprehensible state social programme that guarantees Russian citizens a decent standard of living and social stability at all stages of the reforms. Any measures that have the potential to cause a fall in the population's living standards must be preceded by social protection measures. The movement favours radical reform of the provision of pensions system based on realistic expenditure by different groups of the population.[9] "We care about the misfortunes of all of society, which finds itself in a very grave state, but you will agree that old people, invalids and victims of ecological disasters are the most deprived. The impoverishment of the majority of the people in our country, who have crossed the line into poverty, is well known but pensioners and invalids undoubtedly have the emptiest pockets. Or take unemployment which is advancing upon us increasingly irreversibly. Who, primarily, is being cut back? Once gain it is those who are older and weaker. Just two years ago, 30 per cent of pensioners were working. Under [Soviet] Union law 5 per cent of jobs were firmly assigned to pensioners. This is now being consigned to oblivion. Among third category invalids, capable and desirous of working, just one in six now has this opportunity. The problem of medicines, whose prices have become simply fantastic, is shortening human life. Many people are finding funerals simply beyond their reach."[10]

"Unfortunately, our society is now divided up into a handful of super-rich people and a mass of people who can barely make ends meet. It is a great pity that the latter include people with higher education: engineers, physicians, teachers and many others. I believe it would be fair if the most super-rich shared part of their super-income with the poor. I am not talking of handouts. They degrade people's dignity. True charity is quite different. In our view the state's entire social policy must serve it."[11]

Notes

1 *FBIS-SOV-93-223*, 22 Nov. 1993, from *Pravda,* 19 Nov. 1993.
2 2 according to Vladimir Pribylovsky and Grigory Tochkin, *Russkaya mysl,* 12 Jan. 1994.
3 *FBIS-SOV-93-236*, 10 Dec. 1993, from Ostankino TV, 9 Dec. 1993.
4 *FBIS-SOV-93-227*, 29 Nov. 1993, from *Segodnya,* 26 Nov. 1993.
5 *FBIS-SOV-93220*, 17 Nov. 1993, from *Rossiiskie Vesti,* 16 Nov. 1993.
6 Ibid.
7 *FBIS-SOV-93-223*, 22 Nov. 1993, from *Pravda,* 19 Nov. 1993.
8 Ibid.
9 *FBIS-SOV-93220*, 17 Nov. 1993, from *Rossiiskie Vesti,* 16 Nov. 1993.
10 *FBIS-SOV-93-223*, 22 Nov. 1993, from *Pravda,* 19 Nov. 1993.
11 Ibid.

Liberal Democratic Party of Russia (LDPR)
Liberalno-Demokraticheskaya Partiya Rossii

Foundation. 1989.

Leadership. Vladimir Zhirinovsky (ch.); Akhmed Khalitov (dep. ch.); Aleksei Mitrofanov; Anatoly Kashpirovsky; Mikhail Lemeshev.

Membership. The party has 90 primary organizations and about 100,000 members in Russia and the CIS (Dec. 1993).

History. The party was founded by Vladimir Bogachev after leaving the Democratic Party of Lev Ubozhko and was originally called the Liberal Democratic Party of Russia. Vladimir Zhirinovsky joined Bogachev in 1989. The former had drafted a programme for the Social Democratic Party of Russia. In December 1989 the programme was renamed the programme of the LDPR. At the constituent congress, on March 31, 1990, the Bogachev–Zhirinovsky group consisting of 13 persons began to call themselves the Liberal Democratic Party of the Soviet Union (LDPSS). The congress adopted the party programme and statute and Zhirinovsky was elected chairman and Bogachev chief co-ordinator. It was claimed that the LDPSS had over 3,000 members in 31 regions of the country and was the first opposition party in the USSR.

On June 8, 1990, the LDPSS was one of the initiators of the establishment of a centrist bloc of parties and movements. On Oct. 6, 1990, while Zhirinovsky was attending the Congress of the Liberal International in Helsinki, some members of the Central Committee, headed by Bogachev and K. Krivonos convened an extraordinary Congress, expelling Zhirinovsky for "pro-communist activities" and renamed the party, the Liberal Democratic Party. Zhirinovsky's riposte was to convene an all-Union conference with the rights of a

Congress on Oct. 20, 1990. The Congress expelled the opposition, amended the statute, expanded the Central Committee and established a new ruling body, a five-person Supreme Council. Zhirinovsky was elected party chairman.

During December 1990 and January 1991 Zhirinovsky repeatedly demanded the introduction of a state of emergency and the temporary dissolution of all political parties. On Feb. 27, 1991, the LDPSS participated in the conference "for a great, united Russia", organized by the Communist Party of the RSFSR.

At the Second LDPSS Congress, on April 13–14, 1991, Zhirinovsky was nominated as a candidate for the Russian presidency. The fourth Russian Congress of People's Deputies accepted his nomination. On the eve of the election the party had about 200 members. Zhirinovsky surprised many by obtaining about 8 per cent or 6 million votes. After the election party branches were set up in many Russian cities.

On April 12, 1992, the LDPSS was registered by the USSR Ministry of Justice, with only 146 party members being listed, although by Soviet law an all-Union party required at least 5,000 members to be registered. The third LDPSS Congress took place in Moscow on April 18–19, 1992, with Zhirinovsky re-elected party chairman and with Akhmed Khalitov, a *kolkhoznik*, as his deputy. On Aug. 10, 1992, the USSR Ministry of Justice cancelled the registration of the LDPSS claiming that it had been based on "crude violations of the law and on falsified documents". On Aug. 19, 1991, during the attempted coup, Zhirinovsky delivered a speech from the balcony of the Moskva Hotel, on Manezh Square, in support of the aims of the Extraordinary Committee.

In October 1991 Zhirinovsky submitted documents to the Russian Ministry of Justice applying for registration of the party as the Liberal Democratic Party. On Jan. 16–17, 1993, a conference of the LDPR amended the statutes of the party and nominated Zhirinovsky for election as mayor of Moscow. In February 1993 Zhirinovsky addressed military officers at an officers meeting and participated in events organized by the Communist Party of the Russian Federation.

In the December 1993 parliamentary elections the LDPR scored a dramatic success, securing 22.79 per cent of the vote and gaining the second largest number of deputies in the new State Duma. Although the LDPR won the highest percentage of votes according to party lists, Russia's Choice obtained more seats in the single-member constituencies, thus allowing it to emerge as the party with the largest number of deputies (see Table 6).

The shock result for the LDPR raised concerns both inside and outside Russia. However, as Egar Gaidar stated, "the overwhelming proportion of people today did not vote for fascism. The overwhelming proportion of people were simply expressing discontent, disillusionment, scepticism, readiness to believe any promises to resolve quickly the problems".[4] Nikolai Travkin on the other hand called the preliminary election results a "political disaster which has struck Russia", claiming that the true reason for the LDPR's success was the people's scepticism turning into anger. People voted for Zhirinovsky out of spite following the failures of the current economic policies: "In the President's place I would choose one of the regions where Zhirinovsky had a convincing victory to appoint him governor. In three weeks, not only buses, but also sewer facilities would be at a standstill there ... The mistake Russia's Choice and other centrist blocs, including the DPR, made was that they underestimated Zhirinovsky's party".[5]

Otto Latsis, an economist and former Party journalist, now a highly regarded *Izvestiya* commentator, was alarmed by the West's reaction to the LDPR's success. "The danger in overestimating Zhirinovsky lies in setting off a chain reaction. I dread to think that NATO

Table 6: Election results of the Liberal Democratic Party

The LDPR was the first to collect signatures for the election and put up a party list of 100 candidates. It collected 153,000 signatures in total.

State Duma

Total number of seats: 70[1,2]

Seats obtained on party lists: 59

Seats obtained in single-member constituencies: 11[3]

State Duma Committees headed by the LDPR

— Labour and Social Support (Sergei Kalashnikov)
— Ecology (Mikhail Lemeshev)
— Industry, Construction, Transport and Power (Vladimir Gusev)
— Natural Resources and the Utilization of Nature (Nikolai Astafev)
— Geopolitics (Vladimir Zhirinovsky)

might welcome neighbouring countries like Poland, the Czech Republic and the Baltic republics into the club. The militants here would immediately cry: 'You see the West is still our rival'. That would not only prove fatal to reaching further arms reductions agreements but would also kill off Yeltsin's reform policy. That nearly 23 per cent of the vote went to a man who intends to drop atomic bombs on Germany, if necessary, propagates the idea of a Greater Russia and commands considerable support within the army, may well give cause for more than raised eyebrows in the West. It is a mistake to compare the present situation in Russia with Germany in the 1930s. Those who regard Zhirinovsky as a new Hitler are on the wrong track. Under such circumstances, I would even go so far as to say that the Russian population is less nationalistic than the US population . . . According to my estimates, a maximum of 8 per cent of the electorate can be considered hard core militant Zhirinovsky supporters. The rest voted for the LDPR as a protest."

Vitaly Churkin, Russian Deputy Foreign Minister, and special envoy on Yugoslav affairs, in an interview, stated that he regards Zhirinovsky's electoral success as a "fairly serious signal, one that should be taken into consideration by Russian democrats and by foreign countries, that highly complex processes are taking place in Russia, that the continuing struggle for democracy is taking place under extremely complicated conditions. At the same time, I do not think that it is necessary to react from all sides and with an outcry to every statement Zhirinovsky makes. For example, he spoke about some weapons. So what? What can he actually do? He is a man with a very peculiar and well-known manner of conduct. He is not averse to sensationalist statements; his main concern is to build up his popularity. If each of his statements triggers a minor storm the world over, it will only play into his hands, in my opinion. Therefore, I would suggest that the reactions be calm and prudent because . . .Zhirinovsky is far from being the President and is not even a Russian politician who could influence certain decisions." Asked about Zhirinovsky's statement statement in Bulgaria where he called for the removal of President Zhelev, Churkin replied that "this is precisely one of those cases where commentary is unnecessary. The man simply does not hesitate to resort to such scandalous statements for the sake of popularity. How can you elbow your way to the front pages of newspapers in east European countries, for example? . . . If we were oversensitively react to each of his statements and call a meeting of the General Assembly or the UN Security Council every time, we would look absurd — if we get trapped by this simple political trick. . . . Another matter is that the December elections — and also the way that Zhirinovsky exploited the thesis about the position of Russians abroad — demonstrated that this problem really exists. Therefore, when we raised this question on the premises of the CSCE, the Council of Europe, or the UN, it was not propaganda on our part, as some of our partners in the Baltic countries have been trying to interpret this, but the pinpointing of actually existing sore spots that must be dealt with."[6]

A further comment on the LDPR's electoral appeal was made by Mikhail Poltoranin, head of the Federal Information Centre. "I do not agree with the widespread view that it was the poorest strata of the population who voted for Zhirinovsky . . . Let me tell you about my recent tour of *raions* in Moscow *oblast*. Here is a typical picture. A rich family — and they became rich thanks to the economic reforms — had voted solidly for the LDPR. I asked them why? And they told me: We could not breathe any more — criminal gangs were stifling us with their extortion. If you don't give them what they demand, they threaten to take reprisals against your family. It is as if the authorities did not exist. Zhirinovsky promised strict order . . . Or take another, similar example. Some Korean peasants from Stavropol *krai* told me recently that during the harvest they joined together to hire several armoured carriers with their crews, and in this way defended themselves against ruinous raids by gangsters from the neighbouring north Caucasian republics. The peasants told me that this case was not exceptional and that the struggle for survival has become a way of life there . . . A staggering 37.7 per cent of the population of this traditionally rich *krai* voted for the LDPR. The figure reflects bitter disappointment with the administration's helplessness, as well as an attempt to clutch at the straws of promises . . . One of the major reasons for the voters' protests . . . is that in general the authorities in Russia have become shamefully indifferent to good and evil. Zhirinovsky did not steal the communist electorate, he drew votes from among the confused masses. Leniency towards evil gives cruelty and violence a free rein. And that always leads to the demoralization of society . . . The vote for the constitution was a vote for a strong power and many people saw Zhirinovsky as a strong man."

Programme. Article 5 of the Russian Constitution gives the LDPR most trouble at present. "As long as the constitution talks about national republics and autonomous provinces you can't expect tranquillity in the country. We must abandon the Bolshevik principle of the national-territorial division of the country. Russia within its historic borders (as of the beginning of this century, or at least within the 1977 borders) should consist of 40 or 50 self-governing territorial units without any nationality-based overtones.[7]

Constitutions can be drafted to suit the form of state that has been chosen — presidential or parliamentary. Russia is a multi-national state. The interests of every nationality cannot realistically be taken into account. Look at Georgia. There are three nationalities there and a good constitution. Yet war seems to be endemic there. Russia needs an authoritarian state to impose order. It is like the fight against crime, where the ideal option is the usual procedure. The criminal is arrested and the court grinds on slowly. In our situation today that is not possible. Gangland savagery is rife in our country. We can only stop crime by exceptional measures".[8]

The party's stand on domestic issues is unashamedly populist. On television, during the election campaign, Zhirinovsky promised to index savings bank deposits, provide every one of 200,000 officers with flats and make available an abundance of inexpensive vodka. He called for the elimination of all sovereign states [former USSR republics] which have become members of the UN and for the present tattered peace in the CIS to be transformed into a civil war.[9] He favoured the adoption of the draft constitution: "If it is not adopted a power vacuum will develop and parliament will be illegitimate."

Zhirinovsky has evaded his widely cited pre-election statements about "on the spot execution of criminal gang leaders by firing squads, the Jewish infection on TV, 99 per cent of Russians in the future government, or the restoration of Russia's former borders" and puts them down to the unscrupulousness of journalists. "We are being provoked by being called fascists," he says, and promises that under his regime there will be "neither social nor ethnic discrimination" and that Russian troops will "leave all foreign states, provided that the other countries do the same" while the former republics will be "begging us to let them back in with the status of *guberniya* (province)", due to their economic situation. "We shall transfer to world prices in relations with everybody and, should Russians be discriminated against, we shall just stop supplies." Eastern Europe, and whoever should so wish, may join NATO. Germans and South African farmers may emigrate to Russia. "Both my mother and father are Russian, and father's kin were all lawyers". [This is to counter persistent reports that his father was Jewish.][10]

"Allegations about a split in the ranks of the Liberal Democratic Party are groundless." Zhirinovsky praised the party faction in parliament for supporting the resolution on amnesty which released the leaders of the October 1993 revolt in Moscow from prison. He also stated that two months of his party's activity in parliament had "resulted in certain changes" in Russian foreign policy towards the Serbs. He confirmed his view that the "revived military–industrial complex of Russia can bring the country fantastic profits through selling weapons on the world market". The only thing Russia needs is to "learn to trade properly".[11]

On economic policy, Zhirinovsky has said, "The state is the treasury and the army. If the treasury is empty and there is no army, then there is no state. The treasury really is empty because it has been robbed by those who are seated before you today and declare with horror: How can it be that our state has collapsed . . . our economy has collapsed? But it is they who have done this, all of them except our party. All of them, apart from me, have been and are still in control of the Russian state . . . Throughout all these years, throughout these 75 years it is precisely they who have caused the destruction. We shall change things. Television will be different. We shall remove all commercial advertisements. They will only be allowed in the newspapers. There will be no Snickers, no chewing gum, no beaches. We have eight months of winter. We need fur coats and not your beaches and cooling drinks. You will be able calmly to watch good Russian films. Ninety per cent of all news on our television channels will be only about Russia, in good Russian. You will be presented by Russian presenters with good, kind blue eyes with fair hair. This can all be done quickly."[12]

On economic policy the party claims that Russia does not need radical economic reform. Priority should be given to domestic agricultural producers with imports from abroad being discouraged. The party is against the selling of land.

The LDPR's minimum programme promises to improve living standards by 100 per cent in three or four months. To achieve this, three conditions will suffice: i) have Russia stop providing assistance to all nearby and distant foreign countries ii) suspend defence industry conversion and conduct wide-ranging sales of weapons on the world market iii) put an end to organized crime by destroying all 5,000 gangs in Russia. "What are we doing destroying existing weapons, weapons for which certain countries are willing to pay immediately in hard currency. Saddam Hussein is willing to give us US$10 billion today and pay back Iraq's debt to our country . . . Hussein even told me: I am surprised at your diplomats. I say to them: "Take it, it is your money — but they don't take it."[13]

The LDPR advocates the mixed principle. "We must not artificially break up the state sector and force on the private sector. Let everything develop naturally. For that we must create equal conditions for the state sector and the private sector. In the countryside, let the collective forms of management (collective and state farms, subsidiary enterprises, agricultural firms) and private forms in the shape of private farms, peasant farms, and smallholdings, exist. The state sector in industry should remain in the volume required by the economy. All large plants must be in state hands. In industry, the private sector should extend to small workshops, small factories and plants mainly producing consumer goods. Conversion in the military-industrial complex is harmful and should be stopped. Let existing military plants continue to produce military output . . . The tax system should be directed in favour of producers. Here, of course, it is desirable to reduce the tax to 40–30 per cent . . . the normalization of the economy could serve to increase funds channelled into indexing pensions and grants and opening stores where the poor could use coupons to acquire a minimum of essential foods and goods. Children are also in need of special attention and here it is also essential to step up aid in all directions . . . Payments for various services should be in specific proportion, for instance once every three years each savings account holder should have the right to use 20 per cent of his savings to acquire property and in the subsequent three years would have the right to use 20 per cent to acquire very expensive goods — cars, furniture and so forth."

Russian foreign policy should be based on non-interference in the domestic affairs of other countries and strict prevention of outside attempts to dictate to Russia how it should behave or threaten it with the use of force." We are opposed to rendering any aid in any region outside Russia. That would enable us to save 30 per cent of our material resources and channel them into improving the lives of Russian citizens. We are in favour of the intensified export of arms abroad. We are in favour of taking no part in the blockading of countries which are in our debt, for instance Libya or Iraq, or of those countries which are close to us in spirit, for instance our Orthodox brothers in the Balkans. Our foreign policy must be entirely independent. We must be neutral if that accords with Russia's interests. It is expedient to pass from the centuries old East–West relations to the more profitable, promising and less strained North–South contacts. With this aim in view it is necessary to agree with the leading powers to divide the spheres of influence (economic interests). Latin America and the Caribbean will be the sphere of influence of the United States — by purely economic and political methods, not military; West Africa for Europe's industrialized countries; Afghanistan, Iran and Turkey for Russia; South Asia and Oceania for Japan and China."

"We must focus efforts on the Southern salient — Turkey, Iran Afghanistan, the Caucasus, Central Asia. The endeavours to form military blocs in Central Asia based on ethnic or religious communion must not be encouraged. No matter what kind of union it is — Pan-Turkic or Pan-Islamic — it will inevitably become a source of new political and economic tensions in the region and the world as a whole. In the east it is desirable for us to restore relations with Iraq and Syria and with the Arab world. Iraq should be viewed as Russia's strategic ally in the south. However while supporting its policy of limiting the

United States' influence in the Middle East area, the LDPR stands against Iraq's calls for the elimination of the state of Israel. India should remain the biggest and most reliable friend of Russia in Asia. China should be viewed as a factor for stability in the Far East. We should strengthen co-operation with that nuclear superpower and try to restore our old friendly ties with it. The LDPR would press for the signing of a peace treaty with Japan without any preliminary conditions. It must be remembered that Russia was a victor in the Second World War and territorial claims must not be allowed . . . Relations with Japan should be built on the principle of clearly dividing spheres of influence and maintaining an equitable partnership."

"In the West we must restore economic and cultural relations with eastern Europe. In the long term we could try to create a union of Slav states. The LDPR stands for peaceful co-existence and allied relations in Europe, particularly with Germany. We must maintain ordinary relations with America, remembering that this is our main rival and is not interested in Russia's prosperity and might. Russia's relations with countries in other parts of the globe (America, Africa, Australia, Oceania) are beyond the area of our directly vital interests. However we must firmly press for the repayment of all the debts owed us by Third World countries."[14]

"We must pay proper attention to the development of space and individual types of weapons in order to ensure the fulfilment of Russia's foreign policy tasks. Naturally we do not remove from the agenda the slogan of the defence of Russia throughout the territory of Russia and the former USSR and that brings us close to our country's true patriotic forces . . . we are not by any means saying that we will restore Russia's borders by force. On the contrary we would like to be in no hurry to include a number of territories in Russia, even as *guberniyas*."

Asked about refugees, Zhirinovsky said "It is easy to stop the flow of refugees. All we would have to do would be to threaten the regions from which Russians are being expelled by saying that we would take similar action against representatives of their indigenous nationalities living in Russia. Take Azerbaijan, for example. Some 500,000 Russians once lived there. Now 100,000 are left. But how many Azerbaijanis are wandering around Russia? A million. So, to start with we should expel 400,000 Azerbaijanis from Russia and send them to Baku. And if Azerbaijan lays hands on the Russians there again, we'll send the whole million Azerbaijanis back. That's what we should do in all the other regions, too. One should also not forget the democracy also makes provision for violence."

"I dream that Russian soldiers will wash their boots in the warm waters of the Indian Ocean and switch to summer uniforms for good". Asked about how this differed from Hitler's demands for more space, he replied: "Hitler had his Drang nach Osten, we have our Drang nach Süden . . . The redivision of spheres of influence continues, the chief danger for Russia today is the south. All our problems come from there. It's an unstable region. Volatile, fiery, rebellious. It promises us conflicts and wars that will make Dushanbe and Sukhumi seem like child's play in comparison. This region must be calmed down. The world community itself will ask us to do this."

"All of these areas, the Baltics, Bessarabia, the Caucasus, belong to Russia . . . There's no need to conquer anyone . . . We stop delivering timber to Ukraine and all the mines in the Donets basin will collapse. We stop delivering to Ukraine everything we're delivering today, and in three months it will be on its knees and the Kravchuk government will collapse. We stop our aid, including military aid, to Tajikistan, and Rakhmonov will run to Moscow, getting there by any means of transport, and ask: Admit us to Russia, admit us as the Dushanbe *guberniya*. I implore you."[15] He deems it necessary to pursue a course independent of the West in foreign policy, a policy founded on Russia's national and geopolitical interests.[16]

During a joint news conference with Gerhard Frey, leader of the German People's Union [*Deutsche Volksunion*] Zhirinovsky talked of his attachment to Russian–German friendship. He predicted the emergence of a Moscow–Berlin axis and adds New Delhi — presumably in connection with his book, *The Last Push South*. He believed that the present Russian government will collapse in the autumn. The President would then invite him to Zavidovo and would entrust him with the mandate to form a government. At the very worst he is prepared to head one of the power ministries, or the Foreign Ministry. In three months, according to him, the government of the single unblemished party — the Liberal Democratic Party — would root out 5,000 armed gangs, put an end to military conversion, and completely cut off neighbouring republics. He denied that criminal proceedings had been instigated against him, accusing him of propagating war in connection with his book, *The Last Push South*. He stresses that everything would occur without a single shot being fired. First, Russia would withdraw its troops from the south and then the peoples there, beset by conflict, would ask to be put under Russian domination. "I am only in the capitals for a few hours, Ljubljana, Belgrade, Warsaw, and millions of people are standing there shouting: Russia, Russians, we are behind you. They kiss my hand, throw flowers at my feet, and I have difficulty escaping back to Moscow."[17]

Reacting to the news that the Russian procurator general's office had instituted criminal proceedings under clause 71 of the Russian criminal code, that is, war propaganda, Zhirinovsky states: "I have been telling you for an hour — no violence, not a single shot, and the same is true for all my speeches, I have already said that if there are people with sick minds who claim that my speeches or books contain some kind of call to war, they should be examined by a psychiatrist."[18]

On military policy, Zhirinovsky has said that the army should be sent in to combat banditry. Russia needs a strong, technically advanced, excellently equipped army. It is inadmissible to economize on defence. Military personnel's social problems should be resolved. Servicemen should enjoy a high social status.

Notes

1 65 according to Vladimir Pribylovsky and Grigory Tochkin, *Russkaya Mysl*, 6–12 Jan. 1994.
2 63 registered as State Duma faction *FBIS-SOV-94-010*, 14 Jan. 1994, from *Interfax*, 13 Jan. 1994.
3 6 according to Pribylovsky and Tochkin, *op. cit.*
4 *FBIS-SOV-93-244*, 22 Dec. 1993, from Ostankino TV.
5 *FBIS-SOV-93-240*, 16 Dec. 1993, from *Interfax*.
6 *FBIS-SOV-94-010*, 14 Jan. 1994, pp. 31–33 from *Narodna Obroda*, Bratislava, 12 Jan. 1994.
7 *The Current Digest of the Post-Soviet Press*, Vol. xlv no 48, Dec. 29, 1993, from *Izvestiya*, Nov. 30, 1993.
8 *FBIS-SOV-93-236*, 10 Dec. 1993, from Ostankino TV, 9 Dec. 1993.
9 *Current Digest of the Post-Soviet Press*, Vol. xlv, no. 47, Dec. 2, 1993, from *Izvestiya*, Nov. 26, 1993.
10 SWB SU/1874 17 Dec. 1993, p. B/9.
11 *FBIS-SOV-94-044*, 7 March 1994, from *ITAR-TASS*, 5 March 1994.
12 *FBIS-SOV-93-234*, 8 Dec. 1993, from Ostankino TV.
13 *Current Digest of the Post-Soviet Press*, Vol. xlv, no. 48, Dec. 29, 1993, p. 6.
14 *FBIS-SOV-93-242*, 20 Dec. 1993, from *Interfax*, 17 Dec. 1993.

15 *Current Digest of the Post-Soviet Press*, Vol. xlv No. 48, Dec. 29, 1993, from *Izvestiya*, Nov. 30, 1993.
16 *Krasnaya zvezda*, Dec. 2, 1993.
17 *FBIS-SOV-94-018*, 27 Jan. 1994, from Russian TV, 26 Jan. 1994.
18 *Ibid.*

Party of Economic Freedom (PEF)
Partiya Ekonomicheskoi Svobody

Foundation. May 14, 1992.

Leadership. Konstantin Borovoi (ch.); Irina Khakamada (g.s.).

Membership. Approximately 10,000 persons with 72 regional organizations, including branches in St Petersburg, Rostov, Penza, Yakutsk, Novosibirsk, Khabarovsk, Voronezh, Tambov, Kaluga, Samara, Pskov, Tula, Lipetsk, Saratov, Vologda, Ossetia and Tatarstan.

History. The Party of Economic Freedom was originally organized as the Party of Russian Entrepreneurs (PRE), linked to the financial and economic group of the Russian raw materials exchange. It tends towards liberal conservatism. It was founded on May 14, 1992, at a Constituent Congress in Moscow with about 500 persons attending, predominantly brokers from the Russian raw materials exchange but also representatives of other commercial organizations. Konstantin Borovoi, president of the Russian raw materials exchange, was elected chairman of the PRE. The party was registered in the Russian Ministry of Justice on June 22, 1992.

Borovoi favoured the dissolution of the Russian Supreme Soviet and the election of a Constituent Assembly. In July 1992 the party and the Renewal Union proposed the creation of a council of constructive forces, a round table of all organizations in favour of a market economy. The PEF also collaborates with the society for the defence of those businessmen sentenced unjustly. In September 1992 the Party of Constitutional Democrats stated it was joining the PEF but retaining its organizational autonomy. V. Zolotarev became the third co-chairman of the PEF.

The First Congress of the PEF took place in Moscow on Dec. 5, 1992. The congress ratified the party programme, the statute, confirmed officially the co-chairmen in office and introduced two new posts, general secretary and first secretary. The PEF played an active role in round tables in the spring of 1993 and participated in the organization of the Public Committee in Support of the Constituent Assembly.[1]

In October 1993 the party conference drew up a federal list of candidates for the State Duma and a list of the candidates for single-member constituencies. Following the suppression of the October uprising the party believed it had every chance of winning a considerable number of seats and of ultimately exerting a major influence on the shape of the government and its policy.

The PEF confirmed on Sept. 22, 1993, that President Yeltsin's decree of the previous day, dissolving the Russian Supreme Soviet and calling a referendum on a new constitution, was a necessary act affording the Russian people an opportunity to decide Russia's future by democratic means. The PEF resolutely and vigorously condemned the armed uprising and wholly supported the measures taken by President Yeltsin to suppress it on Oct. 4, 1993.

The Second Extraordinary Congress of the party was held in Moscow on Oct. 6, 1993, and a resolution adopted stated that the "pseudo-centrist forces are bankrupt. The democratic forces supporting the President and the government have gained an opportunity to strengthen substantially their influence". The document stresses that the PEF "advocates the speediest organization of elections to a new Russian parliament and reaffirms the need for nationwide elections to both the State Duma and the Council of the Federation." The party believes that early elections for President of the Russian Federation should be held following the election of the new deputies and it advocates the implementation as soon as possible of reform in regional and local agencies of soviet power.[2]

The PEF aimed to contest the elections as part of the August association [PEF and the Party of Constitutional Democrats (Viktor Zolotarev)].[3] The association also includes a number of public organizations such as the Union of Retired Officers, the Union of Convicted Economic Managers, etc.[4] As a leading candidate, Leonid Shpigel, stated: "We respect the leadership of Russia's Choice with which we have concluded a kind of non-aggression pact. Although we did not succeed in creating a broad, democratic pre-election association, we are not going to take the path of mutual recrimination, boorishness and mud slinging".[5] Borovoi realized that his bloc, if it was separated from the leading democratic forces, would not be able to play a significant role in the new political play that will begin with the upcoming elections. August's members may also be impelled to think this by the results of a telephone poll conducted by the Ostankino TV programme, *Public Opinion*, in which Konstantin Borovoi made a very modest showing. In conversation with a *Rossiiskie Vesti* correspondent he stated: "August will co-ordinate its position with other democratic associations". But is evident that the bloc has set itself the goal of becoming an independent player in the broad political arena, where the niche of a constructive opposition remains empty. Perhaps this goal will also be served by the strong human rights plank in August pre-election programme, which is geared above all to the development of economic freedoms. According to one candidate, more than 30,000 persons convicted on the basis of the obsolete anti-market articles of the 1961 criminal code, which remains in effect in Russia, are now in confinement. According to data provided by the Ministry of Internal Affairs, the number of such "criminals" grew by another 3,500 people last year.[6]

The PEF put forward 83 candidates for election to the State Duma,[7] but the August association failed to collect at least 100,000 signatures by the deadline (Nov. 6, 1993) and hence was barred from participating in the elections.[8]

Programme. The party supports the government's programme of economic reforms, a free economy, and guarantees of the rights and freedoms of the individual enshrined in the Declaration of Human Rights, and stands for press freedom, large-scale privatization and an end to free hand-outs of state property. Khakamada believed the party has about 80,000 supporters. The party is financed by its co-chairman, Konstantin Borovoi, and contributions from commercial organizations, primarily those registered on the Russian raw materials exchange. The party or its leaders fund several publications, including the newspaper, *Srochno v Nomer* (Stop Press).[9]

The main priorities are privatization and the fight against inflation. Privatization should be carried out much more quickly and vigorously. The list of sectors and enterprises taken out of the privatization programme should be sharply reduced and military spending cut considerably — primarily through reduction in arms procurements. Current taxes should be reduced sharply. Differences in taxation in different sectors or branches and types of activity are impermissible. Foreign trade must be liberalized. Protectionalism is permissible only to a very limited extent. Economic regionalization is currently the most effective way of reviving Russia.[10]

Courts should play a key role in the system of state power and that most conflicts should be decided by them, rather than by government or parliament. Present-day social policy should be based not on protecting citizens from the market but on developing their ability to engage in independent activity under the new economic conditions. Russia should remain a strong, integral country with all its components and nationalities enjoying equal rights. There should be no place for separatism and nationalism.

Organization. The Political Council of the party is the main organization and has 43 members, including Vladimir Bukovsky, the well-known dissident, and Aleksandr Ivanov, the poet and satirist. The party and Political Council are led by three co-chairmen: Konstantin Borovoi, Viktor Zolotarev and Svetoslav Fedorov, the eye surgeon. Irena Khakamada, general-secretary, and Leonid Shpigel, first secretary, are responsible for co-ordinating the work of the party. The activities of local organizations is co-ordinated by an inter-regional council, consisting of 33 leaders of regional branches.

Publication. Srochno v Nomer (Stop Press).

Notes

1 *FBIS-SOV-93-198*, 15 Oct. 1993, from *Rossiiskaya gazeta*, 14 Oct. 1993.
2 *Ibid.*
3 *FBIS-SOV-93-204*, 25 Oct. 1993, from *Interfax*, 23 Oct. 1993.
4 *Current Digest of the Post-Soviet Press*, Vol. xlv, no. 43, Nov. 24, 1993, from *Rossiiskie Vesti*, 30 Oct. 1993.
5 *Ibid.*
6 *Ibid.*
7 SWB SU/1817, 12 Oct. 1993, p. B/3, from Rusia TV, 7 Oct. 1993.
8 *Current Digest of the Post-Soviet Press*, Vol. xlv, no. 45, Dec. 8, 1993, from *Izvestiya*, 9 Nov. 1993.
9 *FBIS-SOV-93* 14 Oct. 1993, from *Izvestiya*, 13 Oct. 1993.
10 *FBIS-SOV-93-198*, 15 Oct. 1993, from *Rossiiskaya gazeta*, 14 Oct. 1993.

Party of Russian Unity and Accord (PRUA)
Partiya Rossiiskogo Edinstva i Soglasiya

Foundation. Oct. 16–17, 1993.

Leadership. Sergei Shakhrai (currently Minister for Nationalities and Regional Policy, and formerly chairman of the State Committee for Federation and Nationality Affairs); Ramazan Abdulatipov (formerly Chairman of the Russian Federation Supreme Soviet's Council of Nationalities, then Vice-Chairman of the State Committee on Federation and Nationality Affairs, and currently chairman of the Federation Council and first Deputy Minister for Nationalities and Regional Policies); Aleksandr Shokhin (Deputy Prime Minister, and Economics Minister. (Chairman of the Commission for International Humanitarian and Technical Assistance, and Chairman of the Joint Commission for Social Problems of Servicemen and Members of their Families.); Oleg Soskovets (First Deputy Prime Minister and Chairman of the Commission for Operational Questions, and Chairman of the Commission for Export Control); Konstantin Zatulin (leader of the Association of Entrepreneurs for a New Russia and Minister for Co-operation with the CIS states); Sergei Stankevich (former presidential adviser).

Membership. The PRUA has received the support of the association of Entrepreneurs for a New Russia (led by Konstantin Zatulin).[1] The Association of Socialist Trade Unions (Sotsprof) proposed its candidates for the PRUA list and collaborated in the drafting of the party's social platform. According to Dmitry Semenov, Sotsprof Co-ordination Committee co-chairman, the decision on co-operation with the PRUA was determined by the fact that "the second in command in the Party is Aleksandr Shokhin, the only man in the government with a deep understanding of the essence of labour relations and seriously concerned with the need for reforming them". The other no less important reason that prompted the choice of this party was the agreement that the Scotsprof would be writing the party's electoral programme on social and labour relations.[2]

The party maintains closest contacts with the North Caucasus, Western Siberia, and the Russian North-West,[3] and received the support of voters in 71 regions.[4]

History. The Party of Russian Unity and Accord (PRUA) was created by Sergei Shakhrai in an attempt to attract all those democrats who were becoming increasingly dissatisfied with radical market reform.[5] The PRUA presented itself as an alternative to the radical policies carried out by the Gaidar team, but at the same time, tried to win the support of the "centrist" members in the government, particularly the increasingly popular Prime Minister, Viktor Chernomyrdin. It also tried to obtain the support from President Yeltsin and refused to recognize Russia's Choice as the only presidential bloc.[6] The PRUA said it was ready to emerge in constructive co-operation with the government.

The party's parliamentary strategy was aimed at attracting the votes of the "regions", the area where Russia's Choice seemed to be most vulnerable.[7] The PRUA aimed at merging the political and economic concerns of the regions with those of the Russian Federation as a whole. "We want to create a party that will convey the opinion of regional leaders to the federal authorities", Shakhrai said at the founding congress.[8] Although the party attempted to rely on republican, territorial and regional branches, and reduce the number of Moscow politicians to a minimum,[9] it eventually failed to gain the support of most of the regional votes because it lacked its own mass support base.[10] Its failure was also due to the fact that the regions trusted more their local leaders who most often run independently, than a party inevitably linked with the centre; and due to the difficulty of rallying the divergent interest of Russia's regions.[11]

Although it supported regional interests, the PRUA stressed the need to preserve and strengthen the integrity of the Russian state as a united and multi-federal entity.[12] Shakhrai portrayed himself as the champion of traditional and conservative values, such as the family, labour, property and the fatherland, and said he understood conservatism as the preservation of the Russian state and the rebirth of old Russian traditions.[13]

The party held its founding congress on Oct. 16–17, in Novgorod.[14] The newly elected party leader, Sergei Shakhrai, said the PRUA would aim at merging the interests of the regions with those of the Russian Federation as a whole and mentioned his intention of co-operating with Viktor Chernomyrdin and Oleg Soskovets.[15] At the congress the economic, social and regional platform of the party was presented and approved.[16] Finally, delegates to the congress elected the members of the Federal Council (the party's executive body). They included Deputy Prime Ministers Sergei Shakhrai and Aleksandr Shokhin; Aleksandr Kotenkov, Director of the Russian Federation President's Chief Legal Affairs Administration; Ramazan Abdulatipov; former Chairman of the Russian Federation Supreme Soviet's Council of Nationalities and at the time vice-Chairman of the State Committee on Federation and Nationality Affairs, Sergei Stankevich, adviser to the

Table 7:   Election results of the Party of Russian Unity and Accord

---

Before registration the party collected 222,000 signatures.

State Duma
Total number of seats: 27
Seats obtained on party list: 18
Seats obtained in single-member constituencies: 9

State Duma faction: 30 members

State Duma Committees headed by the PRUA:
— Commonwealth of Independent States Affairs and Contacts with Co-Nationals Committee
   (Konstantin Zatulin)
— Federation Affairs and Regional Policy Committee (Sergei Shapovalov)
— Local Government committee (Anatoly Sliva)

Council of the Federation
Seats: 4 (Mikhail Prusak, Ramazan Abdulatipov, Yury Matochkin and Petr Premyak)

Deputy speaker of the house: Ramazan Abdulatipov (PRUA), First Deputy Minister for
Nationalities and Regional Policies

Members in government
— Sergei Shakhrai, Minister for Nationalities and Regional Policy
— Ramazan Abdulatipov, chairman of the Federation Council and first Deputy Minister
   for Nationalities and Regional Policies
— Aleksandr Shokhin, deputy Prime Minister and Economics Minister
— Oleg Soskovets, First Deputy Prime Minister and Chairman of the Commission for
   Operational Questions, and of the Commission for Export Control
— Konstantin Zatulin, Minister for Co-operation with the CIS states

---

President of Russia; and Vladimir Zaganov, Chairman of Buryatia's Council of Ministers,
as well as representative of other regions. The Federal Council was in charge of drawing
up the party's electoral lists for the State Duma and the Federation Council.

Although the PRUA did not score particularly well in the elections, it did retain important
positions in the federal government (Shakhrai, Shokhin, Soskovets, and Abdulatipov). Its
leaders responded negatively to Russia's Choice calls for the creation of a broad democratic
coalition of parliamentary forces, and instead tried to obtain the support of the independent
deputies of the "New Regional Policy" faction of the State Duma. After the elections the
PRUA attempted to present itself as the centrists' alternative to both the radical democrats
of Russia's Choice and to the nationalists of the Liberal Democratic Party of Russia and
again expressed its support for Viktor Chernomyrdin and his government.[17] The PRUA was
a staunch advocate of the amnesty granted to all those involved in the attempted coup of
August 1991, the Moscow riots of May 1993, and the conservative revolt of Oct. 3–4, 1993.[18]

This came as a surprise to the rest of the democratic forces. Shakhrai justified his position by saying "there was only one effective way for avoiding further confrontation [among the nationalist forces and Yeltsin], and this was through an act of reconciliation". In his view, both sides were to blame for the October events, and now society as a whole will benefit.[19]

Programme. In March 1992, on the eve of the Sixth Congress of People's Deputies, the President instructed Sergei Shakhrai, his chief legal adviser, at the time a Russian state counsellor, to come up with a Constitutional draft proposal. Yeltsin was dissatisfied with the draft being prepared by the Constitutional Commission, because it did not give him (the President) all the powers he wanted. Shakhrai's draft, like the commission's draft, abolished the Congress of People's Deputies and replaced it with a bicameral parliament, but gave the President more rights than did the commission's third draft.[20] This proposal however failed to meet with the approval of the republics, which argued that they were given insufficient powers.[21]

Debate over the constitution continued for another year until the holding of the April 1993 referendum on trust in the President and his reforms. Yeltsin's success in the referendum gave him confidence to speed up the work on the new constitution, and on April 29, the full text of the latest constitutional draft, prepared by a group of legal experts including Sergei Shakhrai, was released. This "presidential" draft again increased the powers of the President in relation to the latest draft being prepared by the Constitutional Commission.[22] But in a clear concession to the regions and especially to the republics, the major opponents to the constitution, this draft included the entire Federal Treaty,[23] and gave Russia's republics a proportionally large number of representatives in the powerful upper house. Including the Federal Treaty in the text of the constitution implied, according to some critics, that the Russian Federation would become a treaty-based federation instead of a constitution-based one, and this in theory could increase the legal status of the regions and republics. The republics however were not given the right to secede.[25]

During the spring of 1993, Yeltsin called a Constitutional Assembly to complete work on the new basic law and instructed this body to discuss and draft the final text. Sergei Shakhrai co-chaired the group of members of the Russian Federation of the Constitutional Assembly together with the Karelian parliament chairman Stepanov. The question of the distribution of power between the constituent members of the Russian Federation and the central government, as well as the status of the regions compared with that of the republics, headed the agenda along with the issue of the division of power between the legislative, the executive and judicial branches. The Constitutional Assembly draft, published in July 1993, described the republics as "sovereign states", and permitted the republics to introduce their own citizenship alongside the Russian one, and their own state language together with Russian. The draft also allowed for separate deals to be negotiated between the Russian Federation and its members, in response to Tatarstan demands that the new Constitution recognized its special status.[26] In response to demands from the regions that they be given the same rights as the republics, the draft stipulated that all members of the federation were equal in their relations with the federal leadership. The entire text of the Federal Treaty was included as part of the draft, but again republican and regional leaders refused to sign it.

Events in Russia in September and October completely altered the situation. Having defeated his opponents in parliament, Yeltsin imposed his last version of the draft to referendum. Alarmed by the increasing power achieved by the regions during the crisis,

Yeltsin decided to reduce many of the concessions given to the regions and republics. The definition of republics as sovereign states was dropped; permission for separate republican citizenship was abolished, the text of the Federal Treaty was excluded, and permission for a special status for some members of the Federation was abolished. Like the July draft it stressed that all members of the federation were equal in their relations with the federal leadership.[27]

The PRUA recommended the adoption of the draft Constitution put forward by Yeltsin in the December 1993 referendum in order "to avoid civil war and prevent the disintegration of Russia" and asked its potential electorate to support it in the referendum. The PRUA, however, was more in favour of the constitutional draft approved by the Constitutional Assembly on July 12 and said that this text should have been submitted to referendum.[28] It objected to the removal of the Federal Treaty from the Basic Law and rejected the provisions "that establish an imbalance between the branches of government".[29]

Shakhrai considers that the possibility of combining parliamentary and governmental positions is expedient and well-justified in the current situation. "In Russia the principle of the division of powers cannot and must not be given absolute priority because it may lead to a tragedy similar to the storming of the White House on Oct. 3–4."[30] He believes that "without making any cardinal changes in the principles of the division of power, we must take our bitter experience into account and build a bridge between the government and parliament, so that understanding and co-operation, not conflicts or confrontation, characterize the work of the supreme authorities".[31]

Shakhrai also believes that regional leaders should be allowed to run for seats in the Federation Council and that Russia's provinces should be represented by their leaders in the parliament's upper house.[32]

Although the PRUA backs the economic reform course of the President, its programme in some respects differs from the current line of the government. It emphasizes socially-oriented market reform and federalization. In Shakhrai's view "federalism, local self-government and socially-oriented market economy are the key elements for the development of a stable Russian state".[33]

The main difference between the PRUA's and Russia's Choice's economic programme is the former's emphasis on social welfare policies. The PRUA deems it necessary "to depart from the strict criteria of financial stabilization" as it is cheaper, according to Shokhin, "to spend some money now for social programmes than to spend much more money later to eliminate the social consequences of anti-inflationary policies".[34] According to Shokhin hidden unemployment affects 6–7 million people. This difficult situation will force the future government to sacrifice financial stabilization for the sake of averting social explosion.[35]

Dmitry Olshansky, professor of political science and PRUA candidate for the State Duma, maintains that Russia's instant entry into the market economy is impossible and that evolutionary reforms should be sought instead. This entails establishing a social partnership among the major economic and social groups. "Reform is for the people and not the other way round", he said.[36]

The party's economic policy is determined by "economic federalism", a concept put forward by PRUA's leader Aleksandr Shokhin. "Economic federalism" entails a reform of the fiscal system and a rational distribution of tax revenues, by which "the centre takes from the regions exactly as much as it needs to carry out its functions".[37] Economic federalism also envisages the existence of a single economic space, which means that individual republics, territories and regions should not be granted special economic conditions.[38] In Shokhin's view, the disparities in the economic space give rise to tensions among regions, and lead to separatist actions and threats.[39] Finally, economic federalism envisages support for the "depressed" and less developed regions, in particular those regions touched by high unemployment,[40] by means of regional development funds and subsidies.[41]

The PRUA supports the privatization process carried out by the government but favours some adjustments. In its view privatization and anti-monopoly legislation contributed to the disintegration of large enterprises[42] In particular, it supports privatizing those enterprises that are "closest to the market" (transportation and sales units) and favours granting state credits to those industries and enterprises that will ensure economic growth. Shokhin however stressed that state support should be channelled mostly through commercial structures, i.e. banks and investment funds.[43]

The PRUA favours some reasonable protectionism from foreign goods in order to support Russia's entrepreneurs, until Russian business becomes competitive in world markets.[44] Shokhin put forward the following measures to protect native producers from foreign competition: introduction of moderate export tariffs, encouragement of the export of Russian capital and Russian technical assistance, limitations on the activities of foreign banks in Russia, and introduction of reasonable duties to weapons exporters.[45] Konstantin Zatulin, leader of Entrepreneurs for a New Russia and supporter of the PRUA, said that he favoured the protection of local producers, because "the country basically finances foreign industry and undermines our own production levels by means of unwise tax policies".[46]

The PRUA supports private land ownership and believes that President Yeltsin's edict on land privatization gives a real impetus to the development of the peasantry's creative energy and the broadening of agricultural production.[47] It believes that the protection of private property should be the duty of the state.

The PRUA stressed the need, within the course of reforms, to direct more aid and social welfare benefits to the poorer sections of the population and to the less developed regions. The PRUA social policy envisages compensations for the socially disadvantaged strata of the population (children, elderly people, and disabled), introduction of minimum wages and protection for the unemployed. The PRUA envisages retraining programmes for those made redundant as a result of the closure of large industrial sectors.

Aleksandr Shokhin stressed the need to introduce regular compensation payments to those who need them.[48] Mr Semenov (co-chairman of Co-ordination Committee of the Association of Socialist Trade Unions) advocated collective salary agreements. In his view, "it is unacceptable that merchants should be allowed to set the prices of goods freely while the cost of the labour force is kept regulated. An important point in the programme is the provision that 'the cost of labour is also negotiable'".[49] The party also gives priority to scientific, technical, educational, and environmental projects, as well as youth association programmes.[50]

The PRUA has portrayed itself as the true defender of the interests of the regions. However, the party also stressed the need to preserve an integral and indivisible state.[51] Shakhrai believes that "a strengthening of the powers of the regions is necessary for the establishment of strong state structures".[51] He also said that his party, which is to represent regional interests, will work "for the idea of preserving a single Russian state".[53] During the September crisis, Shakhrai, a supporter of the provinces' demands, immediately denounced the Council of Members of the Federation as illegitimate. The Council was set up by 70 per cent of the members of the Russian Federation after the banning of Parliament, in an attempt by the regions to take over from the centre the government of Russia.[54]

Shakhrai advocated the passing of laws which consolidate the legal order, and change the civil and penal codes. In his view the State Duma should adopt a civil code, pass the constitutional laws necessary to reinforce Russia's statehood, and create the basis for new democratic elections.[55]

Notes

1 The association stressed however that it would continue supporting the economic platform developed in co-operation with G. Yavlinsky's centre. (*FBIS-SOV-93-217, 23 Nov. 1993, p. 45, from Moskovskie Novosti.* No. 46, 14 Nov. p. B1.)

2 *FBIS-SOV-93-208*, 29 Oct. 1993, p. 37, from *Segondya*, 28 Oct. 1993, p. 2.

3 *FBIS-SOV-93-222.* 19 Nov. 1993, p. 29, from *INTERFAX.* 18 Nov. 1993.

4 *FBIS-SOV-93-225.* 24 Nov. 1993, p. 31, Editorial Report.

5 Alexander Rahr, "Preparation for the Parliamentary Elections in Russia", *RFE/RL Research Report*, Vol. 2, No. 47, 26 Nov. 1993, p. 4.

6 *FBIS-SOV-93-219*, 16 Nov. 1993, p. 32. Editorial Report.

7 Alexander Rahr, "Preparations for the Parliamentary Elections in Russia", *op. cit.*, p. 4.

8 *FBIS-SOV-93-199*, 18 Oct. 1993, p. 45, from *INTERFAX*, Moscow, 15 Oct. 1993.

9 *BBC SWB, SU/1821 B/1, 16 Oct. 1993, from ITAR-TASS World Service*, Moscow, 14 Oct. 1993.

10 *Izvestiya*, 28 Oct. 1993, p. 4.

11 The PRUA, however, did well in a number of republics, gaining 37 per cent of the vote in Tuva; 34 per cent in Kabardino-Balkaria, and 24.5 per cent in Altai Republic. Overall, though, it barely overcame the 5 per cent barrier, leading some observers to conclude that for many Russians the question of federalism was not at the top of the agenda.

12 Alexander Rahr, "Preparations for the Parliamentary Elections in Russia", *op. cit.*, p. 4.

13 *BBC SWB, SU/1824 B/1, 20 Oct. 1993, Editorial Report.*

14 The Congress was attended by 161 representatives of 53 Russian regions (BBC SWB. SU/1824 B/1, 20 Oct. 1993, Editorial Report). Vladimir Saganov, Chairman of Buryatia's Council of Ministers, was the only leader of a Russian republic to attend the congress. According to Saganov the interregional association of Far East regions and the Siberian Agreement would most probably bring their support to the new party (Nezaavisimaya Gazeta, 19 Oct. 1993, p. 1).

15 *Nezavisimaya Gazeta*, 19 Oct. 1993, p. 1.

16 *Ibid.*, p. 1.

17 Shakhrai intended to create a broad parliamentary coalition in support for Viktor Chernomyrdin and his policies (*Kommersant-Daily*, 8 Feb. 1994, p. 3).

18 The voting in support of the amnesty was part of a package of resolutions, which included an amnesty connection with the adoption of a new Constitution, a memorandum of concord, and a resolution which called for the setting up of a commission of inquiry into last October's uprising.

19 *FBIS-SOV-94-048.* 11 March 1994, p. 21, from *Komsomolskaya Pravda*, 10 March 1994, p. 2.

20 This draft called for a strong presidential republic along the lines of the US executive presidency, although the Russian President would be more powerful because he would have the ability to initiate legislation. The President would be elected for a six-year term and appoint his cabinet essentially without parliamentary approval. He would also have veto power over parliamentary legislation, although the parliament would be able to overrule this veto by a two-thirds majority vote. (For further details see: Carla Thorson, "Toward the Rule of Law: Russia",. *RFE/RL Research Report*, Vol. 1, No. 27, 3 July 1993, p. 18.)

21 Vera Tolz "Power Struggle in Russia: The role of the Republics and Regions", *RFE/RL Research Report*, No. 15, 9 April 1993. For more details on relations between the centre and the republics see: Vera Tolz. "Thorny Road towards Federalism in Russia". *RFE/RL Research Report*, Vol. 2, No. 48, 3 Dec. 1993.

22 It also included Sergei Alekseev, formerly the chairman of the USSR Committee for Constitutional Oversight: August Mishin, a specialist on American Constitutional law; and Anatoly Sobchak, Mayor of St Petersburg.

23 For details see Vera Tolz "Drafting the New Russian Constitution" *RFE/RL Research Report*, Vol. 2, No. 29, 16 July 1993, p. 5.

24 For details on the Federal Treaty, see Vera Tolz, "Thorny Road towards Federalism in Russia" *op. cit.*

25 *Ibid.*, p. 5.

26 Ariel Cohen, 'Competing Visions: Russian Constitutional Drafts and Beyond" *RFE/RL Research Report*, Vol. 2, No. 38, 24 Sept. 1993, p. 55.
27 Vera Tolz, "Thorny Road toward Federalism in Russia", *op. cit.*, p. 7.
28 *Nezavisimaya Gazeta*, 28 Oct. 1993, p. 1.
29 *Segodnya*, 27 Nov. 1993,p. 2.
30 *FBIS-SOV-93-203*, 22 Oct. 1993, p. 26, from *INTERFAX*, Moscow, 21 Oct. 1993.
31 *Ibid.*, p. 26.
32 *BBC SWB* SU/1821 B/2, 16 Oct. 1993, from *ITAR-TASS World Service*, Moscow, 14 Oct. 1993.
33 *FBIS-SOV-93-210*, 2 Nov. 1993, p. 35, from *ITAR-TASS*, Moscow, 1 Nov. 1993.
34 *FBIS-SOV-93-222*, 19 Nov. 1993, p. 29, from *ITAR-TASS World Service*, 18 Nov. 1993.
35 *Segodnya*, 20 Nov. 1993, p. 3.
36 *FBIS-SOV-93-225*, 24 Nov. 1993, p. 32. Editorial Report.
37 Shokhin supports the introduction of two types of taxes; federal taxes, collected in order to cover federal expenses, and local taxes, levied at local level and aimed at meeting local needs. (*Nezavisimaya Gazeta*, 19 Nov, p. 1.)
38 *FBIS-SOV-93-215*, 9 Nov. 1993, p. 40, from *ITAR-TASS*, Moscow, 6 Nov. 1993.
39 *FBIS-SOV-93-207*, 28 Oct. 1993, p. 27, from *Kommersant-Daily*, 27 Oct. 1993, p. 3.
40 *FBIS-SOV-93-215*, 9 Nov. 1993, *op. cit.*, p. 40.
41 *FBIS-SOV-93-217*, 12 Nov. 1993, p. 43, from *INTERFAX*, Moscow, 11 Nov. 1993.
42 *FBIS-SOV-93-207*, 28 Oct. 1993, *op. cit.*, p. 27.
43 *FBIS-SOV-93-222*, 19 Nov. 1993, *op. cit.*, p. 29.
44 *Nezavisimaya Gazeta*, Oct. 19, 1993, p. 3.
45 *FBIS-SOV-93-224*, 23 Nov. 1993, p. 31, from *ITAR-TASS*, Moscow, 22 Nov. 1993.
46 *Ibid.*, p. 31.
47 *Rossiiskie Vesti*, Nov. 16, 1993, p. 1.
48 *Nezavisimaya Gazeta*, 19 Oct. 1993, p. 3.
49 *Segodnya*, 27 Oct. 1993, p. 2.
50 *Rossiiskie Vesti*, 16 Nov. 1993, p. 1.
51 *Nezavisimaya Gazeta*, 28 Oct. p. 37.
52 *FBIS-SOV-93-209*, 1 Nov. 1993, p. 26, from *Die Woche*, 28 Oct. 1993, p. 17.
53 *FBIS-SOV-93-206*, 27 Oct. 1993, p. 33, from *ITAR-TASS*, Moscow, 26 Oct. 1993.
54 Vera Tolz, "Thorny Road towards Federalism in Russia, *op. cit.*, p. 6.
55 *FBIS-SOV-93-219*, 16 Nov. 1993, p. 31. Editorial Report.

Russia's Choice Bloc
Vybor Rossii

Foundation. 16–17 Oct. 1993.

Leadership. Egor Gaidar (former first deputy chairman of the Russian Federation Government, and leader of Russia's Choice); Sergei Kovalev (chairman of the Human Rights Commission attached to the Russian Federation President, and human rights activist); Ella Pamfilova (former Russian Federation Minister for social protection of the population); Anatoly Chubais (deputy chairman of the Russian Federation Government and the chairman of the State Committee on Administration of State Property); Andrei Kozyrev (Russian Federation Foreign Affairs Minister); Boris Fedorov (former deputy chairman of the Russian Federation Government and former Russian Federation Finance Minister); Sergei Filatov (Head of the Administration of the Russian President); Mikhail Poltaranin (former leader of the Russian Federal Information Centre and head of the State Duma Committee on Information Policy and Communications); Gennady Burbulis (Chairman of the Strategiya centre).

History. The Russia's Choice (election) bloc, set up on the eve of the December 1993 elections, brought together various democratic movements and associations (led by the Russia's Choice movement) as well as the bulk of the politicians who were closest to President Boris Yeltsin during 1993. It included most of the leading government members, including Egor Gaidar, chairman of the Russia's Choice movement created in July 1993, and leader of the new bloc. The bloc hoped to organize a united democratic front against communist and nationalist forces but failed from the very beginning to obtain the support of democratic parties (the Russian Movement for Democratic Reforms and the Democratic Party of Russia decided to run independently); and from leading democratic figures, who decided instead to create their own political forces and distance themselves from Russia's Choice. (Sergei Shakhrai set up the Party of Russian Unity and Accord, while Grigory Yavlinsky joined Yury Boldyrev and Bladimir Lukin and created a new bloc.) Democratic Russia, the movement that won significant electoral victories in 1990 and 1991, became an important part of the new group.

Democratic Russia (DR) first emerged as an alliance of voters' clubs, electoral support teams and democratic associations which presented candidates to the Russian parliamentary and local elections of March 1990.[2] Its successful campaign strategies resulted in impressive victories: DR's candidates won comfortable majorities in the Moscow and Leningrad soviets, and enough seats in the Russian Congress of People's Deputies, to be able to elect Boris Yeltsin as chairman of the Russian Parliament (the Supreme Soviet) and to approve a bill on the sovereignty of the Russian Federation.[3] These successes, however, did not lead to the transformation of DR into a strong political party.[4]

Democratic Russia was in fact an electoral alliance which brought together people with very different political opinions, ranging from moderate Russian nationalists, advocating a strong Russian state within its "natural borders", to radical intellectuals opposed to the formation of any rigid party structures. They were united only by a common desire to ouster the CPSU from power.[5] DR also suffered from the ambivalent relationship it had with Boris Yeltsin, the only undisputed leader capable of unifying the bloc and transforming it into a powerful organization. After his election as chairman of the Russian parliament. Yeltsin resigned his membership of DR and distanced himself from the movement.

Soon after Yeltsin's election as chairman to the Supreme Soviet it became clear to many DR leaders that a permanent organizational structure was needed to unify the democratic opposition and to enable it to dislodge the CPSU from power. But its leaders could not agree on the type of party they wanted to establish. DR Deputy Nikolai Travkin's decision to create a well-disciplined and vertically structured political party with a single leader met with resistance from other leading democrats such as Lev Ponomarev, Marina Sale, and Ilya Konstantinov, who favoured the creation of a loosely organized and collectively-led social movement.[6] No agreement was reached. Democratic leaders decided to create a social movement out of "Democratic Russia", while Travkin went on with the establishment of his own party, the Democratic Party of Russia (DPR). At the founding congress of Democratic Russia on Oct. 20–21, 1990, the movement stated its opposition to the political monopoly of the CPSU, its commitment to market reform, and its support for the principle of the right of nations to self-determination.[7]

Democratic Russia achieved a series of victories in its attempt to remove the Communist party from power. In early 1991, it managed to introduce direct, democratic elections to a Russian presidency and to the mayors of Moscow and Leningrad. On June 12, 1992, DR candidate, Boris Yeltsin, was elected President of Russia in the country's first democratic elections; and DR's candidates Gavriil Popov and Anatoly Sobchak became the first democratically elected mayors of Moscow and Leningrad respectively.[8] But soon, former disagreements reemerged. In July four Russian leaders (Popov, Sobchak, Vice-President Rutskoi, and Russian Prime Minister, Ivan Silaev) joined five progressive members of Gorbachev's entourage (Aleksandr Yakovlev, Eduard Shevardnazde, Stanislav Shatalin, Nikolai Petrakov and Arkady Volsky) and set up the Movement for Democratic Reforms. The aim of the new movement was to bring together the prominent supporters of radical reform among the old élite with the new democratic élite, in an attempt to split the CPSU and cause its downfall. During the autumn of 1991, DR was further weakened by disagreements between leading intellectuals on the one hand (Afanasev, Elena Bonner, Leonid Batkin, Yury Burtin, and Vyacheslav Ivanov) and the movement's Co-ordinating Council on the other, over the Novo-Ogarevo process.[9]

After the August 1991 coup, the first real splits in the ranks of DR occurred. During the movement's second congress (on Nov. 12, 1991) the DPR, the Christian Democratic Party (led by Viktor Aksyuchits), and Constitutional Democrats (led by Mikhail Astafev) abandoned the movement because they supported the Union Treaty and disapproved of DR's support for the developments that were leading to the disintegration of the Soviet Union. They were followed in their decision by the Social Democratic Party of Russia. In January 1992, the first direct confrontation within DR took place between those leaders who were ready to offer unconditional support to Yeltsin, and the radical intellectuals who believed that Democratic Russia was becoming a tool of the executive power. Intellectuals accused Yeltsin of betraying the cause of democracy by preserving the political and economic power of the old *nomenklatura*. The radicals — among whom Afanasev, Sale, Burtin, and Batkin — were eventually defeated and abandoned the party in March 1992.[10]

The defeat of the radicals meant that the movement had a higher chance of developing into a presidential party. But Yeltsin's contradictory attitude towards the movement prevented it from becoming a strong and valuable supporter of the President. Yeltsin's ambivalence about whether to compromise with, or confront his opponents in the Congress of People's Deputies increasingly weakened DR. In fact, whenever Yeltsin decided to confront his opponents by seeking a popular mandate in a referendum, DR was reactivated. But its will and capacity were seriously undermined whenever he decided to compromise with his opponents in the Congress.[11]

Although DR never materialized into a party, it proved extremely powerful as a social mobilizer. During Yeltsin's electoral campaign DR organized numerous rallies and sent numerous campaign materials to the provinces of Russia: during the August coup it organized three mass demonstrations in Moscow, and during the April referendum its contribution to Yeltsin's success was crucial, since, contrary to 1991, Yeltsin did very little campaigning himself.

In spite of his contradictory attitude towards the democratic forces of Russia, Yeltsin supported various attempts by the democrats to create a broad left-centre alliance in support of his policies. Although a centrist coalition never emerged, the efforts led to the creation of Democratic Choice — an alliance of democratic groupings which expressed their unconditional support for Gaidar's economic reforms. Democratic Choice included various high-ranking officials such as Burbulis, Chubais, Gaidar, and Kozyrev,[12] and became one of the founding groups of the Russia's Choice electoral bloc.

The constituent congress of the Russia's Choice bloc was held in Moscow on Oct. 16–17, 1993, and was attended by representatives of the Democratic Russia movement, Democratic Choice, the Living Ring Union, the Peasants' Party, the Association of Russian Private

Farms and Agricultural Co-operatives (AKKOR), the Council of Work Collectives, and the Servicemen for Democracy movement. At the congress, the bloc reaffirmed its commitment to economic reform, freedom and private property.[13] It also expressed its support for President Yeltsin's policy and for the reformist policies of the government. President Yeltsin was invited to the congress, but decided not to attend.[14]

On the eve of the congress, disagreements emerged between Democratic Russia's leaders and the leaders of the Russia's Choice movement over the structure of the new bloc. Gennady Burbulis, Anatoly Chubais, and other RC leaders insisted on the creation of a movement with rigid organizational structures, i.e. a party, while Democratic Russia's leaders favoured keeping a loose alliance of parties. Russia's Choice leaders eventually managed to impose their views and, after the elections, the bloc developed into a party. Disagreements also emerged regarding the final list of candidates to the State Duma elections. Democratic Russia's leaders were in fact overshadowed by the new leaders of Russia's Choice,[15] but still decided to stay in the bloc.

At a press conference Gleb Yakunin, leader of DR movement, said that although there were no ideological differences between Democratic Russia and Russia's Choice, DR did not intend to become a government party. Instead, it preferred to stay in opposition and criticize eventual corruptions among the democratic ranks. His words were supported by another DR leader, Lev Ponomorev, who stated that Democratic Russia could not go along with undemocratic procedures that might be carried over to the future parliament.[16] He said that in the event of Russia's Choice evolving into a ruling party, DR would not join it.[17]

The unsatisfactory performance of Russia's Choice in the State Duma elections (it did not manage to obtain more than 30 per cent of the votes), and the high number of votes given by the Russian population to the Liberal Democratic Party of Russia, led by Vladimir Zhirinovsky, came as a complete surprise to the leaders of Russia's Choice. They immediately called for the creation of an "anti-fascist" alliance of democratic forces.[18] Zhirinovsky's victory, however, turned out to be less spectacular than it initially seemed. Russia's Choice far outstripped the LDP in the elections of deputies to single-member constituencies. Nevertheless, Russia's Choice leaders, in particular E. Gaidar, admitted that the democrats had suffered a terrible defeat,[19] and after some hesitation decided to pass to the opposition. On Jan. 16, Gaidar resigned from government. He was followed 10 days later by Finance Minister Boris Fedorov, who, after a series of controversial negotiations,[20] also declined the post of Finance Minister. However, four Russia's Choice members stayed in government: Anatoly Chubais, deputy Prime Minister and chairman of the Russian State Property Managing Committee; Andrei Kozyrev, Foreign Minister; Evgeny Sidorov, Minister of Culture, and Viktor Danilov-Danilyan, Environment Minister. In parliament, Russia's Choice managed to agree with other major factions on the chairmanship of the committees of the State Duma, but faced a slight internal defeat when some RC deputies, Andrei Makarov and Boris Fedorov decided to join the new radical faction — the "Union of 12 December". On April 15, the leaders of the Union of 12 December (Boris Fedorov and Irina Kharamanda) expressed their intention of transforming the parliamentary faction into the Liberal Democratic Union.[21]

Soon after the elections, it became clear to Egor Gaidar that the creation of a party on the basis of Russia's Choice was needed in order to "co-ordinate the activities of all democratic forces in Russia",[22] and to counter the rising influence of anti-reformist parties. His aim was to create a force that would champion serious market reform and democratization in Russia.[23] He appealed to all democratic parties and movements, in particular to the RMDR

461

and to the Democratic Russia movement. Leaders of Democratic Russia refused to join the party, arguing that they opposed the creation of a rigid party, and favoured instead the preservation of a loose democratic movement. However, Democratic Russia's regional branches were given the choice to participate in the formation of the new party's grassroots organisations.[24] Close co-operation was established with the parliamentary faction Union of 12 December.

Membership. The bloc includes the Democratic Russia movement (leader — Lev Ponomarev); the All-Russia Association of Privatized and Private Enterprises (leaders — Egor Gaidar, P. Filippov); the Association of Russian Private Farms and Agricultural Co-operatives (AKKOR) (leader — V. Bashmachnikov); the League of Co-operative Workers and Entrepreneurs (leader — Vladimir Tikonov); the Living Ring Union of Defenders of Free Russia and the Radical Democrats faction (leader — Sergei Yushenkov); the Servicemen for Democracy movement (leader — V. Smirnov); the Peasant party (leader — Yury Chernichenko); and the Democratic Initiative Party (leader — Pavel Bunich). The Trade Unions for Reforms and Elections Joint Centre, a bloc of free trade unions not belonging to the Federation of Independent Trade Unions of Russia (FITUR), also supported Russia's Choice.

The Russia's Choice movement organized itself in 54 regions,[25] most often on the basis of the regional organizations of the Republican Party, which divided its support between Russia's Choice and the Yavlinsky-Boldyrev-Lukin bloc. A total of 602 delegates from 82 Russian regions attended the founding congress held in Moscow in October 1993.[26]

Programme. Russia's Choice was the only association that gave virtually unconditional support to Boris Yeltsin in the referendum on the Constitution. The bloc completely supported the draft Constitution and the adoption procedure proposed by Yeltsin, and asked the Russian electorate to vote for it on Dec. 12.[28] Its leaders, however, did not always entirely agree on the principle of the division of powers. While Mikhail Poltaranin opposed the combination of jobs in parliament and government,[29] Egor Gaidar and Sergei Filatov seemed more inclined to support such a combination in order to facilitate the work of the executive. Admitting that the decision to combine the post of deputy and minister was far from ideal, Gaidar nevertheless stated that "the wonderful principle of the separation of powers should not be carried to absurdity", and added that "banning government members from participating in parliamentary work, serves only to heighten tensions between the branches of power".[30] In an interview with *Obshchaya Gazeta*, he was even more emphatic when he said that "any government member, whether or not he is a deputy, *a priori* works with parliament to a considerable extent because otherwise he simply does not fulfil his functions".[31] Sergei Filatov said that "recently [before the October events] there had been no separation of powers. Instead, the alienation of one branch of power from the other was constantly being fuelled, to a high degree of hostility". In order to improve relations between the executive and parliament, Filatov believed that some government structures should be integrated with representative structures, intending by that a combination of posts.[32] Andrei Kozyrev's position was more ambiguous. Speaking at the founding congress of Russia's Choice, he said that the new parliament had to maintain sufficient independence in relation to the executive. It had to oppose the executive professionally and monitor its activities.[33] But on a trip to Murmansk just before the elections, Kozyrev said that it was appropriate, given the circumstances, to combine the functions of minister with the duties of parliamentary deputy. In Russia's specific conditions, Kozyrev thought it is "correct and useful".[34] There was also no agreement regarding the term of the new parliament. While Kozyrev stressed the need of a four-year parliament, Gaidar said that Russia's Choice regarded the coming parliament as temporary, meaning that it had to fulfil its main functions within two years and then dissolve itself.[35]

Russia's Choice economic policy is based on a rapid transition to a market economy and on the adoption of legislation that guarantees private property and private enterprise.[36] Economic reform is seen by Russia's Choice as part of a revolutionary transformation of society that should eventually lead to the elimination of the dominant role of the state in society. According to Gaidar, the main tasks of the new parliament should not be limited to economic transformation but, above all, to reforming the entire structure of the Russian state, in particular "liberating the state from everything it should not be doing under market conditions".[37]

Aware of the lack of support such measures carried among the Russian population, Russia's Choice leaders tried to portray their policies as the only alternative available if total economic disarray was to be avoided. "The way to stability in Russia", said Gaidar, "lies only in the implementation of consistent, calm market reforms. We cannot promise easy ways to solve the problems, but we can only promise what is feasible: government stability and stable legislation that defends private property."[38] Gennady Burbulis, the former Russian state secretary, was even more blunt when he said, regarding the difference between the economic programmes of Russia's Choice and the coalition led by Yavlinsky: "Yavlinsky believes that the collapse of the socialist, monopolistic economy could have been stopped, but we are sure that this collapse was inevitable. We are convinced that the existence of miracle methods for conducting radical reforms in the economy, without fairly difficult tests for the majority of the population — something to which Yavlinsky refers — is either an academic utopia or a social and political myth."[39]

Russia's Choice economic policy rests on three main pillars: lowering of the inflation, privatization of industry, and privatization of land. Anatoly Chubais calculated that, if these reforms are carried out, 1994 could be the year of stabilization when the slump in production ceased, and 1995 the year of economic growth, when recovery began.[40]

Russia's Choice intended to reduce sharply the rate of inflation down to 3–5 per cent by the end of 1994,[41] in order to avoid the total collapse of monetary circulation. Boris Fedorov believes that lowering inflation will guarantee a continued development of production, will encourage the population to save, and will stimulate investments.[42] According to Egor Gaidar, lowering inflation should be achieved by reducing the budget deficit, abandoning preferential credits, reducing import subsidies, and reforming the budget system, including future tax cuts.[43]

Russia's Choice advocates the total privatization of Russian industry, but opposes the granting of massive subsidies to ailing enterprises. Anatoly Chubais warned against the support of industry or agriculture by means of "pouring money into them".[44] In his view such a policy would result in financial explosion and runaway inflation and he cited Ukraine as an example of what happens when "the fine slogans of backing industry, fixed prices, the renunciation of shock therapy, a slow-down of privatization, and state control of the economy" are implemented.[45] In reality they lead the economy to the verge of collapse, he concluded. "If we are to agree today to the crazy demands which the communists and agrarians are continuing to make, calling for an immense injection of all types of financial resources into the country-side, we will end up destroying it." He said that "industry can be backed, any sector of the economy can be backed only through financial policy", adding that only when a financial system is working and inflation is falling can the government seriously consider which industry needs priority treatment.[46] His views were shared by E. Gaidar who noted that "the worst for the industrial sector, the only way to destroy it completely, is to try to make all factories work". Gaidar believes that industrial enterprises should adapt to new market conditions by producing goods that are in demand. In his view, the state should not continue supporting industrial enterprises. Instead, enterprises should look for additional private resources and should lower the costs of production.[47]

Although Gaidar advocated opening up the economy, with tough competition and import of goods,[48] he did seem to be willing to protect some vital sectors of the Russian economy. At a meeting with Russian bankers at Russia's Choice headquarters on November 18, 1993, Gaidar gave them assurances that he opposed an excessive liberalization of the banking sector and said he would limit the access of foreign banks.[49]

RC supports land privatization, but does not insist on accelerated wholesale privatization and the free distribution of property.[50] Talking at a session of AKKOR (Associations of Russian Private Peasants' Farms and Agricultural Co-operatives), Gaidar promised to support the countryside and particularly private farmers by the following methods: relaxation of import restrictions, lowering of duties, and easing of export and import transactions. Gaidar also promised to abolish all compulsory deliveries to the state. The state would purchase essential products, but, in doing so, would provide peasants with an economic stake.[51] He concluded by saying that "The state needs the farmers. They are a very important component of our economic policy. The state resources are not limitless, bur farmers will get priority".[52]

Russia's Choice proposes an ecological revival of Russia based on a considerable reduction of human and industrial damaging influence on the environment. It includes a reduction of harmful gases and a cutback of industrial and agricultural discharges. The programme stresses the need of creating a "a network of regeneration", which entails the cleaning of deteriorated natural systems. Viktor Danilov-Danilyan, a Russia's Choice candidate and Russia's Environmental Minister, said that "legal uncertainty" existed in the field of environmental protection in Russia and stressed the need to create "a legal framework for environmental protection activity in line with the new Constitution". According to Danilov-Danilyan, the framework should regulate the use of natural resources between the federal authorities and the provinces.[53]

Russia's Choice believes that the development of a low inflation and growing economy should be accompanied by the implementation of an effective social policy.[54] Priority should be given to all those who suffered from the recent changes in the economy.

The bloc plans to reorganize the entire financial system of the social scheme, and adopt a selective social support scheme, which targets above all pensioners, invalids, families with children, and particularly those living below the level of poverty.[55] Gaidar stressed the need to introduce a system of universal benefits for those living on low incomes,[56] and added that a new law on indexation and pensions was currently being prepared.[57]

Russia's Choice sustains the view that Russia's high-level defence capability can only be maintained if it is supported by steady economic development. Defence expenditures should be lowered in view of the new geopolitical environment and the reduction of the nuclear threat. Military expenditure, which now represents 5.5 per cent of the GNP, should be kept at that low level, provided Russia's geopolitical interests and world power status are not put in jeopardy.

Russia must close relations with its neighbours in the security sphere in order to solve the conflicts in adjacent territories. According to Gaidar, Russia should participate actively in the strengthening of the UN and the CSCE, and should regard these institutions as adequate instruments for the resolution of conflicts.[58]

Russia's Choice intends to make sure that the Armed Forces occupy a worthy place in the system of state institutions. But at the same time, it advocates effective civilian control of the military institution. "We consider it unacceptable to shift onto the military the political responsibility of decisions made by the country's leadership", Gaidar told *Krasnaya Zvezda*.[59] Russia's Choice also favours a phased transition to a professional army distinguished by a high standard of personnel training and of its technical equipment. The bloc is also concerned with the material conditions of the soldiers and foresees the introduction of specific social protection measures for servicemen. RC is aware that this specific group of state employees does not have and cannot have any other means of income, and this is why their pay must be really high.[60]

Russia's Choice favours the territorial integrity of the Russian Federation, and the granting of equal rights to all regions and peoples, as well as the establishment of clear delimitations between federal, regional, and local ownership of property.[61] Its leaders believe that the danger of an eventual disintegration of the country has disappeared. According to Gaidar, "the centrifugal tendencies which dominated the Russian political scene since the early 1990s were due, to a very large extent, to the power vacuum which existed in Moscow and to the existence of two competing centres of power: first the Union against Russia, and then the Russian legislative against the Russian executive". The new constitution will solve, according to Anatoly Chubais, the acute problem of the inequality of rights among the different components of the federation. By granting equal rights to all components of the Federation, it will stop all desires of succession from Russia.[62]

Foreign Minister Andrei Kozyrev has embodied Russia's Choice foreign policy priorities. Although his policy has not always been very coherent and in recent months he has adopted a more nationalistic stance, which takes greater account of Russia's specific national interests, he is still an advocate of a pro-Western approach. During his first year in office, his policies called for embracing of universal democratic values and for the political and economic integration of Russia into the Western world. He emphasized a tight relationship between a successful pro-Western foreign policy and a healthy fiscal policy. Other leaders of Russia's Choice, Gaidar, Burbulis and Mikhail Poltaranin, particularly concerned with Russia's economic recovery, also emphasized the need to develop close foreign economic relations with the industrialized countries, and worked for the integration of Russia into world economic structures such as the IMF, the World Bank and above all the G-7 group of industrialized nations.[63]

Although at an early stage Kozyrev devoted most of his efforts to the integration of Russia into the community of "civilized nations"[64] and to the recognition of Russia as the legal successor state of the Soviet Union, during 1993 he became increasingly concerned with Russia's relations towards the newly independent republics. As early as February 1992, Kozyrev said Russia respected the sovereignty of the former Soviet Union republics and wished to build relations with them on an equal basis. But he added that Russia would defend its own interests, which included not only economic co-operation but also preservation of a unified army, defence of human rights and protection of the Russian and Russian-speaking population in other CIS states.[65] At a later stage, however, he stated that the best way to protect the rights of ethnic Russians in the republics of the former Soviet Union was by establishing good relations with their host states.[66]

Kozyrev rejects the view that Russia has a specific role or mission in world politics, and believes that its foreign policy should reject all ideological schemes for global imperialism,[67] but he still believes Russia is a great power[68] and, as such, should play an important role in world politics. By this he means that Russia should play a greater role in such international organizations as the UN and CSCE, and should not be isolated from the world community. Kozyrev often stressed the importance of international institutions and believes they should play a role in resolving conflicts in the CIS. Although Kozyrev is an advocate of negotiated, political and international resolution of inter-ethnic conflicts, he does not discard the use of force in extreme situations.[69] He promoted the idea of Russian participation in peace-keeping missions as part of the country's overall diplomatic effort to improve relations with the successor states and to solve inter-ethnic conflicts. In recent months he has even demanded a UN mandate for carrying out these peace-keeping operations.[70]

The creation of legislation guaranteeing property rights is considered a priority by Russia's Choice leaders. The bloc also plans to carry out radical reform of the legal system and adopt a new Civil Code. In the bloc's view, it is also necessary to provide appropriate funding to law-enforcement organs and guarantee social safeguards for the custodians of law.

Notes

1 On 20 Feb. Ella Pamfilova was elected co-chairman of Democratic Russia (*FBIS-SOV-94-036*, 23 Feb. 1994, from *Moscow Mayak Radio Network*, 20 Feb. 1994).

2 The Moscow Association of Voters could be considered the most immediate predecessor of Democratic Russia. Created in the summer of 1989 as a coalition of voters' clubs and electoral support teams, the association organized the 1990 campaign on the basis of radical political, economic and constitutional reform. It was joined by other associations such as the Memorial Society (Memorial), the Interclub Party Group, the Moscow Popular Front, the nationwide network of voters' clubs formed during the 1989 electoral campaign to the USSR Supreme Soviet, and the Interregional Group of Deputies of the USSR Congress of People's Deputies (Yitzhak M. Brudny, "The Dynamics of "Democratic Russia," 1990–1993, *Post Soviet Affairs*, 1993, 9, 2, p. 143).

3 The law declared the RSFSR a sovereign entity whose constitutions and laws would take precedence over those of the USSR.

4 The deputies elected under the DR alliance formed the Democratic Russia parliamentary bloc.

5 The core of the movement, however, was formed by deputies highly critical of the conservative members in leadership and of the conservative majority in the USSR Supreme Soviet. They included historian Yury Afanasev; the future mayor of Moscow, Gavriil Popov; Popov's aide Ilya Zaslavsky; Yeltsin's future adviser Sergei Stankevich; and the current Moscow police chief, Arkady Murashev. (Julia Wishnevsky, "The Rise and Fall of Democratic Russia", *RFE/RL Research Report*, Vol. 2, No. 22, 29 May 1992, p. 24).

6 Yitshak M. Brudny, *op. cit.*, pp. 147–148.

7 At the Congress DR set up its governing bodies: a Co-ordinating Council (48 members) and a Council of Regional Representatives (138 in number). The movement was to be led by five co-chairmen. In January 1991, Yury Afanasev, Viktor Dmitriev, Arkady Murashev, Lev Ponomarev, and Gavriil Popov were elected the movement's first co-chairmen. Soon after the election, Popov and Dmitriev left their posts, leaving the other three as the DR co-chairmen (Yitshak M. Brudny, *op. cit.*, p. 150).

8 Also on that same date, Yury Afanasev was elected a Russian deputy as a result of a by-election in a Moscow constituency; local referendums were held in Moscow and Leningrad, and in both cases DR's proposals won a majority of votes from the population: Moscow's city and oblast administrations were merged and Leningrad was renamed St Petersburg (Julia Wishnevsky, *op. cit.*, p. 25).

9 Intellectuals appealed to Yeltsin to refrain from signing the Union Treaty that was being worked out by

him, Gorbachev, and the heads of eight other republics in Gorbachev's summer resort at Novo-Ogarevo. The Co-ordinating Council of DR, instead, expressed its support for the treaty.

10 Yu. Afanasev, L. Batkin and Yu. Burtin declared their intention to set up a new movement under the name "Democratic Russia — New Wave", while M. Sale decided to remain in the movement, hoping to replace the leadership in the new congress.

11 Yitzhak M. Brudny, *op. cit.*, pp. 162–167.

12 The Democratic Choice bloc, created on July 9 included, among others, the Democratic Russia movement, the Republican Party of Russia (set up in late 1990 on the basis of the Democratic Platform within the CPSU), and the Russian League of Businessmen (Suzanne Crow, Alexander Rahr and Vladimir Socor, eds., "Weekly Review", *RFE/RL Research Report*, Vol. 1, No. 30, 24 July 1992, p. 78). A previous attempt in April 1992 to create an alliance between DR and the Russian Union of Industrialists and Entrepreneurs (RUIE), the DPR and the People's Party of Free Russia, failed because the latter parties refused to express unconditional support for Gaidar's economic policies. As a result these parties created the Civic Union in June 1992.

13 *BBC Summary of World Broadcasts (SWB)*, SU/1820 B/2, 14 Oct. 1993, from *Ostankino Channel 1 TV, Moscow*, 13 Oct. 1993.

14 His press secretary Kostikov said, "politically and intellectually his heart is with Russia's Choice". However, during the entire election campaign, Yeltsin tried to distance himself from Russia's Choice. He did not want to be identified with any particular party or movement and preferred to be seen as the representative of all Russians (*FBIS-SOV-93-199*, 18 Oct. 1993, p. 39, from *Mayak Radio Network*, 16 Oct. 1993).

15 After a day-long bargaining, a common list was drawn up, but the final voting gave pre-eminence to Russia's Choice leaders. It excluded Democratic Russia leaders L. Ponomarev and G. Yakunin, as well as AKKOR leader V. Bashmachnikov (*Current Digest of the Post-Soviet Press*, Vol. XLV, No. 42. 17 Nov. 1993, from Yelena Pstrukhina, "Russia's Choice Splits at Once", *Megalopolis-Express*, No. 41, 20 Oct. 1993, p. 3).

16 *FBIS-SOV-93-201*, 20 Oct. 1993, p. 41, from *Izvestiya*, 19 Oct. 1993, p. 1; *BBC SWB* SU/1822 B/7 18 Oct. 1993, from *ITAR-TASS* news agency, Moscow, 16 Oct. 1993. Whereas Democratic Russia's leaders described the results of the founding congress of the Russia's Choice bloc as "our joint victory", the movement's rank and file were primarily dissatisfied with their own bosses, who failed to ensure the movement's success at the Russia's Choice congress (*BBC SWB* SU/1826 B/2, 22 Oct. 1993, from *Moskovsky Komsomolets*, 20 Oct. 1993, p. 2).

17 *FBIS-SOV-93-201*, 20 Oct. 1993, p. 42, from *ITAR-TASS*, Moscow, 19 Oct. 1993.

18 *BBC SWB* SU/1876 B/1, 20 Dec. 1993, Editorial Report. Russia's Choice's appeal was directed particularly at the Yavlinsky's bloc, the Party of Russian Unity and Accord, led by Sergei Shakhrai, and to the Russian Movement of Democratic Reforms. The Women of Russia were also considered as potential allies. The leaders of the party did not exclude a possible alliance with the communists, but only with the moderate membrs of the party (*FBIS-SOV-93-245*, 23 Dec. 1993, p. 7, from *Komsomolskaya Pravda*, 23 Dec. 1993, p. 2). The coalition of democratic parliamentary forces, however, never materialized (*FBIS-SOV-94-007*, 11 Jan. 1994, p. 45, from *ITAR-TASS*, 10 Jan. 1994).

19 *BBC SWB* SU/1874 B/11, 17 Dec. 1993, from *Izvestiya*, 15 Dec. 1993, p. 2).

20 Boris Fedorov put forward two conditions for staying in the government: he demanded the removal of Aleksandr Zaveryukha from government, and the release of Viktor Gerashchenko from the post of Chairman of the Central Bank (FBIS-SOV-94-012, 19 Jan. 1994, from *INTERFAX*, 18 Jan. 1994).

21 According to *Vesti* the name was chosen deliberately with the goal of rehabilitating a concept of liberal democracy which had been compromised by Zhirinovsky and his Liberal Democratic Party of Russia (*RFE/RL News Briefr* 11–15, April 1994, p. 5).

22 *FBIS-SOV-94-007*, 11 Jan. 1994, p. 45, from *ITAR-TASS*, Moscow, 10 Jan. 1994. On 19 Feb, RC Co-ordinating Council approved the decision and adopted a resolution which expressed support for the proposal to form a new party made by the RC parliamentary group and urged regional Democratic Russia branches to help organize the party (*FBIS-SOV-94-035*, 22 Feb. 1994, p. 29, from *INTERFAX*, Moscow, 20 Feb. 1994).

23 *FBIS-SOV-94-063*, 1 April 1994, p. 24, from *ITAR-TASS*, Moscow, 31 March 1994; and *TRUD*, 10 March 1993, pp. 1–2.

24 *FBIS-SOV-94-035*, 22 Feb. 1994, *op. cit.*, p. 29.

25 In these regions, party organizations were set up independently from Democratic Russia, although these regions already had organizing committees with Democratic Russia members.

26 *Izvestiya*, 19 Oct. 1993, p. 1.

27 *FBIS-SOV-94-026*, 8 Feb. 1994, from *Moscow Radio Rossiya Network*, 8 Feb. 1994.

28 *The Current Digest of the Post-Soviet Press*, Vol. XLV, No. 48, December, p. 5 from *Sevodnya*, 27 Nov. p. 2 — Lawyer Andrei Makarov said "The position of Russia's Choice is absolutely unequivocal. We support the draft constitution and call for all citizens of Russia to vote for it" (*BBC SWB*, SU/1860 B/5, 1 Dec. 1993).

29 *BBC SWB*, SU/1828 B/4, 25. Oct. 1993, from *Mayak Radio*, Moscow, 23 Oct. 1993.

30 *FBIS-SOV-93-202*, 21 Oct. 1993, p. 33, from *Kuranty*, 20 Oct. 1993, p. 4.
31 *FBIS-SOV-93-203*, 22 Oct. 1993, p. 34, from *Obshchaya Gazeta*, No. 14/16, 22–28 Oct. 1993, p. 8.
32 *FBIS-SOV-93-203*, 22 Oct. 1993, p. 36, from *Krasnaya Zvezda*, 22 Oct. 1993, p. 3.
33 *FBIS-SOV-93-199*, 18 Oct. 1993, p. 40, from *ITAR-TASS World Service*, 16 Oct. 1993.
34 *BBC SWB* SU/1860 B/9, 1 Dec. 1993, Editorial Report.
35 *FBIS-SOV-93-203*, 22 Oct. 1993, p. 34, from *Obshchaya Gazeta*, No. 14/16, 22–28 Oct. 1993; *FBIS-SOV-93-211*, 3 Nov. 1993, p. 40, from *ITAR-TASS*, 3 Nov. 1993.
36 Interviewed by *Mayak Radio*, Gaidar said that the most important long-term task was the creation of a reliable legal base for private enterprise and private ownership. This meant reforming the law in order to establish clear-cut and well-defined relations (*BBC SWB* SU/1836 B/1, 3 Nov. 1993, from *Mayak Radio*, Moscow, 30 Oct. 1993).
37 *FBIS-SOV-93-199*, 18 Oct. 1993, p. 39, from *ITAR-TASS World Service*, 16 Oct. 1993; *FBIS-SOV-93-203*, *op cit.*, p. 35.
38 *BBC SWB*, SU/1822 B/6, 18 Oct. 1993, from *ITAR-TASS World Service*, 16 Oct. 1993.
39 *FBIS-SOV-93-199*, 18 Oct. 1993, p. 42, from *Mayak Radio*, Moscow, 17 Oct. 1993.
40 *FBIS-SOV-93-202*, 21 Oct. 1993, p. 31, from *ITAR-TASS World Service*, 20 Oct. 1993.
41 *FBIS-SOV-93-203*, *op. cit.*, p. 35.
42 *Rossyskaya Gazeta*, 6 Oct. 1993, p. 2.
43 *FBIS-SOV-93-201*, 20 Oct. 1993, *op. cit.*, p. 41.
44 *FBIS-SOV-93-219*, 16 Nov. 1993, p. 31, Editorial Report.
45 *Ibid.*, p. 31.
46 *Ibid.*, p. 31.
47 Visiting a car factory near Moscow, Gaidar refused to write off its debts but promised to help it to look for [private] investors (*BBC SWB* SU/1837 B/10, 4 Nov. 1993, from *Russia TV channel*, Moscow, 30 Oct. 1993).
48 *FBIS-SOV-93-203*, *op. cit.*, p. 34.
49 *Izvestiya*, 19 Nov. 1993, p. 4. According to the same source, bankers had threatened Russia's Choice with an election boycott unless its leaders in the government adopted measures that restricted foreign rivals.
50 *Rossiyskiye Vesti*, 17 Nov. 1993, p. 1.
51 *BBC SWB* SU/1870 B/12, 13 Dec. 1993, from *Mayak Radio*, 10 Dec. 1993.
52 *Izvestiya*, 6 Nov. 1993, p. 2.
53 *FBIS-SOV-93-223*, 22 Nov. 1993, p. 30, from *ITAR-TASS*, Moscow, 22 Nov. 1993.
54 *BBC SWB* SU/1870 B/12, 13 Dec. 1993, *op cit.*
55 *Rossiyskiye Vesti*, 17 Nov. 1993, p. 1.
56 *FBIS-SOV-93-222*, 19 Nov. 1993, p. 27, from *ITAR-TASS*, Moscow, 19 Nov. 1993.
57 *BBC SWB* SU/1862 B/7, 3 Dec. 1993, from *Ostankino Channel 1 TV*, Moscow, 30 Nov. 1993.
58 *Krasnaya Zvezda*, 2 Dec. 1993, p. 2.
59 *Ibid.*, p. 2.
60 This was expressed by Sergei Yushenkov in an interview with *Radio Moscow* (*FBIS-SOV-93-228*, 30 Nov. 1993, p. 30, from *Radio Moscow*, 29 Nov. 1993).
61 *FBIS-SOV-93-201*, 20 Oct. 1993, *op. cit.*, p. 41.
62 *BBC SWB* SU/1859 B/5, 30 Nov. 1993, from *ITAR-TASS World Service*, Moscow, 25 Nov. 1993.
63 Alexei G. Arbatov, "Russia's Foreign Policy Alternatives" *International Security*, Vol. 18, No. 2 (Fall 1993), p. 10.
64 In A. Kozyrev's view, "the most important thing was to prevent Russia from dropping out of international relations as a result of the disintegration of the USSR" (Suzanne Crow, "Russia's Relations with Members of the Commonwealth", *RFE-RL Research Report*, Vol. 1, No. 19, 8 May 1992, p. 9).
65 Suzanne Crow, "Russian Federation Faces Foreign Policy Dilemmas", *RFE/RL Research Report*, 6 March 1992, Vol. 1, No. 10, p. 19.
66 Suzanne Crow, "Russia Prepares to Take Hard Line on 'Near Abroad'", *RFE/RL Research Report*, Vol. 1, No. 32, 14 Aug. 1992, p. 22.
67 Alexander Rahr, "'Atlanticists' versus 'Eurasians' in Russian Foreign Policy", *RFE/RL Research Report*, Vol. 1, No. 22, 29 May 1992, p. 17.
68 Suzanne Crow, "Russia Debates its National Interests", *RFE/RL Research Report*, Vol. 1, No. 28, 10 July 1992, p. 45.
69 Jeff Checkel, "Russian Foreign Policy: Back to the Future?" *RFE/RL Research Report*, Vol. 1, No. 41, 16 Oct. 1992, p. 21.
70 Suzanne Crow, "Russian Peacekeeping: Defence, Diplomacy, or Imperialism?" *RFE/RL Research Report*, Vol. 1, No. 37, 18 Sept. 1992, p. 39.

Russia's Future–New Names (RFNN)
Budushchee-Rossii–Novye Imena

History. On Oct. 25, 1993, the Youth Movement in Support of the Party of the People's Party of Free Russia, the Civic Union Political–Economic Association and the Russian Youth League formed an election bloc, called RFNN, and made Oleg Sokolov the movement's leader. The list of candidates to the State Duma includes 150 persons from 40 regions of Russia. Sokolov said that the bloc intended to attract the attention of electors with new names and with the ideas of non-confrontational policy and national statehood. The bloc succeeded in collecting the required number of signatures to participate in the elections.

Leadership. Vyacheslav Lashchevsky (leader of the Russian Youth League); Oleg Sokolov (youth representative of the People's Party of Free Russia); Vladimir Mironov (dir. of the Institute of Politics); Vladimir Zharikhin; Aleksandr Kerimov (lawyer); I. Ivanenko (former ch. of the Russian KGB); I. Vinogradova (former dep. of the Russian Supreme Soviet and leader of the New Russia People's Party in parliament).

Programme. The bloc's programme is based on the recognition of the supremacy of the rights, liberties and vitally important values of the individual and society over the state. In order to achieve this, it claims that it is necessary to restore civil peace and make the state safe for society. The goal should be an efficiently functioning and truly federal, democratic state and the strengthening of its position in the economy. The association favours the formation of an effectively functioning, truly federal, democratic state and the strengthening of its role in the economy.

In economic policy it aims to create a market economy in the interests of broad strata of society, relying on the country's own economic potential. The bloc stands for the market economy but entry to the market must be carried out gradually and not regardless of cost. It will not accept a situation in which vast masses of people are left below the poverty line. It considers that private ownership of land is necessary, but that there must be certain restrictions with regard to its use and its acquisition by foreign citizens.[1]

Foreign policy should be drawn up with strict consideration for Russia's interests as a nation state.

In security policy, the bloc favours raising the armed forces' prestige during the transition to a contract and conscription system of manning the ranks. In order to improve patriotic training, the Russian Youth League was willing to set up organizations in military units. [It is not yet known if the military leadership will permit this.] National security must be ensured not by the level of armament but by the degree of development of the scientific and technical potential.

Social policy is a priority. It radically disagrees with the ultraliberal policy in the socio-economic sphere pursued by Egor Gaidar. In the transitional period to a market economy the state is obliged to take care of those sections of society which for objective reasons cannot adapt quickly and painlessly to the new social conditions. If production begins working there will be money for the social sphere. Therefore, first, it is necessary immediately to create a rational and just system of taxation and ensure that it is observed. This tax system must stimulate production and philanthrophy. Second, it is necessary to reduce the cost of maintaining state functionaries and consequently to reduce the state apparatus itself which now exceeds the former [Soviet] Union apparatus in size [about three times as large].[2] Finally, it is necessary to optimize the conditions for investment, both domestic and foreign, in production. In addition, it is necessary to encourage support for the social sphere, not by state structures but by private structures — it is necessary to create the conditions under which it will be beneficial for them to invest money there.[3]

Notes

1 *FBIS-SOV-93-218*, 15 Nov. 1993, from *Rossiikie Vesti*, 12 Nov. 1993.
2 *FBIS-SOV-93-226*, 26 Nov. 1993, from Ostankino TV, 23 Nov. 1993.
3 *FBIS-SOV-93-218*, 15 Nov. 1993, from *Rossiikie Vesti*, 12 Nov. 1993.

Russian Communist Workers' Party (RCWP)
Rossiiskaya Kommunisticheskaya Rabochaya Partiya

History. The party was founded after the banning of the CPSU and was based on the Communist Initiative Movement. This movement had emerged from the movement of supporters of a Communist Party of Russia within the united platform of workers of the CPSU. The First Initiative Congress took place in Leningrad in three stages, April 21–22, June 9–10 and Sept. 20–21, 1990. Besides the Initiative Movement, members of Unity, the organization of Nina Andreeva and the national bolshevik wing of radical patriots, led by Aleksandr Romanenko, took part in the congress but both these groups were in the minority. The Congress put forward its own candidates for election to the CC, CPSU and the CC, CPRF, elected an organizational bureau, and Viktor Tyulkin and Aleksei Sergeev, among others were elected to it. At the XXVIII Congress of the CPSU, Aleksei Sergeev, a professor of economics, was elected to the CC, CPSU.

The Second Initiative Congress took place in Leningrad on April 20–21, 1991, and in Moscow on June 29–30, 1991. They adopted a motion of no confidence in the "anti-popular course of the anti-communist faction of Gorbachev" and also demanded the resignation of Mikhail Gorbachev as Secretary-General of the CPSU. The Initiative Movement split into two wings after the congress: the radical wing, led by Viktor Anpilov and the moderate wing, led by Richard Kosolapov. As a result two sets of programmatic documents were prepared and at the second part of the congress, the draft programme of the CPSU, prepared by Kosolapov's group, was adopted.

In August 1991 Russian members of the Initiative Movement set up an organizational committee to found the Russian Communist Workers' Party. The Moscow preparatory conference took place on Nov. 17, 1991. The meeting set up a Moscow Organization of Communists, elected an organizational bureau, headed by first secretary Viktor Anpilov, and delegates to the founding congress. The first part of the founding Congress of the RCWP took place on Nov. 23–24, 1991, in Ekaterinburg. It was attended by 525 delegates from all regions of Russia. The Congress adopted a declaration about a programme (based on Kosolapov's draft), elected a CC of 85 full members and four candidate members and a 15 member Central Control Commission. During the autumn the embryonic began to establish the pro-communist movement, Labouring Russia (*Trudovaya Rossiya*).

A plenum of the CC, RCWP in St Petersburg on Jan. 5–6, 1992, elected a CC organizational bureau consisting of several secretaries of the CC. The leading role in the organizational bureau was played by Viktor Tyulkin, CC secretary for organizational questions. The radical wing of the party had grown more influential by the middle of

1992. The July and September plenums of the CC, RCWP approved the "Leningrad" draft programme of the M. Popov group, not the "Moscow" draft of R. Kosolapov. The problem concerning the programme was only taken at the second part of the Constituent Congress, in December 1992, in Chelyabinsk. In May 1992 the Russian Ministry of Justice issued an official warning to the RCWP about its "programme of extreme measures", adopted by the CC, RCWP.

A plenum of the CC in St Petersburg, on Sept. 18–19, 1992, decided to hold the second part of the Constituent Congress in Chelyabinsk and also a decree on preparations for the celebrating of the 75th anniversary of the Great October Socialist Revolution. It also expressed support for the convening of the Second All-People's Veche (Assembly) on Oct. 24, 1992. The second part of the Constituent Congress convened in Chelyabinsk on Dec. 5, 1992. Mikhail Titov and Richard Kosolapov were removed from the CC and it was decided not to join the National Salvation Front. On Feb. 20, 1993, a campaign to collect a million signatures for the holding of a referendum on the adoption of a new Soviet constitution began. This proposed constitution had been drafted by a group headed by Yury Slobodkin, a Russian Supreme Soviet deputy. If the authorities ignored this initiative, the RCWP intended to call for a massive campaign of civil disobedience.

Viktor Tyulkin, secretary of the Organization Bureau of the CC, stated that the CWPR had decided not to participate in the elections to the State Duma, urging a boycott instead. The party has also not decided on its policy towards elections to local government bodies. The party still insists that a referendum should be held on the constitution, drafted by Yury Slobodkin. More than one million signatures had been collected in support of a referendum.[1]

Notes
1 *FBIS-SOV-93-204*, 25 Oct. 1993, from *Interfax*, 23 Oct. 1993.

Russian Movement for Democratic Reforms
Rossiiskoe Dvizhenie Demokraticheskik Reform

Foundation. Feb. 15, 1992.

Leadership. Gavriil Popov (leader) Anatoly Sobchak (Mayor of St Petersburg); Svyatoslav Fedorov (physician and general director of the Mikrokhirurgiya glaza inter-branch scientific technical complex, and public entrepreneur); Oleg Basilashvili (actor); Aleksandr Yakovlev (academician and chairman of the Commission under the Russian Federation President for the Rehabilitation of Victims of Political Repression); Evgeny Shaposhnikov (Air Force Marshal and former head of the CIS forces); Ivan Kivelidi (chairman of the Free Labour Party, chairman of the Council for the Development of Entrepreneurship under the Russian government); Saygali Sharipov (deputy chairman of the Independent Miners Union of Russia); Aleksandr Braginsky (deputy premier of Moscow for public and political relations); Sergei Krasavchenko (economist, first deputy leader of the Russian Federation President's Administration); Nikolai Shmelev (economist, writer and professor); Evgeny Kozhokin (deputy chairman of the State Committee for Federation and Nationalities Affairs, and member of the Russian Free Labour Party); Oleg Gazmanov (composer, singer); Aleksandr Kiselev (scientist, and chairman of the RMDR executive committee); Kirill Lavrov (actor, people's artist); Viktor Nekrasov (chairman of the Russian Seamen's Trade Union); Ilya Roitman (historian, president of the Institute of Politics and International Relations).

History. On July 1, 1991, a series of prominent Soviet politicians — former Politburo members Aleksandr Yakovlev and Eduard Shevardnadze, the head of the USSR Scientific and Industrial Union Arkady Volsky, RSFSR Vice President Aleksandr Rutskoi, RSFSR Prime Minister Ivan Silaev, Mayors of Leningrad and Moscow Anatoly Sobchak and Gavriil Popov, former presidential adviser Stanislav Shatalin, and economist Nikolai Petrakov — issued a formal statement announcing their intention of forming a new political movement, to be called the Movement for Democratic Reforms (MDR). They planned the movement as an all-Union organization and appealed to democratic and reform-oriented forces throughout the USSR — in particular to liberal members of the CPSU — to join them. The MDR was initially intended to be an organized opposition bloc, powerful enough to counter the CPSU. But by the summer of 1991, all hope that the CPSU could be reformed from within, or that the democratic wing of the party might obtain some of its assets as part of a negotiated split had faded, and most liberals had either resigned or been expelled from the organization. Many smaller parties had previously been established to challenge the monopoly of the CPSU, but none were large or influential enough to act as an effective opposition to that 15-million-strong organization. The movement intended to create a broad coalition of democratic forces which would join the new democrats with the liberal members of the Communist Party. At the same time, the aim was to split the CPSU by attracting disaffected liberal party members to the movement.[1]

The statement called for a "qualitatively new step in democratic development" and for the return to "Soviet citizens of what 'has been taken away from them'", including the return of land to the peasantry.[2] It also emphasized the need for the privatization and demilitarization of the Soviet economy. The statement, however, stressed the need to preserve the integrity of the Soviet Union. Although it envisaged a renewed union, "a democratic state emerging from the voluntary union of sovereign nations", it insisted that "the disintegration of the totalitarian system must not lead to the severing of ties that have been naturally established between peoples during the course of history". Unlike Democratic Russia, the MDR supported the Novo-Ogarevo version of the Treaty of the Union, and Mikhail Gorbachev.[3] Within the democratic camp, the reaction to the creation of the new organization was mixed. Democratic Russia's leader, Yury Afanasev, questioned the viability of an all-Union movement at a time when the survival of the USSR was at stake. Other members of the same organization considered the movement unworkable at all-Union level, because democratic organizations in other republics, such as Ukraine for example, would probably not support it. Some members of the democratic movement reacted negatively to the approval given by Mikhail Gorbachev to the new body. For many the real aim was to "create a new communist party for the President", its real function being to act as a vehicle whereby Gorbachev could abandon the CPSU and win re-election as USSR President. Critics argued that the movement was an attempt by the old Communist *nomenklatura* to preserve its position in a post-communist society.[4] Other democratic organizations — such as the Republican Party of Russia, led by Vladimir Lysenko — as well as RSFSR President Yeltsin reacted positively.[5] Nikolai Travkin, leader of the Democratic Party of Russia, although supportive of the new organization, favoured the setting up of a centralized party as opposed to a loose movement. He also set out another condition for his participation in the organization: that all members of the movement abandon the CPSU. As these two conditions were not fulfilled, he decided not to participate in the new movement.[6]

During the attempted coup in August 1991, the MDR proved very successful in gathering most former communists around President Yeltsin, Sobchak and Popov. However, after the aborted coup and the subsequent banning of the CPSU, the primary purpose of the new movement — to create an alternative structure to the CPSU — disappeared. At the MDR's first organizing conference in September, the aim of the movement was already in doubt. Forty-one of the 450 delegates to the conference responded to an appeal by Popov and founded the Russian Party of Democratic Transformation within the MDR.[7] The influence of MDR decreased during the autumn of 1991, as a result of its continued support for the USSR President Mikhail Gorbachev, and its reluctance to accept the disintegration of the Union.

With the dissolution of the Soviet Union, the movement lost one of its central aims, to become an all-Union democratic political force. The movement's central political task became the establishment of strong links with other democratic movements across the former Soviet Union, as well as proposing peaceful and democratic solutions to ethnic conflicts in the former USSR.[8] At the first MDR congress in December 1991, the delegates adopted the movement's charter, elected seven co-chairmen[9] and, after some hesitation, voted in support of the CIS. The International MDR was set up to co-ordinate relations among branches in each of the former Soviet republics. Throughout 1992, the MDR issued a series of statements and appeals for democratic solutions in particular trouble spots such as the Caucasus and Moldova, but its efforts produced little tangible results. At the second congress of the International MDR, held on Dec. 26, 1992, the need to stop "fratricidal wars" became the main theme of discussion, and the defence of human rights within the CIS states became the top priority of the MDR. The congress, consisting of 86 delegates and 46 observers representing all CIS states, stated its primary goal to be the transformation of the CIS "from a mechanism of civilized divorce into a mechanism for the consolidation of the new states".[10] In practice, however, the International MDR had a not very significant impact on relations among democratic political groups in the CIS states. In February 1992, it lost some of its most influential leaders, such as Shevardnadze, Yakovlev and Volsky; while Popov and Sobchak were mainly dedicated to their jobs as mayors of Moscow and St Petersburg respectively, and then became involved in setting up the Russian branch of MDR.[11]

Described as "the free association of parties, organizations, and individuals campaigning for a socially oriented state with a market economy", the Russian MDR initially got the support of the Republican Party of Russia, the People's Party of Free Russia, and the Russian Party for Democratic Transformation, but failed to gain the support of more influential democratic organizations such as "Democratic Russia" or the Democratic Party of Russia, led by Nikolai Travkin. A further blow to the movement occurred in February 1992 when the Republican Party of Russia abandoned the movement. Furthermore, its leaders became increasingly isolated as power in Russia shifted to the Russian Congress of People's Deputies, where the movement had only a few deputies. A debate among the leadership took place over the new role of the movement, since political isolation and lack of a definite constituency were driving the movement increasingly into disarray. At its founding congress, held in Nizhny Novgorod on Feb. 15, 1992, the delegates decided to act as a "constructive opposition" (opposing specific policies of the government, but not attempting to remove the President or the government from office).[12] The ultimate goal of the movement became the adoption of a new constitution to replace the existing structures of the Russian Federation. It called for the limitation of functions of the legislative branch, its non-interference in the executive power, and "early elections of all legislative bodies from top to bottom".[13] In March 1992, together with Democratic Russia, the RMDR proposed the holding of a referendum on the dissolution of the Congress of People's Deputies. The proposal however, was condemned by the International MDR and in May 1992, the Russian MDR finally separated from the International MDR.[14]

During the whole of 1992, the RMDR actively supported President Yeltsin and the course of reforms in his struggle against parliament. By the end of 1992, aware of the lack of legitimacy of the Congress, the movement called several times for the setting up of a Constituent Assembly to draft a new Constitution, and Popov even expressed support for the introduction of presidential rule and the temporary suspension of the legislature. In his view the "solution lay in the summoning of a Constituent Assembly, the adoption of a new Constitution and the calling of early elections".[15]

On the eve of the VIII Congress of People's Deputies, the RMDR joined the conference organized by all democratic parties and movements which had not been invited to the "round table" talks that were taking place between the parliamentary parties and the government. The RMDR signed all conference documents which called for a real "round table" between all political forces, aimed at finding a constructive way out of the political crisis.

On Oct. 9, 1993, the Movement for Democratic Reforms decided to enter the election campaign as an independent political force. Sobchak tried unsuccessfully to rally Grigory Yavlinsky and other democrats to his movement, in order to establish a democratic coalition in opposition to the pro-government bloc Russia's Choice. Yavlinsky instead decided to set up his own movement.

Although during the elections the movement suffered a heavy defeat and did not manage to pass the 5 per cent barrier for proportional representation in parliament, Shaposhnikov said the RMDR "did not plan to dissolve itself". He added that the RMDR would lend its support to Russia's democratic forces and to the reform course.[16] In January, the RMDR urged "all democratic forces not connected with the government to begin talks on the co-ordination of a single new reform platform, to be called the Democratic Alternative".[17]

Programme. The adoption of a new constitution to replace the old Soviet one was announced as the main goal of the movement during its first congress, held in Nizhny Novgorod on Feb. 15, 1992. At the time, the Russian Constitutional Drafting Commission (headed by Oleg Rumyantsev) was drawing up a constitutional project, while Sergei Shakhrai was preparing an alternative draft on behalf of the President.[18] Anatoly Sobchak objected to both these drafts, arguing that they did not adequately defend individual rights nor clearly delineate the separation of powers. He directed the preparation of another draft (based on a document drawn up by the late Andrei Sakharov) which placed more emphasis on human rights and gave the legislature greater powers over the executive branches. The draft also allowed each ethnic group within the Russian Federation to negotiate its status.[19] Sobchak hoped that the MDR would be able to persuade Congress to discuss his draft but this never happened. The RMDR also insisted that the new constitution should be ratified by a constitutional assembly and not by the Congress of People's Deputies, no longer considered legitimate. In the RMDR's view, the Congress lacked a popular mandate and had discredited itself during the constant struggle with the President.[20]

Although Sobchak did not succeed in imposing his draft he became involved in further constitutional projects. In April 1993, he participated together with legal expert Sergei Alekseev (formerly the chairman of the USSR Committee for Constitutional Supervision), August Mishin (a specialist on American constitutional law), and Sergei Shakhrai in the preparation of the second "presidential" draft. The draft, released on April 29, 1993, right after Yeltsin's success in the referendum, was heavily criticized by liberal and conservative politicians alike for its clearly presidential character. Gavriil Popov questioned the balance of power between the upper and lower chambers, and Sobchak himself, co-author of the draft, stated that it would be suitable only for a transitional period, which he estimated could be as long as 10 years.[21] In early June 1993, under Yeltsin's directive, a Constitutional Assembly was called to work out a final draft on the basis of the "presidential" draft and the draft prepared by the Constitutional Commission. The Assembly comprised 750 delegated members representing various Russian institutions and Sobchak co-chaired the group of representatives of political parties, trade unions, mass movements and religious confessions.[22] The Assembly prepared another draft which incorporated many features of the Constitutional Commission version but resembled more the last presidential draft. This version, with some additional changes, became the final one presented by Yeltsin to the Russian population in a referendum.

During the electoral campaign the RMDR urged its voters to support the constitution, although it was aware of the draft's flaws. Gavriil Popov said that although "the draft is not a masterpiece of democracy, it must be adopted in order to avoid a power vacuum".[23] However, the RMDR believed that the draft constitution should serve as the country's fundamental law for the transition period only.[24]

The movement mainly objected to excessive power granted by the Constitution to the President, to the detriment of the legislative and judicial branches of power.[25] Although Gavriil Popov agreed with the idea of Russia becoming a presidential republic, the President being the head of state, he maintained that his powers and those of Parliament should be restrained.[26] Sobchak viewed the new parliament as a temporary body mainly concerned with the drafting of a new constitution. In his own words: "the new parliament has the task, which is of vital importance for Russia, of adopting a constitution."[27]

The RMDR also disagreed completely with the idea that ministers could combine their posts in executive bodies of power with membership in the future Federal Assembly. Popov believed that such practices would revive the old parliament of the Brezhnev era, which overflowed with ministers, judges, and prosecutors devising laws for themselves.[28]

The RMDR strongly disagrees with the economic policy conducted by the Gaidar government. Although it supports the process of economic reforms, the RMDR "favours not a radical but a liberal-democratic reform, more gradual and without stressful disruptions".[29] The movement calls for the abandonment of the government's policy which is preoccupied "with taxes and finances", and advocates the support of production and entrepreneurship.[30]

Interviewed by Russian television, Sobchak stated that "encouragement of production, support of producers, rather than financial reforms, should be chosen as the basis of economic reforms".[31] Popov added that the economic policy presented by the RMDR is an alternative to the present government's course, which "instead of monetarism, places emphasis on production".[32]

The movement therefore supports a gradual transition towards private ownership. Interviewed by ITAR-TASS, entrepreneur Svyatoslav Fedorov explained that the Russian economy would benefit from the development of a high number of private owners and profitable enterprises, and added that raw materials should become the property of independent owners, rather than the state.[33] The energy sector should also be transferred to private hands, so that production costs are reduced and energy becomes cheaper.[34] In his view, the task of the future government should be to integrate Russia into the world economy. Russia should enter the world market "not with spoiled tomatoes, but with cars no worse than the Mercedes and planes no worse than the Boeing".[35]

The RMDR proposes drastic tax reductions and suggests that the budget deficit be reduced by serious cuts in the administrative apparatus of the state, which, according to Aleksandr Yakovlev, poses the principal danger to the reforms.[36] In the view of S. Fedorov, the "enormous army of bureaucrats" absorbs 63 per cent of the entire budget, and is the strongest opponent of reform.[37]

The RMDR supports the introduction of private land ownership and the development of private farming, and proposes carrying out land reform by issuing land vouchers.[38] The movement also favours the preservation and the granting of state support to those existing *sovkhozes* and *kolkhozes* that operate efficiently. It proposes to implement the first stage of agrarian reform more rapidly by giving every Russian one-tenth of a hectare.[39] The RMDR favours allocating 10 per cent of land close to villages and cities to private farmers.[40]

The RMDR believes that the reform process should not be carried out at the expense of the Russian people. Instead, the reforms need to be directed towards the needs of the people. Employees should receive a minimum wage, and in certain sectors of the economy, salaries as well as pensions should be adjusted according to the inflation rate. The RMDR favours the implementation of a programme that guarantees higher education and medical care for every Russian citizen. According to the RMDR a certain minimum percentage of the annual state budget should be devoted, by law, to the financing of education, culture and science.[41]

Before the collapse of the Soviet Union, the Movement of Democratic Reforms advocated the preservation of a renewed Union and in 1991 strongly supported the Novo Ogarevo process. Its disarray after the coup was partly due to its support for the Union and Gorbachev. Although RMDR leaders finally resigned themselves to the emergence of a series of independent states on the territory of the USSR, they always favoured keeping strong ties with them.

At present, the RMDR intends to promote the creation of "a new and equitable union of some of the former republics in the fields of defence, economics and foreign policy". According to Evgeny Shaposhnikov, "we must act so that people in the CIS will live better than they did in the USSR". The RMDR foresees establishing a programme for protecting the rights of "Russians in the nearby foreign countries" which envisages the granting of dual citizenship to Russians, awarding of cultural autonomy to Russians, and the creation of a long-term programme for their resettlement in Russia.[42]

Popov, a strong advocate of a strengthening of ties among the states of the former Soviet Union, albeit by peaceful means, believes Russia should unite with those countries of the CIS "which want to unite". He said that "if we fail to do this within the present generation which speaks a good language and has an identical mentality, the unification process may last for decades".[43]

The RMDR believes Russia's foreign policy should be based on the country's national interests. However, Russia's policies should not infringe on the rights and interests of other people. In Sobchak's words, "[the government] must, among other things, concentrate on a thought-out foreign strategy which would take into consideration the Russian national interests, especially in its relations with the former Soviet republics". With regard to the "near abroad", the movement supports the establishment of a united European state within the CIS framework.

Regarding the role of peace-keeping forces in 1992, Marshal Evgeny Shaposhnikov, commander in chief of the Joint Armed Forces of the Commonwealth of Independent States, highlighted the need to prevent and respond to threats along the "external frontiers" of the CIS. He was referring to the highly explosive Tajik-Afghan border and proposed creating a military force that would police the CIS's external frontiers and prevent the eruption of hostilities, for instance between Afghanistan and Tajikistan or between Turkey and Armenia. Although he favoured setting up a force that would be capable of reacting to particular conflicts along the borders of the CIS, he was reluctant to use such force to settle inter-ethnic conflicts. At that time there was strong distaste among the Russian Armed Forces for involvement in peace-keeping operations in conflicts such as the one between Armenia and Azerbaijan over Nagorno-Karabakh. However, the Armed forces opposed the external participation of the UN, the CSCE or NATO in these conflicts. Shaposhnikov, in particular, rejected the introduction of military force or observers from these international organizations. He believes this is the sole responsibility of the CIS.[44]

In the military sphere, the RMDR advocates the establishment of a world-wide security system as well as an all-European and regional security system. The movement deems it necessary to establish open and effective control over the production and trading of weapons and military equipment. In its view, the revenues from arms sales must be used primarily to resolve the Army's housing problems, and to reintegrate military professionals into the market economy. Revenues should also be devoted to military training programmes.[45]

Shaposhnikov said that he was relieved that the enemy-seeking approach had been removed from the Russian military doctrine. He said that now politicians should be able to resolve all problems by peaceful means and added that if the state needed the army, then it should take proper care of it and provide for its servicemen accordingly.[46]

The RMDR favours a transformation of Russia "from a unitary state with growing disintegrative tendencies to a genuine, and therefore stable, federation. This will permit the acceleration of reforms in Russia". The RMDR envisages Russia as a presidential republic with autonomous Federation components.[47]

Professor Svyatoslav Fedorov, co-ordinator of RMDR, supported the creation of a federal democratic state and stressed the need "to ensure the real separation of functions between the [centre] and the components of the Federation; as well as the clear delimitation of functions at federal level between the President — the leader of the state — and the government — the practical organizer of reforms — and parliament".[48] He recognized, however, that it was necessary to strengthen the centre and free it from the tutelage of the regions, leaving at federal level only those tasks which are essential for the preservation of the state's integrity.[49] Although a new approach must be taken to relations with the constituent parts of the Federation, and more attention must be paid to the Russian interests, this should not be done at the expense of the rights and interests of other peoples on the Federation's territory.[50]

Notes

1 Vera Tolz, "Political Parties in Russia," *RFE/RL Research Report*, Vol. 1, No. 1, 3 Jan. 1992, p. 13; Yitzhak M. Brudny, "The Dynamics of Democratic Russia", 1990–1993, *Post-Soviet Affairs*, 1993, 9, 2, p. 154.
2 Elizabeth Teague and Vera Tolz, "Prominent Reformers Create Opposition Movement", *Report on the USSR*, 12 July 1991, p. 2
3 Vladimir Pribylovsky, *Slovar novyk politicheskik partii y organizatsii Rossii*, Panorama, Moscow, Dec. 1992, p. 14.
4 In spite of the ambiguous reaction from Democratic Russia, the MDR announced its intention to collaborate with the movement. Three members of the latter's co-ordinating council (S. Trube, A. Musykantsky and V. Lysenko), as well as former co-chairman G. Popov, became members of the political council of MDR.
5 Elizabeth Teague and Vera Tolz, *op. cit.*, p. 3. The movement also received the support of the chairmen of the local soviets and executive committees of a series of Russian cities — Ekaterinburg, Novosibirsk and Volvograd (Vladimir Pribylovsky, *op. cit.*, p. 14).
6 Vladimir Pribylovsky, *op. cit.*, p. 14.
7 Popov himself, however, did not join this new organization, which was headed by the people's deputy Aleksandr Kiselev (Vladimir Pribylovsky, *op. cit.*, p. 15).
8 Carla Thorson. "A Loss of Direction for Russia's Movement for Democratic Reforms", *RFE/RL Research Report*, Vol. 2, No. 10, 5 March 1993, p. 12.
9 They included A. Volsky, G. Popov, A. Sobchak, E. Shevardnadze, V. Shostakovksy, S. Shatalin, and A. Yakovlev. Its collective membership included the Republican Party of the Russian Federation, People's Party of Free Russia (Rutskoi's party) and the Russian Party of Democratic Reforms.
10 *Rabochaya Tribuna*, 26 December 1992.
11 In June 1991, Popov resigned as mayor of Moscow in order to work full-time for the Russian MDR (Carla Thorson, *op. cit.*, p. 13).
12 At the Congress, Popov was elected chairman of the RMDR and Sobchak became a member of its Political Council, together with Popov, Aleksandr Kiselev, Aleksandr Braginsky, and Pavel Gusev (R. Medvedev (ed.) *Spravochnik — politicheskie partii, dvizheniya i bloki sovremennoi Rossii*, Nizhny Novgorod, 1993, p. 52). Also at the Congress, the Republican Party of the Russian Federation left the movement because it opposed the single chairmanship of Popov, which it believed threatened to transform the RMDR into a superparty (Vladimir Pribylovsky, *op. cit.*, p. 15).
13 R. Medvedev, *op. cit.*, p. 52.
14 *Ibid.*, p. 52
15 *Ibid.*, p. 52
16 *FBIS-SOV-93-240*, 16 Dec. 1993, p. 23, from *Kuranty*, 15 Dec. 1993, p. 2.
17 *FBIS-SOV-94-001*, 3 Jan. 1994, p. 31, from *Izevstiya*, 31 Dec. 1993, p. 8.
18 For more details on the constitutional drafts see: Vera Tolz, "Russia's Constitutional Debate", *RFE/RL Research Report*, Vol. 2, No. 29, 16 July 1993, pp. 1–12; Ariel Cohen, "Competing Visions: Russian Constitutional Drafts and Beyond", *RFE/RL Research Report*, Vol. 2, No. 38, 24 Sept. 1993, p. 50–56; and Carla Thorson, "Russia's Draft Constitution", *RFE/RL Research Report*, Vol. 2, No. 48, 3 Dec. 1993, pp. 9–15
19 Carla Thorson, "Toward the Rule of Law: Russia", *RFE/RL Research Report*, Vol. 1, No. 27, 3 July 1992, p. 18.
20 Carla Thorson, "A Loss of Direction for Russia's Movement for Democratic Reforms, *op. cit.*, pp. 13–14.
21 Vera Tolz, "Russia's Constitutional Debate", *op. cit.*, pp. 5–6.
22 *Ibid.*, pp. 8–9.
23 *Segodnya*, 27 Nov. 1993, p. 2.
24 *FBIS-SOV-93-223*, 22 Nov. 1993, p. 27, from *ITAR-TASS*, Moscow, 19 Nov. 1993.
25 *Segodnya*, 27 Nov. 1993, p. 2.
26 *FBIS-SOV-93-195*, 12 Oct. 1993, p. 74, from *INTERFAX*, Moscow, 9 Oct. 1993.
27 *FBIS-SOV-93-196*, 13 Oct 1993, p. 60, from *Bild am Sonntag*, 10 Oct. 1993, p. 4.
28 *FBIS-SOV-93-201*, 20 Oct. 1993, p. 40, from *Moscow Programma Radio Odin Network*, 19 Oct. 1993.
29 *Nezavisimaya Gazeta*, 10 Nov. 1993, p. 1.
30 *Segodnya*, 28 Oct. 1993, p. 2.
31 *FBIS-SOV-93-207*, 28 Oct. 1993, p. 29, from *Moscow Russian Television Network*, 27 Oct. 1993.
32 *Ibid.*, p. 29.
33 *FBIS-SOV-93-207*, 28 Oct. 1993, p. 30, from *ITAR-TASS*, Moscow, 27 Oct. 1993.
34 *Rossiiskaya Gazeta*, 17 Nov. 1993, p. 2.

35 *FBIS-SOV-93-207*, 28 Oct. 1993, p. 30, *op. cit.*
36 *Segodnya*, 28 Oct. 1993, p. 2.
37 *Rossiiskaya Gazeta*. 17 Nov. 1993, p. 2.
38 *Izvestiya*, 13 Oct. 1993, p. 4.
39 *Rossiiskie Vesti*, 16 Nov. 1993, p. 1.
40 *Rossiiskaya Gazeta*, 17 Nov. 1993, p. 2.
41 *Rossiiskie Vesti*, 16 Nov. 1993, p. 1.
42 *FBIS-SOV-93-207*, 28 Oct. 1993, p. 29, from *Moscow Russian Television Network*, 27 Oct. 1993.
43 *FBIS-SOV-93-195*, 12 Oct. 1993, *op. cit.*, p. 75.
44 Suzanne Crow, "Russian Peacekeeping: Defence, Diplomacy, or Imperialism?" *RFE/RL Research Report*, Vol. 1, No. 37, 18 Sept. 1992, p. 38.
45 *Krasnaya Zvezda*, Dec. 2, 1993, p. 2.
46 *BBC SWB* SU/1862 B/9, 3 Dec. 1993.
47 *Izvestiya*, 13 Oct. 1993, p. 4.
48 *Rossiiskaya Gazeta*, 17 Nov. 1993, p. 2.
49 *Ibid.*, p. 2.
50 *FBIS-SOV-94-002*, 4 Jan. 1994, p. 15, from *INTERFAX*, Moscow, 30 Dec. 1993.

Russian Social Democratic Centre
Rossiisky Sotsial-Demokratichesky Tsentr

History. The party emerged as group within the Social Democratic Party of the Russian Federation (SDPR), led by Oleg Rumyantsev. It was registered in the Russian Ministry of Justice on January 25, 1993.

The Constituent Congress took place on Nov. 28, 1992, and a programme and statute were adopted. In March 1993 the Council decided to draft a centrist programme. It favours the establishment of independent labour exchanges and accommodation for the homeless. Many programmes are regional programmes. Rumyantsev was actively engaged in setting up *Rodina*, a new centrist faction in the Russian Supreme Soviet. In March 1993 the Centre participated in round tables in the Moscow mayor's office and convened its own round table in the White House involving 30 public organizations.

There are about 500 members, but collective membership is preferred. There are 45 local organizations which form part of the Centre as collective members and are autonomous as regards the solution of local matters. The main agency of the Centre is the conference which convened once a year. The conference elects a Council of Representatives. The Council is elected every three months and has 16 members.

Leadership. Oleg Rumyantsev; Viktor Kulikov (dep.); Valentin Erikaev (dep.); Aleksei Gorbunov (sec.).

Programme. The Centre, led by Rumyantsev, aims to see the evolution of a Greater Russia. It views Russia as a European great power, as a progressive, federal, social, Rechtsstaat, with a decentralized administration but one which is concerned with retaining Russia as a whole. Russian geopolitical interests are to be respected and promoted. This involves expanding treaty relations with Russia's traditional, strategic and historical friends and partners.

Social Democratic Party of the Russian Federation (SDPR)
Sotsial-Demokraticheskaya Partiya Rossiiskoi Federatsii

Foundation. May 4, 1990.

Leadership. Anatoly Golov (ch.)

Membership. 4,000 in 117 organizations in 60 regions of Russia.

History. The origins of the party go back to 1987 when the Democratic Perestroika club (Pavel Kudyukin and Andrei Fadin) was set up in Moscow. Economists from the Mathematical Economics Institute and the Institute for the Economy of the World Socialist System, USSR Academy of Sciences, dominated the club. In January 1988, a Council of the club was elected and became the prototype for the formation of the SDPR. The Council consisted of 15 members with Oleg Rumyantsev and R. Kozyrev as co-chairmen and V. Kardailsky as official secretary. The aim of the club was to discuss the ideology of reform socialism (*perestroika*) and the political experience of the world social democratic movement.

On March 8, 1988, a group of Leningraders (Roman Astakhov, Vitaly Grigorev and Vadim Lifshits), who had left the club, set up the Social Democratic Union. On Feb. 4–5, 1989, at a conference in Leningrad convened on the initiative of Andrei Boltyansky, the Social Democratic Conference was set up. It united various informal groups and clubs in various cities, including parts of the Social Democratic Union, which had already split. On May 21–22, 1989, an inter-city working conference of democratic clubs convened, on the initiative of the Democratic Perestroika club, in Moscow, and set in motion the establishment of a Social Democratic Association. A leadership contest between Leningrad and Moscow resulted in the latter winning. In July 1989, at the social democratic school in Tallinn, the majority of members of the Perestroika club voted for the setting up of the Social Democratic Association.

The founding Congress of the Social Democratic Association (SDA) took place in Tallinn on Jan. 13–14, 1990, with 130 delegates from 70 organizations and clubs participating. Also attending were 10 deputies of the USSR Supreme Soviet, 20 representatives of foreign social democratic parties and about 60 invited representatives from other political movements. It was expected that Yury Afanasev, one of the leading figures of the democratic movement, would take over the leadership of the new party. However, he informed the Congress that he was not prepared to become leader since he was still in the process of defining his relations with the CPSU. Three co-chairmen were elected: N. Tutov (Orenburg), member of the USSR Supreme Soviet; Oleg Rumyantsev (Moscow), co-chairman of the Democratic Perestroika club, and V. Saatpalu (Tallinn), chairman of the Democratic Worker's Party of Estonia.

In February 1990 the SDA convened a conference and prepared the way for the founding of the SDPR. Social democratic organizations were set up in many cities and regions of the Russian Federation: Volgograd, Vladivostok, Novgorod, Tambov, Novosibirsk, Orenburg, Yakutia, Chuvashia, Mordovia and in the Urals. The Constituent Congress of the SDPR took place in Moscow on May 4, 1990. There were 237 delegates from 104 organizations from 94 Russian cities. A section of the St Petersburg delegation, headed by A. Boltyansky, left the Congress and did not join the SDPR. Pavel Kudyukin, A. Obolensky and Oleg Rumyantsev were elected members of the presidium and co-chairmen of the party. The Social Democratic Association was retained, side by side with the SDPR. Many social democrats expected the members of the Democratic Platform within the CPSU to join them. However, after the Democratic Platform left the CPSU in the spring of 1990, it split into three factions. The first, and smallest, joined the SDPR, the second joined the newly established Democratic Party of Russia (DPR) (led by Nikolai Travkin) and the third laid the foundation of the Republican Party of Russia. On Sept. 4, 1990, the SDPR, the DPR and the Democratic Platform outside the CPSU called for a coalition and called on their members to engage in closer co-operation. There were 57 deputies from the social democratic and republican faction in the Russian Supreme Soviet, elected in March 1990. Among these deputies were V. Bragin, V. Varov, L. Volkov, V. Lysenko, O. Rumyantsev, Yu. Ryzov, S. Filatov and V. Sheinis. In some cities social democrats and republics fused. However, the expected united social democratic party never materialized.

There were many reasons for this. The Republican Party of Russia split. One group, headed by V. Shostakovsky, adopted a liberal conservative position, another, led by V. Filin, founded the Social Liberal Party. Rutskoi and Travkin's parties came together with the Volsky–Vladislavlev group which represented the interests of the military-industrial complex and industrial managers and later formed Civic Union.

The Second Congress of the SDPR convened in Sverdlovsk (Ekaterinburg) in October 1990. There were 94 delegates from 62 organizations present. The Congress approved a political coalition with the Democratic Platform and the Democratic Party of Russia as well as the participation of the SDPR in the Democratic Russia movement. The first representatives of the SDPR in Democratic Russia were Oleg Rumyantsev and Vyacheslav Lyzlov, later Leonid Volkov and from the beginning of 1992, Leonid Kudyukin. The party was registered in the RSFSR Ministry of Justice on March 4, 1991.

The Third Congress met in St Petersburg on April 30–May 3, 1991, and adopted a party programme. A Board of 23 persons (with a further 15 places unfilled) was elected as well as a Presidium of three consisting of Professor Boris Orlov, Oleg Rumyantsev and Leonid Volkov, both RSFSR Supreme Soviet deputies. There were 162 delegates representing 2,500 members from 62 organizations. It was revealed that the party had 4,100 members, far fewer than had previously been thought. Clear divisions had surfaced in the party and the three main factions were: the right (social-liberal), centrist and left. The right-wing faction was dominated by the St Petersburg organization while Moscow was most influential in the centrist faction.

In early 1992 the SDPR and some other parties in Democratic Russia (SDPR, People's Party, Peasants' Party, Social-Liberal Association, Young Russia Union) set up the left-centre bloc, New Russia. On May 7–10, 1992, the Fourth Congress took place in Moscow, attended by 103 from over 60 organizations, representing 2,500 party members. The post of chairman was created with Boris Orlov elected to the post. Oleg Rumyantsev, Vladimir Rybnikov and Igor Averkiev were elected deputy chairmen. A 24-member Board was also elected. The composition of the delegates was revealing. Practically all of them were graduates. A questionnaire revealed that 51 per cent of the delegates were supporters of the Social Democratic Centre, 20 per cent of the Social Liberal faction and 12 per cent of the Left Platform. In June 1992 a Political Council of 11 members was elected.

In mid-1992 the SDPR regarded as potential allies those parties which favoured political and economic reform. Among these were the People's Party of Russia (T. Gdlyan), the Peasants' Party of Russia (Yu. Chernichenko), the Christian Democratic Party (A. Ogorodnikov) and the Young Russia movement (D. Glinsky). They all made up the New Russia electoral bloc.

Increasing tension between Orlov and Rumyantsev led, in September 1992, to the removal of Rumyantsev as deputy chairman of the party. One of the grounds of the conflict was differing views on how Russia should develop. Orlov favoured a confederation, but Rumyantsev opposed it. On the issue of the Kurile islands, Orlov supported their return to Japan while Rumyantsev preferred a Russian–Japanese condominium. In December 1992 the social democratic centre, led by Oleg Rumyantsev, split from the party and Boris Orlov resigned as chairman. Rumyantsev consistently defended the geopolitical interests of Russia. "SDPR members who are always talking about sanctions against Serbia and the transfer of the Kurile islands to Japan betray Russian interests.' Igor Averkiev was elected chairman and Vladimir Boldyrev, Pavel Kudyukin and Vladimir Rybnikov, deputy chairmen. Nikolai Pustovetov was elected secretary.

Debate over the way forward for a social democratic party in Russia was often heated. Oleg Rumyantsev, for instance, holds to the view that Christian Democratic, Liberal Democratic, Social Democratic and Social Liberal Parties in Russia enjoy little success. He regards it is important to focus on the divisions in Russian society. The party should therefore concentrate on such traditional institutions as the commune (*obshchina*) and the national council (*zemsky sobor*) in order to retain the wholeness and the organic nature of the Russian state. The development of the state and the its maintenance as a whole are thus of primary importance. Two main concepts of freedom and social justice surfaced in the SDPR. Freedom is understood by many to be *volya*, an anarchic way of life not related to any legal norms. There is also the concept of inner freedom which describes a state in which the person is entirely free from the constraints of external circumstances. These views on freedom find no institutional expression. They are linked to the idea of social justice which favours an egalitarian sharing. Hence European liberalism does not fit easily with either the Russian view of freedom or social justice. The debate with Rumyantsev touched on the role of the individual and what mechanisms should regulate relations between the individual and the state. Should freedom be based on the division of powers, as in Western Europe, or should the individual be subordinated to a dominant statehood?

At the XIX Congress of the Socialist International (SI), in September 1992, the application by the SDPR to permanent membership of the SI was rejected. At the Congress Mikhail Gorbachev was given free rein to expresses his views while the SDPR representative was only given five minutes to report on social democracy in Russia. The SDPR and other CIS social democratic parties were granted guest status, without any reference to their standing in their state.

The SDPR took part in many round tables in the Moscow mayor's office and also in the right-wing Officers' Assembly and conference on the army in post-Soviet society. It was a co-signatory of the Novoarbat agreement of March 9, 1993.

Tension surfaced with the SDPR over the party's attitude to President Yeltsin's referendum of April 25, 1993. A centre-left group, headed by I. Averkiev, party chairman, and P. Kudyukin, deputy chairman, criticized both the President and parliament. They came up with the colourful metaphor: the plague is not any better than cholera. The first number of the social democrat newspaper, *Novaya Sotsialdemokratiya*, which appeared a few days before the referendum, called on Russian citizens to boycott the referendum and called for the founding of an non-aligned movement. On television, Averkiev, advised his listeners to vote no to the question about trust in President Yeltsin.

The result of the referendum revealed how out of step Averkiev and Kudyukin were and this surfaced at the Fifth Extraordinary Congress of the SDPR, which took place in Nizhny Novgorod from May 7–10, 1993. The main beneficiary of this discontent was Oleg Rumyantsev who had founded, in May 1992, the Moscow, and in November 1992, the Social Democratic Centre. Rumyantsev, whose Centre had joined Civic Union, appeared to believe that the Union would topple President Yeltsin. However, this problem was not discussed at the Congress. Heated discussions prevented agreement on an election programme for Russian social democrats. The left wing of the party declined to stand for election to the party leadership and Rumyantsev's supporters consequently did well but Rumyantsev was neither elected chairman nor one of the three deputy chairmen. Anatoly Golov, an engineer from St Petersburg, was elected chairman. The left began discussing setting up their own party.[1] Henceforward the party espoused the market economy and may be called a right-wing social democratic party.

In the run-up to the December parliamentary elections Anatoly Golov, informed a press conference in Moscow that the SDPR had joined the Yavlinsky-Boldyrev-Lukin electoral bloc because of a similarity of views and the priority of maintaining democratic reforms. The party's main task was to create a professional parliament, capable of conducting a real debate with the executive. The party's list of candidates includes many highly qualified economists, lawyers and sociologists. (See the entry on the Yavlinsky-Boldyrev-Lukin bloc.)

Programme. The SDPR believes that in order to restore every citizen's sense of being protected by the state it is necessary to complete the judicial reform and considerably reinforce law enforcement agencies. If spending on re-equipping these agencies is carried out within the framework of the conversion programme, then the spending will not double. State orders for equipment, whose absence is causing such suffering for the defence industry, should be aimed at defending people against ever increasing crime.[4]

In economic policy the party pledges to strive for the inadmissibility of uncontrolled executive power and of officialdom as a whole by establishing "systems-co-ordinated" [*sistemo-soglasovannye*] legislation and the opportunity to press charges against the state for failing to implement the social sections of the budget. "The welfare states long ago introduced the market into the Third World, but few have attained the former's level on this path . . . they are noticeable for the proportion of national wealth channelled into the social sphere. Non-commercial turnover in all Western countries hovers around the one third mark! This alone produces the effect of social equilibrium typical of the societies which we are urged to emulate, without however being in any hurry to explain on what these societies are based. A market is an essential but insufficient condition . . . Economics is not an emotional thing but matters are ultimately decided by the emotions that it engenders in us. The civilized world, in practice, is controlled by investors. It is they who decide which sector to give priority funding to, which projects should be elaborated and which should not . . . They have the power. The SDPR has some means at its disposal to ensure the smooth transition from centralized investment to a system of civilian investment."[3]

In social policy, the party believes in the better utilization of resources to pay for social needs.

"Hitherto as taxpayers we have not had any guarantees that the state would spend the money it receives from us on precisely the needs for which it was supposedly collected from us. Co-ordinated reform of the budgetary and tax system will enable each of us to know what proportion of every ruble we pay is spent on what. What is more, if the distribution of this money is fixed, each taxpayer will, within the limits of his distribution, have an opportunity to control automatically a certain proportion of his deductions. Why should we pay the state as all the money due from us for the maintenance of education, for example, in the form of taxes? Why should we not give a certain proportion of this money direct to the schools where our children study or use our money in another targeted way for what we see as the good of society? Each of us will be able to become an investor and will decide how much money is spent on crèches, how much on kindergartens, how much on schools and how much on higher education establishments. And our system of state control guarantees the country against the theft of funds. It has already been expertly evaluated by the tax inspectorate and a number of international organizations."

"As regards property. The main demand on it by those who do not possess it is that it should work. Property must be in the hands of those people who can really provide us with highly paid work! The present privatization is an interim, semi-kolkhoz compromise. There was no other option under the old Supreme Soviet. It is a phase. It is necessary to go further. Otherwise employment problems will overwhelm our country. Property is not an absolute. Control over its use is a mandatory component of the rule of law state. The freedom of any of us is naturally restricted by our duty not to harm other people. As consumers we need protection against monopoly producers; as workers — from employers' tyranny; and as human beings we need a healthy environment. Our children need education while invalids and pensioners need social protection. Appropriate legislation is needed — anti-monopoly and labour legislation and legislation on non-commercial activity. The real rights of such civil society organizations as consumers' societies, trades unions and charitable organizations must be enshrined alongside the state's supervisory functions in these matters. But these rights are still weak. Thus during the transition period we, not only the deputies, will have to put in some work. Flexible taxation . . . will make it possible to reduce the revenue section of the state's budget as its functions are transferred to civil society. Simply lowering taxes or increasing the budget deficit has already hit society with a social crisis."[4]

Organization. There are 5,600 members with 114 territorial organizations in 356 towns in 54 regions of the Russian Federation. The party is based on the federal principle with a board consisting of 20 or more members from regional organizations, elected at a party congress. This board then elects a Political Council, consisting of 11 members, and is a consulative body for the chairman and the secretariat. There are many journalists among the party members. The SDPR has close contacts with trade unions, especially the new, independent trade unions. These include Sotsprof, the independent miners' union and the union of pilots.

Notes

1 Boris Orlov, 'Die Sozialdemokratische Partei der Russischen Föderation Interessen, Wertvorstellungen, Leitlinien,' *Berichte des Bundesinstituts für ostwissenschaftliche und internationale Studien*, Cologne, no. 44–1993.
2 Yury Khavkin, *Rossiiskaya Gazeta*, 19 Nov. 1993, *FBIS-SOV-93-223*, 22 Nov. 1993.
3 *FBIS-SOV-93-223* 22 Nov. 1993, from *Rossiiskaya Gazeta*, 19 Nov. 1993.
4 Yury Khavkin, *Rossiiskaya Gazeta*, 19 Nov. 1993, *FBIS-SOV-93-223*, 22 Nov. 1993.

Women of Russia
Zhenshchiny Rossii

History. The Women of Russia political movement bloc was founded by the Women's Union of Russia, the Association of Women Entrepreneurs and the Union of Women in the Navy and registered on Oct. 13, 1993. In the December parliamentary elections, Women of Russia fielded 36 candidates for election to the State Duma.

Leadership. Alevtina Fedulova (ch., and ch. of the Women's Union of Russia); Ekaterina

Lakhova (adviser to the President on family and women's affairs); Natalya Malakhatkina (former dep. ch. of the Federation of Independent Trade Unions of Russia); Marina Dobrovolskaya (ch. of the Union of Women in the Navy); Tatyana Malyutina (head of the Association of Women Entrepreneurs); Tamara Chepasova (employee of the Anti-Monopoly Committee); Natalya Gundereva.

Programme. The women's electoral bloc did not come into being in opposition to the men's bloc. Women of Russia is categorically opposed to the assertion that a women's place is in the kitchen and it struggles to destroy stereotypes. Women should enjoy the right to choose. Women of Russia favours a differentiated family policy on the part of the state (all families must be helped, but whether the family has students in it, whether the family has members who are disabled, and so on, must be taken into account). Women of Russia opposes the commercial exploitation of sexuality.[1]

The group argues that at present the women's movement has no other chance of entering state power structures. An analysis of the current situation revealed that the number of women included on party tickets (8.8 per cent of declared candidates) was very limited and that their names were usually placed at the very bottom which actually reduced their chances. "In the opinion of many Russian experts women can only exert a real influence when their representation reaches at least 30 per cent. Of course no one is expecting that kind of success today, but it would be wrong to miss any opportunity. Moreover, the ploy of re-educating many political parties so that sooner or later they recognize the need to nominate women for parliament through party channels, looks more promising. Unfortunately this will not happen in the near future. But the Women of Russia are making their presence felt and do not intend to lose."[2]

"We are completely against a policy based on sexual promise. But it so happens in our state that for many years policy has only been made by men. Of course, some people would say that there were women in parliament. Yes, there were, but they were some kind of decoration, they were just the background. Of course, all our problems are the problems which everyone in our country is facing now, but it is very important for us to separate all these problems. We should know what the state will do and what regions will do in this or that respect."[3]

In economic policy, the movement argues that economic policy should be directed towards human values. Tax regulations should be enforced so that the large enterprises pay taxes to the state to enable the money to be channelled into the social sphere. Laws should be directed at protecting domestic producers and settling realistic prices for food. When planning state policy with regard to the population's incomes it is necessary to proceed not only from the physiological subsistence minimum but also to include in the basket of consumer goods the use by citizens, including pensioners, of such consumer services as laundries, dry cleaners and so forth. This can be achieved by the regulation of taxation policy and its prompt adjustment.[6]

Further reforms of the army and navy are necessary. Women of Russia advocate maintaining the level of combat readiness of the armed forces which will ensure normal life for Russians and deliver them from the threat of attack from abroad.

Priority should be given to social policy. The budget should place more emphasis on the social needs of the people — education, culture, social protection. Protection of childhood, tighter laws against crime, equality before the law — for individuals as well as the state — are some of the problems the organization is hoping to address. Another problem is ante- and post-natal care, shortage of medicines and necessary facilities in medical establishments.

Provision of kindergartens and nursery schools is inadequate. It is important to ensure under market conditions such facilities do not suffer.[7]

Women of Russia advocates a sensible combination of the satisfaction of the population's needs from the state budget and the development of the network of paid services. The movement's priorities are: the accessibility of free, high quality education and medical assistance for all sections of the population in addition to paid provision; a differentiated state family policy and the creation of the economic and legal conditions to ensure a decent family life based on labour; the priority of the interests of the child; guaranteed support for members of the family unfit for work, including pensioners and invalids and also for underprivileged families with one breadwinner, young families, student families, large families, the elderly, foster families, and families with invalids; the preservation of the state system of pre-school and extramural children's establishments with guaranteed access for every family in conjunction with the development of the forms of children's paid education.[8]

Notes

1 *Current Digest of the Post-Soviet Press*, Vol. xlv, no. 43, Nov. 24, 1993, from *Segodnya*, Oct. 23, 1993.
2 *FBIS-SOV-93-200*, 19 Oct. 1993, from *Izvestiya*, 16 Oct. 1993.
3 *FBIS-SOV-93-227*, 29 Nov. 1993, from Ostankino TV, 26 Nov. 1993.
4 24–26 according to Vladimir Pribylovsky and Grigory Tochkin, *Russkaya mysl*, 12 Jan. 1994.
5 2 according to Pribylovsky and Tochkin, *op. cit.* Another one to three independents elected supported the bloc during the election.
6 *FBIS-SOV-93-218*, 15 Nov. 1993, from *Rossiikie Vesti*, 12 Nov. 1993.
7 *FBIS-SOV-93-200*, 19 Oct. 1993, from *Izvestiya*, 16 Oct. 1993.
8 *FBIS-SOV-93-218*, 15 Nov. 1993, from *Rossiikie Vesti*, 12 Nov. 1993.

Yavlinsky-Boldyrev-Lukin bloc (Yabloko)

Leadership. Grigory Yavlinsky, (co-author of the 500-day economic reform programme published in 1990, and Deputy Prime Minister in the government of Russian Prime Minister Ivan Silaev); Vladimir Lukin (former Russian Ambassador to the USA). Yury Boldyrev (formerly Russia's Chief State Inspector and Director of the Supervisory Administration of the Russian President's staff.)[1] Evgeny Ambartsumov (former head of the Supreme Soviet Committee for International Affairs and Foreign Economic relations, and member of the Security Council); Anatoly Adamishin (professional diplomat closely linked to Vladimir Lukin); Nikolay Petrakov (economist and former economic adviser to Soviet President Mikhail Gorbachev); The bloc also includes various young economists from Yavlinsky's Centre for Economic and Political Research (EPI centre): Aleksei Mikhailov, Mikhail Zadornov, Sergei Ivanenko, Aleksei Melnikov and Tatyana Yarygina.

Membership. The Republican Party of the Russian Federation (headed by Vladimir Lysenko and Vyacheslav Shostakovsky), the Social Democratic Party of the Russian Federation (headed by Anatoly Golov), and the Russian Christian Democratic Union (led by Valery Borshchev) form the backbone of the new bloc. Yavlinsky's EPI-centre has also been used as the basis for the development of the bloc's structures.

The bloc has also received the support of the Greens and of the Union of Independents.

The Union of Independents was established in Moscow in October 1993 and consists of all those organizations and groups that were members of Democratic Russia and decided to abandon the movement after it allied with Russia's Choice.[2]

The Republican Party of the Russian Federation

The Republican Party of the Russian Federation was set up in November 1990 by those leaders of the reformist Democratic Platform of the CPSU who had left the Party during the XXVIII Congress in July 1990. At the party's founding congress in Moscow on Nov. 17–18, Vladimir Lysenko, Vyacheslav Shostakovky and Stepan Sulakshin were elected co-chairmen by the freshly elected Co-ordinating Council. The Party's platform, similar to that of the Democratic Party of Russia (headed by Nikolai Travkin) and the Democratic Russia movement, supported the process of democratization and advocated the introduction of a market economy. Its programme was very close to the Social-Democratic Party of Russia led by Oleg Rumyantsev, Leonid Volkov, and Pavel Kudyukin. Attempts to merge with it, however, were unsuccessful.[3] Although it participated in Democratic Russia as a collective member its leaders consistently dissociated themselves from it, and they finally decided to leave the movement in October 1993.[4] The party also joined the Movement of Democratic Reforms, but abandoned it in February 1992. In December 1992 it participated in the creation of a new bloc, Liberal Russia, which includes a number of entrepreneurial parties such as the Russian Party of Free Labour (led by Igor Korovikov).[5]

During the election campaign for the new Federal Assembly, the Republican Party divided its support between Russia's Choice and Yavlinsky's bloc. The party feared it would be unable to collect the 100,000 signatures needed to register a federal list of candidates, and at the Congress held in Moscow on October 19, 1993, 34 regional organizations decided to side with Yavlinsky, while 20 supported the bloc led by Egor Gaidar. This meant that at the federal level the Party joined Yavlinsky, but at regional level, many organizations were allowed to join Russia's Choice.[6] As a result, the Republican Party structures helped both blocs to collect signatures and to allocate candidates among one-mandate constituencies.

The Republican Party also supported the Yavlinsky bloc in some of the republics of the Russian Federation (Dagestan, North Ossetia, Kabardino-Balkaria, Tatarstan) through its regional organizations.[7] It supplied two-thirds of the candidates for deputies in the regional part of the federal list. Of the 170,000 voters' signatures collected by the bloc at the first stage of the elections, 110,000 were collected by the Republicans. The party currently has branches in 65 Russian Federation regions, and a total of 5,000 members.

The Social Democratic Party of Russia (*see* separate entry)

The Social Democratic Party of Russia (SDPR) emerged out of the Association of Social Democrats of Russia on May 4, 1990.[8] It is, in fact, one of the few social democratic associations not to have developed from the CPSU. The party sought to restore the old Russian traditions of social democracy, but abandoned the latter's revolutionary character in favour of the restoration of capitalism. It defined itself as a parliamentary and reformist movement, rejecting all forms of violence and committed to inter-ethnic peace. The SDPR remained small and never managed to obtain broad popular support. It currently has 5,000 members.[9]

The Christian Democratic Union of Russia

The Christian Democratic Union of Russia was established in August 1989 by 80 members of Christian public groups. At the conference in Moscow, former political prisoner, Aleksandr Ogorodnikov, was elected chairman. The party strove for the spiritual and economic revival of Russia, and attempted to combine West European political democracy, Roman Catholic social thinking and Russian religious philosophy. It was subject to numerous splits and never managed to become a serious political contender, and became mostly devoted to charitable work.[10]

History. On Oct. 26, 1993, Grigory Yavlinsky announced the creation of his own election bloc — a democratic opposition to the pro-government forces in the next parliamentary elections. The bloc hoped to gain the support of those voters who rejected Gaidar's "shock therapy" programme, but favoured economic reform. He was joined by former Russian Ambassador to the United States Vladimir Lukin, and by sociologist and former chief inspector of the Russian regions, Yury Boldyrev. The bloc obtained the support of three existing political parties (the Republican Party of the Russian Federation, the Social-Democratic Party and the Russian Christian-Democratic Union) and attracted liberal defectors from Yeltsin's team.[11] They were joined by other dissatisfied Yeltsin's supporters such as the Union of Independents, and were supported by human rights organizations such as the Movement for the Defence of Democracy and Human Rights, headed by Pavlovsky.[12]

Before the elections, the bloc said it might join other democratically-oriented forces in the event that the communist opposition found a strong leader capable of securing victory. But after the surprising victory of communists, agrarians and the Liberal Democratic Party of Russia, the bloc did not join an alliance of all democratic forces.[13] Nevertheless, it has almost always voted in line with Russia's Choice in the State Duma.[14]

The bloc has obtained the implicit support of the liberal press in Russia and of the country's leading intelligentsia, increasingly dissatisfied with Yeltsin's authoritarian methods. In their view, the bloc represents a serious democratic alternative to the pro-government forces.[15]

Programme. The bloc believes that the most important political task in Russia today is the creation of a real and representative parliament, "a parliament capable of inspiring confidence, of contributing to a real distribution of powers, and of carrying out strong and constructive opposition to the government".[16]

The bloc was very critical of the December parliamentary elections, but decided nevertheless to join the race. In Yavlinsky's view, the elections were aimed at strengthening the current government's position. This explains, according to him, the creation of a presidential party such as the Russia's Choice bloc. In his view such situation resembles the Soviet era when political leaders combined governmental and legislative functions: member of the CPSU Central Committee, member of government, and deputy of the Supreme Soviet. Yavlinsky nevertheless admits that "elections to a new parliament are the only opportunity for laying down the foundations of law and legitimacy". "A workable parliament and a democratic government are indispensable for Russia", he said.[17]

Yavlinsky sees the new parliament as a constituent assembly, responsible for the adoption of a new constitution. He does not approve of the idea of holding a referendum on the Constitution concurrently with parliamentary elections and believes this would result in an illegitimate parliament.[18] According to Yavlinsky, Russians should first elect a parliament in charge of discussing and adopting the new constitution, then parliament should prepare a draft constitution and submit it to referendum. If the draft is approved in the plebiscite, the constitution should be adopted by parliament. Thereafter presidential elections on the basis of the new constitution should follow, as well as elections to local government bodies and to a new parliament. In his view the new parliament, responsible for creating a new constitution, "will fulfil a truly historic mission: it will be the founder of a new, democratic Russia".

The bloc leaders could not agree on how to advise their supporters to vote in the referendum on the draft Constitution. Some leaders were "in favour" of the Constitution, albeit with some reservations, while others were "against" it, because the draft cancelled early presidential elections. Nikolai Petrakov, one of the opponents of the draft, clearly stated that "the Constitution cannot be adopted in its present form, since its transitional provisions rule out an early presidential election".[19] Petrakov also objected to the fact that "the draft [gave] sweeping powers to the President who [would] find himself above all branches of government".[20] Yavlinsky for his part, said he would not vote in the referendum but did not want to give any advice to the voters. He believed preparations for the referendum were undemocratic and disliked the President's exorbitant powers, as well as Russia's federal structure.[21]

Another prominent member of the bloc, Viktor Sheinis, believed that the draft was the best of those available, "or at any rate, the least inadequate", and that he would vote for it. Vladimir Lysenko, co-chairman of the Republican Party, advocated the adoption of the Constitution. He said: "everyone should recognize that if a new Constitution is adopted and if a strong central authority emerges then we will preserve our country for our decendants".[22] Vladimir Lukin, for his part, said that if the draft was not approved in the referendum, the new parliament would have to combine the functions of both a representative and a constituent assembly.

The Yavlinsky-Boldyrev-Lukin bloc supports the transformation of Russia's state-owned economy into a market economy, but advocates a modification of the economic reform methods currently applied. "Otherwise, Yavlinsky believes", we could end up with a super-monopolized economy, instead of a market economy."[23]

The bloc believes that the Gaidar team has failed to transform the totalitarian economic system into a real market economy. Although during the past two years there was much talk about liberalization, a monopolistic economy has been maintained. According to Yavlinsky "the government has completed the collectivization of industry, transforming companies into enormous industrial *kolkhozes* where nobody understands who runs them, where the money is, or who works in them. The managers think they are free, but they are still asking for money from the government". Thus, a new system of interests has been created. In fact the money economy has been replaced by barter trade, whereby goods and services are traded without money, creating a giant parallel monetary flow that feeds the inflationary process and evades the Central Bank's control.

Yavlinsky believes that "if we want to have a more or less stable budget and monetary policy, then we have to make a choice: either everything is state-owned and prices are fixed, or there is a free market and free prices. There is no alternative. Gaidar realized that he could no longer manage fixed prices and decided to liberalize prices. However, he should have known that he could not leave a completely monopolistic economy at the mercy of free prices. He should have moved around and continually made adjustments on a trial-and-error basis. This was not done".[24]

The Yavlinsky-Boldyrev-Lukin bloc rejects unpredictability and "shock measures" in economics and politics"[25] and proposes the following options for putting the Russian economy back on its feet: "giving priority to private ownership, de-monopolizing industry, and strengthening ties with the former USSR republics".[26] This means that the scale of the private sector must be substantially expanded, that monopolies should be destroyed as soon as possible, that protection and support for competition should be provided, and that the conditions for cautious land reform should be created.[27]

Yavlinsky strongly opposes the current privatization methods. He believes that the voucher system "which gives 40 per cent of the enterprise's shares to the workforce, 40 per cent to the state and 20 per cent to the director" converts enterprises into a sort of collective farm where no-one is responsible for the management. Yavlinsky believes that a correct privatization process should be accompanied by anti-monopoly policies, and laws protecting private ownership.[28] He proposes that "small enterprises" should be auctioned to the populations of individual regions, and large-scale enterprises should attract investment from foreign industries.[29]

Combating inflation is also a bloc priority, but, contrary to Russia's Choice, for whom financial stabilization is an essential priority, the Yavlinsky bloc believes that inflation cannot be eliminated without institutional changes in the economy: industrial privatization, land reform and de-monopolization. In his opinion, it is impossible to combat inflation under the current economic conditions, characterized by the absence of private industrial ownership, by ill-defined property relations, by a highly-militarized production structure and by lack of competitiveness.[30] The bloc also believes that it is impossible to achieve financial stabilization if there are 10 Central Banks operating in republics of the former USSR, which use the ruble, without having any proper monetary, credit and budgetary policies.

A fundamental tenet of the bloc's economic strategy is the prevention of the outflow of foreign currency, which is currently accumulating in the accounts of Russian enterprises, organizations, and private individuals, abroad. The bloc opposes a free exchange-rate mechanism and proposes a system whereby the government forecasts the exchange-rate and maintains the rate within the confines of the commitments it has taken.[31] The bloc supports Western assistance, but believes that any Western credits not connected with institutional transformations will not pay any dividends. "It is obvious from last year's experience that foreign credits are more like a narcotic than a medicine", Yavlinsky said.[32]

There have been some discrepancies among members of the bloc regarding the role of the state in the transformation of the economy. Although Yavlinsky is aware of the importance of the state in the Russian economy, he believes its role should gradually diminish. In his own words: "We believe that the state should help to develop the market and gradually transfer its functions to new market structures",[33] Petrakov instead believes that the "economic legacy" left by the Soviet Union cannot be transformed into a market economy "on the principles of self-organization, i.e. economic Darwinism". He believes that the state should have an active role in transforming society.[34]

The bloc favours a gradual and carefully thought-out land privatization. Land reform, in its view, requires correct legislation and consideration of the region's social and cultural peculiarities, as well as ecological restrictions. In Yavlinsky's words "in principle all restrictions on the possession of land should be lifted, but regional peculiarities be left intact. It is for the local authorities to settle the problem rationally and peacefully".[35] The bloc believes that the right to own land must be guaranteed above all to those citizens who work the land.[36]

With regard to returning property to those who owned it before the 1917 revolution, Yavlinsky things that the "right to properties should be recognized in principle. But this does not mean that each heir must physically regain such property".[37] Yavlinsky suggests that by recognizing inheritance rights, the government should compensate the owners of property with money or some other equivalent.[38]

The bloc considers that market reforms should be socially oriented. Social guarantees should be provided to all those who are most directly touched by the reforms and cannot immediately adjust to the new rules of the game.[39]

The state must also increase the working possibilities of the labour force and provide basic social benefits to those incapable of working. In particular the bloc's social policies involve: reaching collective salary agreements among the various social groups, making deductions from wages for social needs; introducing partial indexation of wages in non-producing sectors, increasing excises on luxuries; and introducing a property tax.

The bloc deems it absolutely necessary to pay wages promptly, and to create state programmes in the sphere of science, education, culture, and medical service; to amend labour legislation and provide retraining opportunities for the unemployed; and to provide special retraining programmes for servicemen in order to integrate them into the civil life. The bloc also supports private welfare systems, private pension funds, private insurance systems, and private charitable organizations.[40]

Two highly influential figures in Russia's foreign policy, Vladimir Lukin and Evgeny Ambartsumov, are members of the Yavlinsky bloc. Although their views on Russia's foreign policy slightly differ, they share many opinions and in particular they both oppose the "internationalist, pro-Western" foreign policy carried out by Foreign Minister Kozyrev during his first years in office. Lukin, former Russian Ambassador to the USA, believes Russian foreign policy and secutiry should be based on the specifics of Russia's geopolitical position. "Russia continues to be a multi-national Eurasian country, with its interests extending to the key regions of the world: Central and Northern Europe, Asia Minor, the Middle East, and the Asia-Pacific region. Its location both in Asia and Europe largely determines its international interests. Any attempts to force Russia solely into either Asia or Europe are ultimately futile and dangerous."[41] According to Lukin, top priority should be given to Russia's relations with the neighbouring republics of the former Soviet Union, which does not mean however, that Russia should not co-operate with the West and become an integrated member of the international community.[42] "As we discard our past global chimeras and converge with European politics and values, Russia's lasting and natural interest in Europe becomes stronger."[43] But Russia should not necessarily approve of all Western positions, especially if it feels these positions go against its national interests.

Lukin believes that end of the Cold War has created a new situation, whereby the greatest threat to Russia — nuclear destruction — has practically disappeared. In his view however, new threats have appeared which might put in jeopardy the very existence of Russia. The main concern of the Russian state is its increasing encirclement by potentially serious conflicts and its isolation in the world community. Relations have deteriorated with many of its neighbours (Japan, Korea, Central Asia) and in some areas real armed conflicts have erupted, which not only risk spreading onto Russia's territory but threaten the lives of many Russians as well (Moldova, Nagorno-Karabakh, Tajikistan).

In Lukin's view however, Russia's foreign policy should not be based on Russian chauvinism but on "an enlightened understanding of Russia's national interests based upon the notion of self-interest properly understood". Lukin believes that this can only be achieved if democracy and a market economy are developed in Russia. "[Democracy] is the only path that can lead to a revival of a strong Russia that is confident in its security. At the same time it is the only mode that can make Russia safe for the rest of the world." Lukin maintains that if Russia becomes a strong democratic state, it will bring democratization to the republics of the "near abroad". His view of Russia's new mission in the Eurasian heartland is therefore strongly related to the development of democracy in Russia and in the republics. In his words "perhaps that is Russia's new mission: to become the guarantor of stability throughout the Eurasian heartland through its own democratic revival", In Lukin's view, Russia cannot impose its foreign policy on its neighbours by force, but it cannot remain inactive either. Lukin proposes the strengthening of the structures of the CIS as a means of achieving stability in the whole entire region, but stresses the need to protect the interests and rights of Russians and other minorities outside the Russian Federation.[44]

Evgeny Ambartsumov, former chairman of the Committee for International Affairs and Foreign Economic Relations, became very influential in the making of Russia's foreign policy during 1993, particularly with regard to Russia's policy towards the former Yugoslavia and the "near abroad". Ambartsumov is in favour of better relations with the West, but believes that Russia should preserve its leading role in the international community, and should keep its "own sphere of influence". Ambartsumov, as do many other "centrists", regrets the break-up of the former Soviet Union and advocates the close integration of the former Soviet republics. "I was opposed to the break-up of the Union and believed that the consequences of the Minsk accord were not correctly calculated. But to return to the pre-Minsk situation is impossible."[45] Ambartsumov considers that Russia should play a leading role in peace-keeping operations in the former Soviet Union. He believes that these areas form part of Russia's sphere of vital interest, and that the West should recognize Russia's leading role in the area. "Russia must secure from the international community the role of political and military guarantor of stability on all the territory of the former USSR."[46] Russia should also obtain international recognition and financial support for Russia's "blue berets".

The bloc supports close economic collaboration with the former republics of the USSR. Unlike Egor Gaidar, who was in favour of building capitalism in Russia alone, G. Yavlinsky advocated the maintenance of a common market among the former republics of the USSR.[47]

The bloc sees the political settlement of armed conflicts around Russia as a priority task. If the government fails to do this in time, the conflagration will move onto Russian soil. The bloc believes that a defence alliance among the CIS countries is necessary to preserve peace, as well as legal regulations regarding the status of Russian troops abroad. However, the bloc considers the doctrinal enshrinement of the Army's involvement in resolving internal conflicts is clearly wrong. In fact, like most blocs, Yabloko believes it is not the Army's job to supplant internal troops and the militia.[48]

In Yavlinsky's view the question of the federal structure of the Russian Federation — considered as essential — is not properly addressed in the Constitution. He described the current attempt by the authors of the draft constitution to put all localities on an equal footing and to remove the question of sovereignty as "laying mines around a decision, which would trigger off fresh conflicts in the future".[49] He also added that the "question of the federative structure of the state requires a serious discussion and working out of standpoints taking into account the results of the 12 December elections".[50]

The bloc advocates a constitutional rather than a treaty-based Federation. The unity of Russia is the bloc's abiding principle. It cannot be called into question either by a vote in parliament or even by a referendum on certain of its territories. "We are opposed to enshrining the right of succession from the Federation in the constitutions of the Russian Federation and its territories." The uniformity of the budget relationship between Moscow and the regions, and the priority of federal legislation, are the fundamental principles of the federal system.[51]

Lysenko, leader of the Republican Party added, "the peoples of the Federation have already seen for themselves — regrettably, through bloodshed, suffering, and destruction — that it is in our common interest to preserve Russia as a united, strong, federal state. The leaders calling for secession from the Federation are now losing their former prestige. We have lived together for centuries. We will continue to live together in one big family".[52,53]

Notes

1 Julia Wishnevsky, "Corruption Allegations Undermine Russia's Political Leaders," *RFE/RL Research Report*, Vol. 2, No. 37, 17 Sept. 1993.

2 *Nezavisimaya Gazeta*, Oct. 19, 1993.

3 Geoffrey A. Hosking, Jonathan Aves and Peter J. S. Duncan, (eds.) *The Road to Post-Communism — Independent Political Movements in the Soviet Union, 1985–1991*, London and New York, Pinter Publishers, 1992, pp. 101–102.

4 Vera Tolz, Wendy Slater, and Alexander Rahr, "Profiles of the Main Political Blocs." *RFE/RL Research Report*, Vol. 2 No. 20, 14 May 1993. p. 18; *Kuranty*, 21 Oct. 1993, p. 1.

5 Vera Tolz, Wendy Slater, and Alexander Rahr, "Profiles of the Main Political Blocs." *op. cit.*, p. 19.

6 However, according to an article published in *Rossiiskie Vesti* (October 21, 1993, p. 2), the Republican party in Moscow supported Yavlinsky, while its branches in 49 regions of Russia supported Russia's Choice.

7 Interview with Vladimir Lysenko, *Rossiiskaya Gazeta*, Nov. 27, p. 2.

8 At the congress, a 40-member council and its presidium were created. To the presidium were elected Alexander Obolenskii, a former CPSU member and deputy to the Russian Congress of People's Deputies; Oleg Rumyantsev, the Secretary of the Constitutional Commission, and the historian Pavel Kudyukin.

9 Richard Sakwa, *Russian Politics and Society*, London and New York, Routledge, 1993, p. 145.

10 *Ibid.*, pp. 149–150.

11 The majority of the bloc's candidates, including G. Yavlinsky, Yu. Boldyrev and Egor Yakovlev, were previously members of Yeltsin's team. Personal ambitions and overt disagreements led them to create a new democratic opposition.

12 Julia Wishnevsky, "Liberal Opposition Emerging in Russia?" *RFE/RL Research Report*, Vol. 2, No. 44, 5 Nov. 1993, p. 11.

13 Although YABLOKO leaders aware of the need of creating a coalition of democratic forces against the communist-nationalist alliance, they refused to seal an alliance with Russia's Choice, on the grounds that common objectives were a necessary pre-requisite for further association. The bloc favoured forming a coalition with those parties that agreed on the pace of reform (*FBIS-SOV-93-240*, 16 Dec. 1993, p. 21, from *L'Unita*, 15 Dec. 1993, p. 5).

14 It opposed together with Russia's Choice, and the Russian Movement For Democratic Reforms, the granting of an amnesty to all those involved in the attempted coup of August 1991, the Moscow riots of May 1993, and the conservative revolt of Oct. 3–4, 1993; and opposed the resolution on the setting up of a commission to investigate the events of Sept 21 to Oct. 4, 1993.

15 Elena Ovcharenko, of *Komsomolskaya Pravda*, told Ostankino television that her newspaper would support Yavlinsky's bloc because they propose bloodless reforming methods (Julia Wishnevsky, "Liberal Opposition Emerging in Russia?" *op. cit.*, p. 11).

16 G. Yavlinsky, interviewed by *Le Figaro*, 21 Oct. 1993, p. 5.

17 *FBIS-SOV-93-217*, 12 Nov. 1993, p. 44, from *INTERFAX*, Moscow, 11 Nov. 1993.
18 *Nezavisimaya Gazeta*, 3 Nov. 1993, p. 2.
19 *Segodnya*, 27 Nov. 1993, p. 2.
20 *FBIS-SOV-93-222*, 19 Nov. 1993, p. 25, from *ITAR-TASS*, Moscow, 18 Nov. 1993.
21 *FBIS-SOV-93-223*, 22 Nov. 1993, p. 27, from *INTERFAX*, Moscow, 19 Nov. 1993.
22 *Rossiiskaya Gazeta*, 27 Nov. 1993, p. 2.
23 *The Current Digest of the Post-Soviet Press*, Vol. 45, No. 44, 1 Dec. 1993, p. 19, from *Nezavisimaya Gazeta*, 3 Nov. 1993, p. 2.
24 G. Yavlinsky interviewed by *La Repubblica*, 19 Oct. 1993, p. 15.
25 *FBIS-SOV-93-207*, 28 Oct. 1993, p. 28, from *ITAR-TASS World Service*, 27 Oct. 1993.
26 *Krasnaya Zvezda*, 29 Oct. 1993, p. 1.
27 *Rossiiskaya Gazeta*, 27 Nov. 1993, p. 2.
28 *FBIS-SOV-93-211*, 3 Nov. 1993, p. 40, from *Radio Rossii Network*, 2 Nov. 1993.
29 *FBIS-SOV-93-202*, 21 Oct. 1993, p. 31, from *ITAR-TASS World Service*, 20 Oct. 1993.
30 *FBIS-SOV-93-223*, 22 Nov. 1993, p. 27, from *INTERFAX*, Moscow, 19 Nov. 1993.
31 *FBIS-SOV-93-207* 28 Oct. 1993, *op. cit.*, p. 29.
32 G. Yavlinksy interviewed by *Komsomolskaya Pravda*, 9 Nov. 1993, p. 3.
33 *FBIS-SOV-93-222*, 19 Nov. 1993, p. 25, from *ITAR-TASS*, Moscow, 18 Nov. 1993.
34 *FBIS-SOV-93-223*, 22 Nov. 1993, *op. cit.*, p. 28.
35 *FBIS-SOV-93-217*, 12 Nov. 1993, p. 45, from *INTERFAX*, Moscow, 11 Nov. 1993.
36 *Rossiiskie Vesti*, Nov. 17 1993, p. 1.
37 *FBIS-SOV-93-217*, 12 Nov. 1993, *op. cit.*, p. 45.
38 *Ibid.*, p. 45.
39 *FBIS-SOV-93-204*, 25 Oct. 1993, p. 35, from *Moskovsky Komsomolets*, 23 Oct. 1993, p. 1.
40 *Rossiiskie vesti*, 17 Nov. 1993, p. 1.
41 Vladimir Lukin, "Our Security Predicament", *Foreign Policy*, No. 88 (Fall 1992) p. 59.
42 Alexei G. Arbatov, "Russia's Foreign Policy Alternatives", *International Security*, Vol. 18, No. 2 (Fall 1993) pp. 10-11.
43 Vladimir Lukin, *op. cit.*, p. 59.
44 *Ibid.*, pp. 58–68.
45 Suzanne Crow, "Ambartsumov's Influence on Russian Foreign Policy", *RFE/RL Research Report*, Vol. 2, No. 19, 7 May 1993, p. 39.
46 *Ibid.*, p. 41.
47 *Le Figaro*, 21 Oct. 1993, p. 5.
48 *Krasnaya Zvezda*, 2 Dec. 1993, p. 2.
49 *FBIS-SOV-93-217*, 12 Nov. 1993, *op. cit.*, p. 44.
50 *FBIS-SOV-93-207*, 28 Oct. 1993, *op. cit.*, p. 29.
51 *Rossiiskaya Gazeta*, 27 Nov. 1993, p. 27.
52 *Ibid.*, p. 2.
53 This contradicts previous views expressed by Yavlinsky. "I favour a constitutional rather than a contractual federation, but the road to it is very long. Russia has a future only if territories merge into a federation on their own (voluntarily)" (*FBIS-SOV-93-217*, 12 Nov. 1993, *op. cit.*, p. 45).

Table 8: Election results of Russia's Choice bloc

Before registration the bloc collected 200,000 signatures.

State Duma
Total number of seats: 96
Seats obtained on party list: 40
Seats obtained in single-member constituencies: 56

Russia's Choice formed the largest faction in the Duma: 76 members

Mikhail Mityukov (RC) is First Deputy Chairman
Sergei Kovalevev (RC) is Plenipotentiary for Human Rights

State Duma Committees headed by Russia's Choice:
— Defence Committee (Sergei Yushenkov)
— Health Protection Committee (Bella Denisenko)
— Information Policy and Communications Committee (Mikhail Poltaranin)
— Organization of the State Duma Committee (Vladimir Bauer)
— Subcommittee on the Russian Central Bank's credit and monetary policy (Boris Fedorov)[27]

Council of the Federation
Russia's Choice was the only electoral bloc to put forward a list of Federation Council candidates. But many of the recommended candidates were centrists, closer to Prime Minister Viktor Chernomyrdin. Forty candidates recommended by Russia's Choice were elected to the Federation Council. Among those 40, only three (E. Gaer, V. Fateev and L. Kotesova) have openly expressed their allegiance to the bloc and one (K. Titov) is a member of the Russian Movement for Democratic Reforms. Another seven are supporters of centrist forces — they were included in the list probably for lack of candidates. Three elected candidates, not included in the recommended list, openly expressed their support for Russia's Choice and therefore could be included in the bloc. This brings the supporters of Russia's Choice in the Council to 36.

Members in Government
— Anatoly Chubais, deputy Prime Minister and chairman of the State Committee on Administration of State Property
— Andrei Kozyrev, Foreign Minister
— Evgeny Sidorov, Minister of Culture
— Viktor Danilov-Danilyan, Environment Minister

Members in Commissions attached to the President
—Sergei Filatov, Head of the Administration of the Russian President and chairman of Commission for State Prizes of the Russian Federation in Literature and Art
— Kovalev, chairman of the Human Rights Commission attached to the Russian Federation President

---

Table 9:   Election Results of Russia's Future–New Names

Before registration the bloc collected 109,000 signatures

State Duma
Total number of seats: 1
Seats obtained on party lists: none (failed to overcome 5 per cent barrier)
Seats obtained in single member constituencies: 1

State Duma Committees headed by RFNN: none

Council of the Federation

Seats: none

Table 10:   Election results of the Russian Movement for Democratic Reforms

---

Before registration the movement collected 135,000 signatures.

State Duma
Total number of seats: 8
Seats obtained on party list: none (The party did not manage to pass the 5 per cent barrier)
Seats obtained in single-member constituencies: 8

Head of Committees in State Duma:
none

Council of the Federation
Total number of seats: 1 (Konstatin Titov, member of RMDR and also on the list of recommended candidates of Russia's Choice)

Members in the executive branch
— Akeksandr Yakovlev, Acting Chairman of the Russian State Television and Radio Broadcasting Company Ostankino, Head of the Federal Television and Radio Broadcasting Agency, and Chairman of the Commission for the Rehabilitation of the Victims of Political Repression
— Gavriil Popov and Anatoly Sobchak are members of the Presidential Council

---

Table 11: Election results of Women in Russia

Before registration the movement collected 127,000 signatures

State Duma

Total number of seats: 25[4]
Seats obtained on party lists: 21 (8.1 per cent of the vote)
Seats obtained in single member constituencies: 4[5]

State Duma faction: 23

State Duma Committees headed by Women of Russia: none

Table 12: Election results of the *Yavlinsky-Boldyrev-Lukin bloc (YABLOKO)*

Before registration YABLOKO collected 170,000 signatures.

State Duma
Total number of seats: 33
Seats obtained on party list: 20
Seats obtained in single-member constituencies: 13

State Duma faction: 25 members

State Duma Committees headed by YABLOKO:
— Budget, Taxes, Banks, and Finance Committee (Mikhail Zadornov)
— International Affairs Committee (Vladimir Lukin)

Council of the Federation
Seats: 3 (Yury Boldyrev, Boris Nemtsov and Evgeny Krestyaninov)

Adygea[1]

The republic of Adygea is home to 92 nationalities[2] and, according to the 1989 census, had over 454,000 inhabitants. Of these 22 per cent or 95,800 were Adyge. Until 1917 the territory occupied by the Kuban Adygea was part of Ekaterinodar and Maikop departments (*otdel*) of Kuban *oblast*. In 1922 the Adygea autonomous *oblast* was established which also included Russians and Cossacks. In 1924 the Adygea autonomous *oblast* was transferred to the Kubano-Chernomorsky (Kuban-Black Sea) *oblast*, in 1934 to the Severo-Kavkazsky (North Caucasian) *krai*, in 1937 to the Azovo-Chernomorsky (Azov-Black Sea) *krai* and in 1937 to Krasnodar *krai*. In 1991 the autonomous *oblast* was upgraded to a republic. In 1936 Adygea autonomous *oblast* was extended by adding Maikop, and Giaginsky *raion*, and the capital was moved from Krasnodar to Maikop. In 1962 Maikop *raion* was added to the Adygea autonomous republic. Hitherto Maikop *raion* had been part of Krasnodar *krai* and was populated mainly by Russians and Ukrainians. At present Adyge predominate in Teuchezhsky, Shovgenovsky and Koshekhablsky *raions*. In Takhtamukaisky *raion* they are about a third of the population, in Krasnogvardeisky *raion*, about a quarter and in Giaginsky and Maikop *raions* they are insignificant. Russians are the main nationality in the republic, accounting for 295,000 or about 65 per cent of the population. In 1990 there were about 14,000 Ukrainians. Russians and Ukrainians are concentrated in Maikop, Giaginsky and Takhtamukaisky *raions* and make up a large proportion of the population of Maikop. There are also over 10,000 Armenians (including refugees). Most of them live in Maikop and Maikop *raion*. There are also Tatars (2,500), Germans (1,700) and Greeks (1,300).

Many national-cultural movements and societies have been founded in the republic, representing the interests of the various nationalities. The most influential is *Adyge Khase* which, according to its statute, unites citizens irrespective of race, nationality, sex or religious belief. Its main goal is self-determination for the Agyge people, the revival of its history, culture and traditions, and the improvement of ethnic relations among all the nations living in Adygea. Most of its members are from the intelligentsia but there are some workers and peasants. Its newspaper is *Guas* (Herald). It promotes bi-lingualism in the republic, the repatriation of Adyge and the re-establishment of Shapsugsky *raion* in Krasnodar *krai*.

The Union of Cossacks in Adygea was set up at the end of the 1980s and early 1990s as a part of the Kuban Cossack Rada. The Rada regarded the re-establishment of the institute of Cossackdom and the revival of cultural and traditional Cossack life as its primary objective. It gradually became more radical and political and there was discussion about Cossacks leaving Adygea with their land and joining Ukraine.

The Union of the Slavs of Adygea, set up in 1991, represents the interests of the Russian-speaking population. Its statute states that it unites the representatives of the Slav peoples living in Adygea in defence of their civil rights and freedoms. The Union was in many ways a response to the founding of *Adyge Khase* which began as a national-cultural movement. However the goal of a republic, the election of a president and the desire to leave Krasnodar *krai*, politicized both *Adyge Khase* and the Union. Culture was forced to take a back seat. The Russians feared possible isolation from Russia, the loss of their close links with Russia and discrimination.

The German society, *Wiedergeburt* (Rebirth), was established in 1992 to unite Germans, to develop German culture, and to study the language and establish schools and classes where subjects are taught in German. *Wiedergeburt* has close links with Germany and there is a general desire among Adygean Germans to consider moving to Germany.

The Tatar society, *Duslyk* (Friendship), unites Tatars and other nationalities, irrespective of religious belief. Its goals are the maintenance and study of the Tatar language and culture and the spreading of information about Islam.

The Greek society, *Argo*, seeks to promote the Greek language and culture, the revival of nationality and original family names and the return of Greeks to their historical places of habitation. The repatriation of Greeks from Adygea has also been discussed but no decision has been taken.

The Armenian society, *Druzhba* (Friendship), besides promoting the development of Armenian language and culture, has taken upon itself the resolution of conflicts between Armenians and other nationalities in Adygea. In Maikop and Giaginsky *raions*, joint Armenian and Cossack patrols have cut down the incidence of crime.

There are many other societies, for instance the charity, *Istoricheskaya rodina* (Historic Motherland), *Ny khase* (Council of Mothers), the Union of Women of Adygea and the Youth Union of Adygea.

In early 1992 the public movement, *Edinstvo* (Unity), was established in an attempt to consolidate democratic forces. It convened a congress in June 1992 in which Russians, Adyge, Ukrainians, Armenians, Tatars and Germans participated. However, *Adyge Khase*, the Union of Slavs and the Union of Cossacks declined to send representatives. *Edinstvo* lays great stress on round tables in order to bring together representatives of various nationalities. It promotes links with the republican radio and the newspaper, *Sovetskaya Adygeya*.

Ethnic stability in the republic of Adygea depends almost entirely on relations between the two main ethnic groups, Russians and Adyge. However, increasingly deprecatory remarks are being heard. Russians are offended by being called immigrants and conquerors. The transfer of Adygea from Krasnodar *krai* led the Maikop *raion* soviet to vote in 1990 for the return of Maikop *raion*, where Russians make up 84 per cent of the population, to Krasnodar *krai*. Many Russians fear becoming second-class citizens, along the lines of Russians in the Baltic States. Most leading positions in Adygea are occupied by Adyge and Russians seldom have a command of the Adyge language. Not all Russians welcomed the new Adygea flag regarding it as symbolizing the Adyge and Islam. Some Adyge object to the Russian flag since the war against their forebears was conducted under the same flag.

The ataman of the Union of Cossacks of Maikop, A. I. Tarasov, regards the attempts by the Union of Slavs to involve Cossacks in politics and transform them into a political party as fraught with danger. He states that Cossacks seek stability, the revival of Cossackdom and the Russian people and do not wish to interfere with the rights of other peoples. Cossacks refrain from party and political deals. The leadership of the Union of Slavs is regarded as extremist in pursuing the interests of the Russians in Adygea. The decree of the President of the Russian Federation on the reform of the military structure of the frontier and internal forces in the North Caucasus region of the Russian Federation and state support for Cossackdom, published in *Rossiiskaya gazeta*, March 23, 1993, aroused concern among the Adyge, especially over the ownership of land.

There are a small number of Meskhetians (mostly in the Greek village of Goverdovsky) but they regard their stay in the republic as temporary until a solution to the problem of their return to their historic home in Georgia. An increasing number of Russian and

Ukrainian immigrants are finding their way to Adygea. In 1991 there were over 12,000 of them and in the first quarter of 1992 another 3,000 arrived. Most of them are from "hot spots" in the former Soviet Union, industrial workers from the north of Russia and members of the military who have served in the republic and wish to settle there after demobilization. They have caused problems due to their lack of knowledge of the local language and its traditions. In March 1993 there were also about 3,500 refugees from Abkhazia and the indigenous population extends considerable aid to them.

The *Rodina* (Motherland) committee for national policy and society was founded to promote links with the Adyge diaspora, mostly to be found mainly in Turkey, the USA, Israel and Europe. Repatriation has begun, including some families from Syria, Turkey, Jordan and Israel. About 300 families, or 1,500 persons, are expected in the next few years, with many of them having professional skills.

Islam never had deep roots in Adygea, unlike Chechnia and Ingushetia, but it is being promoted officially as the Adyge religion by the republican government. Plots of land have been made available for the construction of mosques in Maikop and the *raions* where previously they had been almost entirely destroyed. The construction of mosques is also being financed by local budgets, local enterprises, the *Adyge Khase* society, the religious society, *Din Khase*, local residents and the diaspora. There are practically no Islamic clergy in Adygea and this has led to young men being sent to Syria, Jordan and other Middle East countries to study.

The Russian Orthodox Church is also increasing in influence, especially as Cossacks regard church-going as one of the obligatory practices of being a Cossack and as churches have also set up Sunday schools. There is an Armenian church in Maikop and it runs the religious society, *Surb Arutyun*.

Notes

1 N. D. Pchelintseva, L. V. Samarina, *Sovremennaya Etnopoliticheskaya i Etnokulturnaya Situatsiya v Respublike Adygeya*, Rossiiskaya Akademiya Nauk Institut Etnologii i Antropologii, Issledovaniya po Prikladnoi i Neotlozhnoi Etnologii, No. 47 (Moscow 1993).
2 *Sovetskaya Adygeya*, July 25, 1992.

Dagestan

The Nogai people inhabit the Nogai steppe which until the revolution of 1917 was treated administratively as a single unit, first of all in Stavropol, later in Terek *guberniya*. Between 1922 and 1937 the steppe was within Dagestan ASSR. Between 1944 and 1957 it was in Grozny *oblast*. A decree of the Presidium of the Supreme Soviet of the RSFSR of Jan. 9, 1957, divided the Nogai steppe into three parts: Kayasulinsky and Achikulaksky *raions* (western part of the steppe) were transferred to Stavropol *krai*; Naursky and Shchelkovsky *raions* (southern part of the steppe) were made part of the Chechen-Ingush ASSR and the Nogaisky and Kizlyarsky *raions* (north, central and south-east part of the steppe) became part of Dagestan ASSR. This decree, the re-establishment of the Chechen-Ingush ASSR and the abolition of Grozny *oblast*, are regarded by the Nogai as an "arbitrary act and bloodless repression".[1] Until 1957 the Nogai were a single ethnos but when they were divided into three parts they lost the status of a unified people.

Unity
Birlik

History. In 1989 the First Congress of the voluntary society, *Birlik* (Unity), was held and declared its main objective to be the unification of the Nogai people into one autonomous unit. Further All-Nogai *Birlik* congresses were held in 1990 and 1992. The congresses adopted the parliamentary path of development and resolution of all Nogai problems, including the achievement of autonomy. Speakers underlined the fact that the Nogai were legally and politically defenceless. A Nogai delegation was received by Boris Yeltsin, chairman of the RSFSR Supreme Soviet, on July 17, 1990, and stressed that the Nogai were deprived of having their own representatives in legal and representative state bodies due to the fact that they were a small minority in the territories they inhabited. They argued that the decree of Jan. 9, 1957 discriminated against them and hence it should be repealed. *Birlik*'s task was to establish departments in all regions where the Nogai lived. On Sept. 20, 1992, Birlik founded *Nogaistan*, an all-Nogai social and political newspaper.

Nogai political activity was centred on Terekli-Mekteb, Nogai *raion*, Dagestan, where *Birlik* has its headquarters and the editorial board of the *Nogaistan* newspaper. A conference marking the 600th anniversary of the Nogai state was held here in November 1991.

A joint congress of the Nogai and Terek Cossacks was held in November 1990, but the expected union of the Nogai and Cossacks did not take place. However, Nogai leaders regard this event as one of the reasons preventing Dagestan declaring national sovereignty. Responses to the Nogai claim for autonomy were mixed. Dagestan responded by saying that sovereignty was inappropriate at present but something should be done about to uphold their cultural autonomy. Checheno-Ingushetia stated that since there were few Nogai in the territory it could not resolve the question by itself. Stavropol *krai* simply passed the Nogai request to the RSFSR Supreme Soviet and it, in turn, proposed cultural autonomy. As the Nogai shrewdly observed, no one knows precisely what cultural autonomy means.

Independence for Dagestan and Chechnia would have had serious consequences for the Nogai, but this danger has since receded. As a consequence the 2nd Extraordinary Congress adopted a gradualist approach to the problem of raising the status of the Nogai territories. It demanded that the autonomy of the Nogai be recognized and that there should be no interference in their constitutional rights. This was forwarded to the leaders of Russia, Dagestan, Chechnia, Ingushetia and Stavropol *krai*. *Birlik* is trying to secure the formation of a Nogai autonomous *okrug* in Neftekumsky *raion*, Stavropol *krai*, that would form a stable Nogai territorial-administrative entity. The Nogai complain that the term Nogai steppe has disappeared from maps and been replaced by Kizlyarsky pastureland. Considerable conflict has arisen over pasture and *Birlik* has succeeded in having some hill areas returned to the Nogai. The Nogai are opposed to private ownership of land and favour the retention of *kolkhozes* and *sovkhozes*. The reason for this is their fear that if a market develops in land outsiders will buy up land and force the Nogai from their land. About 40 per cent of the Nogai live in Dagestan but only about 30 per cent of the land they farm in Dagestan is in Nogai *raion*. The standard of living of the Nogai in Stavropol *krai* is higher but political problems are greater. Their leaders there regard economic advance as the only way to ensure that the national idea survives.

The political options of Birlik are three-fold: autonomy within the Russian Federation, the consolidation of Nogai areas around Nogai *raion* in Dagestan or if Dagestan becomes independent and leaves the Russian Federation, full sovereignty for the Nogai outside the Russian Federation.

Birlik is also to be found in Astrakhan *oblast* and promotes the interests of the Nogai living there.[2]

Notes
1   K. P. Kalinovskaya, G. E. Markov, *Poiski resheniya problem nogaiskoi stepi*, Rossiskaya Akademiya Nauk Institut Etnologii i Antropologii, Issledovaniya po prikladnoi i neotlozhnoi etnologii, no. 44 (Moscow 1993), p. 3.
2   V. M. Viktorin, *Astrakhanskie Nogaitsy*, in ibid.

Kabardino-Balkaria[1]

According to the 1989 census there are 363,494 Kabardin, 70,793 Balkar, 240,750 Russians, 12,826 Ukrainians, 9,996 Ossetians, 8,569 Germans and some other peoples in the republic. The Balkar were deported to Central Asia in 1944 and were only permitted to return in 1956. The decrees on the rehabilitation of peoples who suffered repression (April 26, 1991) and the rehabilitation of the victims of political repression (Oct. 18, 1991) proved difficult to implement, with the most intractable problems being those connected with land. This has been at the root of most of the present conflicts in the republic.

When Soviet power was proclaimed in 1918, Kabarda and Balkaria were placed in the Gorsky (Mountainous) autonomous republic (ASSR). In the early years of Soviet rule Kabarda was reduced to a third of its size by the forced transfer of territory to Karachaia, Balkaria, Ingushetia and Ossetia. In 1921 Kabarda left the Gorsky ASSR and became the Kabarda autonomous *oblast*. In 1922 Balkaria also left the Gorsky ASSR to merge and form the Kabardino-Balkar autonomous *oblast*. In 1936 it was upgraded to the status of an autonomous republic (ASSR). After the deportation of the Balkars, from 1944–56, the territory was known as the Kabarda ASSR. [Research in party archives revealed that 35,958 (9,037 families) had been deported in March 1944 and in 1957-58 35,367 (9,335 families) Balkars returned.] In 1957 it was again the Kabardino-Balkar ASSR.

The main goal of the administration was to secure a higher constitutional status and, on Jan. 30, 1991, the Supreme Soviet adopted a declaration on state sovereignty and renamed the republic the Kabardino-Balkar Soviet Socialist Republic. In March 1992 the Supreme Soviet amended the name to Kabardino-Balkar Republic. In September 1991 the post of President was introduced and a law on the election of the President passed. In December 1991 V. M. Kokov, formerly first secretary of the CPSU *obkom*, was elected President. An important decree was passed in May 1991 on the re-establishment as the borders of the republic those existing on Jan. 1, 1944. This was due to the fact that in 1944 a considerable part of the territory was transferred to neighbouring republics. Many requests were addressed to President Yeltsin and the RSFSR Supreme Soviet about this matter but no reply was received. The Supreme Soviet of Kabardino-Balkaria, in 1991–92, drafted laws on property, leasing, the status of a people's deputy and on citizenship. In November 1991 the Supreme Soviet of the republic accepted the decree of the RSFSR Supreme Soviet introducing a state of emergency in the Chechen-Ingush republic and itself passed a decree banning the illegal distribution of arms among the population of its republic.

In September 1990, a conference, convened on the initiative of Balkar people's deputies, decided to hold a Congress of Balkar people. This took place in March 1991 and was called the first stage of the first Congress. The Congress adopted a decree on the re-establishment and implementation of the political, economic and socio-cultural rights of the Balkar people. This included recovering the land lost in 1944. The second stage of the Congress convened in November 1990 and it proclaimed the Republic of Balkaria and the national sovereignty of the Balkar people. The Supreme Soviet of the republic supported the proclamation of the Republic of Balkaria and set up a commission to elaborate a means of dealing with the consequences of the declaration. However, it refused to recognize as legal the creation of the so-called National Council of the Balkar People (NCBP) as the supreme agency of power of the Balkar people between Congresses (chairman: B. Chabdarov; deputy chairman: T. Ulbashev).

The first step towards the establishment of the NCBP had been the publication of a decree on the holding of a referendum in Balkaria of Dec. 29, 1991. Voters were invited to respond to the following questions: Are you in favour of the proclamation of the sovereignty of the Balkar people and the republic of Balkaria as a subject of the RSFSR? The Supreme Soviet of the republic declared the referendum illegal, but it went ahead and about 95 per cent of those who voted supported the questions. The holding of the referendum against the wishes of the Supreme Soviet changed relations between the NCBP and the Supreme Soviet. The former began actively seeking allies in order to achieve its goal and turned to the Russian Supreme Soviet and the Council of Leaders of the Assembly of Turkic Peoples. The Russian parliament did not reach any decision. The Assembly of Turkic Peoples, set up to counter the Conference of the Mountain Peoples of the Caucasus, does not have any explicitly political goals and regards the achievement of self-determination of all Turkic peoples as its goal. In January 1992, in Makhachkala (Dagestan), the Council of Leaders of the Assembly of Turkic Peoples (chairman: R. Mukhametdinov) adopted a resolution on the proclamation of a Republic of Balkaria and the national sovereignty of the Balkar people. The NCBP was recognized as the only legal body representing the interests of the Balkar people. The Council appealed to President Yeltsin and the Russian Supreme Soviet to resolve the matter of the Balkar quickly. In May 1992, in Makhachkala, the Caucasian-Black Sea Commonwealth of the Assembly of Turkic Peoples, came into being. The founding members were the Renaissance People's Party of Azerbaijan, the Popular Front of Azerbaijan. the Tenglik Kumyksky People's Movement, the Turan People's Democratic Party, the Birlik Nogai People's Movement, the Birlik Party. The republic of Balkaria was represented by the League for the Renaissance of Balkaria, a political party which was registered in November 1991. Its goals were to contribute to the regeneration of the Balkar people and the re-establishment of the state of Balkaria as a subject of the Russian Federation (chairman: Z. Sh. Zukaev).

Adyge Khase is the most influential socio-political Kabardin organization and has been exercising growing influence on the development of Kabarda. It originated from several large meetings, between May 1990 and September 1991, and convened the first Congress of the Kabardin people. *Adyge Khase* was set up to transform the political and socio-economic system in the republic of Kabardino-Balkaria. Its chairman (*tkhamada*) is Dr Z. M. Naloev, a philologist in the Institute of History, Philology and Economics of the Council of

Ministers of the republic. The First Congress took place on Jan. 10, 1992. The Republic of Kabarda was proclaimed and it was stated that the statehood of the Kabardin people was re-established in 1921 through its own efforts when Kabarda first left the Gorsky republic and ceased to have links with Balkar societies. The 1922 unification of Kabardino-Balkaria contravened international law and was void from its inception. The Congress proclaimed the creation of a sovereign Kabardin republic within the historical frontiers of the Kabardin people (according to the frontiers laid down in the Terek estates and land commission of 1863) and the election of a Congress of the Kabardin People (CKP), which functions between Congresses. The latter was to draft a programme of action in line with the demands of the current situation. Congress chairman until January 1993 was Yu. Kh. Kalmykov and since then Zh. M. Gubachikov. The Supreme Soviet of the republic of Kabardino-Balkaria supported the decision of the First Congress of the Kabardin people to proclaim a Kabardin republic and set up a commission to implement the decisions of the Congress. The Second Congress of the Kabardin people took place on May 15–16, 1992, and charged the CKP with the drafting of legal norms and laws to bring into being a republic of Kabarda and a programme to promote the renaissance of the Cherkess (Adyge) people.

The Supreme Soviet of the republic became alarmed at the divisive tendencies of the NCBP and the CKP and in May 1992 published a decree on measures to stabilize the situation, including holding a referendum on whether the Kabardin and Balkars wished to continue to co-habit in one republic. The Supreme Soviet claimed the right to decide if a Congress could be held in future. The NCBP and the CKP were both hostile to the referendum idea. The NCBP decided to appeal to the Russian Supreme Soviet not to permit the holding of a referendum in the republic. Both the NCBP and the CKP advised their peoples to abstain from participation in the referendum.

The entry into the republic of military units from other parts of the Russian Federation and the arrest of the deputy chairman of the CKP and president of the Conference of Mountain Peoples of the Caucasus, Yu. Shanibov, led to the CKP and *Adyge Khase* convening a huge demonstration in Nalchik on Sept. 24, 1992, and which only dispersed on Oct. 4, 1992. Balkars took no part in these events. The meeting presented the following demands to the President, Supreme Soviet and Council of Ministers of the Kabardino-Balkar republic:

i)   convene immediately a session of the Supreme Soviet to discuss its own dissolution;
ii) form a government of national accord;
iii) withdraw Spetsnaz units from the Dom Sovetov (Palace of Soviets) and Russian military from the territory of Kabardino-Balkaria for a month;
iv) cease exaggerating events in connection with the situation in Abkhazia and prevent the prosecution of those participating in the conflict in Abkhazia [CKP members were fighting on the Abkhaz side against the Georgians];
v)   provide the CKP with TV time twice a week;
vi) organize a round table of representatives of socio-political movements and leaders of the republic to analyse current events.

The Supreme Soviet viewed the demonstration as illegal and regarded it as bringing the peoples close to civil war and as a national catastrophe threatening the territorial integrity of the republic. On Oct. 9, 1992, it decreed that the demonstration was an unconstitutional act by the organizers and members of the demonstration whose objective was the violent overthrow of the legally elected agencies of power. The activities of the executive committee and the CKP leadership, attempting to overthrow by force the legally elected agencies of power, were declared unconstitutional and destabilizing the socio-political situation, undermining the unity of Kabardino-Balkaria, separating from the Russian Federation and fomenting an inter-ethnic war. The Procurator-General of the republic was to examine the legality of the activities of the CKP. The majority of the demands of the demonstration were also judged unconstitutional.

The CKP reacted by declaring the Supreme Soviet decree evidence of a right-wing lurch in the policies of the President and the supreme agencies of power in the republic, an attempt to establish a totalitarian regime and to suppress democracy, freedom and thought. The Third Congress of the Kabardin people took place on Nov. 28–29, 1992, and it underlined the deterioration of relations between the CKP and the leadership of the republic. The Congress reaffirmed its goal as the establishment of a republic of Kabarda, to include land, illegally transferred in 1944 to neighbouring republics. The Kabardin republic was to be set up by 1995. Given that the President and the Supreme Soviet of the republic had adopted a confrontational course *vis-à-vis* the CKP and the Congress, the CKP was charged with the task of devising tactics as a constructive opposition.

Tension has surfaced from time to time between Kabardin and Balkars. In December 1991 a Balkar policeman in the village of Yanika killed a Kabardin from the neighbouring village of Shalushka. The Shalushka assembly wanted to exact revenge and the villagers of Yanika appealed to the NCBP to mediate. Russian troops were placed between the two villages. Z. M. Naloev, *Tkhmada* of the *Adyge Khase*, succeeded in finding a solution to the conflict. Another conflict erupted between April 29 and May 3, 1992. On April 29, 1992 a Balkar murdered a Kabardin from the village of Khamidie (Tersky *raion*) in Nalchik. During the night of May 1–2 a group of 60 Kabardin attacked Balkar farms in Tersky *raion*. On May 3 Kabardin attacked the settlement of Novaya Balkaria. The conflict was resolved by the NCBP and the Supreme Soviet of the republic.

During 1992 the NCBP and the CKP attempted to make contact. On Feb. 24 the presidium of the Supreme Soviet of the republic arranged a meeting between a representative of the NCBP (B. K. Chabdarov) and the CKP (Yu. Kh. Kalmykov). It was agreed to co-operate on implementing decisions of the Congresses of the Balkar and Kabardin peoples. Specialist groups were set up to deal with land problems. The first meeting took place on March 23, 1992, and it turned out that the views of the Balkar and Kabardin sides were quite different with both sides maintaining their positions. The borders between Balkaria and Kabarda were laid down in 1709 with the agreement of both sides. The alterations in 1863 were not agreed to by both sides. The Third Congress of the Kabardin people, in November 1992, laid down that the final settlement of the border between the two republics should be based on the finds of an independent specialist commission at an ordinary Congress of the Kabardin people. The NCBP is coming round to the view that the final decision should rest with the state agencies of the Russian Federation.

Russians and Cossacks have also organized themselves politically. The two most important political forces are the Russian Language Congress and the Tersko-Malkinsky department (*otdel*) of Terek Cossackdom. These two organizations defend the rights of the non-titular nationalities to equal participation in the economy and running of the republic. The Russian Language Congress was registered in August 1992 (chairman: V. V. Protasov) and unites Russian speakers in Prokhladny and Maisky and aims to prevent any ethnic group acquiring a monopoly and to retain the unity of the republic. There are other smaller societies, for instance *Rossiyane* (Russians), which unites Russians in Nalchik and seeks to defend members of the organization against injustice and discrimination through legal channels. *Slavyane* (Slavs) represents the interests of the Slav peoples of Kabardino-Balkaria and its objective is to develop political activity among the Slavs.

Cossacks aim primarily to retain the Russian state. The Terek Cossacks are the most influential. The Tersko-Malkinsky department (*obshchina*) of the Terek Cossacks unites Cossacks in *obshchinas* that have sprung up in various villages (*stanitsa*) and towns (chairman-ataman: M. M. Klevtsov). The founding Congress of the Cossack Circle took place on Oct. 19, 1990. The *otdel*'s primary objective is to revive the centuries-old Cossack tradition. The origins of the Russian language movement go back to the wish of the Kabardin and Balkar peoples to have their own state. The founding Congress of the Russian Language Congress, in May 1992, underlined the wish of Russians and Cossacks to remain subjects of the Kabardin-Balkar republic but in the event of the establishment of a republic of Kabarda and a republic of Balkaria, the population of Prokhladny and Maisky *raions* wish to leave the Kabardino-Balkar republic. The CKP reacted negatively to this and a declaration of the executive committee of the CKP of July 5, 1992, opposed the granting of equal status to the Russian language inhabitants of the republic and that the Kabardin people would never assent to the alienation of legally Kabardin land.

Notes
1 I. L. Babich, *Etnopoliticheskaya Situatsyia v Kabardino-Balkarii*, Rossiiskaya Akademiya Nauk Institut Etnologii i Antropologii, Issledovaniya po Prikladnoi i Neotlozhnoi Etnologii, No. 45 (Moscow 1993).

Karachaevo-Cherkessia[1]

Karachaevo-Cherkessia was formed during the 1920s and became an autonomous *oblast* within Stavropol *krai*. On Nov. 30, 1990, it became a republic within the Russian Federation. On Jan. 1, 1992, the population was 430,935, of whom 213,171 were urban and 217,764 were rural dwellers. Russians are concentrated in the cities and dominate the towns of Cherkessia. Karachai predominate in 64 of the 144 towns and villages of their region. Russians account for about 42 per cent of the population, Karachai for 32 per cent, Cherkess for 10 per cent, Abazin for 7 per cent, Nogai for 3 per cent, Ukrainians for 1 per cent, Ossetians for 1 per cent and Greeks for 0.4 per cent.

There are over 20 public organizations in Karachaevo-Cherkessia. The most important are as follows:

i)   *Djamagat*, a republican society of Karachai.
ii) *Djamagat* Democratic Organization, a very radical republican society of Karachai.
iii) All-National Council of Karachai; an organization representing the interests of the democratic organizations of Karachai, and a group of Muslims and Karachai Cossacks.
iv) *Khase* (*Adyge Khase*), an Cherkess republican society.
v)   *Adgylara*, an Abazin republican society.
vi) *Apsadgyl*, an Abazin republican association for contacts with compatriots abroad.

vii) Congress of Abazin and Cherkess peoples.

viii) *Birlik*, a Nogai republican society.

ix) *Verkhnekubansky kazachy krug* (Upper Kuban Cossack Circle), a regional Cossack organization, uniting all Cossack societies (circles) on the territory of the republic.

x) *Slavyane Karachaevo-Cherkesii* (Karachaevo-Cherkes Slavs), a Slav republican society.

xi) *Rus* (Russia), a socio-political movement, uniting the Russian population and the Cossacks.

xii) *Heastrofi*, a Pontiac Greek society in Zelenchuksky *raion*.

xiii) *Masis*, a Cherkess urban cultural society of Armenians.

All these organizations seek to promote the ethnographic development of their members (study of history, language, literature, art, renaissance of cultural traditions, publishing and contacts with other groups). *Rus* is the only organization which has explicitly political goals, but the activities of all the others have become to a lesser or greater degree politicized. The leadership of all societies is almost entirely in the hands of the intelligentsia.

Adyge Khase held its Constituent Congress in November 1989 and was registered in March 1990. In addition to the objectives listed above this organization seeks to promote the renaissance of traditional Adyge culture in the countryside: private farming; higher living standards for its members, for instance by transferring allotments of land to them; the regeneration of traditional crafts and the solution of ecological and immigrant problems. Another important objective is to strengthen links with Adyge outside the CIS. Each member of the society receives a membership card on which is a circle surrounded by 12 stars, symbolizing the original 12 Adyge tribes and the three Adyge peoples, the Kabardin, the Cherkess and the Adyge. *Cherkessky Vestnik* is the society's newspaper. *Adyge Khase* co-operates closely with other Kabardin, Adyge, Shapsug and Abkhaz societies, with the Cherkess Fatherland *Khase*, the Kabardin Congress, the Congress of the Abazin and Cherkess peoples, and the International Cherkess Association. It is a member of the Conference of Caucasian Peoples.

Political objectives were articulated for the first time at the Second Extraordinary Congress in February 1991 when the society was renamed a socio-political society. From 1990 *Adyge Khase* opposed Karachaevo-Cherkessia leaving Stavropol *krai* but in October 1991 had to face the new realities of the situation. Many leaders favoured Cherkess autonomy and a session of soviets of all levels of the former Cherkess autonomous *oblast* voted in favour of this. However, the Russian Supreme Soviet suspended this decision and also the decision to establish an independent Karachaia and Cossack Batalpashinsky department (*otdel*). In March 1992 a referendum was held in Karachaevo-Cherkessia and 76 per cent voted to retain the unified republic. Part of the membership of *Adyge Khase* support the concept of forming a unified Cherkess republic which would encompass Kabarda, Cherkessia, Adygea and the historic Adyge territory on the Black Sea littoral. This would involve the repatriation of Adyge from abroad and the establishment of repatriation centres in Nalchik, Cherkessk and Maikop.

Unlike many other societies, *Adyge Khase* attempts to conduct a skilful policy but has found it difficult to win support from the Abazin and the Nogai when it became clear to the latter that the goal was Cherkess statehood. There have also been conflicts between Adyge and Karachai in the pedagogical institute, with the Adyge demanding their own pedagogical institute.

The *Adgylara* society was established in 1990 and is mainly concerned with the promotion of Abazin culture and language. It stresses a positive attitude towards the religious feelings of believers. Originally the society was involved in general problems affecting the peoples of Karachaevo-Cherkessia (elections to the Russian Supreme Soviet, the transformation of the autonomous *oblast* into a republic, etc.) but gradually Abazin questions took over and the goal of creating their own national-territorial formation was raised. At the Abazin Congress in the autumn of 1991 an Abazin republic was proclaimed. The consequence of this was the proclamation of an independent Karachaia, Cherkessia and Batalpashinsky department. A more modest goal was the setting up of an Abazin autonomous *okrug*. The society wants the return of *auls* (villages) and land which they lost during collectivization.

The *Apsadgyl* society was set up in 1991 and its statutes were adopted at a republican conference in September 1991. It was registered in April 1992. The primary objective of the society is contact and co-operation with compatriots living abroad (the near and far abroad) and help to those who wish to return to their historical home. The search for and return of historical and cultural relics to the republic is another major task of the group.

The *Birlik* Nogai society was founded at a Constituent Congress in March 1990 and it has 3,000 members. Most of these are *sovkhoz* workers and members of the intelligentsia. The society has close links with similar societies in Astrakhan *oblast*, Dagestan, Chechnia and Stavropol *krai*. They share a common name and a common programme. *Polovetskaya Luna* is the newspaper of all the *Birlik* societies. The economic situation of the Nogai is poor and chemical pollutants have led to a growth in illnesses in Nogai *auls*, especially stomach ailments and malaria. The Nogai want *sovkhozes* in their area to be directed by Nogai as they are more conversant with local problems. This has led to discussion about the formation of a Nogai autonomous *raion*. During the election campaign to the Russian Supreme Soviet in March 1990 the society advocated the separation of Karachaevo-Cherkessia from Stavropol *krai* and welcomed the establishment of the Karachaevo-Cherkess republic. There are two main views about the future of the Nogai: one is the formation of an independent national-territorial formation of Nogai in the Nogai steppe; the other is to re-establish on the territory of the present Adyge-Khablsky *raion* the former Ikon-Khalkinsky *raion* which was formerly dominated by the Nogai.

The *Slavyane Karachaevo-Cherkesii* society brings together the Slav population and also the Russian-speaking representatives of other peoples whose traditions are close to those of the Slavs. The society is headed by a *Veche* (council) and its executive agency, the *Duma*. The leader is called a *voevod*. The goal of the society is the renaissance of Slav culture, traditions, the Christian faith and the retention of the Russian state as a whole. There is close co-operation with other societies in promoting traditional forms of ownership, economy, agriculture, crafts and maintaining a single economic space and the territorial integrity of Russia and cultural and economic ties with compatriots abroad. The society has aroused considerable interest among Slavs and Russian speakers, especially those who are unwilling to commit themselves to Cossack goals. Resolving the Karachai problem would improve matters considerably and one proposal is that a decision be taken in 3 to 5 years time on whether the Karachai wish to re-establish the Karachai republic, abolished in 1943. The society actively supports the rehabilitation of Cossackdom, including the return of property they lost during collectivization.

The *Rus* socio-political association of Russians in Karachaevo-Cherkessia was formed in December 1991 and includes Cossacks. Some believe that this organization was formed at the instigation of the local *nomenklatura* as a counterweight to the too-democratic *Slavyane* society and to unify Russians and Cossacks. It is estimated that Cossacks make up 5 per cent of the population. Although the society professes to promote peace, friendship and mutual understanding among all the peoples of the republic, it often represents the interests of Cossacks *vis-à-vis* other nationalities. *Rus* works very closely with Cossack societies and skilfully supports their changing demands. For instance, *Rus* supports the demand to re-establish the Zelenchuksko-Urupsky Cossack republic and to transfer it to Stavropol and the re-establishment of the Batalpashinsky department within its 1917 frontiers, the restoration of the former name of Batalpashinsk to Cherkessia and a moratorium to be placed on the use and distribution of land in Batalpashinsky department. This may be connected with the Cossack desire to return to their traditional *obshchina* use of land and secure the return of land at present being farmed by Karachai. *Rus* enjoys wide support among the Russian community but also official backing as well. In the first quarter of 1992 *Rus* received about 300,000 rubles in donations from 21 state enterprises and organizations in the republic.

The origins of the present self-assertiveness of the Cossacks dates back to 1984 when they held a conference on Cossackdom in the October Revolution and the Civil War. They quickly developed a renewed sense of identity and became a source of support for the *krai* administration in its attempt to prevent Karachaevo-Cherkessia leaving Stavropol *krai*. The Cossacks also wanted to leave Karachaevo-Cherkessia and transfer to Krasnodar *krai*. The first Cossack circle was set up at the Constituent Congress in Zelenchukskaya in June 1990 and over the next year a network of circles was established. Village, rural and urban circles formed part of the Batalpashinsky and Urupsko-Zelenchuksky circles and they in turn formed the Upper Kuban Cossackdom. Each circle is headed by an ataman and the Upper Kuban circle by the supreme ataman.

The programme and statutes of each Cossack circle are almost identical. Cossacks began to wear traditional dress, although without carrying weapons. Women started wearing Kuban hats. Proto-military formations came into being in Cossack villages. A major issue at assemblies and congresses was the return of Cossack land. The return of the Karachai from deportation in 1957 had led to mixed Russian and Cossack villages. After the promulgation of the laws on the rehabilitation of peoples who had suffered repression (April 26, 1991) and the rehabilitation of the victims of political repression (Oct. 18, 1991) Cossack associations began to seek the return of their historic lands, partly to re-establish their communal use of land. Another live issue was the restoration of the Cossack military units. Military patriotic education was expanded. In 1990–92 several public opinion polls were conducted to ascertain feeling about the re-establishment of a Cossack administrative-territorial region. The Third Congress of the Batalpashinsky Cossacks, on Aug. 10, 1991, proclaimed the Batalpashinsky Cossack SSR within the RSFSR and the Congresses of Zelenchuksky and Urupsky Cossacks, on Oct. 30, 1991, proclaimed the formation of the Zelenchuksko-Urupsky Cossack Republic as a part of the Union of Cossack Republics. During the referendum on the future of Karachaevo-Cherkessia only 28 per cent of Cossacks voted in favour of a republic.

The decree of the President of the Russian Federation on the rehabilitation of peoples who had been repressed with reference to Cossackdom of June 16, 1992, was welcomed by many Cossacks. It recognized Cossack circles as legal entities, the right to self-administration was returned, their traditional form of agriculture was recognized, the desire of the government to draft a programme of economic and cultural renaissance of Cossackdom and the recognition of the need to develop relations between the Russian Federation and the CIS on Cossack affairs. Some Cossacks were critical of the fact that the boundaries of the

Cossack territory had not been defined and that the statements on the land question were imprecise. The size of the Cossack population is difficult to determine but the chairman of the council of elders of Batalpashinsky department, during an interview with *Nezavisimaya Gazeta* (June 23, 1992), maintained that there were 230,000 Cossacks whereas the 1989 census recorded only 176,000 Russians in the republic. Cossack organizations in the republic have close links with Cossack organizations in Russia and the CIS, with especially close ties to Stavropol and Krasnodar. *Kazachya Volya* (Cossack Will) is their newspaper. The administrative-territorial formation of Cossacks in Karachaevo-Cherkessia forms part of the Union of Cossack Republics of South Russia. The supreme body is the Union of Cossacks of Russia.

Neastrofi is a cultural and educational society of Pontiac Greeks whose main tasks are to maintain and develop the language and culture and re-establish cultural traditions. As part of this the society defends the interests of the Greek population.

Masis is a society for the development of the language, culture, traditions, religion and art of Armenians in the republic. The society seeks to set up workshops, studios, educational establishments and distribute books and journals. The preservation of historical and cultural monuments is important as is the cultivation of links with Armenians in Armenia, Russian *oblasts* and the other states of the CIS.

There are 73 Muslim organizations in the republic as well as 15 Russian Orthodox. There are also 11 Baptist, Pentecostalist and Evangelical communities. Most of them are registered. Muslim activity is co-ordinated by the spiritual board of the Muslims of Karachaevo-Cherkessia and Stavropol. Considerable religious literature comes from outside the republic, especially copies of the *Koran* which are often distributed free. Finance for the construction of mosques and the training of religious teachers is readily available. The Islamic education of the people (Arabic and the reading of the *Koran*) is being held back by a lack of teachers. Only 48 men in the republic have received theological training, all the others are autodidacts. At present 44 students are studying in Nazran, Grozny and Dagestan (where Islamic institutes has been opened) and also in Central Asia. Children receive instruction at school or in the mosque. At present about 30 schools provide such training. Courses on Islam for adults were originally very popular but the enthusiasm has waned.

The multi-confessional nature of the population of the republic rarely leads to conflict but an exception is the Party of Muslims (headed by M. Bedzhiev in Karachaia). The party favours Karachaia separating from Cherkessia. At a party congress Bedzhiev attempted to have himself proclaimed imam. The spiritual board of the republic immediately condemned this manoeuvre but Bedzhiev's influence remained considerable, especially in Karachaevsky and Malo-Karachaevsky *raions*. Fundamentalism appears to be on the increase.

Note

1 Ya. S. Smirnova, *Karachaevo-Cherkesiya: Etnopoliticheskaya I Etnokulturnaya Situatsiya*, Rossiiskaya Akademiya Nauk Institut Etnologii i Antropologii, Issledovaniya po Prikladnoi i Neotlozhnoi Etnologii, No. 48 (Moscow 1993).

Tatarstan[1]

All-Union Tatar Public Centre
Vesesoyuzny Tatarsky Obshchestvenny Tsentr (VTOT)
Betensoyuz Tatar Izhtimagii Uzege

The VTOT is the largest and most influential Tatar socio-political group and has its headquarters in Kazan. Its activities cover the whole of the CIS and the Baltic States and also the Tatar diaspora outside these countries.

VTOT originated in an Initiative group of 11 persons, elected on June 27, 1988, at a meeting in Kazan State University which was attended by about 200 persons, mainly from the Institute of Language, Literature and History of the USSR Academy of Sciences, Kazan Branch. At a meeting on Oct. 29, 1988, an organizing committee of 70 persons was elected to prepare the convening of an All-Tatar Congress or a Congress of supporters of the Tatar Public Centre (TOT). The Kazan TOT group began establishing links with Tatar groups in other cities, such as Naberezhnye Chelny and Nizhnekamsk. A draft programme was published as theses in November 1988. The advent of *glasnost* in the Soviet Union encouraged the formation of many informal Tatar groups (clubs, folklore groups, language circles, etc.) among Tatars in cities such as Ufa (Bashkortostan), Perm, Orenburg, Ekaterinburg, Ulyanovsk and Saratov. Relations with the Tatar ASSR committee of the Communist Party of the Soviet Union (CPSU) deteriorated in January 1989 mainly due to TOT links outside the region which were seen by local party officials as interference in their internal affairs and tantamount to the promotion of nationalism from Kazan. Pressure was applied from Moscow on the Tatar party committee to restrain TOT activities.

The First Congress of TOT convened in Kazan on Feb. 17–18, 1989, and was attended by 586 delegates from 32 cities throughout the USSR. Delegates were overwhelmingly from the intelligentsia. These included 143 university teachers (including two full members of the USSR Academy of Sciences, one corresponding member, 22 Doctors of Science (DSc) and 118 candidates of science (PhD); 53 heads of institutions and organizations). The main themes of the Congress were the political and economic sovereignty of Tatarstan, the demographic development of the republic, the standard of education in the national language, Tatar, and the prospects for the development of Tatar culture. The delegates formally established the Tatar Public Centre, the people's movement in support of *perestroika* (TOT), adopted a programme and a statute (rules). A 77-member Council was elected, as was a Board of Administration of 21 persons (one DSc, 16 PhDs, 2 retired military officers, one writer and one journalist). Shortly afterwards an Executive Committee was formed with staff working under seven chairperson-co-ordinators, chosen from Board members, with the position of chairperson rotating.

The First *Kurultai* (Congress) adopted 13 resolutions and proposals for submission to a plenum of the CC, CPSU on such topics as the status of the Tatar republic, ways of studying public opinion on the status of the republic, the status of the Tatar language in the republic, the economic sovereignty of the republic, the consolidation of the Tatar nation, the demographic situation in the republic and immigration, the national education system, the ecological situation in the republic, the democratization of religious life, and the Crimean Tatars. TOT's demands for political and economic sovereignty and the upgrading of Tatarstan to a Union republic did not alienate the Russian minority (1989 census: of the total population of 3.6 million, 48.5 per cent were Tatar and 43.3 per cent were Russian). There was wide-ranging consensus in the republic since both Tatars and Russians could see the advantageous of an upgrading of their status.[2]

TOT was registered with the Council of Ministers of the Republic of Tatarstan (officially Tatarstan was an autonomous republic) on July 17, 1989, and the statutes of TOT were published in Russian and Tatar. The movement included the following associations: the S. Marjani society; the Bulgar Al-Jadid club; some Islamic organizations, including informal groups, such as the Saf Islam groups, a Crimean Tatar group and a Jewish group. Later the Ittifaq party joined as an associate member, as did the Kryashen (Tatar) ethnographical cultural and enlightenment society and an Azerbaijani group. The Jewish group left TOT and registered as a separate body in the republican cultural foundation. A Russian language section was founded but never flourished.

The Second TOT *Kurultai* convened in Kazan on Feb. 15–16, 1990, with 637 delegates attending: 375 from Tatarstan (255 from Kazan) and 294 from outside the republic of whom 50 were from Bashkortostan and 154 were from 72 regions and republics of the Russian Federation. There were also 40 delegates from Kazakhstan, 13 from Uzbekistan, seven from Ukraine, five from Estonia. Latvia, Belarus, Azerbaijan and Kyrgyzstan had three delegates each and Tajikistan two. Again the intelligentsia dominated with 81.4 per cent of delegates. 22.9 per cent of delegates were under 40 years of age, 30.6 per cent between 41 and 50 years and 46.5 per cent over 51 years of age. TOT was renamed VTOT (All-Union TOT). A new programme and amendments to the statutes were adopted. A document on the main directives to achieve the sovereignty of the Republic of Tatarstan was adopted as were others the establishment of units within governmental and state institutions of the republic to co-ordinate with Tatars living outside the republic; the status of the Tatar language in the Bashkir SSR, the renaming of the Kazan State Conservatory in honour of the Tatar composer, S. Saiddashev, the creation of an All-Union Tatar newspaper, the December 1990 census to be held in the republic by the All-Union Central Institute of Public Opinion (VTsIOM); representing the interests of the Republic of Tatarstan and the Tatar people in foreign countries and international organizations; and rendering assistance to the Crimean Tatars. The *kurultai* elected an All-Union Council of Representatives (124 persons) and at its first plenum on Feb. 16, 1990, it elected a Presidium (29 persons) and a President. VTOT newspapers are *Millet* and *Izvestiya TOT*.

On March 21, 1992, Tatarstan held a referendum, vigorously opposed by Moscow, on the status of the republic. President Boris Yeltsin advised voters to vote no, but of the 82 per cent of the electorate who voted, 61.4 per cent approved of Tatarstan being proclaimed a sovereign state, while only 37.2 per cent voted against.[3] This revealed that sovereignty and independence was not primarily an ethnic issue and was widely supported by Tatars and Russians alike. After the referendum, Tatarstan leaders stated that they would start negotiating with Russia a new status for the republic. As a result, Tatarstan refused to sign the Russian Federal Treaty, which all subjects of the Russian Federation, except Chechnia and Ingushetia, signed in March 1992. The dispute over what should be regarded as a subject of the Federation was so bitter that three separate treaties, one for the republics, one for the *oblasts* and *krais*, and one for the autonomous *okrugs* and the sole autonomous *oblast*, were signed. Sakha, Bashkortostan and Karelia strongly opposed these procedures but eventually only Chechnia and Tatarstan refused to sign.[4] It was reported in May 1992 that working groups from Tatarstan and Russia had begun drafting a bilateral treaty and that agreement had already been reached that relations between Moscow and Kazan would be special. In November 1992 the Tatarstan parliament adopted a republican constitution which was tantamount to a declaration of independence. Tatar and Russian were to become official state languages with equal status. Tatarstan would establish its own citizenship but citizens would be citizens of Tatarstan and the Russian Republic as well. The draft Russian Constitution, published in July 1993, gave precedence to republics, describing them as sovereign states within the Russian Federation, but the regions were classified as state-territorial formation. Neither term was defined. Finding that many of the republics did not support him in the confrontation with the Russian Supreme Soviet in September–October 1993, President Yeltsin revised the constitution, removing some of the concessions granted to the republics in the July draft. Significantly, the new draft constitution did not include the text of the Russian Federation Treaty and only referred to it twice underlining that where the treaty contravened the constitution, the latter took precedence. References to republics as sovereign states were excised, as was the provision for separate republican citizenship and stressed that all subjects were equal in their relations with the federal agencies of state power. The clause permitting republics to negotiate separate treaties with Moscow disappeared from the final draft. Republics were only granted the right to establish their own state languages alongside Russian and to pass their constitutions. Regions only acquired the right to have statutes.[5]

The results of the Dec. 12, 1993, elections to the State Duma came as a shock to President Mintimer Shaimiev of Tatarstan and the Zhirinovsky factor resulted in Tatarstan and Russia agreeing to do a deal. A treaty on the delimitation of spheres of authority and the mutual delegation of powers was ready for signature by Feb. 12, 1994, as were five other intergovernmental agreements. The treaty was signed on Feb. 15 and came into force on Feb. 24, 1994. The treaty does not mention that Tatarstan is a sovereign state. In the new treaty, Tatarstan is described as a state united with Russia, on the basis of the constitutions of the two states and the treaty on the delimitation of spheres of authority and the mutual delegation of powers. On the other hand, the Tatarstan constitution describes Tatarstan as a sovereign state associated with Russia. Russia, according to the new treaty, recognizes Tatarstan's right to conduct its own foreign policy and foreign trade, to draw up its own budget and levy republican taxes, to establish its own legal and judicial institutions, to manage the natural resources and state enterprises on its territory (except objects of federal ownership which are covered in a separate agreement) and to found its own national bank. Tatarstan is afforded the right to decide republican citizenship matters (the only republic in the Russian Federation which has this right). Tatars are exempt from Russian national service and engage in alternative civilian service. Many economic matters are exercised jointly by the two governments and these include pricing policy, monetary policy, military production on the territory of the republic, including arms sales and the conversion of military enterprises to civilian use. An important issue omitted from the treaty, which was also absent from the Federation Treaty, is how the joint exercise of responsibility for the above matters is to be effected. No mechanism has been set up. Another reason why Tatarstan signed the treaty without gaining satisfaction on a range of issues was the economic pressure applied by Moscow to oblige Kazan to sign.

VTOT was disappointed by the treaty, calling it a step backward from independence for the republic.[6] It rejected it on the grounds that it did not recognize Tatarstan as a sovereign state and therefore contravenes the Tatarstan constitution. It would have preferred Russia to develop into a confederation, that is an alliance of sovereign states acting as a group and not as a single entity. The present Russian administration favours a federation, a group of states which act as one, with there only being one sovereign state, the Russian Federation. In the new environment VTOT may not be able to achieve its objectives.

Organization. VTOT has individual, collective and associated members or participants. Its basic entity is the support group (not less than three persons), then there are local groups (rural, settlement, *raion* and urban) and regional (urban, *raion, oblast, krai*) as well as republican (republican and autonomous republican) branches and central All-Union groups. About 130 branches, of which 93 were from outside Tatarstan, attended the Second *Kurultai*. Each group has autonomy in local decision making while being guided by the programme and statues. *Kurultais* are to be convened not less than once every two years. The Presidium has a number of sub-committees on such matters as the protectionship of citizenship, assistance to refugees, culture and education, and military affairs.

Programme. The programme of the movement regarded the main tasks to be the attainment of Union republican status for Tatarstan; the acknowledgement of the Tatar language as an official language of the republic; the Tatar economy to be rendered self-sufficient and sovereign; and the consolidation of the whole Tatar nation. The major problem among these was the status of Tatarstan within the RSFSR and the USSR, especially the differences between the status of a Union republic and that of as Autonomous Republic. Discrepancies existed between the constitution of the RSFSR which recognized autonomous republics as socialist states and the USSR constitution which only recognized Union republics as socialist states. The adoption by the Supreme Soviet of Tatarstan of the declaration on the state sovereignty of the Tatar ASSR, on Aug. 30, 1990, increased tension between Kazan and Moscow. Tatarstan was the first to make no mention of itself as part of the Russian Federation and to claim the status of a Union republic, in effect proclaiming itself the sixteenth republic of the Soviet Union. Tatarstan opposed the Russian Federation signing the Union Treaty, as proposed by President Mikhail Gorbachev, and insisted that Tatarstan sign as a sovereign state. The Second VTOT *Kurultai*, in 1991, viewed the Russian Federation as developing in a unitary-totalitarian direction.

The declaration of sovereignty was viewed by VTOT as only a juridical act and in order for it to be implemented Tatarstan needed to elect a president and a parliament. Laws were needed on republican citizenship that would permit Tatars living outside the republic to become citizens of the republic; and on privatization of the economy, including private ownership of land with ownership to be restricted mainly to citizens of the republic. A Tatar National Bank should be set up. VTOT assigned great significance to the promotion of Tatar culture, including the preparation of textbooks and language aids. The second programme, adopted by the Second VTOT *Kurultai*, proposed the convening of a *Milli Mejlis* (National Congress) as a means for the achievement of national sovereignty of the whole Tatar nation. Funds were to be raised through a national tax. The *Milli Mejlis* would, through various organizations, promote Tatar culture, education, economy and national cohesiveness. As regards the Tatars in Bashkortostan, VTOT argued that they should have the right of national self-determination. A bicameral legislature (Chamber of the Republic and Chamber of Nationalities) was needed in each republic because of the multi-ethnic nature of the populations.

There was no mention of religion in the first programme but in the second there is a section on Islam in Tatar society which underlines the need to have Muslims participating in the political life of the republic and to raise the level of knowledge about Islam among Tatars. This would involve great emphasis being placed on Muslim culture and the history of Islam; Islamic and Muslim cultural studies at the Academy of Sciences of Tatarstan; the establishment of various Muslim religious educational bodies in Kazan and the expansion of contacts with Muslin countries.

Association of Tatars of Tyumen Oblast (ATTO)
Temen Elkese Tatarlarynyn Assotsiatsiyase

History. A regional branch of TOT, a Tatar cultural centre in Tyumen, the Idegei society and some Tatar clubs (for example, in Tobolsk and Yalutorovsk) emerged in the course of 1989–90. On Sept. 29, 1990, a constituent conference established the Association of Tatars of Tyumen Oblast. In October 1990 a ten-member Committee for the Rebirth of the Siberian Tatars was established. By then, the programme of another organization, the Sybyr Association of Siberian Tatars, was also circulating. On Nov. 24, 1990, the draft programme and statute of ATTO were published in the press. The organizing committee of ATTO decided to hold its inaugural congress in Tyumen on Dec. 14–15, 1990. It was attended by 207 delegates (48 of whom were university graduates). Among the resolutions passed were an address to the USSR Supreme Soviet which proposed that the title of aboriginal population be conferred on the Tatars of Siberia, their nationality should be given as Siberian Tatar and Tatar rural soviets and *raions* should be formed. The Congress rejected a proposal to create a Tatar national region.

Organization. Membership is individual from the age of 16 years. The supreme body is the Congress and between congresses a 44-member Council functions. It in turn elects a presidium of seven persons (President, Vice-President and Chairmen of permanent commissions).

Programme. The programme states that Siberia is the only place on earth where the Siberian Tatars can survive and develop as an ethnos with their language and culture. A distinction between Tatars and Siberian Tatars is made in the document. South Tyumen *oblast* should be recognized as a priority zone for the development of the traditional trades and crafts of the Siberian Tatars. The exclusive right to take development decisions rests with rural executive committees (citizens' gatherings). If there is a conflict of interests over land between the aboriginal nationality and the state, priority shall be given to the former. Priority in the distribution of land should also be afforded members of the aboriginal nationality. Private land ownership should be introduced for them. The alienation of land is only permissible in agreement with the local soviets and a people's referendum but the retention of residential reservation zones is compulsory. During the transition to a market economy social security should be paid to poor Tatar families and large families should be helped. ATTO also has a wide-ranging programme for the development of national consciousness and education among Siberian Tatars. It advocates the establishment of Tatar schools, a Tatar publishing house, the promotion of Tatar folklore, records and CDs, Tatar theatres, folk music companies and modern variety groups.

Azatlyk Union of Tatar Youth (AUTY)
Azatlyk Tatar Yashlere Berlege

AUTY was established at the All-Union Congress (*Kurultai*) of Tatar Youth in Kazan on Oct. 12–13, 1990. The Congress had been preceded by a world festival of Tatar youth at the Idel camp, near Kazan. There were 355 delegates at the Congress (of whom 130 were from outside Tatarstan) from over 30 Soviet cities. The Congress was organized by the youth section of VTOT and it adopted a declaration on the programmatic goals of Tatar youth and resolutions on military service, education and culture, an appeal to the Russian population, and an address to the Supreme Soviet of the Bashkir ASSR on the status of the Tatar language. The Congress elected a Chairman (*Reis*) and a Central Council (*Uzek Shura*) consisting of 39 persons and they in turn elected a ten-member Board (*Idara*).

The Second *Kurultai* took place in Kazan on Oct. 11–12, 1991, and was attended by 135 delegates of whom 65 were from Tatarstan; 20 were from Bashkortostan, four from Moscow, one from Leningrad, six from Chelyabinsk, 12 from Samara, four from Ulyanovsk, two from Astrakhan, one from Chaikovsk, three from Omsk, three from Kazakhstan (Pavlodar), three from Latvia (Riga), three from Azerbaijan (Baku) and three from Ukraine. 24.1 per cent of the delegates were under the age of 18 years, 24.8 per cent between 18 and 22 years and 10.5 per cent over 30 years of age. 25.9 per cent of the delegates were university students; 36.6 per cent were university graduates. The *Kurultai* elected a new 31-member Central Council which in turn elected a ten-member Board.

The resolutions passed were mainly political: territorial claims in the RSFSR, the armed forces of Tatarstan, the establishment of a youth centre in Kazan, the condition of the Tatar population in the Belorussian SSR, preparations for a constituent congress of Turkic youth, and imminent changes in VTOT. *Azatlyk* members must propagate the movement's programme, participate in achieving the programme goals and master the Tatar language. Primary organizations must have at least 30 members. The *kurultai* is the supreme body and must be convened not less than annually, with the *Uzek Shura* acting between *kurultais*. The *Reis* may not be elected for more than two consecutive terms. The decisions of the *Reis* can be revoked by the *Uzek Shura*.

The movement's programme envisages the creation of Tatar states by achieving a just democratic society, the raising of the educational level of Tatar youth and the protection of the rights and interests of the Tatar nation. The promotion of a market economy is another goal. In order to achieve these tasks 14 special programmes, including the mother tongue, history, the training of Tatar businessmen, faith (Iman), Crimea and leisure were set up.

Bulgar National Congress (BNC)
Bulgar Milli Kongressy

History. The origins of the BNC go back to the Bulgar Amateur History Club which was founded on Aug. 27, 1988, in Kazan as the *Bulgar Al-Jadid* (New Bulgar). The club was registered by the Kazan soviet executive committee on March 21, 1989. Other Bulgar clubs, some outside the republic, were also formed. On Dec. 9, 1989, *Bulgar-Al-Jadid* decided to convene a Constituent Congress of the Bulgars of the USSR, in June 1990, in order to establish a Bulgar National Congress. The Constituent Congress of the BNC took place on June 8–9, 1990, in Kazan and was attended by about 150 delegates from 23 Bulgar organizations (including those from Moscow, Kiev, Ulyanovsk, Samara, Astrakhan, Orenburg, Magnitogorsk and several cities of Tatarstan). The congress adopted a programme and statute. The BNC newspaper is *Bolgar Ile*.

Organization. The supreme body is the congress which elects a 30-member Council of representatives. The permanent executive body is the 15-member Board, headed by a President.

Programme. The main goal of the BNC is to achieve the national-state rehabilitation of the Bulgar people along the Volga river, the promotion of the Bulgar ethnic group since during the repression of the Stalin era many Bulgars ceased openly to describe themselves as Bulgars. The BNC would like to see the nationality of Bulgar entered in Bulgars' passports. It also hopes that favourable conditions will be provided to permit the free development of the thousand year old Bulgar-Arabic orthography. Special attention needs to be given to inculcating love and respect towards the name, history and culture of the Bulgar people and to disseminate the unpublished and almost inaccessible Bulgar historical and literary writings and to immortalize the memory of outstanding Bulgars.

A project to preserve and restore Shakhri Bulgar, site of the Volga Bulgar state, where some Bulgar architecture from the 14th century has survived, is of great significance to the group. Among other plans are the establishment of a public education centre in the Bulgar reserve, placing a crescent on the minaret in Shakhri Bulgar, restoring the cemetery next to the minaret and organizing a feast celebration in connection with the embassy of Ibn-Fadlan in 922.

Iman Youth Centre of Islamic Culture
Iman Islam Medeniyati Yashler Uzege

History. The decision to establish *Iman* was taken at a meeting, attended by about 120 persons, held in Kazan university on Nov. 29, 1990. The meeting was arranged by the organizing committee of representatives of the Islamic Cultural Centre in Moscow, the organizing committee of the Association of Islamic Culture of Eastern Europe and the *Azatlyk* Union of Tatar Youth. The guiding body of *Iman* is its organizing committee. The Second *Mejlis* of *Iman* took place on Nov. 22, 1991, with 108 delegates present of whom 46 were from Tatarstan, 25 from Bashkortostan, 21 from the cities and regions of the Volga-Urals region (five from Saratov, seven from Ulyanovsk, one from Izhevsk, four from Samara, two from Nizhny Novgorod *oblast*, and one each from Chelyabinsk and Ekaterinburg), four from Ukraine (one from Kharkov and three from Kiev), two from Moscow, four from Omsk, one from Dagestan and five others (including two from Namangan and two from Tashkent). The *Mejlis* elected an 11-member *Shura* (Council), a *Reis* (Chairman) and three deputies. It addressed appeals to the heads of the member states of the Islamic conference; to the Muslim clergy; to *mufti-khazrat*, the leadership of the republic and public organizations to dissolve the Council for Religious Affairs; to the Ministry of Culture to withdraw plays containing anti-Muslim material; to the Ministry of Education to introduce instruction in Islam; and on the dominance of Christian propaganda in the mass media. *Iman* was registered by the Kazan soviet executive committee on Dec. 25, 1991.

Organization. The supreme body of *Iman* is the *Mejlis* which meets twice a year. The *Mejlis* elects a *Reis* and his deputies and approves a *Shura-i-ulama* (council of preceptors) and a Council which functions between *Mejlis*. Membership is on an individual basis with everyone paying dues.

Programme. Iman promotes the need to study, develop and disseminate the spiritual and cultural values of Islam to resolve problems of the humanitarian and socio-economic development of man. It wishes to unite the efforts of Muslim youth, students and intelligentsia, including the Muslim clergy, representatives of culture, science mass media and public figures in order to ensure the revival of the Muslim spiritual heritage. To this end a wide-ranging Muslim infrastructure is needed in Tatarstan, as is a system of Muslim education. In order to achieve this, *Iman* proposes to organize instruction on the principles of Islam at evening schools (*dini maktab* or schools of faith) and circles; promote charity work and assist "god-pleasing" institutions; organize excursions and visits to Muslim countries, youth exchanges with accommodation in Muslim families and visits to sacred places; organize Muslim youth camps; set up an Islamic information centre, publish a periodical, found a business club and business school, establish contacts with foreign companies; and convene inter-confessional and international conferences and dialogues.

The above activities are common to the Moscow Islamic Centre and *Iman* but the latter has special interests in Tatarstan. It wishes to restore all Muslim religious buildings to believers, to restore the Mukhammadia *medrese* and found later an Islamic university based on the *medrese*, to restore Bulgar Muslim monuments and to revive Muslim missions.

Islamic Democratic Party of Tatarstan (IDPT)
Tatarstan Islam Demokratik Partiyase

History. The first organizational conference of supporters of the IDPT was held in Kazan on March 31, 1991. The constituent *Kurultai* of the party took place in Kazan on Dec. 14, 1991, where 150 delegates represented the 700 supporters of the party. The *kurultai* adopted a programme and a statute and elected a Co-ordinating Council with five chairperson-co-ordinators. The party is not officially registered. The primary organization (not less than three persons) can be set up at places of work or residence. The *kurultai* is the supreme body and convened not less than annually. The Co-ordinating Council functions between *kurultais* and is elected for three years but not for more than two consecutive terms. Party membership is conditional on accepting the principles of the Imam and Islam.

Programme. The party's goal is to implement the inalienable rights of the Tatar people, to achieve the age-old dream of its own statehood and to unite the people under the banner of the ideas of national sovereignty. The party proceeds from the view that the aboriginal peoples of the republic enjoy the status of an aboriginal nation. The Tatar language is the official state language and Russian, the language of inter-ethnic communication. The programme envisages religious liberty, freedom of religious education, propaganda and religious upbringing. It also underlines that no forces have been able to eradicate Islam until Muslims themselves began deviating from true Islam, from the *Koran* and the *Sunna*. Communist ideology is seen as particularly nefarious. The party aims to promote Islamic philosophy, the obligatory teaching of the principles of religion in schools, as well as the Arabic language, and favours the opening of alternative schools. Women should return to the bosom of the family and supplements to family budgets should be paid where necessary. The party opposes the *nomenklatura* and believes that a person's social position should depend on his abilities and social work. The party supports the existence of various types of property, the transfer of state enterprises to individual organizations and persons, and land to the peasants. The republic should own, manage and utilize property on its territory.

Ittifak Tatar Party of National Independence
Ittifak Tatar Milli Baisezlek Partiyase

Ittifak emerged from the radical wing of TOT and initially maintained quite close relations with it. The constituent assembly of Ittifak took place on April 27, 1990, in Kazan. The First *Kurultai* (Congress) was held in Kazan on April 13–14, 1991, and adopted a programme and a statute. There were 83 delegates of whom 31 were from Kazan and 27 from other regions and cities of Tatarstan. The other delegates were from outside Tatarstan. Ittifak was registered by the Ministry of Justice of the Republic of Tatarstan as a republican socio-political organization on Jan. 3, 1992. In 1992 it had 28 branches and was represented in all parts of Tatarstan. Party members must respect the Tatar language, recognize the leading role of the Tatar language in the party's activities and work at perfecting it if their command is unsatisfactory. The basic cell is the group which must have at least three members. The statutes reject democratic centralism. The supreme body is the *kurultai*, which elects a Council of Representatives to function between *kurultais*. A ten-member Party board is elected at each *kurultai* to carry out ideological and theoretical work. A Central Executive Council, which consists of paid officials to run current business, is appointed by the Board. A chairman, assisted by his deputies, elected by the *kurultai*, heads the party.

The primary goals of the party are the revival of the Tatar nation, the re-establishment of the state sovereignty of the Tatar nation and the recognition of the inalienable rights of the Tatar people as subject of international law. Dual citizenship is desirable as is the recognition of the Russian and Tatar languages as official languages. All forms of property, including private, co-operative, state and the forms have the right to exist in Tatarstan. A programme for national revival includes the rehabilitation and preservation of the gene pool of the Tatar nation and the historical heritage of the Tatar people; and the rewriting of history to bring an end to the counterfeit history whose objective is to justify the centuries old physical and spiritual genocide practised against the Tatar people. Ittifak, not surpassingly, totally rejected the treaty on the delimitation of spheres of authority and the mutual delegation of powers between the agencies of power of the Russian Federation and the Republic of Tatarstan, which was signed on Feb. 15 and came into force on Feb. 24, 1994. Fauziya Bairamova, leader of the party, called the treaty a tragedy for the Tatar people and a betrayal of the interests of our children.[7]

Magarif All-Tatar Association
Gomumtatar Magarif Assotsiatsiyase

History. The constituent *Kurultai* took place on Jan. 9–10, 1992, in Kazan. It convened on the initiative of the Second *Kurultai* of VTOT which wished to promote the unification of Tatar national schools. The *Kurultai* was attended by 665 delegates involved in public education. Of these 137 came from outside the republic, mainly from regions of the Russian Federation but also three from Kazakhstan and one delegate from Belarus, Uzbekistan and Moscow. Almost all were university graduates. The *Kurultai* adopted a programme and statute and elected a 41-member Steering Council and a 13-member Central Board. Among many resolutions adopted were those on the establishment of the Tatarstan association for culture and education to achieve state status for the Tatar language; on the establishment of the Tatar Pedagogical University; on an Islamic educational centre; and on the transition to a Latin script. Magarif has not been registered officially.

Programme. The movement's goal is to develop Tatar education. Membership is open to any public union or national education institution in any state which recognizes the programme and statute. The supreme body is the *Kurultai* which convenes not less than once every two years. The *Kurultai* elects a Central Council and it, in turn, elects a President, a Vice-President and a Central Board. Particular emphasis is placed on the role of the state in the development of education. No religious instruction is envisaged at school level but the history of religion should be taught as a separate subject. Upbringing and education should be based primarily on the Turkic, oriental and Islamic cultures with due consideration of the positive experience of Western education. Instruction in higher educational establishments will be mainly in Tatar. At institutions where the medium of teaching is Russian Tatar students will study Tatar all through their university studies. Students of other nationalities will acquire an oral command of Tatar.

Milli Mejlis
Milli Mezhles

The *Milli Mejlis* is an elected body on the territory of Tatarstan. An organizing committee to convene an All-Tatar *Koryltai* was set up in November 1991. Ittifak, the S. Mardjani cultural society, the youth section of VTOT, the *Azatlyk* Union of Tatar Youth, the Islamic Democratic Party of Tatarstan and the committee for the defence of the President of Tatarstan composed the organizing committee. The co-ordinating Council of these organizations decided on Dec. 5, 1991, to convene an All-Tatar People's *Koryltai* and to elect a *Milli Mejlis* at it in January 1992. VTOT was not in favour of quick elections to the *Milli Mejlis* and was not active in the organizing committee. The First *Koryltai* of the Tatar People convened in Kazan on Feb. 1, 1992, with 877 delegates attending (542 from Tatarstan, 12 from Uzbekistan, 11 from Kazakhstan, five from Azerbaijan, two from Estonia, 29 from Bashkortostan, six from Chuvashstan, five from Udmurtia, two from Mari-El and others from many cities and regions of the Russian Federation).

The *Koryltai* adopted a law on the *Milli Mejlis* and as a result 79 persons (including the chairman) were elected to it. Among other documents adopted were a law of the Tatar people, on the state independence of the republic of Tatarstan, an address to the Islamic conference, on recalling people's deputies of the Russian Federation representing Tatarstan, and on the ownership of the riches, mineral wealth, immovable property and industry, on the transfer of the law enforcing agencies (Ministry of Internal Affairs, KGB, Ministry of Justice, Supreme Court and Procurator's Office) to the jurisdiction of Tatarstan, on the establishment of a national bank, on the national flag and anthem of the Tatar people, on promoting with all due measures the development of the religion of Islam, and on the activities of public organizations and parties on the territory of Tatarstan.

The *Milli Mejlis* is not officially registered. The Supreme Soviet of the republic of Tatarstan, on Feb. 7, 1992, stated that a number of acts adopted at the *Koryltai* had no juridical validity and the attempts to usurp the right of exercising state power in Tatarstan, the attempts to resolved unconstitutionally questions of national-state, economic and social development of the multi-national people of the republic of Tatarstan were inadmissible.

Organization. The *Milli Mejlis* claims to be the supreme representative body of the Tatar people. It implements the decisions of the *Koryltai* between convocations. The *Koryltai* is seen as the forum of the entire Tatar people and the only expression of the will of the whole people. The *Milli Mejlis* convenes once every 3–4 months. Deputies are elected at a *Koryltai*: 75 in all with two-thirds from Tatarstan and one-third from outside Tatarstan. The *Mejlis* is elected for two years. Deputies of the Supreme Soviet of Tatarstan can be elected if they acknowledge the programme and law of the *Milli Mejlis*. A similar rule applies to the Supreme Soviet deputies of other states. Local *mejlis* can be established. The executive body of the *Milli Mejlis* is the *Milli Nazariyat* which consists of a chairman (Chief Nazir), two deputies and a few others. Local *mejlis* can set up local executive bodies, *Milli Idara*.

Programme. The goals of the *Milli Mejlis* are to achieve the national sovereignty of the Tatar people and cultural-national autonomy of Tatars living outside the republic, to transfer to the people of Tatarstan all the riches created by its labour, to transfer land to those who work it, to provide assistance to Tatars returning to Tatarstan, to elevate Tatar to become the official state language, to undo the impact of the colonial regime on the Tatar people, to bring all agencies of government, police and justice under the jurisdiction of the republic of Tatarstan, to achieve economic stabilization in Tatarstan and to prevent the construction of nuclear power plants and all ecologically dangerous enterprises as well as the transport, storage and burial of chemical and nuclear waste.

Pure Islam
Saf Islam

This is a closed Muslim group which was already in existence in 1982–83. It is centred on Tatarstan, with other groups in Moscow, St Petersburg and Tashkent. It is not officially registered. Its supporters regard the only true path on earth to be the *Koran*. Those who do not follow have gone astray. *Saf Islam* holds that the state departments of religious affairs violate freedom of conscience. Mufti should not be appointed but be elected by all Muslims. Emirs should be elected by community members from among the most knowledgeable and respected men. The state should provide facilities for Muslims to pray while working or travelling, to publish religious literature, to teach the faith of Islam and Arabic in schools and establish new *medreses*. Muslims should be provided with "clean" meat in shops and markets. Army service, in Tatarstan, should correspond to Islamic needs. Foundations to assist the poor should be established.

Sovereignty Committee
Suverenitet Komitety

The Constituent Assembly to establish a committee to protect and realize the sovereignty of Tatarstan was held in Kazan on Sept. 19, 1990. Participants included public organizations in Kazan, including representatives of the unions of the creative intelligentsia of the republic. The assembly elected a 52-member republican steering Council of the Sovereignty Committee. The constituent *Kurultai* of the Sovereignty Committee took place in Kazan on Nov. 25, 1990, with delegates and representatives from 11 cities and regions of Tatarstan. It adopted a programme and statute and forwarded an address to the Supreme Soviet and Council of Ministers of the Republic of Tatarstan about how to protect and realize the sovereignty of the republic. It also sent an address to the RSFSR Supreme Soviet on the cessation of deputies' activities in the parliament of the neighbouring sovereign state. A 27-member steering Council was elected. The committee's newspaper is *Sovereignty*.

Members can be individual, collective or associates. The basic organization is the primary organization with not less than five members. Regional and city organizations can be set up with their own steering Councils and chairmen. The supreme body is the *Kurultai*. It is a republican body and conducts its activities on the territory of Tatarstan. The statute describes the Committee as a democratic public organization based on a civil initiative to support the transformation of Tatarstan into a fully fledged sovereign state. In order to achieve this goal the Committee advocates the following measures: to mobilize the people of Tatarstan and the official state bodies to secure political and economic independence for the republic; consolidate the Tatar nation and all peoples to achieve sovereignty for Tatarstan; organize the intellectual forces and adopt a new constitution and laws of the Tatar SSR as well as governmental programmes to promote the all-embracing and harmonious development of the republic; draft and adopt a mutually beneficial Union Agreement between the Tatar SSR and the Union (confederation) of Sovereign States; an equal and mutually beneficial agreement (but not federal in character) between the Tatar SSR and the RSFSR; equal and mutually beneficial agreements with other republics, and foreign states; mobilize public opinion to prevent any encroachment on the sovereignty of Tatarstan and infringement of the political and economic rights of the republic and its population; mobilize public organizations to use effectively the mass media to promote and achieve state sovereignty for the republic.

The Committee acknowledges the principles of equality between peoples and their state formations. It is in favour of human rights, irrespective of national origin or place of residence and the revival of the ideals of humanism. It also rejects any manifestation of disrespect for those of other nationalities but recognizes that love for one's own people is a natural feeling for everyone and is an element of patriotism.

Vatan People's Democratic Party
Vatan Khalyk-Demokratik Partiyase

History. The need to establish the party was expressed in the informal newspaper, *Vatan*, in May 1990. The constituent *Kurultai* of *Vatan* took place in Moscow on Feb. 23, 1991, attended by 35 delegates representing Moscow, Nizhny Novgorod and Ulyanovsk. *Vatan* declares itself to be a mass democratic organization of the Tatar nation whose aim is to establish a Tatar democratic state within the USSR. *Vatan* is the party's newspaper. The primary organization is a group of not less than three persons. There are district and regional organizations. The supreme body is the *kurultai* which meets once every three years. Between *kurultais* the chairman and parts of the Central Committee (elected at *kurultais*) act as the leadership body. Membership dues are 1 per cent of wages and salaries. The party is not officially registered.

Programme. The party programme declares *Vatan*'s aims to be the protection of the interests of the Tatar nation and to ensure its cultural and national survival. This can be achieved through the setting-up of a Tatar state (Tatar Union republic) within the USSR on an ethnic territory (for instance, the Idel-Urals States of the 1920s). The creation of this state is vitally important given the "imminent" disappearance of Tatar national culture. The interests of the Tatar national minority residing elsewhere in the USSR and abroad need to be protected. Hence dual citizenship for Tatars is recommended. The Tatar Union state should be set up based on the principle of territory and not according to the size of the Tatar population residing there at present since the national composition of the population is the result of the colonial policy pursued by the Russian-Soviet empire. All peoples have the right to a place in the sun and to establish a national state on their territory. Peoples were originally free and are not dependent on the will of another people but on the will of Allah. Equality of peoples can be achieved by civilized development with each people living on its national territory without any claims to one another's territory. *Vatan* should respect the rights of other nationalities in a reborn Tatar state. The party supports the free market and the transfer of land to those who work it, including private ownership. The party recognizes the importance of Islam for the Tatar people but is against any state ideology and considers all religions equal. *Vatan* does not adhere to communist ideology and is opposed to fascism and racism. The party opposes the creation of an autonomous Soviet German territory in the Volga area and proposes it should be established in Kaliningrad *oblast*. The party should strive to achieve its goals by peaceful means and it therefore rejects violence and terrorism.

Notes

1 Based on D. M. Iskhakov, 'Informal Groups in Modern Tatar Society', unpublished manuscript; V. N. Berezovsky et al., *Rossiya: Partii, Assotsiatsii, Soyuzy, Kluby*, Tom 1 Chast I Spravochnik (Rossiisko-Amerikansky Universitet, Informatsionnoe Agenstvo 'Rau-Press', Institut Massovykh Politicheskikh Dvizhenii, Moscow) 1991; *Ibid*. Chast II.
2 Uli Schamiloglu, 'The Tatar Public Center', *Report on the USSR*, no. 51, 1989.
3 Elizabeth Teague, 'Russia and Tatarstan Sign Power-Sharing Treaty', *RFE/RL Research Report*, Vol. 3, no. 14, April 1994, p. 23.
4 *Ibid*. p. 24.
5 *Ibid*. p. 26; details on the constitution are in Vera Tolz, 'Thorny Road towards Federalism in Russia', *RFE/RL Research Report*, Vol. 2, no. 48, 3 Dec. 1993.
6 *Los Angeles Times*, 18 Feb. 1994.
7 *Segodnya*, 23 Feb. 1994.

THE SLOVAK REPUBLIC

Karen Henderson

When the Slovak Republic became an independent state on Jan. 1, 1993, it already had a democratic parliament containing a diverse spectrum of Slovak parties formed since the "velvet revolution" of 1989.[1] However, while the Czech party system was little changed by the division of Czechoslovakia, in Slovakia there have been notable shifts both in the popular support enjoyed by the parties elected to the Slovak National Council in June 1992, and in the constellation of parties as a whole. This difference between the two republics can largely be explained by the fact that the major cleavage determining voters' choices in the Czech Republic already appeared, in 1992, to be based on economic interests, whereas in Slovakia the subtle interaction of economic and national concerns had left many fundamental questions about the country's political orientation to be resolved after independence was gained. The clearest reflection of the fact that Slovakia had yet to achieve any political equilibrium was the change of government which took place in March 1994, followed by the calling of an early general election to take place at the end of September 1994.

In order to understand the situation of the parties in the prelude to the first free elections in an independent Slovak state, it is necessary to trace their fortunes in the preceding two national elections which took place within the Czech and Slovak Federative Republic. An initial point to be noted, and one which contributed to the break-up of Czechoslovakia, was the fact that a pattern of separate Czech and Slovak parties was established by the first elections of June 1990. Only one party standing in both the federation's republics — the Communist Party of Czechoslovakia — managed to obtain parliamentary representation in each. This was a development which had been presaged in the earliest post-revolutionary days, when the citizens' movement formed separate organizations for the two republics: Civic Forum in Prague, and Public against Violence in Bratislava. While it may have been hoped that the existence of separate Slovak organizations would satisfy Slovak desires for self-expression, in practice it gave impetus for centrifugal political forces in the country as a whole. Elections took place on the basis of proportional representation with a 5 per cent threshold for obtaining seats in the Federal Assembly, but because this threshold was operated independently in each of the two republics, there was no incentive for Czech or Slovak political parties to avoid divisive issues and modify their programmes in order to attract votes in the other republic. Political parties frequently adopted policy stances that were more extreme than those of their supporters, and thereby failed to act as an integrative force in the federation. This phenomenon was clearly illustrated by events in the latter part of 1992, when the leaders of the two largest parties — one Czech and one Slovak — agreed to divide the country despite the

Table 1:   Results from Slovakia of elections to the Federal Assembly of the Czech and Slovak Federative Republic, June 8–9, 1990

	% of Votes	Seats
House of the People		
Public Against Violence	32.5	19
Christian Democratic Movement	19.0	11
Communist Party of Czechoslovakia	13.8	8
Slovak National Party	11.0	6
Co-existence–Hungarian Christian Democratic Movement	8.6	5
Others	15.1	0
(inc. Democratic Movement	*4.4*	*0*
Green Party	*3.3*	*0)*
TOTAL	100.0	49
House of the Nations		
Public Against Violence	37.3	33
Christian Democratic Movement	16.7	14
Communist Party of Czechoslovakia	13.4	12
Slovak National Party	11.4	9
Co-existence–Hungarian Christian Democratic Movement	8.5	7
Others	12.7	0
(inc. Democratic Party	*3.7*	*0)*
TOTAL	100.0	75

Source: Federální statistický úřad, Český statistický úřad, Slovenský statistický úrad, *Statistická ročenka '91 České a Slovenské Federatívní Republiky*, Prague, 1991, pp. 629–630.

fact that almost all opinion polls showed ordinary Czechs and Slovaks to be opposed to such a move.

Initial differences in the orientation of Czech and Slovak voters emerged in the first free elections of 1990, when the Slovak Public against Violence (PAV) obtained a smaller percentage of the vote in its republic than the Czech Civic Forum (about a third for PAV, compared to half for Civic Forum). Additionally, while the Communist Party of Czechoslovakia received a similar percentage of votes in both Slovakia and the Czech Republic (just over 13 per cent), this made it the second most popular party only among the Czechs. The second largest vote in Slovakia went to the Christian Democrats, who enjoyed about twice as much support there as among the more secular Czechs. A consequence of these differences in Slovak electoral preferences was that the citizens' movements — who were in any case not averse to forming a coalition government with other parties — needed Christian Democrat support in order obtain the three-fifths parliamentary necessary for the amending the constitution. Passing a new constitution was one of the main tasks for the first, two-year parliament, and one which, in the end, it failed to accomplish.

Table 2: Elections to the Slovak National Council, June 8–9 1990

	% of Votes	Seats
Public Against Violence	29.3	48
Christian Democratic Movement	19.2	31
Slovak National Party	13.9	22
Communist Party of Czechoslovakia	13.3	22
Co-existence–Hungarian Christian Democratic Movement	8.7	14
Democratic Party	4.4	7
Green Party	3.5	6
Others	7.7	0
TOTAL	100.0	150

Source: Ibid, p. 630.

In the case of the Slovak Republic, it is also particularly important to note the results of the election for the Slovak National Council (SNC). These are more relevant than the equivalent results in the Czech Republic for two reasons: first, because of the operation of a lower threshold (3 per cent), two Slovak parties which had failed to reach the Federal Assembly in Prague gained representation in Bratislava, but second, and more importantly, the SNC, being separated geographically from the national parliament in Prague in a way that the Czech National Council was not, became a more significant autonomous actor in the political development of the country than its Czech counterpart.

The new Slovak government was headed by Vladimír Mečiar of Public Against Violence, and contained 12 other members of the movement, as well as seven Christian Democrats, led by Ján Čarnogurský as First Deputy Prime Minister, and three members of the Democratic party (a revival of the party which had won an outright majority in the last free elections of 1946). However, the most notable feature of the Slovak government, in comparison with the Czechoslovak and Czech governments formed after the same elections, is the number of its members who were still prominent figures in political life four years later: for example, Mečiar and Čarnogurský were the leaders of two of the main parties contesting the 1994 elections whilst Finance Minister Michal Kováč had become the first President of the Slovak Republic. Even so, although Slovak politics demonstrated unusual continuity in its leading personalities, the party system underwent great change. This is perhaps best illustrated by the example of Milan Kňažko, a well-known actor prominent in the November 1989 demonstrations in Bratislava who went on to belong to four different parties in as many years: Public Against Violence, the Movement for a Democratic Slovakia, the Alliance of Democrats and the Democratic Union.

The first disruption to the 1990 party system was the fissure of the citizens' movement PAV. Whereas, however, when the Czech Civic Forum split into three, the members of the new parties and movements remained together in coalition, in Slovakia, the demise of PAV was marked by a far greater degree of conflict on the level of both policies and personalities. In March 1991, Prime Minister Mečiar formed a party faction within PAV —

For a Democratic Slovakia — which laid greater emphasis on Slovakia's national concerns and expressed opposition to some aspects of the economic reforms emanating from Prague. Six weeks later, the Presidium of the Slovak National Council dismissed Mečiar and seven members of his government on the grounds that the government was not functional, and two other ministers (including Michal Kováč) resigned shortly afterwards. Apart from policy differences, Mečiar's populism had worried PAV, together with his contention that he was answerable to the Slovak people and not to the SNC. Yet his dismissal formed one of the turning points in Slovak politics and appeared in many ways to be unwise: not only was the SNC Presidium which had removed him a body whose existence derived from the communist parliamentary system, where the actual deputies met for only a few days each year, but Mečiar's opponents had also clearly been unable to convince the population at large of his unsuitability for high office. In March 1991, opinion polls showed him to be overwhelmingly the most popular politician in Slovakia, and his dismissal triggered mass protest demonstrations outside the SNC of the sort that had not been seen on Bratislava's streets since November 1989. Consequently, although the majority of PAV deputies in both the Federal Assembly in Prague and in the SNC in Bratislava remained with the movement, it appeared that large numbers of its former voters had defected with Mečiar. Thus when Mečiar launched his own Movement for a Democratic Slovakia (MFDS) in early May 1991, it was likely from the outset to be a major electoral force.

The division of PAV left the Christian Democrats (CDM) as the strongest single party in the SNC, and its leader Čarnogurský duly became Prime Minister. Up until this point, Čarnogurský had been a more vociferous proponent of Slovak national interests and aspirations for autonomy than Mečiar, and this was evidently one reason why the CDM had gained more support than PAV in the November 1990 local elections. However, the MFDS gradually outflanked the Christian Democrats on these issues, so that by June 1992, the latter party was generally perceived to be Prague-oriented and pro-federation. This had led to a split in the CDM in March 1992, when about a third of its SNC deputies broke away to form the Slovak Christian Democratic Movement (later Christian Social Union). The reasons for the split were very similar to those that had affected PAV: the breakaway deputies were both more nationalist and less enthusiastic about economic reform.

The third most popular party in the 1990 elections, the Communist Party of Czecho-slovakia, also underwent considerable change. It soon ceased to be the only party represented in both the Czech and the Slovak part of the Federal Assembly, as the Slovak Communist Party became more autonomous and changed its name to the Party of the Democratic Left (PDL). More importantly, however, it went much further towards converting itself into a Western-style social democratic party than its Czech counterpart. One consequence of this was that the Social Democratic Party of Slovakia found it hard to gain a foothold on the political scene: unlike its Czech counterpart, it had difficulties surmounting the 5 per cent hurdle in the 1992 elections and gained representation only in the House of the Nations, where it had fielded its chairman, Prague Spring leader Alexander Dubček, as a candidate.

A remarkable feature of the 1992 elections was that, despite the enormous shifts in the Slovak political agenda which had taken place in the previous two years, the actual results were quantitatively very similar to those of 1990: although Mečiar's MFDS was radically different from Public Against Violence, both were popular movements which had gained around a third of the vote, and the other parties are all recognizable. The CDM lost support as a result of both the customary unpopularity of ruling parties during economic difficulties and its recent loss of members to the Slovak Christian Democratic Movement, which was

Table 3: Slovakian results of elections to the Federal Assembly of the Czech and Slovak Federative Republic, June 5–6, 1992

	% of Votes	Seats
House of People		
Movement for a Democratic Slovakia	33.5	24
Party of the Democratic Left	14.4	10
Slovak National Party	9.4	6
Christian Democratic Movement	9.0	6
Co-existence–Hungarian Christian Democratic Movement	7.4	5
Others	26.3	0
(inc. Social Democratic Party of Slovakia	*4.9*	*0*
Democratic Party–Civic Democratic Party	*4.0*	*0*
Civic Democratic Union	*4.0*	*0*
Slovak Christian Democratic Movement	*3.4*	*0)*
TOTAL	100.0	51
House of the Nations		
Movement for a Democratic Slovakia	33.8	33
Party of the Democratic Left	14.0	13
Slovak National Party	9.4	9
Christian Democratic Movement	8.8	8
Co-existence–Hungarian Christian Democratic Movement	7.4	7
Social Democratic Party in Slovakia	6.1	5
Others	20.5	0
(inc. Civic Democratic Union	*4.0*	*0*
Democratic Party–Civic Democratic Party	*3.7*	*0*
Slovak Christian Democratic Movement	*3.2*	*0)*
TOTAL	100.0	75

Source: Český statistický úřad, *Statistiká ročenka české republiky '93*, Prague, 1993, pp. 439–440.

unable to cross the 5 per cent threshold. However, the Slovak National Party, the Party of the Democratic Left and the Hungarian coalition all demonstrated a relatively stable level of support.

However, this superficial similarity between the 1990 and the 1992 election results belies the shifts that had taken place in Slovak politics. Although the Slovak National Party was the only major group to enter the 1992 elections opening advocating Slovak independence, there was considerable consensus among most of its leading rivals (with the most marked exception of those representing the Hungarian minority) that greater Slovak autonomy and confederation rather than federation were desirable goals, and that economic strategies conceived in Prague were unlikely to be suited to solving the problems of the Slovak

Table 4:   Elections to the Slovak National Council, June 5–6, 1992

	% Votes	Seats
Movement for a Democratic Slovakia	37.3	74
Party of the Democratic Left	14.7	29
Christian Democratic Movement	8.9	18
Slovak National Party	7.9	15
Co-existence–Hungarian Christian Democratic Movement	7.4	14
Others	23.8	0
(inc. Social Democratic Party of Slovakia	*4.0*	*0*
Civic Democratic Union	*4.0*	*0*
Democratic Party–Civic Democratic Party	*3.3*	*0*
Slovak Christian Democratic Movement	*3.1*	*0)*
TOTAL	100.0	150

Source: Ibid., p. 441.

economy. This aspect of Slovak politics had radical effects on the way the Federal Assembly operated, since it meant that the Slovak parties had little in common with those in the Czech Republic. There, the political spectrum was divided largely along the left–right axis more common in the West, and support for the federation was almost universal. Moreover, the victorious Czech Civic Democratic Party under Václav Klaus in particular had radically different views on both economic reform and the structure of the common state from those of Mečiar's MFDS. Given the complex legislative procedures which the Federal Assembly had inherited from the communist 1968 constitution whereby constitutional amendments had to be passed by three-fifths of the deputies elected to each part of it, including the Slovak half of the House of the Nations, the polarization of views between the leading Czech and Slovak parties virtually eliminated any possibility of forming a federal government coalition with a legislative majority on constitutional issues.

Furthermore, the SNC, for which most of the Slovak party leaders had opted to stand, showed an even more marked preponderance of the MFDS among Slovak deputies than the Federal Assembly did, so that Mečiar, on his triumphant return to the premiership of Slovakia, nearly had an absolute majority there. This particular MFDS strength in Bratislava had been occasioned by the fact that their percentage vote for the SNC was slightly higher than for the Federal Assembly elections held on the same day, and this was translated into an even higher number of seats because almost a quarter of the vote had gone to parties that did not reach the 5 per cent threshold (the 3 per cent threshold which operated for the SNC in the 1990 elections having been removed). The fragmentation of the liberal, pro-market side of the political spectrum had contributed to this: if PAV's pro-federation successor party, the Civic Democratic Union, had joined with the Democratic Party–Civic Democratic Party, they would both have gained representation. However, while such tactics would have reduced Mečiar's strength, it would not have overcome the centre-right's fundamental problem, which was weak Slovak support for the policy direction chosen by a large majority of Czech voters.

Once the legislative impasse at federal level had been overcome by dividing the Czechoslovak state, a realignment of the Slovak party system was inevitable, since the Czechs no longer acted as a focus for Slovak national and economic grievances. However, the major cleavage of Slovak politics still appeared to be one of nationalism rather than economics. Throughout 1993, Mečiar's government remained in power either through coalition with the Slovak National Party (SNP) or as a minority government relying of *ad hoc* support from other parties, most notably the Party of the Democratic Left. This arrangement proved unstable above all because both the MFDS and the SNP were affected by major splits. The first was led by Mečiar's Foreign Minister, Kňažko, who left the MFDS in April 1993 and formed the Alliance of Democrats of the Slovak Republic together with seven other disaffected MFDS deputies. Kňažko was openly critical of Mečiar's leadership style, and his defection was precipitated by his dismissal from the government following disagreements about Slovak foreign policy, as well as his refusal at the beginning of the year to support Mečiar's first candidate for the Slovak presidency. At the same time, the only SNP minister in the government, party chair L'udovít Černák, resigned. After lengthy negotiations, the SNP did return to government in a formal coalition with the MFDS in October 1993. However, the SNP was already facing internal divisions between those who continued to emphasize nationalist policies, and those, like Černák, who advocated a shift to right-wing policies aimed at economic reform and aid to small and medium-scale entrepreneurs. In February 1994, Černák was finally ousted from the chair of the SNP, and he left the party with five other deputies to form the National Democratic Party (NDP). This was closely followed by a second split in the MFDS, which occurred when Mečiar forced the resignation of two of his minsters, Foreign Minister Jozef Moravčík and First Deputy Prime Minister Roman Kováč. They formed first the Alternative for Political Realism within the MFDS and then an independent party renamed the Democratic Union of Slovakia, thereby depriving the MFDS of a further eight deputies, and also its coalition's majority.

By this point, Mečiar had lost the support, *intra alia*, of two successive foreign ministers and both his candidates for the Slovak presidency, the unsuccessful Roman Kováč and the successful Michal Kováč. All four had at some point been Mečiar's close allies, yet it was the alienation of President Kováč that finally brought about the ousting of Mečiar's government. On March 9, 1994, the President made his first state of the nation speech to the parliament (now renamed the National Council of the Slovak Republic — NC SR). The speech turned out to be a far-reaching critique of the government. It ranged over the negative image of Slovakia abroad, the problems of the Hungarian and Romany minorities, the slowness of economic adaptation, the failure to attract foreign investment and the rise in crime, and it contained a call for political, national and civic conciliation which criticized Mečiar's autocratic style of government. While Kováč specifically stated that he was not asking the Prime Minister to resign, he emphasized the need either for a broad coalition government or for early parliamentary elections. What he actually achieved was all these things: two days later, the ever more numerous opposition parties finally united to bring down Mečiar's government with a vote of no-confidence, and then went on to form a coalition government under the premiership of Moravčík comprising the Party of the Democratic Left, the Alternative for Political Realism, the Alliance of Democrats, the National Democratic Party and the Christian Democratic Movement; and within a week, an election date of Sept. 30–Oct. 1 had been set. Mečiar had now been ousted as premier for the second time within three years, yet on this occasion, the parliamentary procedure used was far more comprehensible to citizens, and the crowds demonstrating in protest constituted only a fraction of the people that had gone on the streets to support him on the earlier occasion.

The Slovak parties thus approach the 1994 elections with a political spectrum divided between the former government of more nationalist forces, who were suspected of authoritarianism, and the government in power, where all parties from the ex-communist PDL to the Christian Democrats shared a degree of consensus about the need for economic reform and national tolerance. This left the participants in the Moravčík government torn between, on the one hand, a perceived need to prevent Mečiar once again avenging his dismissal by returning victorious to the premiership with a mandate from the electorate, and also, on the other hand, the desire to prevail over their own coalition partners in the debate between left and right which was still to come.

The first problem the parties had to address was that there were a relatively large number of them. At the beginning of May 1994, a total of 38 parties and 19 political movements were officially registered in Slovakia, and any of these (plus any more who registered at least two months before the elections) were entitled to submit a list of candidates if they fulfilled one of three conditions: either they had to have at least one deputy in the SNC on the day the election was formally announced; or they had to have obtained at least 10,000 valid votes in the previous elections; or they had to have at least 10,000 registered members or citizens who had given their signature in support. In reality, however, the major obstacle for most of the parties who were serious contenders in the election was the need to gain 5 per cent of the vote in order to be granted any seats at all. This hurdle cannot easily be overcome by presenting joint lists of candidates with other parties, since coalitions of two or three parties have to cross a higher 7 per cent threshold, and coalitions of four or more parties require 10 per cent of the vote. A further hindrance to party consolidation is the tendency of parties to splinter during the decision-making about mergers and coalitions, as members for whom the chosen electoral partners were unacceptable are prone to leave and form parties of their own.

It is possible to distinguish five main segments of the political spectrum where mergers and coalitions were possible. However, in doing so, it must be emphasized that terms such as left, centre and right have a questionable meaning in a society such as Slovakia, where few parties have any real track record in dealing with the enormous economic problems that actually exist. There are considerable similarities in many of the parties' programmes, so that voters often have to decide between them by assessing the sincerity of politicians' promises and their competence actually to achieve their stated aims.

The left was the first to unite in preparation for the elections, in May 1994, with the formation of pre-election coalition comprising the Party of the Democratic Left, the Green Party in Slovakia, the Social Democratic Party of Slovakia and the Farmers' Movement. This meant that they would enter the elections with common lists of candidates, but, as a coalition of four subjects, their lists would require 10 per cent of the vote to obtain any seats. The PDL was in fact one of the few parties almost certain to have passed the 5 per cent threshold if it had stood alone, but if it had done so, the votes of like-minded parties which failed to reach this level of support would have been distributed as seats to all parties in the NC SR, including the PDL's opponents. An offer to participate in the coalition was declined by the Association of Workers of Slovakia, which decided to run independently in the elections.

The centre part of the spectrum was complicated by the fact that it was largely filled by newly established parties comprising liberally-minded defectors from the nationalist parties, the MFDS and SNP. The Alliance of Democrats of the Slovak Republic and the Alternative for Political Realism merged in April 1994, despite doubts on the part of some AD SR members about the left-wing orientation of APR adherents who had so recently been allies of Mečiar and formed a new party under the APR's chosen name, the Democratic Union of Slovakia. The new party hoped to combine the established membership base of Kňažko's AD SR with the popularity of Moravčík and the APR, yet initial opinion polls indicated that support for the new party was less than the total of the support previously enjoyed by its constituent parts. This proved something of a disincentive to coalition-building for other parties. A further complication for the centre parties were difficulties in distinguishing them programmatically from some of the right-wing parties. This problem was best illustrated by the National Democratic Party, which took a long time deciding whether to accept an offer of list places from the right-wing Christian Democrats or from the centrist Democratic Union, before finally opting for the latter.

The difficulties which the right encountered in presenting a common electoral bloc were linked in part to the problem of defining right-wing values in a post-communist society. The secularization of Slovak society in the communist period weakened the Christian Democrats' appeal to the new class of entrepreneurs and much of the now urbanized population. Therefore, although Čarnogurský's CDM remained one of the few points of continuity in post-communist Slovak politics — it was the only Slovak party which looked certain to gain representation in three successive elections while standing under the same name — there was an unwillingness to cede to its leadership on the part of the more market-oriented right. In the spring of 1994, the Democratic Party merged into a single subject with several other parties who shared similar economic policies, but it refused the offer of places on the CDM's list of candidates. The only grouping which accepted the CDM's offer was the very much less significant Standing Conference of the Civic Institute.

The nationalists were regarded as the main opponent by the left, centre and right, and were generally considered to comprise the MFDS, the SNP and the Christian Social Union. The MFDS and the SNP decided to stand independently, since this seemed likely to maximize their total percentage vote (although the MFDS did join with the small Agrarian Party of Slovakia). However, while this seemed a safe option for the MFDS, the SNP risked gaining no representation at all. This was an even greater risk for the CSU, whch had fallen at the 5 per cent hurdle in 1992 and appeared to have lost rather than gained support in the intervening period.

The Hungarian minority, which constitutes over 10 per cent of Slovakia's population, largely votes for its own parties. The Hungarian parties represent a similar diversity of views to the Slovak ones, with the Hungarian Christian Democratic Movement standing on the right while Co-existence is more strongly nationalist and the Hungarian Civic Party liberal. However, there was considerable pressure for them to unite in coalition (as the HCDM and Co–existence had done in 1992) so that no Hungarian vote should be wasted in the struggle for a strong parliamentary voice.

It was notable that, for all the criticism to which Mečiar and the MFDS were subjected, and however sharply their popularity had fallen after independence, the MFDS nevertheless remained the most popular party in the country. Surveys from the spring and early summer of 1994 also showed Mečiar to be the most popular and trusted politician, just ahead of President Kováč and Prime Minister Moravčík. Therefore, although the 1994 election results were likely to be close, with coalition government continuing in their wake, it seemed probable that Mečiar would remain a leading actor in Slovak politics. The final results

Table 5: Elections to the Slovak National Council, Sept. 30–Oct. 1, 1994

	% Votes	Seats
Movement for a Democratic Slovakia/Agrarian Party of Slovakia	35.0	61
Common Choice (Party of the Democratic Left/Green Party in Slovakia/Social Democratic Party of Slovakia/Farmers' Movement)	10.4	18
Hungarian Coalition (Hungarian Christian Democratic Movement/Co-existence/Hungarian Civic Party)	10.2	17
Christian Democratic Movement (with Standing Conference of the Civic Institute)	10.1	17
Democratic Union (with National Democratic Party)	8.6	15
Workers' Association of Slovakia	7.3	13
Slovak National Party	5.4	9
Others	13.0	0
inc. Democratic Party with Party of Entrepreneurs and Tradespeople	*3.4*	*0*
Communist Party of Slovakia	*2.7*	*0*
Christian Social Union	*2.1*	*0*
TOTAL	100.0	150

of the 1994 elections produced a parliament which was likely to be no more conducive of stable government than that which preceded it. The Slovak party system continued to demonstrate a complexity which defied normal Western criteria of left and right: the political spectrum was divided into a nationalist and non-nationalist party, yet each contained individual parties whose self-identification ranged from right to left.

Directory of Parties

Agrarian Party of Slovakia
Rol'nícka strana Slovenska (RSS)

Address. Magnelová 11, 831 04 Bratislava.

Leadership. Pavol Delinga (ch.)

History. The party was formed in October 1990 to protect agricultural and rural interests, and stood together with the Farmers' Movement in the local elections of that year. It did not stand in the 1992 elections, but formed a coalition with the MFDS for the 1994 elections.

Alliance of Democrats of the Slovak Republic
Aliancia demokratov SR (AD SR)
see **Democratic Union of Slovakia**

Christian Democratic Movement (CDM)
Krest'anskodemokratické hnutie (KDH)

Address. Žabotova 2, 811 04 Bratislava.

Telephone. (07) 496 308.

Fax. (07) 496 313.

Foundation. February 1990.

Leadership. Ján Čavrnogurský (ch.)

Membership. 26,352.

History. The party originated just after the 1989 revolution under the leadership of the former Catholic dissident, Ján Čarnogurský. It gained representation at federal and Slovak level in the 1990 elections, and participated in the coalition governments of both Czechoslovakia and the Slovak Republic. When Public Against Violence split in the spring of 1991, Čarnogurský became Slovak Prime Minister, and remained in this post until the 1992 elections. The CDM entered opposition after the second elections, when the party was disadvantaged by its perceived links with Prague and the departure of its more nationalist wing under Ján Klepáč, so that its electoral support was halved. None the less, it remained one of the few constants on the Slovak political scene: it re-entered the Slovak government after the fall of Mečiar in March 1994, and for the 1994 elections, it offered places on its candidate lists to a number of other right-of-centre parties and groups.

Programme. The party is a member of the European Democratic Union and has links with Christian Democratic and conservative parties in many Western countries. Its economic policy supports the stabilization of the currency, with the eventual goal of full convertibility, a balanced state budget, and continued privatization, including the sale of flats, a second wave of voucher privatization and the creation of equal conditions for every form of agricultural enterprise. Its social policy is based on a combination of the personal responsibility of healthy adult citizens for themselves and their families with solidarity towards those who are unable to take care of themselves for reasons of age or infirmity.

Christian Social Union
Krest'anská sociálna únia (KSÚ)

Address. Karloveská 2, 842 58 Bratislava.

Telephone. (07) 729 141, (07) 792 209.

Fax. (07) 723 960.

Leadership. Ján Klepáč.

History. The union originated in March 1992 from a split in the Christian Democratic Movement over disagreements about a new state treaty and the privatization of state property. A number of CDM members, including 11 of its 31 SNC deputies and four of its ministers in the Slovak government, broke away to form the Slovak Christian Democratic Movement. The new party, which was more nationalist in orientation, stood separately in the 1992 elections, with its own candidates and election programme, but failed to gain any deputies. It was later renamed the Christian Social Union, but failed to unify Christian and nationalist forces in Slovakia, and, standing alone, was unable to gain representation in the 1994 elections.

Co-existence
Együttélés-Spolužitie-Coexistentia (ESWS)

Address. Pražská 7, P.O. Box 44, 814 99 Bratislava.

Telephone. (07) 497 877.

Fax. (07) 497 877.

Foundation. March 1990.

Leadership. Miklós Duray (Ch.).

Membership. 12,000.

History. The party was registered in March 1990, and re-registered in April 1992. Standing in coalition with the Hungarian Christian Democratic Movement, it gained representation at federal and Slovak level in both 1990 and 1992, and nine of the coalition's 14 deputies in the Slovak parliament from 1992 to 1994 belonged to Co-existence. It intended to stand again with the HCDM in the 1994 elections, and after protracted negotiations with the Hungarian Civic Party, a coalition of all three Hungarian parties was formed.

Programme. Co-existence describes itself as a centrist political movement with a conservative and liberal orientation. Its programme lays emphasis on civic equality and the collective and autonomous political rights of national and ethnic communities, including their right to their own schools with mother tongue teaching, and the obligatory use of regional languages (as well as Slovak) for propagating information and in contacts with state officials.

Democratic Party
Demokratická strana

Address. Šancova 70, 811 01 Bratislava.

Telephone. (07) 496 885.

Fax. (07) 496 927

Leadership. Ivan Mikloš (Ch.).

Membership. Over 5,000.

History. The Democratic Party was formed at the end of World War II to counter communist influence in Slovakia, and was dissolved after the communist takeover. It was revived in 1989, and joined the Slovak government after the 1990 elections, remaining in the governing coalition after the break-up of Public Against Violence. However, it gained no representation in the 1992 elections, when it stood together with Václav Klaus's Civic Democratic Party. In early March 1994, it merged with the Conservative Democratic Party, a successor to Public Against Violence and the Civic Democratic Union, and initially adopted its chairman, Pavol Hagyari, who was replaced by Ivan Mikloš before the elections. The Democratic Party also absorbed other smaller groupings, including the Civic Democratic Party in Slovakia and the Movement for Czechoslovak Understanding. After complex negotiations, the Party of Entrepreneurs and Tradespeople, led by Vladimir Randa, accepted places on the Democratic Party's candidate lists.

Programme. The party is the nearest Slovak equivalent to the Czech Civic Democratic Party, and it supports the principles of the market economy, extensive individual and property rights and a strong state that guarantees the security of its citizens. It emphasises rapid voucher privatization and the removal of all state restrictions on foreign investment, as well as the reduction of state interference in all financial and business institutions. It states that its supporters are mainly younger people, and that many have higher education and are running private businesses.

Democratic Union of Slovakia
Demokratická únia Slovenska (DÚ)

Address. Pražská 1, 811 04 Bratislava.

Telephone. (07) 491 208, (07) 498 548, (07) 496 971.

Fax. (07) 491 208, (07) 496 971.

Foundation. May 1994.

Leadership. Jozef Moravčík (ch.)

Membership. Several thousand.

History. The party was formed by the merger of two political subjects: the Alliance of Democrats founded under the chairmanship of Milan Kňažko after he left the MFDS in the spring of 1993, and the Alternative for Political Realism, led by Josef Moravčík, which separated from the MFDS a year later. As a consequence, the party from its inception had in its ranks 19 NC SR deputies, including the Prime Minister Moravčík, and had a high public profile likely to be of assistance in the 1994 elections.

Programme. The Democratic Union of Slovakia declares itself to be a liberally oriented party to the right of centre, promoting the interests of people who want to live in a civil and meritocratic society which respects civil liberties, a pluralistic democracy, a market economy and free enterprise. It has the stated aim of adhering to the idea of political tolerance and avoiding confrontation with political rivals, and it supports the orientation of Slovakia towards European integration.

Farmers' Movement
Hnutie pol'nohospodarov SR (HP SR)

Address. S. Chalúpku 18, 071 01 Michalovce.

Leadership. Jozef Klein (ch.)

History. The movement supports agricultural interests, and gained some representation in the 1990 local elections, but did not stand independently in the 1990 and 1992 elections. In May 1994, it joined the left coalition of the PDL for the forthcoming elections.

Green Party in Slovakia
Strana zelených na Slovensku (SZS)

Address. Palisády 56, 811 06 Bratislava.

Telephone. (07) 323 231.

Fax. (07) 364 848.

Leadership. Jozef Pokorný (ch.)

Membership. c. 2,000.

History. The party was founded shortly after November 1989, but in the 1990 elections it only gained representation in the Slovak National Council, where a lower (3 per cent) threshold operated in this election. It failed to return any deputies in the 1992 elections, but remained one of the strongest non-parliamentary parties. In May 1994, it decided to stand in the left coalition led by the Party of the Democratic Left, although this led to some members leaving to form a new party, the Slovak Green Alternative.

Programme. The Green Party describes the goals of the left electoral coalition as laying the base for the development of a broad social democratic current whose policies derive from left-wing traditions, social democratic values and the principles of "green philosophy". The party believes that a healthy environment, a healthy society and healthy people equal a healthy Slovakia, and also has a strong social accent to its policies. It views a market economy not as the aim but as the means of producing a qualitative growth in the standard of living.

Hungarian Christian Democratic Movement (HCDM)
Magyar Kereszténydemokrata Mozgalom/Mad'arské krest'anskodemokratické hnutie (MKDH)

Address. Žabotova 2, 811 04 Bratislava.

Telephone. (07) 495 164, (07) 495 546.

Fax. (07) 495 264.

Foundation. March 1990.

Leadership. Béla (Vojtech) Bugár (ch.)

Membership. As a movement, rather than a party, it does not have registered members.

History. The party was founded to represent the specific interests of citizens of Hungarian nationality, and in the 1990 and 1992 elections it stood in coalition with Co–existence and obtained representation in both the Federal Assembly and the SNC. Five of the coalition's 14 deputies in the parliament of independent Slovakia belonged to the HCDM, and the two parties stood together in the 1994 elections, including the Hungarian Civic Party in their coalition as well. The coalition had represented the only former opposition parties which did not join the new Moravčík government in March 1994.

Programme. The party gives particular attention to the protection of minority and Christian interests, and supports a functioning market economy and an acceleration of the privatization process. Its national orientation is considered to be more moderate than that of Co-existence, and Bugár is therefore less unpopular among ethnic Slovaks than the Co-existence chairman Duray.

Hungarian Civic Party
Magyár Polgári Párt/Mad'arská občianská strana (MOS)

Address. Žabotova 2, 811 01 Bratislava.

Telephone. (07) 497 684, (07) 497 688.

Fax. (07) 495 322.

Foundation. February 1990.

Leadership. László Nagy (ch.)

Membership. 1,790.

History. The party was created as a political movement under under the name of the Hungarian Independent Initiative in November 1989, and was registered in February 1990. In the 1990 elections, it gained representation by standing on the candidate lists of Public Against Violence. In January 1992, it changed its name and became a political party, but failed to cross the 5 per cent threshold when it stood independently in the 1992 elections. It differs from the other Hungarian parties in Slovakia, Co-existence and the Hungarian Christian Democratic Movement, in its markedly liberal orientaiton, but its only chance of gaining representation in the 1994 elections was through forming a coalition with them.

Movement for a Democratic Slovakia (MFDS)
Hnutie za demokratické Slovensko (HZDS)

Address. Tomášikova 32/a, 823 69 Bratislava.

Telephone. (07) 231 769, (07) 230 144, (07) 231 800, (07) 293 925.

Fax. (07) 224 213, (07) 293 855, (07) 293 867.

Chair. Vladimír Mečiar (ch.)

History. Registered in May 1991, the party had broken away from the citizens' movement Public Against Violence two months earlier, led by the then Prime Minister, Mečiar. Although it entered opposition after Mečiar's dismissal, it retained great popular support, and when the movement obtained 74 of the 150 seats in the Slovak National Council after the June 1992 elections, Mečiar once again became Prime Minister. Although the party had entered the elections with a manifesto supporting the creation of a Czecho-Slovak confederation, the MFDS government rapidly ended up presiding over the division of Czechoslovakia when the Czechs refused even to discuss the possibility of a confederation. In the independent Slovakia, the party lost support as the economy stagnated, relations with the Hungarian minority and the country's image abroad deteriorated, and Mečiar became embroiled in the personal conflicts with his former colleagues which led to two splits in the party and reduced its parliamentary representation from 74 deputies to 56. The fall of the MFDS–SNP government in March 1994 quickly led to the calling of new elections, which the MFDS wanted to take place as soon as possible: for all its difficulties, it was still by far the most popular single party in the country.

Programme. The MFDS defies most normal political categories: while its self-definition is most frequently as a party of the centre, its economic policy has been viewed as left-wing, and its bent towards nationalism as right-wing.

National Democratic Party–New Alternative
Národnodemokratická strana–Nová Alternatíva (NDS)

Address. Námestie SNP 2, 814 11 Bratislava.

Telephone. (07) 334 068, (07) 331 772.

Fax. (07) 332 771, (07) 332 026.

Leadership. L'udovít Černák (ch.)

Membership. Around 3,000.

History. The party began as the National Democratic club in the National Council, which was formed at the end of 1993 by six Slovak National Party deputies who disagreed with the state budget for 1994. Their leader, L'udovit Černák, ceased to be SNP chair in February 1994, and the National Democratic Party was founded at the end of March. After some discussion of an alliance with the centrist Democratic Union of Slovakia, the party's candidates then accepted places on the Christian Democratic Movement's candidate lists, but finally ran with the Democratic Union.

Programme. The party aims to create a free civic society, addressing above all the younger generation, and rejects nationalism as a political direction. Programme aims include realizing a state ruled by law and the free competition of political forces; a free market and prosperity; aid to those in social need; a green Slovakia; and spiritual and moral renewal.

Party of Entrepreneurs and Tradespeople of the Slovak Republic
Strana podnikateľov a živnostníkov SR (SPŽSR)
See Democratic Party

Party of the Democratic Left (PDL)
Strana demokratickej ľavice (SDL')

Address. Gonduličova 12, 816 10 Bratislava.

Telephone. (07) 333 617, 334 515.

Fax. (07) 335 574.

Leadership. Peter Weiss (ch.)

Membership. Almost 50,000.

History. The party has its origins as the Slovak part of the Communist Party of Czechoslovakia. It was strongly influenced by reformist forces within the Communist Party, and in 1991, it renamed itself the Party of the Democratic Left and adopted a new programme; by the end of that year it had left the federation with the Czech communists which had been established after the 1989 revolution. The party inherited a strong base of members and resources from its communist predecessor, and has had no trouble crossing the 5 per cent threshold in any election in which it stood. It entered government in March 1994 as part of the left-right coalition, and formed an electoral bloc with three smaller parties to run in the 1994 elections. Its chairman, Peter Weiss, is one of the most prominent personalities of Slovak politics, although he did not, as party leader, himself accept a post in the Moravčík government.

Programme. The party espouses social democratic aims and the principles of the Socialist International. It believes in the transformation from a centrally controlled to a market economy, but within the limits set by the social acceptability of change. Its social policy also emphasizes the importance of high employment in preserving basic social certainties.

Slovak National Party (SNP)
Slovenská národná strana (SNS)

Address. Vajanského nábrežie 17, 814 99 Bratislava.

Telephone. (07) 325 808, 326 457.

Fax. (07) 325 808.

Foundation. December 1989, registered March 1990.

Leadership. Ján Slota.

Membership. c.7,000.

History. The party won seats in both the federal and Slovak parliaments in the 1990 and 1992 elections, with between 7 and 14 per cent of the vote. Although its support was slightly lower in the second elections, this was partly due to the fact that many of its nationalist sentiments were by then being expressed by other parties, and the eventual division of Czechoslovakia must be seen as a victory for the Slovak National Party, which, alone of the major parties, had supported this solution in its election manifesto. In the independent Slovakia, the party co-operated uneasily with the MFDS government, joining a formal coalition with it in October 1993. However, the party had some difficulties redefining its aims after the achievement of independence, and lost six of its 15 deputies to the National Democratic Party in early 1994. It entered opposition after the fall of the Mečiar government, and decided to fight the 1994 elections standing alone.

Programme. When Ján Slota replaced Ľudovit Černák as chairman in February 1994, the nationalist orientation of the party became more marked. It emphasizes the national rights and interests of Slovaks and the renewal of national pride and patriotism, and supports the establishment of Slovak schools in every local district and the exclusive use of Slovak as an official language. It also appeals for a consistent struggle against criminality, including the reintroduction of the death penalty. Its economy policy favours an effective tax system and full support for private enterprise.

Social Democratic Party of Slovakia
Sociálnodemokratická strana Slovenska (SDSS)

Address. Žabotova 2, 811, 04 Bratislava.

Telephone. (07) 494 623, (07) 494 700.

Fax. (07) 494 621.

Foundation. February 1990.

Leadership. Jaroslav Volf (ch.)

Membership. c.4,000

History. The party has roots in traditional Slovak social democracy and the inter-war Social Democratic Party of Czechoslovakia, which was banned in 1938, and briefly re-emerged after the war before being banned again in 1948. The party remained in illegality until it was revived after the 1989 revolution, and in 1991, it was joined by the Party of Democratic Socialists. The Social Democrats failed to gain representation in the 1990 elections, but when Alexander Dubček left Public Against Violence and led the party into the 1992 elections, his candidacy for the Slovak part of the Federal Assembly's House of the Nations helped them to gain five deputies there. However, their lack of SNC deputies left them with no parliamentary seats in the independent Slovakia, and they were also hit by Dubček's untimely death in autumn 1992. For the 1994 elections, they joined the four-party left coalition of the PDL, which espoused broadly social democratic perspectives.

Standing Conference of the Civic Institute
Stála konferencia občianskeho inštitutu (SKOI)

A small right-of-centre organization not registered as a party, it was able to gain parliamentary representation in the 1994 elections through having accepted places on the CDM's candidate lists. Its best-known representatives, including one-time federal Interior Minister, Ján Langoš, are former members of Public Against Violence and the Civic Democratic Union who did not proceed to join the Conservative Democratic Party and the Democratic Party.

Workers' Association of Slovakia
Združenie robotníkov Slovenska (ZRS)

Address. ul. Horná 83, 974 01 Banská Bystrica.

Telephone. (088) 742 563, ext. 27.

Fax. (088) 745 596.

Leadership. Ján L'upták (ch.)

Membership. 12,860

History. The Association stood as an independent organization on the candidates' lists of the Party of the Democratic Left in the June 1992 elections, and its chair, Ján L'upták, obtained a seat in the Slovak National Council. However, it decided to form an independent party in spring 1994, and was registered as such in April of that year. It refused the offer to stand on the lists of the PDL coalition in the 1994 elections, and presented 94 candidates of its own.

Programme. While not rejecting economic reforms such as voucher privatization, the party has a clear left-wing profile and lays greater emphasis than the PDL on protecting the interests of workers and those lower down in society. Initial opinion poll results after its split from the PDL indicated a considerable constituency for such policies which was confirmed by the election results.

Notes
1 For detailed analysis of the party system in the former Czechoslovakia see: Gordon Wightman, "Czechoslovakia" in Bogdan Szajkowski (ed.) *New Political Parties of Eastern Europe and the Soviet Union.* Longman, Harlow, 1991. pp. 53–92. See also chapter on the Czech Republic in this volume.

SLOVENIA

John B. Allcock

Historically Slovene settlement was dispersed over four parts of the Austrian monarchy — Styria, Carniola, Carinthia and Gorizia. Following the dismemberment of the Austro-Hungarian monarchy in 1918, the first two of these, and southern Carinthia, joined the newly founded Kingdom of Serbs Croats and Slovenes (renamed Yugoslavia in 1929), together with small Slovene-speaking parts of Hungary — Prekmurje and Medjumurje). Partly because of their linguistic identity, the Slovenes within Yugoslavia were able to develop an appreciable degree of *de facto* autonomy between the wars. The division of Yugoslavia after the Axis invasion of 1941 awarded Carinthia to Italy, Styria was absorbed into the German Reich, and the eastern territories returned to Hungary. In the peace settlement of 1945 a Slovene republic was established within the reconstituted Yugoslavia, and Eastern Gorizia was added to the areas that were part of the 1918 settlement. Areas including large numbers of Slovene speakers remained outside of Yugoslavia in western Gorizia/Friuli — including Trieste — and (following a referendum) northern Carinthia.

With a surface area of 20,251 km sq the Republic of Slovenia was the fifth largest of the six republics of the federation (7.9 per cent of the total), with a population (census of 1991) of 1,956,143 (8.2 per cent of the total). The most numerous ethnic group in the republic are the Slovenes, with 89 per cent of the total, followed by the Croats, with 3.2 per cent, and the Serbs, with 2.6 per cent. There is a small but locally significant minority of Magyars in the far north-western (Prekmurje) area, although both these and the Italians in the west have declined steady over the post-war period. These territorial and demographic features are unchanged by secession from Yugoslavia.

Border disputes with both Italy and Croatia have been reactivated since independence. In the case of Italy the reasoning is that the international frontier confirmed by the Treaty of Osimo was concluded with Yugoslavia, not with Slovenia, and should not necessarily be considered binding under the new constitutional order. The dispute with Croatia hinges upon the fact that the border between the two republics was a purely internal administrative convenience within Yugoslavia, and that it does not correspond to the historical border of Slovenia. A new dimension is created by the need to demarcate territorial waters between the two states, which under one interpretation of international conventions could pose serious problems of access to Slovenia's only port, at Koper. These international issues have come to provide the focus of important internal political conflicts.

The first multi-party elections in Slovenia (April 1990) took place before the secession of the republic from Yugoslavia. Although the candidate of the reformed League of Communists (Party of Democratic Reform), Milan Kučan, was elected to the presidency, his success rested upon his personal popularity, and a governing coalition was formed

(DEMOS) from the representatives of six explicitly anti-communist parties. It was recognized from the outset that this coalition was inherently unstable, united only by its hostility to the old order and a preference for taking Slovenia out of the Yugoslav federation. When Slovenia successfully asserted its independence in the "ten-day war" of June–July 1991, the work of DEMOS was done and its days were numbered.

As the first multi-party elections had taken place, and Slovene independence had been secured, under the Communist constitution of 1974 the legislature consisted of three chambers — a Socio-political Chamber, a Chamber of Associated Labour and a Chamber of Municipalities — reflecting the concept of regional and economic self-management. A new constitution passed into law in December 1991 which replaced this structure with a bicameral system consisting of an Assembly (*Skupščina*) and a Council of State (*Državni Svet*). The former consists of 90 seats to which members are elected by a system of proportional representation (the D'Hondt system), with the exception of two seats reserved for members of the national minorities which are regarded as autocthonous (Italians and Magyars). Similar privileges are not extended to the ethnic groups from former Yugoslavia which comprise larger proportions of the population (Croats, Muslims and Serbs).

The Council of State is a curious compromise between a Senate and the old self-management system. The structure has been described by one Slovene political leader as "one and a half chambers". It consists of 40 seats, 22 of which are elected by roughly equal regional constituencies, with the remaining 18 seats being filled by representatives of occupational and interest groups, oddly reminiscent of the old Chamber of Associated Labour in a constitution explicitly intended to function as a "new broom".

Fresh elections were held to this reconstructed legislature in December 1992 (Table 1). Although President Kučan was convincingly reconfirmed in office with 64 per cent of the popular vote (three times that of his nearest rival) the new Assembly had a very different composition from the first, with the Liberal Democratic Party taking 22 seats. A new coalition was put together, composed of the Liberal Democrats, the Christian Democrats, the Social Democrats, the Associated List and the Greens–ESP. Nominally this consists of two distinct alliances which have the Liberal Democrats in common, as the Christian Democrats and the former Communists of the Associated List wished to stress their independence from each other from the outset. (The former were elected on a specifically anti-communist ticket.)

The Council of State is nominally non-partisan, and a kind of "house of elders" whose function is to give independent advice to government. In practice, however, there are clear party alignments in the case of all but two of the regional constituency councillors, as the process by which they are nominated as local representatives tends to be party-oriented. Because institutional change has not yet permeated to the local level, figures associated with the former Communist establishment are far more visible in the Council than in the Assembly.

Unlike the British parliamentary system, but like the US Congress, the Cabinet is not recruited from among the members of the Assembly and Council, but stands outside the electoral system. Cabinet Members are nominated by the Prime Minister (Janez Drnovšek, of the Liberal Democrats), although they are constitutionally accountable to the Assembly. All parties in the ruling coalition are represented in the Cabinet, and there are two ministries held by non-party figures.

A central feature of party life since the collapse of DEMOS has been the process of realignment and consolidation. This is belied by the continuing existence of a number of

Table 1: Results of Elections to the Slovene Assembly, Dec. 6, 1992

Parties in the Assembly	Av. % of vote	Deputies (N = 90)
Liberal Democratic Party	21.39	22
Slovene Christian Democrats	13.86	15
Associated List	12.11	14
Slovene People's Party	8.96	11
Slovene National Party	8.76	11
Democratic Party	4.42	6
Greens of Slovenia	3.29	5
Social Democratic Party of Slovenia	3.11	4
Italian and Magyar national minorities†		2

† Seats reserved for candidates representing these groups

Source: Frane Adam (ed.) *Volitve in politika po Slovensko: ocene, razprave, napovedi,* Ljubljana, Znanstveno in publicistično središče, 1993.

small groupings that have failed to gain representation in the Assembly, and not adequately conveyed by the fact that after the second elections the number of parties with seats in the Assembly remained at nine.

Consolidation takes several forms. To a certain extent the former parties were the personal followings of political leaders, their programmes were hastily thought out and overlapping in content, and they lacked a clear sense of a relationship to a distinct base in either local or functional interests. There has been a process of the merger of like-minded groups, the assimilation of political fragments with no hope of independent representation, the drift of people towards a natural ideological home and a clearer identification of parties both with identifiable programmes and constituencies of one kind or another. The significant "left" fractions are now consolidated into the Associated List, which is still in some respects a marriage of convenience of four "parties". Artisan and smallholder groups have gravitated towards the Christian Democrats. A potential merger has been the subject of protracted discussion which will involve the Democrats, the Greens and some former socialists. As the Democrats are also in discussion with the Liberals, there may be a split in the ranks for the former, which originated very much as the personal following of its charismatic leader Dimitrij Rupel. Not surprisingly the process of consolidation involves in the short term the creation of *more* parties as the bearers of the original identity seek to sustain that vision against the realities of electoral contest. (This has happened both with the Greens and the National Party.)

An important aspect of this process, however, has been the failure of Slovene parties to line up along the traditional European left–right axis. There has been a redistribution of the "left agenda" across several of the parties. Looking at the issue in another way, Jan Markarovič has identified the phenomenon of "left conservatism" as the "Slovene political paradox".[1] Thus a highly interventionist stance in relation to the economy, and caution in relation to privatization, for example, may be linked to a traditionally "right" preoccupation with specifically "national" interest. Conversely, an emphatically "liberal" stance with respect to individual rights may be linked in the Slovene context to opposition to

Catholic traditionalism. "Collectivism" is in many cases a badge of "conservative" political identity. As in Croatia, it is more fruitful to conceptualize the principal political polarities in Slovene politics in terms of traditionalism vs. modernization" rather than "right vs. left" (see page 135–148).

Slovene politics has a closed feel about it, which is partly the result of the extent to which the struggle for personal power occupies the "political class". The war raging elsewhere in former Yugoslavia simple does not feature as a focus of political debate, and the refugee problem is very much a minor issue. There is a great deal of concern about the economic impact of independence, especially in relation to unemployment. The major topic of concern is the process of privatization and its link with the reconstruction of the Slovene economy. This question has a certain piquancy in a country which sets such store by the recent assertion of its independence, and the successful overthrow of Communism, and which now addresses the issue of the role and function of foreign capital, and the economic influence of its managerial class, many of whom owe their positions to their success under the old order.

Directory of parties

Associated List

See "United List"

Democratic Party (DP)
Demokratska Stranka (DS)

Formerly known as the Slovene Democratic League (SDL)
Slovenska Demokratična Zveza (SDZ)
Address. Trg Republike 3/XII, 61000, Ljubljana.

Telephone. 61 1253 032/1253 316.

Fax: 61 1252 203.

Foundation. Jan. 11, 1989, although not registered until March 1990.

Membership. In excess of 2,200.

Leadership. Igor Bavčar (pres.); Dimitrij Rupel, the founder, retains an active and influential role. The DP has six seats in the Assembly.

History. The idea of the League was launched by the sociologist Dimitrij Rupel at a meeting of cultural workers on June 2, 1988. It was seen initially as a loose association of intellectuals rather than a party, and still tends to be dominated by them, together with members of the business and professional élite. It performed well in the elections of 1990, and with eight seats in the Assembly entered the DEMOS coalition. Following the elections of 1992 the SDL merged with a smaller group of Social Democrats, to create the DP.

Organization. DP is well represented in most of the 65 communes of the republic. At the time of the research for this volume the party was engaged in informal discussions with several other parties (Greens, Christian Socialists and the Slovene Party of Small Business) about the possibility of merging.

Programme. The party claims to articulate the "political interests of the Slovene people". The DP was always among the most outspokenly separatist of the main political parties, and its determination to turn its back on Yugoslavia is illustrated by a section of its manifesto which lays out very clearly and explicitly the need to create a Mediterranean orientation, developing transport links on a SW–NE axis (Koper and Gorica to Lendava)– in place of the historic NW–SE axis (Jesenice–Zagreb). The enhancement of the political self-consciousness of Slovenes and the building of a specifically Slovene "system" are given the highest priority, and in this respect a large part of the manifesto is devoted to educational and cultural policy.

Affiliations. Observer status with the Liberal International.

Greens – Ecological Social Party (G–ESP)
Zeleni – Ekološka Socijalna Stranka (Z–ESS)

Address. Komenskega 11, 61000, Ljubljana.

Telephone. 61 1320 106.

Fax. 61 1320 174.

Foundation. Originally formed as Zeleni Slovenija on June 11, 1989, but split in March 1993 and renamed.

Membership. c.2,000.

Leadership. Petar Tancig (pres.); Dušan Plut, the elder statesman of the party now heads its scientific "think-tank"; Dr Božidar Voljč is Minister of Health. The party has five seats in the Assembly.

History. The Greens have been active in Slovenia for more than 20 years, originally in informal non-political groups directed to specific environmental issues, such as the nuclear plant at Krško. The movement acquired a more coherent form during the middle and late 1980s. The party was created with the change of the law in 1989. The Greens won eight seats in the first multi-party elections in 1990, and entered the ruling DEMOS coalition which took the country to independence. The party has remained in the government coalition following the second elections of December 1992. The experience of government has produced tensions between those members who have moved towards an "ethic of responsibility" and those who still adhere to the original "ethic of ultimate ends"; the party split along these lines with all five of its elected representatives joining the new party. The original title is retained by the dissident minority.

Organization. The movement still has a strong sense of local identity. There are groups in more than 40 of Slovenia's 65 communes, each of which is represented in the party's assembly. During late 1993 and early 1994 each of these groups was asked to make a choice with respect to its continuing support of the newly reformed party. This process was not concluded at the time of writing. During late 1993 discussions began over the consolidation of party structure involving a possible merger of the Democrats, some socialist groups and the Greens–ESP. This is likely to be a protracted process, starting with exploratory collaboration in local elections during 1994.

Programme. Although ostensibly an environmental party, a surprising amount of the party's early literature stressed nationalist issues. The party now describes itself as in the "middle of the political spectrum", and sees its function as ensuring that "green" issues remain on the agenda of any new political organization that emerges from the current discussions. The programme of the Greens in the past has been distinguished by a number of very specific and pragmatic legislative proposals, covering economic social security and welfare and cultural life. The general tone of its approach has been collectivist and interventionist.

Affiliations. There are loose links with other Green groups in other European countries.

Liberal Democratic Party (LDP)
Liberalno-Demokratska Stranka (LDS)

Not to be confused with the Liberal Party, or with the Liberal Democratic Party of Slovenia.

Address. Dalmatinova 4, pp. 651, 61001. Ljubljana.

Telephone. 61 312 659.

Fax. 61 312 381.

Foundation. Nov. 10, 1990.

Membership. 14,000.

Leadership. Janez Drnovšek (pres.) and Prime Minister; Bogomir Kovač, Edvard Oven, Jaša Zlobec, Vika Potočnik (vice-pres.); Gregor Golobič (s.g.); the party has four members in the Cabinet: Jelko Kačin (Economic Relations and Development), Miha Jazbinšek (Environment and Regional Planning), Miha Kozinc (Justice), Slavko Gaber (Education and Sport). The party has 22 seats in the Assembly.

History. The party emerged from the former official Communist youth organization, the Federation of Socialist Youth of Slovenia. Early party literature made deferential references to the pre-war Liberal Party, but there is no evidence of a direct relationship. In effect it was an independent party with respect to the League of Communists for some time, and certainly since the growth of interest in "civil society" in the early 1980s. A key event in the crystallization of that distinctive status was the case of the "Ljubljana 4" in 1988. The Liberals were the largest single party in the 1990 Assembly, although in opposition to the DEMOS coalition. After Drnovšek joined the party it began to shake off its specific associations with "youth".

Organization. A key organizational feature of the LDP is its use of non-party expert "think-tanks" in relation to policy formation. Strong support for regionalism is reflected in the party's organization. There is a youth organization (Young Liberal Democrats) and a senior citizens' organization (the "Grey Panthers", originally a separate party).

Programme. The party supports the "essential liberal values" of individual rights and liberties, and it has defended these successfully in relation to proposals to limit family planning and the law on citizenship. It favours stronger regional and local government. Equality of opportunity is to be pursued at a variety of levels, especially with respect to health, education and gender. It largely made the running in shaping the process by which privatization should be undertaken and the reform of the banking system. The party favours integration of the rural economy. The Liberal Democrats are explicitly and staunchly secular.

Affiliations. The Liberal Democrats have active links with the British Liberal Democratic Party, although there is no formal affiliation.

Slovene Christian Democrats (SCD)
Slovenska Krščanski Demokrati (SKD)

Formerly Slovensko Krščansko Socialno Gibanje
Address. Beethovnova 4, 61000, Ljubljana.

Telephone. 61 1262 179; 1210 179.

Fax. 61 1211 738.

Foundation. March 10, 1989.

*Membership. c.*34,000.

Leadership. Lojze Peterle (pres.) Deputy Prime Minister and Foreign Minister; the SCD has three ministerial posts, Andrej Šter (Interior), Jože Osterc (Agriculture and Forestry); Igor Umek (Transport and Communications). The party has 15 members in the Assembly.

History. Claims links to the pre-war *Ljudska Stranka*, but these appear to be largely sentimental. Christian Democracy does not have a strong tradition in Slovenia. The movement is largely the creation of non-clerical Catholic intellectuals. Since the 1990 elections the process of party realignment has brought several other individuals and groups into the SCD fold, most notably Ivan Oman, the founder of the Peasant League.

Organization. The party has a network of branches in just about every commune, but it is unquestionably stronger in rural than urban areas, although it also has strong blue-collar support.

Programme. Central concerns of the Christian Democrats are the protection of human and civil rights, the defence of the "full sovereignty of Slovenia", and the protection of Slovene minorities elsewhere. "Moral renewal" is seen as necessary; this is to be achieved through legislation relating to the family as well as through the building of parliamentary democracy and the protection of the Slovene cultural heritage. The SCD advocates a market economy, but with an "ecological and social filter". Among its economic concerns the party lists the problems of regional underdevelopment within the republic, particularly in agriculture. "Balance" is a recurring theme throughout SCD literature.

Affiliations. The party has active contacts with the British Conservative Party, with Christian Democratic parties in Germany and Italy, and with the Austrian *Freiheitspartei*.

Slovene National Party (SNP)
Slovenačka Nacionalna Stanka (SNS)

Address. Kotnikova 2, 61000, Ljubljana.

Telephone. 61 1224 241.

Fax. 61 1125 207.

Membership. 3,500.

Leadership. Zmago Jelinčič (pres.). The SNP has 11 seats in the Assembly.

Organization. The party benefited to a small degree from the demise of the Slovene Peasant League. It seems to be based very much on a personal following of the charismatic leadership of Jelinčič. It draws most of its support from a working class and lower white-collar constituency.

Programme. The party is well to the right of the Slovene political spectrum. It combines an insistence upon vigorous social security measures, traditional Catholic views on the family and population, and a robust and explicit nationalism. It is the only Slovene party whose manifesto could be said to be "militaristic". The SNP takes a very tough line on the disputed borders with Italy and Croatia, and the related financial issues.

Slovene People's Party (SPP)
Slovenačka Ljudska Stranka (SLS)

Address. Zarnikova 3, 61000, Ljubljana.

Telephone. 61 301 891.

Fax. 61 101 871.

Membership. Claims 35,000, although this should be viewed with caution.

Leadership. Marjan Podobnik (pres.). The SLS has 11 seats in the Assembly.

History. As the title of the party suggests, the SPP claims to be the inheritor of the mantle of Mgr Anton Korošec, who dominated Slovene politics in the inter-war period, although it is not known to what extent there is any real, rather than rhetorical, continuity.

Programme. The programme of the SPP suggests that there could be some real continuity here with Korošec's party. Although it is not an openly clerical party, the SPP does stand for the rather ecclectic mixture of populist/Catholic proposals which characterized the pre-war party: marked individualism, emphasis upon family values, with a stress upon co-operativism and social harmony, and a relatively prominent place given to agriculture and rural affairs. The SPP is a key illustration of the redistribution of the Green agenda in Slovenia.

Social Democratic Party of Slovenia (SDPS)
Socialdemokratična Stranka Slovenije (SDSS)

Address. Komenskega 11, 61000, Ljubljana.

Telephone. 61 1256 115; 1253 145.

Fax. 61 1250 304.

Foundation. Feb. 16, 1989.

Membership. c.4,000.

Leadership. Jože Pučnik (a Vice-President of the Republic); Vitograd Pukl. Has four deputies in the Assembly, participates in the governing coalition, and has one ministerial post (Rado Bohinc — Science and Technology).

History. Emerged from the "Litostroj" factory in February 1987, and grew within the "Socialist Alliance", from which it separated two years later. Largely the inspiration of Franc Tomšič, who has now left to set up an independent Trade Union. The SDPS participated both in the original DEMOS coalition, and in its successor. The party was joined for a time by Janez Janša, after his defection from the Democrats, and indeed for a time he held the portfolio of Minister of Defence for the SDPS. He left the Social Democrats in 1994, however, following disclosures over his misuse of the security services.

Organization. Has a branch organization throughout Slovenia. In spite of its impeccably grassroots origins, the party has been hard pressed in its claim to represent the authentic voice of the left by the recovery of the former Communist United List.

Programme. The party presents itself as a "social democratic party in the traditions of European democracy and the social state". As the other main contender for the left-of-centre ground in Slovene politics is not always easy to distinguish the SDPS from the UL. The latter is perhaps more outspoken in its insistence upon the egalitarian traditions of socialism: the former leans more towards claims as an effective force in modernization (in the process sailing rather close to the Liberals). In fact its modernizing concerns extend into several aspects of its manifesto, including the need to address specifically issues of women's rights, and an outspoken attack on the traditionally Roman Catholic understanding of "demographic policy", which the Social Democrats see more in terms of the problems relating to an ageing society, making explicit comparison with German and Scandinavian models.

United List (UL)
Združena Lista (ZL)

(The party is sometimes referred to as the "Associated List": the title adopted here is taken from its own literature).

Address. Levstikova 15, 61000, Ljubljana.

Telephone. 61 1254 222.

Fax. 61 1215 855.

Foundation. In its present form, April 1993.

Membership. 64,000.

Leadership. Janez Kočijančič (pres.); Vlado Rančigaj, Drago Lipič, Rado Bohinc, Peter Bekeš. Ciril Ribičič remains an active elder statesman. The party has 14 deputies in the Assembly, participates in the governing coalition, and its representatives hold three ministries: Rina Klinar (Labour), Maks Tajnikar (Economics) and Sergij Pelhan (Culture).

History. The United List was created by the merger of four left-of-centre parties, which in turn emerged during or after the first multi-party elections from the former League of Communists of Slovenia (known for a time as the Party of Democratic Renewal — PDR) and the Socialist Alliance. In addition to the PDR, these were the Socialist Party of Slovenia, the Social Democratic League and the Democratic League of Pensioners. In many respects it can be seen as a recreation of the League of Communists under another name.

Organization. The party has branches in all communes and most neighbourhoods. It has developed a bimodal structure of support, with its main support among the manual workers and professional and managerial groups. Its strength is greatest in the west of the country, and in the industrial centres of Celje and Maribor.

Programme. The Slovene left has a long history of the advocacy of both internal party democracy and wider political pluralism. The UL presents itself as a party of reconciliation between diverse social interests. In this respect it explicitly continues the socialist tradition of solidarity, but it also appeals to a perceived "culture of dialogue" in Slovenia. The greater part of its manifesto proposals are concerned with the enhancement of social security and welfare legislation — the creation of a Slovene welfare state — and the defence of the tradition of workers' participation. An attempt is made to tie economic reform to social and economic justice.

Affiliations. It is not known to what extent former republican organizations of the League of Communists might still retain active links. The UL is building active links with the renewed trades union movement in Slovenia.

The following minor parties were registered at the time of the elections of 1992. The information given here is dependent upon the Ministry of Information in Ljubljana, and is not always complete. It is interesting to note the large proportion of these minor parties which explicitly address regional interests.

Christian Democratic Party of Slovenian Styria (CDPSS). Christian Socialists (CS) (currently in discussion with the DP about merger). **Direction — Freedom, Peace and Ecological Development**. Typically known by the acronym of its Slovene title, SMER Svoboda, Mir, Ekološki Razvoj. **Forward** usually known simply by its Slovene title *NAPREJ*. **Freedom Party (FP). General Democracy Movement (GDM). Independent Party (IP). Istrian Democratic Assembly (IDA)** (believed to be a Slovene branch of the Croatian party of this name. **Kramberger's Associated List**. This is the personal following of a wealthy Slovene businessman who has contested the presidency of the republic as an independent. **Liberal Democratic Party of Slovenia (LDPS)** (not to be confused either with the Liberal Democratic Party (LDP) or the following). **Liberal Party (LP),** *Liberalna Stranka (LS)*. Formerly the *Slovenačka Zanatska Stranka*. Not to be confused with the LDP. **National Democrats (ND). Party of Citizens' Equality (PCE)**: *Stranka za Enakopravnost Občanov (SEO)*. **Primorska Union (PU). Progressive People's Party of the Centre (PPPC). Regional Party of Slovenia (RPS). Republican Association of Slovenia (RAS). Slovene Business Party (SBP)**. (Not to be confused with the following: **Slovene Craftsmen's and Tradesmen's Party (LCTP)**: *Slovenska Obrinopodjetniška Stranka (SOS))*. Not to be confused with the former name of the Liberal Party. Has support in several areas at municipal level. **Slovene Ecological Movement (SEM). Socialist Party of Slovenia (SSS)**: *Socialistična Stranka Slovenije (SSS)*. Had representatives in the first multi-party Assembly, but has since lost ground to other left-oriented groups.

Notes
1. Frane Adam (ed.) *Volitve in politika po Slovensko*, Ljubljana, Znanstveno in publicistično središče, 1993.

TAJIKSTAN

Bogdan Szajkowski

After the Bolshevik revolution the northern part of the present territory of Tajikistan became part of the Turkestan Autonomous Soviet Socialist Republic within the Russian Soviet Federative Socialist Republic (RSFSR), while its southern section was incorporated in 1920 into the People's Republic of Bukhara. In the early 1920s the area witnessed the Basmachi revolt against Soviet power. The *basmachis*, with the support of anti-Bolshevik forces from outside, staged a prolonged fight against the Bolsheviks. In the remote areas of Tajikistan, particularly the south-east, the communists managed to establish their control only in 1925. The suppression of the *basmachis* caused considerable population movement and many Tajiks fled to Afghanistan. In October 1924 the Tajik Autonomous Soviet Socialist Republic (ASSR) was created as a part of the Uzbek Soviet Socialist Republic. The south-east region of Tajikistan was on Jan. 2, 1925, designated a Special Pamir Region (later renamed the Gorno-Badakhshan Autonomous *Oblast*). On Oct. 16, 1929, the Tajik ASSR became a full Union Republic within the USSR. Its territory was subsequently enlarged by the addition of the Khojand (Khodzent, currently Leninabad) district. This very prosperous area, in the north of the country, which borders Uzbekistan, became the power base for communist rulers of Tajikistan. It has had an uneasy relationship with the southern part of Tajikistan. Significantly, however, the historic cities of Samarkand and Bukhara, where the Tajiks had lived for centuries, and where they constitute a very significant percentage of the inhabitants, remained outside Tajikistan's borders.

Although the Tajiks are the majority (62.0 per cent) of the population in Tajikistan, the presence of another powerful ethnic group, the Uzbeks (24.0 per cent), adds to the political complexities of the republic.[1] Historically, relations between the two nationalities have always been strained. In recent years, however, these difficulties have been further exacerbated by the alleged mistreatment of Tajiks in Uzbekistan. Tajiks and Uzbeks do not even agree on the size of the Tajik population in Uzbekistan. While official Uzbekistan statistics give a figure of 700,000, the most conservative Tajik estimates maintain the population to be between 3 and 3.5 million. The Tajiks also charge that their ethnic brothers in Uzbekistan have been denied access to higher education and have been forced to list their nationality as Uzbek. Tajik nationalists have laid claim to the Uzbek cities of Bukhara and Samarkand. The tensions between the Tajiks and Uzbeks are also reflected in the regional distribution of Uzbeks in Tajikistan and the political allegiances of these regions. The Uzbeks comprising one-third of the population of the northern Leninabad region (which adjoins Uzbekistan),[2] and the south-western Kulyab region which borders Afghanistan, have been perceived as supporters of the communist authorities in Dushanbe. Whether this is true or not becomes irrelevant; once such a theory prevails, all Uzbeks are tarred by the same brush. Both regions remain centres of support for the communists.

In addition, the tangle of regional loyalties has also played a powerful role in the post-1990 political scene. Both Tajiks and Uzbeks have always been region-oriented peoples and for both ethnic groups clan identification remains one of the strongest social bonds. Much of the political temperature has been generated by inter-clan conflict which has spilled over into the political domain and agenda for convenience purposes and as a way of settling old grievances. For most of the Soviet period, politics in Tajikistan was dominated by three large clans: from Leninabad, Kurgan-Tyube and Kulyab.

Of the seven regions of Tajikistan, three (Leninabad, Kulyab and West Garm) have been and remain the power base for the communists. Leninabad, with its capital city Khojand, is physically isolated from the rest of the country and linked by a single road across the dividing mountains, which is impassable during the winter months. It has closer communication links with Uzbekistan than with the rest of Tajikistan. Leninabad is, however, the most developed of Tajikistan's provinces and the industrial centre of the country. By far the greatest share of its industrial output is of military and military-related equipment. The "Khojand mafia" has traditionally provided Tajikistan with its communist political élite. All communist party bosses since 1943, including Rakhmon Nabiyev, came from this area. The Kulyabi group from the south-eastern region of Kulyab has been closely linked to Soviet power in Tajikistan. Kulyabis dominated the Interior Ministry, the KGB and other high ranking posts — the main routes to lucrative bribes.

The Gorno-Badakhshan region has been the base of support for the Tajik Democratic Party (TDP). The other three regions, Kurgan-Tyube, East Garm and Ramit Valley, represent mixed support for the several political organizations opposed to the communists.

Like in the other Central Asian republics, the Tajik leadership was reluctant to implement many of the reforms advocated by Mikhail Gorbachev's policies of *glasnost* and *perestroika*. However, Gorbachev's anti-corruption drive, aimed in particular at clean-up of the CPSU leaderships in Central Asia, led in 1985 to the removal of the First Secretary of the Communist Party of Tajikistan (CPT), Rakhmon Nabiyev (in power since 1982). He was replaced by Kakhar Makkhamov who became openly critical of the economic situation in the country and admitted the high levels of unemployment and poverty particularly in the southern and eastern regions of Tajikistan. Some relaxation in censorship led to a discussion of injustices under communism in the country and a more open discussion of Tajik history, culture and traditions. During 1989 and 1990 several small unofficial opposition groups, including the *Rastokhez* (Rebirth) Patriotic Movement and the Tajik Democratic Party were established in Dushanbe with the aim of pressing for more concessions from the regime and greater liberalization of Tajik politics.

In February 1990 Dushanbe witnessed large-scale, violent demonstrations, reportedly sparked by rumours that Armenian refugees were to be settled in apartments in preference to local inhabitants, some of whom had been waiting for housing for over 10 years. The perennial shortage of housing was used as a focus for the expression of discontent against the communist regime. The demonstrators demanded both political and economic reforms. In response Makkhamov declared a night-time curfew in Dushanbe and requested military support from Moscow. Some 5,000 Soviet interior ministry troops were despatched to the Tajik capital. They, together with the local civilian militia, suppressed the demonstrations. As a result of a bloody government crackdown 21 people were killed and 565 injured.

The government, which portrayed the Dushanbe riots as mobs of Tajik nationalists against "Europeans", used the demonstrations as an excuse to ban opposition candidates from the elections to the Supreme Soviet in March 1990. In the elections, which took place under a state of emergency, the candidates of the Communist Party of Tajikistan (CPT) won 227 of the 230 seats. On Aug. 24, 1990, in a gesture regarded as a concession to growing Tajik nationalism, the Supreme Soviet issued a declaration of sovereignty. The following November the Supreme Soviet elected Kakhar Makkhamov to the newly created post of President of the Republic — he was opposed only by Rakhmon Nabiyev.

In October 1990 when Tajik supporters of the all-union Islamic Renaissance Party (IRP) tried to organize a republican branch, the Tajik Supreme Soviet promptly proscribed the party. This response appeared to be part of the ruling élite's fear that a specifically Muslim challenge to its monopoly of power would have a far greater chance of success than challenges from the urban-based *Rastokhez* Movement and the Democratic Party of Tajikistan.[3] Despite the ban the party flourished, particularly among rural Tajiks, who make up the majority of the country's population.

Tajikistan was one of the most enthusiastic supporters of the preservation of the Soviet Union. In the March 1991 all-Union referendum on the Union Treaty some 90 per cent of the Tajik electorate voted in favour of a new Union Treaty. The Tajik leadership, including President Kakhar Makkhamov, supported the Moscow *coup* in August 1991. After it failed, demonstrators took to the streets demanding the President's resignation. The protests, organized by the *Rastokhez* Patriotic Movement, the Tajik Democratic Party and the Islamic Renaissance Party, eventually forced his departure on Aug. 31. Makkhamov was replaced by Kadreddin Aslonov as acting president. On Sept. 9, following the declaration of independence by Uzbekistan, the Supreme Soviet of Tajikistan also proclaimed the independence of the Republic of Tajikistan.[4] Mass protests, however, continued unabated and finally led to Aslonov's decision to issue a decree, on Sept. 22, banning the activities of the communist party, renamed the Socialist Party of Tajikistan (SPT), and nationalizing its assets. However, the communist hardliners promptly restored the old *status quo*. On Sept. 23 the communist-dominated Supreme Soviet met in an emergency session, declared a state of emergency and rescinded the ban on the SPT. The deputies also forced the resignation of Kadreddin Aslonov and elected Rakhmon Nabiyev in his place.

The election of the already discredited communist boss and the restoration of the communist party served as a focal point for continued demonstrations. Opposition forces took to the streets again and forced Nabiyev to concede to many of their demands. On Oct. 2 the Supreme Soviet revoked the state of emergency, suspended the SPT again and subsequently legalized the previously banned Islamic Renaissance Party. On Oct. 6 Nabiyev stepped down from the post of acting president for the duration of the presidential election campaign in which he was one of seven candidates. In the election, held on Nov. 24, Nabiyev received 58 per cent of the popular vote. He secured the presidency as the result of an overwhelming support from his traditional power base, the Leninabad and Kulyab regions. Nabiyev's main opponent, Davlat Khudonazarov (Chairman of the Union of Cinematographers), who was supported by the main opposition parties, won 30 per cent of the vote. The fairness of the election was contested by the opposition, but the complaints were not upheld by the electoral commission and Nabiyev assumed office in early January 1992. Within days the ban on the SPT was lifted for the second time and the party resumed its activities under its original name of the Communist Party of Tajikistan. Although following the presidential election there was a lull in public protest in Dushanbe, mass discontent soon began to surface in the autonomous region of Gorno-Badakhshan.[5] In December 1991 the supporters of the local autonomy movement, the *Lali Badakhshan* Movement, demonstrated in Khorog, the capital of Gorno-Badakhshan, demanding that the region's status be upgraded. The Badakhshani protest at the beginning of March 1992 moved to Dushanbe after the arrest, on March 6, of Maksud Ikramov, the mayor of Dushanbe and a fellow Badakhshani, on what were widely believed to be trumped-up charges of accepting bribes.[6] The protesters were joined by other opposition groups including the IRP, TDP and *Rastokhez*. The protesters demanded the release of Ikramov, and the resignation of Nabiyev and the Speaker of the Supreme Soviet, Safarali Kenzhaev (who allowed Ikramov to be arrested in the Supreme Soviet chamber), the dissolution of the Supreme Soviet, the holding of genuinely multi-party elections, and the adoption of a new constitution.[7]

After several weeks of demonstrations the protesters forced President Nabiyev to begin negotiations. In the middle of April an agreement was reached that included some concessions to the opposition. The agreement, however, was nullified by the hardline Supreme Soviet, which refused categorically to consider any opposition demands. The demonstrators responded by kidnapping 19 Supreme Soviet deputies, which forced the government back to the negotiating table. The release of the hostages led to another agreement granting some concessions to the opposition parties and the resignation of Safarali Kenzhaev.[8]

In April and May, Dushanbe was the scene of 50 days of non-stop demonstrations by the opposition. To counteract this, President Nabiyev appealed to his supporters from the Kulyab region to express their disapproval over the removal of Kenzhaev. They promptly streamed into Dushanbe and staged counter demonstrations. At the same time Nabiyev requested the Supreme Soviet to grant him emergency powers. Under the emergency regulations, on May 2, he created a National Guard, consisting primarily of young men from Kulyab, answerable directly to him. On May 3 Kenzhaev was restored to his former post in the Supreme Soviet. The extreme tension spilled over into violence. On May 10, some 12 protesters were shot dead as they marched towards the headquarters of the KGB in Dushanbe. Following the shooting, the head of Tajikistan's National Guard, Major-General Bakhrom Rakhmanov, defied Nabiyev and defected to the opposition. This forced the President to reach agreement with his opponents. On May 11, Nabiyev reluctantly agreed to the formation of a coalition government, termed the "Government of National Reconciliation", in which the opposition was given eight of the 24 ministerial posts, including the internal affairs and defence portfolios. The compromise, however, satisfied neither side, least of all Nabiyev and the leaders of the Leninabad region.[9] The agreement also stipulated the dismantling of the National Guard and the surrender of all weapons to the authorities. While some firearms were surrendered, the Kulyabis were able to take their weapons home after the National Guard was dissolved. To all intents and purposes the agreement left the communist power structure largely intact.

The legitimacy of the Government of National Reconciliation was rejected by the Leninabad and Kulyab regions right from the beginning, on the grounds that the Supreme Soviet had approved the government without being quorate — the representatives from these regions had simply refused to attend the parliament's session. On May 23 Leninabad's regional leadership announced that it would only obey those decrees and government orders that it decided were legal.[10] It also threatened to join the *oblast* with Uzbekistan. In the

Kulyab Nabiyev's supporters, reinforced by the armed members of the former National Guard, organized a formidable militia force, the Tajik Popular Front (TPF), under the leadership of Sangak Safarov. They strengthened their position locally by eliminating the small pockets of support for the coalition government. Bloody clashes continued throughout the summer. At the end of May the Kulyabis moved to eradicate Nabiyev's opponents in the neighbouring and strategically important region of Kurgan-Tyube, the stronghold of the Islamic democratic movement. The two provinces have been traditionally at odds with each other for a number of social, ethnic, historical as well as political reasons. Kurgan-Tyube is a region of disparate Tajik and Uzbek family groups. For a period after World War II it was a destination for forcibly resettled people, in many cases whole villages, which perhaps explains why this area has developed as a centre of Islamic activity. Moreover, in the 1980s the Kulyabi authorities had attempted to merge the two regions into one administrative unit dominated by Kulyab.

During the first half of 1992 the situation in Tajikistan became increasingly unstable as a result of the slow cantonization of the country with leaders of the various groups organizing their power bases in the various regions of the country and claiming the allegiance of local clans. The situation soon turned into civil war with the supporters of the coalition government accusing Nabiyev's supporters of trying to restore communism and the latter charging the democratic forces with wanting to instal Islamic fundamentalism. By the end of the summer the casualties were estimated at over 50,000 people dead and some 500,000 displaced as refugees. Most of the refugees were arriving in Dushanbe, with an estimated 65–75,000 crossing into Afghanistan.

Fighting broke out once again in Dushanbe between Nabiyev's supporters and a coalition of democratic and Islamic groups in August 1992. Opposition demonstrators in Dushanbe stormed the presidential palace at the end of August, but Nabiyev escaped and went into hiding. On Sept. 6, however, he was stopped by rebel forces on his way to Dushanbe airport and forced to sign a formal resignation. The Supreme Soviet took over presidential responsibilities and its chairman, Akbarsho Iskandarov, assumed the duties of acting president with the support of a coalition of secular and Islamic groups. Following the forced resignation of Nabiyev fighting intensified and at the end of October 1992 his supporters from the Kulyab region attempted a *coup* against Iskandarov and the coalition government, with the aim of reinstating Nabiyev and the former communist government. They seized key government buildings in Dushanbe and announced that Nabiyev's government had been restored. The *coup* was led by Safarali Kenzhaev, the former chairman of the Supreme Soviet, whose policies had sparked opposition protests earlier in the year and who had been forced to resign in March. Following several days of bloody street battles the capital was retaken by troops loyal to the coalition government.[11] Although the pro-Nabiyev forces were ejected from Dushanbe they blockaded the city for over six weeks. Acting president Akbarsho Iskandrov and the coalition government found themselves under increasing pressure as the economic and social repercussions of the blockade and international pressure to find a solution to the civil war began to mount. Russia, Kazakhstan, Kyrgyzstan and Uzbekistan, apparently convinced that a pro-Islamic government in Tajikistan represented a threat to their own internal stability, issued on Sept. 5 a thinly veiled threat to the coalition government in Dushanbe. It urged the Tajik government to protect the inviolability of its borders with Afghanistan and said that the signatories retained the right to take "all necessary measures" to ensure compliance if the Tajik government could not or would not take the necessary steps to protect the border itself.[12]

On Nov. 10 Iskandrov and the government resigned in order to allow the Supreme Soviet to choose a new chairman and government at its next meeting. A session of the Supreme Soviet which met on Nov. 16 in Khojand in the Leninabad province ended in chaos with delegates unable to agree on who should chair the meeting and who should be allowed to be present at the session. Abdulmalik Abdullodzhanov, the acting prime minister, walked out of the session hall, together with the members of government. The following day the deputies again failed to agree on the agenda. In an attempt to break the deadlock Iskandrov convened a meeting of parliamentary deputies, representatives of various ethnic and political groups and officers from Russian Border Troop detachments stationed in Tajikistan. During the meeting he suggested that the Supreme Soviet introduce martial law and called for a two-year ban on all mass meetings and strikes and the setting-up of a Tajik army. He also issued an appeal to other CIS states to send peacekeeping forces to Tajikistan. Iskandarov's proposals were rejected and when the Supreme Soviet convened on the third day (Nov. 18) it voted to accept his and the government's resignation. It also dismissed the entire presidium of the Supreme Soviet. The deputies voted to abolished the post of President of the Republic and elected Imamali Rakhmanov, the chairman of the Kulyab executive committee (who until recently ran a state collective farm near Kulyab), as the new chairman of the Supreme Soviet. Crucial in Rakhmanov's election was the support he received from the Tajik Popular Front and Sangak Safarov. On Dec. 2 the Kulyabi group with support from Leninabad deputies secured the administrative merger of the Kulyab and Kurgan-Tyube regions into one Halton province.

Renewed fighting again broke out in several parts of the country. The town of Yavan was seized by troops opposed to Iskandarov and the Kulyab forces recaptured mountain ranges near the town of Nurek, site of a large power station guarded by Russian troops. The Kulyab military formations next marched on Dushanbe which they captured in early December. A new government approved by the communist-dominated Tajik Supreme Soviet on Dec. 2, 1992, consisted mostly of communists from the Kulyab region. Most opposition figures either went underground or fled abroad, many to Afghanistan, whose government remained sympathetic and supportive to the democratic-Islamic opposition throughout the civil war in Tajikistan. The opposition became increasingly dependent on Afghanistan and Afghan *mujehadin* groups, some of whom established training camps for their "brothers from Tajikistan". The Tajik forces loyal to the coalition government regrouped in Afghanistan and began striking across the frontier into southern Tajikistan.

As the regime consolidated its position it became increasingly repressive and intransigent, refusing to negotiate with the opposition. In March 1993 Tajikistan's State Prosecutor applied to the country's Supreme Court to ban the four groups that constituted the anti-communist coalition: the Democratic Party of Tajikistan, the Islamic Renaissance Party, *Rastokhez*, and the *Lali Badakhshan* Movement, on the grounds that they violated their own charters and engaged in terrorist activities. In order to emasculate what remained of the opposition inside Tajikistan the regime embarked on a wholesale campaign of coercion. On Feb. 5, 1993, several members of the opposition were arrested in Dushanbe on charges of causing the civil war in 1992. Among them was Mirbobo Mirrakhimov, who headed Tajikistan's State Radio and TV under the coalition government, several of his colleagues from the TV administration, the deputy chief of police of Dushanbe and two leaders of the Islamic Renaissance Party.[13] The regime also laid criminal charges against the popular leader of the Muslim community in Tajikistan, Kazi Ali Akhbar Turadzhonzoda, for his support of the anti-communist opposition. On Feb. 12, the pro-regime official

Muslim religious establishment replaced him by Fatjhullo Sharifov, *imam-khatib* of a Friday mosque in the Gissar Valley, a stronghold of pro-regime forces. As the regime consolidated its position, the persecution of anti-communist personalities increased. On Apr. 14, Davlat Khodonazarov, the unsuccessful candidate of the democratic opposition in the November 1991 presidential elections, was arrested and charged with attempting to overthrow the constitutional order and inciting civil war. The charges were especially ironic since he had repeatedly tried to reconcile the warring factions during the fighting during the second half of 1992.[14]

Resistance to the communist government in Dushanbe continued, despite the regime's claims that its forces had taken control of several strongholds of the pro-Islamic opposition. At the end of February there were major clashes in the Ramit Gorge, some 50 kilometres east of Dushanbe. The level of fighting decreased only after the arrival, in March, of Commonwealth of Independent States (CIS) peacekeeping contingents from Kyrgyzstan, Russia, Kazakhstan and Uzbekistan.[15] Government troops finally captured the Ramit Gorge in the middle of March.

In April 1993, despite an amnesty issued by the Tajik Supreme Soviet on March 12, granting exemption from criminal prosecution to persons who had illegally crossed Tajikistan's borders before Dec. 31, 1992, between 75,000–90,000 Tajik refugees remained in Afghanistan.

In parliamentary by-elections held on June 13, 1993, at the district level, to replace legislators who had been killed or who had fled the country during the civil war, no opposition groups were allowed to nominate their candidates. The name of only one candidate nominated by the Communist Party appeared on the ballot. Following the by-elections the Supreme Court on June 21 banned the four principal opposition parties: the Democratic Party of Tajikistan, the Islamic Renaissance Party, *Rastokhez* and the *Lali Badakhshan* Movement, and ordered their assets to be confiscated.

On June 23 the Tajik parliament met in Dushanbe for the first time for over a year and adopted several resolutions aimed at strengthening the pro-communist forces. It decided that all decrees issued by Akbarsho Iskandarov were illegal, and removed immunity from two opposition deputies, Kazi Ali Akhbar Turadzhonzoda (former Chief Mufti of Tajikistan) and Takhir Abdujobar (leader of the Rastokhez Movemet), both in exile. It also decided to indict them on criminal charges for "guiding the terrorism and civil war in Tajikistan".[16]

During the latter part of 1993 the government allowed for the creation of three political parties which in essence are an extension of the ruling Communist Party of Tajikistan. The People's Party of Tajikistan is headed by the first deputy chairman of the Tajik Supreme Soviet, itself an unreformed communist establishment. The Party of Economic Freedom, which claims to represent the interests of northern Tajikistan, is led by the former prime minister, Abdulmalik Abdullodzhanov. The People's Democratic Party is headed by Abdujalil Homidov, the leader of the Leninabad region.

In August 1993 the Russian Federation became directly involved in the search for a peaceful solution to the on-going conflict. Russian Foreign Minister Andrei Kozyrev issued an appeal for negotiations between the government in Dushanbe and opposition forces who had become increasingly successful in launching military raids across the border from Afghanistan. Although Kozyrev's appeal was rejected by the Tajik government, the leader of the Islamic Renaissance Party who had fled to Afghanistan, agreed to begin negotiations.

A delegation of the Tajik Supreme Soviet met on Dec. 2, 1993, the Co-ordinating Centre of Tajik Democratic Forces in Moscow comprising members of the Tajik opposition in exile in the Russian capital. The talks, which continued till April 14, 1994, resulted in an agreement on the agenda for further negotiations. The agenda included cessation of fighting, repatriation of Tajik refugees in Afghanistan and the participation of all Tajiks regardless of political persuasion in the constitutional process in Tajikistan.

Some progress towards a peaceful resolution of the conflict was made during the second round of talks between the Tajik government and opposition which took place in Teheran between June 18–28, 1994. The negotiations were conducted under the auspices of the UN and were attended by mediators and observers from Russia, Iran and Pakistan. The aim of the negotiations was to agree on a cease-fire as a first step to further negotiations leading to the creation of a new constitutional system. The opposition demanded that as a precondition of a cease-fire the government should release political prisoners and grant an amnesty for exiled opposition leaders. The minister of labour, Shukhurdzhon Zukhurov, who headed the government's delegation, suggested that these conditions could be met, albeit not immediately. Interestingly Zukhurov argued that an obstacle to an immediate amnesty was the government's inability to guarantee the safety of those involved with the opposition.[17]

On Sept. 17, 1994, Tajik government forces took control of Tavildara region, east of Dushanbe. On the same day representatives of the government and opposition signed a temporary cease-fire agreement in Teheran during the third round of talks. The cease-fire is to be monitored by UN observers and last until Nov. 5. During that period a referendum on a new constitution and presidential elections are to be held.

The willingness to negotiate with the opposition reflects the growing divisions within the regime between the Kulyabi group and the dominant Khojand élite. While the Kulyabis, who gained access to power on the strength of their militias and subsequent control of the military, want to preserve the *status quo*, the Khojand élite appears more inclined to seek a new context for the preservation of its traditional claim to the leadership of Tajikistan.

A major problem facing the Tajik regime has been the exodus of Russians and other Slavs. Before the collapse of the Soviet Union and the civil war over 600,000 Russians lived in the republic, many occupying key positions in ministries and industry. In June 1994 Russian sources, citing official statistics, estimated that altogether only 120,000 Slavs remain in Tajikistan, including not more than 80,000 Russians. Approximately 2,000 people, overwhelmingly Russians and other Slavs, have been leaving Tajikistan each month. The exodus has continued despite numerous concessions to Russian-speakers made by the Tajik government, including dual citizenship. Apparently most Russians find the political situation too tense and economic prospects too bleak to stay.[18]

Behind the conflict in Tajikistan are many forces in what is an extremely complex but ultimately discernible struggle for power. On the one hand are those associated with new political ideas, including democracy, nationalism and Islam, long repressed by hardline communist rule, while on the other are those who prefer the system as it was. To this one should add the struggle between regions that have long benefited from communist rule and those that have not. The break-up of the Soviet Union has not "caused" the war in Tajikistan; rather the Soviet system fostered the corruption and instituted the repression of national sentiments, regional loyalties and religious beliefs, a combination that finally exploded into violence of the civil war. All groups in the conflict see the break-up as a chance to avenge the repression or to seize what, in their eyes, has long been denied them.[19]

Directory of Parties

Communist Party of Tajikistan (CPT)

Foundation. 1924.

Leadership. Rakhmon Nabiyev; Kakhkhor Makhkamov.

Membership. 80,000 (claimed in December 1993).

History. Ruling party since 1924. Although nominally an independent party it was in fact an extension of the Communist Party of the Soviet Union and of Soviet policies. One of the most conservative parties in Central Asia, the CPT managed to survive virtually intact despite the policies of *glasnost* and *perestroika*. The Communist Party of Tajikistan supported the Moscow August 1991 *coup*, but following the failure of the *coup* it was renamed the Socialist Party of Tajikistan in early September and declared itself a new organization. In response to mass protests its activities were banned and assets nationalized by presidential decree on Sept. 22. The following day, however, the communist-controlled Tajik Supreme Soviet rescinded the prohibition. As a result of popular protests the party was banned again in October 1991. After the election of Rakhmon Nabiyev to the presidency the ban was lifted in January 1992 and the original name was reinstated. In 1994 the party officially celebrated the seventieth anniversary of its foundation.

Islamic Renaissance Party (IRP)

Foundation. June 1990.

Leadership. Mullah Mukhamadsharif Himmatzoda (leader) Davlat Usmon (dep. leader).

Membership. 10,000

History. The party was originally a branch of the all-Union Islamic Renaissance Party and was formed at the same time as the union-wide party. The IRP has frequently been labelled "fundamentalist" by other groups in and outside Tajikistan, although its leaders have persistently denied accusations that its aims include the formation of an Islamic state based on *Sharia* Law. It was refused permission to hold its founding congress in Dushanbe in October 1990 and was subsequently proscribed by the Presidium of Tajikistan's Supreme Soviet. It took an active part in organizing the mass protests that followed the August 1991 Moscow *coup* which forced the resignation of President Kakhar Makkhamov and led to the suspension of the Communist Party of Tajikistan. The party was legalized on Oct. 2, 1991. It participated in the Government of National Reconciliation (May 11 – Nov. 10, 1992).

On June 21, 1993, the party was banned by the Supreme Court of Tajikistan and its assets confiscated. The court found it guilty of violating its own charter by forming military formations, causing the civil war, and killing or taking hostages. At the beginning of 1993 the party's leadership fled to Afghanistan from where it has been operating since. In August 1993 Mukhamadsharif Himmatzoda said in Kabul that he is prepared to negotiate with the Tajik government.

Programme. The return of spiritual values to politics and society, elimination of official atheism, immorality and corruption.

Lali Badakhshan Movement (*Badakhshan Ruby*)

Foundation. Late 1980s.

History. *Lali Badakhshan* was formed in the Gorno-Badakhshon autonomous *oblast*, in the remote mountainous area of the eastern region of Tajikistan as an autonomous movement of the Pamiri people. The area, acquired by the Russian Empire only in 19th century, has a long history of disputed sovereignty between Russia and Afghanistan with which it shares common border to the west. The Pamiris, who adhere to the Isma'ili sect of Shia Islam, insist that they are not really Tajiks but a separate nationality. The Movement supported the democratic opposition to the communist establishment in Dushanbe. After the collapse of the Government of National Reconciliation and the reassertion of communist power *Lali Badakhshan* was banned by the Supreme Court of Tajikistan and its assets confiscated on June 21, 1993. The court found it guilty of violating its own charter by forming military formations, causing the civil war, and killing or taking hostages.

Party of Economic Freedom

History. Formed in November 1993, the party claims to represent the interests of northern Tajikistan. Its leader, Abdulmalik Abdullodzhanov, is a former prime minister closely associated with the current regime in Dushanbe.

People's Democratic Party
Hizb-i Khalq-i Demokrati

Address. 7355700 Khojand, Dzerzhinskaya 45.

Foundation. December 1993.

Leadership. Abdujalil Homidov.

History. Headed by Abdujalil Homidov, the leader of the Leninabad region, the party claims to represent northern economic interests. Leninabad has been traditionally the power base of Tajikistan communist regime. Formed after the June 1993 ban on opposition parties, the foundation of this party was something of a window dressing exercise by the communist government in order to give the impression that Tajikistan has a multi-party system.

People's Party of Tajikistan

Foundation. August 1993.

Leadership. Abdulmadjid Dostiev (ch.)

History. Formed after the June 1993 ban on opposition parties, the foundation of this party was something of a window dressing exercise by the communist government in order to give the impression that Tajikistan has a multi-party system. The People's Party is led by the first deputy chairman of the Tajik Supreme Soviet, itself an unreformed communist establishment.

Programme. The party aim is to unite all forces in favour of a secular democratic state and the transition to a market economy.

Affiliation. Pro-communist.

Rastokhez (Rebirth) Patriotic Movement (RPM)

Foundation. August 1990.

Leadership. Takhir Abdujaborov, Khalifabobo Khamidov, Holizade Abdulkadyrov, and Khamidullo Khabibullaev.

History. The *Rastokhez* movement which grew out of the nationalist awakening brought on by *glasnost*, was established early in 1990 as a nationalist-religious group with particularly strong support among intellectuals in Dushanbe. Its members were prominent in the 1990 February demonstrations that served as a focal point of expression of opposition to communist rule in Tajikistan. The demonstrations were ruthlessly suppressed by the authorities. As a result of its participation in the February events, *Rastokhez* was refused registration and thus was unable to put forward candidates in the March 1990 elections to the Supreme Soviet. Nevertheless, it continued to attract popular support. The Movement's first official congress took place in January 1991. *Rastokhez* was registered in June 1991. It took an active part in organizing the mass protests that followed the August 1991 Moscow *coup* which forced the resignation of President Kakhar Makkhamov and led to the suspension of the Communist Party of Tajikistan. It participated in the Government of National Reconciliation (May 11 – Nov. 10, 1992).

On June 21, 1994, the Movement was banned by the Supreme Court of Tajikistan and its assets were confiscated. The court found it guilty of violating its own charter by forming military formations, causing the civil war, and killing or taking hostages.

Programme. Revival of Tajik culture and traditions suppressed during communist rule. Fundamental political and economic reforms.

Affiliation. Nationalist-religious party favoured by intellectuals.

Tajik Democratic Party (TDP)

Foundation. August 1990.

Leadership. Shodman Yusupov. (First Secretary of Central Committee), Maksud Ikramov, Davlat Koudonazarov.

Membership. 15,000 (1991) — mostly academics and intelligentsia, as well as a large number of former communists.

History. The party, which is modelled on the Russian Democratic Movement, was involved in the 1990 February demonstrations which resulted in a bloody government crackdown against the emerging opposition to communist rule in Tajikistan. As a result of its participation in the February events it was refused registration and thus was unable to put forward candidates in the March 1990 elections to the Supreme Soviet. Nevertheless, it continued to attract popular support. It was officially registered in June 1991. The

TDP took an active part in organizing the mass protests that followed the August 1991 Moscow *coup* which forced the resignation of President Kakhar Makkhamov and led to the suspension of the Communist Party of Tajikistan. It participated in the Government of National Reconciliation (May 11 – Nov. 10, 1992).

On June 21, 1993, the party was banned by the Supreme Court of Tajikistan and its assets were confiscated. The court found it guilty of violating its own charter by forming military formations, causing the civil war, and killing or taking hostages.

Programme. The creation of a democratic, multi-party, secular state structure, and free-market based Western oriented economy.

Affiliation. Pro-Western, secular nationalist.

Notes
1 According to the 1989 census the ethnic composition of Tajikistan was as follows: Tajiks 62.3 per cent, Uzbeks 23.5 per cent, Russians 7.6 per cent, Tatars 1.4 per cent, Kyrgyz 1.1 per cent, Ukrainians 0.7 per cent, Germans 0.6 per cent, Turkmen 0.3 per cent, Koreans 0.2 per cent, Others 2.30 per cent. More recent estimates suggest the following figures: Tajik 64.9 per cent, Uzbek 25 per cent, Russian 3.5 per cent (declining because of emigration), others 6.6 per cent.
2 According to the 1989 census.
3 Bess Brown, "Whither Tajikistan?". *RFE/RL Research Report.* vol. 1, no. 24 (June 1992). p. 1.
4 The official name — Republic of Tajikistan — was adopted on Aug. 31, 1991.
5 This autonomous *oblast* in the remote mountainous area of eastern Tajikistan is inhabited by the Pamiris, who adhere to the Isma'ili sect of Shia Islam. Badakhshanis insist that they are not really Tajiks but a separate nationality. The region has been a centre for the *Lali Badakhshan* Movement, demanding greater autonomy for Gorno-Badakhshan and its eventual independence.
6 Maksud Ikramov in September 1991 refused to enforce the state of emergency declared by the Tajik Supreme Soviet and ordered the removal of the giant statue of Lenin from the centre of the capital. His arrest was seen as belated revenge by the communists, offended at the removal of the statue.
7 Bess Brown, "Whither Tajikistan?". *op. cit.* p. 3.
8 *Human Rights and Democratization in the Newly Independent States of the Former Soviet Union*, Compiled by the Staff of the Commission on Security and Co-operation in Europe, Washington, DC. January 1993. p. 225.
9 Keith Martin, "Tajikistan: Civil War without end?". *RFE/RL Research Report.* vol. 2, no. 33 (August 1993). p. 20.
10 Bess Brown, "Whither Tajikistan?. *op. cit.* p. 4.
11 *Human Rights and Democratization in the Newly Independent State of the Former Soviet Union. op. cit.* p. 226.
12 Keith Martin, "Tajikistan: Civil War without end?". *op. cit.* p. 22.
13 *RFE/RL News Briefs*, Vol. 2, no. 8, 1993. p. 9.
14 *RFE/RL News Briefs*, Vol. 2, no. 8, 1993. p. 9.
15 *RFE/RL News Briefs*, Vol. 2, no. 17, 1993. p. 8.
16 The CIS peacekeeping contingents from Russia, Kyrgyzstan, Kazakhstan and Uzbekistan were despatched to Tajikistan in accordance with an agreement concluded at the January summit of CIS heads of state.
17 *RFE/RL News Briefs*, Vol. 2, no. 28, 1993. p. 6.
18 *RFE/RL News Briefs*, Vol. 3, no. 28, 1994. p. 6.
19 *RFE/RL News Briefs*, Vol. 3, no. 26, 1994. p. 7.
20 *Human Rights and Democratization in the Newly Independent States of the Former Soviet Union. op. cit.* p. 231–2.

TURKMENISTAN

Bogdan Szajkowski

Bolshevik power was first extended to Turkmenistan in April 1918 when the Turkestan Autonomous Soviet Socialist Republic was declared in the area. The republic, however, was short-lived. In July nationalists, supported by British forces, overthrew the Bolshevik administration and protected by a British garrison established their own government which lasted until 1920. After the British withdrew, the Red Army under the command of a Russified Kyrgyz, General Frunze, took control of the area. On Oct. 27, 1924, the Soviet regime created the Turkmen Soviet Socialist Republic. In 1925 it entered the Soviet Union as a constituent republic of the USSR.

The political, social and economic development of post-Soviet Turkmenistan is closely linked with the personality of Saparmurad Niyazov,[1] formerly the First Secretary of the former Communist Party of Turkmenistan and the chairman of the republic's Supreme Soviet (since Jan. 7, 1990). On Oct. 27, 1990, he was elected, by direct ballot, as President of Turkmenistan. Niyazov was unopposed in the election and received 98.3 per cent of the votes cast. He is the only leader of any of the Central Asian republics to have remained in office throughout the Gorbachev *perestroika* period and the disintegration of the USSR.

Turkmenistan declared sovereignty within the Soviet Union on Aug. 22, 1990. In a nationwide referendum on the independence of Turkmenistan (and the policies pursued by Saparmurad Niyazov) in October 1991, according to official results 94.1 per cent of the country's electorate voted in favour for secession. Turkmenistan was thus the only republic of the former Soviet Union in which the people voted on independence before a formal declaration was made.[2] On Oct. 27, 1991, Turkmenistan declared independence from the Union of Soviet Socialist Republics and changed its name from the Turkmen Soviet Socialist Republic to the Republic of Turkmenistan.

On May 18, 1992, the parliament (at that time still called the Supreme Soviet) unanimously adopted a new constitution. The document abolished the post of vice-president and allowed for strong presidential rule. It states that "Turkmenistan is a democratic, law-based and secular state, in which the administration of government is exercised in the form of a presidential republic". The President is both the head of state and the head of government whose members he appoints, and Supreme Commander of the Armed Forces. It empowers the President to issue laws, except those altering the constitution or criminal code, and to appoint judges and the heads of local administrations. The President also decides what legislation the *Majlis* (parliament) will consider.

The constitution establishes the separation of powers — "The state is based on the principle of the separation of powers — legislative, executive and judicial, which operate independently, checking and balancing one another". It guarantees freedom of religion and the separation of church and state, the right to privacy, freedom of movement, the right of all citizens to use their native language and even equal rights between men and women. The constitution shows somewhat scanty regards for individual rights and liberties — some 30 articles and statutes, including those envisaging the creation of Constitutional Court and concerning the freedom of the press, were removed from the document before it was adopted. Article 27 guarantees "freedom of meetings, rallies and demonstrations", however, "within the framework provided by the current legislation". According to President Niyazov, "These freedoms are all observed at present, although during the transitional stage the state must regulate the functioning of these concepts in the interest of society as a whole. . . . We did not smash the former power structure all at once, which could have created a power vacuum and led to disturbances. We chose the path of steady, gradual transformation. . . . Moreover, our government has resolutely suppressed attempts to pursue destructive notions on the crest of the wave of pseudo-reform and *glasnost*."[3]

The constitution also provides for the new legislative and representative structure of the republic. According to it the new legislature, which replaced the Supreme Soviet, the unicameral *Majlis* (Assembly), consists of 50 deputies elected by district constituencies for a five-year term. In practice the *Majlis* is essentially a rubber stamp for the President: votes are unanimous, as during the communist days.

The constitution creates a new "highest representative organ of popular power", the *Khalk Maslakhaty* (People's Council). It is composed of the President, the deputies to the *Majlis*, the "people's representatives" (60 separately elected officials) one elected from each electoral district, Cabinet ministers, the chairs of the Supreme Court and the Supreme Economic Court, the Procurator General and the heads of local administration. The members of the People's Council serve a five-year term, without compensation. The *Khalk Maslakhaty* meets infrequently (as rarely as once a year) on the initiative of the President, the *Majlis*, or when called by one-third of the Council's members. The Council possess considerable power: it advises on constitutional issues, forms recommendations on economic, social and political issues, and can declare war and ratify treaties. According to official explanations, the People's Council is a traditional Turkmen institution of a supervisory nature. It apparently harks back to the tribal assemblies of Turkmenistan's past. In reality, the body is little more than a rubber stamp for the president. Its exact role *vis-à-vis* the *Majlis* and the President is unclear in terms of constitutional formulations. A report published by the Commission on Security and Co-operation in Europe of the Conference on Security and Co-operation in Europe (CSCE) states that "opposition leaders with whom the Commission met expressed doubts and apprehension about both the People's Council . . . since the People's Council has powers greater than the *Majlis*, they fear it will only fortify Niyazov's power".[4]

The new constitution also establishes a Council of Elders, allegedly a regeneration of a traditional governing body dating back to the days before Russian colonization. At that time, each region elected an elder, with whom the people of the region consulted on local matters, and who represented them in a larger, nationwide council. The CSCE report quoted earlier states that opposition leaders "claimed that the rebirth of the Council of Elders was a particularly cynical way for Niyazov to co-op Turkmen national ideas so cherished by the opposition. In the old days, opposition leaders explained, foreign visitors often commented on the fair and even democratic system (relative to that time) that existed among the Turkmen nomads with their Council of Elders, one elected from each area. Now, it is felt, Niyazov is exploiting the idea; the members of the current Council of Elders are chosen by Niyazov and are virtually all former Communist Party *apparatchiks*. Opposition groups managed to get three people on the Council, but all were expelled when they attempted to speak".[5]

In the presidential elections held on June 21, 1992, in which Saparmurad Niyazov was the sole contender, he received 99.5 per cent of the popular vote. Niyazov was nominated a candidate under a resolution passed by the *Majlis* on May 18 granting it the exclusive right to nominate presidential candidates. The President never had to face an opponent in the election because apparently he ensured that there was no registered opposition party to nominate one.[6] Moreover, when at the end of May the opposition movement *Agzybirlik* nominated its leader, Nurberdy Nurmamedov, and appealed for the postponement of the elections so that its candidate could have the opportunity to make his case before the people, the request was refused. The manner in which the sole candidate was nominated and the outcome of the elections was more typical of the former USSR, and drew critical comments outside Turkmenistan about the lack of democratization of Turkmen political life. Some critical observers suggest that the President enjoys genuine popularity which could be explained by the absence of inter-ethnic friction and visible social tensions,[7] and Turkmen cultural traditions.[8] In a rare sign of dissent from within Turkmenistan's ruling élite in August 1992 the Foreign Minister, Abdy Kuliyev, resigned his post apparently in reaction to growing "personality cult" of Niyazov. The presidential elections were followed by elections to the *Khalk Maslakhaty* held between Nov. 24 to Dec. 7, 1992. With a turnout of 99.5 per cent, 50 regional representatives to the People's Council were elected — all supporters of the president.

In November 1993 several reports from within the ruling DPT and Turkmenistan's government suggested that Niyazov was to be made president-for-life. This reputedly caused the Foreign Minister, Khalykberdy Atayev, to resign in protest. He, however, continued to act as Foreign Minister. In December 1993 the *Majlis* voted to extend Niyazov's presidency until 2002 without re-election in order to allow the President to implement his 10-year programme of economic reforms. This appears to be rather unsophisticated way of circumventing the constitution which clearly stipulates that the president of the republic is directly elected by universal adult suffrage for a five-year term and may only hold office for a maximum of two terms. The parliament's decision was then put to a nationwide referendum on Jan. 15, 1994. The voters were asked to support the exemption of the president from having to seek re-election, which under the constitution should be held in 1997. According to official results, 99.99 per cent voted in favour. (Only 212 out of 1,959,637 registered voters voted against.) The regime explained the referendum and its results in terms that it ensured "political stability" and "the continued implementation of economic reforms".

The creation, registration and operation of public organizations, including political parties, is governed by several articles of the constitution and a Law on Public Organizations. Article 28 spells out the grounds on which political parties can be prohibited by the government, including those parties which "encroach on the health and morals of the people". The vague wording of the article causes concern that any opposition to the government could be seen as an encroachment on the "health and morals of the people", especially in view of the fact a law passed in October 1991 declared that demonstrations and hunger strikes in public places were illegal because, among other things, they were a threat to "public health". The constitution prohibits the creation of political parties on a national or religious basis.[9] The Law on Public Organizations, passed on Nov. 12, 1991, states that political parties and trade unions must be created by a founding congress in which at least

1,000 people must take part. Any organization wanting to operate publicly must have a charter stating its tasks and aims, conditions for membership, procedures for amending the charter, etc. The charter must be registered with the Ministry of Justice. The Ministry can, however, refuse registration if a charter is at variance with other provisions of the law. Thus, though the Law lays out many rights that will be available to any public organization or political party, including engaging in political work and publishing newspapers, the law also reserves for the government the right to refuse registration and hence to prevent any group from acting or publishing legally.[10]

Turkmenistan, despite official claims to the contrary, is essentially a one-party state. The ruling Democratic Party of Turkmenistan is the only one with any power in Turkmenistan and rules the country in much the same fashion as did the Communist Party. Political power remains in the hands of the Communist Party *nomenklatura*, and the overall direction of the political process under the control of President Saparmurad Niyazov. Not one opposition political group has been registered or officially exists. A handful of Western-oriented intellectuals in Ashgabat and Mary (formerly Merv) have attempted to form opposition parties, but they have been constantly harassed by the authorities, and, denied their own media or access to official organs they have little chance to explain their views. Two unregistered groups, the Democratic Party and the *Agzybirlik* movement, comprising dissident intellectuals with little support, are the only groups that openly voice opposition to President Niyazov and the ruling DTP. Consequently, their impact on the rest of the society is virtually non-existent. Opposition leaders have been routinely placed under house arrest or detained in prison. Baroness Margaretha of Ugglass, Chairman-in-Office of the CSCE and the Minister for Foreign Affairs of Sweden, wrote in a report on her visit to Turkmenistan in April 1993 that despite repeated reminders through different channels, the government of Turkmenistan was unwilling to accommodate her request for a meeting with opposition representatives. "In fact . . . personalities whom we had planned to meet during our stay were detained by the authorities and consequently prevented from seeing us."[11] Turkmen officials, including President Niyazov, argue that repression of what little opposition exists in the country is necessary in order to ensure political stability and thus make the country attractive to foreign investors.[12] Although some contested elections to various posts in the *Majlis* have taken place, the contests were essentially between personalities and not between political programmes.

Official pronouncements state that the Democratic Party of Turkmenistan aims to build an "independent and democratic law-governed state". In July 1992 while attending the Helsinki Summit, President Saparmurad Niyazov declared that Turkmenistan is "a rule-of-law, democratic state", and that the country was "building its power structure on the basis of the supremacy of the constitution, respect for law, commitment to democratic values and human rights". However, as the CSCE Commission report states: "Unfortunately, Turkmenistan's record on these matters is not good; it is considered by most observers to be the least 'reconstructed' of all the former Soviet republics. None of the republic's opposition groups is registered, nor are they allowed to have headquarters. (Commission staff met with opposition leaders in a private apartment in Ashgabat.) Demonstrations, hunger strikes and other forms of even non-violent protest have been virtually banned. . . . Opposition members are routinely arrested, fined and subjected to other, sometimes violent forms of harassment."[13]

Prohibiting democratization is made easier for Niyazov by the fact that the level of political awareness is extremely low in Turkmenistan, lower even than in the other Central

Asian republics. The old clan structure is particularly strong. Opposition groups claim that the people who control the government and the court system are all from Niyazov's tribe, and hence all from the same region. The President has also allowed a cult of personality to develop around him, similar to the personality cult of Stalin during the 1930s and 1940s. This cult is underlined by the independent economic policy *vis-à-vis* Russia and the neighbouring Central Asian states pursued by the Niyazov regime. Understandably the personality cult, in addition to cultural and historical traditions, also has socio-economic basis — the citizens of Turkmenistan since 1993 receive free gas, electricity and water supply. (The possibility of free bread in 1996 has also been mentioned.) With the continuous Western investment in the country and its substantial energy resources (natural gas and petroleum in particular), Niyazov's policies and personality cult are unlikely to change in the foreseeable future.

In various pronouncements President Niyazov has given his vision of the party system in Turkmenistan. In February 1992 he stated that he would like veteran communists to form a new communist party, the secretaries of the district party committees to set up a peasant party, and everyone else to joint the ruling Democratic Party of Turkmenistan.[14] At the August 1992 plenum of the DPT he repeated these political goals. While calling on the DPT to lead a "united, national social movement" that would help to achieve "the rebirth of an independent Turkmenistan" and "civil harmony", he noted that some of the prerequisites for the introduction of a multi-party system were in place.[15] On closer examination, however, it would appear that the sort of multi-party system envisaged by the president would resemble closely the "bloc" or "hegemonic" party system that prevailed for example in Poland, Czechoslovakia and Bulgaria during the communist rule. In other words, a mass, dominant party in power with smaller parties claiming to represent the interests of social groups such as the peasantry, serving as appendages. Such system of course dwarfs real opposition, prevents the formation of civil society and the development of democracy.

Directory of Parties

Agzybirlik (Unity of Voice) Movement

Foundation. September 1989. Banned Jan. 15, 1990.

Leadership. Shiraly Nurmyradov, Nurberdy Nurmamedov, Aman Goshayev, Hurdaiberi Khalliyev, Akmukhammed Velsaparov.

Membership. Small, consisting of predominantly urban intellectual élite.

History. Established in September 1989 as a "popular front" style organization concerned with the status of the Turkmen language, cultural discrimination against the native population of the country, ecological damage done to the republic by over-production of cotton and poor water supply, and economic issues. Initially the group did not present itself as a political opposition and was in fact officially registered in October 1989 with the Turkmen Academy of Science. Difficulties with the government began in January 1990 when *Agzybirlik* wanted, for the first time in Soviet history, to commemorate the battle of

Geok-Tepe, when the Turkmen were forcibly incorporated into the Russian Empire. The government opposed the move and the organization was banned on Jan. 15, 1990.[16] Despite the ban the movement held its founding congress in February 1990. Since then *Agzybirlik* has adopted more general opposition platform. The movement has been bitterly persecuted by the regime and its members routinely harassed, dismissed from jobs, imprisoned, kept under house-arrest and sometimes even shot. The movement's leader, and much respected writer, Shiraly Nurmyradov, was arrested in the autumn of 1990 and sentenced to seven years' imprisonment on trumped-up charges of defrauding a woman of money. After numerous protests from international human rights groups and democratic activists in Russia, he was released in April 1992 and sent into exile. He now lives in Moscow where in his words he is "without a motherland, without citizenship, without a residence permit and without a job". Although probably the most influential of the dissident groups, *Agzybirlik* is small in numbers. It comprises dissident urban intellectuals and opponents to President Saparmurad Niyazov's regime. It has little popular support and is not considered even by Russian observers as overtly nationalistic.

Programme. Advocates the creation multi-party democratic system.

Affiliation. Pro-Turkish orientation.

Publication. Dayanch ("Support" or "Foothold") news-magazine published jointly with the Democratic Party. The magazine is published in Moscow and smuggled into Turkmenistan.

Democratic Party

Foundation. December 1990.

Leadership. Durdymurat Hoja-Mukhammedov (ch.).

History. The Democratic Party emerged from *Agzybirlik* and it has similar aims, though it claims to be more concerned with the establishment of democracy in Turkmenistan. At the time of Turkmenistan's declaration of independence in October 1991, it gave it only qualified support arguing that independence at that time would only serve to strengthen the position of the totalitarian regime. Its founding congress in October 1991 had to be held in Moscow, as the Turkmen authorities refused permission for it to be held in Turkmenistan. Like *Agzybirlik* it is an unregistered group comprising small number of intellectuals opposed to the Niyazov's regime. It enjoys minimal popular support.

Programme. The construction of working democracy in Turkmenistan. Consolidation and uniting of all democratic parties in Central Asia, with the help from democratic groups in Russia.

Publication. Dayanch ("Support" or "Foothold") news-magazine published jointly with *Agzybirlik.* The magazine is published in Moscow and smuggled into Turkmenistan.

Democratic Party of Turkmenistan (DPT)

Address. 744014 Ashgabat 14, Gogolya 28.

Telephone. (3632) 25 12 12.

Foundation. Dec. 16, 1991.

Leadership. Saparmurad Niyazov (leader); Durdymurad Khodzamukhamedov (ch.).

Membership. 116,000 (1991).

History. The Democratic Party of Turkmenistan is a successor to the former Communist Party. The Communist Party of the Turkmen Soviet Socialist Republic was suspended immediately after the Moscow *coup* in August 1991. It was officially dissolved at its 25th Congress on Dec. 16, 1991. It changed its name into the Democratic Party in November 1991, distancing itself from its predecessor's "mistakes". It then became the ruling party.

Programme. According to its programmatic statements, the DPT serves as the "mother party", dominating all political activity in the republic and engendering a loyal political opposition.[17]

Affiliation. Ruling party.

Publication. Syyasy sokhbetdesh (Political Symposium), weekly organ, cir. 14,500.

Peasant Justice Party

The creation of the party was foreshadowed by President Saparmurad Niyazov in February 1992 when he stated that he would like veteran communists to form a new communist party, the secretaries of the district party committees to set up a peasant party, and everyone else to joint the ruling Democratic Party of Turkmenistan.[18] Although the registration of the Peasant Justice Party was reported by *Moskovskie novosti* on July 5, 1992, evidence from independent observers in Turkmenistan suggests that if such a party does exist it likely to have minuscule membership and a very weak organization. This observation appears to be supported by President Niyazov's pronouncement in December 1993 when he announced that a second party, the Peasant Justice Party, would eventually be granted official registration, as the first step towards a multi-party system.

Three other unofficial and unregistered political organizations exist in Turkmenistan. The **Movement for Political Reforms** is connected to the reform movement begun in Moscow. Like its Moscow counterpart, it contains many former Communist Party members, and the group appears willing to compromise more with the Niyazov regime in the hope of "reforming from within". The group remains small, though two of its members are deputies in the *Majlis*. The **Genesh** (Conference) is a coalition of several opposition groups, including *Agzybirlik*, the Democratic Party and the Movement for Political Reforms. Established in August 1991, the coalition does not have its own separate programme, but appears to be more of a loose forum to co-ordinate the opposition groups.[19] The **Islamic Renaissance Party** is the remnant of the all-Union Muslim party in the former USSR.

Notes

1 Saparmurad Atayevich Niyazov was born in 1940 in Ashgabat and grew up in an orphanage. In 1967 he graduated from the Leningrad Polytechnical Institute as an electrical engineer. He rose through the ranks of the Communist Party. In 1976 he finished the Senior Party School of the Communist Party of the Soviet Union. In 1980 he was elected First Secretary of the Ashgabat City Party Committee and in 1985 became the

First Secretary of the Turkmenistan Communist Party. In 1990 he was elected the Chairman of the Supreme Soviet of Turkmenistan and shortly after the first holder of the newly-created post of President.

2 Bess Brown, "Turkmenistan Asserts Itself". *RFE/RL Research Report*. vol. 1, no. 43 (October 1992). p. 17. Interestingly the percentage of the electorate who voted in favour of independence was only slightly fewer than the 95.7 per cent who voted in Gorbachev's referendum for the preservation of the Soviet Union in March 1991.

3 *Nezavisimaya Gazeta*, Oct. 20, 1992, quoted in Christopher J Panico. "Turkmenistan Unaffected by Winds of Democratic Change". *RFE/RL Research Report*. vol. 2, no. 4 (Jan. 22, 1993). p. 7.

4 *Human Rights and Democratization in the Newly Independent States of the Former Soviet Union*, compiled by the Staff of the Commission on Security and Co-operation in Europe, Washington, DC. January 1993. p. 181.

5 *Ibid.*

6 Bess Brown, *op. cit.* p. 28.

7 The ethnic composition is as follows: Turkmen 73.3 per cent, Russians 9.8 per cent, Uzbeks 9 per cent, Kazakhs 2.5 per cent, others including Tatars, Ukrainians, Azerbaijanis, Armenians and Baluchis 5.4 per cent.

8 Bess Brown, *op. cit.* pp. 28–29.

9 *Human Rights and Democratization in the Newly Independent States of the Former Soviet Union, op. cit.* p. 181.

10 *Ibid.* p. 182.

11 Conference of Security and Co-operation in Europe. "Report by the Chairman-in-Office on Her Visit to the Participating States of Central Asia". Ministry for Foreign Affairs, Stockholm, May 21, 1993.

12 *Human Rights and Democratization in the Newly Independent States of the Former Soviet Union, op. cit.* p. 181.

13 *Ibid.* pp. 183–184.

14 Christopher J Panico. *op. cit.* p. 6.

15 *Ibid.*

16 *Human Rights and Democratization in the Newly Independent States of the Former Soviet Union, op. cit.* p. 179.

17 Christopher J Panico. *op. cit.* p. 6.

18 *Ibid.*

19 *Human Rights and Democratization in the Newly Independent States of the Former Soviet Union, op. cit.* p. 179.

UKRAINE

Andrew Wilson

Political parties first began to appear in Ukraine in the 1890s, when Ukrainian territory was divided between the Habsburg and Romanov empires. Ukrainian parties were strongest in Austrian Galicia, where political conditions were relatively free and Ukrainian national consciousness was underpined by the local Uniate Church (to this day support for Ukrainian nationalism remains strongest in Galicia). The largest Galician party was the national-clerical National Democratic Party (NDP) formed in 1899. This had two smaller rivals: the secular Ukrainian Radical Party established in 1890 and the Marxist Ukrainian Social Democratic Party, which first appeared in 1899. In Russian Ukraine the first true political party was the Revolutionary Ukrainian Party set up in 1900. The party's supporters amongst the tiny Ukrainian intelligentsia were however divided between advocates of nationalism or socialism, Ukrainian independence or federation with Russia, and the RUP split into nationalist (the Ukrainian Peoples' Party) and socialist (two Social Democrat groups) groups in 1905.

All Ukrainian political parties in Russia declined in the post-1906 reaction, but re-emerged to lead the attempt to establish an independent Ukrainian state in 1917–21. Two parties dominated the three Ukrainian governments of the period, the Ukrainian Party of Socialist Revolutionaries, whose support base lay amongst peasants and the rural intelligentsia, and the Ukrainian Social-Democratic Workers' Party, the main party of leftist Ukrainian intellectuals. However, all Ukrainian governments of the period were precarious. Kiev fell to Soviet force of arms, and Galicia (where the NDP set up a West Ukrainian Peoples' Republic which united with the Kiev-based government in January 1919) to the Poles, resulting once again in the partition of Ukrainian lands. Most of central, southern and eastern Ukraine came under the control of the Ukrainian SSR established in December 1919, which in turn became a constituent part of the USSR following the Union Treaty of December 1922. By the mid-1920s the Communist Party of Ukraine (CPU) had eliminated all traces of opposition in the Ukrainian SSR, although it absorbed the remnants of two independent leftist parties, the *Borotbisti* and *Ukapisti*.

Western Ukrainian territory was divided between three states; Galicia and Volhynia went to Poland, Transcarpathia to Czechoslovakia, and northern Bukovyna (Chernivtsi) to Romania. In Galicia opposition to foreign rule was originally led by the main parliamentary party and successor to the NDP, the Ukrainian National Democratic Union, but after 1929 the UNDO increasingly lost ground to the more radical underground terrorist organization, the Organization of Ukrainian Nationalists (OUN). However, it was the Nazi–Soviet pact rather than the OUN that united western Ukrainian territories to the Ukrainian SSR in 1939–40. The OUN, which by now had a militant neo-fascist ideology, made its mark

577

after the German invasion of the USSR in 1941 when it helped form the Ukrainian Insurgent Army, whose military campaign to establish Ukrainian independence was only finally extinguished in the mid-1950s. The OUN, however, continued to exist in exile.

The CPU then maintained tight political control over Ukrainian life until 1989. Nevertheless underground opposition groups continued to be formed; most notably the Ukrainian Peasants' Workers' Union (1959–61), the Ukrainian National Front (c.1962–67), and the Ukrainian Helsinki Group (1976–c.1980). In the 1960s as much wider circle of intellectual opposition, the so-called *shestydesiatnyky* ("generation of the 1960s") movement was tolerated by Petro Shelest, first secretary of the CPU from 1963 to 1972. However, his successor, Volodymyr Shcherbytskyi, first secretary until September 1989, kept a much tighter reign, ensuring that Ukraine remained relatively quiet even during the early Gorbachev years.

Opposition groups only began to revive in 1988–89, after most Ukrainian political prisoners were released in 1987. Most were based in Galicia or in Kiev. The main group in this period was the Ukrainian Helsinki Union (UHU), the direct successor of the UHG. The UHU's leaders were mainly nationalists, but they continued the continued to operate in the civic traditions established by the *shestydesiatnyky* and the UHG. They placed as much emphasis on human rights and a rule of law as on Ukrainian national revival. The UHU therefore soon lost its more radical members, who forced a series of ultra-radical groups in 1989–90 (the UNP, DSU, UCDP, and UPDP — see below). They then formed the Ukrainian Inter-Party Assembly in mid-1990, which copied the tactics of the Citizens' Congress in Estonia, and refused to recognize the legitimacy of the Ukrainian SSR. More moderate nationalists, along with reformist communists and liberals formed the Ukrainian Popular Movement for Perestroika (*Rukh*) in September 1989, which for a time presented a formidable united opposition to the CPU. Its front organization, the Democratic Block, won 27 per cent of the seats in the March 1990 elections to the Ukrainian parliament.

After the elections the CPU could no longer hold back the process of party-formation, especially after Article 6 of the USSR constitution was abolished in spring 1990. Moderate nationalists formed the Republican and Democratic parties, while centrist groups established a Green Party, two Social Democratic parties and the Party of Democratic Revival of Ukraine, formed by members of the former Democratic Platform of the CPU. At this stage, as the CPU still continued to exist, no new left-wing or regional parties began to emerge.

From the winter of 1990–91 onwards, however, the CPU was under increasing strain as Moscow's authority began to collapse and elements in the CPU, led by the chairman of parliament, Leonid Kravchuk, began to try and forge an alliance with local centrists and nationalists, which was consummated unexpectedly quickly as a result of the collapse of the August 1991 coup attempt in Moscow. The CPU was now cut adrift and a majority were forced to throw in their lot with the nationalists. Ukrainian independence was proclaimed almost unanimously (346 votes to 1) on Aug. 24, and the CPU was formally dissolved on Aug. 30. With the left in dissaray, independence was confirmed by 90.3 per cent of the population in a referendum held on Dec. 1, 1991. On the same day, Leonid Kravchuk was elected as the first president of modern Ukraine, with 61.6 per cent of the vote, easily beating the candidates of *Rukh* (Viacheslav Chornovil, 23.3 per cent), the Republicans (Levko Lukianenko, 4.5 per cent), the PDRU (Vladimir Griniov, 4.2 per cent and Ihor Yukhnovskyi, 1.7 per cent), and the tiny Peoples' Party of Ukraine (Leopold Taburianskyi, 0.6 per cent).

Table 1: Party Representation in 1990 Parliament

Right:	Centre: 40	Left:
Rukh: 40	PDRU: 36	To August 1991 – CPU: 239
URP: 12	SPDU: 2	After August 1991 – PPU:c44
DemPU: 23	USDPU: 1	SocPU: 38
UCRP: 1	PPU: 1	
UCDP: 1		
DSU: 1		

The first free elections of the modern era were held in Ukraine in March 1990. Of those elected 122 (out of 450) joined the opposition group, the People's Council, while the Communist faction became known as the "group of 239". The rest were independents. After the banning of the CPU in 1991 party representation stabilized as set out in table 1.

Despite the nationalists' seemingly strong position in the wake of independence, a series of splits diminished their influence in 1992. *Rukh* divided in two after its third congress in spring 1992. Its more radical members formed the Congress of National Democratic Forces in August 1992, whilst the moderates remained with Chornovil. Several leading nationalist parties, such as the Republicans and Christian Democrats, also split in 1992. The centre, however, solidified, with the formation of the New Ukraine coalition in January 1992. The moderate left also revived, with the formation of the Socialist Party of Ukraine in October 1991, and the Peasants' Party in February 1992.

Most importantly, however, the nationalists' position was weakened by the rapidly deteriorating economy and by the recovery of party conservatives, once the shock of August 1991 began to wear off. As a result, a whole series of left-wing parties and regional groups were formed from the summer of 1992 onwards, particularly in eastern Ukraine and in the Crimea, both largely Russophone regions whose historical links with Ukraine are somewhat tenuous. In the Donbas, the main groups were the Civic Congress, and Labour and Liberal Parties; in the Crimea, the Party of Economic Renaissance and the separatist Republican Movement. In the Crimea a series of Crimean Tatar groups also emerged after the mass return of the Tatars began in 1989–90. Regional groups also appeared amongst the Rusyns of Transcarpathia and the Romanians of Chernivtsi.

Moreover, in 1993 the unity of the so-called "party of power" was undermined by a series of splits. The Communist Party of Ukraine was formally revived in June 1993, and rapidly recovered its position as the largest party in Ukraine. On the other hand, ex-Prime Minister Leonid Kuchma formed his own Interregional Block for Reforms in January 1994, which was pro-Russian but also pro-market.

These trends — the stagnation of the nationalist camp (and the consequent rise of the extreme right), the splits in the old "party of power", and the strong revival of leftist parties in eastern and southern Ukraine — were confirmed by the parliamentary elections of March – April 1994 and by the presidential elections three months later.

The left bloc won the largest number of seats in parliament (see Table 2), with at least 127 out of the 337 deputies elected (37.6 per cent of the vote), mainly from the east and south. Nationalist parties won a mere 54 or 55 seats (16 per cent) in western and central Ukraine, while centrist parties picked up 33 seats (9.8 per cent). The remaining deputies were formally non-party, although some were informal party supporters. The eastward shift in Ukraine's centre of political gravity was confirmed by the presidential elections, in which the more nationalist incumbent, Leonid Kravchuk, with 45.1 per cent of the vote, was defeated by Leonid Kuchmna, the former prime minister and leader of the Interregional Bloc for Reforms with 52.1 per cent. In contrast to Kravchuk, Kuchman preferred to see Ukraine's future in a "Eurasian alliance" with Russia. In a sharply polarized election, Kuchmna dominated the east and south, winning every *oblast* in the southern coastal region and to the east of the river Dnieper. Kravchuk won every *oblast* further to the west, bar one.

The other candidates in the first round of voting (when Kravchuk won 37.7 per cent of the vote and Kuchman 31.3 per cent) were the leader of the Socialist Party and the new chairman of parliament, Oleksandr Moroz (13 per cent), the pro-market liberal Volodymyr Lanovyi (9.3 per cent), the independent businessman Valerii Babych (2.4 per cent), the former chairman of parliament and leading nationalist, Ivan Pliushch (1.3 per cent), and the education minister, Petro Talanchuk (0.5 per cent).

Table 2: Results of 1994 Parliamentary Elections

Far Right: 11–12	*Mainstream Right: 43*	
CUN: 6–7	Rukh: 27	
UNA-UNSO: 3–4	URP: 9 (+ 1 supporter)	
UCRP: 2	DemPU: 6	
Centre: 33	*Party of Power: 77*	*Left: 127–145*
IBR: 20	LabPU: 6	CPU: 79
PDRU: 4		CPC: 5
New Wave: 3		PPU: 18–36
CDPU: 2		SocPU: 25
SDPU: 1		
LibPU: 1		
CGU: 2		

Only 338 constituencies out of 450 produced a result as the law required both a turnout of 50 per cent or more and at least a 50 per cent vote for the leading candidate for the results to be valid. Moreover, the large number of nominally non-party candidates made the results difficult to classify. The "party of power" means those directly associated with the Ukrainian government.

Table 3: Results of the Spring 1994 Elections to the Crimean Soviet (94 out of 98 elected)

'Russia' Block: 54
Medzhlis: 14
CPC: 3
PERC: 2
RusPC: 1

Directory of Parties

Christian Democratic Alliance of Romanians in Ukraine (CDARU)

Foundation. Nov. 26, 1991.

History. The CDARU represents the interests of the estimated 190,000 Romanians and Moldovans who live in the Chernivtsi region of western Ukraine (20 per cent of the local population). The Alliance's official programme calls for greater cultural and linguistic autonomy for the Romanian minority, but some of the CDARU's radicals have openly called for Chernivtsi to be rejoined to Romania, which ruled the region from 1918 to 1940. In October 1993 the local authorities attempted to suppress the main paper supported by the Alliance, *Plai Romanesc*, accusing it of fermenting separatist sentiment. One deputy elected in spring 1994, Ivan Popesku, is reportedly close to the CDARU.

Publication. Plai Romanesc.

Christian Democratic Party of Ukraine (CDPU)
Khrystiiansko-demokratychna partiia Ukrainy (KhDPU)

Foundation. June 20, 1992.

Address. 123217, Kiev, vul. Draizera, 11/85.

Telephone. 5467676.

Leadership. Viktor Zhurakivskyi.

Membership. 30,095 claimed January 1994.

History. The CDPU was formed as a result of a split in 1992 with the more nationalistic Ukrainian Christian Democratic Party, based in western Ukraine whose supporters are mainly Uniate catholics. The CDPU on the other hand represents Orthodox Christians in central and eastern Ukraine, a majority of whom are Russian-speakers. It stands for liberal reforms and the creation of a market economy. In spring 1994 it won two seats in the Ukrainian parliament, one in Transcarpathia and the other in Odesa.

Civic Congress of Ukraine
Grazhdanskii kongress Ukrainy

Address. 340000, Donetsk, a/s 3540.

Telephone. 0622 357464.

Foundation. June 1992.

Leadership. Aleksandr Bazeliuk and Valerii Meshcheriakov.

Membership. 2,100.

History. The Civic Congress grew out of several movements for regional autonomy that appeared in eastern Ukraine in the wake of Ukrainian independence in 1991, and was formally constituted at two congresses in June and October 1992. As such it paved the way for the strong revival of left-wing forces in the region in 1993–94, for whom it has provided intellectual leadership. The CCU stands for a federal Ukraine, the use of Russian as a parallel state language in eastern and southern Ukraine, and close economic and political ties with Russia. It is, however, not as firmly against market reforms as rival leftist groups in eastern Ukraine. Its main support is in Donetsk, Luhansk and Kharkiv. The Congress won a pair of seats in the spring 1994 elections.

Publication. Occasional *Grazhdanskii kongress.*

Communist Party of the Crimea (CPC)
Kommunisticheskaia partiia Kryma (KPK)

Address. 333017, Simferopol, ul. Budennogo, 24.

Telephone. 256051.

Foundation. June 18, 1993.

Leadership. Leonid Grach.

Membership. 30,000, September 1993.

History. The Communist Party did not stay banned in Crimea for long. Local organizations began to reform in late 1991, and combined into the Union of Communists of Crimea in June 1992. The Union was led by Leonid Grach, the last head of the local Communist Party before the August 1991 putsch. In June 1993 the Union formally renamed itself the CPC. The CPC is relatively unreconstructed, and stands for a revived USSR and state control of the economy. It is a constituent part of the Communist Party of Ukraine, and would like to become part of a revived CPSU. The CPC had close links with the Russian White House before it was stormed in October 1993, and with the Russian Communist Party. Grach came fourth in the January 1994 presidential elections in the Crimea, with 12.2 per cent of the vote. The party won four seats in the all-Ukrainian elections of March 1994, but only three in the simultaneous elections to the Crimean parliament. Despite close co-operation between the CPC and the "Russia" Block before the elections, Crimean president Meshkov did not grant the CPC the positions its leaders expected, and the party went into opposition in the Crimean parliament.

Publication. Weekly *Kommunist Kryma* (formerly *Nash golos*).

Communist Party of Ukraine (CPU)
Komunistychna partiia Ukrainy (KPU)

Address. 252024, Kiev, prov, Vynohradnyi, 1/11.

Telephone. 2934044.

Foundation. June 1993.

Leadership. Petro Symonenko.

Membership. 122,560 claimed January 1994 (true figure closer to 46,000).

History. The Communist Party of Ukraine was formally banned in August 1991, but a campaign for its revival began as early as the summer of 1992, culminating in two restoration congresses in Donetsk in March and June 1993. The party claims to be the "legal successor" to the old CPU, but avoided declaring the June congress the "29th" congress of the CPU, and has been unable to claim former CPU property. The party was officially registered in October 1993, the day after Yeltsin's troops bombarded the White House in Moscow. Unlike similar revivalist parties in Poland and Lithuania, the CPU remains aggressively anti-capitalist and anti-nationalist. It stands for the restoration of state control over the economy, and for some kind of confederative union between Ukraine and Russia. The CPU's populist nostalgia rapidly gained it support in economically troubled industrial areas of eastern Ukraine, especially in the Donbas (Petro Symonenko is the former second secretary of the CPU in Donetsk). The CPU emerged as the largest party in the Ukrainian parliament after the March–April 1994 elections with a total of 94 seats (nearly all in eastern and southern Ukraine), setting the stage for further sharp conflict between Ukrainian east and west.

Publication. Periodical *Kommunist*.

Congress of National Democratic Forces (CNDF)
Kongres natsionalno-demokratychnykh syl (KNDS)

Address. 252024, Kiev, vul Prorizna, 27.

Telephone. 2280772.

Foundation. Aug. 2 1992.

Leadership. Mykhailo Horyn.

History. The CNDF is an umbrella organization representing those Ukrainian parties and organizations of a national democratic orientation, including the URP, DPU, UCDP, UNCP and a variety of like-minded social organizations, including the Union of Ukrainian Students and the Ukrainian Language Society *Prosvita*. It stands somewhat to the right of *Rukh*, arguing for "the national character of Ukrainian statehood", and Ukrainianization of the state, schools, armed forces and public administration. It also stands for a unitary state system, and opposes concessions to ethnic minorities in eastern Ukraine, Crimea and Transcarpathia. The CNDF supports strong national defence and the retention of nuclear weapons in the face of Russian threats to Ukrainian security. The CNDF wants Ukraine to leave the CIS and lead an anti-Russian "Baltic–Black Sea Alliance". In the economic sphere, the CNDF supports the creation of a "society of property owners", but in the short-run favours a policy of national preference for Ukrainian enterprises, and opposes "wild privatization". In 1992–93 the CNDF was generally supportive of President Kravchuk (at considerable political cost to its member parties), but by 1994 the relation between the two was becoming more strained. The CNDF faction *Derzhavnist* (Statehood) has 25 members in the new parliament in 1994.

Congress of Ukrainian Nationalists (CUN)
Kongres Ukrainskykh natsionalistiv (KUN)

Address. Kiev, vul. Kreshchatyk, 21/111.

Telephone. 2292425.

Foundation. Oct. 17–18, 1992.

Leadership. Slava Stetsko.

History. CUN was established by the émigré Organization of Ukrainian Nationalists in 1992 as a means of attracting various small right-wing groups into its ranks. Many in the OUN leadership feared that the organization's name was still controversial, while others preferred to maintain a semi-underground existence. An umbrella organization was therefore seen as the best means for the OUN to return to active politics in Ukraine. CUN has therefore absorbed other rightist groups, such as Mariia Oliinyk's "United Ukraine" group in Donetsk, while indirectly supporting a variety of independents. CUN's programme commits the organization to support democratic nationalism and a strong nation-state independent in all respects from Russia. CUN is in favour of Ukraine's immediate departure from the CIS. Economically, CUN veers between the strongly pro-capitalist orientation of its émigré members, and a recognition of the need for state protection for the enfeebled Ukrainian economy.

CUN was officially registered in January 1993. Although Stetsko was prevented from standing in Stryi, Lviv, in the spring 1994 elections, CUN's association with the wartime OUN won it considerable support in nationalist western Ukraine, and it elected six or seven deputies to the new parliament.

Publication. Weekly paper *Shliakh peremohy*.

Democratic Movement of the Donbas (DMD)
Demokraticheskoe dvizheniia Donbassa (DDD)

Foundation. December 1990.

Leadership. Dmitrii Kornilov.

Membership. 2–3,000.

History. The DMD was formed in the largely Russian-speaking Donbas in December 1990 to campaign against the implementation of the 1989 Ukrainian Language Law (which made Ukrainian the official state language). The DMD opposed Ukrainian independence in the autumn 1991 referendum campaign, and calls for "an autonomous Donbas within a federalised Ukraine", local state status for the Russian language and dual citizenship between Russia and Ukraine. The DMD also has good links with the Russophile Independent Miners' Unions under Yurii Boldyrev. Because Ukrainian electoral law attempts to prevent overtly regional groups from standing for parliament, the DMD was instrumental in creating the broader Civic Congress of Ukraine in mid-1992, into which it then largely subsumed its efforts. However, the DMD still exists as a ginger group of Russophone intellectuals.

Publication. Occasional *Nash Donbass*.

Democratic Party of the Crimea (DPC)
Demokraticheskaia partiia Kryma (DPK)

Foundation. June 1993.

Leadership. Anatolii Filatov.

Membership. c.200.

History. A centrist party, based mainly in rural regions and amongst the Yalta intelligentsia, the DPC favours a policy of national reconciliation in Crimea, and has allied itself with moderate Crimean Tatar groups such as the OCNM (*see* below). The DPC favours Crimean autonomy, but believes the peninsula should remain part of the Ukrainian state.

Democratic Party of Ukraine (DPU)
Demokratychna partiia Ukrainy (DPU)

Address. 252006, Kiev, vul. Chervonoarmiiska, 93, Flat 14.

Telephone. 2685743.

Foundation. Dec. 15–16, 1990.

Leadership. Volodymyr Yavorivskyi.

Membership. 3,000 in December 1992.

History. The DPU is the main party of the nationalist Ukrainian intelligentsia, many of whom were the original founders of *Rukh*. It supports a civic, territorial conception of nationalism, although it favours a unitary state and opposes autonomy for Ukraine's ethnic minorities. Under the party's first leader, Yurii Badzio (1990–92), the party moved to the right, and forged a close alliance with the URP (*see* below). There was even talk of a formal merger between the two. However, Badzio was replaced by Volodymyr Yavorivskyi at the party's second congress in December 1992, who moved the party back into the political centre and away from merger with the URP. The DPU supports strong national defence, Ukrainian departure from the CIS, and a social market economy. The DPU had 23 deputies in the 1990–94 Ukrainian parliament, but poor organization meant that its representation collapsed to six in 1994.

Publication. Occasional periodical, *Demokrat*.

Green Party of Ukraine (GPU)
Partiia zelenykh Ukrainy (PZU)

Address. 242024, Kiev, vul. Liuteranska, 24.

Telephone. 2935236.

Foundation. September 1990.

Leadership. Vitalii Kononov.

Membership. 2,500.

History. Because of public reaction to the 1986 Chornobyl accident, the environmental association *Zelenyi svit* ("Green World") was one of the first opposition groups to emerge in the late 1980s. It held its first congress in October 1989, which decided to establish a separate party for explicitly political activity. The GPU, initially supported by elements within the CPU, first proposed a leftist programme of "ecosocialism", but some fell under the influence of more right-wing elements. Although the GPU is informally linked to the centrist New Ukraine group, it is a firm supporter of Ukrainian independence. Despite broad public support, the GPU has never been effectively organized, and was originally little more than a federation of like-minded local groups. Kononov, elected leader at the party's third congress in October 1992, has attempted to shake up the GPU's organization, but with little success. Despite significant but shallow public support, it was unable to elect any of its members to the 1994 parliament.

Publication. Weekly *Zelenyi svit.* (now suspended).

Interregional Bloc for Reforms (IBR)
Mizhrehionalnyi blok reformiv (MBR)

Foundation. Jan. 21, 1994.

Leadership. Leonid Kuchma and Vladimir Griniov.

Membership. Not fixed.

History. Kuchma, Ukrainian prime minister from October 1992 to September 1993, and former deputy chairman of parliament Griniov (both Russian-speakers) announced the formation of the IBR in December 1993. Its political base was the PDRU and New Ukraine movement, headed by Griniov, the Union of Ukrainian Industrialists and Managers, headed by Kuchma, and a variety of business and party structures in eastern and southern Ukraine, including the Crimea. The MBR's slogan is "Strength to the state, prosperity to the people, reason to power!", and its definition of its order of priorities is "the individual — the locality — the region — the country". According to Kuchma therefore, the IBR has three main planks to its programme; more power to the Ukrainian regions, market reforms and a strategic alliance between Ukraine and Russia. Despite quarrels between Kuchma and Griniov (Griniov is more in favour of a market economy), the IBR managed to elect 25 supporters in the 1994 elections, nearly all from the east-central regions of Kharkiv (Griniov's base), Dnipropetrovsk (Kuchma's home town), and Chernihiv.

Labour Congress of Ukraine (LCU)
Trudova kongres Ukrainy (TKU)

Address. 252055, Kiev, vul. V. Vasylevskoi, 27.

Telephone. 2961378.

Foundation. June 1993.

Leadership. Anatolii Matvienko.

Membership. No fixed membership.

History. The LCU was founded by leading members of the Ukrainian establishment as a left-leaning party of "constructive centrism" that might help to take some of the steam out of the left-wing revival in 1993. Matvienko is a former head of the Ukrainian *komsomol*, and head of the parliamentary committee on youth and sport. The LCU was supported by five other deputies, and reportedly has the backing of parliamentary chairman Ivan Pliushch, the Ukrainian Union of Industrialists and Managers, headed by Leonid Kuchma, and the official trade unions under Oleksandr Mril. The LCU was officially registered in September 1993. In the 1994 elections it kept a low profile, but indirectly supported many of the "party of power".

Labour Party of Ukraine (LabPU)
Partiia truda Ukrainy (PTU)

Address. 340016, Donetsk, a/c 3327.

Telephone. 0622 632630.

Foundation. December 1992.

Leadership. Viktor Landyk, Nikolai Azarov.

History. Commonly characterized as the party of "red directors" in the Donbas, the LabPU was indeed founded by the Interregional Association of Industrialists, the main lobby for east Ukrainian industry, in December 1992. The party had a strong position on the local councils of Donetsk and Luhansk, and long-standing links with the old official trade unions. In June 1993, after a damaging wave of strikes in the Donbas, President Kravchuk attempted to win the region's support by appointing the LabPU's two leaders, Valentyn Landyk and Efym Zviagilsky (the former mayor of Donetsk), as deputy prime ministers in Kiev (Azarov runs the party on their behalf while they are in Kiev), and in October 1993 Zviagilsky was promoted to the position of acting prime minister. The LabPU purports to be a centrist party, standing for "the equality of all forms of property", and "the union of state and market forms of regulation of the economy", but under the influence of Landyk and Zviagilsky the Ukrainian government moved sharply to the left from summer 1993 onwards, placing more emphasis on state regulation and "economic stabilization" and delaying measures to promote privatization and credit control. The party also supports closer links between Ukraine and the CIS, and a "system of several state languages in Ukraine". The party's three main leaders were all (re)elected as deputies in 1994, along with three others, but in the Donbas as a whole the party lost out to the more effective populist campaign of the Communist Party.

Liberal Democratic Party of Ukraine (LDPU)
Liberalno-demokratychna partiia Ukrainy (LDPU)

Address. Kiev, vul. Bratyslavska, 40, flat 110.

Telephone. 5197970.

Foundation. November 1990.

Leadership. Volodymyr Klymchuk.

Membership. Less than 100.

History. In 1990 centrist intellectuals founded both a Liberal Democratic Party and Liberal Democratic Union, although most members of the latter eventually joined the PDRU. Unlike Vladimir Zhirinovsky's misnamed equivalent in Russia, the LDPU supports genuinely centrist positions. It favours a managed transition to a market economy, greater stress on individual rights, a federalized Ukraine, and friendly relations with Russia. In the December 1991 presidential elections, the party supported the PDRU's Vladimir Griniov.

Publication. Occasional *Polslova.*

Liberal Party of Ukraine (LibPU)
Liberalna partiia Ukrainy (LibPU)

Address. 340055, Donetsk, vul. Artema, 74a.

Telephone. 0622 355787.

Foundation. June 1993.

Leadership. Ihor Markulov.

Membership. 40,000 claimed autumn 1993.

History. The LibPU was founded in Donetsk by maverick local businessman (and adviser to President Kravchuk until 1993), Ihor Markulov, in August 1991, although it did not hold a formal party congress until June 1993. The party is backed by ex-CPU and *komsomol* money, which has allowed it to adopt a high profile, with Markulov making a series of extravagant promises to finance personally the restructuring of both the national and local economies. Like the IBR, the LibPU stands for market reforms but also supports greater autonomy for the Ukrainian regions and economic union with Russia. In the Donbas Markulov has attempted to form an alliance of convenience with the local independent trade unions, and has promised to broker a programme of regenerative investment. However, his ostentatious personal style did not go down well in the 1994 elections, with the party only winning a single seat.

Publications. Periodicals *Liberalna hazeta* and *Vzgliad.*

Medzhlis (*see* OCNM below)

Milli Firka (National Party)

Foundation. August 1993.

Leadership. Ilmy Umerov.

Membership. Less than 100.

History. The Milli Firka is a radical Crimean Tatar group named after the party that attempted to establish an independent Crimean Tatar republic in 1917–18. It rejects all idea of compromise with the authorities in the Crimea or in Kiev, whom it describes as "occupying powers". The Milli Firka seeks to establish an ethnic Crimean Tatar republic in the Crimea, in which the Crimean Tatar language, culture and religion would predominate. The party also supports direct extra-parliamentary methods of struggle where necessary. To date, however, Umerov has accepted subordination to the much larger *Medzhlis*. Umerov became a Crimean deputy in March 1994.

National Fascist Party of Ukraine

Foundation. December 1993.

Leadership. Fedor Zaviriukha.

Membership. 100.

History. An avowedly nationalistic party based in Lviv, the National Fascist Party stands for the establishment of a "Greater Ukraine" within the borders of the medieval state of the Kievan Rus, that is including substantial neighbouring territories in Belarus, Russia and Poland.

National Movement of the Crimean Tatars (NMCT)
Natsionalnyi dvizheniia Krymskikh Tatar (NDKT)

Address. Simferopol, s. Chistenkoe, ul. Sovetskaia, 15.

Foundation. April 1987.

Leadership. Vashtii Adburaiimov.

History. The NMCT is the oldest Crimean Tatar organization, with roots going back to the protest movements of the 1960s. Nevertheless, its first formal meeting was in April 1987 when the vast majority of Crimean Tatars were still in exile in Central Asia. The NMCT is the most moderate of the three main Crimean Tatar organizations, favouring co-operation and dialogue with the Crimean authorities, and rejecting the claim by the *Medzhlis* and OCNM to Tatar sovereignty over the whole of the Crimea. The long-standing leader of the OCNM, Yurii Osmanov, was murdered in November 1993 and replaced by Vashtii Adburaiimov as leader at a special congress in December 1993. Adburaiimov formally allied the NMCT with Yurii Meshkov's "Russia" block for the spring 1994 elections, but the NMCT was soundly defeated in the special elections for the Crimean Tatars, winning only 5.5 per cent of the vote and no seats.

Publication. Areket.

New Ukraine
Nova Ukraina

Address. 252025, Kiev, vul. Velyka Zhytomyrska, 15.

Telephone. 2283014.

Foundation. June 1992.

Leadership. Vladimir Griniov.

History. The roots of New Ukraine lie in the campaign begun in September 1991 by the main centrist Ukrainian party, the PDRU (*see* below), to unite all centrist and pro-market forces in Ukraine. The result was the announcement of a "coalition of politicians and industrialists" in January 1992 that included the PDRU, the Social Democrats, some Greens, the LDPU and reform-minded managers, and declared itself in favour of "capitalism with a human face". Two New Ukraine stalwarts have briefly held the position of minister for economic reform since 1992, Volodymyr Lanovyi from March to July 1992, and Viktor Pynzenyk from October 1992 to April 1993. However, New Ukraine's push for market reforms has had little effect, despite the movement's 50–60 strong faction in the 1990–94 parliament. At New Ukraine's second congress in March 1993, the leading Russophile Vladimir Griniov replaced PDRU leader Volodymyr Filenko as chairman. Consequently, Griniov largely subsumed New Ukraine in the IBR.

New Wave
Nova khvylia

Foundation. Autumn 1993.

Leaders. Viktor Pynzenyk and Ihor Yukhnovskyi.

History. New Wave was founded by several leading centrist deputies in Lviv in autumn 1993 as a democratic and pro-market alternative to the rising tide of extrme nationalism in the region. The high profile of many of its leading members, including the former minister of economics in the national government, Viktor Pynzenyk, allowed the movement to elect four deputies in Lviv in spring 1994 (and win 10 per cent of the local vote), and prevent the nationalists making a clean sweep in Lviv.

Organization of the Crimean Tatar National Movement (OCNM)
Organizatsiia Krymskotatarskogo natsionalnogo dvizheniia (OKND)

Address. 333270, Simferopol, ul. Samokisha, 8.

Foundation. August 1991.

Leadership. Rejep Khairedinov.

Membership. 600–800.

History. The OCNM is the largest of the three main Crimean Tatar parties, whose roots go back to a founding meeting in May 1989 in Uzbekistan. Most mainstream Crimean Tatar activists are members of the OCNM, including Mustafa Cemiloglu and Refat Chubarov, head and deputy head of the Crimean Tatar parliament or *Medzhlis* elected in 1991 (the *Medzhlis* is a representative body, the OCNM its equivalent as a political party). The OCNM stands for "the restoration of national statehood" for the Crimean Tatars in their historic homeland, although the movement is avowedly secular and places heavy emphasis on liberal rights and a rule of law. Rejep Khairedinov was elected leader of the party at its third congress in January 1993. The *Medzhlis*/OCNM's position as the main Crimean Tatar political organization was confirmed in the March 1994 elections to the Crimean parliament, when the *Medzhlis* won 89.3 per cent of the Crimean Tatar vote and 14 out of 14 of the seats reserved for the Tatars.

Publications. (Through the *Medzhlis*) papers *Avdet, Kirim Sedasi*, and *K'yrym*.

Organization of Ukrainian Nationalists in Ukraine
Orhanizatsiia Ukrainskykh natsionalistiv v Ukraini (OUNvU)

Address. 290017, Lviv, vul. Aralska, 1, flat 6.

Telephone. 0322 750220.

Foundation. Jan. 30–31, 1993.

Leadership. Ivan Kandyba.

History. In early 1991 several leading OUN veterans and former political prisoners in Galicia formed a committee for the relegalization of the OUN. After they discovered that the émigré leadership of the OUN (in Ukraine, CUN) was reluctant to return to open political activity in Ukraine, the committee held a conference on its own initiative in Lviv in January 1993, which called on the three émigré factions of the OUN to unite and return to Ukraine. The émigré OUN disowned the initiative, leading to yet another split in the ranks of the Ukrainian far right, after the Lviv group proclaimed themselves "the OUN in Ukraine". However, "The OUN in Ukraine" was soundly defeated by CUN in the spring 1994 elections. Despite fielding 11 candidates in Lviv, it only managed to win 1 per cent of the vote, compared to CUN's 13.5 per cent.

Publication. Weekly *Neskorenna natsiia*.

Party of Civic Accord of Ukraine

Foundation. Dec. 25, 1993.

Leadership. Ihor Kozhevin.

Membership. 20,000.

History. The Party of Civic Accord is a centrist non-nationalist party that supports radical economic reforms, the abolition of the system of local councils in Ukraine, and its replacement by a federal system of local self-government.

Party of Democratic Rebirth of Ukraine (PDRU)
Partiia demokratychna vidrodzhennia Ukrainy (PDVU)

Address. 252024, Kiev, vul. Liuteranska, 11, Flat 3.

Telephone. 2283870.

Foundation. December 1990.

Leadership. Volodymyr Filenko.

Membership. 3,000.

History. The PDRU grew out of the Democratic Platform of the CPU, formed in the run-up to the 28th Congresses of the CPU and CPSU in 1990. After the relative triumph of party conservatives at both congresses, 28 Ukrainian deputies left the CPU on July 27, 1990, and formed an initiative group to create the PDRU (which eventually claimed the support of 36 deputies). In the economic sphere, the PDRU combines both a pro-market liberal element and a social-democratic wing from eastern Ukraine (several east Ukrainian branches defected to the SDPU in 1993), while in the political sphere the party favours decentralization, and the maintenance of healthy links with Russia and the CIS (most of its members are Russian-speaking), whilst opposing nationalist policies of Ukrainianisation. The PDRU was the main founder member of the centrist New Ukraine coalition. The party's drift towards the political centre in 1992–93 cost it support in eastern Ukraine, however. In 1994 it was almost wiped out, winning only four seats, three of which were in Zaporizhzhia. Filenko was defeated in Kharkiv. Its place has largely been taken by the IBR.

Party of the Economic Rebirth of Crimea (PERC)
Partiia ekonomicheskogo vozrozhdeniia Kryma (PEVK)

Address. Simferopol, vul. Ushynskoho, 2/46.

Telephone. 0652 290633.

Foundation. May 20, 1993.

Leadership. Vladimir Sheviov, Vladimir Egudin and Vitalii Fermanchuk.

Membership. 30,000.

History. PERC held its first conference on Nov. 1, 1992, and constituted as a political party at a congress in Simferopol in May 1993. It is backed by local import/export and tourism business interests, and had a strong presence in the Crimean soviet in 1993 (up to 60 out of 196 deputies). Widely regarded as the local "party of power", PERC also operates an all-Ukrainian party in alliance with the New Ukraine movement. It supports market reforms within the framework of an economically independent Crimea, but is a pragmatic centrist party. In 1993 it was responsible for formulating plans for Crimean fiscal independence and a Crimean central bank, both of which were due to be implemented in early 1994. PERC's relations with the local communist party and Republican Movement are poor. The party's close association with the existing Crimean leadership under Mykola Bagrov led to a heavy defeat in the March 1994 Crimean elections, when the party was reduced to a residue of two seats (plus a further four business "supporters").

Peasants' Party of Ukraine (PPU)
Selianska partiia Ukrainy (SelPU)

Address. 35200, Kherson, vul. Maiakovskoho, 6, flat 29.

Telephone. 05522 24452.

Foundation. January 1992.

Leadership. Serhii Dovhan.

Membership. 65,970 claimed January 1994.

History. The roots of the PPU lie in traditional rural CPU organizations, which established first the Peasants' Union of Ukraine in September 1990, and then the PPU in January 1992. Most collective farm chairmen and heads of agro-industry prefer to remain "non-party", but nearly all support the PPU in practice. In 1992–94 most of the 44 collective farm chairmen in the Ukrainian parliament supported the PPU, which has been a powerful force maintaining the flow of huge subsides to the agricultural sector and obstructing plans for land privatization since 1991. Agriculture ministers, Volodymyr Demianov and Yurii Kurasyk, are widely seen as patrons of the party. In alliance with the CPU and SPU, the PPU polled strongly in spring 1994, winning 18 seats in conservative rural areas. It dominates the faction "Rural Ukraine", which claims 36 members.

People's Party of Crimea (PPC)
Narodnaia partiia Kryma (NPK)

Foundation. Nov. 13, 1993.

Leadership. Viktor Mezhak.

Membership. less than 1,000.

History. The PPC is one of several offshoots from the Republican Movement of Crimea (*see* below), originally formed as a more moderate alternative to Yurii Meshkov's Republican Party of the Crimea. The PPC stands for a confederation between Crimea, Russia and Ukraine rather than outright Crimean independence or simple reunion with Russia. Mezhak, however, withdrew his candidacy for the Crimean presidency in favour of Meshkov, and in January 1994 the PPC joined with Meshkov's Republican Party to form the "Russia" block, which routed PERC in the Crimean elections of Spring 1994, winning 54 out of 94 seats. The "Russia" block was only an electoral arrangement, however, rather than a proper political party, and underlying tensions between the PPC and RPC made it difficult for the block to operate as a single faction in the Crimean soviet.

Peoples' Party of Ukraine (PPU)
Narodna partiia Ukrainy (NPU)

Address. Dnipropetrovsk a/s 1235, vul. Naberezhna Lenina, 1.

Telephone. 0562 588032.

Foundation. Sept. 22–23, 1990.

Leadership. Lepold Taburanskyi.

Membership. 4,200.

History. Taburianskyi is a maverick deputy, whose PPU consists almost entirely of employees at the Olimp factory in Dnipropetrovsk, of which he is director. Taburianskyi stood in the presidential elections on December 1991, but only won 0.6 per cent of the vote.

Republican Movement of the Crimea (RMC) — Republican Party of the Crimea (RPC) Republikanskoe dvizheniia Kryma (RDK)

Foundation. Aug. 23, 1991.

Leadership. Yurii Meshkov.

History. The RMC was formed in August 1991 by local deputy Yurii Meshkov to campaign first against Ukrainian independence and for the maintenance of the USSR, and then in favour of Crimean independence. The RMC's petition campaign to force the Crimean authorities to hold a referendum on Crimean independence collected 246,000 signatures in mid-1992, forcing the Crimean soviet to agree in May 1992, only to back down in the wake of Kiev's furious reaction. Thereafter the RMC quarrelled increasingly with the Crimean soviet, led by Mykola Bagrov, and fell victim to a series of internal splits (the Russian Party of Crimea and Peoples' Party of Crimea left the RMC in 1993 – *see* below). The RMC then formalized itself as a political party (the RPC), and organized a second petition campaign in summer 1993 to force the resignation of Bagrov and the local soviet, which resulted in the collection of 195,000 signatures, but the campaign was frustrated by the Crimean authorities, who simply invalidated a sufficient number of signatures for the petition no longer to have legal force.

The campaign to elect a Crimean President in the winter of 1993–94 proved the RPC's salvation. Meshkov was the best-known opposition candidate to the increasingly unpopular Bagrov, and Meshkov secured adequate revenge for earlier slights by soundly trouncing Bagrov in the poll held on Jan. 31, 1994, winning 72.9 per cent of the vote to Bagrov's 23 per cent. Meshkov's "Russia" group, dominated by the RPC, then won 54 out of 94 seats in the March 1994 elections to the Crimean soviet, while simultaneously urging local voters to boycott the all-Ukrainian elections held on the same day.

The RPC's political platform is dominated by the single theme of securing Crimean independence, while its economic policy is a mixture of populist measures (lowering the price of bread), lower taxes to attract foreign (Russia) investment, and plans for Crimean economic independence, but the party's campaign proposal to return Crimea to the rouble zone was quickly forgotten after the elections.

Rukh

Address. Kiev, vul. Shevchenka, 37/122.

Telephone. 2249151.

Foundation. Sept. 8-10, 1989.

Leadership. Viacheslav Chornovil.

Membership. 50,518 claimed January 1994.

History. The first attempt to unite all Ukrainian opposition groups in a "Popular Front" modelled on similar groups in the Baltic republics was crushed by the CPU in the summer of 1988. The second attempt therefore brought in moderate elements from the CPU and Writers' Union of Ukraine over the winter of 1988–89, and resulted in the publication of a draft manifesto in February 1989. At this stage, *Rukh* (the Ukrainian for "movement") still accepted the leading role of the CPU, Ukraine's "socialist choice", and refrained from any direct mention of Ukrainian independence. This pattern was largely confirmed by the movement' first congress in September 1989, which elected the writer Ivan Drach as leader. The autumn of 1989 also marked the resignation of the CPU's veteran conservative leader, Volodymyr Shcherbytskyi, and the beginning of the campaign for republican elections, which allowed *Rukh* to slowly expand its influence. *Rukh*'s high-water mark was in March 1990, when the movement's front organization, the Democratic Block, won 27 per cent of the seats in the elections to the Ukrainian parliament.

Thereafter, *Rukh* lost its role as the sole opposition group. Other political parties began to appear, and *Rukh* fell increasingly under the control of its nationalist wing. The various elections and referenda of 1991 showed no advance on *Rukh*'s 1990 position, and the movement effectively split at its third congress in February–March 1992, with the more nationalist wing leaving to found the CNDF in August 1992. Viacheslav Chornovil was left in charge of a rump *Rukh*, which formally turned itself into a political party under his leadership at its fourth congress in December 1992. Chornovil's *Rukh* takes a centrist-nationalist line on most questions. It supports market reforms and a liberal democratic state united around territorial rather than ethnic patriotism, but supports strong national defence and Ukraine's immediate departure from the CIS. Chornovil's *Rukh* formed a faction of 27 deputies after the spring 1994 elections.

Publication. Weekly *Narodna hazeta*, and numerous local periodicals.

"Russia" Block

Foundation. December 1993.

Leadership. Yurii Meshkov.

History. The "Russia" Block was founded by the Republican Party of Crimea, the People's Party of Crimea, and numerous smaller pro-Russian groups in December 1993 to contest the January 1994 presidential elections in Crimea. It stands for an independent Crimea in close political association with Russia, the reintegration of Sevastopol into the Crimean republic, and an undivided Black Sea fleet under Russian control. The Block followed up its success in the presidential elections by winning 54 out of 94 seats in the new Crimean parliament elected in March–April 1994 (four seats remained vacant).

Russian Party of the Crimea (RusPC)
Russkoi partiia Kryma (RPK)

Foundation. Sept. 25, 1993.

Leadership. Sergei Shuvainikov.

Membership. c.1,000.

History. Shuvainikov's RusPC is a splinter group from Meshkov's RMC (*see* above). It is more radically anti-Ukrainian than the RMC, and is supported by Vladimir Zhirnovsky's Liberal Democratic Party in Russia. Whereas the RMC includes both Russians and Russified Ukrainians amongst its supporters, the RusPC is mainly a party of ethnic Russians. Moreover, unlike the RMC, the RusPC favours outright union between Crimea and Russia, rather than an independent Crimea. Shuvaninikov came third in the January 1994 Crimean elections with 13.6 per cent of the vote, but by then his party was beginning to fall apart amongst accusations of bad faith and personal corruption. The party won only one seat in the Crimean parliament in the spring 1994 elections, where it is in official opposition to the "Russia" Block.

Publication. Occasional *Rossiiskii Krym*.

Social Democratic Party of Ukraine (SDPU)
Sotsial-demokratychna partiia Ukrainy (SDPU)

Address. 252032, Kiev, vul. Tolstoho, 16, flat 24.

Telephone. 2935919.

Foundation. May 1990.

Leadership. Yurii Zbitniev.

Membership. 1,300.

History. Ukraine's small social democratic movement first emerged in 1988, when various all-USSR groups were first active in Ukraine. In 1989–90, however, the Ukrainian groups cut their ties with sister organizations in the rest of the USSR, and organized a founding congress in May 1990. However, the congress resulted in a split, with the SDPU representing those who supported Ukrainian sovereignty and a post 1959 German-style conception of social democracy. At the fifth SDPU congress in Luhansk in September 1993 the party moved back towards the left, announcing its departure from the centrist New Ukraine coalition, and increasing hopes for eventual reunion with the USDPU (*see* below). The SDPU won two seats in the 1990 election and one in 1994.

Publication. Occasional *Sotsial-demokrat Ukrainy*.

Social National Party of Ukraine (SNPU)
Sotsial-natsionalna partiia Ukrainy (SNPU)

Foundation. December 1991.

Leadership. Yaroslav Andrushkiv.

Membership. c.200.

History. The SNPU is an openly neo-fascist and ethnicist party based in Lviv, which favours the expansion of the Ukrainian state to include all the territory controlled by the early medieval kingdom of Kievan Rus. The party has a paramilitary wing, and its symbols and uniforms are none too subtly reminiscent of the Nazi party. SNPU thugs were prominent in the (unsuccessful) attempt by radical nationalists to take over the Lviv branch of *Rukh* in October 1992, and were rapidly recruiting new members as the economic and political situation deteriorated in 1993–94. The SNPU was prominent in organizing the paramilitary committees "In Defence of the Honour of the State and the Nation", set up in Galicia in the wake of the September 1993 Massandra Agreement between Ukraine and Russia that radical nationalists considered tantamount to national betrayal. Its 19 candidates in Lviv in the spring 1994 elections won 2.5 per cent of the local vote.

Socialist Party of Ukraine (SocPU)
Sotsialistychna partiia Ukrainy (SocPU)

Address. 242034, Kiev, vul. Malopidvalna, 21, flat 41.

Telephone. 2916063.

Foundation. October 1991.

Leadership. Oleksandr Moroz.

Membership. 29,000 in December 1992.

History. The Socialist Party of Ukraine was the first would-be successor to the banned CPU, formed a mere two months after the August 1991 coup. Its leader is Oleksandr Moroz, the former head of the CPU majority in the Ukrainian parliament. Moroz steered the SocPU away from open nostalgia for the old system, but throughout 1992–94 adopted a populist position attacking the "introduction of capitalism" and the "growth of national-fascism" in Ukraine, and calling for the reintroduction of state direction of the economy, price controls, and "socially just privatization". The party condemns "national isolationism", and supports at the very least closer economic and political ties with the CIS. Its more radical members support a restored USSR. However, unlike the revived CPU the SocPU is on the whole reconciled to the fact of Ukrainian independence. In June 1993 the SocPU formed a coalition entitled "Working Ukraine" with the PPU and smaller left-wing groups, and the close co-operation of the revived CPU. The SocPU claimed the support of 38 deputies in the Ukrainian parliament in 1992–93 while it enjoyed the advantage of being the only organized leftist successor to the Communist Party of Ukraine. Its pre-eminence on the left disappeared with the rise of the restored CPU in 1993–94, but it still won 14 seats in the 1994 elections. By summer 1994 it controlled a faction of 25 deputies. Moroz was elected chairman of the Ukrainian parliament in April 1994.

Publication. Weekly *Tovarysh*.

Statehood and Independence for Ukraine (SIU)
Derzhavna samostiinist Ukrainy (DSU)

Address. Kiev, vul. Kurska, 20, flat 14.

Telephone. 2422183.

Foundation. April 7–8, 1990.

Leadership. Roman Koval and Volodymyr Shlemko.

Membership. 530 in December 1992.

History. The DSU was formed as a radical splinter from the Ukrainian Helsinki Union in 1990 by a former political prisoner, Ivan Kandyba, who wished his party to be a reincarnation of the OUN. The DSU stands for a powerful Ukrainian nation-state within its ethnographic borders, i.e. including territories in Poland, Belarus and Russia. Membership is not open to non-Ukrainians and former members of the CPU. At the third DSU congress in December 1992, the party's one deputy, Volodymyr Shlemko, replaced Kandyba as leader, but Shlemko increasingly quarrelled with his deputy Roman Koval, the editor of the main party paper, who began to call for the "ethnic cleansing" of Russians and Jews from Ukraine. Koval's colleague, Anatol Shcherbatiuk, was arrested in autumn 1993 for repeating such calls, and the DSU formally split at its fourth congress in December 1993 between supporters of Koval and Shlemko. Shlemko's group in effect merged with the organization OUN in Ukraine (*see* above).

Publications. Weekly *Neskorenna Natsiia* and journal *Napriam*.

Subcarpathian Republican Party (SRP)

Foundation. March 1992.

Leadership. Vasyl Zaiats.

History. The SRP argues that the Slav population of the Transcarpathian region in western Ukraine form a distinct ethnic group as Rusyns. Its origins lie in the Society of Carpatho-Rusyns, established in February 1990, which originally confined itself to cultural goals, but after November 1990 began a campaign for Transcarpathian autonomy, endorsed by 73 per cent of local voters in a referendum on Dec. 1, 1991. Since then Kiev has repeatedly delayed plans to make Transcarpathia at least a "free economic zone", resulting in the formation of the SRP in 1992, whose more radical members have openly called for Transcarpathia to be returned to Hungary, which ruled the region until 1918, and from 1938–45.

Ukrainian Christian Democratic Party (UCDP)
Ukrainska khrystiiansko-demokratychna partiia (UKhDP)

Address. Lviv, vul. Turianskoho, 10a, flat 4.

Telephone. 0322 331325.

Foundation. April 21–22, 1990.

Leadership. Vasyl Sichko.

Membership. 7,000.

History. The UCDP was one of the very first nationalist groups to emerge in Galicia, traditionally the main base of support for the Uniate Church. The group first appeared in November 1988 as a Christian Democratic "Front", but turned itself formally into a political party at a congress in April 1990. Despite its ecumenical programme, the UCDP has in practice always been a mono-confessional (Uniate) party, confined to Galicia. The Orthodox wing of the party split away in June 1992 to create the rival Christian Democratic Party of Ukraine (*see* above). Moreover, party leader Sichko's autocratic style led to a second split among the party's Galician supporters in 1992. Sichko's group remains the official registered version of the UCDP. The party has in the past adopted an ultra-nationalist position, boycotting the 1989 and 1990 elections as the "act of an occupying power" (although the party had one "sympathiser" deputy, Zinovii Duma). The UCDP is a member of the CNDF.

Publication. Occasional *Za viru i voliu.*

Ukrainian Civic Congress of the Crimea (UCCC)
Ukrainskyi hromadskyi kongres Kryma (UHKK)

Foundation. Nov. 28, 1993.

Leadership. Serhii Lytvyn and Ihor Banakh.

History. The UCCC was formed in the autumn of 1993 by Kiev and the local Ukrainian community in the Crimea (24 per cent of the population) in order to oppose the separatist RMC under Yurii Meshkov. (Ihor Banakh is also chairman of the "Crimea with Ukraine" movement.) The UCCC demands that the Crimean law and constitution be brought into line with that of Ukraine as a whole, and, having condemned the January 1994 Crimean presidential elections as "unconstitutional", called, unsuccessfully, on local Ukrainians to boycott the vote. The UCCC was unable to elect any deputies in the spring 1994 elections either to the Ukrainian or the Crimean parliament.

Ukrainian Conservative Republican Party (UCRP)
Ukrainska konservatyvna respublikanska partiia (UKRP)

Address. Kiev, vul. Volodymyrska, 189/6.

Telephone. 2293056.

Foundation. June 6–7, 1992.

Leadership. Stepan Khmara.

Membership. Less than 1,000.

History. Stepan Khmara was deputy leader of the URP from 1990–92, during which time he constantly argued with his more moderate colleagues and gained a reputation for obdurate nationalism. After Khmara and his supporters were forced out of the URP at the party's third congress in May 1992, they created a rival party one month later. Khmara's UCRP is violently anti-Russian, but, unlike the URP, is also strongly opposed to compromise with former communists such as Leonid Kravchuk, whom Khmara had persistently hounded as a "traitor" to Ukrainian national interests. Khmara has been a leading advocate of a nuclear Ukraine, and of support for ethnic Ukrainians in neighbouring Russian territories such as the Kuban. Khmara secured revenge against Mykhailo Horyn, leader of the URP, by defeating him for a seat from Lviv in the Ukrainian parliament in spring 1994. The UCRP elected one other deputy.

Publication. Occasional *Klych.*

Ukrainian Inter-Party Assembly
(*see* Ukrainian National Assembly below)

Ukrainian Nationalist Union (UNU)
Ukrainska natsionalistychna spilka (UNS)

Foundation. Nov. 3–4, 1990.

Leadership. Dmytro Korchynskyi, Viktor Melnyk and Oleh Vitovych.

*Membership. c.*100.

History. The UNU was formed as a splinter group from the student group SNUM (Union of Independent Ukrainian Youth) by radical nationalists who wanted to replace SNUM's "democratic nationalist" ideology with a neo-fascist doctrine derived from the Ukrainian nationalist philosopher, Dmytro Dontsov. Having cut their teeth in student politics, the leaders of the UNU became the leading force in the main ultra-nationalist group, the UNA, after 1991 (*see* below).

Publication. Weekly *Zamkova hora.*

Ukrainian National Assembly (UNA)
Ukrainska natsionalna assembleia (UNA)

Telephone. 228024.

Foundation. September 1991.

Leadership. Yurii Shukhevych.

Membership. 14,000 claimed in February 1993.

History. The UNA was originally the Ukrainian Inter-Party Assembly (UIA) formed on 30 June–1 July, 1990. The UIA was formed by the UNP, UPDP, UNU and others as a radical alternative to moderate nationalist groups such as the UHU, and rejected all participation in the institutions of the Ukrainian SSR, which they saw as part of "an occupying regime". Instead the UIA organized a petition campaign for the re-establishment of the Ukrainian Peoples' Republic of 1918, which they planned to reconvene as a rival government. The UIA claimed to have collected 2.8 million signatures by April 1991 (nearly all of these were in western Ukraine), but its campaign was overtaken by the declaration of Ukrainian independence in August 1991. The UIA therefore reconstituted itself as the Ukrainian National Assembly, in effect a political party, in September 1991 (by then the UIA was to all intents and purposes dominated by the UNU in any case). The UNA has a national-corporatist ideology, and supports the building of a "neo-imperial" Ukrainian state, independent of both Russia and the West. Initially the UNA, which despised the "weak" and inexperienced democratic nationalists, was a strong supporter of national communists such as President Kravchuk, but by mid-1993 they were disillusioned with his regime, which they castigated for corruption and subservience to foreign capital. The UNA's slogan in 1994 was "Vote for the UNA and you will never be troubled to vote again".

The UNA also has a notorious paramilitary wing, the Ukrainian Self-Defence Forces (UNSO), which claims to have 5,000 men under arms. UNSO gained a high public profile in 1992–94 by sending its paramilitaries to participate in the Transnistria and Abkhazian conflicts, and by a series of violent attacks on separatist organizations back home in Ukraine. Moreover, like the IRA, UNSO has gained popularity by posing as the defender of the common man against mafia corruption. In November 1993 the Ukrainian parliament amended the criminal code to specifically outlaw paramilitary groups, but UNSO carried on its activities regardless. The UNA-UNSO secured a major breakthrough in the spring 1994 elections, when the radicalization of the public mood in nationalist western Ukraine resulted in the election of three of its members. Moreover, UNA-UNSO candidates also performed well in Kiev, where four of its candidates progressed to the second round of the elections.

Publications. Weeklies *Holos natsii* and *Ukrainski obrii*.

Ukrainian National Conservative Party (UNCP)
Ukrainska natsionalno-konservatyvna partiia (UNKP)

Foundation. October 1992.

Leadership. Viktor Rodionov.

History. The UNCP is a small right of centre party, formed as the result of a merger between the Ukrainian National Party and Ukrainian Peoples' Democratic Party in June 1992. The party is a member of the CNDF.

Ukrainian National Party (UNP)
Ukrainska natsionalna partiia (UNP)

Foundation. Oct. 21, 1989.

Leadership. Hryhorii Prykhodko.

Membership. Less than 100.

History. The UNP broke many taboos when it appeared as the first (underground) non-communist political party in Galicia in October 1989. Its extreme nationalism (the UNP refused to recognize the Ukrainian SSR, called for the "right to bear arms", and the expansion of the Ukrainian state to her natural "ethnic borders") consciously echoed the 1930s OUN. In 1992 the UNP merged with the UPDP to create the Ukrainian National Conservative Party, a member of the CNDF (*see* above).

Publication. Periodicals *Klych natsii* and *Ukrainskyi chas.*

Ukrainian Peasants' Democratic Party (UPDP)
Ukrainska selianska demokratychna partiia (USDP)

Address. 252054, Kiev, vul. Chkalova, 52, Flat 61.

Telephone. 2241792.

Foundation. June 9, 1990.

Leadership. Serhii Plachynda.

Membership. 4,000 in March 1993.

History. The UPDP was created to challenge the domination of the Ukrainian countryside by conservative collective farm chairmen and agro-industry bosses. However, it failed to have much impact outside Galicia, and remained tiny in comparison to the PPU (*see* above). Moreover, Plachynda's radical brand of Ukrainian nationalism limited the potential appeal of the party. The UPDP is a member of the CNDF.

Publication. Occasional *Zemlia i volia.*

Ukrainian Peoples' Democratic Party (UPDP)
Ukrainska narodno-demokratychna partiia (UNDP)

Foundation. June 1990.

Leadership. Oleksandr Bondarenko.

History. The UPDP enjoyed temporary popularity in 1990 as a haven for radical nationalists disillusioned with parliamentary parties such as the URP. It opposed all participation in the "colonial" institutions of the Ukrainian SSR, and was one of the main founders of the UIA in summer 1990. Most of the party's members were then absorbed into the UIA or drifted away. A rump UPDP merged with the UNP in 1992 to create the Ukrainian National Conservative Party (*see* above).

Publication. Occasional *Nezalezhnist.*

Ukrainian Republican Party (URP)
Ukrainska respublikanska partiia (URP)

Address. 252024, Kiev, vul. Prorizna, 27.

Telephone. 2230306.

Foundation. April 29–30, 1990.

Leadership. Mykhailo Horyn; Levko Lukianenko (hon. chair.).

Membership. 13,000.

History. The URP was the first modern non-communist political party to be officially formed in Ukraine, in April 1990, and the first to be officially registered, on Nov. 1, 1990. The URP was the direct successor of the Ukrainian Helsinki Union (1988–90), itself a revival of the Ukrainian Helsinki Group (1976–*c*.1980). Throughout the early 1990s it has been the best organized nationalist party in Ukraine, despite lacking the intelligentsia support enjoyed by the DPU (*see* above). The party bases its ideology on the conservative Ukrainian philosopher, Viacheslav Lypynskyi, and supports "the Ukrainian character of national statehood", while advocating a tolerant approach to the civic rights of ethnic minorities. However, the party has always had more radical elements within its ranks, including Stepan Khmara, the party's deputy leader until 1992 (*see* the UCRP above). Since independence the URP has been a strong supporter of the Ukrainian authorities, and stands for resolute national defence, immediate departure from the CIS and a strong, unitary, presidential republic. Economically, the party supports the creation of "a society of property owners", but opposes "socially unjust privatization", and favours a policy of priority support for national industry. The party was the main founder of the CNDF. Despite strong local organization and fielding a total of 130 candidates, the URP performed poorly in the 1994 elections, as it was tainted by its too often uncritical support for the Ukrainian authorities. Only nine party members (and one supporter) were elected, while party leader Mykhailo Horyn was embarrassingly defeated by Khmara in Lviv.

Publications. Weekly *Samostiina Ukraina*, monthly journal, *Rozbudova derzhavy*.

Union for Democratic Reforms (UDR)
Obiednannia demokratychnykh peretvoren (ODP)

Foundation. December 1993.

Leadership. Serhii Ustych and Volodymyr Prykhodko.

History. The UDR was founded in the western Ukrainian region of Transcarpathia in December 1993 to represent local *nomenklatura* and business interests. The Union's leader is Serhii Ustych, deputy head of the regional council and head of the committee to establish a free economic zone in Transcarpathia. The Union has links with Vasyl Durdynets, former first deputy chairman of the Ukrainian parliament and a native of Transcarpathia. Two to three independents elected in Transcarpathia in spring 1994 are reportedly close to the UDR.

Union in Support of the Republic of Crimea (USRC)
Soiuz v podderzhku Respubliki Kryma (SPRK)

Foundation. Oct. 1, 1993.

Leadership. Sergei Kunitsyn.

History. The USRC represents traditional industrial interests in the Crimea. It had 20 deputies in the local soviet in 1993, and two deputies in the Kiev parliament (Yakob Apter and Sergei Kunitsyn). During the Crimean election campaign over the winter of

1993–3 Apter was killed in a road accident, and replaced by Kunitsyn as party leader at an emergency congress in December 1993. The USRC takes a relatively moderate line towards relations with Kiev and with local Ukrainians and Crimean Tatars. In spring 1994 the USRC formed *Yednist*, a coalition between the Crimean Tatar *Medzhlis* and moderate centrist parties, but the coalition made little impact on the 1994 elections, winning less than 3 per cent of the vote.

United Social Democratic Party of Ukraine (USDPU)
Obiednana sotsial-demokratychna partiia Ukrainy (OSDPU)

Foundation. May 1990.

Leadership. Oleksandr Alin.

Membership. 1,000.

History. After the split at the founding congress of the Ukrainian Social Democrats in 1990, the USDPU was formed by the more left-wing faction, who based their social democracy on the pre-1917 tradition of the Ukrainian Social Democratic Workers' Party. The USDPU has remained a small group of left-leaning intellectuals, however, and in 1993 was trying to rebuild its bridges with the SDPU in order to expand its influence. In 1993 the party had the support of one Ukrainian deputy, Volodymyr Moskovska, from Kharkiv.

UZBEKISTAN

Bogdan Szajkowski
Krystyna Vere-Bujnowski

Uzbekistan became a Soviet Socialist Republic in 1924 and included what is now Tajikistan. In 1936, seven years after Tajikistan became a Soviet republic in its own right, the region of Karakalpak was incorporated into Uzbekistan as an "autonomous republic". The 1989 USSR census shows that Uzbekistan, with about 20 million people, is the most heavily populated of all the Central Asian republics. Among the many ethnic groups in Uzbekistan there are 12 with populations of 100,000 or more. Uzbeks are the largest group, making up 71.4 per cent of the population and four out of five Uzbeks (over 11 million people) live in rural areas. There are well over a million and a half Russians (8.34 per cent), nearly a million Tajiks (4.71 per cent) and nearly 2 million Tatars, Kazakhs and Karakalpaks. The predominant religion is Islam, particularly in the countryside, and 9 per cent of the population follow the Eastern Orthodox tradition.

The new republic is the third largest cotton producer in the world and has important mineral and energy resources including gold, aluminium, coal, petroleum and natural gas. Before independence, Uzbekistan was reliant on internal trading within the USSR and suffered heavily in post-war economic crises, not least because of the Soviet policy of underpricing its raw materials. In 1991, after the break-up of the Soviet Union, Uzbekistan was left with a considerable trading deficit and although it was in Uzbekistan's interest to attract foreign investment, the Soviet debt was a disincentive for Western entrepreneurs. When in late 1992 the successor states relinquished claims to Soviet assets in return for the Russian Federation taking on the USSR's debts, the path was cleared for Western finance to invest in Uzbekistan's considerable natural resources.

It is in this context that political reform since 1989 has been systematically discouraged and since 1992 actively repressed. A stable political order is a key factor in attracting and keeping foreign investors and Islam Karimov, President since 1990, has constantly cited the need for stability as the justification for increasingly repressive political measures. Stifling the opposition has the effect in the short term at least of removing threats to Karimov's personal power and so the economic interests of the people and the personal ambition of the President are intertwined.

Like other Central Asian states, Uzbekistan has remained under the control of the communist party or its successor. Parliamentary elections were held in February 1990 under the Soviet system. In Uzbekistan a third of the deputies of the 500-seat Supreme Soviet were elected unopposed and a quarter of the seats were reserved for communist-controlled organizations. The presidential elections which followed in March were held within the

Supreme Soviet and Islam Karimov, the leader of the Uzbekistan Communist Party, was duly elected. He retained a dominant hold on the country, and in a national referendum in March 1991 achieved a 98 per cent vote from the people of Uzbekistan for the continuation of the USSR.

Six months later, however, the attempted coup by hardliners in Moscow failed and on Aug. 31, 1991, the Supreme Soviet voted for an independent sovereign state. In the referendum of Dec. 29, 1991, 98 per cent of voters confirmed the desire for complete sovereignty. On the same day, direct presidential elections were held for the first time and the fact that an opposition leader, Mohammed Saleh, was allowed to stand as a candidate appeared to be a clear indication that pluralist politics had been sanctioned by the ruling People's Democratic Party (PDP), the successor to the Uzbekistan Communist Party. Saleh was the leader of *Erk*, the Freedom Party, which had been allowed to register as a *bona fide* political party probably because it had only a small membership. At its peak it had 5,000 members compared with the communist party's half a million. Karimov could not have thought that Saleh presented a serious challenge. Another opposition group *Birlik* (Unity), which was founded in November 1988, was reputed to have almost as many members as the communist party at that time and could thus be regarded as a significant force for democratic change. *Birlik* was refused registration and could not field a candidate to stand against Karimov, nor was it allowed access to national media to campaign against him. At the time of the election *Erk* and *Birlik* were in disagreement about political strategy and so there was no credible or effective opposition to Karimov.

Islam Karimov won 85.9 per cent of the votes cast and Mohammed Saleh polled 12.45 per cent. Saleh claimed the elections were not fair since the PDP controlled the election process, the administrative procedure and access to the broadcasting media. The CSCE were indeed sceptical about the freedom of choice given to voters but they commented that there was considerable support for the incumbent president. Although they found no evidence of coercion they did speculate on the role that fear could play on the Uzbek electorate.[1]

In the event, the contested presidential election did not herald the beginning of a multi-party system. *Birlik* has never been allowed to register as a political party, even when re-registration was called for by the Supreme Soviet in March 1993. Despite its best attempts, *Birlik* was finally prevented from being eligible because it had no address by the deadline of Oct. 1, 1993, the government having confiscated its headquarters. It was allowed to continue as a registered "social movement" but was finally banned completely in 1993. No other opposition group has been allowed to register as a political party and *Erk* was refused re-registration in October 1993. It suffered a similar fate to *Birlik*. *Erk* was made homeless when the fire authorities investigated the premises a week before the Oct. 1 deadline and pronounced the building unsafe.[2] Although opposition parties have been banned or refused registration, from March 1992 a number of groups have been allowed to register as political parties. These seem indistinguishable from the satellite parties under the old system which were subordinate to, or protégées of, the ruling communist party. Under the new constitution, elections were due to be held in 1994 when the unicameral Supreme Soviet would become the National Assembly or *Mejlis* and would be reduced from 500 seats to 250. Even though parliament endorsed this move on Dec. 28, 1993, so far no date has been set for such elections.

Erk's loss of favour coincided with its increasingly harmonious relationship with *Birlik* and with two other opposition parties, the Islamic Renaissance Party and *Adolat*, the Party for Justice. They agreed to bury their differences in order to fight off the increasing threat to their individual survival. Several leading opposition figures had been harrassed, even beaten up and left seriously injured. In spite of their alliance, the opposition groups remained vulnerable to attack, the preferred method being to pick on individuals and physically molest them or to bring them to trial on flimsy charges and evidence. Abdurrahim Pulatov, the leader of *Birlik*, has been beaten and left with a fractured skull. His brother Abdumanob, who leads the Uzbek human rights movement, was abducted from a conference in Bishkek, Kyrgyzstan, by Uzbek secret police. He was put on trial for insulting the honour and dignity of the president, sentenced and immediately amnestied. Other leading figures were put on trial in 1993 on the same charge. They were found guilty and sentenced to between one and three years' imprisonment but released under the terms of an amnesty granted by Karimov in September 1992. Six people found guilty of conspiring to set up an alternative parliament (*Milli Mejlis*) and a court of law, apparently serious charges, were also released under the amnesty. Mohammed Saleh was implicated in the *Milli Mejlis* case and left the country before he could be arrested. A policy of systematic intimidation was being vigorously pursued from May 1992.[3]

This coincided with the unrest in Tajikistan which eventually descended into civil war and Karimov made it clear that the need for stability was paramount so that the events in Tajikistan would not be repeated in Uzbekistan. As well as harrying the opposition, Karimov began to draw greater powers to the presidency. For example, the President was responsible for all appointments to governorships of local regions and *oblasts*; the PDP-controlled Supreme Soviet passed a law setting up a Presidential Council which has the power to oversee directly all areas of administration and ensure the implementation of policy.

It is difficult to reconcile the overt centralization of power with the passing of a new constitution on Dec. 8, 1992, which embraces such fundamental liberal values as freedom of speech, thought and belief, freedom of association and freedom of assembly. On closer inspection, however, the constitution reveals that citizens' rights and liberties are not only curtailed to the extent that they infringe on those of others, which would be a central tenet of any liberal theory of justice, but they are also suborned to the "legitimate interests" of the state. Individual rights and liberties are thus at the mercy of the guardians of the state: the government and the President. The constitution is sufficiently vague to necessitate a strong body of constitutional law. Failing this, the executive arm of the state retains a monopoly on the interpretation of the constitution. Legislation that would prescribe the rights and liberties of the individual and provide protection from the incursion of the state has not been forthcoming. The development of legitimate opposition to the incumbent government is also curtailed. For example, although the constitution allows for freedom of assembly it does not revoke an earlier law which forbids external gatherings. Thus, any form of open-air assembly, including popular demonstrations, is illegal whether or not arranged by political or social movements.

Of course, in order to protect its citizens the state must safeguard itself. A strong state is more likely to offer effective protection than a weak one and it is more likely to meet the needs of its people. Paradoxically even the liberal state needs to centralize power in order to be strong. A state that cannot rely on its legitimacy in the eyes of its citizens is even less likely to grant individual liberties however much the constitution appears to uphold them and the most repressive measures can be justified in the name of stability.

Islam Karimov has repeatedly endorsed the value of stability and the dangers of social and political disorder. His overriding concern is to limit the influence of political dissidents and religious fundamentalists, these in his view being the greatest threat to the socio-political order. Thus though he is prepared to pursue a liberal economy and constitution there is no guarantee of political liberalization. Whereas on the one hand Uzbekistan needs to develop a liberal economy in order to safeguard the long term interests of rulers and ruled, the pace of change must be slow enough to allay the fears and uncertainties of citizens, not only because their welfare is important in itself but also to prevent disaffection and unrest. The prevention of instability appears to have been at the root of Karimov's every move. It is a different question to ask, however, how much this is prompted by real concern for the welfare of Uzbeki citizens and how much by personal ambition.

The paradox becomes perceptible when, alongside plans to develop the constitution, new laws on citizenship and attempts at economic liberalization, the Uzbek government promotes an increasingly systematic clampdown on the voice and activities of opposition movements and a corresponding increase of the powers of the presidency. Karimov's pursuit of social stability may yet contain another paradox. If relatively moderate opposition groups are proscribed and the outlets they offer for popular political expression are dammed then it is conceivable, as Mohammed Saleh has pointed out, that extremist opposition movements will capture the aspirations of the people. Karimov is gambling on the fact that the political culture that existed under old Soviet rule has not substantially changed. This gamble will probably come off in the short term but events in neighbouring states and the effects of economic liberalization forced on Karimov as a political expediency may have unsettling and unforeseen effects on the population he strives to govern.

Directory of Parties

Adolat (Justice)

Foundation. 1992.

History. A small group of Muslims based in Namangam and reputed to have extensive influence in the local area. Eleven of its members were arrested in March 1992 and are still held. The party was banned from its inception.

Programme. It aims to combat the influence of the official Muslim leadership of the Chief *Mufti*, Mohammed Sadik Mohammed Yusuf, who is said to be under the dominance of the state President, Islam Karimov.

Birlik (Unity) People's Movement (BPM)

Address. c/o Union of Writers of Uzbekistan, 700000 Tashkent, ul. Pushkina 1.

Telephone. (3712) 337921.

Foundation. First came into being in November 1988 and held its first conference in May 1992.

Leadership. Abdurrakhim Pulatov (ch.); Pulat Akhunov (co-ch.); Shukhrat Ismatullaev (co-ch.).

Membership. At the height of its popularity and before the government clampdown on opposition groups, *Birlik*'s own estimate of its numbers was one and a half million. It was reputed to have at least half a million members but by November 1992 Pulatov admitted to only a few thousand, the rest having been intimidated into renouncing membership.

History. Birlik was originally founded on a programme of establishing Uzbek as the state language, following the relaxation of Russian-dominated rule under Gorbachev. It has also advocated a "Commonwealth of Turkestan". The movement was an umbrella organization for individuals rather than groups and contained both democrats and nationalists. After independence, it has been unable to shake free from the iron rule of Islam Karimov and the PDP and was banned as a political party. It was registered as a social movement but this did not allow it to take a legal part in any political proceedings. It tried to register as a political party when re-registration was called for in October 1993, but failed because the government had removed it from its headquarters and it therefore had no address. Both Pulatov and Ismatullaev have been badly beaten in different attacks and Akhumov is in jail.[4]

Programme. It supports democratization, economic reform along liberal lines, political pluralism and secularism of the state. It supports other groups on the basis that they should be allowed to participate openly in an open society, even though it may not agree with all their ideas.

Erk (Freedom) Democratic Party (EDP)

Foundation. 1990.

Leadership. Muhammad Salih (ch.); Samad Muradov (g.s.).

Membership. In 1991 it had 5,000 members, mainly urban intellectuals. They include ex-members of the Supreme Soviet. *Erk*'s membership has declined because of the government's clampdown.

History. Mohammed Salih and other founder members of *Birlik* left because they did not agree with using violence for political ends. The party was allowed to register as a political party in 1991, probably because it would be proof of the PDP's intention to move towards multi-party politics. Its small and select membership would pose no real threat to the ruling PDP. Saleh ran as a presidential candidate in the elections on Dec. 29, 1991, when he came a poor second to the incumbent president. *Erk* and *Birlik* decided to co-operate in 1992 after President Karimov started to clamp down on opposition groups. In 1993 parties were told they had to re-register and *Erk* was prevented from doing so because like *Birlik* it had no address. A few days before the Oct. 1 deadline, the fire department closed down *Erk*'s offices as a fire risk. Salih is now in exile having been implicated in a conspiracy to found an alternative parliament and *Erk* is proscribed.

Programme. Supports non-violent democratic reform.

The Free Peasants' Party (FPP)

Leader. Mirazaali Mukhammejanov.

Membership. Numbers not known. Mainly farmers and farm workers from the Fergana valley. Some members around Tashkent and Bukhara.

History. Appears to have been affiliated to *Birlik*. Not registered as a political party.

Programme. The FPP seems to be close in spirit to *Erk*.

The Forum for Democratic Forces

Foundation. Probably in May 1992.

Membership. *Birlik*, *Erk*, *Adolat* and the Islamic Renaissance Party.

Leadership. Shukrulla Mirsaidov[5] is a leading member.

History. Founded as an umbrella organization in response to the government's clampdown on opposition forces. The forum was an attempt to create strength in unity.

Islamic Renaissance Party (IRP)

Foundation. 1990.

Leadership. Abdullah Utayev (ch.).

Membership. The number of members is not known, it is believed to include both moderates and fundamentalists.

History. After its inauguration as a party in 1990 it was refused registration and was banned by the government in 1991 along with all other religious political parties. Its main support comes from the Fergana valley which is heavily agricultural and populated mainly by ethnic Uzbeks. Utayev has been in jail since Dec. 6, 1992. He has not been heard of since June 1993.

Programme. The IRP wants to make Islam a fundamental part of the political system. It wants an independent voice for Islam and maintains that the Chief *Mufti* is too much influenced by the government.

Istiqlal Yoli (Independence Path)

Foundation. June 12, 1994.

Leadership. Shadi Karimov (ch.).

History. Shadi Karimov is a former member of *Birlik* and *Erk* and has said that he wants to co-operate with Islam Karimov but would want to advocate some changes which have not yet been specified. He has publicly criticized Mohammed Salih who is still in voluntary exile and opposition figures suspect that this is another government sponsored party.

The New Movement For Democratic Reform Of Uzbekistan

Foundation. May 1992.

History. Officially registered as a social movement.

Programme. It aims to counter Muslim opposition groups which are banned by advocating the official Muslim line.

People's Democratic Party (PDP)

Address. 700163 Tashkent, ul. Uzbekistanskaya 43.

Foundation. Nov. 18, 1991.

Leadership. Islam A. Karimov.

Membership. In 1993 it was said to have 340,000 members.

History. Formerly the Communist Party of Uzbekistan, it remains the ruling party. Karimov is President of Uzbekistan.

Programme. Ostensibly committed to extensive economic reform, including privatization, it has followed a slow course arguing that there should be a period of adjustment to allow the people of Uzbekistan time to assimilate the drastic changes brought on by economic liberalization. It has been forced to accelerate the pace of reform by foreign investors. It has advocated a multi-party state and has passed a new constitution encompassing liberal values. This programme is at odds with its suppression of opposition parties and its compliance in the extension of presidential powers.

The People's Movement "Turkestan"

Foundation. July 1991.

Leadership. Bakhrom Hazip.

History. Seems to have been involved with *Birlik*.

Programme. Advocates the unification of those states which were formerly Turkestan — Uzbekistan, Kazakhstan, Kyrgyzstan, Tajikistan and Turkmenistan. Has contacts with similar groups in the other Central Asian states. Hazip was beaten up in April 1992, and was arrested when he summoned the police for help.

The "Samarkand" Movement

Leadership. Uktam Bekmuhammedov (ch.).

Membership. A small membership consisting of Tajiks living in Uzbekistan.

Programme. Advocates the cultural and linguistic rights of Tajiks settled in Uzbekistan.

The Party of Social Progress of Uzbekistan

Leadership. Fayzulla Ishkanov.

History. Officially registered as a political party, the PSP is government supported and is rumoured to have received financial assistance from the government to set itself up.

The Uzbekistan Society for Human Rights

Address. c/o The Uzbekistan Writers' Union 700000 Tashkent, ul. Pushkina 1.

Telephone. (3712) 337921.

Foundation. February 1992.

Leadership. Abdumanob Pulatov; Mikhail Ardzhinov.

History. Pulatov has taken an active part in opposition politics, he was a founder member of *Birlik*, along with his brother. The society has been active too, in drawing attention to violations of human rights by the Karimov government. It has participated in international conferences on human rights, most spectacularly in 1992 when Pulatov was abducted from a conference in Bishkek by the Uzbek secret police. In 1993, there was another bid to abduct Pulatov from the same conference being held in Kazakhstan, but this time the Kazakh authorities publicly thwarted the Uzbek attempt.

Programme. To advocate human rights and to publicize violations of human rights by the government and state institutions of Uzbekistan.

Vatan Tarrakiyets (The Fatherland Progress Party)

Foundation. August 1992.

Membership. About 4,000.

Leadership. Usman Asimov.

History. Asimov was a founding member of *Birlik* but in 1991 he accepted a post on the Presidential Council, Karimov's committee for overseeing the implementation of government policy. The party is officially registered and has government support.

Programme. Advocates parliamentary democracy and a market economy.

Notes

1 *Human Rights and Democratization in the Newly Independent States of the Former Soviet Union*, compiled by the staff of the Commission on Security and Co-operation in Europe, Washington D.C., January 1993, p 207.
2 *RFE/RL Research Report*, vol. 3 no. 1, 7 January 1994.
3 Yalcin Tokgozoglu "Uzbek Government Continues to Stifle Dissent" *RFE/RL Research Report* vol. 2 no. 39 (October 1993). The article gives details of further cases of intimidation and suggests that a campaign is being carefully contrived at the same time to enhance Karimov as a great leader. This appears to be a familiar and recurring theme in the Central Asian states as their leaders show reluctance to accept the path toward political reform.

4 Akhunov was first sentenced to one year's imprisonment in 1992 for accusing Karimov of complicity in the Moscow coup attempt. He claimed to have written evidence. Instead of releasing him under the amnesty of September 1992, as most of the other political figures have been, in February 1993 the authorities sentenced Akhunov to a further three years for being found in possession of narcotics in his cell. See *RFE/RL Research Report*, vol. 2 no. 39.

5 Shukrulla Mirsaidov was Karimov's vice-president. In June 1993 Mirsaidov was arrested and tried for corruption. He was given a three-year prison sentence but immediately released under the September 1992 amnesty. He has since narrowly escaped a car bomb left outside his home.

YUGOSLAVIA

(The Socialist Federal Republic of Yugoslavia)

John B. Allcock

Although the former Socialist Federal Republic of Yugoslavia ceased to exist on April 27, 1991, the pattern of successor states that will eventually replace it is still by no means clear in mid-1994. The "Third Yugoslavia" — the Federal Republic of Yugoslavia — which was formally inaugurated in April 1991 is widely regarded as inherently unstable and has failed to secure general international recognition. War continues in Bosnia-Hercegovina. Somewhere between a quarter and a third of the territory of the independent Croatian republic is controlled by the secessionist Serb forces of the so-called "Republic of Serbian Krajina". The future status of Macedonia and Kosovo is regarded by many observers as incomplete. Even Slovenia has not achieved its aim of complete extraction from Yugoslavia, as the final apportionment of the international debt of the former federation awaits the end of hostilities, and the process of "normalization" of the Slovene economy remains impossible for as long as it is cut off from a substantial section of its former and natural markets.

Under these circumstances a chapter on party development within the former Yugoslavia is not a piece of sentimental "Yugo-nostalgia". In every case the configuration of parties that have emerged in the separate republican polities continues to bear the stamp of the struggles *within* Yugoslavia which brought them to birth. The provision of a separate historical narrative for each of these states prior to the break-up of Yugoslavia would result in tedious and unnecessary repetition. In particular, this shared history provides the substratum upon which rest the characteristics of rule by the Communist Party of Yugoslavia (later renamed the League of Communists) since 1945, as well as the more recent struggle for the realization of new democratic political forms.

Of primary importance in this respect is the location of Yugoslavia across one of the principal historical fault-lines of Europe. The boundaries between the Roman and Greek traditions of Christianity, between Christianity and Islam (in particular, between the Austro-Hungarian and Turkish empires), between the Mediterranean world and that of the Slav cultures and peoples, all have divided in one way or another the South Slav peoples, who in 1918 came together in the Kingdom of the Serbs, Croats and Slovenes.

This complex cross-cutting of lines of cultural identity and strategic orientation left the Yugoslav peoples in many respects without natural and positive forces of cohesion. Consequently many observers have seen in the Yugoslav state an entirely artificial creation imposed upon the region, which suits the interests of powerful outsiders rather than serving the real needs and ambitions of its peoples. Yugoslavia has been described as a creature of the Versailles Conference, the inherent weakness of which was testified to by the collapse of that state (renamed "Yugoslavia" by King Aleksandar, in 1929) under the impact of invasion by the Axis powers in April 1941. In February 1945, however, the conference of the Great Powers at Yalta reaffirmed the perceived necessity of a unified Yugoslav state, but recognized its position of marginality, in the celebrated Stalin–Churchill "50/50" formula, which acknowledged the joint legitimate interest in Yugoslavia of both the Western powers and the Soviet Union. Those who take this view of Yugoslavia are able to ask, with some point, whether the events of 1991–93 do not represent a second and definitive failure of the Yugoslav experiment.

To pose this question in this way, however, is to neglect some very important facts, historical and contemporary. This view overlooks the role of very long-term indigenous forces encouraging the unification of the South Slav peoples. It conveniently sets aside the fact that in the Versailles settlement the Great Powers blessed an agreement which had already been negotiated between representatives of the "Yugoslav Committee" — the government of Serbia and other interested parties. There have been significant historical tendencies working towards the economic, cultural and political cohesion of the South Slav lands. Furthermore, the current "Balkanization" of the region has meant that its component parts are thought by many to be too small to stand as viable independent units in a world increasingly shaped by large states, trans-state groupings and international corporations. It has been argued that the Yugoslav peoples need each other if for no other reason than to provide an institutional means of protecting their diverse individuality in a world in which far more powerful groupings could consume them all. The force of this argument is implicitly acknowledged in the fact that all of the successor states of Yugoslavia see their future as assured only within the context of an expanded European Union. Bearing in mind the fact that all but the most optimistic commentators measure this process in decades rather than years, in the shorter term the existence of some form of more local integration which might replace the defunct Yugoslavia while not carrying the force of historical necessity at least represents sound common sense in the kind of world we now confront.

There is no requirement in this context that an attempt be made either to argue the case for any particular configuration of states which will replace Yugoslavia, or to predict their future. At the time of writing, the future political possibilities for the South Slav peoples are far from clear. One thing can be said with confidence, however, and that is that the condition of "Balkanization" was not the exclusive property of the state called Yugoslavia, whose disappearance can now be expected to result in stability in place of disorder and division. "Balkanization" afflicts also its component parts. Consequently, the process of its disintegration, in which one state has been replaced by a nest of smaller ones, has resulted in the replication on a smaller scale of the self-same processes which characterized Yugoslavia itself. The problem will outlast the useful life of this volume, and this fact also is underlined by the provision of a common framework for the account of political developments in the former components of the Yugoslav federation.

One significant feature distinguished Yugoslavia from the majority of other states in eastern and central Europe. When Yugoslavia emerged from war in 1945, the victorious partisan movement, led by Josip Broz "Tito", had earned a valuable capital fund of legitimacy which has shown signs of exhaustion only in recent years. This is not to deny the importance of the complex civil war between the communist forces, the Serbian royalist "chetniks", and several brands of domestic collaborationist forces, as a continuing source of bitternesss within historical memory. Nor does its recognition mean that one is prepared to ignore the brutal way in which the superficial trappings of democracy devised by the Tito–Šubašić agreeement on 1945 were swept aside within a year, to be replaced by communist authoritarianism. Even so, the partisan experience endowed the regime in Yugoslavia with both a legitimating mythology (which allowed its rule to sit relatively lightly upon its citizens) and a tremendous source of *esprit de corps* (which reinforced its own solidarity and conviction of its right to rule).

That wartime experience continues to have a lively impact upon the current political scene in three ways. First of all, it has intensified the difficulties of political change. The ousting of communism in Yugoslavia has not been experienced as the sloughing off of an unnatural and foreign system of domination, and a return to "normality". We are witnessing a *real and intense* crisis of Yugoslav political culture. This is reflected, at the very least, in the continuing vigour with which the various successors to the League of Communists cling to political life, and indeed, have earned a significant measure of electoral success. Communism has not even been definitely "deposed" throughout the former Yugoslav federation, let alone "eliminated" as a political force. Former luminaries of the LCY occupy prominent positions in the political system everywhere, even in Slovenia, where both the state President and the Prime Minister are former senior Communist politicians (Kučan and Drnovšek). Reconstructed versions of the League of Communists are a power in Montenegro and Serbia, and share power in coalition in Macedonia. Socialist parties, even where not in power, remain a significant force in opposition. What is more, it is generally recognized that beyond the parliamentary process the old *nomenklatura* retain a *de facto* share of power which is out of all proportion to the nominal changes that have taken place since 1990. What is most interesting is the fact that virulently anti-Communist movements have nowhere been strong enough to present an effective challenge to the legitimacy of these vestiges of the old order.

Secondly, the manner in which communist revolution was intertwined both with a "war of national liberation" and an inter-ethnic civil war in the period 1941–45 has meant that the formation of present-day political groupings is burdened with a history of peculiar and bitter emotional intensity, which makes the containment of political struggle within a framework of democratic politics extremely difficult. In addition, there is a tradition of political violence among the Yugoslavs (far older than the wartime experience, but reinforced by it) which to a greater or lesser extent lurks beneath the surface of newly devised forms of democratic party politics in every republic. The *prima facie* illegitimacy of political violence cannot be taken for granted in any part of former Yugoslavia in the way in which it can in many other European countries.

This ties in closely with the third sense in which the experience of the war is relevant to the contemporary scene. After 1945 the armed forces enjoyed a particularly privileged position within the Yugoslav system. It is no exaggeration to say that their importance as a political force was in many respects comparable to that of any one of the individual republics. Within the Praesidium of the League of Communists, the armed forces were represented on exactly the same level as were the republican delegations; and although excluded from the federal collective presidency, the Yugoslav National Army (YNA) always had an effective voice in the conduct of affairs.

More significantly, the Yugoslav military was always consistently committed to a particular vision of the nature of Yugoslavia. This ideological standpoint was most strongly identified, not so much with the economic characteristics of the communist system, nor even with a specifically "bolshevik" view of the nature of the Party, as with the central dogmas regarding the nature of federation, and above all the nature of the relationship between

617

nations and nationalities within that federation. The old wartime Titoist slogan of *bratstvo i jedinstvo* (brotherhood and unity) provided the key to this. (The fact that "brotherhood and unity" could act as ideological screens behind which to hide particular interests, especially national interests, is beside the point in the present context.) Consequently, although it was always highly politicized, the JNA saw itself as the principal guardian of "the system" not defined by reference to any specific set of economic or even political institutions, but rather by reference to the sacrosanct status of the federation itself.

This feature of Yugoslav politics accounts in large measure for the fact that the secession of Slovenia and Croatia in 1991 was never amenable to negotiation along the lines of the separation of Slovakia and the Czech Republic. Any reconstitution of states in the space of former Yugoslavia would have challenged at a fundamental level this ideological definition of the federation — and its institutional bearers.

A great deal of what has been written about the disintegration of Yugoslavia since 1991 has taken for granted the claim that the federation foundered primarily upon the rock of nationalism. In particular, a disproportionate measure of the blame has been laid at the door of "Greater Serbian" aspirations. This view tends to rely far too heavily upon extrapolation from the disproportionately Serb origins of military officers, and sets aside too readily the significance of the structural position of the military within Yugoslav society, and the militarization of Yugoslav political culture.

A further important general characteristic of the communist experience has a direct bearing upon the recent development of multi-party politics in Yugoslavia and its successors. It is fundamentally mistaken to equate communism in the region with a monolithic political orthodoxy, which is to be contrasted with the diversity and debate that are the supposed characteristics of democracy. The communist movement has a long and highly fraught tradition of *internal* dissent in Yugoslavia. Party discipline has been a precarious achievement throughout the greater part of its history. When Josip Broz was nominated to the post of Secretary-General of the Yugoslav Communist Party in 1937 it was quite specifically with the remit of "tidying up" the Cold Comfort Farm of political factionalism for which the party had become a by-word. National divisions were especially problematic from the beginning; but internal conflict was by no means confined to these.

This trend of internal dissent continued strongly into the post-war period. In many ways the regime set up in 1946 was a model of communist orthodoxy, and the Tito regime was regarded by the West as particularly obdurate. The expulsion of Yugoslavia from the Cominform in 1948, as a consequence of the refusal of the Yugoslav leadership to accept discipline from Moscow, came as a shock to all observers. The dispute also placed the most enormous strains on *internal* party discipline, and in the years which followed there was a protracted struggle to root out the *ibeovci* (supporters of the *Informbiro*), the marks of which are still carried by sections of the communist movement to this day, especially in Montenegro.

Party discipline was strained still further by the campaign of the forced collectivization of agriculture upon which Yugoslavia embarked the following year, partly as a means of demonstrating the socialist credentials of the regime, partly with the intention of subordinating agriculture to the already agreed policy of rapid industrialization. For a variety of reasons this attempt collapsed, and was definitively abandoned in 1953. In 1950, again to some extent as a direct response to the dispute with the Soviet Union, the first steps were taken in the creation of Yugoslavia's celebrated system of "workers' self-management" (*radničko samoupravljenje*). The accommodation of this ideological novelty was one of the reasons behind the constitutional reform enacted in 1953. These events brought with them the most intense intra-party discussion over the characteristics of socialism and the nature of the real political possibilities open to Yugoslavia, and above all over the nature of the Party itself.

The severity of these divisions became briefly apparent in 1953–54, when the Vice-President of the Party, and one of its leading ideologists, Milovan Djilas, broke ranks with the publication of a series of highly critical articles in the party paper *Borba*. These pieces, together with his subsequently published book, *The New Class*, mounted a thoroughgoing moral and political critique of the emergent leadership stratum, and ensured his political disgrace and imprisonment. Djilas became a *cause célèbre* as a "dissident": but the attention paid in the West to his personal dissent has diverted attention from the deeper and more widespread party disunity which his gesture both expressed and precipitated.

During the same period Tito also led Yugoslavia into its prolonged involvement with the Non-Aligned Movement. In the inevitable period of revaluation that has followed Tito's death in 1980 there was a tendency to dismiss the NAM as a quirky personal obsession of the Marshal. This is to say the least partly misplaced as a judgement on Yugoslavia's relationship to the NAM. It is vital to acknowledge the part which this foreign policy stance played in relation to Yugoslav domestic politics. The Communist Party had been compelled to come to terms with the delicacy of the problems posed by the ethnic diversity of the region early in the war. It moved rapidly from the mainstream CP line of denigrating nationality as a bourgeois distraction from the essential unity of the working class and, particularly under the influence of the Slovene ideologist Edvard Kardelj, came to build recognition of national diversity into the main framework of the country's ideological and political structure. As early as the first meeting of AVNOJ (the Anti-fascist Council for the National Liberation of Yugoslavia), in November 1942, the need for a federal solution to the problems of political order in any post-war settlement was accepted. Indeed, the Yugoslav state came to be defined as an association of nations, in which respect the communist predeliction for collectivist concepts in politics was extended and not challenged. The putative unity of the "working people" of the country was legitimately qualified by their division into *nations*, without being undermined by any recognition of their diversity as individual *citizens*.

This capacity to incorporate a recognition of the central importance of nationality into the ideological orthodoxy of Yugoslav communism thus simultaneously added to the effectiveness of its legitimacy, while sowing the seeds of future national conflicts. It is to the first of these purposes that involvement in the NAM centrally related. The policy of using a world platform to insist upon the right to self-determination of peoples, and the significance of the anti-colonial struggle, not only underlined publicly the determination of the Yugoslav party to maintain its independence from Moscow: it also entrenched at the domestic level the primary political importance of the nation. Non-alignment provided an ideological parable on the international plane of the correctness of the regime's stance with respect to national identity within Yugoslavia.

The central features of the "Yugoslav road to socialism" — workers' self-management, decentralization and adhesion to the NAM — laid down in the 1950s therefore worked in two directions. They served to buttress the communist regime; but they also at least potentially served to legitimate particular potential forms of dissent, in relation to both the nature of a socialist polity and the importance of nationality.

The mounting economic problems faced by Yugoslavia during the early 1960s added to the pressures for diversity within the country's politics. The steps taken to extend regional decentralization and to introduce "market socialism", in the form of the new constitutional law of 1963, and the economic reform package of 1965, brought with them new conflicts. The severity of these is suggested by the dramatic dismissal of Aleksandar Ranković from his position as head of the internal security services in 1966, accused of abuse of his powers.

In many respects the reform programme was a resounding success. The late 1960s were a period of unrivalled prosperity for most Yugoslavs; and this new economic freedom was accompanied by a measure of political liberalization. This was expressed in publications as diverse as the Catholic paper *Glas Concila* and the philosophical journal *Praxis*, as well as in much more open political debate *within* the League of Communists itself. Public acknowledgement of this new toleration was marked by the change of the name of the former Communist Party of Yugoslavia to the League of Communists of Yugoslavia (LCY).

These halcyon days were relatively short-lived. By the end of the decade the return of severe economic difficulties found the regime feeling exposed and threatened once again by outspoken dissent, and the participation of Yugoslav students in the international movement of unrest during 1968 was met with a very heavy-handed response. When reaction to the country's economic problems began to take the form not only of a demand for radical economic liberalization, but linked this to the demand for a massive extension of national independence, the result was a vigorously enforced return to centralized political control by a variety of means.

The most widely reported and dramatic of these movements of dissent was the MASPOK (*masovni prokret* — mass movement) in Croatia during 1971–72. The party replied with the suppression of the cultural organization *Matica Hrvatska*, which had been revived in 1967, and which had become increasingly significant as the medium of expression of Croat nationalism. It also led to a thorough purge of the Croatian LCY, and most notably to the expulsion from the party of its republican secretary Savka Dabčević-Kučar and Prime Minister Mika Tripalo. (The former has returned to active political life, and now heads the Croatian People's Party.)

Whereas press and academic attention were caught by the events in Zagreb, the same process was repeated at a more discrete level throughout the federation. In Slovenia, for example, the pro-reform Kavčić was also removed, and in Macedonia the Milosavljevski fraction was ousted on similar grounds.

The disturbed period of 1968–72 did produce "reform" in the Yugoslav system, but in the form of a retrenchment of Stalinism. This was concealed for some time by the externalities of the reform process, and in particular by the new constitution introduced in 1974, and the now infamous Law on Associated Labour (typically known by its Yugoslav acronym, ZUR — *Zakon o udruženom radu*). The former created an outward show of radical democratization and decentralization. The new constitution thus apparently conceded the Croatian case, by devolving a far greater measure of responsibility to republics and municipalities, and by involving citizens in the complex set of institutional mechanisms known as the "delegate system" (*delegatski sistem*). The latter supposedly elaborated and developed the existing system of self-management. It gradually became apparent, however, that behind the screen of these radical measures lay the reaffirmation of control by the LCY (even if at the cost of reducing the party itself to a federation of republican parties). There followed a *de facto* repoliticization of the economy, the relative marginalization of technical and managerial expertise, a reduction in inner-party democracy and the recapture of the political system by representatives of the partisan generation and their nominees — a return to *nomenklatura*. There was a perceptible enhancement at the same time of the position of the military in politics. These measures together heralded the arrival of the "leaden years" (*olovne godine*) in Yugoslav political life, which featured a reduction in the diversity of opinion and the freedom of its expression both within the party and more generally.

Institutional controls of this kind turned out to be ineffective in Yugoslavia (as elsewhere) as means of containing the pressures created by the country's real complexity. The situation was exacerbated in 1979 by the effects of the first "oil shock" upon the Yugoslav economy, which began to expose serious weaknesses. While it was possible to some extent to contain conflict during the lifetime of Josip Broz — for all the demystification which was set in motion after the death of "Tito", there is no denying the real political force of his personal hold on politics — the continued imposition of political cohesion became rapidly impossible after his death in May 1980. By 1983 it emerged that Yugoslavia was in very acute economic difficulties. These had been concealed behind heavy foreign borrowing, but this had not been used to fund modernization or restructuring, and consequently had not resulted in compensating gains in productive capacity or corresponding growth in exports. The retrenchment of political interests within the economy had in fact exacerbated the problems of economic irrationality. Yugoslavia was not paying its way on a massive scale. The seriousness of this state of affairs was not publicly known until the assistance of the IMF was sought in the management of the country's US\$20 billion external debt, in 1983.

Throughout the 1980s successive governments struggled to manoeuvre the country towards at first "stabilization" and then economic restructuring, in the face of the determined resistance of a large section of the Communist political establishment, and hampered by the sometimes extreme conflicts of regional interest, to which the new emphasis on the power of the republics gave free rein. Things finally came to a head in December 1988, when the government of Branko Mikulić resigned over its failure to secure acceptance of a reform package. This was the first resignation of any government in post-war Yugoslavia, and is significant if for no other reason in that it raised the possibility that governments could be held accountable for their performance, and needed to generate their own legitimacy. Mukulić was succeeded by Ante Marković, who was distinguished not only by the way in which his own economic reform programme attracted both domestic and foreign respect, but by the way in which he saw the necessity of linking economic reform to the creation of democratic politics, as a means of relegitimating the political system.

The debate about the economy, the need to move away from various forms of politicization and towards the creation of proper markets for all the factors of production, fiscal reform and monetary responsibility, was complicated by equally important conflicts over the proper character of Yugoslavia's political structure. The most intractable issue here was that of nationality. It has already been suggested that the roots of this problem lay deep within the history of Yugoslavia. The problems did not stem simply from the facts of the ethnic diversity of the country, but more particularly from the features of a political system which insisted that the unit of political account is *the nation* and not the citizen. (The commitment of the communists to the centrality of the nation in politics was underscored by the fact that three new "nations" were in significant measure created under the auspices of the LCY — the Macedonians, the Montenegrins and the Muslims.) The collectivist straightjacket of Yugoslav ideology rendered the entire problem of political rights and the relationship between ethnic groups in terms of the need to protect or balance the rights and claims of *nations*; and the federal structure of the country made matters particularly intractable through its tendency to identify the full recognition of national identity with control of a nation quasi-state.

Two problems came to be persistently difficult in this regard, both touching upon the position of Serbia and of Serbs within the federation. As the largest of Yugoslavia's constituent ethnic groups, with 8.4 million of the Yugoslav population of 23.9 millions in the census of 1991, the Serbs made up 35 per cent of the total. Only 6.3 million of these (75 per cent) lived within the republic of Serbia itself. A quarter of all Serbs in Yugoslavia were resident in other republics, particularly in Croatia (where somewhat more than half a million of them made up 11 per cent of the republic's population) and in Bosnia and Hercegovina (where 1.4 million of the republic's 4.5 million inhabitants were Serbs). In addition to this, the republic of Serbia is itself the host to substantial national minorities. The largest of these is the Albanians, whose 1.7 million represent about 11 per cent of the population of the republic. These are largely concentrated in the former Autonomous Province of Kosovo, bordering Albania itself, in the south-west of Serbia. There are also some 370,000 Hungarians, generally located in the north, in the former Autonomous Province of the Vojvodina. The status of Autonomous Provinces granted to these ethnically distinctive areas, before the imposition of the revised Serbian constitution in 1990, was fiercely resented by Serbs.

The position of Serbs was thus doubly problematic. A quarter of Serbs increasingly regarded themselves as second-class citizens within other republics, dominated by other nations within Yugoslavia; and at the same time the privileged status of the Autonomous Provinces meant that they felt that they even lacked standing within significant areas of "their own" republic. Attempts to extend the arm of the Serbian state into other republics where there were substantial Serb minorities naturally aroused hostility there — especially in Croatia. On the other hand, the attempt to enforce Serb control within the Autonomous Provinces created its own problems; and correspondingly, the efforts of the Albanians to enhance their own situation by transforming the Province in which they constituted more than 80 per cent of the population into a fully-fledged republic were met with aggressive Serb resistance. After the outburst of Albanian unrest in Kosovo in 1981 the area has remained under a state of virtually permanent armed occupation by either federal or republican security forces, with particularly serious disorder breaking out in 1987 and 1989.

The debates about the economic future of Yugoslavia coincided with the debate about nationality in important ways. In particular, the sometimes extreme differences in levels of economic development between the republics led to sharp differences in their views about economic structure and policy. The economically more advanced and wealthier republics of Slovenia and Croatia came to look with greater favour upon competition, the market and the depoliticization of economic life. The economically less advanced and poorer areas generally remained attached to socialist concepts of economic solidarity and *dirigisme*. These contrasts tended to become identified with the differences between the interests of the various nationalities inhabiting these regions. Consequently the defence of economic interest came to be expressed through demands for greater republican autonomy, even to the point of secession from the Yugoslav federation.

So powerful were these fissiparous tendencies that they affected the League of Communists itself. Following the constitutional reform of 1974 the LCY gradually decomposed to the point where it was itself no more than a federation of eight loosely allied parties. At the 14th Congress of the party in Belgrade in January 1990 it collapsed altogether.

In the light of these developments, it is clear that it can not be said in any meaningful sense that the LCY "permitted" the growth of political diversity. It was itself caught up in political processes making for pluralism which it was powerless to resist. It was to an appreciable extent the victim of devices which it created with the intention of perpetuating its own hegemony. The simultaneous need to both enact and to legitimate drastic processes of economic reform, and to cope with the consequences of the disintegeration of the ruling League of Communists, left little room for alternatives to a rapid movement towards multi-party democracy in 1990.

In the struggle to secure the elections to the republican Assemblies, in the pattern of party activity which was created surrounding that electoral contest, and in the results which they produced, can be traced not only the post-war (and even pre-war) history of dissent *against* communist rule, but also the complex story of the internal struggles of the LCY itself.

Furthermore, it is clear that the process of political differentiation in Yugoslavia was not confined to the development of a multi-party system. Possibly even more important than this was the process of the "republicanization" of politics, by which the federation gradually decomposed into a number of barely-related sub-systems. This was plainly reflected in the pattern of party organization, in that during the round of pre-disintegration elections only Marković's Alliance of Reform Forces among the principal parties made any pretence of operating across the entire federation.

The depth of this disintegrative process is indicated by the referenda conducted in Slovenia and Croatia, which led to declarations of their secession from the federation (Slovenia) or their intention to move in that direction (Croatia), on June 26, 1991. The subsequent intervention of the YNA in Slovenia in the attempt to overrule that move underlines two central features of the Yugoslav situation — the collapse of effective control by the federal government, and that fact that the future of the Yugoslav peoples was not decided, at least in the short term, through the ballot box. Developments subsequent to June 1991 are discussed in chapters which deal with each of the newly independent republics that have since emerged from the former federation.

Although the federal constitution of Yugoslavia enacted in 1974 now no longer describes the institutional framework of any of the successor states of the federation, it will be useful to consider some of its features as framing both the transition to multi-party politics and providing a background to some specific features of later political practice. While this document suggested a wide variety of freedoms which were at the disposition of its citizens, in effect these excluded the freedom to form competing political parties. Among those things which constituted the "inviolable foundation of the position and role of man" were found "democratic political relations, which enable man to realize his interests" (*Ustav SFRJ*, Basic principles, II, 1974). Article 153 insisted that "the freedom and rights of man and citizen are limited only by the equal freedom and rights of others and by the constitutionally affirmed interests of the social community". These general declarations were both counter-balanced by others and circumscribed in practice, precisely by the statement that: "The League of Communists of Yugoslavia . . . has become the organized leader of the ideal and political powers of the working class in the building of socialism and in the realization of the solidarity of working people and of the brotherhood and unity of the nations and nationalities of Yugoslavia" (Basic principles, VIII). In spite of the much-publicized unique features of "the Yugoslav way", the League of Communists of Yugoslavia secured for itself the same privileged position, on the basis of its claim to play a "leading role", as did communist parties elsewhere in eastern Europe.

Within the criminal code of the federation the delineation of offences such as "counter-revolutionary activity" (Article 114), the commission of "hostile propaganda" (Article 118), and especially "association for the purposes of hostile activity" (Article 136), gave ample scope for interpretation in such a way as to suppress any attempt at the organization of opposition. These laws were even used in order to suppress relatively innocuous groups, such as the *Praxis* group of philosophers. Article 133, which made possible prosecution for "verbal delicts", was particularly effective as an instrument for silencing opposition, and regularly earned for Yugoslavia the opprobrium of civil rights organizations. Internal party discipline, of course, regularly sanctioned the removal those within the ranks of the LCY who were regarded as subversive of party order.

Elections were a standard feature of the Yugoslav political scene throughout the post-war period, and under the 1974 constitution provision was made for a complex array of electoral choices at neighbourhood (*mjesna zajednica*), municipality (*općina*) and republican levels. The possibility that elections might be contested by more candidates than there were seats available, within the complex Yugoslav system of "delegations", antedated the formation of competing parties. Furthermore, it was not uncommon for candidates both to compete and be elected (certainly at the lower levels of government) who were not party members. (See Amendment XXVI to the federal constitution, enacted in 1988.) The absence of legitimate organized competition within elections, however, meant that the system could at best be described as a form of "managed democracy".

The first steps towards the creation of new parties were taken *within* the framework of the 1974 constitution, when the Slovene Peasant League registered as an "association" *within* the Socialist Alliance of Slovenia, in May 1988. In January the following year Dimitrij Rupel's Slovene Democratic League was launched on a similar basis, and in February the Zagreb-based Association for a Yugoslav Democratic Initiative was set up under the same provisions. This practice was declared "unconstitutional" by the Praesidium of the Socialist Alliance, but their judgement was never put to the test of the courts.

The Marković government began the process of institutional reform in earnest by announcing its intention to make possible multi-party elections, following its nomination in May 1989, by which time the League of Communists was faced with a rash of emerging "associations". Significant progress towards liberalization with respect to the expression of opinion was made when Article 133 of the Criminal Code was abolished in December 1989; nevertheless, legislation to facilitate the creation of competing political parties was first enacted at the *republican* rather than the federal level. The Slovenes once again jumped the federal gun by passing their own new Law on Political Associations, on Dec. 27, 1989.

On Jan. 20, 1990, the League of Communists finally began its ill-fated and long deferred 14th Congress. The proposal that there should be reform of the law relating to political association was approved, although several other Slovene proposals for political reform were rejected. This led immediately to the withdrawal of the Slovenes from the LC, and its rapid collapse. The failure of the reconvened Congress of the LCY later in March both confirmed its fate, and underlined the absolute necessity for reform. Legislation in the other republics followed in anticipation of any unifying federal legislative framework, the Croatian Assembly leading the way on April 25. The process of legitimation was not underwritten at the federal level until July 25, 1990, with the passage of the Law on the Association of Citizens. The last of the republics to pass appropriate legislation was Serbia, in September.

The round of elections to republican Assemblies under the new laws was initiated by the Slovenes in April 1990, and concluded in December by the Serbs, Montenegrins and Macedonians. Multi-party elections never took place to the federal Assembly. This sequence of events is particularly important, as the juxtaposition of new *republican* legislatures which had been legitimated by popular elections, and a *federal* Assembly which in lacking such legitimacy was unable to exert any moral authority over the decisions of supposedly "subordinate" bodies, must rank highly among the factors which hastened the collapse of Yugoslavia.

The new federal law declared that "citizens may freely and voluntarily join together for the purposes of founding associations, social organizations and political organizations within the territory of the SFRY" (Article 1). It specifically forbade that such bodies should take as their aim the overthrow of the constitutional order, the threatening of the territorial integrity or independence of the country, or the infringement of the constitutionally guaranteed freedoms of citizens. Neither was it permitted to organize for purposes of inciting national, racial or religious hatred (Article 2). Otherwise no limits were placed upon the legitimate purposes of associations within the meaning of the act. Secret organizations were forbidden, as it was necessary for all political parties to be registered. Article 6 defined the basic provisions which had to be made in the statute of all associations (the statement of their purposes; nature and responsibility of their administrative organs; duties of their officers and arrangements for the disposition of property, and so on).

The most important restrictions placed upon political associations were of a formal kind. They should be constituted by a minimum of ten citizens who are eligible to vote (Article 9); registration must be undertaken in accordance with certain specified particulars (Articles 11–13); and it is possible for associations to be *excluded* from the register for infractions of procedure (Article 14). Provisions were outlined for the winding up of associations (Articles 18–21): especially important to note here is the fact that they were obliged to adhere to their stated and registered purposes (Article 20). The remaining articles detailed penalties which may be exacted in the event of infraction of the provisions of the law.

Although enacted over the period of a year, occasionally in advance of the passage of federal legislation, and by individual republican Assemblies, the various republican laws were all remarkably similar in form and provisions. There were some interesting features upon which it is appropriate to comment. The law in Bosnia and Hercegovina, for example, outlawed "association on the basis of national or religious membership" where these were not already governed by the law on religious bodies; and provisions of this kind are typical. Although the letter of this type of regulation was usually respected nowhere did it prevent parties from forming *de facto* precisely along national or religious lines. The intentions of the law in this respect are clear. The key to its demonstrable failure lies in the fact that the restriction was applied to the *statement of the aims* of political associations and not to their *conduct*. The abolition of the law on verbal delicts made it possible for political figures to engage in all kinds of racial, ethnic or religious abuse or incitement on the hustings, but provided that these things were not contained in the statement of their party's *aims*, they could not be prosecuted.

The procedure governing registration was invariably complex, and invariably spelled out in great detail, and adhesion to these provisions was a strict precondition for permission to operate. In none of the republics, however, were these elaborate formal provisions an effective deterrent to the foundation of large numbers of parties, the majority of which had little if any chance of securing representation in the Assemblies.

Provisions for the conduct of elections are also worthy of comment in this context. Elections were an established element of the Yugoslav system even within the single party order. Amendment XXVI to the federal constitution specified that these must be "direct, universal and secret". The handling of elections was historically one of the prerogatives of the Socialist Alliance. Under the system of multi-party elections, however, this task was delegated to "electoral commissions" which were set up in each republic upon the announcement of an election to the Assembly. Although managed by republican officials, these commissions were composed of representatives of the parties themselves, who took on routine tasks such as the staffing of polling stations and the telling of votes. (This is in contrast with the British system, for example, where the volunteers who run the electoral process are generally recruited from the ranks of professional civil servants.) Following the elections allegations were made about the failure to make adequate provision in some areas to protect the secrecy of the vote, through proper screening of the booths. This is a relevant concern where the members of the electoral commissions who staff the polling booths were themselves active members of the parties contesting the election. Aspects of electoral practice of this kind may be of particular importance in restricting the free expression of opposition to locally dominant parties, above all where there is an element of patronage in politics.

Arrangements for the republican Assembly elections of 1990 appear to have worked fairly well, and the majority of problems which were reported stemmed from inexperience, and in theory could be remedied with ease. The most serious problems stemmed from the fact that not all republics had verified electoral registers in advance of the elections. Polling cards were sent out to voters, the presentation of which was intended to be the prerequisite of voting. Since it was rapidly recognized that the lists were seriously defective, it was announced that electors would be permitted to vote on production of either a valid passport or an identity card. Not altogether surprisingly, significant numbers of citizens in some areas rapidly grasped the opportunity which these problems offered to engage in multiple voting. The issue was particularly serious in some areas of Macedonia.

A major feature of the electoral system adopted throughout Yugoslavia, which is essential to an understanding of the development of party politics there, was the adoption of the simple majority principle. Provision varied to some extent between republics. Parties presented separate lists of candidates constituency by constituency. In other words, named representatives were elected for each and every constituency, and not selected in proportion to the party's vote from a list offered to the republic as a whole. Voting took place over several rounds. If any candidate secured an absolute majority of votes cast within a constituency in the first round, there was no need for further rounds. If no candidate secured the necessary absolute majority, a second round was held in which the leading candidate in the first round stood again, but could be contested by only one other candidate. The second candidate might be simply the one with the second largest number of votes, or be decided by agreement among several of the losing candidates in the first round.

An important consequence of this system was, of course, that the victorious candidate in each case always received the votes of more than half of the electorate in the constituency. That person was not necessarily the *first choice* of the majority of voters, however, since the candidate with the largest number of votes after the first round might be defeated in the second round by a candidate who was a lower-ranking choice for the majority of those who cast their votes in the second round, but was nevertheless acceptable as a compromise candidate.

Where the newly independent republics have introduced modifications to this system in post-independence legislation these changes are discussed in separate chapters devoted to the new states.

Although detailed consideration of recent political developments is given in the relevant chapter for each of the successor states of the former Yugoslavia, there are a number of features of party development which if not common to all are at least of general relevance, and which can be set out here.

The practical process of establishing political parties outside the ruling League of Communists of former Yugoslavia was managed at first through the device of setting up "political associations", which were registered within the Socialist Alliance of the Working People of Yugoslavia (SAWPY). This body was a classic popular front organization that operated throughout the federation, providing a vehicle through which communist influence could be assured within a number of "democratically" elected bodies, the agency through which the process of "delegation" was handled, and an all-purpose medium of agitation and mass mobilization.

By these means the first independent body with expressly political aims in post-war Yugoslavia, the Slovene Peasant League, was set up by Ivan Oman (together with its associated youth organization) in May 1988. In a similar manner a group of academics from Zagreb and elsewhere created the Association for a Yugoslav Democratic Initiative, under the leadership of the eminent Zagreb economist, Branko Horvat, in the spring of 1989. Whereas the aims of the Slovene organization were limited to the advancement of agricultural interest within the republic, the Democratic Initiative set out explicitly to work for the realization of a democratic multi-party system throughout the whole Yugoslav federation. Its well-connected and articulate support had an influence far greater than its minimal electoral success might suggest. It provided both a forum within which ideas about the future development of the system could be aired and examined, and was the seed-bed out of which a number of other independant parties of a variety of kinds were subsequently to emerge.

The device of using the SAWPY as a stalking horse for the creation of political parties explains the fact that so many of them now trace their origins to this organization. Former association with the Alliance turned out to have remarkable benefits in many cases, in that those parties that are able to count themselves among its legatees often found themselves far better endowed than the majority of their competitors with accommodation and the other material prerequisites of effective party organization.

The process of party formation in Yugoslavia is also illuminated by brief reference to older patterns of political activity in the region. It is important to acknowledge that for some areas of Yugoslavia the experience of multi-party politics is entirely novel, whereas for others the task of party formation and organization can draw upon older models. The regions of Yugoslavia that were formerly incorporated into the Austro-Hungarian Empire — Slovenia, Croatia and the Vojvodina — have historical experience of the election of representatives to the Diets of either Vienna or Budapest. The former kingdom of Serbia also had its own *Skupština*, around which parties were formed during the last quarter of the nineteenth century. The greater part of southern Yugoslavia — namely Bosnia and Hercegovina, Macedonia, the Sandžak of Novi Pazar, Kosovo and Montenegro — had no proper acquaintance with modern party politics until after the formation of Yugoslavia in 1918. The flowering of freely competitive party life was even then rather brief. The royal dictatorship which King Aleksandar imposed in 1929 terminated that freedom, and the elections of 1935 and 1938 were orchestrated as a highly artificial competition between a "Yugoslav National Party" and a "United Opposition". The short period of nominal return to party pluralism in 1945–46, before the realities of communist hegemony became fully apparent, contributed little to qualifying that pattern.

These early years have left a direct legacy to contemporary political actors in several ways. First of all, several of the current parties can trace either direct or symbolic continuity with earlier bodies. The most important of these, of course, are the continuing legatees of the communist movement. Even before the formation of Yugoslavia, communist parties were relatively successful in Macedonia and Montenegro. The first inter-war parliament contained 58 Communist deputies. Communism *does* have very long indigenous roots in this part of the Balkans, so that it cannot be in any way dismissed as some kind of exogenous imposition on the region which is likely to disappear under conditions of a presumed non-communist "normality". In each of the newly independent states a significant "social-democratic" party can still be found which is the direct legatee of this tradition. These went through a process of refurbishment between 1989 and 1991 that has varied in its impact from the more or less cosmetic (Serbia) to the dramatic and thorough (Croatia and Slovenia). Communist parties thus reconditioned form the governments in Serbia, Montenegro and Macedonia, and provide a significant oppositional force in Slovenia. Leaving aside the case of Bosnia-Hercegovina, where war makes it difficult to discuss party life in any meaningful sense, only in Croatia has the exaggeratedly anti-communist tone of nationalism managed to marginalize avowedly socialist parties.

The inter-war period also saw in Yugoslavia the rise of vigorous populist movements of a markedly nationalistic character. These have returned dramatically onto the contemporary stage, although not always in the same guise. The Croatian Peasant Party, which dominated Croatian politics after the First World War, still functions in Zagreb after 50 years in Canadian exile. Both metaphorically and literally senilized, the CPP is no longer the force in Croatian politics which it was, although its performance and support to date sugget that it will continue to have an effective voice in Croatia. It is not far-fetched to suggest also that its spirit of romantic nationalistic collectivism still flourishes in Tudjman's Croatian Democratic Union. Although the mantle of Serbian nationalism is now worn by Milošević's Socialist Party of Serbia (SPS), and not by the resuscitated Radical Party of Nikola Pašić (now the National Radical Party), much of the former Radical rhetoric still functions, and the methods adopted by the SPS owe as much to Pašić as they do to the communists. Macedonia's IMRO (Internal Macedonian Revolutionary Organization) is in many respects a similar type of organization.

The most remarkable continuity in party life across the hiatus of the war is, indeed, the persisting importance of *nationality* as the dominant organizing principle of Yugoslav politics, either explicitly or implicitly. Thus the Bosnian Party of Democratic Action took over almost exactly where the pre-war Muslim Organization left off; the Democratic League of Kosovo carries on the work of the former *Džemijet*, and the Christian Democratic Party in Slovenia has continued in important respects to carry the banner of Mgr Korošec's Slovene People's Party (although without the latter's massive popular support). Very few of the parties currently in contention for power are not, in effect, national parties. Before the disintegration of the federation only Ante Marković's Alliance of Reform Forces made any attempt to operate consistently in all republics (and even the ARF was organized as a network of republican parties.)

The *de facto* significance of nationality is obscured by the surface of ethnic neutrality which many of them adopt. For example: almost *all* the Slovene parties are effectively *Slovene* parties — except where they carry some other designation; and the Liberal Party and Democratic Party in Macedonia have little active support outside the Macedonian Slav community.

Nationality is, even so, not the only significant point of division between parties in former Yugoslavia. The observer can not fail to be bewildered, and possibly even amused, by the sheer number of parties which "sprang up like mushrooms after rain" following the liberalization of the law on freedom of association in Yugoslavia in 1989. More than 200 separate political organizations are listed in the chapters on the successor states to Yugoslavia. "Rates of fragmentation" vary, with the Slovenes being content to field a baker's dozen of parties in the proper sense of the term, whereas the Macedonians (with a similar population) find that they need nearly 60! Perhaps the record for the entire eastern European region is held by the Montenegrins, whose 649,000 inhabitants were offered a choice of no fewer than 22 parties in the elections of 1990. Of course there is some truth in the humorous response to this of many — including the Yugoslavs themselves — who explain this political cornucopia by reference to the novelty of the electoral process. One frequently hears it said that "three men in a *bife* are a political party".

This kind of response might be taken as suggesting that the phenomenon of fragmentation is an ephemeral result of the novelty of the parliamentary contest, and that these numbers might quickly be reduced. Not only is there no evidence of consolidation, however, but there are reasons for believing that acute fragmentation is a more deep-seated structural feature. The growth of a multiplicity of parties reflects the cross-cutting of a multiplicity of possible principles of organization within Yugoslav politics. Political life within each of the republics is fissured by a series of lines of cleavage which do not reinforce but cut across each other. Consequently, even *within* each of the nationalist camps there is invariably a cleavage between what might be called "modernist" and "traditionalist" stances. Croatian nationalism (to take just one example) is not entirely encapsulated within Tudjman's CDU, which is counterposed by the "modernist" Croatian People's Party, led by Savka Dabčević-Kučar. Within those republics in which the Roman Catholic church is strong, the anti-communist forces are acutely divided between clericals and anti-clericals. Thus within Slovenia this is a very active fault-line, separating groups such as the Slovene Christian Democrats (where clerical influence is strong) from the secular intellectuals who have dominated Dimitrij Rupel's Slovene Democratic League. Montenegrin politics is splintered into groups representing varying shades of opinion regarding the relationship of Montenegro to Serbia. This issue has been reflected in the vocabulary of Montenegrin politics, which distinguishes between *zelenaši* (those who favour greater autonomy from the Serb state) and *bijelaši* (those who wish to tie Montenegro more closely to Serbia). Identically, attitudes towards union with the Albanian republic cut through Kosovar politics.

The rural/urban divide is still the focus of important clashes of interest throughout all of the former Yugoslavia, and every state has at least one peasant party. The significance of *locality* as a focus of political identity is witnessed both by the relatively large number of parties which operate within very circumscribed areas, and by the remarkably large number of independent candidates who have stood for election. These might also be said to represent a metropolitan/local split (which is *not* necessarily the same as the rural/urban division). Although several of the independent candidates were successful both in the elections of 1990 and in subsequent contests, study of the election results does not really reveal the importance of this phenomenon. The listing of parties, however, includes mention of the place of registration of every organization. It is worth noting that in Bosnia and Hercegovina, to take just one example, of the 23 minor parties which did not send representatives to the republican Assembly in 1990, only five were registered in the capital, Sarajevo.

If one takes all of these observed lines of political cleavage — Communist/anti-Communist; nationalist/non-nationalist; modernist/traditionalist; secular/clerical; rural/urban; local/metropolitan — one is faced with a theoretical matrix which is capable of generating without difficulty the kind of hyper-plurality of parties which we now find in Yugoslavia and its successor states.

Partly as a consequence of this acute fragmentation, a further central characteristic of the party scene in former Yugoslavia is the acute instability of party strength. This may be a result of the process of the disintegration of Yugoslavia, or a reflection of the relationship between party leaderships and members.

Several indigenous commentators have remarked upon the fact that Franjo Tudjman's CDU is best regarded as a "movement" rather than a "party". Its *raison d'être* has been framed entirely by the exigencies of independence and the ensuing war, and it would be highly unlikely to repeat its earlier victories in future elections. Any opportunity to develop a "normal" politics within Croatia will see its natural and necessary fission, and indeed it has already experienced one dramatic split in the spring of 1994. The overwhelming predominance of the Democratic League as a force in Kosovar politics has the same character. Parties which owe their existence to the struggle for independence from the Communist-dominated Yugoslav federation are acutely vulnerable to any change in the terms of politics. (Such organizations have been compared with some justice to the Congress Party in India.)

Coalitions, and sometimes parties which depend upon participation in a successful coalition for their prominence, are particularly vulnerable. Depending upon the particular axis which dominates party debate at any one time, the grouping of allies within coalition groups can shift radically. One illustration of this is the DEMOS coalition of six parties which ousted the communists in the first Slovene elections. Its government failed to survive a motion of no confidence in April 1992, which reflected rather than heralded its internal fragility. The two principal pillars upon which this coalition was built were the defeat of the communists and the securing of Slovene independence. The first of these was secured by the elections, and the second was guaranteed by the declaration of independence on June 26, 1991. A succession of important policy and legislative questions, especially the Slovene citizenship bill, the question of abortion, and above all matters relating to economic policy, revealed its fragility and suggested alternative possible party groupings. Its mission accomplished, the grouping which swept the board in 1989 had disappeared within two years.

An important factor underlying both fragmentation and instability is the absence of personal loyalty to parties on the part of their members. Possibly the most dramatic illustration of this instability is found in Macedonia, where MAAK (the Movement for Pan-Macedonian Action), which was hailed both within Yugoslavia and abroad as the respectable voice of moderate Macedonian nationalism, suddenly found itself completely eclipsed at the polls by the plebian IMRO. In 1994 it barely survives as a party.

This is a factor which is acknowledged both by party professionals and commentators on the party scene, and is reflected both in the experience of electoral contest and in opinion polls. The professionals often bemoan the relative ignorance of the electorate. Yet an examination of party manifestos reveals that these are often far from helpful as a guide to what parties stand for, contenting themselves with vague and high-sounding phrases and rarely outlining specific legislative proposals. With the more nationalistic parties their specifically national programme is often present either in semi-coded form, or as a kind of "hidden agenda" which is communicated more through word of mouth than through formal policy statements.

The converse of the instability of electoral support can also be seen in the inconstancy of political leaderships. Crucially, the ideas to which parties apparently commit themselves during election campaigns are little use as a guide to how they will behave in office, when the demands of securing coalition solidarity may weigh more heavily than any sense of ideological commitment. A factor of no little significance also in this respect is the number of parties which have the character of "followings" rather than organizations formed around stable political programmes or the interests of classes. The attachment of leaders to parties is by no means secure, and prominent defectors characteristically take with them a dowry of personal electoral support.

A combination of these factors seems to account at least in part for the strange incongruity noted by Croatian political scientists between the ideological commitments of individual voters, measured by independent questionnaire studies, and the actual programmes of the parties to which they report an allegience.

Whereas it is possible in most of the independent states emerging from former Yugoslavia to hypothesize some probable stable trends or configurations in the political process, in every case notions of incipient patterns of behaviour, structure or loyalty need to be accompanied by a caveat concerning the overall fluidity of party systems throughout the region.

Furthermore, politics in the successor states of former Yugoslavia must be examined for the extent to which and the sense in which it might be possible to talk about the emergence of political "pluralism" in the Balkans. It is frequently assumed that a multi-party system and pluralism in politics are synonymous terms; but in fact this is not so. There are two important senses in which it is necessary to distinguish between the two ideas in this context.

In several cases, when we examine the scene region by region, what we observe is a series of one-party states. This is particularly the case in those areas still directly implicated in war or threatened immediately by armed struggle. In the so-called Republic of the Serbian Krajina (the secessionist areas of Croatia) there is nothing which could be called meaningfully a multi-party system. The various fragments of Bosnia-Hercegovina are, from a political point of view, fiefs of particular ethnic parties. The extraordinary conditions which prevail in Kosovo have endowed the DLK with a very peculiar position *vis-à-vis* the majority Albanian population. To some extent this is created by the local conditions of the break-up of the federation, in that ruling parties take power who are either the direct legatees of the former LC and its monopoly (as in Montenegro and in Serbia) or the effectively unchallenged bearers of the independence process, as in Croatia. There is some reason to believe that this pattern is becoming attenuated over time.

A more significant sense in which "pluralism" needs to be distinguished from the existence of a party contest centres upon the notion of a *plurality of centres of power*, which can include the control of economic or cultural capital in institutions which are both formally and practically differentiated from the political system in a narrower sense. The privatization of formerly socially-owned or state resources is to some extent under way in each of the states, but it is clear that the real extent of this varies enormously, from the nominal in the case of Montenegro to the considerable in Slovenia. The true effectiveness of this has also been questioned at two levels. In some sectors and in some regions the creation of *de jure* independent institutions is believed to go along with the continuing importance of *de facto* informal control. This observation has been made both with respect to Croatia and Serbia. Alternatively, the frequency of the "management buyout" as a mechanism for the transfer of ownership and/or control of resources often leaves in place, in effect, the same élite figures, working within the same political and economic culture, although dressed in new institutional clothes. While warning of the potential importance of these processes for the future development of politics throughout the region, it is still too early to comment in detail on its actual significance in relation to the establishment of parliamentary, multi-party democracy.

Finally, no realistic consideration of parliamentary politics in the area of former Yugoslavia can be complete without explicit acknowledgement of the continuing importance of war and the threat of war. More specific comment on the relevance of this is made in chapters on the newly independent states that emerged from the former Socialist Federal Republic or Yugoslavia republics. It is appropriate to note, however, that in one way or another recent, actual or anticipated violence colours political life throughout the entire region.

YUGOSLAVIA

(Federal Republic of Yugoslavia)

John B. Allcock

The Federal Republic of Yugoslavia, consisting of two republics of the former Socialist Federation of Yugoslavia — Serbia and Montenegro — was created by the promulgation of a new constitution in April 1992. There are no political parties which can be appropriately considered "Yugoslav" (i.e. federal) parties. Although the Serbian Radical Party makes a limited impact in Montenegrin politics, it is clearly a Serbian organization (and not just an organization of Serbs). Consequently this volume does not include a Directory of Parties section for Yugoslavia. Details of parties operating in the constituent parts of the Federal Republic of Yugoslavia can be found in the separate entries for Serbia and Montenegro. For details of party political development prior to April 1992, see also the chapter on "Yugoslavia — The Socialist Federal Republic of Yugoslavia" on pages 615–632, and individual country entries for successor states to the Yugoslav federation.

In April 1992 a new constitution was promulgated, establishing the "Third Yugoslavia" or Federal Republic of Yugoslavia (FRY). The 1992 constitution does provide for a Federal Assembly in Belgrade, necessitating some general comment about the framework within which parties operate at the federal level.

The Federal Assembly (*Skupština*) consists of two Houses, the Chamber of Citizens and the Chamber of Republics. Elections take place for 138 territorial constituencies within the former, whereas the latter is composed of 40 members, 20 drawn from each republic reflecting the party composition of the republican Assemblies. The President of the federation is elected by the Assembly, and not directly by the electorate.

The range of responsibilities of the federation is relatively narrow, but covers some very important matters: the federation is a single market and is served by a single monetary system; transport and communications, health and safety, international relations and defence are all within federal competence.

There have been some significant conflicts between Montenegrin and Serbian representatives within the Assembly, and the former have generally been staunch defenders of local autonomy. In July 1993 the most severe of these conflicts surfaced over a proposal to abolish republican ministries of Defence, Foreign Affairs and Foreign Economic Relations. The balance of representation means that the Federal Assembly is more often than not a forum within which to extend the conflicts proper to Serbian politics. Nevertheless, the Serbs need the federation. The FRY has always set great store in international relations upon its claim to be the legitimate successor state to former Yugoslavia. Without the federation this claim would collapse. It is widely believed that Milošević cherishes the ambition to create an expanded federation, which would take in at least part of Bosnia–Hercegovina, the Republic of Serbian Krajina and probably also Macedonia. It is worth noting that the federal constitution contains provisions for the accession of additional republics. The existence of a constitutionally separate Montenegrin state within the federation is important if this project is not to be dismissed as "Greater Serbia".

The first direct elections to the Chamber of Citizens were held in May 1992, although these were boycotted by several opposition parties. The *doyen* of the Serbian literati, Dobrica Ćosić, took on the Presidency. A wealthy expatriate, Milan Panić, was appointed as federal Prime Minister. By December serious conflict had developed between the federal and Serbian governments, particularly over the conduct of the war in Bosnia–Hercegovina. Fresh elections were called for both the federal and republican Assemblies in December. Panić was defeated in the Serbian presidential contest by Milošević, after which he was dismissed as federal Prime Minister, and the Socialist Party of Serbia was able to form a new federal government in coalition with the Montenegrin Democratic Party of Socialists, which took office on Feb. 3, 1993. The results of these elections are summarized in Table 1.

Although Ćosić was re-elected as federal President, Milošević was able to force his dismissal in June in connection with allegations that he had plotted a *coup d'état* in Serbia with senior military officers. He was replaced by a non-entity, Zoran Lilić.

There is still some uncertainty as to whether the apparatus of parliamentary government at the federal level in Yugoslavia is a mere smoke-screen behind which is concealed the agency of the Socialist Party of Serbia. At the time of writing, however, federal power may have been used to embarrass the Serbian Presidency, but has yet to succeed in thwarting its aims on any vital issue.

Table 1: Results of Elections to the Chamber of Citizens of the Federal Assembly, December 1993*

Party	Seats N = 138
Socialist Party of Serbia	47
Serbian Radical Party	34
DEPOS	20
Democratic Party of Socialists	17
Democratic Party	5
Socialist Party of Montenegro	5
National Party	4
Democratic League of Magyars of Vojvodina	3
DP/DLMV†	2
DP/DLMV/Civic Party†	1

Notes: * The second chamber (the Chamber of Republics) is not elected directly by citizens.
    † Joint candidates

Source: *Politika*

Serbia

A semi-independent principality of Serbia was created from Ottoman territory following a successful rebellion by the Serbs in 1813. This underwent a series of enlargements throughout the nineteenth century. The most substantial of these was the gains made as a result of the Balkan wars, when the Sandžak of Novi Pazar, Kosovo and Macedonia were acquired. Serbia was effectively fully independent as a kingdom after 1868. After World War I Serbia joined the new Kingdom of Serbs, Croats and Slovenes (renamed Yugoslavia in 1929), ruled by the Serbian Karadjordjević dynasty. At this time also the territories known as Bačka and the Banat, north of the Danube and formerly part of Hungary, but settled largely by Serbs, were acquired.

Following invasion by the Axis powers in 1941, Serbia was dismembered, with large areas in the south under Bulgarian occupation (including Macedonia) and those areas with predominantly Albanian populations being attached to the Italian client state of Albania. A truncated Serbian state was set up, nominally still under the monarchy, but under an indigenous military governor, backed by German occupation forces. Bačka was annexed by Hungary, and the Banat (with its large German minority) directly by the German Reich.

Following the reunification of Yugoslavia in 1945 a Serbian republic was created, but containing an "Autonomous Province" of the Vojvodina, which included Bačka, the Banat and Srem (formerly regarded as a part of Croatia). The largely Albanian areas of the south-west, "Kosmet" (a neologism combining Kosovo and Metohija) were an "Autonomous region" until 1968, when as "Kosovo" they were granted the same status as the Vojvodina. The autonomy of both of these provinces was abrogated in the revised Serbian constitution of 1990.

With a surface area of 88,361 km sq the Republic of Serbia is the largest of the six republics of the former federation (34.5 per cent of the total), with a population (census of 1991) of 9,916,068 (41.5 per cent of the total). The most numerous ethnic group in the republic are the Serbs, (63.7 per cent), followed by the Albanians (estimated 11.2 per cent) the Magyars (3.1 per cent) and the Muslims (2.6 per cent). There are also locally significant minorities of Croats, Montenegrins and Romanies.

The ethnic structure of the republic was reflected before 1990 in the creation of two Autonomous Provinces within the republic. Kosovo, in the south-west and adjacent to Albania, covered 10,887 km sq (about 12 per cent of the territory of the republic); the Vojvodina in the north covered 21,506 km sq (about 24 per cent). Containing nearly 1.7 million of the 2.2 million Albanians resident in former Yugoslavia, Kosovo is thought to be nearly 85 per cent Albanian in its population. (The Albanians boycotted the census of April 1991, so these figures are estimates.) With a rate of increase of roughly 30 per cent over the decade 1981–1991, the Albanian population in Serbia was the fastest growing demographic group in Yugoslavia. Because of its very special political situation Kosovo is discussed in greater detail in pages 651–655 below.

The Vojvodina contained the majority of Yugoslavia's Magyar minority, who are especially numerous in the area known as Bačka. Their numbers declined at an accelerating rate over the intercensal period, as have the numbers of Croats living in Serbia. Numbers of national minorities in the republic generally fell in this interval, with the exception of Albanians, Muslims and Romanies. The presence of all of these is politically sensitive in Serbia.

635

A distinctive feature of the Serbs' situation in former Yugoslavia was their dispersal. The census of 1991 recorded more than 8.3 million Serbs, of whom only 6.3 million (75 per cent) lived within the Republic of Serbia. The diaspora of more than 2 million Serbs resident in other republics of the federation (especially Bosnia-Hercegovina and Croatia) gave to Serbs a particularly keen interest in the integrity of the federation and consequently (in a period in which relations between republics and between the republics and the federation were becoming ever more strained) a disproportionate potential for making an impact upon the political process throughout most of Yugoslavia.

The political relevance of Serbs and of Serbian politics was enhanced by two factors. The Communist *partisan* movement had recruited with particular effect among Serbs from other republics in 1941–45; and ethnic minorities in all republics had both incentive and opportunity to use federal institutions as an avenue of social mobility throughout the post-war years. Taken together, these two factors heightened the commitment of Serbs to the Communist system, and placed them in positions of special vulnerability when the continuing future of both party and federation came under challenge.

Although the 1974 constitutional changes have been recognized subsequently as allowing a partial "restalinization" of the Yugoslav system (and hence a strengthening of the hand of this "old guard" in which Serbs were relatively over-represented) the lurch towards the creation of a market economy and the growing republicanization of politics after the IMF intervention of 1983 were perceived as very threatening, both in Serbia (with its rather obsolete and protected industrial sector) and among the stratum of career political functionaries everywhere. Under these circumstances, the constitutional and economic position of Serbia, and the position of Serbs in general, emerged as potent ideological symbols masking a struggle for the defence of the old Communist order.

Under the 1974 constitution (following the death of President Tito in 1980) the federation has been headed by a collective Presidency of eight members — one representing each of the republics and Autonomous Provinces. In relation to several areas of economic reform, Serbia could often count upon a relatively cautious Presidency, acting as a brake upon the commitment to modernization of Croatia, Slovenia and the Vojvodina. On other matters, especially reform of the League of Communists (LC) itself, the Serbian interest was often outvoted — deserted by its "own" provinces.

Serbian politics took a crucial turn in 1987 when, in the middle of a prolonged economic crisis, Slobodan Milošević took over the leadership of the Belgrade LC. His political project was a bold one, combining a paradoxical attempt to relegitimate the leadership of the LC through advocacy of "anti-bureaucratic revolution". This involved cutting loose from the outworn political vocabulary of Yugoslav politics, and using the anxieties about falling living standards and diminished personal security — expressed in plain language — to demand a reinforcement of the powers of the federation against those of established republican élites. In May 1989 Milošević became President of the Serbian Presidency.

Milošević rapidly stumbled upon the potency of the weapon offered by the position of the Serb diaspora, and anxieties of Serbs within Serbia itself. The addition of an edge of Serb nationalism to his "anti-bureaucratic" populism gave him a ready audience and political allies in other republics in his fight against the decay of the federation. It also offered him the means of strengthening Serbia's hand at the federal level. In October 1988 the leadership of the LC in the Vojvodina was brought down, largely as the result of mass demonstrations orchestrated by Milošević supporters. In December and January 1989, a similar result was achieved in Montenegro; and in March 1989 the leadership of the

Kosovo LC was also purged (culminating in the show trial of Azem Vllasi) in the attempt to secure its compliance. An attempt in December 1989 to intervene in Slovene politics failed ignominiously. Cumulatively, these events tended to entrench a view of Yugoslav politics as a contest between Serbia and the rest.

The centrepiece of Milošević's strategy within Serbia was the revision of the republican constitution, re-establishing the primacy of Belgrade over the Autonomous Provinces, promulgated in September 1990. His insistence upon Serbia becoming "master in its own house" was given greater force by the growing sense of Serbia's isolation within the federation. Multi-party elections in Serbia were held under this new constitution to a unicameral *Skupština* in December 1989. Milošević's Socialist Party of Serbia (the renamed League of Communists) secured a sweeping victory, posing as the defender of Serbia's interests within the federation, and with his personal standing boosted by the achievement of constitutional reform.

Slobodan Milošević has often been falsely depicted outside the country either as a rabid Serb chauvinist, or as a die-hard Communist. In fact this is to misunderstand seriously the agility with which he has balanced extremes, isolating and fragmenting the opposition in the process. While appealing to a sense of Serb nationalism, Milošević has been able to represent Serbs as the true custodians of the general *Yugoslav* interest. In this he has distanced himself both from the romantic Serb isolationism of Vuk Drašković (1990 version) and the monarchist fractions, and the iron-fisted centralism of Šešelj's Radicals. While advocating a continuing economic role for an interventionist state and a gradualist approach to economic reform, he has also argued for movement towards a market economy and away from the monopoly of "social property". Here he has positioned the Socialist Party of Serbia neatly between an uncontrolled gallop into capitalism (as he portrayed Ante Marković's programme) and the defence of state socialism mounted by the League of Communists–Movement for Yugoslavia. The strong strain of pragmatism in his politics has enabled him to portray all other aspirants to political power in Serbia as bigots, dilettantes or opportunists.

The difficulty of putting together a coherent opposition under these circumstances is indicated by the violent shifts of stance which Drašković's SMR and the various factions of Democrats have adopted in the search for electoral support. The Western press has typically misunderstood the situation, looking in vain for a potential moderate opposition that might offer a more acceptable alternative to the SPS.

The hold of the SPS on Serbian politics has not been achieved solely by the use of political argument. Since 1989 Milošević has been able to secure effective control over the principal media of mass communication, allowing an exclusion of dissenting voices which surpasses that of the former one-party Communist state.[1] He has also been prepared to use open violence to intimidate opposition, and to build up a substantial paramilitary police force — which is also believed to constitute an important independent asset in any potential conflict with the Army. This police force figured strongly in the suppression of anti-government demonstrations in Belgrade in June 1992 and the seizure of the Federal Ministry of Internal Affairs in December 1992, during the struggle for power between Milošević and the federal Prime Minister Milan Panić. The deployment of force has been a constant feature of government control over Kosovo throughout the period under review.

In fact the most distinctive feature of the opposition scene in Serbia, especially since the outbreak of war in former Yugoslavia, has been the rise of radical nationalist parties, often linked to irregular armed units. Drašković's Serbian Movement for Renewal, Šešelj's

Table 2: Result of Elections to the Serbian Assembly*

Parties	(250 seats)		
	Dec. 1990	Dec. 1992	Dec. 1993
Socialist Party of Serbia	194	101	123
Serbian Movement for Renewal (DEPOS)	19	49	45
Serbian Radical Party		73	39
Democratic Party	7	7	29
Democratic League of Magyars of Vojvodina	8	9	5
Democratic Party of Serbia		7	
Party of Serbian Unity		5	
Party of Democratic Action (SDA)	3		2†
Alliance of Peasants of Serbia	2	3	
Alliance of Reform Forces of Vojvodina	2	2	
Party of Yugoslavs	1		
Democratic Reform Party of Muslims	1	1	
National Peasant Party	1		
Serbian Democratic Party	1		
Association for a Yugoslav Democratic Initiative	1		
Party of Democratic Action (PDD)	1		
Democratic League of Croats in Vojvodina	1		
Independents	8		

Sources: Politika
Notes: * The Serbian Assembly has only one Chamber
† In 1993 in coalition with the Democratic Party of Albanians

Serbian Radical Party and Željko Raznjatović (Arkan)'s Movement for Serbian Unity have all been openly associated with *četnik* formations of one kind or another that have played an active role not only in the conduct of war in Croatia and Bosnia–Hercegovina, but in the intimidation of other opposition groups within Serbia (especially where these have been vocal in their opposition to war). In many cases (particularly with "Arkan", who is wanted internationally by the police on charges of armed robbery) these formations are believed to be connected with criminal organizations. This strand of violence gives a character to Serbian politics which is absent from other republics of former Yugoslavia, unless under war conditions. The culture of violence emerges even within the *Skupština*, the proceedings of which are not infrequently interrupted by fist-fights between deputies.

A potentially significant feature of the constitutional changes in Serbia has been reform of the system of local government, replacing the former communes (*opštine* — of which there are 136) with 29 districts (*okruzi*). For electoral purposes these have been grouped into nine regions, returning approximately 25 deputies each to the Assembly (with the exception of Belgrade, which returns 46). An intriguing feature of the drafting of these electoral regions is the obvious element of gerrymandering with respect to the ethnic distribution of the population. The Vojvodina is divided into two, and these areas are linked to parts of the solidly Serb Šumadija and the Morava Valley. The Sandžak, with its large Muslim population, is treated similarly, yoking its two halves to the most ethnically pure parts of south-western Serbia. The electoral impact of Kosovo is reduced by carving off two portions of solid Albanian settlement and merging these with the more "reliable" environs of Leskovac. As a relatively novel feature of the system, however, the effects of this transparent attempt to ensure as far as possible permanent Serb domination throughout the republic have yet to be fully evaluated.

Directory of Parties

Because of the very large number of parties registered in Serbia (111 contested the elections of December 1993) it is necessary to restrict the number covered by full entries here. All parties which have been represented since December 1990 are included: the rest given briefer mentions. Because of the specific political conditions prevailing within the former Autonomous Province of Kosovo, a supplementary section following the main entry for Serbia deals with the unregistered parties which competed in the unofficial elections to the Assembly of the "Republic of Kosova". Registered parties which have contested the official elections are listed in the main section, even though these may also have fielded candidates in the unofficial elections.

Association for a Yugoslav Democratic Initiative (AYDI)
Udruženje za Jugoslovensku Demokratsku Inicijativu (UJDI)

Address. Aberdareva 1, 11000, Belgrade.

Telephone. 11 332-982.

Foundation. November 1989.

Leadership. Nebojša Popov (pres.); Žarko Puhovski.

History. Initially the Association saw itself as a movement, the function of which was to promote the process of democratization in Yugoslavia. In the early phase of its development, therefore, it operated as a "political association" within the Socialist Alliance. Having secured a seat in the 1990 elections it began to take on the characteristics of a party, but retains much of its ambiguous nature.

Programme. The central concerns of AYDI are the promotion of human and civil rights within the framework of a democratic politics. It has been a staunch critic of the war in Bosnia, and active in the canvassing of peaceful solutions to the war.

Civic Alliance (CA)
Gradanski Savez (GS)

Address. Vlakovićeva 1–3, 11000, Belgrade.

Telephone. 11 630-409.

Leadership. Vesna Pešić (pres.).

History. Emerged from AYDI.

Organization. Secured two seats in the republican Assembly in the 1993 elections. Its support is concentrated among the educated urban population, especially in Belgrade.

Programme. The Alliance has a strong emphasis on civil liberties and civil rights, although this appears to contradict several of the key elements of the platform of DEPOS, especially with respect of Kosovo.

Affiliations. Participates in the DEPOS coalition.

Democratic Alliance of Croats in the Vojvodina (DACV)
Demokratski Savez Hrvata u Vojvodini (DSHV)

Address. Trg Lazara Nešića 1/X, 24000, Subotica.

Telephone/fax. 24 51-348.

Foundation. July 15, 1990.

Leadership. Bela Tonković (pres.).

Organization. The party secured the election of one of its representatives to the republican Assembly for the Subotica area in 1990, with the support of the DCMV. Its members are drawn primarily from the Croat minorities known as *Bunjevci* and *Šokci.*

Programme. The DACV advocates the protection of individual rights, and those of all national and religious minorities, especially rights to linguistic and literary expression, and reform of the judicial and educational systems. It gives a strong emphasis to private enterprise in the economic sphere.

Affiliations. No formal affiliations, but in fact works closely with the DUMV, the NPP and the Social Democrats.

Democratic Union of Magyars of Vojvodina (DUMV)
Demokratska Zajednica Vojvodanskih Madara (DZVM)

Address. Trg Oslobodenja 11, 21100, Ada.

Telephone. 24 852-248.

Foundation. March 31, 1990.

Leadership. Agošton Andraš (pres.).

Organization. As its title suggests, the party represents the interests of the Magyar population of the Vojvodina, and has secured the election of five of its members to the republican Assembly, three to the federal Assembly, and three others in coalition with other parties. All of these are for seats in that region. At the time of writing the DUMV is undergoing schism into two groups, and an important axis of division is the question of whether or not the party should support an autonomist platform for Magyars, analogous to the position taken by the DLK in Kosovo.

Programme. The party's programme stresses the protection of individual and collective rights, and especially those which have a bearing upon cultural and linguistic minorities. It has been strongly critical of Serbia's participation in war in other republics.

Democratic Party (DP)
Demokratska Stranka (DS)

Address. Terazije 3/IV, 11000, Belgrade.

Telephone. 11 338-078; 345-184.

Fax. 11 623-686.

Foundation. Feb. 3, 1990.

Leadership. Zoran Dindić (pres.). The party now has seven seats in the republican and five in the federal assemblies.

History. The party was founded by Dragoljub Mićunović, a respected academic, and provided a major component of the opposition at the time of the elections of 1990, securing seven seats in the republican Assembly. It vacillated at length over the role of Serbia in the war in Croatia and Bosnia, finally settling on a strongly nationalistic position, and split in 1992. (Personal differences between Dindić and Mićunović were also significant, and antedate the war.) The latter has withdrawn from leadership. A secessionist group set up the Democratic Party of Serbia (see below).

Programme. The Democrats demand the strengthening of public confidence in the state through vigorous action against corruption. They also take a strong line on "welfare state" measures to protect the lower-paid. The party supports state control of the major resources and the continuation of a measure of both public and social ownership (reversing its original position of strong commitment to the market). The DP is vigorously nationalistic. Since the elections of December 1993 it has been in coalition with the SPS, and programmatic differences between the two appear to be nominal.

Democratic Party of Albanians (DPA)
Partia Demokratike Shqiptare (PDS)
Demokratska Partija Albanaca (DPA)

Address. Selami Halači bb., Preševo.

Foundation. Aug. 23, 1990.

Leadership. Ali Ahmeti (pres.).

History. Little is known of this group other than the fact that it operates among the Albanian community in Preševo, on the Macedonian border. In particular, how it differs politically from the PDA in the same city is unclear. It did secure two seats in the republican Assembly in 1993, working in coalition with the Muslim PDA (*qv*).

Democratic Party of Serbia (DPS)
Demokratska Stranka Srbije (DSS)
Not to be confused with the DS

Address. Smiljaničeva 33, 11000, Belgrade.

Telephone. 11 459-179; 822.

Fax. 11 444-6240.

Foundation. July 24, 1992, following a split with the DP.

Leadership. Vojislav Kostunica (pres.).

Organization. Secured seven seats in the elections of 1993.

Programme. Monarchist and reputedly near-fascist, the DPS has been an outspoken supporter of the Bosnian Serbs. In fact, it demands the unification of all Serbs (in which they include Montenegrins) in a single state. In the economic field the party differs from the DP by advocating minimal state intervention and the opening-up of the economy to international competition. (Under conditions of international economic sanctions this latter point is of rhetorical interest only.)

Democratic Reform Party of Muslims (DRPM)
Demokratska Reformska Stranka Muslimana (DRSM)

Address. Koritnik 3, 29000, Prizren.

Telephone. 29 22-322; 31-281.

Leadership. Azar Zulji (pres.).

Organization. The party secured the election of one member to the republican Assembly in 1990 and in 1992, but lost its seat in 1993. The extent to which it is able to function effectively beyond its base in Prizren is not known. It is reputed to be left-wing in orientation.

Democratic Movement of Serbia (DEPOS)
Demokratski Pokret Srbije (DEPOS)

Formerly known as the Associated Serbian Democratic Opposition (ASDO)
Udružena Srpska Demokratska Opozicija (USDO)

Address. Maršala Birjuzova 13, 11000, Belgrade.

Telephone. 11 685-490.

Foundation. Aug. 31, 1992, in the run-up to the elections of December.

Organization. Formally a coalition of four opposition parties: the MSR led by Vuk Drašković; the CA, led by Vesna Pešić; the SLP, led by Nikola Milošević; the ND, led by Dušan Mihailović (*see* separate entries for these parties). The coalition secured 45 seats in the 1993 elections, although this has since been depleted by the secession from the alliance of the ND.

Programme. DEPOS has criticized the government strongly for its connivance at corruption and war profiteering. It has taken a strong line on Kosovo, and during the 1993 election campaign advocated the construction of 150,000 new flats in support of the Serb colonization programme there. While criticizing the SPS for its conduct of the war, it demands the unification of all Serb territories (in which it includes Macedonia) in a single state. It is unclear how these demands are to be reconciled with the first item in its manifesto, which was the lifting of international sanctions against Serbia, or with its acceptance of a multi-ethnic Bosnia! Government monopolization of the mass media has been a repeated target of DEPOS.

National Peasant Party (NPP)
Narodna Seljačka Stranka (NSS)

Address. Nušićeva 17, 11000, Belgrade.

Telephone. 11 3227-791.

Foundation. May 20, 1990.

Leadership. Dragan Veselinov (pres.).

Organization. The extent to which this party operates beyond its base in Pančevo is unknown. It secured the election of one member for Pančevo in the elections of 1990.

Programme. The principal concerns of the party are economic. Here it advocates very emphatically the defence of private property and the free movement of private capital, although within a mixed economy. It has a special concern for agriculture, and advocates the payment of reparations to those who suffered under the collectivization and nationalization programmes. Several specific reforms are advocated, in the area of social security and working conditions, including the development of free trade unions.

New Democracy (ND)
Nova Demokratija (ND)

Address. Ho Ši Minova 27, 11000, Belgrade.

Telephone. 11 135-804.

Leadership. Dušan Mihailović (pres.).

History. This party entered the DEPOS coalition in 1992. Following the 1993 elections, however, it left the coalition using its six votes to support the minority SPS government. Its nationalism is fairly outspoken.

Peasants' Party of Serbia (PPS)
Seljačka Stranka Srbije (SSS)

(Formerly Party of the Alliance of Peasants of Serbia:
Stranka Saveza Seljaka Srbije)

Address. Maršala Tita 81, 11000, Belgrade.

Telephone. 11 789-235.

Foundation. Oct. 26, 1990.

Leadership. Milomir Babić (pres.).

History. No information is available about this party other than the fact that they secured two seats in the elections to the republican Assembly in 1990, which they held in 1992 but lost the following year.

Party of Democratic Action (PDA)
Partija Demokratsko Delovanje (PDD)
Partia e Aksionit Demokratik (PAD)

This is not to be confused with the principal party of Bosnian Muslims, the English title of which is the same.

Address. 15 Novembra 74, Preševo.

Leadership. Riza Haljimi (pres.).

Foundation. Aug. 23, 1990.

Organization. The PDA appears to operate exclusively in the area of Preševo-Bujanovac-Medveda, in the extreme south of Serbia, where they succeeded in electing a member to the republican Assembly in the election of 1990. The population of the area is largely Albanian, and it is among Albanians that it finds support. How it differs politically from the DPA is unclear.

Programme. The programme of the PDA starts out from the observation that its home area is among the poorest in Serbia. It sees parliamentary democracy as a way out of the extreme "degradation" of Albanian culture, which is a victim of the "arbitrariness" of the state, and towards respect for national minorities. While strongly pursuing the defence of Albanian culture, its programme expresses concern for the position of women, and demands the "complete rooting-out of blood-revenge".

Party of Democratic Action (PDA)
Stranka Demokratske Akcije (SDA)

This is not to be confused with the similarly-named party above.

Address. E. Redžepagića 54, 36300, Novi Pažar.

Telephone. 20 25-626; 25-667.

Foundation. Aug. 11, 1990.

Leadership. Sulejman Ugljanin (pres.).

Organization. The party secured the election of three representatives to the republican Assembly in the elections of 1990, all from the Sandžak region. In coalition with the DPA it secured two seats in 1993. It is the Serbian branch of the principal party of Bosnian Moslems (*see* chapter on Bosnia). The extent to which it functions independently of the parent organization is unknown.

Programme. Whereas in general the programme of the party in Serbia mirrors that of its parent in Bosnia, it does give greater place to the expression of concern over the rights of minorities, and in particular includes advocacy of the "complete cultural autonomy of the Sandžak".

Party of Serbian Unity (PSU)
Stranka Srpskog Jedinstva (SSJ)

Address. Ljutice Bogdana 3, 11000, Belgrade.

Telephone. 11 4441-600; 4441-667.

Foundation. Oct. 26, 1993.

Leadership. Željko Ražnjatović "Arkan" (pres.).

History. The party emerged as a rather opportunistic creation on the eve of the 1992 elections, when its candidates stood nominally as a "group of citizens" — i.e. as independents — making a particular bid for control in Kosovo, where the elections were boycotted by the Albanians. The gain of five seats on this occasion was not matched in the 1993 elections, however, by which time it had acquired the trappings of a proper party.

Organization. The party is heavily centred upon the personality of its founder, "Arkan". It is more influential as a paramilitary organization than a conventional political party, with a long record of engagement in the dirtier parts of the war in Croatia and Bosnia, as well as in Kosovo.

Programme. The PSU has worked closely with the SPS for a time. Arkan is prone to wildly contradictory, off-the-cuff statements intended to have an immediate popular appeal to the audience of the moment, so that it is hard to speak of a "programme" in any normal sense of the term. Sentimental rhetoric about family values and the Orthodox faith are standard.

Party of Yugoslavs (PY)
Stranka Jugoslovena (SJ)

Address. Jevrejska 16, 11000, Belgrade.

Telephone. 11 626-208.

Fax. 11 628-357.

Foundation. Sept. 20, 1990.

Leadership. Borislav Kosijer (g.s.).

Organization. The party secured one seat in the 1990 elections. Although previously represented in several of the republics of the former Yugoslav federation, in effect it now operates only in Serbia and Montenegro.

Programme. As its name suggests the party grew up as the voice of those who regarded themselves as of "Yugoslav" ethnicity.

Serbian Liberal Party (SLP)
Srpska Liberalna Stranka (SLS)

Address. Akademski trg 11, 11000, Belgrade.

Telephone. 11 634-256.

Foundation. May 12, 1991.

Leadership. Nikola Milošević (pres.).

Programme. The party is committed to the typical liberal programme of personal and economic freedom, within a framework of parliamentary democracy.

Affiliations. The SLP is a partner in the DEPOS coalition.

Serbian Movement for Renewal (SMR)
Srpski Pokret Obnove (SPO)

Address. Terazije 3/X, 11000, Belgrade.

Telephone. 11 342-918.

Foundation. July 20, 1990.

Leadership. Vuk Drašković (pres.).

History. The party emerged during 1989 largely as the personal following of Drašković, a charismatic figure who made his name as a writer and poet of a highly emotional and nationalistic colour.

Organization. The SMR is represented in the majority of the republic's communes, and also has branches in other republics of Yugoslavia as well as among the Serb diaspora abroad. The extent of this network is unknown, but is certainly large. The party secured the election of 19 members to the republican Assembly in the elections of 1990, and became the senior partner in DEPOS during the 1992 election. In 1993 it secured 36 seats.

Programme. The SMR set out as a highly vocal advocate of the "Great Serb" ideal, hard to distinguish on a policy basis from other nationalistic groups, with the exception of the greater specificity with which it spelled out demands for the maintenance of what it considered to be the historic rights of the Serb people, and the methods by which these were to be secured. It has apparently reversed its former policy on Bosnia, and now supports a unified, multi-ethnic Bosnia, but how this squares with other statements about a future Serb state is unclear. The party demands the restoration of the monarchy, the defence of the cyrillic script and other symbols of the Serbian past. Its programme includes the consolidation of Serbian domination in Kosovo (by various means, including the massive ejection of Albanians) and in Macedonia. Anti-Islamic and anti-Papal invective is prominent. It is strong on privatization, and emphatic about the need for a more independent media and the subordination of the state to the rule of law.

Affiliations. The lynchpin of the DEPOS coalition.

Serbian Radical Party (SRP)
Srpska Radikalna Stranka (SRS)

Address. Francuska 31, 11000, Belgrade.

Telephone. 11 625-231.

Foundation. Feb. 25, 1991.

Leadership. Vojislav Šešelj (pres.).

History. The SRP first attracted attention when it successfully contested a by-election to the Serbian Assembly in June 1991.

Organization. The party very much has the character of a "following" surrounding its leader, Šešelj, who refers to himself as *Vojvoda* — the traditional Serbian title for a military leader. The party has its own paramilitary wing, which has been active in the war both in Croatia and Bosnia, as well as in thuggery against domestic opposition. The relationship between the party and the armed units is unclear. It became the major opposition party briefly after the 1992 elections, and went into a short-lived coalition with the SPS, but suffered a severe setback in the 1992 contest. Since then it has been further weakened by the desertion of its elected representatives; estimated by mid-1994 to be down to 29.

Programme. The SRP is among the most vociferous and aggressive advocates of a "Great Serbia" — which its literature indicates is intended to encompass all of the Yugoslav federation without Slovenia — although the character envisaged for this state appears to be federal, as it insists that Serbia should not interfere in the affairs of the Serbian Republic of Bosnia–Hercegovina or the Republic of Serbian Krajina. The movement is known to be engaged in terrorism and arms running on a large scale. Its pronouncements are rhetoric rather than a coherent programme and the majority of its efforts appear to be devoted to extra-parliamentary action.

Affiliations. The SRP is one of the few Serbian parties which is actively represented among Serbs outside Serbia.

Socialist Party of Serbia (SPS)
Socijalistička Partija Srbije (SPS)

(Formerly League of Communists of Serbia:
Savez Komunista Srbije)

Address. Bulevar Lenjina 6, 11000, Belgrade.

Telephone. 11 627-084.

Foundation. In its present form, July 16–17, 1990.

Leadership. Slobodan Milošević, President of the republic of Serbia; Mihailo Marković, Vice-president of Serbia; Mirko Marjanović, Prime Minister of Serbia. Since the party is the principal partner in the governing coalition most of the ministers are party nominees. It currently has 123 seats in the republican Assembly, and 47 in the federal Assembly, where it also dominates federal ministries.

Organization. The party is effectively organized at local and municipal levels throughout the republic. It has massive real estate and other resources. It also continues to exercise the kinds of informal control of other organizations, especially the press, which have been associated with Communist Party practice for a long time.

Programme. While acknowledging the importance of its links with the Communist movement in the past, the programme of the SPS stresses that this is not "given forever, and must be constantly subjected to critical re-examination". In this respect, it emphasizes the importance of the democratic electoral process. The party advocates a "democratic socialism", which excludes racial, religious or national hatred. The manifesto stresses "responsibility" and stability. While giving place to the need to create markets for all factors of production, it sees a continuing role for the state in the economy, is opposed to unregulated "enrichment" and privatization, and advocates solidarity, participation and the defence of the system of social security. It has recently waged a vigorous campaign against economic criminality as the cause of increasing social differentiation.

Affiliations. The extent to which real co-operation between former republican organizations of the LCY is sustained under present circumstances is unknown.

In addition to these parties with established electoral success, it is worth mentioning the following because of its impact on political debate and the attention which it has attracted outside Serbia.

League of Communists–Movement for Yugoslavia (LC–MY)
Savez Komunista–Pokret za Jugoslaviju (SK–PJ)

Address. Bulevar Lenjina 6/XVI, 11000, Belgrade.

Telephone. 11 145-678; 659-526.

Foundation. Feb. 27, 1991.

Leadership. Dragomir Drašković (pres.).

History. This group, often known as the "party of the generals" is a fragment of the former LCY that is devoted to a relatively hardline communism linked to a strong affirmation of the integrity of the 1974 constitution. If and when necessary, these aims are to be furthered by the appropriate use of military force. It is centred around a number of mainly retired senior officers (especially former defence chief Admiral Branko Mamula) and at one time was believed to have the backing of a substantial section of the Veterans' Association. Mirjana Marković, the wife of Slobodan Milošević, is believed to be linked to it. Although at one time it was regarded as the focus for a possible military coup and a force to be reckoned with, it has subsequently emerged as a group of the disillusioned and nostalgic old guard.

The following minor parties either contested the elections of 1990 or have appeared since then. Information has been obtained from the Serbian Ministry of Information and the Serbian press. Unless otherwise stated the place of registration is Belgrade.

All-Serbian Alliance (ASA): *Svesrpski Savez* (SS). Not to be confused with the following. **Alliance of All Serbs of the World (AASW):** *Savez Svih Srba Sveta* (SSSS). Note the way in which two parties have chosen to play on the monogram included in the Serbian coat of arms. Although this group has made no impact in Serbia itself, it is a significant force in the Krajina. **All-National Democratic Front of Vojvodina (ANDFV):** *Svenacionalni Demokratski Front Vojvodine*. Registered in Novi Sad. **All-Serbian National Movement (ASNM):** *Svesrpski Narodni Pokret* (SSNP). Registered in Novi Sad. **Association of Albanians, Serbs, Montenegrins and Other Citizens for a United Republic of Serbia and Yugoslavia.** *Udruženje Albanaca, Srba, Crnogoraca i Ostalih Gradana za Jedinstvenu Republiku Srbiju i Jugoslaviju*. Registered in Kosovska Mitrovica. **Association of Natives of Serbia (ANS):** *Udruženje Starosedelaca Srbije* (USS). **Belgrade Citizens' Party (BCP):** *Beo-Gradanska Stranka*. Not to be confused with the following. **Belgrade Party (BEST):** *Beogradska Stranka* (BEST). **Christian Democratic Party (CDP):** *Demohriščanska Stranka* (DHS). **Citizens' League of Serbia** (CLS): *Gradanski Savez Srbije* (GSS). **Citizens' Movement for Subotica:** *Gradanski Pokret za Suboticu*. Also known as the **Doves of Subotica. Citizens' Party (CP):** *Gradanska Stranka* (GS). Registered in Novi Sad. Not to be confused with the GP, or with the following. **Citizens' Party of Serbia (CPS):** *Gradanska Stranka Srbije* (GSS). Registered in Uroševac. Not to be confused with the similarly-named party above. **Communist Party of Yugoslavia (CPY):** *Komunistička Partija Jugoslavije* (KPJ). Not to be confused with the following. **Communist Party of Yugoslavia in Serbia (CPYS):** *Komunistička Partija Jugoslavije u Srbiji* (KPJS). **Democratic Alliance of Bulgarians in Yugoslavia (DUBY):** *Demokratski Savez Bugara u Jugoslaviji*. Registered in Niš. **Democratic National Party (DNP):** *Demokratska Narodna Stranka* (DNS). Registered in Pančevo. **Democratic Party (Davidović–Grol) (DP(D–G)):** *Demokratska Stranka (Davidović–Grol)* (DS(D–G)). The reference here is to the Democratic Party of pre-war years, which was allowed to function briefly after the war in the "popular front" period. **Democratic Party of Romanies of Yugoslavia (DPRY):** *Demokratska Stranka Roma Jugoslavije* (DSRJ). Registered in Aleksinac. Not to be confused with the following. **Democratic Political Party of Romanies of Yugoslavia (DPPRY):** *Demokratska Politička Partija Zajednice Roma Jugoslavije* (DPPRJ). Registered in Kragujevac. **Democratic Union of the Centre (DUC):** *Demokratska Unija Centra* (DUC). **Democratic Women's Movement (DWM):** *Demokratski Pokret Žena*. Registered in Kragujevac. **Economic Movement for Serbia (EMS):** *Ekonomski Pokret Srbije* (EPS).

Farmers' Party (FP): *Zemljoradnička Stranka* (ZS). Registered in Valjevo. **Grand Rock 'n Roll Party:** *Velika Rockn'Roll Partija.* The Yugoslav equivalent of "Screaming Lord" Sutch! **Green Party (GS):** *Zelena Stranka* (ZS). **Householders' Party (HP):** *Domaćinska Partija* (DP). Not to be confused with the Democratic Party. **Labour Party (LP):** *Partija Rada* (PR). Not to be confused with the Liberal Party. **League for Pančevo – Party for Moderate Progress (LP–PMP):** *Liga za Pančevo – Stranka Umerenog Napretka* (LP–SUN) Registered in Pančevo. **League of Serbian Families (SPAS):** *Savez Porodica Srbije* (SPAS). Registered in Mladenovac. **League of Social Democrats of Vojvodina (LSDV):** *Liga Socijaldemokrata Vojvodine* (LSDV). Resistered in Novi Sad. **League of Workers of Serbia (LWS):** *Savez Radnika Srbije* (SRS). Not to be confused with the Serbian Radical Party. **Liberal Party (LP):** *Liberalna Stranka* (LS). Believed to be quite distinct from the SLP. Registered in Valjevo. **Morava League (ML):** *Moravska Liga* (ML). Registered in Jagodina. **Movement for the Protection of Human Rights (MPHR):** *Pokret za Zaštitu Ljudskih Prava* (PZLjP); also known as the "Human Rights Party" — *Stranka Ljudskih Prava.* Not to be confused with the following. **Movement for the Protection of Citizens' Property Rights (MPCPR):** *Pokret za Zaštitu Imovinskih Prava Gradana* (PZIPG). **Movement of Vlachs and Romanians of Yugoslavia (MVRY):** *Pokret Vlaha i Rumuna Jugoslavije* (PVRJ). Registered in Zaječar. **Movement "Vojvoda Vuk":** Pokret "Vojvoda Vuk". Registered in Kragujevac. **Muslim Bosnian Organization (MBO):** *Muslimanska Bošnjačka Organizacija* (MBO). Registered in Novi Pazar, but a branch of the Sarajevo party of the same title. **National Farmers' Democratic Party (NFDP):** *Narodna Zemljoradnička Demokratska Stranka* (NZDS). Registered in Mladenovac. **National Front of Yugoslavia for Serbia (NFYS):** *Narodni Front Jugoslavije za Srbiju* (NFJS). **National Party (NP):** *Narodna Stranka* (NS). **National Radical Party of Nikola Pašić (NRPNP):** *Narodna Radikalna Stranka Nikole Pašića* (NRSNP). **National Unity League (NUL):** *Liga za Nacionalno Jedinstvo* (LNJ) **Natural Law Party (NLP):** *Partija Prirodnog Zakona* (PNZ). **New Communist Movement of Yugoslavia (NCMY):** *Novi Komunistički Pokret Jugoslavije* (NKPJ). **Old Radical Party (ORP):** *Stara Radikalna Stranka* (SRS). **Party of Bunjevci and Šokci (PBS):** *Bunjevačka i Šokačka Stranka* (BSS). Registered in Subotica. **Party of Businessmen and Private Initiative (PBPI):** *Stranka Privrednika i Privatne Inicijative.* **Party of Foreign Currency Savers (PFCS):** *Stranka Deviznih Štediša* (SDS). **Party of Independent Entrepreneurs (ZaPIS):** *Stranka Samostalnih Privrednika* (ZaPIS). **Party of Independent Democrats of Serbia (PIDS):** *Stranka Samostalnih Demokrata Srbije.* Registered in Niš. **Party of National Concord (PNC):** *Stranka Narodne Sloge* (SNS). **Peasant–Workers' Party of Serbia (PWPS):** *Seljačko–radnička Stranka Srbije* (SRSS). **Pluralistic Socialism Party (PSP):** *Stranka Višepartijskog Socijalizma* (SVS). Registered in Kruševac. **Popular Independent Party of Vlachs (PIPV):** *Narodna Samostalna Stranka Vlaha* (NSSV). Registered in Kladovo. **Progressive Party (PP):** *Napredna Stranka.* **Radical Party (RP):** *Radikalna Stranka* (RS). Not to be confused with either the SRP or the Republican Party. **Radical Party of Unification (RPU):** *Radikalna Stranka Ujedinjenja* (RSU). **Reform Democratic Party of Vojvodina (RDPV):** *Reformska Demokratska Stranka Vojvodine* (RDSV). Registered in Novi Sad. **Republican Club (RC):** *Republikanski Klub* (RK). **Republican Party (RP):** *Republikanska Stranka* (RS). Registered in Arandelovac. **Serbian Democratic Party of Serbia (SDPS):** *Srpska Demokratska Stranka Srbije* (SDSS). **Serbian Fatherland League (SFL):** *Srpski Otadžbinski Savez* (SOS). **Serbian National Party (SNP):** *Srpska Narodnia Stranka* (SNS). Registered in Priština. **Serbian National Revival (SNR):** *Srpska Narodna Obnova* (SNO). Not to be confused with the SMR of Drašković. Registered in Nova

Pazova. **Serbian National Union (SNU)**: *Srpska Nacionalna Unija* (SNU). Registered in Kragujevac. **Serbian Party of Rights (SPR)**: *Srpska Partija Prava* (SPP). **Serbian Party of St Sava (SPSS)**: *Srpska Svetosavska Stranka* (SSSS). Not to be confused with the AASW. **Serbian Royalist Block (SRB)**: *Srpski Rojalistički Blok*. Not to be confused with the following: **Serbian Royalist Movement (SRM)**: *Srpski Rojalistički Pokret* (SRP). **Serbian Youth–New Serbia Movement (Pride)**: *Srpska Omladina–Pokret Nove Srbije* (PONOS). Registered in Kragujevac. It is readily possible to confuse the following group of "Social Democratic" fractions (*). **Social Democratic Alliance of Serbs/Yugoslavia (SDAS/Y)**: *Socijaldemokratski Savez Srbije/Jugoslavije* (SDSS/J)(*). **Social Democratic Movement of Serbia (SDMS)**: *Socijaldemokratski Pokret Srbije* (SDPS). Registered in Niš (*). **Social Democratic Party (SDP)**: *Socijaldemokratska Partija* (SDP)(*). **Social Democratic Party of Romanies in Serbia (SDPRS)**: *Socijaldemokratska Partija Roma u Srbiji* (SDPRS)(*). **Social Democratic Party of Serbia (SDPS)**: *Socijaldemokratska Stranka Srbije* (SDSS)(*). **Social Democratic Party of Yugoslavia (SDPY)**: *Socijaldemokratska Partija Jugoslavije* (SDPJ)(*). **Socialist National Party of Yugoslavia (SPY)**: *Socijalistička Narodna Stranka Jugoslavije* (SSJ). **The Užice Movement (UM)**: *Užički Pokret* (UP). Registered in Užice. **Vojvodina Party (VP)**: *Vojvodanska Stranka* (VS). Registered in Zrenjanin. **Women's Party (WP)**: *Ženska Stranka* (ŽS). **Workers' Party of Serbia (WPS)**: *Radnička Partija Srbije* (RPS). **Yugoslav Democratic Party (YDP)**: *Jugoslovenska Demokratska Stranka* (JDS). **Yugoslav Economic Radical Party (YERP)**: *Jugoslovenska Ekonomsko-radikalna Stranka* (JERS). Registered in Beli Potok. **Yugoslav Working Class "Josip Broz Tito"**: *Jugoslovenska Radnička Klasa "Josip Broz Tito"*. Registered in Novi Pazar. **Zora–Citizens' Association for a Better Grocka (Zora)**: *Zora – Udruženje gradana za bolju Grocku (Zora)*. Registered in Grocka.

Kosovo

Although Kosovo is constitutionally a part of Serbia, its historical development and political conditions are distinctive, and the position of the region is sufficiently vital to the future of the whole of former Yugoslavia to merit more extended attention in this survey.

Largely because of its specific ethnic structure the region was marked out for special constitutional status as early as the Jajce conference of AVNOJ in 1943. As an "Autonomous Region" (subsequently an "Autonomous Province") within the Republic of Serbia, its status varied through the post-war period. In the years immediately following World War II the Albanian population were subjected to heavy pressure to assimilate as Serbs or to accept designation as "Turks" (on the basis of the predominance of Islam among Albanians) and to emigrate to Turkey. Estimates vary as to the numbers of Albanians who were compelled to leave the region during the 1950s, but the number may be as high as 200,000. At the same time, the land reform programme was partly utilized in order to reinforce the representation of Serbs and Montenegrins.

Following the constitutional reform of 1963, and with added impetus after the purging of Ranković in 1967, Kosovo participated in the general process of the decentralization of politics within Yugoslavia. The constitution of 1974 almost left the region with the status of a *de facto* republic, enjoying specific representation in the collective Presidency of the federation, and having an organization of the League of Communists that carried effective republican status. Even so, the management of the relations between this overwhelmingly Albanian region and the South Slav federation was always difficult, especially after widespread disorder in 1968 and 1981.

As conflict deepened over the future of the federation during the late 1980s, and the Serbian LC became the principal voice favouring a strong federal government, conflict between Belgrade and Priština intensified. In the debate about the future constitutional order of Yugoslavia, the Kosovars became increasingly vocal in their demands for outright acknowledgement as a republic within a confederal structure. Consequently an early objective of Slobodan Milošević, having assumed the leadership of the Serbian LC, was to reduce the constitutional odds against the Serbian view by asserting clear control over the republic's two Autonomous Provinces — Kosovo and the Vojvodina. In 1988 the process was begun of amending the Serbian constitution to this effect — incidentally by-passing the federal constitution in the process.

Following a period of increasing disorder in the province, the Serbian Assembly suspended the operation of the provincial government in Kosovo on June 26, 1990, and on July 5 dissolved the Provincial Assembly. The Presidency of the Autonomous Province resigned in protest. The promulgation of the new Constitution on Sept. 28, 1990, included the change of name of the Province to "Kosovo and Metohija", although under the new provisions their separate identity was purely nominal. The Albanian member of the federal collective Presidency resigned in March 1991, and the functions of the provincial Presidency were suspended. The new federal constitution of April 1992 confirmed the change of status of the provinces.

The former members of the Kosovo Assembly set themselves up as an "Assembly-in-Exile", and on Sept. 26–30, 1991, organized a referendum on the independence of a Kosova Republic, which returned a massive positive vote. Illegal elections were organized on May 24, 1992, creating a new government and assembly-in-exile for the "Republic of Kosova". The Democratic League of Kosova secured a substantial majority of the 130 seats, and Ibrahim Rugova (leader of the DLK) was elected as President.

The parallel government has attempted to create a series of unofficial institutions and agencies, replacing those systematically dismantled by the Serbian state. There have been wide-ranging dismissals of Albanians from official posts throughout Kosovo, and their replacement by Serbs and Montenegrins. A massive police and army build-up in the region has ensured the continuing repression of protest, and throughout 1993 and 1994 expectations rose that the policy of non-violent resistance would erupt into open armed struggle.

Although the struggle for independence has come to be associated outside Kosovo largely with the DLK (and in many respects it shares characteristics with Tudjman's CDU as a "movement" rather than a party), the Democratic League is far from constituting the sole political voice for Albanians from the region. There is lively party contention within the Albanian community; and other ethnic groups have developed their own parties. In the nature of the case, party politics is even more closely patterned upon ethnic lines than elsewhere in former Yugoslavia, with no significant groups emerging which are capable of bridging effectively a diversity of ethnic groups.

The majority of Albanians have boycotted all aspects of the political process organized from Belgrade — local, republican and federal elections — and do not participate in the official Assemblies at any of these levels.

Table 3: Results of the Unofficial Elections of May 1992 in Kosova

Party	% of vote	Seats (N = 130)
Democratic League of Kosova	76.44	96
Parliamentary Party of Kosova	4.86	13
Peasants' Party of Kosova	3.15	7
Albanian Demo-Christian Party	3.10	7
Independents	3.29	2

Source: Kosova Information Centre, *Albanian Democratic Movement in Former Yugoslavia, Documents: 1990–1993*, Prishtina, 1993.

Directory of Parties

The following political organizations are known to operate in the Kosovo region, although they are not registered officially with the authorities in Belgrade for obvious reasons. They all have a record of success in the unofficial elections organized in the "republic of Kosova". This is known to be an incomplete list of political organizations in Kosova, as 22 bodies offered candidates in the elections of May 1992.

Officially registered parties which have contested elections organized by the Republic of Serbia are reported in the main body of the directory for Serbia.

Albanian Demo-Christian Party (ADP)
Partia Demokristiane Shqiptare (PDS)

History. Founded in September 1990. Its title suggests affiliation to the Christian democratic tradition, but paradoxically most of its members are believed to be Muslims, although the party was founded specifically among the Catholics of Peć. The PDS gained seven seats in the unofficial elections of May 1992. The extent to which it has real links with Christian Democrat organizations elsewhere is unknown, and its programme suggests a strongly paternalistic approach to the state, and a developed interest in environmental questions, without reference to the traditional Catholic individualism and concern for family issues.

Democratic League of Kosovo (DLK)
Lidhja Demokratike e Kosovës (LDK)

Address. Beogradska bb., 38000, Priština.

Telephone. 38 27-660.

Foundation. Dec. 23, 1989.

Membership. Claims 700,000 in Kosovo alone, with up to 1 million including branches elsewhere.

Leadership. Ibrahim Rugova (pres.). Rugova is Chair of the Co-ordinating Council of Albanian Political Parties in Kosova and former Yugoslavia, and president of the unofficial government.

History. Following the formation of an Association for a Yugoslav Democratic initiative in 1989, as a forum for more general democratic discussion in Yugoslavia, a Council for Civil Rights was formed in Kosovo. This was a direct response both to the immediate past history of violent protest against Serb rule in the province, and to the prospect of a changed Serbian constitution, abolishing the Autonomous Provinces. The League rapidly emerged as the principal political expression of Kosovo Albanians. Although there are several parties based in Kosovo the DLK has always been a kind of "first among equals" among the groupings.

Organization. Although based in Kosovo the League has more than 30 branches, some of which are in other republics, and some in other countries.

Programme. The DLK identifies the basic cause of the problem of Kosovo as economic backwardness, and proposes that the most effective way out of this is via the creation of a market economy. The League's position is officially that of accepting "equal federal or confederal" status for Kosovo as a republic within Yugoslavia. It is widely believed that many within the party would prefer to see either an independent state, or union with Albania, either of which are perhaps accommodated within the phrase: "It is the right of Albanians in their ethnic lands to communicate and co-operate through forms they consider most suitable." The DLK advocates multi-party democracy with the full equality of all citizens before the law, the abolition of restrictions on the press and other civil rights, and the abandonment of all forms of "nationalistic and bureaucratic manipulation of the nationality problem", believing that it is possible for all nationalities resident in Kosovo to live together peaceably.

Affiliations. It is known that the League has extensive links with the Albanian diaspora in Western Europe (especially Switzerland) and the USA. These are a vitally important source of funding. It is believed that there are also strong links with political groups in the republic of Albania, but nothing definite is known about the nature of these or their significance.

Parliamentary Party of Kosovo (PPK)
(Sometimes known as the Liberal Party of Kosovo (LPK))
Partia Parlamentare e Kosovës

Founded in the summer of 1990. Led by Veton Surroi. The party publishes its own journal, *Koha* (Time), which has become quite influential as a forum for discussion of Kosovar political opinion. Contact address, Sunčani Breg, Lamela 10, Priština. Tel. 38 49-236 or 43-999. Described as a party of the "modern European centre", it has links with Liberal organizations elsewhere in Yugoslavia. With 13 representatives in the unofficial Assembly, the PPK is probably the most significant of the political groupings outside of the DLK.

654

Peasant Party of Kosovo (PPK)
Partia Fshatare e Kosovës (PFK)

Founded Jan./Feb. 1990. Has seven seats in the unofficial Assembly.

Social Democratic Party (SDP)
Partia Social-demokrate (PSD)

Led by Shkëlzen Maliqi. The party insists that it is not a specifically Albanian organization. It is not known to what extent it is linked with other social democratic groups elsewhere in former Yugoslavia. Founded in January–February 1990. A group of Western-oriented intellectuals provide its core. Maliqi in particular is known as a moderate and effective communicator of the Albanian case outside Kosovo. The fact that the SDP gained no seats in the unofficial elections indicates that it is more influential outside Kosovo than within it.

Turkish Peoples Party (TPP)

Led by Sezair Shaipi, and based in Priština. Two Turkish representatives were elected to the unofficial assembly, with the active co-operation of the DLK, with which the TPP co-operates closely.

Notes
For a thorough study of Serbian politics, see Mark Thompson (ed.), *Forging War: the Media in Serbia, Croatia and Bosnia–Hercegovina*, Article 19 International Centre Against Censorship, 1994.

Montenegro

Montenegro is a small semi-independent state that survived the general Ottoman occupation of the Balkan peninsula, and sustained intermittent armed resistance against Turkish hegemony since the fifteenth century. Ruled from the end of the seventeenth century by a dynasty of prince bishops, Montenegro became a kingdom in 1851. The monarchy was abolished in 1918 when Montenegro joined the Kingdom of Serbs, Croats and Slovenes (renamed Yugoslavia in 1929). Montenegro was placed under an Italian governor after the invasion of 1941, and became a republic within the Yugoslav federation in 1945.

With a surface area of 13,812 km sq the Republic of Montenegro is the smallest of the six republics of the former federation (only 5.4 per cent of the total) with a population (census of 1991) of 648,483. The most numerous ethnic group in the republic are the Montenegrins, with 61.8 per cent of the population, followed by Muslims, with 13.9 per cent, the Albanians, with 6.2 per cent, and the Serbs, with 3.5 per cent. The Muslims are generally concentrated in the west and south-west of the republic, and the Albanians in the south. These form continuous areas of Muslim settlement with the Sandžak of Novi Pazar in neighbouring Serbia, and of Albanian settlement with the former Autonomous Province of Kosovo and with Albania itself. The proportion of Montenegrins in the population at the census of

1981 was 68.5 per cent, and the decline relative to the various Muslim groups has become something of a political issue in the republic. Nearly 6 per cent of the population in 1991 declared themselves to be "Yugoslav".

Montenegrins were typically staunch supporters of the Yugoslav federation, and generally allied themselves with the Serbian attempt to preserve the union even by force. Montenegrin units within the Yugoslav National Army were very active in particular in the war in Croatia. Even so, when the EC laid down criteria for acceptance as an independent state, in January 1992, the Montenegrin constitution (adopted in November 1990) was hastily amended in order to meet the EC's requirements for recognition.

Following a referendum in March 1992, in April Montenegro joined with Serbia in establishing a "Third Yugoslavia" — the only one of the former republics of Yugoslavia to do so. Its constitution was amended again in October 1992 to bring it into line with the new federal constitution.

Possibly even more than in Serbia, Montenegro was slow to move in the direction of multi-party elections, having very strong links with the Communist system. Montenegrins were statistically heavily over-represented in the higher reaches of the League of Communists (LC), government and especially the armed forces. The first freely contested elections took place only in December 1990, and illustrated clearly this relative entrenchment within the old order. The Communist candidate for the republican presidency, Momir Bulatović, was elected (although with a narrow majority), and the LCM secured an absolute majority (83) of the 125 seats in the republican Assembly (*Skupština*). Following the constitutional restructuring of October 1992, a new presidential election was held on Jan. 10, 1993, which once again returned Bulatović to power (representing the former Communists, now renamed the Party of Democratic Socialists). The results of these elections are summarised in Table 4.

With more than 30 parties registered within this tiny state of 600,000 people. Montenegro must present the most fragmented party structure in eastern Europe. Following the break-up of former Yugoslavia there has been a certain consolidation, however, with several previously separate, minor ethnic parties collaborating in a Democratic Action Party, and a merger between the extreme National Party, led by Novak Kilibarda, and the former Socialist Party of Montenegro, to form a New Socialist Party of Montenegro.

Political debate in Montenegro in the main revolves around the issue of the relationship between the republic and Serbia within the Yugoslav federation. (A very old axis of division within Montenegrin politics is that separating the *zelenaši* (Greens) from the *bijelaši* (Whites): the former are stout defenders of Montenegrin independence, while the latter are advocates of close political and cultural attachment to Serbia.) The bringing down of the republican government in January 1989 by demonstrations organized by supporters of Slobodan Milošević — incidentally bringing Bulatović to power — was an example of the resurgence of this historic issue.

Several manifestations of the strength of autonomist sentiment in Montenegro contrast with this evidence of Montenegrin subordination to the will of Belgrade. In October of the same year the remains of former King Nikola (deposed in 1918) and other members of the royal family were returned to Cetinje for reburial, amid massive popular demonstrations. In October 1993 the Archimandrite Antonije Abramović was installed as head of an autonomous Montenegrin Orthodox Church, at a ceremony in the Ostrog Monastery, severing historical ties with the Serbian Church and providing occasion for acute controversy.

Table 4:   Results of Elections to the Montenegrin Assembly (December 1990) and to the Presidency (January 1993)

Party	Seats
Montenegrin Assembly	
League of Communists of Montenegro	83
Democratic Party of Socialists	
Alliance of Reform Forces†	17
Democratic Coalition¶	13
National Party	12
Total	125

Election to the Presidency, 10 January 1993:	
Momir Bulatović (DPS)	63.3%
Branko Kostić	36.7%

Source: Secretariat for Information, Republic of Montenegro
Notes: * The Montenegrin Assembly has only one Chamber
   † The Alliance of Reform Forces in Montenegro was created through a coalition of three parties; the Liberal Alliance; the Socialist Party and the Party of Socialists
   ¶ The Democratic Coalition was created through a coalition of the Party of Democratic Action, the Democratic League and the Party of Equality (itself a fusion of three small parties)

Throughout the process of Yugoslavia's disintegration, and in spite of Bulatović's former status as a client of Milošević, co-operation between the republics has been strained, to the point at which in 1993 the Montenegrins attempted to secure the stationing of UN observers on the border with Serbia, in order to demonstrate that international sanctions were not being breached. Montenegrin opinion was outraged by the proposal canvassed in July 1993 that republican ministries of Defence, Foreign Affairs and External Economic Relations should be abolished and replaced by unified federal ministries.

Although Montenegro shares with all the other republics of former Yugoslavia the characteristic of ethnic diversity, inter-ethnic relations have never deteriorated to the point reached elsewhere in former Yugoslavia. (In this respect the situation resembles more closely that in Slovenia.) Party political activity is divided along ethnic lines: several minority parties collaborate in a Democratic Coalition of Muslims and Albanians in Montenegro. Because many Montenegrin Albanians are Roman Catholics, however, the solidarity of the coalition revolves around broad issues of civil and minority rights.

Directory of Parties

Alliance of Reform Forces for Montenegro (ARFM)
Savez Reformskih Snaga za Crnu Goru (SRSCG)

Emerged from a Democratic Forum of opposition parties set up in Montenegro in 1989, and registered in December 1990. As a party it was created by the merger of three parties: the Liberal Alliance of Montenegro (LAM); the Socialist Party (SP) and the Party of Socialists of Montenegro (PSM), which initially came together under the banner of Ante Marković's reform programme, and was strongly oriented towards the maintenance of the Yugoslav federation and the creation of a market economy. In the elections of 1990 the ARF secured 17 seats in the Assembly. Since the disintegration of the federation, however, the Alliance has unravelled, largely over the issues of the role of Montenegro in the war, and the independence of the republic *vis-à-vis* Serbia. There has been a realignment of its components, with the PSM joining the ardently unitarist National Party to form the New Socialist Party of Montenegro.

Democratic Coalition (DC)
Demokratska Koalicija (DK)

Foundation. Formed after the elections of December 1990 through the collaboration of three parties: the Party of Democratic Action; the Party of Equality; the Democratic League.

Leadership. Lekë Lulgjuraj (sec.); Mehmet Bardhi; Asim Dečević.

Organization. The party has 13 representatives in the republican Assembly. It is not clear to what extent the coalition entails the subordination of the specific aims of its individual components. Explicitly it remains a coalition, and is not a new party.

Programme. It is possible to identify the platform of the new Coalition in relation to its formerly independent components. All expressed strong concern for the building of a "legal state", a market economy and a pluralistic democracy. All were especially firm about the protection of human and civil rights. All were vocal on issues of the position of national minorities. Nevertheless, each in different ways, explicitly or implicitly, addressed problems of the inadequate political representation of the interests of Muslim or Albanian citizens in the republic.

Affiliations. The Party of Democratic Action is the principal Muslim party in Bosnia and Hercegovina. The Democratic League is the leading Albanian political organization based in Kosovo.

Democratic Party of Socialists (DPS)
Demokratska Stranka Socijalists (DSS)
Formerly League of Communists of Montenegro (LCM)
Savez Komunista Crne Gore (SKOG)

Address. Jovana Tomasevića bb., 81000, Podgorica.

Foundation. July 1948, the date of its first Congress. Registered under the present law, July 24, 1990.

Leadership. Momir Bulatović (pres.) President of the republic; Milo Djukanović is Prime Minister.

Organization. The apparatus of Communist party organization is very much intact in Montenegro, and the DPS retains in its hands the real estate and other resources appropriate to its former position as the sole party.

Programme. As with the other reformed Communist parties, the DPS presents itself as standing in the "European tradition of democratic socialism", fighting for the "humanistic ideas of socialism". Its programme strongly stresses the unification of all interests, of gender, nationality, religion, and region. It accepts a mixed economy and pluralistic democracy. The party has supported the participation of Montenegro within the new Yugoslav federation, but staunchly resists any notion of outright union with Serbia. Its policy statements are distinguished by their extreme vagueness.

Affiliations. It is not known to what extent there remain effective links between the several republican Communist organizations in their reformed mode.

Liberal Alliance of Montenegro (LAM)
Liberalni Savez Crne Gore (LSCG)

Foundation. Jan. 1, 1990.

The Liberal Alliance was one of the small parties which came together under the banner of the ARF before the break-up of Yugoslavia. It has remained in existence under the leadership of Slavko Perović. Registered initially in Cetinje, it takes a firmly pro-independence stance.

National Party (NP)
Narodna Stranka (NS)

Foundation. May 12, 1990

Under the leadership of Novak Kilibarda, the party won 12 seats in the Assembly in 1990. The National Party was probably the most uncompromisingly Serbian of the parties in Montenegro, being aggressively and explicitly in favour of the "Great Serb" ideal, and seeing Montenegrins simply as one branch of the Serbian people. In many respects, including its anti-Communism, the NP resembled Drašković's MSR in Serbia itself. In 1992 it merged with the Party of Socialists of Montenegro (still with Kilibarda as its leader), under the title the New Socialist Party of Montenegro.

New Socialist Party of Montenegro (NSP)
Nova Socijalistička Crne Gore (NSS)

Formed in 1992 from the union of the National Party and the Party of Socialists of Montenegro, this party is now the primary voice of unitarist sentiment in Montenegro, and the most vocal voice in opposition. Led by Novak Kilibarda and Radoje Kontić. It gained five seats in the federal Chamber of Citizens in December 1992, and joined the Socialist Party of Serbia to create a governing coalition, with Kontić as Prime Minister.

The following minor parties either contested the elections in 1990 or have appeared since then. Altogether 31 political parties were registered in October 1992. Information has been obtained primarily from the Montenegrin Secretariat for Information. All are registered in Podgorica, unless otherwise indicated.

Association for the Advancement of Democratic Processes (AADP) *Udruženje za Unapredjenje Demokratiskih Procesa* (UUDP) Should be considered a movement rather than a party. Registered in Nikšić. **Democratic Action Party (DAP)** *Partija Demokratsko Delovanje* (PDD), or *Partia e Aksionit Demokratik* (PAD). An Albanian group linked to the party of the same name based in Preševo in the Serbian part of the Sandžak. Not to be confused with the Sarajevo-based PDA. **Democratic League of Albanians of Montenegro (DL)** *Demokratski Savez Albanaca u Crnoj Gori* (DS) *Lidhja Demokratike e Shqiptareve te Malit te zi* (LD). This is a branch of the principal Albanian political organization, based in Kosovo. Works within the Democratic Coalition following the elections of 1990. For additional information see the entry under Kosovo pp. 651–655. **Democratic Party (DP)** *Demokratska Stranka* (DS). The party was created too late to participate in the 1990 elections, so there has been no real test of its strength, but for a time it appeared to be a serious rival to the ARFM as the voice of moderation and reform in Montenegro. **Democratic Socialist League (DSL)** *Demokratski Socijalistički Savez* (DSS). Another fraction to emerge from the "Socialist Alliance". **Ecological Movement of Montenegro (EMM)** *Ekološki Pokret Crne Gore* (EPCG) The Montenegrin version of the Greens. **Independent Organization of Communists (IOC)** *Nezavisna Organizacija Komunista* (NOK) Registered in Bar. **Montenegrin Federalist Movement (MFM)** *Crnogorski Federalistički Pokret* (CFP) Registered in Cetinje. **Party of Democratic Action (PDA)** *Strank Demokratske Akcije* (SDA). This is a branch of the principal Muslim Party of Bosnia and Hercegovina. Works within the Democratic Coalition, following the election of 1990. Registered in Rožaj, with support drawn principally from the Montenegrin portion of the Sandžak. **Party of Equality (PE)** *Stranka Ravnopravnosti* (SR) Merged with the Democratic Coalition following the election of 1990. **Party of National Equality (PNE)** *Stranka Nacionalne Ravnopravnosti* (SNR). **Party of Socialists of Montenegro (PSM)** *Partija Socijalista Crne Gore* (PSCG). Another fraction to emerge from the "Socialist Alliance". Merged with the ARF after the elections of 1990, subsequently merging with the National Party forming the New Socialist Party of Montenegro. **Serbian Radical Party**

(SRP) *Srpska Radikalna Stranka* (SRS) This is simply the Montenegrin branch of the Serbian party of the same title. It has no representation in the Assembly, but is a significant voice at the extreme end of Serbian nationalism. **Socialist Party (SP)** *Socijalistička Partija* (SP) Merged with the ARF following the elections of 1990. **Social Democratic Party of Montenegro (SDPM)** *Socijaldemokratska Stranka Crne Gore (SDSCG).* **Yugoslav National Party (YNP)** *Jugoslovenska Narodna Stranka* (JNS).

The following sections on "The Croatian Republic of Herceg-Bosna" and "The Serbian Republic of Bosnia–Hercegovina" are included here for the purposes of presenting material as comprehensively as possible. No commitment is made by the author or editor of this volume for the justice or otherwise of claims for independence or recognition.

Croatian Republic of Herceg-Bosna

Although the predominantly Croat areas of Bosnia–Hercegovina set up a "Croatian Republic of Herceg-Bosna" on July 7, 1992, it was a relatively transient affair, and does not merit a separate directory entry here. On Aug. 28, 1993, an Assembly was held in the village of Grude, composed of Croat representatives formerly elected to the Sarajevo Assembly. This declared the capital of the "Republic" to be Mostar, although this was never effectively implemented, and the decision was quickly overtaken by events, in the form of the internationally backed agreement to create a new federation, uniting the Croat-held areas of Bosnia and Hercegovina with those under Presidential control.

Political leadership in the short-lived "Republic" was firmly in the hands of the local branch of the Croatian Democratic Union (CDU), headed by Mate Boban. Organizationally the region behaved as a dependency of Zagreb, and its pretentions to independence lasted for just as long as it suited the interests of the Tudjman government. The contrast between the pliant and subordinate relationship of Grude to Zagreb, and the dogged defiance of Belgrade by the Serb Assembly in Pale, is noteworthy.

Serbian Republic of Bosnia and Hercegovina

On March 27, 1992, a "Serbian Republic of Bosnia and Hercegovina" proclaimed its independence from Bosnia and Hercegovina, thus completing a process of withdrawal from the former Yugoslav republic which can be traced to the non-co-operation of Serb representatives with other parties to the governing coalition during 1991. As early as April of that year localities in the republic with substantial Serb populations began to declare their autonomy from the republic, beginning with the "Municipal Community of Bosanska Krajina", centred on Banja Luka, which announced its intention to unite with the autonomous Serb areas of Croatia. Several such areas quickly emerged, especially in eastern Hercegovina and the area to the east of Sarajevo, known as the Romanija. Throughout 1991

661

evidence also began to accumulate of the stockpiling of weapons by Serbs in anticipation of civil war. It was not until September, however, that regular and serious armed clashes developed.

On Oct. 24, 1991, the Serb deputies elected to the republican Assembly met in Pale as the "Assembly of the Serb Nation of Bosnia and Hercegovina", and proposed a referendum on the creation of a common Serb state. This was duly held Nov. 9–10, anticipating the official government referendum on the constitutional status of the republic, which was not held until Feb.–March 1992. On March 27, 1992, the formation was announced of the "Serbian Republic of Bosnia and Hercegovina" (SRBH).

Although the Serbs in Bosnia had therefore dissented from the creation of an independent Bosnian state outside the framework of the Yugoslav federation, they were not included in the foundation of the "Third Yugoslavia" in April 1992. Consequently (unlike with other secessionist fragments of the former federation – the "Republic of Serbian Krajina", the "Republic of Kosova" and "Herceg-Bosna") the SRBH has remained in a limbo, not fully recognized as a state either internationally or among its allies within the former federation, and yet powerful enough to be included as a player in international negotiations over the future of Bosnia and Hercegovina.

In many respects this situation is a creation of the UN and EU negotiators who, between July 1992 and Feb.–March 1994, seemed to put their weight behind a succession of schemes that would have partitioned Bosnia and Hercegovina between three ethnic states.

In relation to Yugoslavia, the federal army intervened actively on the side of the Serbs, supporting their declared aim of remaining within Yugoslavia, to the point at which (in August 1992) federal involvement in the republic was formally declared to have ceased, and a separate army of the SRBH was created. This ambiguity is deepened at the level of political parties, since the SRBH is the only region of the former Yugoslavia outside of Serbia in which Serbian-based parties play a significant role. Formally, both the Party of Serbian Renewal and the Serbian Radical Party, for example, maintain an active presence in the Serb-held areas of Bosnia. Informally, irregular forces linked to Serbian parties have played a significant role in the war, especially as instruments of terror supporting "ethnic cleansing".

The image of politics in the SRBH which is presented to the outside media might convey the impression that Radovan Karadžić's Serbian Democratic Party (SDP) is the sole voice of the region's Serbs. Although it is undoubtedly the case that the SDP *does* have the backing of the great majority of Bosnian Serbs, there is a significant line of differentiation between those parties which are based primarily within Bosnia and Hercegovina and those which are not. The differences have been largely masked by the conduct of the war and the recurrent issue of the acceptance or rejection of international plans for the "cantonization" or division of Bosnia and Hercegovina into separate states or quasi-states. On this issue Bosnia's Serbs have largely remained in solid support behind Karadžić.

It remains impossible to speak with any confidence, however, of the nature of party support or organization within the SRBH. There have been no elections to the Pale assembly, which remains an assembly of those Serb members initially elected to the Sarajevo Assembly in November 1990, and there has been no serious test of the extent to which the SDP retains the overwhelming electoral support it secured on that occasion.

Directory of Parties

League of Communists – Movement for Yugoslavia (LC–MY)
Savez Komunists – Pokret za Jugoslaviju (SK–PJ)

This is the local committee (based on Banja Luka) of the Belgrade "Party of Generals". If anything it has more influence in Bosnia and Hercegovina than in its "home territory", although even here its significance is marginal. It can be contacted through its Belgrade base.

Serbian Democratic Party of Bosnia and Hercegovina (SDPBH)
Srpska Demokratska Stranka Bosne i Hercegovine (SDS BiH)

Fax. 71 786–022; 783–260.

Foundation. July 12, 1990.

Leadership. Radovan Karadžić (pres.), Mončilo Krajišnik, Gen. Ratko Mladić, Biljana Plavšić and Miodrag Simović.

Organization. With the support of around 30 per cent of the vote in the 1990 elections, drawn from those areas with substantial Serb settlement, the party won 72 seats in the bicameral Assembly of Bosnia and Hercegovina. It remains the moving spirit behind the creation of a separate Serb Republic in Bosnia. It is the governing party of the secessionist republic. By virtue of wartime conditions, however, its organizational structure and operations are *ad hoc*. It is important to note that the SDP is the *only* significant party within the "Republic" which is not a branch of an organization based in Serbia itself. It is this, as much as the details of any policy platform, that provides the basis for its popular support.

Programme. The SDP is explicitly the political voice of Serbs living in Bosnia and Hercegovina. In the pre-war period it advocated the development of multi-party democracy, toleration and respect for the rights of minorities, and legality in the conduct of the affairs of the state. Its programme had little to say about economic affairs beyond the abolition of a maximum size for land holdings. It defended the Serbian position in Kosovo; and sought to protect and develop Serbian cultural institutions, especially the Orthodox church. More recently its exclusive pre-occupation has been the conduct of the war, and the aim of creating an independent Serb republic.

Serbian Movement for Renewal – Bosnia-Hercegovina (SMR–BH)
Srpski Pokret Obnove – Bosna i Hercegovina (SPO–BH)

This is the local representation of Drašković's party. It was the only Serb party other than the SDP to gain seats in the elections of 1990, and its elected representative (Jović) plays an active part in the Pale Assembly. It remains unclear to what extent it may have managed to retain any significant support or coherent local organization since the outbreak of the war. Contact can be established through the Belgrade office of the SMR.

663

Serbian Radical Party of Bosnia-Hercegovina (SRPBH)
Srpska Radikalna Stranka Bosne i Hercegovine (SRSBH)

The party was established in Bosnia and Hercegovina in May 1993, with branches in Banja Luka, Prijedor and Bijeljina. It has no independent existence, but is the local arm of political operations of Šešelj's SRP in Serbia. It experienced difficulty in formation precisely because of its lack of genuine local support. Contact can be arranged through the Belgrade office of the SRP.

Socialist Party of the Serbian Republic (SPSR)
Socijalistička Republika Srpska (SPRS)

Address. Direct contact is difficult as a result of the war, but an approach can be made through the headquarters of the original "parent" organization in Belgrade.

Foundation. Formerly the republican branch of Milošević's SPS, it only became a constitutionally distinct entity in April 1994.

The party's centre of operations in Banja Luka. The core of its support is drawn from former army officers and state functionaries. It was set up as the local arm of Milošević's operations in Bosnia and Hercegovina, and is credited with the attempt in the summer of 1993 to initiative a military mutiny in Banja Luka, with the aim of destabilizing Karadžić's position in the republic. The open rift between Serbia and the SRBH over the international contact group's plan for a territorial settlement in Bosnia in the summer of 1994 undermined its position, and it is doubtful whether it has a future as a serious political force.

Notes
K. Milešević, "Marginalije o Be Haizborima '90", *Revija za sociologiju*, Vol. 22, 3–4, 1991.

The following section on the "Serbian Republic of Krajina" is included here for the purposes of presenting material as comprehensively as possible. No commitment is made by the author or the editor of the volume for the justice or otherwise of claims for independence or recognition.

Republic of Serbian Krajina

The early expressions of Croatian determination to increase republican autonomy, moving from a "federal" to a "confederal" Yugoslavia, aroused misgivings among the republic's half-million Serbs. These anxieties intensified as Croatia moved towards independence. The "first-past-the-post" system adopted for the elections of April–May 1990 in Croatia, and the collapse of support for the former Communists, directly or indirectly resulted in a diminution of the representation of minorities in the *Sabor*. Several of the changes introduced (either innocently or with manipulative intent) by the new CDU government were taken as signalling a sharp move towards chauvinism in Croatian politics. President Tudjman and his advisers frequently overlooked early warning signs and the need to allay Serb fears of marginalization.

During the summer of 1990 Serbs responded to proposals to amend the constitution by forming their own "Serbian National Council", intended to co-ordinate resistance to constitutional change and campaign for greater cultural autonomy. A referendum was organized on this issue in August which was accompanied by serious disorder in areas with Serb majorities along the Bosnian–Croatian border. Croatian police were barricaded out of some municipalities; and by December several of these had declared their autonomy from Croatia.

A vicious circle of deteriorating community relations and political misjudgement set in during 1991. The creation of Serb paramilitary formations was matched by the creation of Croatian units, especially those attached to Dobroslav Paraga's Croatian Party of Rights, usually known by their Croatian acronym, *HOS* — *Hrvatske Oružane Snage* (Croatian Armed Forces). In January the Zagreb government refused to implement a federal order banning armed paramilitary groups. This had been intended to head off the foundation of the Croatian National Guard, but was used to give credence to Serb claims that the Croatian government openly tolerated *HOS*, represented as a resurgence of the wartime *Ustaša* movement.

The decision of the *Sabor* the following month that republican legislation took precedence over federal legislation appeared to commit Croatia almost irrevocably to deepening conflict, eventual secession, and the relegation of Serbs to the position of a minority group within a republic "of the Croatian people".

Insurrectionary and terrorist actions by Serb groups spread to central and eastern Slavonia, and deepened Croat determination not be be bullied by the agents of Belgrade. The tendency to dismiss the grievances and fears of local Serbs as the result of external manipulation was reinforced by the intervention of the federal army, whose supposedly neutral acts of interposition in local conflicts all too frequently tipped the balance in favour of the Serbs.

Although the break-up of Yugoslavia is often dated from the outbreak of Slovenia's "Ten-Day War" in June–July, it is clear that by mid-1991 there was already widespread insurrection in Croatia. By October three areas had been wrested by Serb forces from Croatian government control, and declared themselves to be autonomous regions: the area around and to the north of Knin; western Slavonia; and Baranja and western Srem. These adopted the name *Krajina*, claiming historical continuity with the Austro-Hungarian *Vojna Krajina* (*Militärgrenze*, or frontier march) against the Ottoman empire set up in the seventeenth and eighteenth centuries. In December 1991 these areas were declared to constitute an autonomous state — the "Republic of Serbian Krajina" (RSK). In spite of attempts to extend their territory and consolidate Serb control through the expulsion of their non-Serb inhabitants, it has never been possible to make all three areas territorially contiguous, and communication between them remains circuitous.

In January 1992 a UN-sponsored cease-fire was negotiated between the Croatian National Guard and the Serb-Yugoslav forces, following which a United Nations Protection Force (UNPROFOR) was installed, dividing the RSK and adjacent areas with Serb majorities under the control of the Yugoslav People's Army (YPA) ("pink zones") between four UN Protected Areas (UNPAs). Although the YPA subsequently withdrew from these areas there has been no significant progress towards their envisaged demilitarization, and fighting between Serb and Croat forces has continued intermittently, especially in Sectors North and South.

In the face of continuing military uncertainty the Krajina Serbs have pressed ahead with their project of creating an autonomous state. To this end elections were held on Dec. 12, 1993, to an Assembly of 84 seats (the first to encompass all areas of the Krajina, although partial elections had been held earlier) contested by around 350 candidates representing 12 parties. They have been dismissed both within Croatia and by many external observers as falling far short of the normal canons of democratic practice. The main Croatian parties could not have taken part, as to do so would have constituted recognition of the RSK. On this ground even the Serbian National Party abstained: indeed, they are regarded as hopelessly compromised accommodationists by Serbs from RSK. Non-Serb inhabitants felt discouraged from participation, and there were allegations of irregularity in some areas, especially in the conduct of the presidential contest. Voting had to be repeated in the municipalities of Benkovac and Knin on Dec. 26 because of misconduct in the first round.

Although the Serbian Democratic Party of Krajina, with 31 seats, emerged as the strongest group in the Assembly the presidential race was won not by its candidate (Milan Babić) but by an independent, the former police chief and leader of a paramilitary organization from Knin, Milan Martić. Seven candidates contested the presidency; and as none secured the requisite majority a second round was held on Jan. 23 1994. The results of the election are summarized in Table 5.

The existence of a plurality of parties in the Krajina, which conveys the impression of a multi-party electoral contest, conceals the fact that parties are closely associated with specific regions, which should be regarded as party fiefs. In many cases they have the character of personal followings.

Table 5: Elections to the Unofficial Assembly of the "Republic of Serbian Krajina", December 1993

Party	Seats N = 84
Serbian Democratic Party of Krajina	32
Serbian Radical Party	16
Serbian Democratic Party of the Serbian Lands	16
Serbian Party of Socialists	6
Social-Democratic Party	4
Independents	10

Source: Ministry of Foreign Affairs, Republic of Serbian Krajina.

Directory of Parties

Serbian Democratic Party of Krajina (SDPK)
Srpska Demokratska Stranka Krajine (SDSK)

Led by Milan Babić, and centred upon Knin, the party has 32 seats in the unofficial Assembly. The party, and Babić in particular, takes a strongly anti-communist line, and are dogged defenders of an independent future for the Krajina. The first President of the break-away "Republic", Babić was forced from office because of his opposition to the UN-sponsored cease-fire in early 1992. Standing against Martić for the presidency again in 1994, he was defeated, although the SDP is the largest party in the unofficial Assembly. This has created an uncomfortable situation in which the main elected party is seriously at odds with the President. An uneasy coalition has endeavoured to reconcile these contradictions.

Serbian Democratic Party of Serbian Lands (SDPSL)
Srpska Demokratska Stranka Srpskih Zemalja (SDSSZ)

The party has 16 members in the unofficial Assembly. It is unclear how this group is distinguished by its policies from other nationalist political organizations. It does not appear to be dependent upon the support of any Serbian-based organization, even though two minor parties in Serbia have similar titles. Based primarily in Slavonia.

Serbian Radical Party (SRP)
Srpska Radikalna Stranka (SRS)

The local branch of the party of the same name run by Vojislav Šešelj, in Serbia. Has 16 members in the unofficial Assembly. The Speaker of the Assembly, Branko Vojnica, is from the SRP.

Social Democratic Party (SDP)
Socijaldemokratska Stranka (SDS)

Has four seats in the unofficial Assembly, but no additional information has been obtained.

Socialist Party of Serbia (SPS)
Socijalistička Partija Srbije (SPS)

This is the local organization of the Serbian party of the same name. It has six representatives in the unofficial Assembly. Although Milan Martić is not directly affiliated to any political party, as the protégé of Milošević he is closely linked to the SPS. Personal rivalry between

Martić and Babić provides a significant axis of politics in the region. Martić is a former senior police official with close links to the Serbian political and security hierarchies. Martić has been seen as the moving spirit behind the negotiated cease-fire with the republican authorities in Croatia, and in moves to reach an accommodation with them, in line with the SPS position in Serbia. Consequently the SPS in the Krajina has been strongly criticized by the more intransigent, separatist groups in the region.

BIBLIOGRAPHY

Frane, Adam. (ed.) *Volitve in politika po Slovensko* Znanstveno in publicisticno sredisce, Ljubjana, 1993.

Businessman's Guide to Central Asia. Prepared by the Central Asia Research Forum. School of Oriental and African Studies, University of London. (unpublished and undated paper)

Conference on Security and Co-operation in Europe. "Report by the Chairman-in-Office on Her Visit to the Participating States of Central Asia". Ministry for Foreign Affairs, Stockholm, May 21, 1993.

Hosking, Geoffrey A., Aves, Jonathan and Duncan, Peter J. S. *The Road to Post Communism. Independent Political Movements in the Soviet Union 1985–1991* Pinter, London, 1992.

Human Rights and Democratization in the Newly Independent States of the Former Soviet Union Compiled by the Staff of the Commission on Security and Co-operation in Europe, Washington, DC. January 1993.

Kipel, Vitaut and Kipel, Zora. *Byelorussian Statehood* Belarusian Institute of Arts and Science, New York, 1988.

Medvedev, Roy. (ed.) *Spravochnik — politicheskie partii, dvizhenia i bloki sovremennoi Rosii* Nizhny Novgorod, 1993.

Bucur-Ion, Micu *Paride Politice 1993* Rompress, Bucharest, 1993.

Pribylovsky, Vladimir. *Slovar novyk politicheskik partii i organizatsii Rossii* Panorama, Moscow, 1992.

Pribylovsky, Vladimir. *A Guide to Political Parties in the Newly Independent States* Panorama, Moscow, 1994.

Report of the CSCE Rapporteur Mission to Kazakhstan and Kyrgyzstan. Secretariat of the Conference on Security and Co-operation in Europe, Prague. CSCE Communication no. 149. Prague, 24 April, 1992.

Szajkowski, Bogdan. (ed.) *New Political Parties of Eastern Europe and the Soviet Union* Longman, Harlow, 1991.

Zaprudnik, Jan. *Belarus at the Crossroads* Westview Press, Boulder, Colorado, 1993.

INDEX

671

B

INDEX